D0105778

Ombudsmen and Others

Ombudsmen and Others

citizens' protectors in nine countries

Walter Gellhorn

Harvard University Press
cambridge · massachusetts · 1967

Second Printing

Distributed in Great Britain by Oxford University Press, London
Library of Congress catalog card number: 66–23465
Printed in the United States of America

for Kitty Gellhorn
who ably shared all
the work underlying
this book

Preface

Scholarly work builds on foundations others have laid. That is certainly true about the work leading to the present volume. American and foreign colleagues have written about lessening the irritations governmental operations sometimes create. Their writings aroused desire to learn more about non-judicial means of resolving disagreements with officials' actions or failures to act. Having first studied what was in print, Kitty Gellhorn and I devoted fifteen months to observations and interviews in the nine countries the following chapters chiefly discuss. Those countries drew us because their programs seemed likely to hold particular interest; but of course they are not the only ones that have been doing things worth learning about.

Our purpose at the outset was to gather material that might possibly be relevant to the needs of the United States. Every modern country, whatever be its constitutional structure, is marked by greatly expanded governmental activities and, consequently, by greatly multiplied opportunities for friction between governmental personnel and others. Since that condition is common to all, each country can perhaps be instructed by the experiences of others even though national institutions are themselves rarely directly transferable. In another book, *When Americans Complain,* I have sought to analyze whether citizen-official conflicts in the United States might advantageously be approached in ways observed elsewhere.

The studies now presented could not have been made had not scholars and officials in many lands been well disposed to give intellectual assistance. Listing all who submitted to interviews, participated in conferences, or otherwise provided documentary or oral enlightenment would consume numerous pages and might possibly embarrass a few among the many. Throughout this book appear informal comments by men and women not directly identified because, when interviewed, they were assured of confidentiality. I am deeply obliged to all upon whose experience I have drawn.

I am especially indebted to the following persons who, in addition to enlightening me in other ways, kindly read my papers in their semi-final form. Of course these readers share none of the responsibility for what now at last appears, but all of them helped me greatly: *Denmark*—Prof. Bent Christensen, Judge Sv. Gram Jensen, Prof. Carl Aage Norgaard; *Finland*—Prof. Paavo K. Kastari, Prof. Veli Merikoski, Prof. Kauko Sipponen; *Japan*—Prof. Otis Cary, Prof. Takeo Hayakawa, Prof. Koichi Inomata, Mr. Richard W. Rabinowitz, President Nobushige Ukai; *New Zealand*—Dean Colin C. Aikman, Sir Guy Powles, Mr. John R. Robson; *Norway*—Prof. Torstein Eckhoff, Supreme Court Advocate Tore Engelschion, Mr. Audvar Os; *Poland*—Prof. Stanislaw Ehrlich, Prof. Emanuel Iserzon, Prof. Jozef Litwin; *Sweden*—Mr. Alfred Bexelius, Judge Anders Bruzelius, Prof. Nils Herlitz, Judge Ulf Lundvik, Judge Bertil Wennergren; *U.S.S.R.*—Prof. Harold J. Berman, Prof. Merle Fainsod, Prof. John N. Hazard, Prof. Boris Krylov, Prof. Glenn G. Morgan; *Yugoslavia*—Prof. Borislav T. Blagojević, Mr. Peter V. Djordjević, Miss Sanja Milić, Prof. Eugen Pusić, Prof. Nikola Stjepanović.

Work in foreign lands would have been altogether impossible without capable, cooperative interpreters and translators. Chief among our well qualified and congenial aides were Willi Barenthin (Sweden), Kirsti Coward (Norway), Hans Bro Nielsen (Denmark), Adam Rybczinski (Poland), Kaarlo Sarkko (Finland), and Yozo Yokota (Japan).

Statistical data in various chapters were constructed from official reports or from information especially compiled for use here.

Columbia University, the Rockefeller Foundation, and the Walter E. Meyer Research Institute of Law supported the nine "country studies" now presented. I am keenly grateful for the material aid they provided.

Preface

Parts of the chapters that follow have been published in the California, Columbia, Harvard, McGill, Michigan, Pennsylvania, Stanford, and Yale law reviews, whose editors I thank for their cooperation.

The field work on which this book rests was completed in 1964 and 1965. Correspondence has kept the material reasonably precise and complete until the forepart of 1966. Changes in detail have probably occurred here and there since then, but none of any great significance are known as of the time the book goes to press.

Walter Gellhorn

August, 1966

Contents

Introduction 1

one **Denmark** 5

Creation of the Office, 7. Controls over Administration, 8. The Ombudsman's Duties and Powers, 10. The Sources of the Ombudsman's Business and How He Disposes of It, 18. An Attempt to Appraise, 33.

two **Finland** 48

A Page or Two of History, 49. Choosing the Watchmen, 50. Relationship to the Executive, 53. Relationship to the Courts, 57. Relationship to Non-judicial Administration, 64. Complaints, 65. Action on Own Initiative, 75. Inspections, 78. Presenting General Proposals, 80. The Educational Force of the Watchmen's Work, 83. Concluding Observations, 85.

three **New Zealand** 91

New Zealand and Its Governance, 93. The Creation of the Ombudsman, 101. The Ombudsman Statute and Some Questions It Has Raised, 103. The Ombudsman's Decisions and Some Questions They Have Raised, 127. The Impact of the Ombudsman's Work, 142. Concluding Observations, 152.

four **Norway** 154

The Genesis of the Ombudsman System in Norway, 154. Choosing the Ombudsman, 158. Limitations upon the

Ombudsman's Power, 159. What the Ombudsman Does Do, 171. The Ombudsman's Work Methods, 185. Concluding Observations, 191.

five **Sweden** **194**

How It All Began, 194. Sweden's Governmental System, 195. The Selection of the Ombudsman, 202. The Ombudsman's Powers, 205. The Nature and Sources of the Ombudsman's Work, 208. Private Complaint Cases, 210. The Ombudsman's Inspection, 218. The Relationship of the Press to the Ombudsman's Work, 227. The Ombudsman as Unofficial Adviser, 231. Relationship of the Ombudsman to Other Public Watchmen, 231. The Ombudsman's Relations with the Courts, 237. Appraising the Ombudsman's Work, 239.

six **Yugoslavia** **256**

Political Structure, 256. Economic and Social Organization, 259. The Yugoslav Law on General Administrative Procedure, 264. Judicial Review, 269 The Constitutional Court, 273. Non-judicial Correctives, 278. The Power House, 287. Concluding Observations, 290.

seven **Poland** **295**

The Code of Administrative Procedure, 296. Citizens' Complaints to Higher Authorities, 303. The Prokuratura, 314. The Press and Radio, 321. The Supreme Chamber of Control, 327. The Party, 329. Concluding Observations, 332.

eight **The Soviet Union** **336**

The Legislature, 337. Judicial Review, 338. Administrative Procedure, 340. The Right to Complain, 342. The Historical Background of the Procuracy, 344. The Procuracy's Review of Subordinate Legislation, 350. The Procuracy's Review of Administration, 355. Some Concluding Comments, 366.

nine **Japan** **372**

The Existence of Formal Remedies, 372. The Uses of Personal Influence, 381. The Administrative Management Agency, 385. The Civil Liberties Bureau of the

Ministry of Justice, 404. Counseling by Local Governments and Prefectures, 413. Some Concluding Observations, 416.

ten **Common Strands in the Fabric of Controls** **421**

Personnel Issues, 422. Bringing Critics into Action, 426. Conducting Inquiries, 431. The Aftermath of Inquiry, 433. Enforcing the Critics' Views, 436. A Final Word, 438.

Index **441**

Ombudsmen and Others

ABBREVIATIONS

Am. J. Comp. L.	American Journal of Comparative Law
Am. J. Int'l L.	American Journal of International Law
Anglo-Swedish Rev.	Anglo-Swedish Review
Bur. of Lab. Stat. Report	Bureau of Labor Statistics Report
Can. B. Rev.	Canadian Bar Review
Colum. L. Rev.	Columbia Law Review
Curr. Dig. of the Sov. Press	Current Digest of the Soviet Press
Fed. Prob.	Federal Probation
Harv. L. Rev.	Harvard Law Review
How. L. J.	Howard Law Journal
Int'l & Comp. L. Q.	International and Comparative Law Quarterly
Int'l Rev. Admin. Sci.	International Review of Administrative Sciences
J. Indian L. Inst.	Journal of the Indian Law Institute
J. Int. Comm. of Jurists	Journal of the International Commission of Jurists
J. Pol.	Journal of Politics
J. Pub. L.	Journal of Public Law
Minn. L. Rev.	Minnesota Law Review
N.Y.U. L. Rev.	New York University Law Review
N.Z. J. Pub. Admin.	New Zealand Journal of Public Administration
N.Z. L. J.	New Zealand Law Journal
N.Z. L. R.	New Zealand Law Reports
Ore. L. Rev.	Oregon Law Review
Ore. Rev. Stat.	Oregon Revised Statutes
Parl. Affairs	Parliamentary Affairs
Pol. Sci.	Political Science
Pol. Sci. Q.	Political Science Quarterly
Pub. Admin. Rev.	Public Administration Review
Pub. L.	Public Law
Pub. Serv. J.	Public Service Journal
Rutgers L. Rev.	Rutgers Law Review
Scand. Stud. in Law	Scandinavian Studies in Law
Tul. L. Rev.	Tulane Law Review
U.C.L.A. L. Rev.	University of California at Los Angeles Law Review
U. Ill. L. F.	University of Illinois Law Forum
U. Pa. L. Rev.	University of Pennsylvania Law Review
U. Toronto L. J.	University of Toronto Law Journal
Wis. L. Rev.	Wisconsin Law Review
Yale L. J.	Yale Law Journal

Introduction

The countries discussed in the following chapters have asked themselves: How best can we inquire fairly and quickly into asserted official impropriety or insensitivity? The answers they have given to that question are markedly diverse. Some are rather more satisfying than others. All reflect resolute coping with a major problem no contemporary government, including that of the United States, can ignore.

Although current, the problem itself is far from having been freshly discovered. Nor is it the sole concern of countries that count themselves "modern" and "enlightened." Every social grouping, no matter how primitive, maintains channels through which questions and complaints flow. The patriarch whose word is law within his clan, the potentate whose subjects have no voice in their governance, the tribal council that deliberates beneath the sacred tree, the sophisticated organizations that exercise power in industrial nations—all are concerned with the good order of the societies they rule.

This necessitates their knowing about the doubts that unsettle stability. Could rulers be omnipresent, they might reinforce their conception of "good order" by directly intervening in every conflict before it could become a clash. That being impossible, they may do the next best thing: they may make themselves readily accessible to disputants so that controversy can be ended by authoritative decision instead of by sheer test of strength. Even that much is impracticable when social groupings are large and controversies numerous. Then the no longer accessible rulers must rely on agents to be true expositors of their will. Exercising the rulers' power, not their own, the agents determine the rights and wrongs of matters committed to their consideration. Grand Vizier, tax collector, policeman, judge—in sum, everyone who exercises governmental power—is simply a ruler's spokesman.

Agents can be incompetent instead of wise, ruthless instead of vigorous, disloyal instead of dedicated, corrupt instead of upright. That is why rulers have been slow to confide uncontrolled capacity to act in their stead. Helping rulers detect and correct subordinates' shortcomings has, throughout history, been the work of supervisory officials and revisory courts. Safeguarding subjects against blunders may at first have been merely incidental to protecting rulers against faithlessness. In the eighteenth century, for example, a long-absent Swedish monarch, having lost touch with his tax gatherers and other employees, and moved more by desire to insure himself against embezzlement than by desire to insure his countrymen against oppression, named an overseer of officials. Only much later, after power had passed from the hands of absolutists, did the emphasis of administrative oversight change. Then the possibility of wrongs against the ruled rather than against the ruler became the chief concern—and it continues until this day to be the main focus of the modern Swedish Riksdagens Justitieombudsmän, the Parliamentary Commissioner for Justice, when he inquires into the conduct of official business. In the twentieth century, somewhat similarly, the Soviet Union's prosecuting attorneys were first charged to exercise "the function of general supervision" over the whole of public administration, not to forestall despotism but to safeguard the ruling Communist Party's revolutionary gains. During the past decade, however, the prosecutors have more closely resembled people's tribunes than smiters of faithless servitors.

In states where power is widely diffused the antinomy between the interest of the ruler and the ruled is theoretically indiscernible to the extent that self-government prevails. In actuality, however, self-government is becoming something of a rarity. The areas reserved for *self* government tend constantly to contract, while *majority* government expands. A majority can be a tyrant at times. Moreover, in any given instance even those who approve the majority's rule may be dismayed by its application. Further, so long as control by popular vote remains a reality, a majority may be short-lived. Those who, in combination, shape the policies governmental officials apply must therefore remain mindful that official inequities or iniquities, if tolerated today when they press on others, may tomorrow oppress yesterday's rulers. Thus everyone, whether or not in momentary ascendancy, shares a long-range interest in nurturing even-handed, effective, and honest law administration; the rulers and the ruled alike benefit from devices that correct governmental mistakes and help prevent their occurring again.

Modern administration is complicated and forceful. Controls over official action have had to match its complexities. Internal review of decisions—that is, review by higher-ranking administrators—aims at assuring consistency and at coordinating the work of lesser functionaries who deal only with segments of a total problem. Bringing an uncommitted intelligence to bear on what administrators have done—that is, judicial review whether in administrative courts as in France or in general courts as in America—aims at assuring adherence to proper standards of administrative judgment and conduct. Fiscal superintendence—that is, auditing by an authority independent of the rest of the official establishment—aims at preventing dissipation of public funds and at misuse of the power that springs from access to a large treasury. When functioning at maximum efficiency, these controls singly or collectively constitute strong bulwarks against improprieties. But, like most human institutions, they do not invariably work as well as they should; and sometimes making them work at all requires exertions disproportionate to a citizen's concern for good government. They do not fill every need.[1]

Recent decades have seen intensified search for cheap and easy means of inquiring into asserted deficiencies. This has not been an entirely governmental phenomenon, to be sure. The humble in bygone times may have thought themselves helpless to resist unfairness at the hands of the powerful, but not so in "the century of the common man." Once upon a time, for example, workers quaked when bosses drew nigh. Nowadays few employers dare behave like despots, benevolent or otherwise; their employees can challenge despotic decisions through elaborate grievance procedures provided by collective bargaining agreements. No entrepreneur in what is sometimes mistakenly thought still to be a free enterprise society would have the temerity to

[1] More particularized discussion of the inutility of ponderous processes for checking official abuses or mistakes appears in Gellhorn, *When Americans Complain,* Chap. I (1966).

respond to critics by roaring, like Commodore Vanderbilt, "The public be damned!" Instead, businessmen devote substantial resources to "adjustment bureaus" that seek to eliminate dissatisfactions rather than simply override them. Public utility companies, legal monopolies without direct competitors, preserve good will by quick action on complaints of defective service; large staffs devote themselves to customers' relations and to suitable remedial efforts. Private disagreements can of course be remitted to more formal procedures if need be. Disputed employer-employee contractual rights, if remaining in controversy after discussion, can be adjudicated by arbitration or otherwise. Outraged customers can go to court or to a regulatory agency if complaints have been ignored. But nobody regards formal decisions about the merits as anything other than a last resort.

So it must be with government as well. Heavy machinery need not be used on the great bulk of citizens' discontents and uncertainties about official actions. The main batteries of governmental power can be held in reserve, to be used sparingly when lighter machinery has failed. The lighter machinery, if fully suited to its work, should enable complainants to carry grievances beyond the official persons or organs they implicate.[2] Confidence in the grievance-handler's objectivity may largely determine the acceptability of the final result.

The grievance-handling mechanisms these pages describe are not the only ones that ingenuity and imagination might be able to construct. New designs are under active consideration in many lands, including the United States, for use nationally or locally. The experiences of nine countries are detailed here because they can perhaps suggest steps others might wish to take—or to avoid.

[2] G. R. Pipe, "Congressional Liaison: The Executive Branch Consolidates Its Relations with Congress," 26 *Pub. Admin. Rev.* 14, 24 (1966): "If an objective and intensive examination of constituent problems can be established in a more formal sense than is now the case, this would nullify the need for ombudsmen."

|one|

Denmark

In 1955 Denmark's first Ombudsman—the Folketingets ombudsmand, or Parliamentary Commissioner, to give him his proper title—took office and began to function. This was 146 years after a similar activity had commenced in Sweden and 36 years after a Finnish version had appeared. For most of the world, however, interest in the ideas behind the ombudsman institution was all but non-existent until Denmark's Ombudsman came on the scene. Then, suddenly, the institution began to attract attention not only in the Western world, but also in Asia and Oceania.

This spate of interest may be attributed in part to the enthusiasm with which the Danish Ombudsman himself—Professor Stephan Hurwitz[1]—has described his work and its fruits. Mindful from the first that his own countrymen were insufficiently aware of the powers and possibilities of his newly created office, Professor Hurwitz energetically engaged in a campaign of public education in his homeland.[2] Early successes as a lecturer abroad created a lively demand for appearances

[1] Hurwitz was the Professor of Criminal Law at the University of Copenhagen when elected to be the Ombudsman. A member of a highly regarded family, he had long been prominent in public and cultural affairs, though without political identification. Newspapers had often sought his views concerning matters of current moment and he had written influential articles for popular consumption. He had been recognized as an energetic and resourceful leader of Danish émigrés during Germany's occupation of Denmark in the 1940's. His professional advice was widely sought by business interests, public authorities, and reformist groups. He was identified with all manner of socially useful activities. He was, in short, a well known "community figure" long before he became Ombudsman.

[2] Today, instruction about the Ombudsman has become a routine element of a required course on Danish institutions given in all primary schools.

by him in distant places. Responding to that demand, he widened the range of his expository and exhortatory efforts, almost as though he were an apostle of a new faith or, perhaps, the salesman of an export commodity. His persuasive speeches and writings,[3] well supported by the writings of other enthusiasts,[4] transformed an ancient institution into one seemingly designed specifically to meet current needs.

Speechmaking and writing of articles may explain why persons in far-off lands know about a Danish governmental activity, but they do not explain why that activity has aroused such enthusiasm. For that explanation one must look to the Danish Ombudsman's actual accomplishments. These indeed have been substantial. The office has been a marked success, well deserving the applause given it.

At the same time, foreign enthusiasm has perhaps occasionally run ahead of the information at hand. The Ombudsman of a country other than Denmark recently remarked, "The ombudsman institution is certainly justifying its existence, but it isn't as great a thing as some people outside Scandinavia apparently believe. Professor Hurwitz is a man of magic—or perhaps I should describe him as a man with magic eyes who has bewitched the world. Because he has aroused so much admiration, the office he holds has seemed to be even more significant than it really is. If expectations about what ombudsmen can accomplish become too greatly inflated, their genuine achievements may be

[3] An interview during a British Broadcasting Corporation program had an extraordinary impact upon opinion in Britain. It is published as "The Danish Ombudsman and His Office," 63 *The Listener* 835 (1960). Professor Hurwitz's writings about his office appear in French, German, and Italian, as well as in Danish and English. Articles by him in English include "Control of the Administration in Denmark: The Danish Parliamentary Commissioner for Civil and Military Government Administration," 1 *J. Int. Comm. of Jurists* 224 (1958) and [1958] *Pub. L.* 236; "Denmark's Ombudsman," 1961 *Wis. L. Rev.* 170; "The Folketingets Ombudsman," 12 *Parl. Affairs* 199 (1959); "Public Trust in Government Services," 20 *Danish Foreign Office J.* 11 (1956); "The Scandinavian Ombudsman," 12 *Pol. Sci.* 121 (1960). A brochure written by him, *The Ombudsman: Denmark's Parliamentary Commissioner for Civil and Military Administration,* was published in Copenhagen in 1961 by Det Danske Selskab.

[4] The leading work in English is B. Christensen, "The Danish Ombudsman," 109 *U. Pa. L. Rev.* 1100 (1961). See also I. M. Pedersen, "The Danish Parliamentary Commissioner in Action," [1959] *Pub. L.* 115, and "The Parliamentary Commissioner: A Danish View," [1962] *Pub. L.* 15, as well as the same author's "Denmark's Ombudsmand" in D. C. Rowat, ed., *The Ombudsman: Citizens' Defender* 75 (1965); H. J. Abraham, "A People's Watchdog Against Abuse of Power," 20 *Pub. Admin. Rev.* 152 (1960). And see K. C. Davis, "Ombudsmen in America," 109 *U. Pa. L. Rev.* 1057 (1961). Among foreign writings, an especially noteworthy contribution has been made by J. G. Steenbeek, *De Parlementaire Ombudsman* (Haarlem, 1964).

forgotten when the inflated expectations explode. For myself, I fear that the ombudsman idea may have been a bit oversold by those who are enthusiastic about it."

The present sketch of the Danish Ombudsman's functioning attempts to describe briefly what he does and how he does it, and also to gauge its significance.

1|Creation of the Office

The Danish Constitution of 1953 empowered the Folketing (Parliament) to provide by statute for the appointment by it "of one or two persons who shall not be members of the Folketing to control the civil and military administration of the State."

The committee upon whose recommendation this action was based had stated the objective in view as "the establishment of increased guarantees for the lawful conduct of the government's civil and military administration." Existing guarantees, the committee asserted, were widely regarded as insufficient in view of "the extraordinary expansion of the administration" during the past several decades. Legislative power had been extensively delegated to administrative authorities, and this in itself "makes it natural that there be more stringent supervision and that Parliament be allowed better access than at present to follow the administration's use of its extensive powers." To that end the committee thought that "a Parliamentary Commissioner arrangement similar to the Swedish prototype" should be created.

Despite some degree of opposition, spearheaded by civil service groups and local governments, the committee's views were adopted. A 1954 statute created the office of a single Parliamentary Commissioner, to deal with both civil and military administration.[5] While

[5] Act No. 203, June 11, 1954.

The Ombudsman is elected by the Folketing after every general election; but he may be dismissed whenever he "no longer has the confidence of the Folketing," which may then choose a successor (Sec. 1). While the Folketing lays down general rules to guide his activities, he is otherwise "independent of the Folketing in the performance of his duties" (Sec. 3)—an independence that has been scrupulously observed. His relationship with the Folketing is maintained through an annual report and through contact with a special seventeen-member committee which comprises repre-

not wholly ignoring "the Swedish prototype," the Danish Parliament improved upon rather than slavishly copied what had previously existed in Sweden and Finland.[6]

2|Controls over Administration

Before the duties and powers of the Ombudsman are described, the pre-existing body of legal controls over public administration may be quickly outlined.

Denmark has a strongly centralized governmental system. Ministers exercise ultimate administrative power over the departments they head. They are politically answerable to (though they themselves need not be members of) the unicameral Parliament, sitting in Copenhagen.

Approximately 1,400 local governments carry on activities within the small country. Denmark's population is roughly the same as Georgia's; Georgia's land mass is more than three times greater than Denmark's. Administration is complicated because apart from the mainland peninsula of Jutland projecting northward from West Germany, Denmark's territory is scattered over some five hundred islands, of which about a hundred are inhabited.

---

sentatives of all major parties seated in the Folketing. He brings to that committee's notice his recommendations concerning changes in existing statutes or regulations, as well as "any mistakes or acts of negligence of major importance" (Parliamentary Directives, Arts. 11, 12). The Ombudsman has attended most of the committee's sessions, by its invitation.

The statute fixes the Ombudsman's salary at the same level as a Supreme Court judge's and makes generous pension provision under a statute applicable to members of the Cabinet (Sec. 12). The Ombudsman's salary is exceeded, in the civil public sector, only by those of the President of the Supreme Court, the Permanent Secretary of the Foreign Ministry, the Postmaster General, and the head of the state railways. In fact an additional nonstatutory allowance has been provided for the present Ombudsman because the statutory salary would have caused a steep drop in his income.

Section 13 authorizes the Ombudsman to engage and dismiss his own staff, whose number and salary are to be determined, however, by the Folketing's Committee for Procedure. The committee has thus far wholly accepted the Ombudsman's recommendations. The salary scale for the Ombudsman's assistants approximates that of the Ministry of Foreign Affairs for its resident officials; this is somewhat above the general civil service level.

[6] Discussion of the ombudsman systems in those two countries may be found in chapters five and two, respectively. The ombudsmen in New Zealand and Norway were subsequent creations.

The work of the towns and rural districts is largely financed by the central government, whose statutes and regulations have established minimum standards for local authorities' direction of education, hospital, library, and social welfare activities. The central government directly provides the courts, the police, and the main highway network. Public utilities such as waterworks, electric power, and gasworks as well as some public transport are usually owned and operated by local authorities, singly or in a cooperative organization. Local governments also have responsibility for town-planning with its attendant restrictions on land use. Population movements during the present century have made some of the old boundary lines meaningless (as has been true in most Western countries). Considerable effort has been made, through voluntary cooperation, to achieve a functionally necessary regionalism or metropolitanism in place of the parochialism of the past, but local pride and vested interests have thus far prevented large-scale rationalization of administration. Supervision of the budgets, expenditures, borrowings, and decisions of municipal governments is exercised in general by the Ministry of the Interior. County (or provincial) governments similarly supervise the rural district councils. The provincial administrations are in turn answerable to the Ministry of the Interior.

Few national administrative determinations are immune from being appealed within the administration itself. The power of initial review is lodged in an official superior to the one who made the challenged decision. Usually the final reviewing officer is, nominally, the Minister himself. A few independent adjudicatory bodies—such as the Tax Court and the Disablement Insurance Tribunal—have been created, but for the most part an appeal is handled simply as an element of administration, just as was the original decision from which an appeal has been taken.

Until 1964 administrators were almost entirely free from statutory prescriptions of procedure. Then an Administrative Procedure Act[7] for the first time required that parties to an administrative proceeding, either local or national, be fully informed of the documentary materials and evidence bearing upon the case and that they be afforded an opportunity to comment orally or in writing before a decision is made.

[7] Act No. 141, May 13, 1964, effective October 1, 1964.

Judicial review is available in the ordinary courts. Denmark, unlike Sweden and Finland, has no special administrative courts. A party aggrieved by a final administrative decision may sue for its annulment or modification. If monetarily injured, he may seek to recover damages from the State. An official who has assertedly abused his powers may be prosecuted before the courts, which also have power to pass upon the propriety of disciplinary sanctions, including removal from office.

While the scope of Danish judicial review seems at first glance to be broad,[8] it is in fact somewhat limited. When considering exercises of discretion, Danish courts ordinarily confine themselves to questions of ultra vires. So long as the administrator has jurisdiction over the subject matter and has not been shown to have been improperly motivated, the courts cannot candidly inquire whether he exercised his discretion arbitrarily.[9]

Furthermore, inactivity seems not to concern the courts; they will not, for example, order an administrator to make a determination even when he has been unreasonably slow in acting upon a matter before him. The courts themselves act slowly on appeals from administrative orders, and their proceedings are rather costly, so that close questions may be abandoned rather than put to the test.

All these factors have discouraged recourse to litigation, which has been small in proportion to the volume of administrative decisions that, in theory, are judicially reviewable. "Where it operates," a prominent scholar has written, "the control of the courts is excellent; its operation, however, is sporadic."[10]

3|The Ombudsman's Duties and Powers

Persons within the Ombudsman's jurisdiction. The 1954 statute that created the Ombudsman confined him to supervising "civil and military central government administration" exclusive of the courts. His jurisdiction extended to "ministers, civil servants and all other persons

[8] The Danish Constitution (Sec. 63) empowers courts to determine all questions concerning the limits of power conferred upon a public authority.

[9] The 1953 Constitution explicitly broadened the scope of review in cases involving the valuation of private property taken for public purposes.

[10] Christensen (note 4 above), at 1103.

acting in the service of the State" except those engaged in judicial administration.[11] Those who act "in the service of the State" include not only officials who control or command, but all those who are on the national payroll, such as university professors, museum curators, clergymen, and ballet directors (all of whom have been principals in cases acted upon by the Ombudsman). The civil employees of the national government in Denmark number only slightly more than a hundred thousand altogether, including the many office, maintenance, and manual workers who are unlikely to have any contact with the public at large.

The Ombudsman's jurisdiction was broadened to embrace, commencing in 1962, local officials as well when acting "in matters for which recourse may be had to a central government authority."[12] The activities of elective bodies ("local government councils") remained beyond the Ombudsman's reach ordinarily, though he was empowered to "take up a case for investigation on his own initiative," even if it grew out of a collective action of a local council, "provided that the case involves a violation of material legal interests." The statute cautioned the Ombudsman to "take into account the special conditions under which local governments operate," thus reflecting residual support of the concept of local autonomy.

In terms of power, the Ombudsman today could perhaps, if he chose, deal with virtually every high level or low level exercise of governmental authority outside the courts. In terms of political tact, he appears to proceed very gingerly when dealing with local affairs. Municipal governments' hot opposition to extending the Ombudsman's authority caused Parliament to enact a somewhat confused statute, conferring power more grudgingly than the Ombudsman himself had urged.[13] In the circumstances, he has seemingly not been disposed to

[11] Act No. 203, June 11, 1954, Sec. 4.

[12] Act No. 142, May 17, 1961. As to the local government situation in Denmark, see P. Meyer, "The Development of Public Administration in the Scandinavian Countries Since 1945," 26 *Int. Rev. Admin. Sc.* 135, 145 (1960).

[13] See S. Hurwitz, "Scandinavian Ombudsman," 12 *Pol. Sci.* 121, 133 (1960), noting that national and local authorities often work together (as, for example, in tax matters) and, even when working separately, engage in similar activities. Citizens cannot understand, the Ombudsman argued, why he should be able to deal with a complaint against the administration of, say, a school or hospital operated by a national authority, while a precisely similar complaint against a locally administered school or hospital should be beyond his reach. Since in the end he could not order anyone to do anything, but could only make recommendations, the Ombudsman did

test the outermost limits of his authority.[14] Spokesmen for an organization of local governments declared during an interview in 1964, however, that opposition to the Ombudsman's supervision of local activities has now all but vanished.

As indicated above, the Danish Ombudsman has no power to deal with judicial administration. This exception is a major departure from "the Swedish prototype," for much of the Swedish Ombudsman's energies are devoted to policing the judiciary. In Denmark complaints about the behavior of judges can be lodged either with the presidents of the several courts or with a special Court of Complaints, founded in 1939. That court has other functions, however, such as deciding whether closed cases should be reopened because newly discovered evidence or some other development may have undermined the existing judgment. Apparently the Court of Complaints is little used by persons who have been offended by judges; the number of complaints received by that body annually is said to be on the order of six, while court presidents are thought to receive perhaps ten additional complaints that a judge has been unnecessarily sharp-tongued or dilatory. Few disciplinary decisions have been rendered by the Court of Complaints. In recent years one judge has been dismissed because of a tax delinquency wholly unrelated to his judicial work. Another has been censured for interfering with newspaper reporters' efforts to observe proceedings in his court. Many of the approximately 215 judges in active service have had considerable experience in the Ministry of Justice before being appointed to the bench. Confidence in their probity is universal, so far as one can gauge the matter on the basis of personal interviews with all manner of occupational groups. The severest criticisms encountered during conversations in 1964 were that one judge "is said to drink too much, but he is a very clever judge who handles his work well, anyway" and that "some of the

---

not see how his "subsequent control may constitute an interference with local autonomy." So he advocated a flat grant of power to look into governmental activities at all levels.

[14] Taxes, schools, and public assistance programs are examples of local matters "for which recourse may be had to a central government authority," and therefore clearly lie within the Ombudsman's jurisdiction. The condition of town streets and sidewalks, the setting of wage rates for local authorities' employees, and the direction of municipally owned public utilities are examples of matters dealt with entirely locally and, therefore, probably not suitable for the Ombudsman's attention under the statute as now drawn.

judges in the community courts other than the City Court of Copenhagen are not very competent professionally, though all are thoroughly honest." These comments were more than offset by flattering appraisals.

The nature of the Ombudsman's responsibility. The statute and Parliament's accompanying "general directives" command the Ombudsman to inform himself constantly about the manner in which all officials within his jurisdiction perform their duty.[15]

The Ombudsman, it must be stressed, has no statutory power to change a decision he finds to be improper. He can comment on the quality of administration, but not directly overturn the results of poor administration. Later discussion will make clear, however, that the Ombudsman's suggestions do frequently have the effect of reversing or modifying determinations he has found to be unsound.

The Ombudsman's formal powers. If he believes that misconduct in public service has occurred, the Ombudsman may order the public prosecutor to investigate further or to commence a criminal proceeding in the ordinary law courts;[16] or, if he chooses, he may order that disciplinary proceedings be commenced by the appropriate authority. In point of fact, he has not once during the eleven years of his activity ordered either a prosecution or a disciplinary proceeding, though in a few instances he has requested prosecutors to carry on investigations.[17]

15 The statute provides in Section 5 that the Ombudsman is to "keep himself informed" as to whether persons subject to his supervision "commit mistakes or acts of negligence in the performance of their duties." Section 3 authorizes the Parliament to give the Ombudsman general rules to guide his activities. Article 3 of the Directives adopted by the Parliament on February 9, 1962, expands the statute somewhat by saying: "The Parliamentary Commissioner shall keep himself informed as to whether any person comprised by his jurisdiction pursues unlawful ends, takes arbitrary or unreasonable decisions or otherwise commits mistakes or acts of negligence in the discharge of his or her duties . . ."

16 Though Section 9 of the statute grants a general power to order prosecution, the Parliamentary Directives (Art. 9) place an explicit limitation on the Ombudsman's power to proceed against a Cabinet member: "If the Parliamentary Commissioner, on having made an investigation, finds that a Minister or a former Minister should be held responsible under civil or criminal law for his conduct of office, he shall submit a recommendation to that effect to the Folketing Committee on the Parliamentary Commissioner's Office."

17 No such an investigation (the precise number of which has not been ascertained, though they are known to be very few) has eventuated in a prosecution. Although the Ombudsman has never ordered a disciplinary proceeding, apparently some have occurred as a consequence of his inquiries and perhaps directly in response to his suggestion. Reflections of his offering a "suggestion" without making an "order" appeared in two interviews during 1964. In both instances subordinate officials were found by their superiors to have been at fault and, though not dismissed, were told that they would never be promoted to higher posts.

Chiefly the Ombudsman has acted in the far milder manner contemplated by Section 9 of the statute: "In any case, the Parliamentary Commissioner may always state his views on the matter to the person concerned."[18]

At first glance this may seem to be a sword without a sharp cutting edge. As wielded by the Danish Ombudsman it has proved to be a potent and versatile weapon. He himself has written that the power to voice his opinion "enables the Commissioner to exercise a guiding influence on the administration and provides him with the legal basis for initiating oral or written negotiations with the ministers or the services concerned in order to have decisions which he considers erroneous corrected or, if this cannot be done, to achieve revision of the general procedure."[19]

Furthermore, the Ombudsman has not hesitated to express criticism even when the outcome of a particular case has not been at stake. A reviewing court must (at least in theory) disregard a "harmless error." Not so the Ombudsman, who points out deficiencies of method, judgment, or personal manners in the hope of discouraging their later occurrence. Nor does the Ombudsman confine himself to stating his views about what administrators are legally required to do. Instead he freely states what he thinks they would be well advised to do. Unlike the courts, a leading commentator has remarked, the Ombudsman "is not required to base his judgment solely on legal considerations; rather, he may include in his opinions more discretionary reflections on the justification and expediency of the conduct of administrative agencies, without having to disguise them in the garb of traditional legal analysis."[20] The Ombudsman has, for example, explicitly said that an official organ cannot be criticized for what it has done or failed to do in the particular matter under discussion, because its acts were consonant with existing law—and then has outlined what he believes would be a better practice for the future.[21]

[18] The Directives (Art. 9) say essentially the same thing: "Even if the subject matter of a complaint gives the Parliamentary Commissioner no occasion for action, he may always state his views on the matter to the person whom the complaint concerns."

[19] S. Hurwitz, "The Folketingets Ombudsmand," 12 *Parliamentary Affairs* 199, 202 (1959); and see also the same author's "Scandinavian Ombudsman," 12 *Pol. Sci.* 121, 124 (1960).

[20] B. Christensen, "The Danish Ombudsman," 109 *U. Pa. L. Rev.* 1100, 1116 (1961).

[21] The Ombudsman's contributions to administrative procedure reform are dis-

The Ombudsman sometimes nimbly oversteps the dividing line between passing upon the merits of a specific decision and suggesting methodological improvements. One of his recent reports, for example, discloses a textile importer's complaint that he had been forced to pay excessive customs duties on seven lots of nylon between July 29, 1959, and June 21, 1961.[22] As to five lots imported before 1961, the complaint was groundless. As to the two lots imported in 1961, however, a more troublesome question appeared because the applicable tariff rate had been reduced before the importation occurred. The Department had denied the importer's claim for a refund because he had paid at the pre-existing (and higher) rate without protest, no samples of the imported goods now remained available for quality analysis, and an overpayment if it had in fact occurred was attributable to the importer's having neglected to provide all the information needed by the customs authorities. The Ombudsman, having reviewed a rather extensive file, concluded that the importer's factual presentations had not been so gravely deficient as to justify rejection of his claim. Without deciding that a refund should be made in any specific amount, the Ombudsman therefore requested the Department to reconsider the once rejected claim. This it agreed to do, and there the matter ended. In a technical sense, the Ombudsman did not overturn a decision he had found to be erroneous; the overturning was done by the Department itself. Realistically, of course, the Ombudsman's muscle provided the push.

Sometimes the muscle is not so clearly evident, but its presence is nevertheless strongly suspected. A ministry dismissed a civil service employee with loss of pension rights because of his faithlessness. Subsequently another administrative organ denied him an old-age pension, as was apparently statutorily correct in view of the conditions of his past employment. The Ombudsman, when besought to relieve the former

---

cussed in I. M. Pedersen, "The Danish Parliamentary Commissioner in Action," [1959] *Pub. L.* 115, 116–120.

For an example of a substantive suggestion, see Folketingets Ombudsmands Beretning for Året 1962 (Annual Report for 1962), at 36: A complainant asserted that an administrative organ had denied him cash sickness benefits because it had misinterpreted the health insurance law. The Ombudsman concluded that he could not criticize the interpretation given the statute, but he urged the Ministry of Social Affairs to consider whether the act should not be amended at the first opportunity in order to clarify the conditions of eligibility for benefits.

[22] Folketingets Ombudsmands Beretning for Året 1962, at 27.

civil servant's plight of being pensionless in a country where not having a pension is indeed phenomenal, found nothing he could criticize. He neither publicly demanded a change in the rulings nor appealed for mercy in the penniless man's behalf. Soon afterward, however, the ministry relented. It substantially restored the civil service pension benefits previously ordered to be forfeited. Civil servants who tell this story ascribe the change to the Ombudsman's mediatory efforts. The correctness of their belief has not been officially confirmed, but its very existence is significant.

A more generalized administrative determination came under scrutiny when a convict complained that he had been unable to cast his ballot in a recent parliamentary election.[23] A registered voter may vote at his place of registration or, if he will necessarily be absent on election day, by previously depositing his ballot at another registration office. A prisoner requested permission to leave the penitentiary so that he might vote at a nearby registration office. The prison administration denied permission because escorting a stream of prisoner-voters to the nearest town was impracticable; as to some strictly confined prisoners, excursions beyond prison walls were entirely out of the question. The Ombudsman, having received this explanation, said that the prison directorate could not be criticized for its decision. He added, however, that he thought the rules about prisoners' voting should be altered. Since Denmark does not regard loss of civil rights as an element of punishment for crime, the Ombudsman urged that prisoners should be encouraged to function as citizens to the fullest extent feasible. The Minister of Justice, to whom the Ombudsman had addressed these remarks, agreed with the position taken. He promised that he would be mindful of the Ombudsman's views when subsequently discussing the possible enlargement of absentees' voting opportunities.[24]

The power of persuasion. One should not conclude that the Ombudsman broods in splendid isolation and then "states his views" to a rapt audience of officials. On the contrary, many of his pronouncements merely record conclusions previously reached jointly by the Ombudsman and the administrative organs involved.

[23] See the report cited in note 22, at 23.

[24] The problem of absentee voting affected hospital patients in the same manner as penitentiary inmates; patients, like prisoners, lost their votes if unable to deposit them in person. Despite the Minister's assurance in 1962 that the problem would be well considered, no change in the pertinent statutes had been made as of the end of 1965.

Sometimes, indeed, they might best be described as negotiated settlements, representing not what the Ombudsman may initially have proposed but, rather, what the administrators have been ready to accept. Mutual enlightenment and persuasion may beget conclusions agreeable to the officials and the Ombudsman alike, though perhaps not entirely to the taste of either. So far as the record may show, the Ombudsman simply made recommendations that were accepted; the record may not show with equal clarity whether the recommendations were modified to make them palatable.

The bargaining process, some cynics say, produces a spurious air of accomplishment. It creates, they contend, a misleading image of the Ombudsman as a fount of wisdom from which flow inspired ideas gladly adopted by all concerned.

That is too harsh a view. Discussion before pronouncement has been a functionally sound choice. It has encouraged cooperation and receptivity. The Ombudsman, a man of tact, believes that persuasion is more enduringly forceful than edict. He realizes, too, that Denmark's able civil servants possess a valuable store of experience which can fortify his own judgment; he is humble enough to realize that one man cannot possess all human knowledge. Hence the negotiations that precede his recommendations are genuine opportunities for illumination and not merely for compromise.

The discussions have another value. They have decreased the Ombudsman's workload because administrators who have come to understand and approve his approach have, in later instances, taken suitable steps without his having had to prompt them in each instance. So, for example, one of the Ombudsman's assistants recently remarked that the national police administration "has become quicker than we are. Cases have started with a complaint to the Ombudsman; a request has been made to the police for information; they have immediately investigated; and, after the investigation, they have reported not only the facts they have found, but what they propose to do unless the Ombudsman disagrees. Instead of having to belabor the cases, we have been able to close them."

Similarly, though on a different plane, the Ministry of Social Affairs recently revised the work methods of one of its bureaus in order to strike at slow action on difficult cases. "We knew from past experience," a Ministry spokesman declared, "that what seem to us to be troublesome decisions do not necessarily seem so to an outsider, and we also knew that the Ombudsman had been severely critical of what he regarded as undue delay in some of our other proceedings. So we developed new criteria for identifying the tough cases, which now go at once to senior personnel without first being put to one side by somebody who dreads having to tackle them."

"Preventive therapy" of this kind, perhaps stimulated by the Ombudsman but, in an immediate sense, voluntarily initiated by the administrators themselves, is especially valuable. Self reform has deeply penetrating and usually lasting consequences.

4|The Sources of the Ombudsman's Business and How He Disposes of It

The statute and directives under which the Ombudsman functions authorize him to proceed upon the basis of a complaint, upon his own initiative, or by direct inspection of official operations. All persons in the service of the State must furnish information and "produce such documents and records as he may demand for the performance of his duties."[25]

Inspections. Inspections do not bulk large in the Ombudsman's work.

Perhaps because of his own long-standing interest in penology, Professor Hurwitz has spent considerable time inspecting places of detention, where persons in custody have been enabled to confer with him privately.[26] A veteran prison administrator said in 1964, "The inmates

[25] Parliamentary Directives, Feb. 9, 1962, Art. 3(4). Whether the Ombudsman can demand to see the "internal working papers" of a ministry is unclear. Some authorities maintain that they are not "documents or records" which must be produced if requested. Some ministries have in fact been including them along with more formal materials, when the Ombudsman's office has asked to see a case file. Members of the Ombudsman's staff have expressed doubt that their production could be compelled, and the matter is unlikely to be put to the test. Denmark, unlike Sweden, does not have a sweeping requirement that the files of official bodies be open to general inspection by the public.

As for "secret" documents—as in military or foreign affairs matters—a member of the Ombudsman's staff has been given "top secret clearance" so that pertinent papers may be consulted when deemed necessary; for instance, in connection with a complaint that a permit to work in Greenland had been wrongfully withheld, a personnel security file was made available in this manner.

[26] Section 6 of the statute creating the Ombudsman provides, additionally, that

look forward to his visits. It makes a nice change for them. They enjoy talking with him even if they have to invent a complaint."

The Ombudsman agrees that most prisoner complaints have proved to be unmeritorious, but he nevertheless believes that "these talks may well be considered important, since apart from the value they may have for the person confined, they may afford grounds for examining questions of more general interest."[27] Specific "questions of more general interest" that came to light through inspections and that would not equally have come to light by a written complaint could not be pinpointed in 1964. No doubt, in any event, the prisoners' conversations with a nationally important personage do have psychological value, for they may allay the feeling that prisoners have been wholly rejected and forgotten by society.

Apart from institutional inspections (which are somewhat a misnomer, for the institutions are usually not so much inspected as simply visited to facilitate personal conversations), the Ombudsman has also briefly visited military barracks. The infrequency of complaints by soldiers is said to have been a surprise, and he therefore thought it desirable to make himself personally accessible to military personnel. He paid four visits to military bases in 1963, looking at sleeping quarters, infirmaries, and eating places and also conversing with soldiers, who seemed to him to be reasonably well contented.[28]

So far as can be determined, he has never inspected an administrative organ, national or local. During an interview in 1964 the Ombudsman expressed doubt that random sampling of administrative operations by pulling case folders from the files, would reveal anything useful. His remark reinforced the strong impression that Pro-

---

"any person deprived of his personal liberty is entitled to address written communications in sealed envelopes to the Parliamentary Commissioner." It has become a fairly open secret, however, that this pledge of privacy does not mean a great deal, because the Ombudsman asks the authorities to comment on the communications he has received, or he sends the authorities copies of his replies to his correspondents; hence both the identity of complainants and the nature of their complaints become known in fact. The Ombudsman's action in this regard is consonant with his duty, under Section 7(3) of the statute, to provide officials an opportunity to respond to criticism.

[27] S. Hurwitz, *The Ombudsman* 15.

[28] Folketingets Ombudsmands Beretning for Året 1963, at 7. After an inspection by the Ombudsman, the Army is said to have declared all-out war against cockroaches in military kitchens. The Ombudsman also used his influence with the state railways to obtain free transportation for soldiers while on leave.

fessor Hurwitz, unlike his Swedish counterpart, is skeptical about the value of routine inspections.[29] In any event, his annual reports call slight attention to this phase of his work, and it seemingly consumes only a small portion of his energy.

Initiative. Although empowered to proceed on his own initiative, the Ombudsman rarely commences an investigation except upon complaint. During the five years 1960–1964, inclusive, the Ombudsman's office docketed 5,745 cases, of which only about 60 were launched on his initiative.

The qualitative importance of those few cases was, however, high.

In what is perhaps the most illuminating of his various published discussions, the Ombudsman has described at length six cases under the heading, "Some Examples of Cases of Special Interest."[30] Two of the six were self-initiated: "Because of widespread newspaper discussion of the case the Parliamentary Commissioner decided in 1955 to make an investigation of the Royal Veterinary and Agricultural College's treatment of a thesis . . ." and "In May 1958 Ejnar Blechingberg, Commercial Adviser at the Danish Embassy in Bonn, was charged with espionage . . . The case was debated in Parliament in February 1959 and thereafter the Parliamentary Commissioner found it expedient—on his own initiative—to investigate the steps taken by the Ministry of Foreign Affairs since 1940 relative to Blechinberg, and his position in the Foreign Office."

As these two examples may suggest, the matters into which the Ombudsman has inquired without having been bidden to do so tend to be scandalous and to have aroused public disquietude. "In such cases," a prominent scholar has written, "the Ombudsman's activities assume a special character. In each, his main business has been to get to the bottom of the case, to segregate the core of truth from the exaggerations and controversy, and to try to put an end to the affair. In most cases he has been successful, and his recommendations have often resulted in new regulations and procedures designed to prevent the recurrence of such episodes."[31]

[29] Sweden's and Finland's experience with inspections is discussed below at pages 218 and 78, respectively. The ombudsmen in those countries favor inspection trips; the writer shares Professor Hurwitz's skepticism.

[30] S. Hurwitz, *The Ombudsman* 31.

[31] B. Christensen, "The Danish Ombudsman," 109 *U. Pa. L. Rev.* 1100, 1124 (1961).

The low number of avowedly self-initiated cases obscures the fact that the Ombudsman often goes far beyond the confines of a complaint, once an investigation has commenced. Danish lawyers give the Ombudsman very considerable credit, for example, for having speeded the final determination of tax matters. This he achieved by proposing procedural and organizational changes after a sweeping study of tax administration. The study was undertaken after a single taxpayer had complained about a seemingly unconscionable delay in obtaining a needed ruling. Investigation of that complaint broadened into a general survey. Statistically, the matter is still recorded as a complaint case. Realistically, it might well be included among the Ombudsman's self-initiated probes.

The same may be said of numerous other cases. What may at first have seemed to be narrowly personal grievances were later perceived to have implications that overshadowed the initial episodes. So, for example, a correspondent's complaint that a letter to the Ministry of Education had been unanswered led, in the end, to an examination of internal controls and suggested changes in supervisory practices. In the most literal sense all of this may have been "initiated" by the disgruntled correspondent, but in truth he had probably never imagined that annoyance about one mislaid letter might cause a comprehensive inquiry into a ministry's work methods.

Complaints. The Ombudsman is not obligated to spring into action whenever a complaint reaches his desk. The statute (Sec. 6) requires a complainant to identify himself[32] and to lodge his complaint within a year after his grievance arose;[33] action by the Ombudsman must be withheld if available administrative remedies have not been exhausted; the Ombudsman may determine, in all events, "whether the complaint gives sufficient grounds for an investigation." The Parliamentary Directives provide, additionally, that complaints should ordinarily be

[32] In a few instances a complainant has requested that his identity, though revealed to the Ombudsman, be withheld from the official or organ complained against. If the Ombudsman concludes that the request should not be honored, he simply writes the complainant that he may withdraw the complaint or allow his name to appear, whichever the complainant may prefer.

[33] The Ombudsman notes that he can decide to proceed on his own initiative if a complaint has been barred by time, but he is not likely to do so in the absence of some "exceptional circumstance." Similarly, he can, if he chooses, proceed on his own initiative in respect of the subject matter of an anonymous complaint. So far as has been discovered, he has never yet chosen to act on an untimely or anonymous complaint, so one must guess at what circumstances he might deem to be exceptional.

written and supported by evidence (Art. 4), that the Ombudsman should take no action on a complaint beyond his jurisdiction or tardily filed, other than to refer it to the appropriate authority and "give the complainant reasonable guidance" (Art. 5), and that the Ombudsman may simply inform the complainant that "he finds no reason to take action in the matter" if he believes that a complaint is "unfounded" or that its subject matter is "insignificant" (Art. 6). Further, a "Supervisory Board"—actually, a standing committee of the parliament—has been established by Danish law to deal with the treatment of patients in mental hospitals, alcoholism centers, and other institutions; the Ombudsman is directed to refer to that board all complaints "about the treatment of persons deprived of their personal liberty through any procedure other than the administration of criminal justice" (Art. 5), thus enabling him to slough off a type of case that has bedeviled ombudsmen in other countries (though the Board seems now to be falling into the habit of asking the Ombudsman to investigate after all).

These limitations have kept the Ombudsman's work within manageable dimensions, though new cases come in at the rate of more than a thousand per year.[34]

During the five years 1960–1964, inclusive, the Ombudsman took up for investigation only 856 cases, constituting but 14.9 percent of the 5,745 matters registered at the Ombudsman's office in that period. Readiness to investigate seems to be declining.[35] The increasing proportion of dismissals perhaps reflects the Ombudsman's sharpened awareness of what he can feasibly do.[36] Assuredly it also reflects a statutory change that has enabled him since 1959 to ignore complaints

[34] Total new matters registered in recent years have been as follows: 1961—1,065; 1962—1,080; 1963—1,130; 1964—1,370.

[35] In 1956, the first full year of the Ombudsman's service, 50.4 percent of the cases filed were investigated. In 1964, the figure had fallen to 12.4 percent.

[36] The Ombudsman has acknowledged a tendency to dismiss summarily complaints that relate to "certain groups of discretionary administrative decisions . . . where as a rule experience has proved that the Commissioner is not able to criticize. As examples of such groups may be mentioned, complaints concerning the amount of maintenance fixed by an administrative authority, refusal of a petition for free legal aid in lawsuits against private persons, refusal of application for reduction of tax assessment and petitions for mercy. To these groups may be added complaints about the degree of disablement fixed in workmen's compensation cases . . ." Hurwitz (note 30 above), at 18.

about decisions still susceptible of being reversed by a superior administrative authority.[37]

The actions taken upon cases docketed in recent years is summarized in Table I, which reveals how exercising judgment at the threshold enables the Ombudsman to concentrate his energies on relatively few cases.

Table I. Disposition of matters registered

	1962	1963	1964
Total registered	1,080	1,130	1,370
Considered on the merits	152	151	170
Dismissed	928	979	1,200
(a) filed tardily	41	54	68
(b) outside jurisdiction (pertaining to judiciary, local councils, private persons, etc.)	281	313	394
(c) administrative remedies not exhausted	181	166	240
(d) anonymous or meaningless	28	38	38
(e) Ombudsman found no basis for complaint or subject matter was trivial though within his jurisdiction	293	254	281
(f) inquiry rather than complaint	119	124	146
(g) withdrawn by complainant	36	28	32
(h) initiated by Ombudsman and then dropped without action	3	2	1

To say that a case is "considered on its merits" is not to say that the Ombudsman has in every instance found grounds for criticizing the officials involved. In fact, criticisms of particular occurrences or general suggestions for future improvement (both of which may appear in the same case) were made in less than 30 percent of the cases closed

[37] The amendment was embodied in Act No. 205, June 11, 1959. The relationship of investigations to new filings, expressed in terms of percentage, was 37.3 in 1957. In 1958, the percentage was 26.5. This fell to 20.7 in 1959, and it has continued downward since.

after investigation during the years 1960–1964. Less than one in twenty of the total number of matters registered gave rise to censure or representations by the Ombudsman.

The Ombudsman's remarks, while not staggeringly numerous, have grown out of cases involving a very large number of governmental authorities. The cases carried to a conclusion in recent years have related to fifteen ministries, thirty-nine national administrative authorities, and five local organs, as well as the police and prosecutors.

Table II. Official establishments involved in cases determined after investigation

	Ministries	Other national agencies	Local agencies
1962	12	31	0
1963	15	39	4
1964	14	26	5

Those chiefly involved in each year were the Ministry of Justice and the Ministry of Finance. The former generated sixteen cases in 1962, eleven in 1963, and seventeen in 1964. The Ministry of Finance was the object of inquiry in twenty-five cases in 1962 and fifteen in both 1963 and 1964. The conduct of police and prosecutors was brought into question in nine of the 1962 cases, fifteen of the 1963 cases, and seventeen of the 1964 cases. The Ministry of Defence was involved during these three years in a total of twenty-four cases, and state prisons in thirteen. In 1964 no ministry (except Justice and Finance) or other administrative body gave rise to more than ten cases.

The types of problems dealt with in recent years have been summarized in Table III, which shows that the substantive content of official decisions is the largest single cause of serious complaint. This is especially noteworthy because the ombudsman system has sometimes been represented as necessary chiefly to control bad manners rather than bad judgment. In fact, as the figures below disclose, the administrators' judgment arouses far more controversy than does their behavior.[38] The second largest cause of serious complaint has been

[38] This is not a new development. Figures compiled by the Ombudsman for the years 1957–1960, inclusive, show in summary that 46.2 percent of all the cases taken up for investigation in that period related to official decisions, while only 6.3 percent had to do with official conduct. Hurwitz (note 30), at 21.

Table III. Nature of issues involved in cases determined after investigation

	1961	1962	1963	1964
General questions	11	14	10	10
Decision	56	49	53	58
Case handling	44	33	31	33
Delays	22	19	28	32
Behavior, statements, etc.	23	15	7	13
Civil service—appointment, discipline, wages, pension, etc.	18	22	22	24
Total	174	152	151	170

summed up by the term "case handling," which includes all aspects of administrative procedure, but excludes complaints about alleged slowness, which have been tabulated under the heading of "delays."

Civil servants as complainants. The final entry in the immediately preceding table, showing civil service disputes as a substantial ingredient of the Ombudsman's caseload, deserves particular attention.

When the ombudsman system was first proposed in Denmark, civil servants and their organizations were energetically opposed. Existing review mechanisms, they contended, provided ample protections against mistake. To create an overseer of public administration would be simply to invite harassment by cranks and malcontents. Ultimately, too, it might lead to debasing personnel safeguards that had, over the course of many years, created a professional, responsible, trustworthy Danish civil service envied by less favored countries.

When the ombudsman statute was enacted despite this opposition, it embodied clauses intended to mollify civil servants. Anonymous complaints were proscribed (Sec. 6) in order to lessen the risk of irresponsible accusations.[39] The new law also provided (Sec. 7) that a civil servant involved in a matter of interest to the Ombudsman "may always demand that the matter shall be referred to treatment under the provisions of the Civil Servants (Salaries and Pensions) Act,"

[39] The Ombudsman can still, if he elects, take up "on his own initiative" a matter reported to him anonymously. Experience has persuaded him, however, that the writers of anonymous complaints are almost invariably "crackpots."

which meant in effect that he could insist upon being investigated by the agency in which he served rather than by the Ombudsman.

This provision, added to the original bill upon the demand of civil service groups, has never been used. "In the beginning," the president of a major organization recently said, "we were suspicious. As a matter of fact, we were scared. But we have found that we were mistaken." Instead of fleeing from the Ombudsman, civil servants have fled to him. Many of their cherished "protections" had in fact not been legally enforceable through the ordinary courts, and Denmark has had no administrative court specially empowered to deal with personnel disputes. The Ombudsman's capacity to inquire into every type of official lapse was quickly seized upon by public servants who thought they had been ill treated by their superiors. Thus it has come to pass that over 13 percent of all the cases fully investigated by the Ombudsman in 1962, 1963, and 1964 involved controversies about personnel matters.[40] The share of his time devoted to this type of problem seems all the more remarkable when one recalls that the group from which the cases arise numbers only a little more than 100,000 in a population of 4,500,000.

Another aspect of the Ombudsman's relations to civil servants deserves mention. When the statute was being considered in 1954, many low-ranking public employees opposed it because they feared the Ombudsman's weight would fall mainly on them. They were the ones who met the public face to face. They were the ones, they thought,

[40] Many of these are petty. In 1962, for example, the Ombudsman criticized an administrative authority for having answered an employee's letter by telephone instead of in writing. And he criticized another body for not giving a civil servant a copy of an adverse report about his work, though the report had been shown him. Folketingets Ombudsmands Beretning for Året 1962, at 38, 51. A more serious matter arose during the same year when a highly ranked official (near retirement age) was removed from an important technical post on the ground of alleged incompetence. Without reference to the issue of competence, which was seriously controverted, the official seems to have been markedly incompatible with associates. He was finally released from his post, but on full pension. This was in the nature of an agreed settlement. His attorney has expressed belief that had the Ombudsman not been involved in the case, the official would simply have been discharged without pension. No appeal from that action would have been possible.

In one interesting case the Ombudsman concluded that a civil service employee had been discharged in violation of applicable regulations. Besides criticizing the administrative action, he recommended that the discharged employee be given free legal aid to sue for damages. This was done and a settlement was made out of court; the wrongfulness of the discharge was acknowledged and damages were paid. See Hurwitz (note 30), at 25–26.

against whom the public would complain, even when they were simply carrying out their standing orders. To avoid being involved in controversy, they forecast, many civil servants might refer matters to their superiors, thus delaying final action and destroying initiative at subordinate levels. These fears appear to have been wholly set at rest. The Ombudsman has declared that most complaints addressed to him have been made quite impersonally against the administrative organ concerned, rather than against individuals whether of high or low rank.[41] Many of the decisions in cases he has taken up for investigation have stated explicitly that while no basis has been found for criticizing the civil servant whose actions have been in question, the Ombudsman has nevertheless desired to comment on a general administrative practice that, in his view, should be revised for the future; thus he has taken pains to avoid blaming an individual official for following paths others have mapped for his use. The president of the largest civil servants' organization unequivocally concluded, during a recent conversation, that the possibility of a citizen's complaining to the Ombudsman has not deterred civil servants from exercising appropriate judgment in matters within their authority. "We thought," he said, "that inflexibility, uncritical insistence upon rules, bureaucratic rigidity, and efforts to obtain advance approval were going to increase after the Ombudsman had found a few occasions to criticize officials. But we have been proved wrong. The civil service in Denmark has had a good tradition and the Ombudsman has not weakened it."

Sources of complaint. The Ombudsman's annual reports identify agencies against which complaints have been made, but do not describe the complainants. Persons close to the Ombudsman have estimated that civil servants have initiated about 5 percent of all the cases received in recent years, that 10 percent of the complaints have come from persons in detention either before or after conviction of crime, that 5 percent of the complainants have been inmates in public institutions of one kind or another, and that attorneys have signed about 5 percent of the complaints and have perhaps prepared another 5 percent to which their clients' names have been attached. The remainder have come from "the public at large," without any significant occupational or geographical grouping that has been noted.

[41] Hurwitz (note 30), at 22.

The attorney's relationship to the Ombudsman's work warrants a few additional comments.

Spokesmen for the advocates' association, to which every Danish lawyer must belong, tended in 1964 to minimize the Ombudsman's significance. As one of them said, "He is chiefly concerned with petty problems that don't affect businessmen. When a businessman has a problem, his lawyer sends him to the right office in the right ministry, and that will take care of the problem without going to the Ombudsman." Another remarked: "From our point of view, the Ombudsman is valuable mainly because we lawyers can refer quarrelsome people to him and get them out of our own offices, where they take up a lot of time but produce few fees."

Other practitioners' comments suggest that these reactions may not be representative. Several prominent advocates, interviewed separately, described their own recourse to the Ombudsman in behalf of clients who remained dissatisfied with final administrative acts for which judicial review had been unavailable. All agreed that the Ombudsman's accessibility had diverted no clients from them, but had instead given lawyers an additional avenue of redress. One of them, indeed, expressed surprise upon being told that attorneys were not the chief source of the Ombudsman's business. He proceeded to describe cases filed by him in which the Ombudsman, without criticizing decisions previously rendered, had made "clarifying statements" the "clients found very satisfying and regarded as valuable for public relations purposes." In another instance an administrative determination adverse to the client had remained unmodified but had been quietly ignored by officials in future years, a result the attorney attributed to questions asked by the Ombudsman. Another lawyer, after recounting a somewhat similar case that had had a favorable outcome, added: "As a matter of fact, I have found that just having the Ombudsman reject a complaint, saying that he finds nothing to criticize, sometimes helps me with a client. It serves at least to persuade the client that we have done everything we can, and puts an end to what might otherwise be a continuing doubt."

While so narrow a sampling of professional experience permits no confident conclusions, evidence is at hand that alert members of the bar can and do use the Ombudsman advantageously.

The Ombudsman's staff. Constant reference to "the Ombudsman" might suggest to the unwary that he singlehandedly copes with all the problems referred to him. He does in fact utter the final word in each instance, but he has able assistance in preparing to do so.

The Ombudsman's staff consists of seven lawyers and five clerical employees. The present Chief of Office and a senior assistant have been associated with the Ombudsman from the first. Three junior staff members joined the office immediately upon receiving their law degrees. Two others were "borrowed" for three years from permanent posts elsewhere. The demand for lawyers is greater than the available supply in Denmark. Moreover, the salary scale of Danish government employees is not impressive. The demand for their services coupled with their low official salaries has induced many legally trained civil servants to hold more than one job. Sometimes both their jobs are in the public sector. Sometimes they work in an attorney's office or serve as counsel to a private organization. Most of the Ombudsman's assistants are nominally part-time employees because they have dual employment.[42] They seem nevertheless to work at a full-time pace.

Attachment to the Ombudsman's office is apparently regarded as a desirable assignment. A former chief of office has become a member of the High Court, and junior staff members have also moved on to attractive positions after service with the Ombudsman had given them broad exposure to governmental activities.

Staff conferences do not occur, nor do staff assistants generally have other direct associations with the Ombudsman. They consult the Chief of Office about difficult problems occasionally, but the Ombudsman's organization seemingly lacks informality and the personal touch despite its smallness. No doubt exists, however, about whose is the dominant personality at work in that establishment. The Ombudsman does not permit actions to be taken in his name. Even when he is on

[42] No rules have been laid down concerning possible conflicting interests arising from a staff member's dual employment. A few problems have in fact occurred, but have been disposed of informally. As for the Ombudsman himself, the governing statute (Sec. 12) forbids his holding any public or private office except with the consent of a Folketing committee; and the Parliamentary Directives (Art. 16) instruct him that if he "finds that a case involves circumstances which may give rise to doubt about his complete impartiality," he must inform the Folketing committee, which will then "decide who is to perform his functions."

vacation, papers must be sent to him by post for his consideration and personal signature.

Processing complaints. Each incoming complaint is passed to the Ombudsman personally as soon as it has been numbered and entered in the official register.[43] He may jot down brief directions in the margin, or point out some special aspect that has aroused his interest. The file then passes to the Chief of Office for another quick glance before being assigned to a staff member. Each staff assistant receives, in turn, all the cases registered during a calendar week, an average of about twenty. Specialization according to areas of governmental activity or types of complaint has not been encouraged.

Cases that are clearly not cognizable by the Ombudsman (such as those, for example, pertaining to judges or to private legal problems) are quickly disposed of, as are those the Ombudsman has decided not to investigate because their subject matter is unappealing. The staff member simply drafts a letter for the Ombudsman's signature, informing the complainant that the matter will not be pursued.

In many other instances, a telephone call to the agency concerned provides the basis for speedy action. Thus, for example, an agency may disclose that the complainant has not yet utilized his right of administrative appeal. In that event the Ombudsman may transmit the complaint to the agency (notifying the complainant that this has been done) or may advise the complainant to pursue the available remedies; the complaint to the Ombudsman will in either event be dismissed as premature.[44]

In other cases, a telephone call about a complaint against official lethargy may elicit information that the desired action has in fact already occurred; or it may reveal that the agency's non-action was caused by the complainant's failing to reply to the agency's request for additional data.

[43] A few complainants have chosen to present themselves at the Ombudsman's office without reducing their complaints to writing. The governing statute and the Parliamentary Directives do not flatly require complaints to be written, though the Directives do say (Art. 4) that they "should, as far as possible, be submitted in writing and be accompanied by the complainant's evidence."

[44] The Ombudsman infrequently requests that he be informed of the cognizant agency's action on a case he has referred to it. His annual reports have suggested several times that an administrative decision adverse to a private party should be routinely accompanied by information about appellate processes and other available remedies. The suggestion has not yet been widely accepted.

In all such matters, the staff member summarizes the complaint and the information he has informally obtained, proposes a suitable disposition of the case, and drafts a letter to the complainant for the Ombudsman's signature. The file then passes from the assistant to the Chief of Office and, if he approves, to the Ombudsman for final action.

Approximately half of all the complaints filed with the Ombudsman have been reviewed and finally disposed of in some such manner within a fortnight after their receipt.

Each staff assistant has full responsibility for developing the facts in the cases assigned to him. This may necessitate obtaining the official files bearing upon a complaint, but, more frequently, a simple informative statement is sought from the official or agency concerned in the complaint. When issues of fact are present, the agency's statement is usually sent to the complainant for his rejoinder, upon which the agency will in turn be given opportunity to comment. In these exchanges, the officials always have the last say. Occasionally complainants have been invited to come to the office for personal conference, but nothing in the nature of an adversary hearing or a confrontation of complainant and accused official has ever occurred. Though the statute (Sec. 7) gives the Ombudsman the power to draw upon judicial assistance in order to compel the giving of testimony and the production of evidence, no occasion has yet arisen for taking that step.

When written observations or documentation have been sought, responses to staff inquiries have usually been made within a month; if no reply has been received within two months, a second inquiry occurs routinely. Approximately 25 percent of the Ombudsman's cases have been closed in less than two months but in more than two weeks.

Most of the remaining cases have been decided between two and four months after filing, though some have dragged on for as much as a year, long after all the facts have been gathered, while discussions have proceeded about what recommendations should be made.

The individual staff members work with a considerable degree of independence and with opportunity to develop their own "contacts" within ministries, so that needed information can be speedily obtained. They are allowed to take far more initiative than their counterparts in other Scandinavian ombudsmen's office, though the final product of their labors remains entirely subject to approval by the Ombudsman, who may return a file with a request for more data or a completely fresh approach.

His decisions ordinarily take the form of a letter addressed to the complainant, restating the complaint, reviewing the facts found (and, when pertinent, the applicable legal principles), and announcing the Ombudsman's conclusion. Copies of the letter are sent as a matter of course to any official personally involved in the matter as well as to the administrative bodies concerned. If the conclusion contains a criticism or a proposal for the future, a covering letter particularly directs attention to it.

Troublesome cases. One especially troublesome type of case has consumed considerable staff energy while producing results of somewhat uncertain value. When inquiry has disclosed that a case is beyond his statutory competence or involves an indubitably legal though arguably unwise exercise of official discretion, the Ombudsman has nevertheless sometimes chosen to explain the complaint at length and to discuss its significance in such a manner as to disclose his opinion about the merits.[45] Several ministry officials expressed strongly adverse sentiments about the Ombudsman's indulgence in lengthy dicta. "He upsets us most," one spokesman asserted, "when he writes about something we have done, says he cannot criticize us for having done it, and then proceeds to criticize exactly the thing he said he had no power to criticize."

Substantial staff effort has been devoted, also, to cases cognizable by the courts though submitted instead to the Ombudsman as complaints against official determinations. Though every administrative remedy must be utilized before a complainant may turn to the Ombudsman,[46] the continuing availability of judicial review affects the Ombudsman's competence not at all. True, he will never consider a complaint concerning a matter already before a court, whether or not the court has yet reached a decision. And when the judges have spoken finally, he follows their lead. Often, however, complainants address

[45] For discussion and examples, see Christensen (note 4), at 1108.

[46] The Ombudsman may, however, take up a case on his own initiative at any stage of an administrative proceeding. Moreover, if a complaint has to do with official behavior or methods rather than with the content of the action taken by a subordinate official, it can be acted upon by the Ombudsman even though some administrative channel may remain open.

themselves to him instead of the courts simply in order to save time and expense. He cannot then slough off their complaints as untimely.

Still he must recognize that his conclusions are indecisive so far as they deal with legal questions. His interpretations of statutes defining administrative powers or prescribing administrative methods, for example, may be held erroneous if the same issues are subsequently brought before the courts. Quite properly reluctant to be overruled by later judicial decisions, the Ombudsman has pressed his staff to make thorough legal studies before recommending action.

His final actions in cases of this type have been diverse. Sometimes, when sufficiently confident, he has stated a flat judgment. Sometimes he has expressed a much more tentative belief, coupling this with a reminder that the matter is still open for judicial consideration and suggesting that the case be taken to court, at public expense if the complainant be needy.[47] Sometimes he has simply stated mildly that he is dubious about the administrative agency's authority to act as it has done, perhaps adding a suggestion that parliamentary clarification would be desirable.[48] Questions of ultra vires are rarely easy for the staff or for the Ombudsman. Often, when unable to come to a firm conclusion, he ends a discussion by "declaring that the question is doubtful and that it is for the courts to make the final decision."[49]

5|An Attempt to Appraise

A "cult of the personality" has grown during the incumbency in office of Stephan Hurwitz (though not by his choice). Expressions of doubt about the accomplishments of his office seem virtually to be attacks

[47] Article 6(2) of the Parliamentary Directives states that the Ombudsman may, if the subject matter of a complaint brings it within judicial reach, "give guidance to the complainant with that possibility in view," and if the complainant intends to commence a law suit against a public authority or official in respect of any matter within the Ombudsman's competence, the Ombudsman may in appropriate instances "recommend that the complainant be granted free legal aid."

[48] Specific examples of these various approaches to questions of legal authorization appear in Hurwitz (note 30), at 26–28; and see also Christensen (note 4), at 1113, 1117–1118.

[49] Hurwitz, "Scandinavian Ombudsman," 12 *Pol. Sci.* 121, 131 (1960).

upon the sacrosanct. This attempt to appraise the Danish Ombudsman must therefore be prefaced by the unusual statement that the appraisal is of an institution and not of a man.

Publications. The Ombudsman's relations with journalists have been cordial almost beyond belief. What he himself has characterized as "the extremely friendly attitude of the press"[50] has led to extensive newspaper coverage of his decisions. These have usually been described admiringly and have almost invariably been attributed to Professor Hurwitz by name, rather than to the Ombudsman as an official. He has consequently become very strongly identified in the public consciousness as a noble righter of wrongs. Even the Ombudsman's staff has been surprised by the enthusiasm with which relatively minor matters have been set forth in the daily press. Nobody with whom the matter was discussed in 1964 blamed Professor Hurwitz for the journalistic exuberance, but a number of sober observers, sympathizing with the Ombudsman's purposes and admiring his achievements, thought that publicity was sometimes almost too intense.

If any fault there be, it seems not to be the Ombudsman's. Danish law, unlike Sweden's, does not embody a "publicity principle" requiring that the Ombudsman lay bare to the public everything he officially knows.[51] The Ombudsman has taken advantage of his power not to name names, express alarm, and tell all every time a public servant lapses from absolute perfection.

Decisions have been announced with sufficient "blurring" (as one staff member put it) to protect both the complainant and the officials from needless personal embarrassment. An outstandingly able Danish judge, warning against regarding all promulgators of adverse discretionary decisions as "sinister power-seeking representatives of the New Despotism," has urged the public to realize that "even cases where administrative decisions are set aside or criticised are not necessarily evidence of bad faith or deliberate error. They ought, in the normal case, to be dealt with in the same spirit as when a judgment is set aside by an appellate court."[52] That seems clearly to be the Ombudsman's

[50] Hurwitz, "The Folketingets Ombudsmand," 12 *Parl. Aff.* 199, 208 (1959).

[51] Compare N. Herlitz, "Publicity of Official Documents in Sweden," [1958] *Pub. L.* 50.

[52] I. M. Pedersen, "The Parliamentary Commissioner," [1962] *Pub. L.* 15, 21, 23.

view. His press releases have been uninflammatory. They have had a personalized focus when this was necessary to make a point, as when the then head of the University of Copenhagen was criticized for evaluating his son-in-law's doctoral dissertation. But in the generality of cases the Ombudsman has dealt with problems, not with people.

The same is true of the annual reports to the Folketing. They are sober in tone. Individuals are often represented by an initial rather than by a patronymic. The cases that are discussed in detail are a conscientious sampling of the year's work and not a jungle of single instances amidst which the misguided or the malicious might pretend to find the seeds of scandal.[53]

Educational force of Ombudsman's work. The ombudsman institution is designed for educational as well as corrective purposes. Eliminating an isolated imperfection is a worthy objective, but the achievement becomes truly significant if the correction of one error induces avoidance of others. Since awareness of what the Ombudsman has done is a necessary precondition to its being powerfully influential, inquiry into the circulation of his opinions is appropriate here.

The favorable press relations described above have promoted dissemination of the Ombudsman's actions in colorful cases. The Ombudsman makes an effort, too, to reach specialized publications. Decisions particularly affecting the police forces are sent to the editor of a periodical circulated among policemen, and matters of interest to customs officers are similarly directed to a magazine devoted to that branch of public service. "Technical" and generalized issues remain to be studied, if they are to be studied at all, only in the pages of annual reports which appear in print in the autumn of the year after the one to which they pertain.

Until 1964, only 1,700–1,800 copies of the annual report were printed. In that year the number rose to 3,600 because, the Ombudsman's jurisdiction having been extended to certain municipal activities, the report was for the first time sent to every local council in Denmark. The mailing list includes the members of the Folketing, all sitting

[53] The 1963 report, for example, describes only forty-one cases at length; the 1964 report describes only thirty-five. Each annual report contains a comprehensive cumulative index covering all the reports since the first, so that the document becomes a useful research tool and source book for future reference, and not merely a record of transient interest.

judges, each ministry and administrative authority, every police chief, many high-ranking officials, and the top-level provincial administrators.

As every law professor well knows, students' attentiveness and receptivity are variables. Some minds seem impervious to even the most piercing professional thoughts. The Ombudsman, as educator of officialdom, sometimes similarly encounters mental impermeability that blocks the easy circulation of his ideas. His official writings are nevertheless widely and respectfully read. Supreme Court judges "almost always read each report carefully though it has no instant impact on our work"; a provincial governor reads "all the headlines in the report and, in depth, all the cases that bear on my own work, and I think that is what almost all superior civil servants do"; a copy goes to every unit in the Ministry of Justice, where it is circulated among approximately ten professional staff members for a perusal that "is not at all routine. The higher up you go in the ministry, the more carefully you read the Ombudsman's report"; in the Finance Ministry, "most high officials really read the reports and most academical civil servants [that is, those with university training, who constitute the corps of professional public officials] at least run through them."

The question then arises whether the lessons the reports attempt to teach are well learned by the report's readers. Some enthusiasts for ombudsmanism have given too easy an answer. They have contentedly supposed that whenever an ombudsman has spoken, all officials have listened. They have imagined that whatever an ombudsman has said should be done has in fact been done for evermore. The realities of life are different. The reformer's lot is not easy, and the Ombudsman is a would-be reformer.

The Ombudsman's work has indubitably had a tonic effect upon public administration. A number of administrators frankly acknowledge that laziness has diminished because during the past decade an outsider has been in a position to criticize. Work methods have in some instances been rationalized at the behest of superior officials, impressed by the Ombudsman's suggestions concerning other organizations. Moreover, staffs that had like aging humans become too "set in their ways" have sometimes been liberated from their bondage by the Ombudsman's fresh approach. The director of a maximum security prison, for example, gives the Ombudsman large credit for his staff's increased receptivity to proposed changes. "Some of our habits were justifiable only because they were easy. Then conservatism—reluctance to try anything different—made us look for other reasons to justify the existing practices. Now the staff is more likely to deal with the real merits of suggestions instead of resisting them simply because they are new," he said.[54] The head of another large organization commented in a somewhat similar vein: "The Ombudsman, coming from the outside, sometimes sees things that are perfectly obvious, but that we have stopped noticing because they are constantly before our eyes."

Despite the Ombudsman's generally wholesome influence, however, some of his triumphs are more apparent than real.

In one much publicized case seven years ago, for instance, the Ombudsman told the police they had no right to keep the fingerprint record of an arrested person who had subsequently been absolved. The Ombudsman's advice was taken in that particular instance; the fingerprints of the complainant were destroyed. But the police have nevertheless continued to take fingerprint impressions and to retain them whether or not the persons suspected have afterward been released as innocent. The Ombudsman's decision has had no lasting consequence beyond the case to which it pertained. "The matter is

[54] The staff's formerly resistant attitude first brought it into conflict with the Ombudsman in an extremely petty matter. A prison rule forbade smoking in workshops. To facilitate the rule's enforcement each prisoner was allowed to possess only one pipe, which had to be left in plain sight in the prisoner's cell when he was at work elsewhere. A prisoner complained to the Ombudsman. Himself an avid pipe-smoker who knew that a pipe loses its savor if too constantly in use, the Ombudsman counseled against restricting pipe ownership, saying that smoking in workshops could be prevented by other means.

Soon afterward prisoners complained that the prison commissary had rejected their request that powdered coffee be made available for sale; they desired to prepare coffee in their own cells at other than meal hours. The staff had voted against granting the request because hot water could not be made constantly available to the inmates. The Ombudsman deemed this unreasonable; he suggested, instead, that hot water be supplied at specified times when it was not needed for other institutional purposes and when most prisoners were in any event allowed to circulate outside their cells.

In a third episode a prisoner wrote the Ombudsman that bathing facilities were inadequately maintained, an objection that had apparently not seemed tenable to the staff members to whom it had first been voiced. When the prison director himself inspected the facilities after the Ombudsman had made an inquiry, he concluded that the complaint was indeed well founded. Suitable corrective steps were then promptly taken.

This succession of incidents, insignificant in themselves, apparently affected staff attitudes profoundly.

still under study," was the euphemistic reply of a high police official when recently asked whether the Ombudsman's opinion had affected police practices.

Similarly, the Ministry of Justice has resisted the Ombudsman's repeated urging that its adverse decisions be better explained, instead of being baldly stated conclusions as at present. Early in 1964 the Minister did at last appoint a committee to study the feasibility of adopting the Ombudsman's ideas.

Failure to formulate the reasons underlying an administrative judgment has been a prolific cause of complaint to the Ombudsman; often the Ombudsman's explanation of a previously incomprehensible decision has seemingly sufficed to make it acceptable.[55] In any event, whenever the Ombudsman has asked for elucidation of a determination concerning which he has received a complaint, the Ministry has had to articulate its reasoning and has been unable merely to say, as did an official during a recent interview, "Maybe ten things are involved at the same time; it isn't easy to explain just what each of them contributed to the final result; judgment is more subjective than objective." Sooner or later every ministry encounters what Julius Stone calls the insistence that "even logically uncompelled choices are to be made with reasons publicly examinable."[56] The Ministry of Justice appears to a foreigner to have been unduly slow to heed the Ombudsman's

[55] See Hurwitz (note 30), at 20: "Since in many instances the administration gives no reasons for its decisions, and since the complainant does not often have sufficient knowledge of the basis for the decision in question he often does not understand it. In many instances, by giving a detailed explanation of the whole matter, it has been possible for the Parliamentary Commissioner to make the complainant understand that the treatment of the case and the decision taken, gives no occasion for criticism."

And see also I. M. Pedersen, "The Danish Parliamentary Commissioner in Action," [1959] *Pub. L.* 115, 121: "Quite often it is very difficult for [applicants] to grasp the principles behind the exercise of discretion especially if the subject is complicated and highly technical. In such circumstances a quick answer and a politely worded letter giving detailed reasons for the decision may not reconcile an applicant to an adverse decision, but it may lessen his irritation considerably and convince him that his case has been given careful attention. And as conditions of modern life seem to necessitate an ever-expanding administration it becomes increasingly important to establish good relations between officials and the public."

[56] J. Stone, "Reasons and Reasoning in Judicial and Juristic Argument," 18 *Rutgers L. Rev.* 757, 769 (1964).

The Ministry of Social Affairs has, alone among the ministries, been under statutory command for the past thirty years to state the reasons for its decisions in a major area of administrative activity. A spokesman for that ministry described the requirement as "burdensome," but added his belief that the decisions are better because of the necessity of formulating reasons.

counsel about giving explanatory statements. But the fact remains that the Ministry dragged its heels (rather than clicked them) after the Ombudsman had spoken.

A similar intransigence appeared when the Ombudsman recommended that reports of police investigations into traffic accidents be readily shown to the persons involved, as is done in some but not all localities. The Ministry of Justice rather brusquely replied that it had considered the suggestion, but saw no reason to change existing practices. The matter remained under negotiation for several years while the Ombudsman unsuccessfully sought acceptance of his views.[57]

Repeated suggestions that administrative agencies provide fuller information about their internal procedures, so that the availability of appellate opportunities might become better understood, have generated few if any discernible advances. This has been one of many procedural proposals put forward by the Ombudsman, who has been especially keen to maintain a high level of rectitude in administrative practices. His ideas in the field seem eminently sound; his efforts to create, as it were, a common law of administrative procedure deserve applause.[58] But administrators, when asked pointblank whether their own methods had been changed, often responded simply (though not persuasively) that the Ombudsman's suggestions were not pertinent to their agencies' proceedings.

Sometimes, of course, change comes slowly, not in a sudden rush. Perhaps, therefore, the enduring influence of the Ombudsman's proposals can not yet be fully gauged, for some that have seemed to have narrow effects may in fact gain added support as time passes. An administrative procedure act of 1964 embodies two ideas adumbrated by the Ombudsman's criticisms in previous years, and possibly those criticisms hastened the new enactment.

[57] The matter is discussed in the Ombudsman's annual reports for 1961 (at 152–154), 1962 (at 15–16), and 1963 (at 14).

[58] Pedersen (note 56), at 117–120, points out that Danish administrative law has laid down few procedural rules to guide administrators. Among the Ombudsman's contributions in this field, the author notes, have been criticizing (1) an agency counsel's failure to disclose documents in the case file; (2) a tax board's entering an adverse decision without affording opportunity for argument; (3) use of ex parte evidence; (4) an appellate board member's sitting in review of a decision in which he had participated at a lower level; (5) advising about processing auto drivers' license suspension cases; (6) suggesting that applicants be informed of the cause of delay in acting on their cases; (7) proposing that an unsuccessful license applicant be advised that denial of the license may be judicially reviewable.

Candor requires the statement, nevertheless, that until the present many of the Ombudsman's suggestions have been unproductive. While his proposals for legislative development (growing out of his consideration of particular cases) have not been ignored, some have been shelved without action. The Ombudsman has on the whole been rather unpugnacious when his advice has been unheeded. He has said that if one of his recommendations is not adopted and if he "feels that it is of appreciable importance that a change or correction be made," he can then "report the matter to Parliament which may take up the question with the Minister responsible."[59] In fact he has almost never sought to enlist parliamentary support when agreement has not been negotiable. One may speculate that the reasons are twofold: first, that he has been unsure of winning; second, that he has concluded that cooperative relationships with the major administrative organs will in the end bring more victories than would a heavily wielded bludgeon.[60]

Since nobody enjoys being worsted, the Ombudsman exercises a fairly cautious judgment about getting into fights he will probably lose. An especially astute Danish observer, discussing instances of nonconformity with the Ombudsman's proposals, made this concluding comment: "The Ombudsman is a devoted man, acting without partisan bias, neither for nor against the government in power. But at the same time he exercises what you might call a political judgment about what the ministries and civil servants will take from him. His work would fail if they did not, at bottom, support it. Knowing that, he does not go very far up paths they are unwilling to follow. The reason you do not find more cases of non-compliance than you do is that the Ombudsman does not often give advice unless he believes it will likely be taken."

The Ombudsman's big reach. The remark just quoted suggests that the Ombudsman prudently conserves his powers of persuasion. It should not be read, however, as an intimation that the Ombudsman

[59] Hurwitz (note 30), at 11. The governing statute provides (Sec. 10) that if the Ombudsman "informs the Folketing . . . of a case, or if he brings up a case in his annual report, he shall, in such information or in his report, state what the person concerned has pleaded by way of defence."

[60] His attitude in this respect, one may note in passing, has caused confusion or uneasiness in some quarters. A high official of a teachers' union, for example, declared that his organization regarded the Ombudsman as "Ministry-minded." It would therefore not have recourse to him if access to the courts were possible, despite the expense involved in seeking judicial redress.

has been timid. As a matter of fact, some doubt may be expressed as to whether he has not undertaken to do too much rather than too little. He has, for example, sometimes come close to entering into competition with the Organization and Methods Office of the Finance Ministry, an internationally known body whose aid has been widely sought to improve the internal structures of governmental agencies. If what is needed is simple advice that an official should maintain a record of cases in his office to enable him to detect undue delays (advice given not long ago to a branch of the Education Ministry), the matter no doubt lies within the "common sense" competence of a generalist like the Ombudsman. If more searching investigations of organization or methods seems desirable, perhaps the Ombudsman should not make them himself (as he has done),[61] but should instead call upon the specialized staff agency created for just such purposes. In one instance he approached doing so; the Ombudsman proposed to a Minister that a study be made of a subordinate unit, the Minister requested the Organization and Methods Office to do the job, and the study was successfully completed.

Another staff agency with which the Ombudsman has almost competed is the Revision Department, an examiner of official accounts that reports to the Folketing concerning the propriety of all expenditures of public funds. Upon complaint of the Royal Danish Automobile Club the Ombudsman allowed himself to be drawn into a long-simmering controversy about the propriety of spending certain motor taxes (the "road millions," as they had become popularly known) for purposes unrelated to automobile traffic. The matter had already been extensively discussed in the Folketing and the issue seemed, in any event, entirely suitable for consideration by the Revision Department. Undaunted, the Ombudsman proceeded to study the merits, concluding that no criticism by him was in this instance suitable. Had he reached the contrary conclusion, confusion and conflict would have been the most likely products of his labor. Since the Ombudsman is empowered

[61] Compare Hurwitz (note 30), at 30: The Ombudsman has not only investigated complaints about delay, "but has also undertaken a more detailed investigation of the whole system for the dispatch of current business in that office, with a view to the possibility of achieving a reduction in the time usually involved, by changes in the methods hitherto followed in the disposition of such business. As a rule these investigations have resulted in a recommendation from the [Ombudsman] to the responsible Minister suggesting that an attempt be made to implement the necessary changes in method or system."

to look into the actions of all "persons acting in the service of the State," no doubt he can concern himself with officials' disbursements of public moneys. Since, however, a professional agency exists for that specific task, his undertaking the assignment may be a misapplication of energy.

Overextension may unfortunately be an inherent element of the ombudsman system. Those who vaunt the system greatly stress the importance of the Ombudsman's personality and his directly participating in every phase of official superintendence. This emphasis upon personalism may discourage the Ombudsman's using other governmental resources, lest he seem to have adopted "bureaucratic methods" and to be "passing the buck." In plain fact, however, a single official, aided only by a handful of assistants, cannot encompass all of organized society's problems. Ombudsmen everywhere tend to stretch themselves as close as possible to the unrealistic limits fixed by uninformed public desire. While unwillingness to stretch at all would be deplorable, willingness to stretch too far has its perils, too.

A problem of Danish public administration may perhaps serve illustratively. Child welfare programs of every kind are locally and somewhat inexpertly administered in Denmark. While the Ministry of Social Affairs is at the apex of the governmental pyramid, its involvement in decisional processes is sporadic and its superintendence of a traditionally communal activity has not been insistently firm. In recent years the methods of local bodies and various other aspects of child care have attracted the Ombudsman's interest. He has been in no position, however, to make the extensive surveys that might yield full insight into the problems of this branch of public administration. Improving the organization, standards, and procedures of child care agencies lay beyond his capabilities realistically, because in the nature of things his contributions would perforce be episodic rather than comprehensive.

At hand for possible use in matters of this nature is a tax supported institution—the Socialforskningsinstituttet, or Social Research Institute—specifically designed to conduct field researches and make empirical studies. This organization, staffed by persons with civil service status on the Ministry of Social Affairs' payroll but having its own independent board of directors, can function as a national bureau of applied social research or, perhaps one might even say, as a social ombudsman. When resources like this fortunately exist, the Ombudsman might be well advised to use them rather than rely chiefly on his own capacity to draw valid general conclusions from sometimes extremely limited data.

Despite the breadth of his initial jurisdiction—which, it will be recalled, embraced every phase of national administration, military as well as civil, other than the judiciary—the Ombudsman has sought to add to his domain. He has been somewhat dissatisfied with the 1962 statutory grant of limited power to oversee local administration; probably his authority in that respect will be further enlarged in the course of time. In 1964 he became enmeshed in controversy with the legal profession because he had entertained complaints against lawyers who had been designated and paid by the Ministry of Justice to serve impecunious clients. In his view they were "persons acting in the service of the State" and therefore within the Ombudsman's reach. He even intimated that lawyers as a class might be regarded as suitable objects of his concern since they perform a public function with a status derived from law. Discussion between the Ombudsman and the chairman of the Bar Association produced a retreat but not a complete surrender. The Ombudsman did agree that future complaints should in the first instance be handled by the Bar Association and he did withdraw any pretense of present jurisdiction over the entire profession.[62]

[62] A letter from the Ombudsman to the Advokatrådet, dated June 10, 1964, reads in part as follows: "At a meeting with the chairman . . . we agreed upon the following lines concerning the Ombudsman's jurisdiction over lawyers:

"We agreed to avoid bringing the question to a head, but to consult one another if doubtful issues arise.

"From my point of view it was essential to seek agreement that the Ombudsman could sometimes be of assistance in dealing with complaints against the conduct of lawyers who had been designated to render free legal aid to clients.

"If such cases arise hereafter, the Ombudsman will in each instance refer the complaint to Advokatrådet, with a request to be informed about what is then done in that matter. Should problems emerge that seem suitable for special discussion, this can be arranged at the time.

"As for the conduct of members of Advokatrådet in general, I am willing to disclaim jurisdiction (as, in fact, has been the actual practice in the past), but I should nevertheless like to be informed about Advokatrådet's attitude toward complaints that may arise, so that I may be in a position to initiate negotiations with Advokatrådet if special reasons appear.

"These understandings should eliminate the possibility of future conflict, but each question that may arise can be taken up for negotiation if the circumstances of a particular case warrant."

What the Ombudsman does best. The Ombudsman's greatest effectiveness appears in cases that involve departures from accepted norms, and not in cases where he must deal with clashes of values. He can usefully dispose of dissatisfactions engendered by an official's having strayed from common patterns of rightful conduct. Such cases, important though they may be to the persons immediately concerned, are likely to have petty dimensions.[63] They touch individuals and not society in the broad. In a sense, the Ombudsman is at his best when, like an American labor arbitrator, he deals with concrete grievances involving a claimed disregard of established rights. When cases lose personal focus, when they involve the community, the Ombudsman's touch is far more tentative and the chance of producing a concrete result is greatly lessened.[64]

63 Examples taken at random from the Ombudsman's report for 1962: (1) A disabled person applied in January for special public assistance in order to obtain a telephone. A favorable decision on his application was made in March, but was not communicated to him until June, negotiations between the public authority and the telephone company having meanwhile occurred. The Ombudsman thought that the time lapse was in this instance justifiable, but that the applicant should have been more speedily informed about what was happening (p. 38). (2) A prisoner complained that money taken from his cell so that the police could investigate whether he had gained it legally, had not been returned to him until nine months after the police investigation had in fact ended without producing any evidence of illegality. The Ombudsman said that the prisoner's property should have been returned more promptly, and the police apologetically agreed (p. 30). (3) An institutional employee had made a written request that had been forwarded by her immediate superiors to the ministry concerned. The ministry made a negative response to the request. The employee was informed of this by telephone. She complained to the Ombudsman that she was entitled to have a written rejoinder to her written letter. The Ombudsman agreed (p. 38).

64 The 1962 report provides a good example at 52. Professor Steen Eiler Rasmussen, one of Denmark's leading authorities in the field of city planning, complained to the Ombudsman that Copenhagen had not been forced to adopt suitable plans, as required by law, for developing the Slotsholmen area, in which are located the parliament building, the stock exchange, and many public offices and in which a new governmental office structure had been commenced. Contending also that the Ministry of Housing could not impartially review decisions of the Copenhagen municipal authority concerning state-owned sites, he urged that such decisions be referred to an external board of experts. The Ombudsman wrote a long essay on the history of city planning laws and their administration in Denmark, reviewed the literature on the subject, found long-standing discord between law and practice, concluded that he could not criticize the absence of planning for Slotsholmen, and requested the Minister of Housing to broaden the terms of reference to an already existing study committee so that it might consider how area planning should be done. As for the suggestion that the Ministry of Housing should give way to some other appellate body, the Ombudsman engaged in a political science discussion, concluding that inevitably the State may have a proprietary interest in matters that must in the end

Estimates of the Ombudsman's success. In the manageably narrow cases—the ones that involve applying accepted principles to unclear facts and the ones in which a sage jurist can enunciate new principles that commend themselves so quickly that they seem to have been accepted already as "natural justice"—the Ombudsman's work seems to have been almost spectacularly successful from the standpoint of citizen and official alike.

"The Ombudsman is squeezing the arrogance out of government," said a prominent social scientist. "Decisions are quicker all down the line," said an attorney. "The Ombudsman is a safety valve and all of us feel more satisfied than we did before," said the head of a major women's organization. "The civil service exercises power more justly, it is prompter, its methods are fairer," said a business leader.

"The Ombudsman has done us a lot of good. The public is likely to accept his decision and to stop grumbling at us after he has upheld us, as he does most of the time," said a ministry official who is also an official of a superior civil servants' union. "We have about 20,000 cases a year here, and there is bound to be some dissatisfaction with decisions. The Minister personally interviews complainants one day each week, seeing about twenty of them on each of those days. We all work hard on complaint cases, and still the dissatisfaction remains. Then people go to the Ombudsman, whom they regard as sitting on top of all the ministries. He gives his opinion and that's the end of the matter. Everybody seems to be satisfied once he has spoken," said an official in a second ministry. "Some persons have come in here again and again and have gone away without ever feeling they had received justice. Then they want to know where else to go and we suggest the Ombudsman. He makes a decision, maybe exactly the same as ours, but they respect him and accept what he says as just and as final," said yet a third ministry official.

Since remarks like these, uttered with obvious sincerity by both private persons and public servants, are commonplace and since contrary sentiments are simply not heard, perhaps they should be accepted

---

be decided by public authorities of one kind or another, but the authorities should not be deemed incapable of making just decisions on that account.

One's imagination staggers at the thought of the Ombudsman's deciding otherwise than he did. He could not singlehandedly remake Copenhagen or supplant one appellate authority by another that would have to be endowed with powers not yet in existence.

unhesitatingly. Their rather intangible underpinnings do nevertheless raise tiny uncertainties. For example, the business leader quoted above had never heard of a businessman who had turned to the Ombudsman; he personally knew nobody of any description who had done so; and he could not think of a single thing that might in any way serve to illustrate the asserted improvements in civil servants' justice, promptitude, or methods. The governmental spokesmen who say that the Ombudsman's words transform malcontents into cooing doves have no evidence of this fact other than that complainants fall silent. This quietude, for all anyone surely knows, may reflect despairing realization by still disgruntled passengers that they have reached the end of the line without yet arriving where they had wanted to go.

In the absence of any scientific sampling of the opinions of unsuccessful complainants, estimates like those quoted above may be accepted. But they remain only estimates until confirmed by fuller evidence than is now available.

An outsider, scantily acquainted with Denmark, is poorly situated to offer a confident evaluation of what the Danish Ombudsman has accomplished. A few diffident impressions are, however, offered in conclusion.

First, ombudsmanship works in small ways its wonders to perform. Too exalted expectations are a disservice to the institution. The Ombudsman can be important without constantly dealing with important matters, just as judges are important though they deal chiefly with picayune conflicts. An Ombudsman's accomplishments are likely to be interstitial. He cannot create a solid structure of public administration. He can only do a bit of patching and sewing of minor rents in a basically sound fabric.

Second, the Ombudsman's greatest role is that of teacher rather than governor. He does not command. He persuades. Like most teachers, he will have to repeat his lessons often for the benefit of the slow learners; and even then some of his pupils will fail to absorb them. In any event, he cannot perform the work of an entire faculty. He succeeds as he does in Denmark because that country's civil servants have many other good teachers, notably their own colleagues and the high traditions of Danish officialdom.

Third, the Ombudsman should not be viewed as an acceptable substitute for parliamentary or ministerial responsibility. Because he is so readily identifiable, so embraceable as a kind of father-figure, some of his countrymen may call upon him for too large tasks of statesmanship; and, being devoted to rendering public service, he may be tempted to respond. The broad contours of public administration—how much power is to be conferred, for what purposes, upon whom, to be exercised by what means—are primarily questions for political determination. No matter how able an ombudsman may be, no matter how venerated he may be by the public, he cannot supplant the political processes that in the end control the administration of public affairs.

No panacea for the cure of governmental ills exists. The greatest injustice to the Ombudsman would be to regard him as the possessor of a cure-all.

|two|

Finland

To their own great loss, Americans are scantily acquainted with the friendly people and delightful scenery of Finland. Despite Finland's geographical and cultural remoteness, however, students of government in the United States have become increasingly curious about that small country's long experience with nonjudicial watchmen against governmental aberrations.[1] Knowledge of Finland's experience may assist others' searches for simplified safeguards against official mistakes and misdeeds.[2]

[1] "Small country" is, of course, only a relative term. Finland's area is larger than that of New York, New Jersey, all the New England states, and Maryland in combination, or than that of Eire, Scotland, Wales, and England together. Almost a tenth of its surface is covered by lakes, however, and part of its territory is in the as yet unproductive Far North. The population totals only about four and a half million, of whom roughly half a million live in the largest city, Helsinki. The next two largest cities in the nation have populations of a bit less than 150,000.

[2] Finnish experience has not been much discussed in English language publications. The main papers are P. K. Kastari, "The Parliamentary Ombudsman; His Functions, Position, and Relation to the Chancellor of Justice in Finland," 28 *Int. Rev. Admin. Sc.* 391 (1962), and "The Chancellor of Justice and the Ombudsman," in D. C. Rowat, ed., *The Ombudsman: Citizen's Defender* 83–113 (1965); D. C. Rowat, "Finland's Defenders of the Law: The Chancellor of Justice and the Parliamentary Ombudsman," 4 *Canadian Public Administration* 361, 412 (1961). See also B. Chapman, *The Profession of Government* 245–259 (1959); S. V. Anderson, "The Scandinavian Ombudsman," 12 *American-Scandinavian Rev.* 403 (1964). In 1965 the Ombudsman's office itself published an informative booklet, *The Position and Functions of the Finnish Parliamentary Ombudsman.* For general background material, see V. Merikoski, *Précis du Droit Public de la Finlande* (1954).

1 | A Page or Two of History

Finland, for six centuries a part of the realm of Sweden, was ceded to the Russian Empire in 1809. Accorded the special status of grand duchy within the empire, it continued to have its own laws, its own autonomous administration, and its own state church. The Czar, an autocratic ruler in Russia itself, was simply the Grand Duke of Finland and thus subject to constitutional restrictions as had been the King of Sweden previously.

Somewhat ironically, the people of Sweden wrought major changes in their constitution almost at the moment when Finland ceased being directly governed by it. The discarded and outmoded terms of the Swedish Constitutional Acts of 1772 and 1789 were nevertheless carried over into the new Grand Duchy of Finland. They provided the framework of government until more than a century later, when Finland's national independence was granted by the Russian Bolsheviks.

One of the Swedish institutions that continued in the Grand Duchy was the office of Chancellor of Justice. In origin the Chancellor was a royal appointee, charged with the responsibility of overseeing the King's servants. In time he became the chief prosecutor, commanded by his royal master to ferret out faithless officials. Although in Sweden the importance of this post declined after 1809,[3] it flourished in Finland with no change in powers or responsibilities despite acquiring the title of Procurator, by which a similar office was known in Russia.

Unable to resist engulfment by physical force, Finns sought to keep their Russian overlords in place by insistently strict observance of legality in all governmental relationships. The basic laws to which such devoted attention was paid had not been particularly enlightened or well designed in the first place, nor had they been improved by age. But they did have the great virtue of being known quantities, not subject to change without notice by czarist fiat. Watchfulness against disregard of the old laws fostered what Jan-Magnus Jansson, a leading Finnish political scientist, recently characterized as a kind of antiquarian spirit among Finland's lawyers. Although this antiquarianism

[3] See Chap. 5. Compare S. Rudholm, "The Chancellor of Justice," in Rowat, ed., *The Ombudsman* 17.

may not have opened the doors to the future, it did help to keep them closed against the loss of political autonomy.

During the decades immediately preceding World War I the Russian government exerted great pressures to end Finland's privileged position within the empire. A few Chancellors of Justice and local judges withstood those pressures. They heroically obstructed the enforcement of "imperial legislation" they considered incompatible with the Grand Duchy's basic laws. The jurists' intractability proved to be perhaps the main impediment to easy realization of czarist plans. Pertinacious scrutinizing of legal questions became, indeed, almost a patriotic obligation in the troubled days when encroachment upon the laws might have been the prelude to ethnic subjugation. Legal technicalities often frustrated, though they could never entirely block, the mighty and increasingly hostile government of the Czar.

That period left its stamp on now independent Finland. Legal precision, perhaps at first merely a tactic, has become a firm national policy, an ingrained habit, almost an obsession for whose perpetuation Finland's official watchmen are responsible.

Finland's independence did not alter the position of the Chancellor of Justice. The new government simply restored the ancient title and changed the personnel; the first post-Russian appointee traveled to his job all the way from Siberia, where he had been exiled some years previously for resisting the authority of a Russian incumbent. When a constitution was later adopted in 1919, it not only preserved the Chancellor's office substantially as it had been, but also created the parallel office of Parliamentary Ombudsman, to perform much the same work and with many of the same powers. History and tradition had linked the Chancellor with the Government, that is, with the executive branch. Henceforth a separate guardian against executive misdeeds was to be at the legislature's disposal.

2 | Choosing the Watchmen

Manner of appointment. The President alone appoints the Chancellor, "who must possess a mastery of the Law."[4] He serves until retirement

[4] Finland Const. Art. 37.

unless the President removes him sooner for the good of the nation, an eventuality that has not yet arisen. The Chancellor himself can be prosecuted if he exercises his functions "in a manner contrary to law."[5]

Parliament alone chooses the Ombudsman, who is required only to be "a person distinguished in law."[6] He is elected by simple majority vote to serve for four years. During that term he is irremovable; moreover, no provision has been made for prosecuting him were he to misuse his office. When his four-year term ends, Parliament may shunt him aside, as has occurred twice since World War II.

The watchmen's powers. The Chancellor "must see that authorities and officials comply with the law and perform their duties so that no person shall suffer injury to his rights."[7] The Ombudsman, conformably with Parliament's instructions, "shall supervise the observance of the laws in the proceedings of courts and other authorities."[8] The Chancellor "shall have the right to assist at the sessions of the Council of State [that is to say, the Cabinet] and those of all tribunals and public departments, and he shall have access to the minutes of the Council of State and its Ministries, of the tribunals and other public authorities."[9] The Ombudsman "shall have the same right as the Chancellor of Justice to assist at the sessions of the Council of State and of tribunals and other public departments, to have access to the minutes of the Council of State, and its Ministries, of the tribunals and other authorities."[10] The Chancellor and the Ombudsman receive the same high salary, equal to that of the presidents of the Supreme Court and the Supreme Administrative Court. If the President were to decide that a member of the Cabinet should be tried before the Court of Impeachment, the Chancellor would serve as prosecutor; if the Parliament were to make the same decision, the Ombudsman would carry out the prosecution. If the President or a member of the Supreme Court or the Supreme Administrative Court were to be impeached, either the Chancellor or the Ombudsman could prosecute.

This careful matching of Tweedledum with Tweedledee does finally come to an end, however. The Chancellor is declared to be the

[5] Finland Const. Art. 47.
[6] Finland Const. Art. 49.
[7] Finland Const. Art. 46.
[8] Finland Const. Art. 49.
[9] Finland Const. Art. 46.
[10] Finland Const. Art. 49.

"Supreme Public Prosecutor" with responsibility for supervising all prosecutors throughout the Republic.[11] On the other hand, the Ombudsman is instructed to prosecute an impeached Chancellor,[12] while the Chancellor has no similarly explicit authority to proceed against the Ombudsman.

The watchmen's prestige. Despite the close resemblances just noted, the Chancellor's prestige has undoubtedly exceeded the Ombudsman's. His office is the older and more glamorous, for the Ombudsman never enjoyed the status of popular hero as the Chancellor occasionally did in Russian times. Once appointed, the Chancellor serves continuously despite changes in the country's political complexion. Superficially, therefore, he seems less tinctured by partisanship than is the Ombudsman, whom a vociferously partisan assemblage elects quadrennially.[13] As a newcomer during the early days of the Finnish republic, the Ombudsman modestly remained inconspicuous and, consequently, was largely overlooked by a public already accustomed to turn to the Chancellor for protection. Though entitled to attend Cabinet meetings, the Ombudsman refrained from doing so, while the Chancellor rather ostentatiously kept close watch over the highest governmental circles. Generally the Chancellor has come from the Supreme Administrative Court or the Supreme Court and sometimes has returned to his former tribunal to be its president. The Ombudsman, by contrast, has typically been drawn from a slightly lower level of professional attainment, since the short term of his office makes it unattractive to professors, judges of the highest rank, and similarly secure persons. On several occasions the then incumbent Ombudsman has welcomed appointment to the Supreme Administrative Court. This has been regarded as a promotion because, though the Court's members have a smaller income, their tenure is assured. One unusually

[11] Finland Const. Art. 46.

[12] Parliamentary Directives §4.

[13] Usually two names are put forward to be voted upon in Parliament. No all-party consensus is sought before the balloting begins. The vote is taken in closed session, but, according to informed observers, the requisite majority is quickly obtained because voting proceeds on party lines, though party activists have been shunned as nominees.

In the beginning, the election of the Ombudsman was an annual affair. The term of office was lengthened first to three years and, more recently, to four in an effort to enhance the efficiency of the office and de-emphasize the Ombudsman's dependence on the electors' favor.

successful Ombudsman resigned in order to accept a professorship of law, but most have had to be content with lesser distinctions when leaving that post.

The ranking of the two offices may possibly change. The Chancellor seems less venerated today than in the past. His close ties with the Government may taint his independence, or at least be thought to do so. Moreover, his role as the Government's legal counsel may close his mind to questions that may later arise concerning the validity of governmental actions. A former Chancellor, remarking that no ministry had ever rejected his advice, added candidly that his advice might not have been relied on so completely if his opinions had vacillated. Realization of that fact, he acknowledged, had handicapped him somewhat when a citizen later asked him to deal with what the citizen regarded as an illegal act. "If the act had been done in accord with advice I had given, I was not eager to find anything wrong with it afterward," he admitted. The Ombudsman is not similarly inhibited, simply because governmental proposals are not discussed with him at an early stage as they are with the Chancellor.

Whatever may be the popularity rating of their respective offices now or in the future, the Chancellor and Ombudsman in 1966 were considerably respected and concededly non-political. The Chancellor, Jaakko Enajarvi, had earned the high regard of lawyers during his fifteen years as a member of the Supreme Court. The Ombudsman, Risto Leskinen, after substantial judicial experience, had headed the law preparation division of the Ministry of Justice and, on a part-time basis, had been secretary of the Constitutional Committee of Parliament. Members of Parliament, favorably impressed by his work, sought him out to be Ombudsman when a vacancy occurred. He is well liked within the legal profession, one of whose chief spokesmen described him as "an able general specialist."

3 | Relationship to the Executive

Executive organization. Defining Finland's governmental system in a few words is not easy. Most functions of administration are lodged in ministries headed by Cabinet ministers, individually and collectively answerable to Parliament. At the same time administrative tasks are performed by a number of central offices and boards that are outside the official hierarchy of the ministries, though ultimately answerable to the Cabinet or to a minister and, through that channel, to Parliament. Finally, the nation's President is elected for a fixed term and his continuance in office is therefore not dependent upon parliamentary support. His position has gained in stature over the years, at least partly because cabinets have been short-lived, no party having won an absolute majority of the seats since 1917.[14] He has power under the Constitution to issue decrees not inconsistent with acts of Parliament, and he is directed to "supervise the administration of the State."[15] In exercising his powers the President must act in consultation with the Cabinet, but is not legally bound by its views.

Pre-auditing questions of legality. All proposals to be acted upon by the Cabinet, whether upon the initiative of the President or of a minister, are submitted to the Chancellor and to the Ombudsman for their prior scrutiny. The Ombudsman would like to take seriously his duty and opportunity to consider the legality of proposed decrees, regulations, and legislative suggestions; but, to be blunt, in this respect he is not taken seriously by others. He receives the agenda only forty-eight hours in advance of the meeting at which decisions are to be made, thus having scant opportunity for thorough study of the tens and sometimes hundreds of items on the agenda.

The Chancellor, on the other hand, really does play an important part at this stage. Although he receives the official agenda just as tardily as the Ombudsman does, ministerial officials who are responsible for preparing papers for Cabinet consideration—or, often, only for their own minister's decision—consult him well in advance concerning troublesome questions. His opinions and suggestions have tremendous weight. Proposals about whose legality he has expressed doubt are simply withdrawn for further study. He has no voice in shaping policy, but of course questions of law cannot always be neatly separated from questions of policy. When the Chancellor does unequivocally declare that the law stands in the path of a proposal, even

[14] In the first forty-five years after independence was gained in 1917, Finland had forty-seven cabinets. J.-M. Jansson, "A Century of Finnish Government," in *Introduction to Finland* 42, 54 (1963).

[15] Finland Const. Art. 32.

the President must pay heed to his counsel.[16] While the Ombudsman has not attended a meeting of the Council of State since 1923, the Chancellor or his Deputy is present at every session, not as a member of the Cabinet with the right to vote, but as a legal censor who sits slightly apart and who expresses his disapproval of the conclusions reached by the Cabinet or the President if he regards them as indisputably unconstitutional.

Legal flexibility has been achieved by the ingenious Finnish device of constitutional "exceptions." A legislative proposal the Chancellor regards as inconsistent with the Constitution need not be abandoned. Instead, it can be submitted to the Parliament for adoption by a special vote, in the same manner as an amendment to the Constitution. So far as is known, the Cabinet has never ignored the Chancellor's advice to proceed by way of an "exception," which has the effect (if Parliament acquiesces) of bypassing the Constitution on an ad hoc basis without permanently altering it.[17] Approximately six hundred laws have been enacted by the special "constitutional procedure" since 1919; some of these have involved such basically important matters as the mode of presidential election during the years of World War II and the legislative delegation of broad powers in times of crises.[18]

[16] Finland Const. Article 45 provides: "If it should happen that a decision taken by the President and to be executed by the Council of State is found to be contrary to law, the Council, after hearing the opinion of the Chancellor of Justice, shall request the President to withdraw or modify his decision, and, if the President nevertheless adheres to his decision, the Council must declare that the decision cannot be enforced."

Finland Const. Article 47 states in part: "If in the exercise of their functions the Council of State or any of its members act in a manner contrary to law, it is incumbent upon the Chancellor of Justice to make representation upon the subject and at the same time indicate in what respect the act is illegal. If no heed is taken of such representation, the Chancellor of Justice shall have his opinion recorded in the minutes of the Council of State, and he shall also have the right to advise the President of the matter. If the illegality is of such a nature as to involve a prosecution against a member of the Council of State . . . and if the President orders such a prosecution to take place, it shall be carried out by the Chancellor of Justice. If the President finds that there is no ground for an indictment, the Chancellor of Justice shall be free to report on the case to Parliament . . ."

[17] Discussion of "the peculiar Finnish system" appears in P. K. Kastari, "Guarantees of Fundamental Rights and the Constitutional Principle," in *Jahrbuch des Öffentlichen Rechts der Gegenwart* 438, 450–452 (1964), and in the same author's "The Constitutional Protection of Fundamental Rights in Finland," 34 *Tulane L. Rev.* 695, 697 (1960).

[18] The need for constitutional procedure is finally determined not by the Chancellor, but by the Constitutional Committee of Parliament, which is said to be quicker than the Chancellor to discern possible incompatibility between a Cabinet proposal and

The watchmen's independence. Frequent and intimate association between the Chancellor on the one hand and, on the other, the President, the ministers, and ministerial staffs leads some Finnish lawyers to doubt the Chancellor's detachment. Expressing a sentiment many others share, a leading constitutional authority has written that the Chancellor serves the government of the day "in much the same sense as does a so-called crown jurist, who should be wholly objective, but who is frequently partisan in his representations."[19] The Chancellor's presence at Cabinet meetings, another prominent scholar remarked during a recent conversation, "covers the Government with a cloak of what looks like legality—and of course that makes it very difficult for him to admit later that he was looking out of the window when legally dubious matters were being dealt with. Instead he defends himself by defending the Government."

Even so, direct clashes between the Chancellor and leading political figures have occurred. Some years ago, for example, a Chancellor persuaded the President that a minister should be prosecuted because he had improperly prepared a Cabinet working paper. More recently a Chancellor prosecuted the directors of a government insurance fund for authorizing low cost loans to build apartment houses in which some of their friends (including fellow officials) hoped to reside. Among the directors were the Prime Minister, Cabinet members, and the President of the Supreme Administrative Court. Some, but not all, of the defendants were fined. The Prime Minister resigned. When fully examined in court, however, the affair seemed far less scandalous and perhaps more "political" than at first had been supposed.

The very fact that the prosecution was initiated may show that the Chancellor is indeed as independent as he is supposed to be. On the other hand, the Chancellor who launched that prosecution was turned out of office afterward upon reaching retirement age, although a permissible extension of three years had been granted his predecessors. When asked whether the insurance fund case had had any permanent consequences, the former Chancellor glumly replied not long ago: "Yes. I lost my job." If his appraisal is correct, future chancellors may be unenthusiastic about demonstrating their detachment.

the Constitution. The Constitutional Committee, the bulk of whose members are not lawyers, utilizes the services of a board of consultants, highly respected jurists whose advice has been closely followed.

[19] P. K. Kastari, "The Parliamentary Ombudsman: His Functions, Position, and Relation to the Chancellor of Justice in Finland," 28 *Int. Rev. Admin. Sc.* 391, 394.

The Ombudsman, who is less closely linked with the executive branch, is presumably uninhibited in dealing with transgressors in high places, though he must have Parliament's consent before he can prosecute a minister personally. In 1952 the Ombudsman, acting on his own initiative, went before Parliament (where he has the privilege of the floor) to seek the indictment of two Cabinet members and two former Ministers for imprudent use of public funds to the advantage of a private business enterprise with which one of them was connected. After lengthy parliamentary consideration, prosecution was authorized. The Cabinet members immediately resigned their offices. The Ombudsman himself served as prosecutor. Two of the four defendants were convicted. The prominence of those whom the Ombudsman had denounced underscored his unconcern for governmental sensibilities.

Soon afterward, a high-ranking official of the Defense Ministry, who had his minister's support, was dismissed and deprived of pension rights after prosecution by the Ombudsman. Only a few years ago the Ombudsman caused a flurry when he gave a sharp "reminder" to the Minister of Justice about his legal duties. Since the Minister happened to have been the Ombudsman at an earlier period in his own career, he received the rebuke with rather marked ill grace.

Episodes like these do not prove that the Ombudsman is totally immune from pressures to which the Chancellor is exposed. They do perhaps suggest, however, that detachment from the executive branch frees the Ombudsman from the personal pangs and embarrassments the Chancellor might feel when attacking an old colleague.

4 | Relationship to the Courts

The watchmen's duty to safeguard legality is all inclusive. Both the Ombudsman and the Chancellor are required to concern themselves with judges as well as with other law administrators. As elsewhere, "judicial independence" is valued in Finland.[20] A nice line must

[20] Finland Const. Art. 2 provides in part that "The judicial power shall be exercised by independent tribunals . . ." Finland Const. Art. 91 forbids ousting a judge "except by a lawful trial and judgment" and also forbids transferring him to another post without his consent, except as part of a general reorganization of the judiciary.

therefore be drawn between supervision, which is regarded as a Good Thing, and interference, which is of course Bad.

Judicial organization. Seventy-three rural district courts and thirty-five city courts, manned by two hundred professional judges, are responsible for the trial of civil and criminal cases. Four courts of appeal, with a total of seventy-five judges, hear appeals. The Supreme Court, with a president and no fewer than twenty-one members who sit in three sections, has final appellate jurisdiction in civil and criminal matters.

The Supreme Administrative Court—a president and no fewer than thirteen nor more than twenty-five members—has comprehensive power to decide administrative appeals, not only from the decisions of inferior administrative authorities and from the "provincial courts" to which later reference will be made, but also from the decisions of the highest authorities, including the Council of State.[21]

In addition, professional judges are part of the personnel attached to specialized tribunals such as military courts, water courts, and a social insurance court. Steps have been successfully taken to reduce the risk of political favoritism in selecting the judiciary.[22] The professional judiciary is generally respected.

Access to Finland's well-manned courts is neither difficult nor costly. Filing fees are very low. A litigant need not engage an advocate

[21] See V. Merikoski, "Legality in Administrative Law: Some Trends in Evolution and Practical Experiences," 4 *Scand. Stud. in Law* 127, 138–140 (1960); J. Uotila, "Improving Public Administration in Finland," 27 *Int. Rev. Admin. Sc.* 1 (1961). Decisions of the Cabinet and ministries are appealable only on legal grounds, while appeals against the exercise of discretion (as well as on legal grounds) can be considered when other administrative authorities are involved. Professor Merikoski's study shows that recognition of the Cabinet's discretionary powers does not greatly limit the court. From 1932 to 1955 the Supreme Administrative Court received 106,123 appeals, of which it transferred only 726 to the Cabinet because they involved the exercise of discretion. Of these, more than half (389) had to do with peddlers' licenses. The use of motor vehicles provided the next largest number. Others had to do with such epochal matters as appointments of doormen at cafes and permission to take crayfish from public waters for breeding purposes.

[22] The President of the Republic has been authorized by Article 87 of the Constitution to appoint the Presidents of the Supreme Court and the Supreme Administrative Court. He also appoints the members of the Supreme Court and the presidents of the courts of appeal, but only upon the recommendation of the Supreme Court. Similarly, the Supreme Administrative Court recommends the persons whom the President appoints to sit in that body. The Supreme Court recommends the appointees to the courts of appeal, and it directly appoints many of the lower court judges and the chairmen of other courts. City court members are elected by the appropriate municipal council, usually on party lines, but sometimes with considerable reliance on the judiciary's advice.

(a status that had been attained in 1964 by only 330 lawyers throughout the entire country[23]) nor one of the two or three hundred practitioners of lesser rank.[24] Instead he may appear in his own behalf or through any representative he may choose. In matters related to public administration, personal hearings before the courts are a rarity since most issues are determined on the basis of the relevant papers without the necessity of briefs or arguments on behalf of the appellant.

In circumstances so favorable to affected persons' use of appellate judicial processes whenever dissatisfied, one might suppose that the judges could cure their own aberrations without external policing. Finland apparently believes otherwise. The Chancellor devotes much attention to the judges. For many years the Ombudsman, though equally empowered to delve into the functioning of the judiciary, seemingly regarded that field as already occupied. Since 1962, however, the Ombudsman has been taking a noticeably keener interest in the courts.

Prosecuting the judges. A Special Prosecutor who is appointed by the Supreme Court with the Chancellor's concurrence is attached to each of the four courts of appeal. His task is to proceed against lower court judges in suitable instances.[25]

Prosecutions of judges are not at all rare. Sixty-one prosecutions were begun against judges in 1960; in 1961, the figure was eighty-nine; in 1962, ninety; in 1963, one hundred and forty-eight; in 1964, one hundred and eighteen. Few of these were for serious offenses. Most of them fell within section 40.21 of the Finnish Penal Code: "An official who commits an error in office through carelessness, omission, imprudence, lack of understanding, or lack of skill shall be sentenced to a fine or suspension from duty unless the error be so minor that a

[23] The Union of Finnish Lawyers, *Law and Lawyers in Finland* 5 (1964).

[24] The Union of Finnish Lawyers, *The Future Supply of Lawyers in Finland and the Demand for Their Services* 17–18 (1960), shows the following occupational distribution of the 3,670 Finnish lawyers who were professionally active in 1957.

Private law practice	561
Judiciary	636
National administration	1252
Local administration	229
Commerce and industry	736
Organizational activity	146
Law teaching	51
Other	59

[25] He also conducts prosecutions of higher level nonjudicial administrators when directed to do so by either the Chancellor or the Ombudsman.

reminder be deemed the appropriate sanction; if the circumstances warrant, he may be removed from office."

A substantial portion of the prosecutions derives from routine review of periodic reports showing sentences imposed and fines collected in each court. The Deputy Chancellor and his subordinates examine these to detect errors, whether or not appeals have been taken.[26] A judicial blunder sufficient to cause an eyebrow to lift brings prosecution of the erring judge.[27]

Most other prosecutions are based upon errors discerned by a court of appeal (or, more rarely, the Supreme Court) when reviewing a lower court's judgment. The Special Prosecutor, who also reviews the "prisoner lists" and "fine lists" supplied by the trial judges, commences a number of cases on his own motion. Very rarely a more serious episode comes to light, usually through information communicated to the Chancellor; a few years ago, for example, a judge was prosecuted and dismissed because he had exacted improper fees for judicial proceedings and another judge lost his job when insobriety affected his courtroom demeanor.

The very frequency of prosecutions may reduce their significance. One of the court of appeal prosecutors, himself a former judge, commented flatly: "A conviction does not affect a judge's career. Of course if he committed an offense knowingly, that would be another matter. And I suppose a judge would have a dim future if he were frequently prosecuted, because this would suggest habitually sloppy work or mental laziness. Prosecutions do, however, keep judges on their mark because a mistake may hit them in the pocketbook."[28]

[26] Both the Chancellor and the Ombudsman are authorized by law to attend the executive sessions of any and all courts. Neither one of them ever exercises this power, however.

[27] In 1960, 44 of the 61 prosecutions of judges were initiated upon the basis of this routinized examination by the Chancellor's staff of lists the judges were required to file. The comparable numbers in later years were as follows:

1961	23:89
1962	19:90
1963	47:148
1964	20:118

[28] As in other Scandinavian countries, Finland imposes fines on a sliding scale related to income; a fine means losing a stated proportion of a certain number of days' wages or salary. Instead of being subjected to a fine after being convicted, a judge may simply be given a "reminder," which is in effect a censure without financial consequences, though of course it remains as a blot on the judge's record.

Some judges, however, appraise prosecutions more harshly than did the prosecutor. A distinguished jurist recently recalled with some asperity that he himself, when a very young judge, had been prosecuted for imposing too severe a fine upon a petty lawbreaker. "I paid back the extra amount as soon as the mistake was called to my attention," he said, "but nobody could pay back to me the shame of being prosecuted." Another judge, highly regarded in legal circles, remarked that judges were under scrutiny too constantly, although he fully favored having some checks upon his own and his colleagues' work. "Our trouble," he declared, "is that everybody is supervising us. The country would be better off if some one body, whether it be the court of appeal or its prosecutor or the Chancellor or the Ombudsman, had the entire responsibility. And some way should be found for detecting and correcting mistakes without this constant prosecuting. If prosecution were reserved for big things, it would be a real whip instead of a damned irritation."

In general, however, the present system seems to be accepted resignedly. The newspapers pay no attention at all to the routine prosecution of judges. A leading law professor, interviewed in the company of an appellate judge and a practicing lawyer, asserted with their seeming accord that a judge is unhurt by a prosecution, which is "more in the nature of a nuisance than a real embarrassment." Other judges with whom the matter was discussed expressed similar views. They insist, too, that they ignore the Chancellor's opinions unless based upon explicit statutory provisions of acknowledged relevance. Supreme Court judges recount with satisfaction their rebuff to the Chancellor a few years ago when he criticized them for increasing the severity of a sentence imposed by a lower court without affording the defendant an opportunity to be heard. "We had the power to do so, and it was none of his business if we chose to exercise it," a member of the Supreme Court recently declared with strong feeling. "If the Chancellor thought we were doing wrong, let him try to prosecute us. He didn't dare do that. So he should have kept his thoughts to himself, and that is what we told him."[29]

Analysis of the list of those prosecuted during a recent three-year period shows that most of the judicial defendants were inexperienced

[29] In this instance, it is only fair to add, the Chancellor had the last word. In 1963 Parliament amended the law to require the hearing the Chancellor had recommended.

young men presiding over rural assizes. Some, indeed, were serving their initial apprenticeship immediately after completing law studies. Prosecution is a rather harsh means of supervising the work of novices and of providing in-service training. It may also be inefficient, for knowledge that a punishment has been imposed is not formally communicated to other judges, who may therefore fail to learn of their colleague's sad experience unless they hear about it from gossips. The present system, as traditionally administered by the Chancellor, puts a high premium on attention to detail in recording the sentencing of penal offenders, but virtually overlooks the rest of judicial work. No attention at all seems to be paid to the administration of civil justice, save as the appellate courts may deal with erroneous judgments from which an appeal has been taken.[30]

Beyond argument, a judge should never impose fines and jail terms that exceed the limits provided by law, and of course a court's records should be up-to-date and accurate. These are not the entirety of good judging, however. The Chancellor's fixation on those phases of judicial work may have nurtured legality in a narrow sense, but it has also been deadening in a way. Great judging requires soaring spirit far more than it requires devotion to the clerical detail which now fills so large a part of a Finnish judge's life.[31]

Reopening closed cases. Both the Ombudsman and the Chancellor have a second major activity in relation to the judiciary. When a judgment has become final and no longer appealable because time limitations have been exceeded, either of these two officers may request the Supreme Court or the Supreme Administrative Court (as the case may be) to annul the prior decision and to reconsider the matter. The request may be based on newly acquired evidence or on equitable

[30] The court of appeal's special prosecutor periodically "inspects" trial courts, but all agree that, until now, these inspections have concerned themselves almost exclusively with fiscal matters, notably the accounting of proceeds of sales of tax stamps that must be affixed to various formal documents. This is but another symptom of the somewhat mechanistic approach taken to "supervision" of judges' work.

[31] Conversation with judges in small cities has produced this composite picture of a trial judge's work week: He sits in court to hear cases for one day, from ten until five. He spends the next day and perhaps a portion of the following day preparing "protocols," or records of the matters heard. He devotes two days to compiling lists and reports of all kinds. In most places he is inadequately assisted by clerical staff or typists, and in some places by none at all. As one judge of fifteen years' experience observed, "It's a very dull job." And as a youthful assistant added: "The only thing I am sure of learning here is how to type."

considerations. These cases are to be differentiated from the far more numerous interventions in matters still open to the conventional processes of review or appeal.

The Chancellor filed an average of 102 petitions to annul and reconsider during the five years 1960–1964, inclusive; 95 percent of his requests were found to be meritorious. The Ombudsman's similar requests were far less numerous, and somewhat less well received by the two supreme courts.

In these cases the Chancellor and the Ombudsman function as protagonists of legality rather than of the affected parties, for they may act quite without reference to the parties' own wishes[32] The Ombudsman's cases pertain to official or judicial omissions or maladroitness that have produced still correctible injustice.[33] In matters of these kinds, however, the Ombudsman and the Chancellor may be said to work as investigators for the courts, rather than as investigators of the courts. Petitions which in other countries might be addressed directly to judges are usually, in Finland, first sifted by these high non-judicial officials. Petitions found meritorious are passed along to one of the appropriate supreme tribunals, which retains full power to decide what, if anything, should next be done.

[32] In 1958, for example, the Chancellor successfully petitioned for cancellation of a final divorce decree, obtained by the parties' collusion. The wife of a high military official had committed an embezzlement and was about to be exposed. To avoid endangering the husband's social standing, the couple falsely testified that they had been separated for more than two years and that cause for divorce existed. The Chancellor, as the nation's chief prosecutor, prosecuted the couple for perjury and, as guardian of legality, asked the Supreme Court to annul the decree of divorce.

[33] Examples from the Ombudsman's 1963 report: (1) A court imposed a fine on Y. E. K. for disobeying a summons to stand trial. On the date set for trial Y. E. K. was in detention elsewhere. His request to be transported to court had been denied by his jailer, who had been unable to confirm the prisoner's statement that he had been summoned. On the Ombudsman's request, the Supreme Court reopened Y. E. K.'s case and set aside the fine previously imposed. (2) A. H. was convicted of a crime, and was sentenced to pay a fine and damages. On appeal, the judgment was affirmed. Subsequently, the Ombudsman became persuaded that A. H. had been mentally irresponsible when the criminal acts had been committed. The Supreme Court agreed, and the judgment against A. H. was set aside. From the 1962 report: A. D., held in prison following his conviction, requested that the minutes of his trial be sent to him there so that he could appeal. The papers reached the prison on the day after A. D. had been released from detention. Instead of being forwarded to A. D., they were returned to the court. Before A. D. had obtained the minutes, the time to appeal had expired. At the Ombudsman's request, the time for taking an appeal was extended.

5 | Relationship to Non-judicial Administration

The watchmen's overlapping duties. The Chancellor and the Ombudsman share the duty and the power to oversee all branches of governmental administration at every level, from the lowliest clerk of a rural commune to the loftiest military officer or central bureau chief. In order to balance workloads somewhat, Parliament has made the Ombudsman primarily responsible for safeguarding legality in the military services and in places of detention. The Chancellor, though still capable of dealing with complaints about those matters, in fact passes them along to the Ombudsman. Otherwise, the two watchmen have an overlapping duty to enforce official compliance with law.[34]

Despite the broad opportunity thus presented for conflict between these high offices, no friction seems to have occurred. Past and present officeholders have stated that neither of the officials will deal with a complaint already under study by the other. While they could act successively upon the same matter and have occasionally done so wittingly or unwittingly, they have so rarely reached contrary conclusions that specific examples of discord could not be recalled during interviews in 1964. The harmony of their opinions and actions is seemingly spontaneous; the Chancellor and the Ombudsman do not consult one another regularly, though conversations occurred at one time between the then officeholders, who happened to be friends of long standing. Each ordinarily goes his separate way without informing the other.

[34] The Chancellor has the responsibility, unshared by the Ombudsman, of being Supreme Public Prosecutor; in that capacity he supervises all public prosecutors throughout the land, other than the Ombudsman himself (so far as that official may be regarded as a prosecutor). Periodic reports are submitted to the Chancellor, showing in detail the actions taken in each prosecutor's office. These sometimes reveal mistakes which lead to a reprimand or a prosecution of a prosecutor. Prosecutors turn to the Chancellor for advice when in doubt whether a prosecutable offense has been made out by the evidence at hand. Either the Chancellor or the Ombudsman can order that a prosecution be initiated. Interestingly, however, neither can override a prosecutor's decision to prosecute; the prosecutor's belief about where his duty lies must be given full play, though the prosecutor may later suffer if his belief be regarded by the Chancellor as too glaringly ill founded. Moreover, the Chancellor has a so-called "absolute power of devolution," which means that he can himself supplant a prosecutor in a pending case and can assume personal responsibility for it. By exercising the power of devolution, the Chancellor could conceivably take over a prosecution of which he disapproved, and could then proceed to drop it.

Good judgment or good luck has thus far prevented any collisions.[35]

In respect of public administration in general, both the Chancellor and the Ombudsman may investigate on the basis of specific complaints, upon their own initiative, or through personal inspections of institutions or offices. If they detect improprieties they may admonish, prosecute, or seek disciplinary measures as circumstances may suggest.

6 | Complaints

Sources and volume of cases. While in theory the Ombudsman is "the people's man," the public at large seems to prefer dealing with the Chancellor.

In numbers alone, the Ombudsman is the leader. In 1963, for example, the Ombudsman received 1,029 complaints, as against only 479 complaints addressed to the Chancellor (who referred 73 of these to the Ombudsman because they dealt with the military services or places of detention); in 1962 the respective figures were 753 and 598 (of which 105 were transferred to the Ombudsman).

These gross figures are, however, somewhat misleading for two reasons. First, in each of the years about seventy additional cases went to the Chancellor (but none to the Ombudsman) from other organs of government which had learned of seeming delinquencies through complaints by the public or through their own observation. Second, and more significant in the present context, the Ombudsman drew most of his complaints from a very small segment of the entire population, namely, prisoners in various places of detention. Persons interviewed in 1964 insistently repeated that the Ombudsman has chiefly been of use to those held in penal institutions. Among those who expressed this view were spokesmen for business groups, local governments, welfare officers, lawyers, trade unions, and civil servants. Even

[35] In its 1920 instructions to the Ombudsman (still in force today), Parliament told him that he was not to "interfere with the activities of the Chancellor." No similar words were addressed to the Chancellor concerning his "interfering" with the Ombudsman, but the absence of such an instruction has made no discernible difference in the officers' relationships.

patients in mental institutions, who are eager "clients" of ombudsmen in other countries, infrequently complain to the Ombudsman in Finland. Officials of the Medical Board remarked simply: "The Ombudsman is not well known to the people at large. Our patients," they added with just a touch of pride, "complain to President Kekkonen himself."

The experience of the large Riihimäki penitentiary, in which only first offenders are confined, somewhat confirms the opinion that the general public is little aware of the Ombudsman. Riihimäki inmates, fresh from civilian life as it were, rarely write the Ombudsman though free to do so without prison censorship. But a prison official observed that "the volume of complaints from the nearly 40 percent of these same men who, unfortunately, will be back in some other prison increases very dramatically as they become 'better educated' by being confined along with older, more experienced convicts. The Ombudsman's word-of-mouth advertising occurs chiefly behind bars, I am sorry to say."

Because statements concerning Finnish experience were inconsistent with observations made in other countries, objective verification was sought by ascertaining the identity of two hundred complainants plucked at random from the Ombudsman's list for the year 1962. Of these two hundred (some of whom filed several complaints in the course of the year), one hundred twenty-five were prisoners of one sort or another; sixty-four might be described as "ordinary citizens"; six were conscripts who objected to treatment by their military superiors; three were schoolteachers; one was a lawyer; and one was a member of Parliament. This sample strongly supports the opinion that the Ombudsman is much more "the prisoners' man" than "the people's man."

Yet, when that has been said, one still notes that 37.5 percent of the Ombudsman's cases came from persons not in detention. This is a substantial share of the whole. The present Ombudsman, more actively than most of his predecessors, has encouraged schoolteachers to expand their students' awareness of his existence. Perhaps in time his office will gain fuller recognition than it has thus far had.

Even now, complaints to the Ombudsman are becoming diversified. Civil servants have little need for his services in personnel matters such as dismissal or disciplinary action, because these are cognizable by specific tribunals to which access is easy. Their organizations have, however, recently turned to the Ombudsman to enforce higher public officials' duty to bargain collectively. They have also encouraged their members to complain about systematic evasions of personnel regulations by local authorities. Municipal officials have complained against what they regard as overbearing conduct by central offices. Despite the organized businessmen's view that the Ombudsman is of no direct use to them, individual businessmen do in fact complain, as has happened for example in connection with the award of bus franchises and the denial of certain licenses. Though practicing lawyers say the Ombudsman is useful only to poor people who cannot pay for professional advice, some lawyers do approach him in behalf of clients, perhaps especially in connection with complaints of wide application. Thus an attorney, acting for a client, was recently successful in complaining to the Ombudsman about policemen's having off-duty private employment regarded as objectionable because of potential conflicts of interests.

Complaints to provincial courts. One very good reason, indeed perhaps the main reason, why neither the Ombudsman nor the Chancellor is overwhelmed by citizens' complaints is that grievances are readily redressed elsewhere, notably in the "provincial courts." These tribunals, at least one of which sits in each province, are catch-all appellate bodies. They are not regarded in Finland as full-fledged courts because they may be (but rarely are) presided over by the provincial governor, and because the three members in each of these tribunals may be assigned purely administrative duties when not fully occupied by judicial work. They function in fact, however, in the same spirit and manner as courts, although their judgments issue in the form of decisions of the provincial administrations in whose name they act. When a citizen's views clash with those of lesser officials (and, after all, most officials with whom citizens come in frequent contact are within the category of "lesser"), the provincial courts are in a position to resolve the clash dispassionately, for the members of those courts have only tenuous links with the administrators.[36] With

[36] The statistics of the three provincial courts that sit in Turku will serve to exemplify the absence of pro-official bias. In 1963 these three tribunals disposed of 5,287 cases. Of these, 369 were dismissed because of untimeliness or nonprosecution

few exceptions, provincial courts' judgments are further reviewable in the Supreme Administrative Court.

The provincial courts do more than siphon off bona fide grievances of individual citizens. They serve also as a forum for the airing of local controversies that might lose their point if they were removed to distant Helsinki for examination by the Ombudsman or Chancellor. Complaints against local officials are within the jurisdiction of both those high dignitaries, but neither one receives many of this type. They are much more likely to find their way to the provincial courts. In one rapidly growing town, a few determined traditionalists have taken nearly thirty cases to the provincial court during each of the past several years, seeking thus to prevent or at least postpone an urbanization they deplore. In the larger city of Turku, an elected official cheerfully commented: "Every time our Council meets, you can be sure that somebody will complain to the provincial court the next day, with copies to the local newspapers. Usually this is just a partisan tactic, having little to do with either legality or efficiency. I sometimes wish we were in the position of the Helsinki municipal council, which does its work month after month without anybody's noticing it at all. But on the other hand ours is a relatively painless way of conducting political warfare."

Complaints to local prosecutors. Finally, citizens may and do complain directly to local prosecutors concerning asserted misbehavior by other officials. Prosecutors, unlike the Ombudsman and the Chancellor, cannot "give a reminder" to an official in the form of a reprimand or advice for the future. They can only prosecute wrongdoers. In an informal manner, nevertheless, they do sometimes chide a public servant for rudeness or lack of diligence without prosecuting him. In this way, without ever putting a name to it, they do in fact though not in theory give a reminder from time to time.

Complaints to prosecutors in the more populous provinces are said to average about five a week, while other and even pettier cases occasionally go to prosecutors in the cities and town. These usually pertain

---

by the appellant. In the 4,918 decisions on the merits, the initial administrative decision was reversed or modified in 2,663 cases, the matter was remanded for further proceedings in 334 cases, and the challenged decision was affirmed in 1,921 cases. Reversals, modifications, and remands thus constituted more than 60 percent of the courts' decisions. This is said to be a typical year's record.

to isolated acts of clear though not easily proved impropriety (such as use of excessive force by an arresting policeman) or to delay in handling papers. Altogether, the eleven provincial prosecutors probably deal with no more than 1,500 complaints per year. Whatever the precise figure may be, the provincial prosecutors do unquestionably handle many cases that could have been referred to the Chancellor or the Ombudsman had the complainants so chosen. This fact is clearly reflected in judicial statistics showing the total number of prosecutions of judges and officials (other than military personnel) during the years 1960–1964, inclusive. The courts during these five years entertained an average of 222 prosecutions against public servants. Of these, only 132 at the very most were (on the average) commenced at the behest of the Ombudsman, the Chancellor, or the special prosecutors of the four courts of appeal, leaving a balance of 90 that may be attributed to other prosecutors' responses to the complaints made directly to them.[37]

The processing of complaints. Neither the Ombudsman nor the Chancellor has a large staff. Two full-time and six part-time assistants are available to the Ombudsman.[38] The Chancellor is aided by a Deputy Chancellor, who can act in his place in matters the Chancellor

[37] The pertinent figures from which the above conclusions are drawn may be summarized as follows:

	1960	1961	1962	1963	1964
Total prosecutions commenced	183	191	221	273	243
Prosecutions of judges	61	89	90	148	118
Other prosecutions by Chancellor	27	24	18	16	20
Other prosecutions by Ombudsman	11	15	9	6	9

Some of the "other prosecutions" attributed to the Chancellor and the Ombudsman probably in fact include a few cases involving judges and may therefore already have been included under the heading "Prosecutions of judges."

In addition to the cases involving civilian officials, civilian courts entertained the following numbers of prosecutions directed against military personnel for what might be called official misconduct: 1960, 17; 1961, 15; 1962, 10; 1963, 14.

[38] Because the demand for lawyers exceeds the supply now available in Finland and because the salaries attached to some positions are unrealistically low, the holding of multiple jobs is not unusual. This sometimes has consequences of uncertain merit. One of the Ombudsman's assistants is also employed in the Ministry of the Interior, which administers police affairs. Complaints to the Ombudsman concerning police administration are likely to be referred to this staff member because of his specialized background, which the Ombudsman deems an asset. The director of the national police force praises the Ombudsman's sound understanding of police problems, based on good advice received from his part-time assistant. The possibility of divided loyalties has apparently not suggested itself as yet to the Ombudsman, the police director, or the staff assistant.

chooses, and by six full-time staff lawyers and one part-time assistant. Seventy to 80 percent of the staff's time is devoted to complaint work, most of which is supervised by the Deputy Chancellor, while the Chancellor concentrates on Cabinet matters and his duties as Supreme Public Prosecutor. In contrast the Ombudsman personally reviews the final action on every complaint, whether that action be a letter rejecting the complaint or a decision to prosecute.[39]

Both offices tend to ask for files in a great many cases, in order to ascertain the facts when complaints cannot be dismissed out of hand. This process is time consuming. Although less cumbersome means of checking the accuracy of a complainant's statements could be devised, neither office has encouraged its staff members to proceed informally or to take any great personal initiative. Neither office has the time or the resources for interviewing witnesses or conducting anything resembling trial hearings when conflicting evidence exists; under Finnish law, in fact, taking testimony under oath is impossible except in formal proceeding in tribunals. Local police officers and, infrequently, magistrates are pressed into service as field investigators, to take statements from persons who may have relevant information. Even when the conduct of policemen is the very fact in issue, the Ombudsman can command the help of no investigators other than the defendant's fellow officers. Although the Chancellor can request a local prosecutor to investigate in his behalf, the ties between prosecutors and police are even closer in Finland than in the United States, and sometimes the head of the police force and the prosecutor are one and the same.

Before "giving a reminder" or otherwise making a finding that might adversely reflect on the person complained against, both the Chancellor and the Ombudsman afford him a chance to explain or object—not a formal hearing but, rather, an opportunity to justify, excuse, or minimize.[40]

[39] Parliament elects a Deputy Ombudsman, who serves only when the Ombudsman is on leave or is incapacitated. He thus adds no numerical strength to the Ombudsman's staff.

[40] Parliament has instructed the Ombudsman, before commencing a prosecution, to give to the affected person "the possibility, if he so wishes, to present his opinion in the matter in a given time." The comparable instructions to the Chancellor say that if investigation of a complaint shows that an official action is "against law or otherwise erroneous, the guilty person, if not already heard in the matter, shall have an opportunity to submit an explanation and thereafter he will be legally prosecuted if the error is not of such nature that the matter can be concluded by a reminder . . ."

Action on complaints. Predictably, most complaints prove to be unfounded. Dissatisfaction with an official's action may be perfectly genuine and yet have no justification. During a four-year period, 1960–1963, action favorable to the complainant's position was taken in only 8.6 percent of complaint cases disposed of by the Ombudsman. In 1964, when many old cases were concluded without positive action upon the complaints, the figure fell to 5 percent.

Table IV. Ombudsman's action on complaints

	1960	1961	1962	1963	1964
Total of cases decided	955	947	805	787	1,513
No action found appropriate because	871	865	730	727	1,437
a) matter pending in court	32	19	30	29	28
b) situation changed	8	22	7	5	8
c) matter outside Ombudsman's jurisdiction	42	36	38	88	112
d) insufficiently persuasive evidence	168	174	136	98	232
e) no error apparent	573	574	496	476	1,003
f) miscellaneous reasons	48	40	23	31	54
Action taken in support of complaint	84	82	75	60	76
by					
a) prosecution	8	15	9	6	8
b) disciplinary proceedings	3	0	0	0	0
c) admonition to official	22	22	37	24	28
d) suggestion or instruction for future guidance	21	15	14	10	14
e) official himself took suitable action after Ombudsman's inquiry	30	30	15	20	26

During the four-year period 1960–1963, only 5.7 percent of the citizens' complaint cases handled by the Chancellor were found to be meritorious.

Negative action on a complaint, however, does not necessarily leave the complainant wholly dissatisfied, for the communications he receives from the Ombudsman or the Chancellor sometimes enable him

Table V. Chancellor's actions on citizens' complaints

	1960	1961	1962	1963
Total of cases decided	635	539	493	406
No action found appropriate because	591	512	467	385
a) matter pending in court	10	5	6	2
b) obviously trivial	22	9	4	3
c) within another official's competence	29	26	20	20
d) no impropriety found	530	472	437	360
Action taken in support of complaint	44	27	26	21
by				
a) prosecution	6	7	7	4
b) disciplinary proceedings or admonition to official	13	8	8	8
c) suggestion or instruction for future guidance	14	8	9	9
d) official himself took suitable action after Chancellor's inquiry	11	4	2	0

to understand and perhaps accept a decision previously resisted. One senses, however, that the Finnish watchmen of legality do not take as great care as their Scandinavian counterparts to enlighten complainants.

The tables set forth above do not show the totality of the watchmen's work. Some of that work is not responsive to complaints, but is wholly self-initiated. The tables omit, too, those complaints initiated not by the public at large but by the Cabinet, one of the superior courts, or some other official. During the years 1960–1963, 80.5 percent of these complaints led to some form of action by the Chancellor, as against the 5.7 percent of citizens' complaints which produced positive results.

Despite the infrequency of corrective actions against individual officials, many administrators testify that the Ombudsman's and Chancellor's investigation of complaints has substantial preventive effect. One high-ranking prison administrator, for example, believes that the

Table VI. Chancellor's actions on officials' complaints

	1960	1961	1962	1963
Total of cases decided	123	71	70	69
No action found appropriate because	22	20	14	9
a) evidence inconclusive	8	8	7	1
b) no merit on face of complaint	10	8	3	5
c) should be referred elsewhere	3	1	4	3
d) settled otherwise	1	3	0	0
Action taken in support of complaint	101	51	56	60
by				
a) prosecution	6	2	2	2
b) disciplinary proceeding or admonition to official	2	7	1	2
c) suggestion or instruction for future guidance	93	42	53	56

behavior patterns of guards has been greatly affected by their knowledge that prisoners have ready access to the Ombudsman. Further, his own administration has often been influenced by the Ombudsman's suggestions that aim at eliminating future complaints. "We do not always think the Ombudsman is right, but if he feels strongly about the way things should be done, we go along with him as a practical matter. At the same time," he added, "the Ombudsman listens to us, too. Before he criticizes, he gives us a chance to discuss; and after discussion he has changed his mind occasionally, just as we have. As a matter of fact we senior officials are glad the Ombudsman exists. He takes a lot of cranks off our backs, because they write to him instead of continuing to badger us. And he helps us superintend a scattered staff. We can't keep our eyes on them continuously no matter how hard we might try. They know, though, that the Ombudsman may be watching when we are not, and they take him seriously."

Police officials in widely separated cities were in accord that the Ombudsman's and the Chancellor's occasional fault finding did have a continuing impact upon policemen's conduct. "We have not had a single prosecution or reminder during my eleven years here," said the chief of police in an industrial city, "and I hope we can keep it that way. But we have had inquiries about matters that had been sent to the Chancellor or the Ombudsman, and so we are well aware that complaints can be made. Of course, too, we have all heard about the prosecution of K. [a police chief in another city] for unnecessarily keeping a sick man in jail. That is very much on our minds because we have not in the past had any good system for dealing with sick prisoners. After what happened to K. we can't continue to be easy going. We are working on that problem right this minute."

Another senior official, commenting on proceedings initiated by the Chancellor as well as the Ombudsman, remarked that even a "reminder" growing out of a prosecution remains on a policeman's record as a black mark until it has been expunged by five years of unblemished service. It impedes promotion and preferment. He was asked whether he agreed with the opinion of one of his superiors that policemen's conduct is not changed by the activities of the two official watchmen. "Don't let anyone tell you," he advised, "that police officers don't care about those fellows in Helsinki. We sometimes think they should spend more time on bigger men than we are, because we already have a lot of supervision over us and the big shots don't. But we know they can and do concern themselves with us, and that makes us careful."[41]

In all likelihood, however, this kind of chain reaction to the handling of complaint cases does not occur with equal intensity throughout the civil administration. An effort was made in 1964 to confirm the supposition that the Ombudsman is especially useful in connection with social welfare matters. Not a shred of evidence was found to support that view. Officials familiar with both central and local administration of laws concerning children, alcoholics, home relief recipients, maternal welfare, and rehabilitation doubted that either the Chancellor or the Ombudsman has had substantial impact on these features of the "welfare state." They agreed that supervision by the Ministry of Social Affairs was energetic and respected and that many

[41] The speaker was no doubt correct in saying that awareness of the Ombudsman encourages policemen to be careful, but of course carelessness does still exist. The Ombudsman's report for 1963 reports a prosecution and fining of a police officer who had failed to withdraw a "Wanted By The Police" notice after a person to whom the notice referred was in fact no longer wanted; as a result the person referred to was later picked up and detained briefly by police in another city. Another policeman was fined and ordered to pay damages because he had struck a person he had arrested.

decisions of public welfare agencies could be and were reviewed by the provincial courts as well. They agreed, too, that welfare administrators have actually been prosecuted in the past for errors in administration. They simply rejected the idea that their work was likely to entangle them with the Ombudsman or the Chancellor; it was not that they were undisciplined in their official activities, but that their discipline and inspiration came from other quarters.

Huoltaja, a monthly magazine published by the Ministry of Social Affairs, provides confirmation of a sort. This periodical, whose pages are devoted to welfare questions of all kinds, is sent to members of each "social board" in every community in the nation. The issues of *Huoltaja* from January, 1958, through September, 1964—eighty-one issues in all—were leafed through in order to find references to the Ombudsman. Only one such reference occurred throughout the entire period. The fact remains, nevertheless, that the Ombudsman does receive fairly numerous complaints pertaining to the work of welfare authorities, whether or not those authorities are sensitive to what affects them.[42]

7 | Action on Own Initiative

Neither the Chancellor nor the Ombudsman must wait for complaints. Both can and to some extent do take up matters on their own initiative.

The figures available in the Chancellor's office are unrevealing because they show chiefly the results of the routine checking of judges' and prosecutors' lists and reports, to which reference has been made in previous pages. Conversations with the Chancellor's office suggest that other self-initiated cases are so rare as to be virtually nonexistent.

[42] The following figures are derived from the Ombudsman's annual reports for the years 1960–1964, inclusive:

	1960	1961	1962	1963	1964
Complaints arising from orders to be detained in a closed institution (which would include alcoholic treatment centers and workhomes in which nonsupporting parents may be confined)	72	61	67	18	48
Complaints arising from other actions of welfare officials	42	30	27	11	70

As one staff member put it, "You can't rely on the newspapers for valuable leads. They are too inaccurate. If there is anything really back of a news story, we think that sooner or later someone will file a complaint. We are too overworked as it is without going out to look for more cases."

The Ombudsman is more ready to explore possible problems without first being asked. His annual reports show that he himself initiated an annual average of about twenty-five inquiries apart from inspections, which will be discussed in the following section. These have led in each year to one prosecution or disciplinary proceeding, an average of nine proposals to guide officials, and one corrective action by an administrative body then under investigation.

One can sympathize with the Ombudsman's and the Chancellor's reluctance to reach out for new business, since both offices have difficulty in keeping abreast of their current workload. The Ombudsman's backlog of unfinished cases rose from 159 in 1960 to 174 in 1961, to 226 in 1962, and to 544 in 1963; but a determined effort reduced the number of pending matters to 245 at the end of 1964. The Chancellor's backlog mounted from 150 in 1960, to 234 in 1961, and to 401 in 1962, then was reduced slightly to 359 at the end of 1963 and rose once more to 373 in 1964.

The watchmen's unwillingness to proceed unless someone has cried for help is, however, especially unfortunate in Finland. Parliament and its committees have no power under that country's constitution to investigate administrative functioning. Citizens rarely call upon their parliamentary representatives for assistance in dealing with government. In fact, after seven centuries of existence under foreign domination, Finns tend not to be very outspoken about dissatisfactions; even in ordinary commercial affairs, let alone governmental ones, many Finns keep their grievances to themselves rather than articulate them forthrightly. "Many of us Finns," a professor asserted recently, "do not speak with open mouths." These circumstances should perhaps caution the official watchmen against too heavy reliance on complaints and too great detachment from the news and rumors of the day.

During a recent period the Helsinki newspapers gave great prominence to two stories that would almost certainly have led ombudsmen elsewhere to launch an inquiry. A large hospital construction contract had been awarded to the higher of two apparently equally reputable bidders, the press declared. The unsuccessful bidder, perhaps fearful of antagonizing officials from whom future contracts might be sought, seemed disinclined to contest the matter. Nobody complained to the Ombudsman or the Chancellor, and neither of them initiated an investigation. In the second case, a schoolgirl had written and published an article critical of her teachers. She was reprimanded and slightly penalized by her school. The press, perhaps sensing an issue of civil liberties, devoted considerable space to the teacher-pupil controversy. The schoolgirl made no complaint, however, and there the matter ended so far as the watchmen were concerned—though the Central Board of Education subsequently reviewed the case on its own motion and upheld the girl.

These two episodes suggest what appears to be a general condition. The watchmen are not invariably inert; at times, on the contrary, they have strongly intervened upon their own motion.[43] Still the unfolding scene does not strongly attract their attention. Consequently they have far less impact on society than does, say, the Swedish Ombudsman, whose repeated interventions over the years have helped mold public opinion concerning such diverse things as free speech, freedom of religion, police restrictions, and penology.[44] The Finnish watchmen, ordinarily concentrating on the routine of law administration and relying on the initiative of complainants whose grievances may be relatively insignificant, miss opportunities to provide social leadership in areas where it seems needed.

[43] Upon the basis of press reports in 1963, for example, the Ombudsman inquired into the assertedly inefficient functioning of a national educational examining body, whose activities importantly affected many young persons. The administration of the examinations and the publication of their results are said to have given far greater satisfaction in 1964. An earlier Ombudsman had acted upon his own initiative to denounce a work stoppage by civil servants—an action still hotly resented in some circles. A former Chancellor asserts that he "looked into" all newspaper reports of "scandal or wrongdoing," though this fact is not reflected in his annual reports. He does point to the termination of a road race on highways near Helsinki after he had called attention to its dangers. Another former Chancellor recalls the promulgation of certain air transport regulations after he had raised questions about gaps in the existing body of controls, a matter into which he had inquired because of a newspaper article.

[44] See A. Bexelius, "The Swedish Institution of the Justitieombudsman," 27 *Int. Rev. Admin. Sc.* 243 (1961). Compare Chap. 5.

8 | Inspections

The Chancellor, who in earlier years personally inspected governmental offices throughout the nation, no longer has time to inspect even offices of the prosecutors who are immediately subordinate to him. The provincial prosecutors regularly visit, in his behalf, the prosecutors and police administrators of the smaller units of government, and their inspection is said to be thorough. The Chancellor's office as such, however, inspects only reports that are filed with it. Hence the Chancellor may, in this context, be characterized as an inspector of documents.

The Ombudsman, by contrast, engages in extensive personal inspections of prisons, police headquarters, courts, and various institutions in scattered locations. His reports show a five-year average of seventy-two such inspections, ranging from a low of thirty in 1960 to a high of ninety-six in 1962 and 1964.[45] The present Ombudsman has been a markedly more energetic traveler than his immediate predecessor.

These figures lose some of their luster, however, when one discovers that only twenty-four days including travel time were devoted to the ninety-six inspections completed in 1962; the ninety-three inspections of 1963 required only thirty-four days, again including travel time; and twenty-seven days sufficed for the ninety-six inspections in 1964. Questions inescapably arise concerning the thoroughness and utility of such hurried and random on-site studies of public administration. When interrogated, officials who have been inspected in recent years were unable to recall any benefits to them in terms of fresh attitudes toward their work. The Ombudsman believes, nevertheless, that his visits do have beneficial effects. He misses no opportunity to stress the dangers of slowness in handling public business. In his opinion this conversational emphasis has a real, though not precisely measurable, influence on the future behavior of the judges and other officials he meets during his travels.

45 These figures are slightly larger than those found elsewhere in the same reports from which Table VII has been compiled. The discrepancy can be explained in this way: in one branch of his report the Ombudsman has counted as one inspection his visiting several establishments under a single control, such as a visit to a police jail in connection with a visit to the superior official responsible for the jail's administration; elsewhere, these have been listed as two separate inspections.

Table VII. Inspections by Ombudsman

Nature of institution inspected	1960	1961	1962	1963	1964
Prisons and work camps	15	7	8	12	11
Equipment for transporting prisoners	0	0	3	3	0
Jails—city and town; police lockups	0	11	12	0	9
Police stations—towns	3	6	11	7	0
Offices of Länsman (police chief, prosecutor, general law administrator in less populous districts)	1	5	17	20	17
Police-highway patrol stations	3	0	5	5	13
Welfare institutions	2	3	5	2	12
Welfare offices	0	2	0	0	0
Military installations	2	3	13	25	9
Border authorities	0	0	1	2	6
Provincial governments	1	1	6	2	4
Country judges	1	1	10	11	11
Offices of national administrative organs	2	4	3	3	3
Municipal offices	0	0	2	1	1
Totals	30	43	96	93	96

The Ombudsman has been specifically instructed by Parliament to conduct "inspection tours in order to make himself acquainted with matters pertaining to his official functions; he shall especially visit prisons and ask for information about the care of prisoners as well as other matters concerning them."[46] This narrow focus is historically explicable by the fact that many political prisoners were in detention when the parliamentary instructions were formulated in 1920 and concern about their treatment was widely felt. Continuing that same focus today is less explicable. Finland has a modern and humane prison administration.[47] Technical inspectors frequently examine penal

[46] Service Regulations of the Parliamentary Ombudsman, Art. 10 (Jan. 10, 1920).
[47] See, e.g., V. Soine, "Finland's Open Institutions," 28 *Fed. Probation* 19 (Dec. 1964).

institutions of every type. The Ombudsman now seems to serve chiefly a psychological purpose; prisoners like to talk with him about their sentences and their family problems, and perhaps they occasionally have something interesting to tell him about prison disciplinary practices or administrative problems other than the perennial favorite in every institution, namely, food. No Ombudsman has asked for a change in Parliament's instructions, although a non-traditionalist may conclude some day that prison abuses can be controlled without forcing the Ombudsman personally to spend so much time behind bars instead of behind his desk.

The present Ombudsman's apparent intention of paying more visits to military installations than did his predecessors is highly commendable. Finland, unlike Sweden and Norway, has no separate ombudsman to deal with problems of military personnel. Thus the legal protection of soldiers as well as civilians is in the Ombudsman's hands. Soldiers are entitled to write or speak to the Ombudsman without going through military channels,[48] but they rarely do so, possibly because they may fear covert reprisals or perhaps simply because they are unaware of their privilege.[49] The Finnish army, somewhat Prussian in its tradition, long resisted civilian intrusion. The Ombudsman is attempting to effect a change in attitude and to make his availability to military personnel a reality instead of the myth it has largely been until now. In 1963 he approached the General Staff, requesting that information about the Ombudsman be included in the orientation program for recruits. His recent inspection trips to military bases have enabled him to "show the flag" if nothing more.

9 | Presenting General Proposals

Both official watchmen have been instructed to note the need for new laws and not to content themselves with enforcing those already en-

[48] See P. K. Kastari, "The Parliamentary Ombudsman," 28 *Int. Rev. Admin. Sc.* 391, 395 (1962).

[49] Action by military authorities was involved in only five complaint cases throughout 1963. See P. K. Kastari, "The Chancellor of Justice and the Ombudsman," in Rowat, ed., *The Ombudsman* 65–66.

acted.[50] Both men have accordingly felt free to present general proposals to the Cabinet, to individual ministers, and to the Parliament. They have, in fact, acted somewhat as law reform commissions, calling attention to desirable changes in fields that would not otherwise be likely to attract much public notice. Thus, for example, the Chancellor in late 1964 sent the Minister of Justice a number of suggested statutory clarifications bearing on criminal trials and sentencing procedures. The frequency with which he had detected judicial errors in these areas suggested that some of the fault might lie with poorly formulated laws rather than with the men who had erroneously applied them.

In general, no more is done than to raise a question. The formulation of suitable legislation is left to others. Thus, in his report for 1962, the Ombudsman called the Ministry of Justice's attention to a complaint received repeatedly from persons serving sentences in prison: they thought they had not received proper credit for time spent in detention after trial but before being transported to the penitentiary. The matter had been handled by the Supreme Court as long ago as 1956, but the decision was adverse to the prisoners' view. The flow of complaints continued. The Ombudsman, after six years of responding to written and oral grievances, finally wrote mildly: "Since the present condition of affairs seems to me unsound, I feel it proper to bring the problem to the Ministry's attention so that it can consider whether legislative or other remedial steps should be taken."

In the same annual report the Ombudsman disclosed that the social welfare administration had altered its explanation of a formula for computing old-age pensions. The change was made after the Ombudsman had told the administration that the explanatory wording previously in use had raised false hope among pensioners and had consequently spawned unnecessary complaints with which the Ombudsman had had to deal.

[50] The instructions to the Ombudsman tell him (Art. 8) to "point out imperfections in Acts of Parliament and decrees as well as unclear or conflicting provisions, especially those that have caused various interpretations, hesitation, or other trouble in jurisdiction or administration, and to make proposals for their elimination." The instructions to the Chancellor say (Art. 14) that if he has "noticed that the administration of law in some respect has caused criticism or that new legislation in some field is necessary," he should express his opinion about such matters in his annual report or otherwise.

The Ombudsman and the Chancellor advance general proposals rather diffidently.[51] They seem especially reluctant to frame fully elaborated ideas for legislative study. In this they differ somewhat from their colleagues elsewhere in Scandinavia, especially in Denmark, where the Ombudsman sometimes presents his suggestions in such detail that they may be readily incorporated in statutes or regulations. The more modest Finnish approach has the virtue of leaving full responsibility in the hands of those who are directly charged with formulating legislative proposals. On the other hand, a suggestion that a problem deserves to be considered is far less forceful than a suggestion of a particularized solution.

Moreover, the watchmen's annual reports to Parliament, embodying their ideas for the future as well as their account of past activities, do not arouse much excited attention. They are referred to the Constitutional Committee, whose secretary masters their contents but whose members are not thought to be extremely diligent readers. The Ombudsman and the Chancellor are sometimes invited to confer with the Committee informally. The Chancellor's reports are usually simply received and approved without comment.

The Ombudsman includes in his report a list (sometimes very lengthy) of parliamentary resolutions the Cabinet has not carried out as expected. This has enabled the Constitutional Committee to inquire into the reasons why a particular suggestion has attracted no response, or even to commence an open battle with a lethargic minister or the Cabinet as a whole. This, however, has little to do with the Ombudsman's own ideas. Political realities have kept most of them outside the legislative arena. They have either been accepted as "noncontroversial" or have quietly gathered dust. The present Ombudsman, a former secretary of the Constitutional Committee who remains in contact with members of Parliament, may prove to be a more vigorous and more adroit lobbyist than his predecessors.

[51] Examples: In 1961 the Chancellor wrote the Ministry of Justice that the use of tape recorders to record courtroom proceedings created some dangers of diminishing the completeness or accuracy of trial minutes. No affirmative suggestions were made and no follow-up seems to have occurred. In 1962 the Ombudsman very mildly suggested to the Ministry of Social Affairs that it might be a good idea, before ordering a person to be confined in a closed workhouse because he had not supported his family, to give him an opportunity to "say what he thinks about the proposed order and to include a short remark about this in the minutes of the directorate."

10 | The Educational Force of the Watchmen's Work

In law administration as in medicine an ounce of prevention is worth a pound of cure. When an official error occurs, it should of course be corrected. If correction of one forestalls another, the value of the correction is many times multiplied.

Both the Chancellor and the Ombudsman can claim significant accomplishments as educators. For example, the Ombudsman advised the Ministry of Justice concerning the rights of a specific complainant who had been returned to prison because of misconduct while on probation; apparently at the Ombudsman's suggestion, this advice was then generalized in the form of instructions circulated to all prison administrators. Similarly, when the Chancellor has bluntly told a Minister that his staff should note the result of a particular case handled by the Chancellor's office, the invariable consequence has been a ministerial communication for subordinate officials' future guidance. Ombudsman's rulings that may have general significance are published in police magazines, one for higher ranking officers and one for the police force in general, giving the rulings an impact far beyond the isolated cases that occasioned complaints. In 1963 the Ombudsman concluded that the Ministry of Finance had disregarded pertinent statutory directions concerning collective bargaining with civil service organizations. Mindful that bargaining sessions were about to commence in various units of the Ministry of Social Affairs, he requested the head of that ministry to issue a bulletin incorporating for his subordinates' information the Ombudsman's admonition to the Finance Minister. The Minister's quick compliance with this suggestion warded off what might have been a widening controversy.

Without minimizing the educational value of moves like these, one must nevertheless note that the watchmen's work is usually more redressive than instructive. Awareness of the Chancellor's and the Ombudmsan's actions is inadequately disseminated. Their judgments are, more often than not, little known islets in the vast sea of public administration.

Both officers view their annual reports to Parliament as their chief channel of communication to officialdom and to the world at large. Their expectation that these reports will be read and pondered is not wholly mistaken. A random sampling of administrators in different parts of Finland showed in 1964 that some do indeed say they read the reports carefully—a child welfare officer here, a provincial prosecutor there, a rural district administrator somewhere else, a judge of a provincial court in yet another place. But the readers are more than offset by the non-readers. A number of judges remarked evasively that they "thumbed through the reports occasionally"; a senior provincial administrator declared that "we get a couple of copies each year, and of course anybody who wants to read them is welcome to do so"; a major ministry believes that few of its officials in the field receive or read the reports, "though we do have several here in the ministry somewhere and we probably have a copy in the library that could be consulted if someone were individually interested." In short, close study of the Ombudsman's and Chancellor's judgments has not become a conventional part of official life, but is, rather, a matter of individual initiative.

To some extent this reflects sheer unavailability of the documents in question. Until recently the Ombudsman's annual report appeared in an edition of about 700 copies. In 1963, however, 2,047 copies were printed in Finnish and 725 in Swedish.[52] About 1,700 copies were sent to various public offices and institutions, the remainder being sold to or otherwise distributed among libraries, scholars, newspapers, and interested persons in Finland and abroad. So restricted a circulation means that general awareness of the reports' contents can be achieved only through supplemental publicity.[53] Some ministries, seemingly more alert than others to find interesting lessons in the reports, occasionally issue bulletins and staff communications that distill general directives from the Ombudsman's or the Chancellor's reactions to particular occurrences. Chiefly, however, the reports are received in silence.

[52] The Constitution of Finland provides in Article 14 that "Finnish and Swedish shall be the national languages of the Republic. The right of Finnish citizens to use their mother tongue, whether Finnish or Swedish, before the courts and the administrative authorities, and to obtain from them documents in these languages, shall be guaranteed by law . . ." About 7.4 percent of the population of Finland according to the 1960 census is Swedish speaking. Of the 189 professorships at the University of Helsinki 23 are designated as "Swedish," and students may use their mother tongue in work with all professors.

[53] Of course the determination of an individual matter is made known by letter to the immediately affected official or organ long before the annual report appears.

The silence extends to the public press. Finnish newspapers pay little attention to the general work of either the Ombudsman or the Chancellor. Of course when major officials are enveloped by political scandals, as in the rare instances when the watchmen have proceeded against Cabinet ministers, newsmen's excitement becomes intense. A few general problems—motion picture censorship and governmental labor relations, for example—have been mentioned by the press. For the rest, as a former Ombudsman remarked, "the day by day activities pass unnoticed. They don't have enough sex and crime ingredients to interest the papers."

The newspapers' inattention to the Chancellor and the Ombudsman handicaps the work of these officials. In other countries the ombudsmen have been able to arouse a certain amount of journalistic fervor about the importance of what they are doing. As a consequence, their prosecutions, reprimands, and recommendations are widely reported in the daily press and thus come to the notice of many officials who would not receive or read an annual report. More than that, the journalists' response to what the ombudsmen do creates, in turn, a larger public response to their efforts.

The press appears not to be unfriendly to the Chancellor and the Ombudsman, nor are they unfriendly to the press. They are simply aloof. As shown in an earlier section of this discussion, newspaper reports cause little stir in the watchmen's offices, nor do those offices make much effort to arouse the newspapers' interest. Possibly the fruits of their work would become more impressive if, as in Sweden, journalists could be made aware of its significance and could be aided in following it closely.[54]

11 | Concluding Observations

Veli Merikoski, one of Finland's best know legal scholars, has effectively discussed his country's mutually complementary efforts to guar-

[54] The Finnish Official Documents Act of 1951 broadened the opportunity to utilize materials in the Ombudsman's or Chancellor's possession. In a recent instance the Ombudsman has himself protected and enforced the newspapers' right to know and to inform their readers; he directed the Helsinki municipal government to reveal the names of applicants for appointment to a staff vacancy.

antee legality of administrative action and, simultaneously, to nurture governmental effectiveness. "The provisions which ensure that decisions shall be just," he has written, "cannot be made so stringent that the decisions will be considerably delayed. This means that the demand for guarantees of legality cannot be allowed, in administration, to push aside altogether the demand for prompt and elastic action—that is to say, for efficiency . . . The trend towards efficiency which is felt in administration makes it impossible to reach perfection in the field of preventive guarantees of legality. Even if such guarantees were to be made as strong as possible, the imperfections inherent in all human institutions would not allow a total suppression of faulty decisions."[55]

Finland has highly developed its means of correcting those faulty decisions that have not been totally suppressed. Few official determinations that affect private persons are unchallengeable. The Supreme Administrative Court has broad powers of review and its members possess both the independence and the professional capability to exercise those powers meaningfully. Moreover, the ordinary courts of law have capacity to deal with administrative improprieties—not only with the graver kinds that would be regarded as malfeasance in any country, but also with lesser faults that would be regarded elsewhere as noncriminal ineptitude or slothfulness.[56] To assure that such matters can be brought within judicial reach an unusual provision of the Finnish Constitution authorizes private parties, quite independently of the prosecutor's office, to commence a criminal action against a public official.[57] Judges as well as other law administrators are personally liable to those injured by their mistakes, but the injured person often has the option of suing the state, which is financially able to pay whatever damages may be awarded and which must then reimburse itself as best it can from the actual wrongdoer.[58]

[55] V. Merikoski (note 21 above), at 127, 128, 129.

[56] See Penal Code §40.21, quoted at page 59 above.

[57] Finland Const. Art. 93(2); see Merikoski (note 21), at 133.

[58] This "protection" is not an unmixed blessing, according to some Finnish lawyers. Officials who fear the possibility of having to pay damages sometimes fail to exercise their judgment vigorously, it is said; the public interest may suffer from overcaution as much as from overaggressiveness and often may suffer even more. Furthermore, disbursing officials are said to be unduly rigid in passing on claims against public funds; if a claimant is underpaid, he can sue to recover the full amount of his claim, but if the claim has been honored and the auditor of accounts later concludes that an overpayment has occurred, the disbursing official must reimburse the public treasury. Lawyers think this leads disbursing officials, anxious to avoid all risk of

With so many legal safeguards available today, the question arises whether the Chancellor and the Ombudsman are still needed—as undoubtedly they once were—to be the public's watchmen against official mistakes. Nobody in Finland appears to have doubts on that score. Public servants and private persons alike speak cordially about their two official complaint bureaus. Their mere existence is generally regarded as a valuable shield against oppression—in much the same way as a nation's military force is usually thought to be a shield against aggression.

"Little Man" and "Big Government" are among the most widely accepted clichés of our times. Brawny allies like the Chancellor and the Ombudsman may fortify Little Man's supposedly constant and necessary efforts to avoid being crushed by Big Government. That seems to be the conception now underlying these two offices.

A considerable discrepancy may be noted between conception and reality. Neither the Ombudsman nor the Chancellor has sprung quickly to the defense of basic rights in time of trouble since Finland achieved independence. Both of them have become righteously wrathful about a person's being fined a penny more than the permitted maximum, or being detained in jail an extra day because the jailer has misread the calendar. Nobody, however, recalls their taking an unpopular stand in defense of larger civil liberties when these have been under heavy pressure, as unfortunately they have been more than once.

Even in smaller issues with a civil liberties cast, the Ombudsman shows no marked eagerness to range himself on the citizen's side. For example, the Ombudsman's help was sought in 1964 by a conscript whose superior officers had forbidden his publishing an article favoring general nuclear disarmament and pacifism. On the basis of rather vaguely identified "principles," the Ombudsman deemed this restriction upon the citizen-soldier to be permissible. The Constitution says that "Finnish citizens shall enjoy freedom of speech and the right to print and publish . . . without interference,"[59] except that this provision does not prevent "the establishment by law of restrictions which are necessary . . . as far as persons on military service are

---

personal liability, to reject claims they really regard as probably valid, with the result that litigation is often necessary to settle accounts that should have been uncontested.

[59] Finland Const. Art. 10.

concerned.[60] No such restrictions had been established by statutory law, if that is what the Constitution means "by law." Obviously an inexpert foreigner cannot pretend to debate finer points of constitutional law with a distinguished Finnish jurist. All that can be said here is that the Ombudsman's analysis revealed no libertarian inclinations.

Another 1964 example may be of interest. A motion picture importer complained that the Film Inspection Office—the film censorship board—had been biased and had disregarded laws applicable to its work. After extensive correspondence the Ombudsman concluded that the Office had indeed been prejudiced and, moreover, had entrusted some of its censorial activities, quite improperly, to a clerk or bookkeeper. He then admonished the Office to behave itself better in the future and also sent a copy of his decision to the Cabinet, to whom he vaguely suggested the desirability of taking steps to guide the Office in order to ensure the legality of its later proceedings. His reactions seem mild when compared with his and the Chancellor's stern insistence upon precision in other areas of general significance.

In 1962 a number of complainants reported that they had been confined in a workhouse and had been forced to labor for their families' support, without having been accorded an opportunity to be heard. The records of the workhouse falsely showed, they asserted, that a hearing had been held. Investigation proved their charges to be well founded; the records were untrue. But the Ombudsman remarked, without any great display of indignation, that the workhouse had no statutory duty to give a hearing anyway, so its inaccuracy could be overlooked.[61] He did suggest, in restrained terms, that hearings might be desirable in the future. Had the Ombudsman thought of himself as the citizen's champion against naked governmental might, he would assuredly have driven this point home with all the force he could command.

In the same year a resident of a rural community complained to the Ombudsman that municipal officials had "warned" him that he must improve his manners in dealings with his neighbors. The complainant, who apparently shared Mr. Justice Brandeis' feeling that "the

[60] Finland Const. Art. 16.

[61] This tolerance of inaccurate records may be contrasted with the prosecution of City Judge P—— in the preceding year. The minutes of a trial for violation of liquor laws had been defectively compiled by Judge P—— though apparently without prejudice to the convicted defendant, who did not appeal. The judge was convicted of imprudence in office and was reprimanded.

right to be let alone" is the right "most valued by civilized man,"[62] argued to the Ombudsman that public officials had no competence to intrude into his personal affairs. The Ombudsman, having inquired into the matter, agreed that the local authorities had acted beyond the limits of their power. But he dropped the issue there, without either a stern admonition or an eloquent essay that might perhaps have reinforced the sorely beleaguered right of privacy.

None of this suggests that the Ombudsman is supernumerary or that the Chancellor is unimportant. The Chancellor would be important if he never received or acted on an individual complaint; his service as legal adviser to the Cabinet would alone justify his existence. With little to distract him, the Ombudsman can concentrate on citizens' complaints and in doing so he doubtlessly performs a valuable social function.

In the end, nonetheless, one comes away with the feeling that in dealing with the problems of Little Man and Big Government, both offices have lacked verve. Their potentialities have been only partly realized. "Legality" has been given so technical a signification that the public at large has no warm feeling for what they do. Technicality is not in itself to be derided. Formalities create normalities in law administration. "The history of liberty," as Mr. Justice Frankfurter well said, "has largely been the history of the observance of procedural safeguards";[63] and this is true even as to those safeguards that appear to the layman to be "mere technicalities." At some point, however, formal correctness becomes formalism and technicality becomes pettifoggery. That point seems very close to being reached in Finland today.

The public at large is unlikely to burst into cheers when the Chancellor reports, for example, the recent prosecution and reprimanding of youthful Judge Edward Andersson. Andersson had penalized one Paavo Lehti for disregarding a summons to appear in the court of Espoo. Unfortunately the summons was written on a printed form that bore the address of the old courthouse from which Andersson's court had recently moved. The location of the new courthouse had, however, been printed in the newspapers, it was posted on the door of the abandoned courthouse, and it was not a closely guarded

[62] Olmstead v. United States, 277 U.S. 438, 478 (1928).
[63] McNabb v. United States, 318 U.S. 332, 347 (1943).

secret in Espoo. Lehti had not explained his absence by saying that he had been unable to find the court to which he had been summoned. Yet Andersson was prosecuted. When the court of appeal refused to convict him, an appeal was taken to the Supreme Court, which finally agreed that the young judge had committed the crime of "imprudence" when he had punished Lehti for ignoring the summons.

A succession of cases like that one might justify the thought that Finland's watchmen were watching for the wrong things, or at any rate were using too powerful magnifying glasses in their search for flyspecks.

Major lapses from governmental rectitude are, fortunately, not matters of constant occurrence in well ordered countries like Finland. The Ombudsman and the Chancellor cannot be criticized, therefore, for failing to achieve daily sensations by exposing arrogant administrators, bungling bureaucrats, grasping governors, and oppressive officials. If other countries were, however, to seek lessons in Finland's experience, they might conclude that the citizenry's guardians need bold initiative and keen awareness of the implications of individual episodes even more than they need a passion for detail.

three

New Zealand

"When the Government in early 1961 circulated a proposal to transplant the ombudsman from Scandinavia to Wellington," a top-ranking New Zealand official recently recalled, "my Department was strongly against the whole idea. We regarded it as just a political maneuver and, as a matter of fact, we may have been right at the time. But now, after nearly three years of experience, we are just as strongly in favor as then we were opposed. The Ombudsman has proved to be a good thing for the citizen—and for the Department, too."

" 'OMBUDSMAN' BILL SHEER HUMBUG," proclaimed a banner headline in the official organ of the New Zealand Public Service Association, whose 48,000 members in governmental posts make it the largest employee organization in New Zealand. The proposal, the *Public Service Journal* continued in September, 1962, "is half baked. It panders to sectional prejudices—those directed against officialdom. If it works at all, it will cause confusion and disgruntlement . . . It is the public servant, and only he, who is to be harassed and hounded as part of the policy of halting the welfare state in its tracks . . . The Commissioner will be a party creature—an apologist for the Government while in office and the spy of the appointing party when in opposition."[1] Three years later the same periodical exulted, in its most prominent news columns, that the Ombudsman's annual report had once again exonerated the Public Service from any charge of malpractice and had found fault with relatively few decisions. "In one respect," the Journal added, "the Ombudsman has proved to be an even better

[1] 49 *Pub. Serv. J.* no. 9, p. 2, cols. 1, 2, 3 (1962).

friend of the Service than these figures suggest. He has laid down precedents for investigating some of the administrative acts of the State Services Commission regarding individual public servants—and has issued some sharp rebukes to the Commission . . . It is becoming increasingly clear that the office of Ombudsman is not necessarily the trap for public servants which many of us feared when it was first established. Indeed, the present incumbent is making it probable that public servants will make more and more use of the office for settlement of otherwise unappealable grievances."[2]

A close analyst of the proposal to create a Parliamentary Commissioner for Investigations told the legal profession in 1962 that the office would probably be unattractive to men of talent: "very few persons would accept appointment, and those few would be least suitable."[3] On the very day the proposal became law later in that year, the New Zealand legislature unanimously elected Sir Guy Powles, K.B.E., C.M.G., to be the first holder of the newly created post. After having been a successful lawyer and soldier, he had served for eleven years as the High Commissioner of Western Samoa when it was a United Nations trust territory in New Zealand's charge, and had then become New Zealand's first High Commissioner (or ambassador) in India. A former Attorney General had remarked that the appointee should be "a very wise, a very mature, a very tolerant person."[4] Despite the earlier fear that only the "least suitable" would accept appointment, Sir Guy fully met the qualifications just quoted. An Australian law professor has well described him as combining "an intimate knowledge of his country's government and leading political and administrative personalities with a profound belief in freedom and democracy; he is shrewd, tolerant, good-humoured, imbued with a sense of the value and limits of his office, and quite without vanity or self-importance."[5]

[2] 52 *Pub. Serv. J.* no. 6, p. 1, cols. 1, 2, 3 (1965).

[3] C. E. Purchase, "The Parliamentary Commissioner for Investigations," [1962] *N.Z.L.J.* 321, 322.

[4] Quoted in J. F. Northey, "A New Zealand Ombudsman?" [1962] *Pub. L.* 43, 51.

[5] G. Sawer, *Ombudsmen* 32 (1964). But compare J. F. Northey, "New Zealand's Parliamentary Commissioner" in D. C. Rowat, ed., *The Ombudsman: Citizen's Defender* 135 (1965): "Sir Guy, who is 58, has had wide experience . . . If any fault can be found in his qualifications, it is on the administrative side. His lengthy service abroad denied him an up-to-date knowledge of New Zealand's public administration and upon appointment he was virtually unknown to many of the senior officials with whom he must deal."

These sharply contrasting observations—somewhat resembling the "unretouched BEFORE and AFTER photographs" with which advertisers of reducing pills and other nostrums beguile potential purchasers —suggest a triumphal march more than a governmental activity. The present chapter addresses itself to the question of whether the "BEFORE and AFTER photographs" tell all.

1|New Zealand and Its Governance

The "ombudsman concept" is very simple. It means only that a citizen aggrieved by an official's action or inaction should be able to state his grievance to an influential functionary, empowered to investigate and to express conclusions. Such a functionary does not operate in a vacuum. Knowledge of an ombudsman's surroundings is prerequisite to understanding how he works.

The country. New Zealand is a decidedly prosperous country, roughly the size of New York, New Jersey, and Pennsylvania in combination. Its population numbers about two and a half million. A member of the British Commonwealth of Nations, it governs itself as a constitutional monarchy. Queen Elizabeth II, the Head of State, is represented by a Governor-General. Actual power rests in the unicameral Parliament, the eighty-member House of Representatives, elected triennially. Two political parties, National and Labour, have held all the seats in that body during more than three decades past.

The Cabinet. The majority party—at present, the National—forms the Government. The Cabinet, comprising fifteen ministers in addition to the Prime Minister, puts forward virtually all the legislation adopted by Parliament. Its members are the political heads of the forty-three Departments of State.[6] Each Minister is directly responsible for law administration in the Departments he controls.

The Departments. The chief executive of a Department is its Permanent Head, a high-ranking public servant responsible to the

[6] The number of Departments is given as 41 in *Report of the Royal Commission of Enquiry on the State Services in New Zealand* 18–19 (1962). The "Schedule of Departments and Organisations to Which This Act Applies," annexed to the Parliamentary Commissioner (Ombudsman) Act 1962, lists the larger number of 43 under the heading of "Government Departments."

controlling Minister, but neither appointed nor removable by him.[7] Departmental determinations are, in the main, communicated in the name of the Permanent Head or his delegate; "New Zealand has not preserved the fiction that the Minister himself has taken the decision."[8]

Departmental personnel from top to bottom are within what is, in American official jargon, "the classified civil service." Appointments, job ratings, and salaries are determined by the State Services Commission, whose judgments in these matters have been statutorily removed from Cabinet control.

Non-departmental administration. Functioning outside the departmental structure are administrative organizations designed for limited though highly important purposes. They include such bodies as the National Roads Board, which decides upon the location and type of new highway construction projects, and the Earthquake and War Damage Commission, which administers a State insurance fund in aid of disaster victims. Twenty-two organizations, including those just named, have been affected by the 1962 statute that created the Ombudsman. Some are subject to ministerial control though unconnected with any department.[9]

Parliamentary control over administration. The House of Representatives is the supreme authority in New Zealand. Its powers are limited not by law, but only by tradition and judgment. Ministers and those whom they direct are subject to challenge, rebuke, and revision by the House as a whole.[10]

Even so, while the Opposition or a private member can occasionally ask an embarrassing question, few wrongs are righted as a result of

[7] Permanent Heads and Deputy Permanent Heads are chosen by a statutory board composed of two Permanent Heads and two members of the State Services Commission. "We receive an expression of opinion by the Minister when a vacancy occurs," a member of the board recently said, "but there is no political yes or no by him or anyone else." The two Permanent Heads who sit on a selection board are chosen by the Minister from a panel of eight elected by the Permanent Heads themselves.

[8] Northey (note 5 above), at 127.

[9] Northey (note 5), at 130: "Relatively small areas of the economy have been committed to tribunals that function outside the normal departmental organization and are in no way controlled by a Minister or his department."

[10] The present Government has in fact sought to strengthen parliamentary control and to enlarge the capacity of private members to inquire into administrative actions. Improvements in the system of parliamentary control are well discussed in C. C. Aikman and R. S. Clark, "Some Developments in Administrative Law (1964)," 27 *N.Z.J. Pub. Admin.* 45, 55–60 (1965). The innovations have been especially effective in respect of examining the expenditure of public moneys.

members' thrusts at ministers. When a constituent complains to his member, the member's usual first step is to send the complaint to the cognizant minister, with a request for his comment. The minister in turn asks the Department to draft a reply; the reply ordinarily tells the member (and, through him, the complainant) that the minister finds no cause for changing the decision. Only rarely do the member's representations induce a minister to reject the departmental view of the matter.[11] The minister's stand, as the dean of the Victoria University law faculty has said, is usually "impregnable because he and his departmental officers alone have full possession of the facts."[12] Agreeing that "rightly or wrongly, the minister can plead superior knowledge as a way of disarming criticism," the present Minister of Justice has candidly added that New Zealand's markedly insistent party discipline "has perhaps made accountability of the executive to Parliament something less than a full-blooded truth."[13]

The House of Representatives also maintains a bipartisan Petitions Committee (and, when needed, two such committees) to consider what are somewhat sentimentally called "appeals to the highest court in the land." These include prayers for relief from determinations of public organs and claims for monetary compensation, as well as proposals for general or special legislation, the latter not being pertinent to this discussion. After hearing the petitioner's evidence and receiving such material as the department involved may choose to submit, the Committee rather speedily formulates a recommendation. "Committees," the Auckland law faculty's dean has observed, "tend to be more sympathetic than the Administration towards the petitioner; in fact it is sometimes said that they have been irresponsible. Invariably, the recommendation of the Committee is adopted by the House; the resolution, together with fuller reports from the departments concerned, is then carefully considered by a Cabinet Committee and finally by Cabinet itself. At this level the departmental view is more likely to prevail. It is understood that about half of those petitioners in respect

[11] Northey (note 5), at 128. Compare G. Powles, "The Citizen's Rights Against the Modern State, And Its Responsibilities To Him," 13 *Int. & Comp. L. Q.* 761, 766 (1964): "On the floor of the House the Minister is usually expected to support his department, but in the process of advising Ministers on their answers the organs of the administration are sometimes compelled to reconsider dubious decisions."

[12] C. C. Aikman, "The New Zealand Ombudsman," 42 *Can. B. Rev.* 399, 416. (1964).

[13] J. R. Hanan, "Any Complaints?" *The Australian,* Nov. 26, 1964.

of whose petitions the Committees make a 'most favourable recommendation' receive some kind of award . . . Committees realise that only petitions supported by such a recommendation have any prospect of adoption by the Government. This causes them to support rather more warmly than might otherwise be justified a petitioner who has a genuine grievance . . . It is recognized that a committee which has no financial responsibility . . . is likely to make a most favourable recommendation in cases which may not entirely merit such support."[14]

Members of the House with whom the work of the Petitions Committee was recently discussed were of two minds about its utility from the standpoint of persons aggrieved by administrative acts. Two prominent members of the Opposition declared that the Committee could function effectively if the Government were required to explain every rejection of a committee recommendation; they acknowledged, however, that they had not advocated that step when they themselves had been Cabinet members. Others felt that the Committee, while useful as a "last resort tribunal" to deal with unusual episodes (not long ago, for example, a "most favourable recommendation" was made in a matter that had been pending since the 1930's), had little value in reducing the frictions of day-to-day government. This view is supported by available statistics,[15] as it is by the experience of legislative committees elsewhere.[16]

The judiciary and its relation to administration. The tradition of an independent judiciary is solidly entrenched in New Zealand. Judges, appointed permanently until reaching the compulsory retirement age of 72, can be removed only by the House of Representatives.[17] The

[14] Northey (note 4 above), at 49; and see also Northey (note 5), at 128–129.

[15] Committee recommendations "For Consideration" or "For Favourable Consideration" are regarded as gentle equivalents of rejection. During the years 1950–1956, only 47 out of 303 petitions were recommended "For Most Favourable Consideration." Of those involving money claims, compensation was received in only a fourth of the "most favourable" group. During the five years preceding 1964, only 17 out of 253 petitions were recommended "For Most Favourable Consideration." Six of these recommendations were substantially accepted by the Government, four were partly approved, and seven were rejected. See Powles (note 11), at 766–767.

[16] Compare W. Gellhorn and L. Lauer, "Congressional Settlement of Tort Claims against the United States," 55 *Colum. L. Rev.* 1 (1955).

[17] Informal pressures initiated by the Bar did, however, cause the resignation of an ill-tempered judge in 1921, while two Magistrates have in more recent years been nudged into retirement earlier than they had planned, because of complaints concerning their conduct. No formal procedures for discipline or admonition exist, other than the ultimate (and unused) sanction of removal from office.

Court of Appeal (three judges) hears appeals from the Supreme Court. Thirty-six Stipendiary Magistrates conduct both civil and criminal trials of lesser importance. Honorary Justices of the Peace may try certain minor offenses in rural areas and, particularly on Saturday mornings, in the cities. In addition, specially appointed judges preside over, respectively, the Court of Arbitration (in labor relations matters), the Compensation Court (in workmen's compensation cases), the Land Valuation Court, and the Maori Land Court.

Quite apart from the judiciary, more than sixty administrative tribunals and authorities pass upon individual cases at both the trial and appellate levels.[18] While some of the matters committed to tribunals may be regarded as petty, their decisions almost surely dispose of more money and property each year than do the judgments of the Supreme Court.[19]

Moreover, the tide has run strongly and rather uncritically in the direction of committing fresh duties to tribunals instead of courts. In 1963, for example, an Indecent Publications Tribunal was created partly to assure consistent decisions and partly on the perhaps mistaken assumption that identification of obscenity is a task fully within the competence of "experts" though not of jurists.[20] In 1964, when New Zealand commenced the important social step of awarding compensation to persons injured by physical crimes, the task of determining the

[18] An admirable report on New Zealand's administrative tribunals was published in 1965 by the Department of Justice under the title *The Citizen and Power: Administrative Tribunals.* It brings together data concerning the tribunals' membership, relationship to other organs, procedure before, during, and after hearing, and amenability to judicial review. An earlier work edited by the present Secretary for Justice (that is, the Permanent Head of the Department of Justice) provides valuable background material; see J. L. Robson, *New Zealand: The Development of Its Laws and Constitution* (1954).

[19] G. S. Orr, *Administrative Justice in New Zealand* 81 (1964).

[20] Compare W. Gellhorn, *Individual Freedom and Governmental Restraints* 21 (1956): ". . . administrators who make decisions concerning such abstractions as 'obscenity' . . . are not experts, though they may sometimes be specialists. No well defined educational process or routinized training has equipped them, as distinct from judges and jurors, to determine the delicate issues of philosophy, aesthetics, psychology . . . It is precisely here that administrative judgment is most subject to miscalculations, distortions, and delusions." And compare the conclusion, after exhaustive study, stated by W. B. Lockhart and R. C. McClure, "Literature, The Law of Obscenity and the Constitution," 38 *Minn. L. Rev.* 295, 320 (1954): "No one seems to know what obscenity is. Many writers have discussed the obscene, but few can agree upon even its essential nature." See also M. L. Ernst and A. V. Schwartz, *Censorship: A Search for the Obscene* (1964).

facts was committed not to courts, which are certainly used to dealing with crimes and compensation, but to a Criminal Injuries Compensation Tribunal.[21] The astute Chief Justice, who was then Solicitor General of New Zealand, has sardonically observed a "reluctance on the part of Parliament to bother the courts with small issues and an unwillingness to trust them with large."[22]

The shunting aside of the courts is perhaps explicable in part by the incapacity of judges in other days to keep in tune with the times.[23] Believing that modern judges do not share their predecessors' deficiencies, many New Zealand lawyers now urge that additional adjudicatory responsibilities should be carried by the courts in the first instance. "If a policy admits of expression with sufficient certainty to make principles to be stated by the draftsman or extracted by the judge," the present Chief Justice contends, "then the courts ought to be trusted to apply it. If not, then the politicians should give the task to a tribunal or, preferably, think again. The need for trained and experienced detachment in decision must be weighed against the desirability of special knowledge or lay participation in the area of dispute."[24]

As yet, this opinion has not gained the ascendancy. On the contrary, the courts have not only been precluded from applying new policies directly, but have been narrowly limited in their power to review the decisions of the newer tribunals that do apply them. In many instances an appeal from a tribunal lies not to a court, but to an "authority"—often a single person—who may review and revise without restraint, and whose judgment is, as a practical matter, unreviewable elsewhere

[21] The tribunal is described in Orr (note 19), at 61–63. See also B. J. Cameron, "The New Zealand Criminal Compensation Act, 1963," 16 *U. of Toronto L. J.* 177 (1965), and "Compensation for Victims of Crime: The New Zealand Experiment," 12 *J. Pub. L.* 367 (1963).

[22] H. R. C. Wild, "The Place of the Administrative Tribunal in 1965," a paper delivered at the Third Commonwealth and Empire Law Conference, held in Sydney, Australia, on August 26, 1965.

[23] Compare Wild (note 22), at 5: "The insistence of some judges on the letter rather than the object of legislation has encouraged the tribunal system . . ." But compare Orr (note 19), at 79: "In so far as any tendency can be discerned, it is to create a special appeal authority where the number of appeals is thought to justify this course, but otherwise to assign the task to either the Magistrate's Court or the Supreme Court. However, a special authority may be constituted in cases where, despite the limited number of appeals, special qualifications are deemed necessary."

[24] Wild (note 22), at 7.

either as to the law or the facts.[25] In a lesser number of cases judicial review is provided as to questions of law or, very rarely, as to the merits of the administrative decision.[26] No clear pattern emerges; one is inclined to think that the availability and scope of judicial review have been determined by accident fully as often as by design.[27]

Whatever may be the true explanation, the courts in fact rarely have the experience of dealing with administrative decisions; the reported cases over a recent ten-year span include only fifty-six court proceedings that involved administrators or tribunals.[28] Less than a third of these attempts to rectify grievances related to Departments or ministers, the balance having to do with ad hoc tribunals and special bodies.

The situation is not, however, as bad as this discussion may make it seem. The caseloads in most of the tribunals and appeal authorities are

[25] As to the limited effectiveness of "prerogative writs" as a means of surveillance over the exercise of statutory powers, see Orr (note 19), at 107 et seq. But see Waterside Workers' Federation v. Frazer, [1924] *N.Z.L.R.* 689, 701–703; Re Otago Clerical Workers' Award, [1937] *N.Z.L.R.* 578.

[26] Even when statutes have empowered them to engage in "full review," New Zealand judges have been reluctant to pass upon the merits of determinations made by others who are presumed to have specialized knowledge. For examples, see Orr (note 19), at 80. Wild (note 22), at 5, commenting on cases of this type, remarks that the legal profession as a whole has very shortsightedly "shown too little readiness to tackle the problem of adapting legal institutions to modern requirements. This curious policy of self-denial on the part of many lawyers is matched by occasional examples of judicial restraint amounting almost to abdication of function in the field of administrative law." He cites a judge's refusal to review the discretion of a licensing agency because "none of the regular courts of the country can have that special knowledge" which the judge attributed to the licensing appeal authority—one lawyer. And see also C. C. Aikman, "Some Developments in Administrative Law (1959)," 22 *N.Z.J. Pub. Admin.* 59–62 (1960).

[27] Former Solicitor General Wild remarked recently, for example, that if the Trade Practices Commission were to command an economically important business to terminate relationships the Commission regarded as unduly restrictive, an appeal would lie only to a one-man Appeal Authority and no farther. If the Motor Spirits Licensing Authority were to suspend a gasoline filling station's license, the suspension order could, by contrast, be appealed first to the Appeal Authority (again, one man) and thence to the Supreme Court and yet again to the Court of Appeal.

And see G. S. Orr, "Administrative Justice," [1965] *N.Z.L.J.* 83, 85: "An aggrieved litigant in the Magistrate's Court, if the matter in dispute is of the value of £50 or more, may appeal as of right to the Supreme Court. Compare this situation with that of a company which earlier this year sought from the Price Tribunal a price increase amounting to £150,000 per annum. The decision when issued simply stated the increase granted (it was considerably less than that sought); *no* reasons were given. There is no right of appeal."

[28] Powles (note 11) at 769, 772. The grievants gained some measure of relief in 40 percent of the cases that were taken to court.

small.[29] The person who conducts a hearing can himself consider and formulate the decision.[30] The appeal authorities are in many instances Magistrates or Judges of one of the special courts, and are thus presumably dispassionate and well trained. They may serve in several different bodies, deftly changing their "expertness" to fit the needs of the day; the late Sir Francis Frazer, a prominent lawyer trained also as an economist, was at one stage of his career the Transport Appeal Authority, the Industrial Efficiency Appeal Authority, and the Sea-Fisheries Appeal Authority, and occupied his remaining idle moments by being also the chairman of the Goods Services Charges Tribunal and the chairman of the War Pensions Appeal Board.[31]

The state of administrative justice nevertheless causes considerable concern in New Zealand. A decade ago one of the country's most highly regarded public servants recognized that administrative tribunals gain strength from continuing contact with a special field and, being unencumbered by pompous traditions, can adopt cheap and speedy procedures. But, he asserted, "administrative tribunals tend in practice to be less independent than the ordinary courts and display a lower standard of objectivity and impartiality."[32] This opinion is widely shared, though supporting evidence has rarely been adduced. Because of uneasiness concerning the largely untrammeled power of administrative adjudicators, lively professional discussion has occurred concerning possible improvements and protections.[33]

While focused at first chiefly on the more obviously adjudicatory bodies, the discussion helped set the stage for a more general con-

[29] So, for example, the Police Appeal Board, presided over by a Stipendiary Magistrate, sat during only five days in the fiscal year 1964–1965, considering the grievances of seven appellants from disciplinary or other personnel decisions. Report to the House of Representatives on the N.Z. Police, Appendices to the Journals of the House (1965), H. 16.

[30] See Northey (note 5), at 130.

[31] Robson (note 18), at 127.

[32] *Ibid.*, at 126.

[33] A significant beginning was made by R. B. Cooke, "The Changing Face of Administrative Law," [1960] *N.Z.L.J.* 128, proposing an Administrative Court which could not only review the legality of administrative determinations, but also revise decisions it deemed unwise. A scholarly work by G. S. Orr, cited in note 19 above, further stimulated discussion of the administrative court idea and also put forward proposals for an administrative procedure act. See also the same author's article cited in note 27 above and his "An Administrative Court," the Scott Memorial Lecture for 1965, N.Z. Inst. of Pub. Admin. For criticism of the Orr thesis, see Aikman and Clark (note 10)), at 64–69.

sideration of the citizen's relationships with officials. In 1960, for example, a former Minister of Justice reacted negatively to advocacy of an administrative court, but at the same time declared his belief that "the further one gets away from the point where policy is made to the point where it is administered over the counter in the district offices all over the country, the greater is the need for some method of review to ensure that the citizen is getting a fair deal."[34] What was really needed, he asserted, was not a new court or more judicialization. What was needed was an independent *administrative* means of reviewing exercises of power.

Thus was the curtain raised on political developments that led to New Zealand's adopting the ombudsman concept.

2|The Creation of the Ombudsman

In November, 1960, the National Party, then the Opposition and about to contest a general election, issued a statement of policy embodying the former Minister's view. Good government, the Party's election statement said, "requires the co-operation of the people in accepting as fair and reasonable the decisions of the administration. To ensure that members of the public in dealing with Departments of State have the right and opportunity to obtain an independent review of administrative decisions, the National Party proposes to establish an appeal authority. Any person concerned in an administrative decision may have the decision reviewed. The procedure will be simple . . . The appeal authority will be an independent person or persons responsible not to Government but to Parliament . . ."

The National Party having been returned to power at the end of 1960, the newly designated Minister of Justice, J. R. Hanan, became responsible for putting flesh on the bones of this campaign promise. To the Department of Justice fell the task of advising him and his colleagues in the Cabinet. By great good fortune, the energetic and scholarly Secretary for Justice, J. L. Robson, was already well informed concerning the Scandinavian ombudsman institution, espe-

[34] [1960] *N.Z.L.J.* at 137, quoted in Aikman (note 12), at 400.

cially as it had been developed in Denmark.[35] Hence the policy choices the Cabinet would face could be quickly sketched. As early as February, 1961 the Minister of Justice had declared again the Government's resolve to create a New Zealand institution akin to the ombudsman—"not of course merely copying the idea from other countries but adapting it to conditions here."[36]

Remarkably little external interest or pressure pushed the Government in that direction. A single questioner in the House of Representatives asked in August of 1961 whether the Government still meant to introduce a bill along the lines the Minister had indicated. He was answered affirmatively. So far as can now be ascertained, nobody else seemed to care.

Meanwhile, however, the Department of Justice proceeded with its work. A detailed draft was circulated among the various departments for comment, and the views of two professors were sought. A further draft, incorporating the suggestions received, came before the Legislation Committee of Cabinet, was searchingly examined and somewhat revised there, and was submitted to the House of Representatives at the end of August, 1961. Neither the House nor the press gave it a warm reception, partly because the revised bill seemed somewhat anemic. No action was taken at that session of the House.

Before the House met in 1962, the Department of Justice had pressed successfully for Cabinet reconsideration of various limitations

[35] Dr. Robson, then Deputy-Secretary of Justice, had attended a United Nations seminar in Ceylon in 1959, along with then Minister of Justice Mason. At that seminar a paper prepared by the Danish Ombudsman was read and discussed, though its author was not present. Brief references to the discussion were subsequently made in New Zealand by Mr. Mason and Dr. Robson; see [1959] *N.Z.L.J.* 221; 22 *N.Z.J. Pub. Admin.* 79 (1960). But these gentlemen were not proselytizing. It is plain, moreover, that the National Party had adopted the "appeal authority" idea before rather than after assuming office. Hence one cannot accept the suggestion put forward by a New Zealand author: "When the National Party defeated the Labour Party at the polls and took office at the end of 1960, the previous Attorney-General, a highly respected but elderly lawyer, was replaced by an equally highly respected but much younger man whose ear the Secretary for Justice would appear to have gained." A. G. Davis, "The Ombudsman in New Zealand," 4 *J. Int. Comm. Jur.* 51, 52 (1962). Similarly, the available evidence does not support the assertion of Sawer (note 5 above), at 25, that "the idea of having such an officer at this time was due largely to personal contacts and enthusiasms" of Messrs. Mason and Robson. The present Minister of Justice disputes Prof. Sawer's opinion concerning the origin of the idea, but adds: "Dr. Robson's familiarity with the institution, however, had important consequences at the drafting stage of the legislation." Hanan (note 13).

[36] Quoted in Aikman (note 12), at 401.

upon the proposed ombudsman's authority. A fresh bill, clearly reflecting the Government's desire to provide the ombudsman adequate power to accomplish his mission, was introduced early in the 1962 session. At a committee hearing on the bill the Public Service Association (the main organization of public servants) attacked the proposal in principle and in detail. The Law Society, the Constitutional Society, and an individual attorney suggested changes, but were generally favorable. That was the extent of expressed public reaction.

During discussion in the House, a few Opposition members scoffed at the notion that an administrative investigator would be useful, but debate was in a markedly low key. In the end, the House made only one change in the bill. The Government had proposed that the new statute be cited as "the Parliamentary Commissioner Act 1962"; and Section 2 provided that "There shall be appointed, as an officer of Parliament, a Commissioner for investigations, to be called the Commissioner." The House amended: The Act as finally passed on September 7, 1962, is to be cited as "the Parliamentary Commissioner (Ombudsman) Act 1962" and it creates "a Commissioner for investigations, to be called the Ombudsman." While the Act never again uses the word ombudsman, but consistently refers to "the Commissioner," the Scandinavian designation is the one that has prevailed in common usage. New Zealand acquired an addition to its vocabulary as well as a new official.

This is rather unspectacular legislative history. It has been recounted here because its very calmness reveals how little the Ombudsman was a response to excited clamor. No scandals had shaken confidence in public administration. No example of maladministration was cited in the House or elsewhere to show the need for a new safeguard. No festering abuses were thought to necessitate drastic surgery. The Ombudsman was created not to clean up a mess, but, rather, simply to provide insurance against future messes.

3 | The Ombudsman Statute and Some Questions It Has Raised

Appointment, tenure, and perquisites. The Ombudsman is, in theory, to be "Parliament's man" and not an agent of the executive. The statute provides that the Governor-General is to appoint him upon each Parliament's recommendation; this means that his normal term is three years (the life of a Parliament), though of course he may then be reappointed; in any case, he is to remain in office until a successor has been appointed (Sec. 4).[37] The Parliament may choose anyone it wishes, for the statute sets forth no qualifications for the office other than that the appointee must not be a member of Parliament (Sec. 3).

The method of appointment is unusual in New Zealand and may, in fact, be unprecedented. Cynics say that since the Government controls the votes of its partisan supporters, it can in fact dictate the choice of the Ombudsman. The form of election seems, however, to reflect a genuine resolve to stress the Ombudsman's detachment from the ordinary processes of political appointment. At the same time, the Ombudsman's limited term of office causes some New Zealanders to see a threat to his independence.[38] Experience in Denmark, which has the same pattern as New Zealand, should reassure them somewhat. A notably independent Danish Ombudsman has held office continuously since 1954, having been re-elected by successive Parliaments quite without reference to partisan considerations.

Unlike the Scandinavian countries, which have set their ombudsmen's salaries at the topmost salary level of the public service, New Zealand chose to pay its ombudsman somewhat less than judges and a very few department heads. The choice, once having been made, is probably irreversible; personal sensibilities would be bruised if the ombudsman were now to be elevated still further in the governmental hierarchy. This is unfortunate because the ombudsman's salary does

[37] Removal or suspension from office is possible only "upon an address [to the Governor-General] from the House of Representatives, for disability, bankruptcy, neglect of duty, or misconduct" (Sec. 5). The provision is the same as that pertaining to Supreme Court Judges.

[38] When this topic was discussed in New Zealand in 1965, a number of persons called attention to a remark by Minister of Justice Hanan when presenting the original version of the ombudsman bill in 1961: "His position comes up for review every three years, so that in effect it is easier to get rid of him than it would be to get rid of the Controller and Auditor General or a Judge. He will be in a very powerful position to criticize Government administration, and our Government might appoint a man who was not the concept of what an Ombudsman should be for, say, a Socialist Government which might want a quite different type of individual." (New Zealand) Hansard for Aug. 29, 1961, 1806. The Minister adheres to the view that the best way to disarm suspicion of the Ombudsman is to make impossible any Government's choosing somebody for the purpose of embarrassing a successor Government. The fact that no political advantage can be gained by, as it were, leaving a spy behind enemy lines will in his opinion encourage selection of persons who can command the confidence of all, thus making for stability rather than frequent changes.

to some extent serve as a status symbol; the higher his status, the more likely his success. Furthermore, a higher salaried judge or public servant might be unwilling to become the Ombudsman, were a future Parliament to decide that he would be its first choice.

Once in office, the Ombudsman is largely independent. His salary cannot be diminished (Sec. 7). He is not subject to the superintendence of the House or any of its committees. For "housekeeping purposes" he is attached to the Legislative Department, whose Permanent Head is the Clerk of the House of Representatives. He is not, however, in any degree an element of that department in the sense of being directed by its officials; the Department, on the contrary, is subject to being investigated by him, like any other Department of State. The only discernible controls over him lie with the Prime Minister (who determines the number of staff members the Ombudsman may appoint) and the Minister of Finance (who approves their salaries and the terms and conditions of their appointments).

Matters within the Ombudsman's jurisdiction. The Ombudsman's principal function, Section 11 of the statute declares, is "to investigate any decision or recommendation made (including any recommendation made to a Minister of the Crown), or any act done or omitted, relating to a matter of administration and affecting any person or body of persons in his or its personal capacity . . ." A Schedule annexed to the Act lists the Departments and other public organs whose affairs may properly concern the Ombudsman. The list is lengthy, but it notably omits administrative tribunals and appeal authorities; it includes, as one of the draftsmen of the law put it, "all the bodies we thought the public regarded as part of the country's day to day administration."

Acts of ministers. The authority to investigate recommendations made to ministers deserves special note. During Cabinet discussions, considerable difference of opinion arose as to whether the Ombudsman should be empowered to review decisions made by ministers themselves. To allow him to do so, some said, would be to undermine the principle of accountability to Parliament. On the other hand, if all actions taken by ministers were to be exempt from later examination by the Ombudsman, a scheming or timid administrator could immunize himself against investigation simply by obtaining his minister's approval of every debatable action. The compromise solution was to put a minister's decision beyond the Ombudsman's reach, but to allow him to inquire into the departmental recommendations upon the basis of which the minister had presumably acted. Thus the possibility of an official's using a minister as a screen or shield was overcome, while at the same time the parliamentary purists were content to observe that ministerial responsibility to the House had been unimpaired.[39]

The differentiation seems to have worked out comfortably enough in practice thus far, though by any realistic analysis the Ombudsman expresses an opinion concerning the soundness of a decision when he evaluates the soundness of the advice on which it rests. In 1964, for example, he acted upon the complaint of two British schoolteachers who had been induced to come to New Zealand for service. Part of the inducement had been the promise of low rent in State-owned houses; but soon afterward the Cabinet had raised the rent. "The original decision to raise the rents of Public Service pool houses," the Ombudsman wrote, "was taken by Government and was thus not within my jurisdiction to investigate—nor were the subsequent decisions of Government on this matter. I was, however, bound to investigate the recommendations made by the Department of Education which formed the basis of the Minister of Education's submissions to Cabinet." Those recommendations, he found, had been put forward in good faith, but were nonetheless defective.[40]

[39] Minister of Justice Hanan, who was not among those perturbed by the possibility of the Ombudsman's looking at a minister's decision, has discussed ministerial responsibility as follows (note 13): "It means that a department is subject to the direction of its minister, and that the minister is accountable to Parliament not only for his *personal* acts or decisions but also for the acts or decisions of his department.

"By 'accountable' is not meant 'personally responsible for' but 'subject to examination.' . . .

"Why then should it impair the principle of ministerial responsibility if the Ombudsman discloses that the act complained of was the act of the department and not that of the minister? The recognition of the right of the minister to direct his department remains unimpaired, as does the accountability of a minister to Parliament . . ."

During the debate on the bill that became the Ombudsman Act Mr. Hanan, commenting on the provision relating to departmental recommendations, had said: "If the Minister follows that recommendation, then criticism of the recommendation will in effect be criticism of the decision. If he does not follow the recommendation, then that fact will doubtless be stated by the Commissioner. In either event the Minister in the light of the Commissioner's findings will eventually be called upon to justify his action in Parliament and that is where the Minister should be called upon to account for administrative acts." Quoted in Powles (note 11), at 756–766.

[40] Case No. 752, Ombudsman's Report 1964, at 29. This or a similar case may have occasioned the following remark by the Assistant Director of Education, quoted in Aikman and Clark (note 10), at 50: ". . . if [the Ombudsman] found it necessary to explore the confidential territory that lay between a permanent head and his Minis-

The risk of too sharp a clash between the Ombudsman and the Cabinet is somewhat lessened by Section 15(5) of the Act, which provides in part that a Minister may request a conference in relation to any matter the Ombudsman is investigating and, further, that whenever an investigation relates to any recommendation made to a minister, the Ombudsman must consult that minister "after making the investigation and before forming a final opinion . . ."

A Cabinet member, asked recently whether he thought that the Ombudsman's power to inquire into departmental recommendations had discernibly affected him or any of the departments for which he had responsibility, answered: "Yes, in two ways. At first I thought that more things might be passed up to me for initial decision, without the department's taking responsibility. That has not happened, as a matter of fact. Many of the recommendations that do come to me, though, seem to me to be better worked out, more carefully considered than they used to be; and this is partly because they can now be scrutinized elsewhere. The second change is that when I am myself interested in a matter—for example, because of representations by Members—I am likely to have a number of conversations with my people before they make any recommendation at all. I'm not disposed to have recommendations made that may later force me to justify having disregarded them. So I sometimes persuade the department to give me the advice I want to accept."

"A matter of administration." The Ombudsman is to investigate acts *relating to a matter of administration,* as distinct from a matter of policy. The Ombudsman himself refers to this as a "notoriously difficult distinction" and acknowledges that he has not been able to "construct any guiding principles," being forced "merely to decide, upon common sense grounds, each case as it arises."[41]

Agreement upon what is commonsensical is just about as rare as agreement upon what is a matter of administration. Some of the Ombudsman's decisions have been strongly criticized because, in the critics' view, they dealt with matters that should have been left to political controls.

---

ter and to disclose to his complainants the recommendations of Departments to Government, that in time would destroy the confidence between Minister and Department that was essential in a democracy."

[41] Powles (note 11), at 775.

Cases No. 10 and 334, for example, grew out of complaints that the Department of Health had too actively sought to influence voters in a local referendum on whether the public water supply should be fluoridated. The matter of fluoridation having been left to local option, the Ombudsman concluded that "direct active campaigning by a Government Department in the local referendum was wrong." The Department's activities, though undertaken conscientiously, "exceeded the proper functions of furnishing information or of pursuing normal health education activities." The Ombudsman advised the Department to refrain from similar activism in future, unless otherwise specifically directed by the Minister of Health.[42] Obviously the Ombudsman regarded the cases as involving "administration." Others thought that they had to do with general direction of the Department's affairs and were therefore within the realm of "policy" for which the Minister was responsible. A confident conclusion concerning this disagreement is not easy, because the Ombudsman's report of the cases necessarily omits certain Cabinet documents which he perused, but was not free to publish.

Case No. 719 necessitated another difficult choice. Several citizens had expressed belief that the Department of Internal Affairs had failed to effectuate the provisions of the Civil Defence Act. The Ombudsman pressed for information, taking the view that a "matter of administration" must include a "failure to administer." Conversations between the Ombudsman and cognizant officials explored the Department's plans for informing the public, developing regional and local activities, and so on. Not content with progress after the elapse of several months, the Ombudsman wrote the Director of Civil Defence that "by now sections 10–13 of the Civil Defence Act should be put into active administration and execution"; the Department was under a duty to administer the Act and, if it needed more staff or funds, "it was the duty of the Director to make the appropriate representation to his Minister." Soon afterward "a firm start was made in administering the relevant sections of the Act." A year later the Ombudsman took another look at the situation and "became satisfied that the Department had the matter of central administration of civil defence well in hand."[43]

[42] Ombudsman's Report 1964, at 32–33.
[43] Ombudsman's Report 1964, at 35–36; Report 1965, at 30.

The Minister of Justice, a strong supporter of the Ombudsman, has doubted whether the jurisdictional boundary had been observed in the cases just summarized. The Ombudsman's comments, he remarked, "seem to indicate that he is assuming a general supervision over Government administration which was not really intended when the office was set up."[44]

A similar observation might perhaps be made concerning Cases No. 883 and 910, in which the Ombudsman considered whether the Prisons Administration had improperly sold prison-made furniture to non-governmental purchasers. His report notes: ". . . the Department reviewed the sales policy in the light of the information gathered in connection with the investigation and, with the approval of the Minister of Justice, it was determined that sales should in future be restricted to: . . . As this policy appeared to me to be fair and reasonable and would mean an end to the sales most objected to by the complainants, I made no formal recommendation."[45]

Cases of this type have a significance beyond their particular facts because they have engendered fear in some quarters that the Ombudsman's solitary judgment has begun to shoulder aside the more traditional political processes. The fear is no doubt overblown, because, as will be shown, the Ombudsman can never do more than express an opinion, having no power at all to issue commands. Overblown or not, concern does exist and has been strongly expressed by thoughtful persons, not all of whom are officials.

Perhaps a "policy" is transmuted into a "matter of administration" when a general principle is administratively applied to a specific "person or body of persons in his or its personal capacity" (in the words of Section 11 of the Ombudsman Act). When, however, an issue is of concern to the public at large, as distinct from identifiable individuals upon whom it particularly focuses, then possibly it should be left to political controls rather than to the Ombudsman's evaluation. Were

[44] Hanan (note 13). The Civil Defense decision was also criticized in House debate and by academic writers. See Aikman and Clark (note 10), at 51; Aikman (note 12), at 419.

[45] Ombudsman's Report 1964, at 38–39. These cases differ somewhat from those just discussed in that the original complainants did have a personal interest in their outcome. In one instance, the complaint alleged a misuse of the complainants' designs; the complainants also asserted that the Prisons Administration had engaged in unfair competition with them. The Ombudsman seems, however, to have gone beyond the specific in order to deal with the general. His report discusses "sales policy" in the broad.

that test to be utilized in New Zealand, matters like those just discussed—departmental campaigning in a local referendum, languid civil defense administration, entry of prison-made products into the channels of commerce—would be deemed beyond the Ombudsman's concern because they affect society as a whole, not a person or body of persons.

The cases just considered may be contrasted with Case No. 666, involving the purchaser of a State-owned house. The purchase agreement provided that the purchaser would himself occupy the dwelling and, if he desired to sell within seven years, would offer it first to the State agency from which he had bought the property. Subsequently the purchaser was transferred to a job in another area. He obtained permission to lease the premises for three years. When he applied for an extension of that permission, he was told that the extension would be granted, but that the seven-year period affecting re-sale of the property would be extended correspondingly. Since the original agreement contained no such provision, the purchaser complained to the Ombudsman. Upon receiving the Ombudsman's representations, the State agency "reviewed its policy covering the pre-emption period of letting and decided to discontinue this requirement."[46] Here, unlike the cases previously discussed, action by public officials did have an individualized impact. An identified person's contractual obligations had been redefined. His interest in the redefinition was wholly distinct from the citizenry's collective interest in housing regulations, a fact that cannot be obscured by the opaque word, "policy."

Matters reviewable elsewhere. Section 11(5) of the Act says that the Ombudsman cannot investigate an administrative act which could be reviewed "on the merits of the case" by any court or administrative tribunal.[47] This puts beyond his jurisdiction many matters that a litigant might wish to turn over to him, in preference to bearing the expense and other burdens of pursuing appellate remedies.

[46] Ombudsman's Report 1964, at 65.

[47] The exclusion of jurisdiction in respect of this kind of case is to be contrasted with the discretion granted the Ombudsman by Section 14(1) to refuse to investigate a complaint if he finds that the complainant has an adequate remedy or right of appeal, under law or administrative practice. This refers, for example, to the possibility of a complainant's seeking review by an official within the administrative hierarchy itself, rather than by an independent body like a court or tribunal. It may also refer to review procedures that do not involve "the merits of the case," but would nevertheless suffice to deal with the particular matters complained of.

The theory behind the exclusion seems defensible enough: If the citizen's disagreement with officials can be reviewed "on the merits" by somebody who is independent of the officials and empowered to overrule them, the citizen has protection enough. No need exists for yet another reviewer in the person of the Ombudsman, and not much can be said in favor of "cheapened justice" (so the theory runs).[48]

If the sole issue to be considered is the substantive soundness of a decision affecting a private interest, and if that issue can be fully examined by a specially experienced or qualified organ designated by the legislature, then indeed the issue should ordinarily go to that organ rather than to the Ombudsman. But if the citizen's grievance pertains to the procedures or behavior of the administrators whose decision has affected him, the matter has a different cast. The experienced and qualified organ may have special insights into the technicalities of the subject involved, but its assumed expertness relates to decisional content only. Problems of public administration in the large come before the Ombudsman more frequently than before any tribunal or appeal authority. As to those problems, he is the expert, not they. In theory he may not be precluded from looking at matters of that type while appellate channels remain open, but in practice he stands aside.

Moreover, as a practical matter, use of statutory remedies after the administrative process has been completed is sometimes impracticable. The expense of going to an external tribunal or court may be prohibitive, so that an aggrieved citizen may abandon a contest even when still believing his cause to be just.[49] Why should such a person be barred from reporting his grievance to the Ombudsman, taking the risk that the Ombudsman might not pursue the matter at all or might

[48] Compare Ombudsman's Report 1963, at 6: "I doubt whether Parliament intended the Ombudsman to be a cheap alternative method of pursuing lawful claims against the Crown, and I have advised several complainants accordingly."

[49] The Ombudsman's reports themselves illustrate this likelihood. See, e.g., Case No. 760, Ombudsman's Report 1964, at 51–52 (remission of income tax was granted by the Commissioner of Inland Revenue; the applicant, a necessitous widow, could probably have achieved the same result by proceedings in the probate court to vary the terms of her late husband's will, "but was in such straitened circumstances that she could not afford the necessary costs"); and see also Case 607, *ibid.*, at 37–38 (a "land agent and farmer in a small way of business" incurred out-of-pocket expenses of £2,229 "to fend off an unjustified tax demand of £2,409" and he recovered only £378 of these costs in the end).

As best can be determined, thirty to forty persons a year are trying to take their cases to the Ombudsman instead of to a court or tribunal.

pursue it differently from the way the affected party would himself have chosen? Surely a distinction can be drawn between cheaper justice and cheapened justice. No other country that has adopted the ombudsman system has insisted as unqualifiedly as has New Zealand that judicial remedies be pursued to the end, no matter what the cost or the nature of the issue.

Some, but not many, doubts have begun to stir about the wisdom of placing appealable matters altogether outside the Ombudsman's jurisdiction. The present Commissioner of Inland Revenue, for example, discourages his subordinates from insisting that every debatable issue be tested out in formal appellate proceedings. The opportunity to litigate is of course meant for the taxpayer's protection, but the Commissioner correctly perceives that the protection is sometimes illusory. He therefore directs his staff not to contest small matters, instead of taking a tough position that will force the taxpayer to choose between surrender or a disproportionately costly war. One gathers the strong impression that the Commissioner would not oppose extending the Ombudsman's jurisdiction beyond its present limits. He is, however, a far from ordinary tax administrator.[50]

[50] The small revolution that has occurred in recent years in the Inland Revenue Department is itself interesting enough to justify a brief digression.

On May 28, 1964, the Commissioner wrote to every staff member a personal memorandum emphasizing the Department's objectives. A few quotations will give its flavor:

> "When I joined the staff of this Department as a cadet, it was impressed on me, as it was on all officers, that, firstly, I was a Revenue Officer and, secondly, that it was a breach of duty on the part of a Revenue Officer to make assumptions in favour of the taxpayer. The ideal of service was not really brought to our notice . . .
>
> "A moment's reflection should be enough to convince all that those earlier objectives are now completely untenable . . .
>
> "So we will have *Service* with *Human Understanding* and *Effectiveness* in carrying out our function of administering the Taxes Statutes. You will notice that the word 'efficiency' has not been used. This is done advisedly because it is effectiveness we want with its implication of understanding rather than the narrowness of pure technical efficiency . . .
>
> "Study Groups in some eight of our branches . . . have examined the implications and effect of errors and complaints, the reactions of the public to these, and ways and means of remedying them . . ."

Another staff communication, October 2, 1964, said in part:

TAXPAYERS *ARE* PEOPLE

"We are trying to help people—
by removing the mysteries of taxation;

Not only are fully appealable matters beyond the Ombudman's grasp, but so also are the tribunals and appeal authorities themselves. Their procedures and conduct cannot be made the object of complaint to him because these bodies are not upon the statutory list of public organs within his jurisdiction. A recent report of the Department of Justice, after noting that the tribunals' procedures are various and inconsistent, nevertheless doubted that New Zealand should emulate the United Kingdom in creating a Council on Tribunals to better the functioning of these adjudicatory agencies.[51] "It would be preferable," the Department wrote, "to charge the Ombudsman with the task of examining the working of our tribunals. This is not to suggest that he be given jurisdiction over the actual decisions of the tribunals or to act as a sort of appellate authority but simply to suggest that the Ombudsman be given power to investigate the procedure of any tribunal and to make recommendations for improvements. In our view this would be a natural and legitimate extension of his present function."[52]

---

by giving an information service to aid them in their dealings with us, and in understanding taxation;

by liberalising our rulings and procedures.

"We are making—

a planned, sustained and determined effort to do away with unreasonable and petty small-minded interpretations of both the law and our instructions.

"We want you—

to handle cases with speed, with reasonableness and with every possible courtesy and consideration. You must not strain the law purely in order to protect the revenue."

A stream of information bulletins has brought taxpayers information concerning their rights as well as obligations. Believing that statutory "tax incentives" are really meant to influence social conduct, the Commissioner has issued special bulletins and announcements about ways in which tax credits can be earned. Small taxpayers are told about new developments through prominent advertisements in newspapers—like this one on August 7, 1965, in the N. Z. Herald (Auckland), p. 11, cols. 7–8: "SPECIAL TAX REBATE FOR SOME SALARY AND WAGE EARNERS—

"If in the year ended 31/3/65 your total income was . . . *and* you had . . . *and* your . . . , you may be entitled to a special tax rebate. If you consider that you qualify under the above headings, application should be made in person or by writing to your local tax office."

[51] See The Tribunals & Inquiries Act of 1958. See also H. W. R. Wade, The Council on Tribunals, [1960] *Pub. L.* 351, and *Administrative Law* 204 et seq. (1961); J. A. G. Griffith and H. Street, *Principles of Administrative Law* 139, 140, 199, 205 (3rd ed. 1963).

[52] Department of Justice (note 18), at 15. The great variety of procedures among tribunals and appeal authorities is disclosed in some detail by the same report at xxvi-xlvii. The Report also notes that some tribunals act on evidence not disclosed to the affected parties, adding: "We are not in a position to say whether such a procedure

The military. The Danish and Finnish ombudsmen can receive complaints concerning military as well as civilian officials; in Sweden, Norway, and West Germany special ombudsmen have been appointed to deal with military affairs. Section 11(5 of the New Zealand statute forbids the Ombudsman to investigate any matter relating to a member of the armed forces if it involves "the terms and conditions of his service" or any "order, command, decision, penalty, or punishment given to or affecting him."

The Ombudsman reported in 1965 that this had prevented his dealing with twenty-eight cases, most of which, had they arisen in some other Department, would have been within his jurisdiction. He noted that about a fifth of the complaints he had received from civilian employees of the State had been found to be justified, and he saw no reason why the same proportion of well-grounded complaints might not be anticipated also in the armed services.[53]

Labour Party spokesmen, who in the beginning had been dubious about having an ombudsman at all, have more recently been urging that the Ombudsman's jurisdiction should embrace the military. Defence Department officials with whom the matter was discussed seemed unperturbed by the thought that the Ombudsman's power to deal with servicemen's grievances may be broadened. Meanwhile, perhaps stimulated by cases the Ombudsman has forwarded, the Department is reviewing and revising existing procedures for investigating compaints and redressing wrongs; the procedures vary, without apparent reason, among the three military services.

Local authorities. Local bodies are entirely outside the Ombudsman's jurisdiction. As an officer of Parliament, he investigates officials and organs answerable to it. Local authorities are neither responsible nor accountable to the national legislature.

While the structural differentiation between national and local administration is plain, a strong current is running in the direction of empowering the Ombudsman to deal with at least some classes of local affairs. Local administration, which often affects citizens more sharply than does most national governmental activity, has already occasioned

---

is justified in the circumstances and we can only suggest that the procedure should be looked at afresh."

[53] Ombudsman's Report 1965, at 8.

many complaints the Ombudsman has had to ignore.[54] Private organizations and public officials freely state the opinion that fewer controls, lesser judicial review, and more frequent crudities are to be found in local than in State administration, and that the need for the Ombudsman's services is therefore all the greater.

A number of mayors and local councilors with whom this topic was discussed readily conceded that citizens' grievances could advantageously be sent to the Ombudsman. One mayor hotly dissented, saying: "In my community, *I* am the Ombudsman and nobody else is needed." His opinion was challenged by the mayor of a larger city, who contended that members of local councils (municipal legislatures)— often, according to him, "untrained, unperceptive, irresponsible, and uninformed"—are poor mechanisms for dealing with grievances; "personalities, influences, animosities, and ambitions infect local much more than central decisions."

Even if so harsh a judgment were to be rejected, a strong case could be made for extending the Ombudsman's jurisdiction. Hundreds of special purpose bodies, many of them elected, function independently of municipal governments and with little national control.[55] Some of them, an experienced observer commented, "act like a law unto themselves." Though salaries at the local level often exceed those for posts of at least equal responsibility in the central administration, the repute of national public servants is undoubtedly the higher. "If anyone needs policing," said the executive head of a nationwide organization, "it is not the people here in Wellington, but the local and regional officials who deal with citizens in their day-to-day affairs—and who don't have the same degree of professionalism we have come to take rather for granted in the major Departments."

[54] Ombudsman's Report 1965, at 75, shows that nearly a fifth of all complaints made to the Ombudsman between October 1, 1962, and March 31, 1965, pertained to "unscheduled organisations," that is, administrative bodies outside his jurisdiction. A large share of these were local authorities. In an address in 1964 the Ombudsman declared that in cases involving "a conflict between public interest and private right"—such as land ownership, water rights, flood damage through public works, and so on —"I have received a greater number of complaints of this kind against local bodies, that were outside my jurisdiction, than against agencies of central Government." Powles (note 11), at 785.

[55] In 1965 New Zealand was said to have 918 local authorities, roughly two thirds of them having "non-territorial functions" such as electric power distribution, drainage, education, and hospitals. The *Dominion* (Wellington), July 16, 1965, p. 2, col. 1.

Some counter-current exists, too. First among the contributors to it is, of course, the amalgam of parochialism and fear that makes for strong political opposition to any possible lessening of local autonomy.

Second is the belief in some quarters that the Ombudsman would be overburdened were local as well as national problems to flow to him. "We would need several ombudsmen, not one, to deal with grievances involving local authorities," one Department Head thinks, "because the areas of contact with the individual citizen are so much more numerous and so much broader at the local level." A highly influential journalist agrees; while local authorities should be made amenable to somebody's observation, "we must be sure not to overload the Ombudsman. There will be no gain for anyone if his office becomes computerized." A Cabinet member, who had on one occasion advocated extending the Ombudsman's power, now takes a different view because, as he put it, "this simply must remain a one-man job if it is to be wholly effective and I'm not sure that the Ombudsman could handle more cases than he already has on his plate." The Ombudsman does not share this particular concern. He has reported that "a single personal Ombudsman could, with a larger staff than I have but still reasonably small, effectively handle more cases than are now dealt with by the New Zealand Office."[56] More specifically, he recently expressed belief that his caseload could be multiplied by four, to a total of about 3,000 per year, if suitable staff assistants were provided to handle details and to undertake necessary legal research.

Even if localism and fear of overwork were to be overcome, delicate thinking would still be needed to fit the Ombudsman into the pattern of local control. Reports to Parliament about municipal disagreement would be inappropriate. Denmark has met a similar problem by directing its ombudsman not to concern himself with the acts of locally elected legislative bodies as such, even when they have a strongly administrative flavor, but to report to those bodies any criticisms he sees

[56] Ombudsman's Report 1965, at 9. The Ombudsman's staff in mid-1965 consisted of three professional employees (a lawyer, an administrator, and an investigating officer) and two clerical employees. He also utilized the part-time services of another lawyer and another typist. Section 24 of the Act empowers him, with the Prime Minister's prior approval, to "delegate to any person holding any office under him any of his powers under this Act, except this power of delegation and the power to make any report under this Act." No such delegation had in fact occurred as of early 1966.

fit to make concerning officials within their respective territorial jurisdictions.

A beginning may be made in New Zealand by enlarging the Ombudsman's ability to deal with the administrative activities of authorities whose local operations are financed by the national treasury.[57] Education boards and hospital boards are the most prominent examples. Their decisions, as a high official of the Department of Education acknowledged not long ago, "can be quite as oppressive as any other, and fully as hurtful in their effects upon individuals as those made by State agencies." Since many persons regard these boards as "disbursing agents of the State" even though their members are locally chosen, political opposition to bringing them into the ombudsman system may be weak.

Moreover, while the boards make day-to-day decisions independently, they are already amenable to guidance by central administration through generalized rules and policy directives. This occasionally enables the Ombudsman to make his influence felt obliquely. Case No. 829, for example, was initiated by a permanent employee of an education board, who complained that he had been dismissed for misconduct without being afforded a fair hearing. The Ombudsman could not take up the case because the acts of education boards are outside his jurisdiction. But, upon reading the existing regulations, he concluded that the non-teaching staff of education boards were inadequately protected against unjustified disciplinary action. "I recommended to the Director of Education," he later wrote, "that the regulations governing the employment of such staff should be amended to provide . . . for a written charge . . . and for a right to a hearing before a responsible and impartial investigator. I have been informed by the Director of Education that the proposal has been welcomed, and that action is being taken with a view to drafting amendments that will meet with the approval of the employing authorities and the employee organisations."[58] The Ombudsman's ingenuity in addressing himself to the Director of Education while ignoring the education board no doubt failed to solace the original complainant; but it did lead to future

[57] This possibility is discussed in G. Powles, "The Ombudsman and Local Government," 1965 *Local Body Rev.* 252.

[58] Ombudsman's Report 1964, at 30–31.

safeguards for education board employees whose problems are supposedly not among his worries.

What the Ombudsman can do. The Ombudsman recently asserted that a full quarter of his effective working hours must be devoted to resolving his own doubts about jurisdiction.[59] That fact alone shows how ticklish are some of the problems suggested by previous sections of this paper.

In the cases he finds to be within his jurisdiction and that he does investigate, the Ombudsman is free to consider whether the administrative action in question was (1) contrary to law; (2) unreasonable, unjust, oppressive, or improperly discriminatory, or was based on a law or practice that could be characterized in that way; (3) based wholly or partly on mistake of law or fact; or (4) just plain "wrong," to use the unadorned word in the statute. He can also examine the propriety of the purposes and grounds underlying an exercise of discretion.[60]

This is indeed a broad scope of inquiry, far broader than that typical of the Scandinavian countries, where the ombudsmen concern themselves with the permissibility of administrative acts, with maladministration, in short; they rarely reappraise the evidence or suggest revised exercises of discretion.

New Zealanders, learning that their Ombudsman has deemed approximately 16 percent of the investigated complaints to be well founded, have expressed surprise that their public servants are so frequently at fault. They had heard, when the proposal to create an ombudsman was being debated, that only about 10 percent of the Scandinavian complaints had been held justified. New Zealand has no cause to be alarmed. The Scandinavian statistic indicates the percentage of justified complaints among the whole number of complaints received; the New Zealand statistic shows the percentage of justified complaints among those that were actively investigated. Actually, fewer than 9 percent of total complaints received in New

[59] Even after that time expenditure, he does not always persuade everyone else that his jurisdictional analysis is sound. See Ombudsman's Report 1965, at 8, 30, 35, 37. The statute contains two references to possible court proceedings to determine jurisdictional boundaries, Sections 11(7) and 21, but they have never been used and, if a foreigner's analysis of New Zealand law has any validity at all, they are useless, as a practical matter.

[60] Ombudsman Act, Sec. 19(1) (2).

Zealand are upheld (as is shown in Table VIII). Since the New Zealand ombudsman's power to express personal preferences is somewhat greater than his Scandinavian counterparts', the statistical evidence is by no means discreditable to New Zealand public servants. Precise statistical comparison is, in any event, quite impossible because the various ombudsmen have differing jurisdictional limitations as well as differing standards of judgment.

The record of the Ombudsman's first two and a half years of work is summarized in Table VIII.[61]

Table VIII. Action on complaints, Oct. 1962–Mar. 1963, inclusive

	Number	Percent
Total received	1,843	100.0
Declined — no jurisdiction	672	36.5
Declined — Section 14(2)[a]	31	1.7
Discontinued — Section 14(1)[b]	94	5.0
Withdrawn by complainant	105	5.7
Investigated and rejected	706	38.3
Investigated and upheld	161	8.7
Still under investigation	74	4.0

[a] Section 14(2) of the Act permits the Ombudsman to decline to act on complaints that relate to matters older than a year, or that relate to matters he regards as trivial, or that are frivolous or vexatious or not made in good faith, or that involve matters in which the complainant has little personal interest. So far as can be ascertained, almost all the declinations under this section have thus far been on the last stated ground.

[b] Section 14(1) authorizes the Ombudsman to discontinue an investigation if he thinks the complainant should pursue some other remedy or if he concludes that, "having regard to all the circumstances of the case, any further investigation is unnecessary."

Table VIII indicates that fewer than ten out of a hundred complaints are finally deemed to be meritorious. Those are the ones in which Section 19(3) of the statute authorizes the Ombudsman to recommend (1) further consideration; (2) rectifying an omission; (3) canceling or varying the decision; (4) altering any practice upon which the administrative action was based; (5) reconsidering any law

[61] The material in this table is largely derived from Ombudsman's Report 1965, at 73–74.

upon which it was based; (6) giving reasons for the decision; or (7) taking "any other steps" he thinks fit. He sends his report and recommendations—not his commands, for he has no power to command—to the administrative body concerned, with a copy to the appropriate minister. Then, if the administrative body does not act to his satisfaction within a reasonable time, the Ombudsman "in his discretion, after considering the comments (if any) made by or on behalf of any Department or organisation affected, may send a copy of the report and recommendations to the Prime Minister, and may thereafter make such report to Parliament on the matter as he thinks fit."[62]

That is the extent of the weaponry at the Ombudsman's disposal. He cannot revise what has been done administratively. He cannot direct that an omitted step now be taken. He cannot prosecute or discipline offenders against good order.[63] He can only write and persuade.

The power of the pen appears to have been adequate. In only one case has his recommendation been directly rejected. He advised the National Roads Board to pay £40 to the owner of a motor car damaged because notices had not been suitably posted to warn of a known defect in the highway; the Board refused to go higher than £25 and there the matter rested.[64]

It would be incorrect, however, to suppose that the Ombudsman's views are always swallowed without a murmur. Unlike Jove, he does not hurl thunderbolts from on high. Administrative authorities have sometimes stuck by their guns, and the Ombudsman has then concluded that they were right after all, thus averting a clash.[65] Sometimes, too, the Ombudsman can perceive that he and a minister are on a collision course, and he chooses to avoid the collision.[66] An outspoken

[62] Ombudsman Act, Sec. 19(4).

[63] Section 15(6) of the Act provides that if the Ombudsman, during one of his investigations, believes "there is evidence of any breach of duty or misconduct on the part of any officer or employee of any Department or organisation, he shall refer the matter to the appropriate authority."

[64] Case No. 106, Ombudsman's Report 1962, at 14.

[65] E.g., Case No. 98, Ombudsman's Report 1963, at 13; with which compare the same case, Ombudsman's Report 1964, at 68.

[66] E.g., Case No. 1760, Ombudsman's Report 1965, at 17: An importer complained that he had been refused permission to transfer his import license from one make of motor car to a more popular make. From the papers at hand, the Ombudsman perceived that "the decision complained of was that of the Minister of Customs himself, made after having before him all relevant submissions by the applicant (which were put to him directly) as well as by the Department, and in addition the Minister had also heard the complainant in person." Concluding that the complainant had already

opponent in the House of Representatives sneered recently, "The Ombudsman talks a lot about not being flouted, but he is canny about 'discovering' some reason not to push along when somebody is likely to challenge him. He knows how not to get into battle." A more kindly disposed Department Head, commenting on matters of this type, remarked: "The Ombudsman had military experience, you know. He has enough sense to try to pick favorable terrain for a fight. You can call it maneuvering if you like, or running away from a wrestling match if you don't like it. I call it, simply, recognition of the old saw about discretion being the better part of valor."

More important, as a matter of normal operations, is the Ombudsman's prudent awareness that he may be mistaken. Administrative reactions to tentatively formulated recommendations can enlighten his judgment and save him from error. Hence, before he makes his final pronouncement, he often consults those to whom the pronouncement will be addressed, thus obtaining a preview of its acceptability. A number of administrators spoke warmly of this practice, saying that it made them feel less the objects of censoriousness and more the Ombudsman's partners in correcting defects. The Ombudsman, on his side, readily acknowledges that preliminary discussions have frequently influenced the tone and content of recommendations. In one recent instance he had prepared a series of four admonitions to an administrative agency. As to the first, he learned that remedial steps had previously been taken; as to the second, the practice had been different from what he had supposed and was in any event in the process of change; as to the third, he became convinced that the criticism he had had in mind was unjust; and as to the fourth, a proposal similar to the one he had drafted was already under active study. Naturally, his final recommendations were reshaped in the light of this information; and, as reshaped, they were entirely acceptable though a different outcome would have been likely had they been announced in their original form.

How matters reach the Ombudsman. Section 13 of the Act provides that anyone, including persons in custody and patients in mental hospitals (whose letters must be forwarded unopened), may complain

had adequate consideration by the Minister, the Ombudsman "determined not to proceed with an investigation into the acts or recommendations of the Customs Department in the matter."

to the Ombudsman in writing.[67] A filing fee of one pound ($2.80) is required "unless, having regard to any special circumstances, the Commissioner directs that no fees shall be payable."

While the sources of complaints have not been categorized for purposes of precise statistics, surprisingly many of the cases included in the Ombudsman's several reports were initiated by substantial businessmen, lawyers, and accountants.[68] On the other hand, few complaints have been filed by inmates of mental institutions and virtually none by persons in prisons or other places of detention. This is noteworthy because these two groups bulk large in the caseloads of all the Scandinavian ombudsmen.

A prison administrator, asked to explain why New Zealand prisoners were so uncomplaining, answered frankly: "They haven't yet learned about taking their grievances to the Ombudsman. And we haven't been eager to educate them." Another possible explanation is that New Zealanders, unlike Scandinavians, must pay for the privilege of writing to the Ombudsman. This requirement probably weighs heavily on prisoners and other impecunious persons.[69]

From the very first, the proponents of the ombudsman institution in New Zealand have insisted that, as the National Party's election policy declared in 1960, "To avoid frivolous appeals, a reasonable fee should be charged." Frivolous appeals have certainly been made to the Scandinavian ombudsmen, whose services are gratuitous. Notwithstanding the filing fee, they have been made in New Zealand, too. Perverse and empty complaints, however, can usually be identified quickly. They can then be disposed of without greatly burdening the Ombudsman or

[67] Section 11(2) of the Act also authorizes the Ombudsman to investigate upon his own initiative. This authority is rarely and, at least thus far, insignificantly used. During the fiscal year 1964–1965, the Ombudsman took up only three matters on his own motion, two as a result of newspaper stories and one because he had personally observed what he regarded as inadequacies in the form to be filled in by a person wishing to license his motor vehicle. Cases No. 1267, 1563, 1245, Ombudsman's Report 1965, at 26, 27, 38.

[68] For example, Cases No. 927 (manufacturer of agricultural chemicals), 954 (commercial aviation company), 1166 (importer of textiles), 1216 (timber importers)—Ombudsman's Report 1965, at 13–15. Cases No. 666, supra note 47, and 815 (Report 1964, at 66) are good examples of attorneys' successful use of the Ombudsman after other remedial efforts had failed.

[69] But compare Northey (note 5), at 138: The "modest fee . . . will, it is expected, be sufficient to discourage the frivolous and the crank, but not be so high that genuine complaints will be inhibited."

anyone else. If a nation is to have a grievance commissioner at all, much is to be said for allowing complaints, whether "frivolous" or not, to flow to him freely. Channelizing grievances is more socially valuable than discouraging them by a price tag. The New Zealand Ombudsman, replying to a direct question, recently said that he perceived neither need for nor advantage in the present filing fee requirement.

Public servants, who have been among the Scandinavian ombudsmen's best customers, have begun to bring a substantial number of problems to the New Zealand Ombudsman. These have pertained chiefly to retirement pay, appointments, and termination of employment during the probationary period. Disciplinary matters involving officials are thoroughly reviewable elsewhere by well understood procedures, and have played no part in the Ombudsman's workload. Local and national officers of the Public Service Association, having overcome their initial hostility to the Ombudsman, have actually suggested that individual members take their cases to him, but the Association has not as yet represented them in these matters. The Railway Officers Institute, which is the collective bargaining agent of the national railways' salaried staff and office workers, has adopted a somewhat more prickly attitude. It has criticized the Ombudsman for receiving a complaint filed by a railway employee, asserting that the Institute alone should decide how and where to press its members' unresolved grievances.

Most interestingly, some alert officials have considered whether the Ombudsman might not be able to help them climb over hurdles. One Department head, for example, commented not long ago on the misfortune of retired public servants whose pensions have remained stationary while living costs have risen. "Former staff members have been complaining very vigorously," he said, "and I really sympathize with them. But I haven't any means of making the adjustments they have requested. One of the men was especially insistent a few days ago that I did have discretionary authority. I disagreed, but I finally suggested to him that he go to the Ombudsman, to see if the Ombudsman can find a power I haven't discovered. I hope he does."

How the Ombudsman proceeds. If the matter complained of seems to lie within the Ombudsman's jurisdiction and if he chooses to investigate, his invariable first step is to communicate the complaint to the head of the public organ involved. The head is requested to comment or to provide pertinent information. In the beginning the Ombudsman never writes directly to the officer involved.

Section 15 of the Act gives the Ombudsman scant procedural direction. His investigation is to be conducted in private; he may obtain information and make inquiries as he thinks fit, without any hearing, except that before making a report which "may adversely affect any Department or organisation or person," he should give the affected body or person a chance to appear before him.

In general, the Ombudsman moves ahead by correspondence with the complainant, the governmental agency involved, and others who may have knowledge of the matters involved. Occasionally he makes on-site inspections, somewhat like a jury's taking a view, but the Act does not require him to make inspections routinely.[70] He interviews witnesses in his office and elsewhere, but informality is certainly the keynote throughout. Moreover, the Ombudsman varies his investigatory technique as circumstances may suggest. So, for example, when a complainant alleged that the Department of Education had been less generous to him than to other similarly situated graduate students, the Ombudsman requested the students named by the complainant to complete a questionnaire providing sufficient information to permit a valid comparison between their and the complainant's situation; their answers showed that the complaint was unsound.[71]

Until now, the Ombudsman has never employed a procedure akin to that of a trial.[72] This, he asserts, has been no loss. His reports show,

[70] The Norwegian and New Zealand ombudsmen are not duty-bound to make inspections; the Swedish, Finnish, and Danish ombudsmen must periodically examine the premises of governmental agencies and institutions. Both the Norwegian and New Zealand ombudsmen have expressed gratification at not being compelled to make physical inspections unrelated to matters already being investigated.

Section 23 of the New Zealand statute authorizes, but does not command, the Ombudsman to "enter upon any premises occupied by any of the Departments or organisations named . . . and inspect the premises and . . . carry out therein any investigation that is within his jurisdiction."

[71] Case No. 1120, Ombudsman's Report 1965, at 17, 18: "All the students cooperated, and in the event I found that there were valid and essential distinctions between the positions or awards of the students who had obtained suspension, and the position of the complainant, and these justified the different treatment accorded by the Department."

[72] Section 15(3) of the Act explicitly states that the Ombudsman may inquire as he sees fit and need not "hold any hearing, and no person shall be entitled as of right to be heard . . ." At the same time, his power to conduct a hearing if he wishes seems

however, that avoidance of confrontation and cross-examination does sometimes prevent his making a confident finding concerning alleged wrongdoing.[73]

Power to obtain evidence. The Ombudsman's power to obtain documentary evidence is what sets him apart from other inquirers into administrative acts in New Zealand. "Crown privilege," which permits officials to withold information whose disclosure might harm the public interest, has often forestalled judicial review and, even, effective review by administrative appeal authorities. Moreover, as previous pages have shown, questioning by members of the House loses force because the questioners do not have access to the files. A prominent legal scholar has expressed belief that the Ombudsman's ability to get at evidence others cannot reach is, indeed, the "main justification" for creating his office.[74]

As for the Ombudsman, his reach is very long indeed. Under Section 16 of the Act he may require "any person" to produce any relevant "documents or papers or things . . . which may be in the possession or under the control of that person." Section 17 says that the Attorney General (who, for many years past, has been the same person as the Minister of Justice) may certify that information should not be given because it might prejudice security, foreign relations, or the investigation of a crime, or because it might expose Cabinet deliberations or Cabinet proceedings that need to be kept secret. If he does so certify, then the Ombudsman is not to press for that information. Otherwise, "the rule of law which authorises or requires the withholding of any

---

clear. Section 16 of the Act authorizes him, among other things, to "summon before him and examine on oath" any official and any complainant and, with the Attorney General's prior approval, any other person. A person required to attend before the Ombudsman is entitled to the same fees and expenses as a witness in court; fees and expenses have in fact been paid on five occasions, when the Ombudsman requested persons other than governmental employees to come to his office in Wellington so that he might interview them.

[73] See, e.g., Case No. 802, Ombudsman's Report 1964, at 54: A public contract had been awarded to someone other than the lowest bidder, who reported an oral explanation allegedly given him by a named official; the complainant suspected that improper influence had deprived him of the contract. The Ombudsman's investigation satisfied him that "there was no evidence whatsoever of dishonesty or bad faith on the part of anyone concerned in the matter" and that the official contracting agencies had "acted prudently and correctly in all respects." The report notes, nevertheless, that the named official "denied making the observation attributed to him by the complainant, and it was impossible to determine the truth of this particular allegation."

[74] See Aikman (note 12), at 407.

document or paper, or the refusal to answer any question, on the ground that the disclosure of the document or paper and the answering of the question would be injurious to the public interest shall not apply in respect of any investigation by or proceedings before the Commissioner."

As a consequence, the Ombudsman can and does regularly request that the entire official file be turned over to him to assist his investigation. Granting so unrestricted a power to delve into departmental records was stubbornly opposed by officials and ministers during the drafting of the Act; the issue was not settled finally until a party caucus made the choice, largely on the ground that the Ombudsman would not command public confidence if Crown privilege were to remain as an impenetrable screen. Sharing the hoary faith of the British civil service, many public servants continued to feel that any outsider's examination of files, including "internal working papers" and "minutes," would gravely impair staff efficiency and candor; officials would become overly cautious and formal in communicating with one another, they asserted, if their every comment might later be scrutinized by alien eyes.

In 1965 an effort was made to ascertain whether experience had confirmed or disproved these views. Without exception the interviewed public agencies maintained that the Ombudsman's access to informal staff notes and other working papers had not had the feared adverse effects.

One Department Head said: "I do detect a shade more caution and restraint than in the past. But this really does not have any functional significance. We have had men who sometimes became a bit too free with their remarks—'We should hit this fellow and hit him hard'—that sort of thing. Well, that is discouraged now, I'm sure. But omitting a few colorful phrases here and there does not change the content of the recommendations the superior receives. If anything, getting rid of the loose language makes the recommender think a bit more clearly about what he means to say, and that is a distinct gain."

Another Department, far from skeletonizing its records, took steps to add to them after the Ombudsman came into being. In modern offices many decisions are made over the telephone or the lunch table, instead of after an exchange of correspondence. A perceptive Department Head wrote his chief aides: ". . . I want you to give thought to the question whether our methods and systems are adequate in the event of a complaint being made to the Ombudsman about any action or inaction of ours. I think it really gets down to a question whether our system of recording is adequate.

"It would be wrong to introduce methods and systems simply because we now have an Ombudsman. The test really is this: What are the demands of good administration? . . .

"A lot of our policy work is transacted orally and it seems to me that the major question is whether more of this work should not be recorded in minutes. Too much recording would be an almost insufferable burden, but I am inclined to think that we ought to do more than we do. Would one of our files read, say, five years from now yield an intelligible, coherent story without too much effort on the reader's part? . . ."

Rather extensive inquiry among administrators uncovered no indications at all that the Ombudsman's examination of official papers had had disadvantageous side effects. Perhaps discussion of the topic may be fittingly closed by the Ombudsman's own response when he was asked whether he was aware of any problem in this respect. "I have heard it said," he answered, "that expression of opinion may be inhibited. But why should a man write a silly thing for inclusion in a file? If silliness has been discouraged, what's the loss?"

4|The Ombudsman's Decisions and Some Questions They Have Raised

Facts and judgment. His office, the Ombudsman has briskly declared, was "established for the purpose, not only of checking administrative abuses and of righting of wrongs, but also of actually reviewing administrative decisions—of securing the making of changes."[75] How far, as a practical matter, can a generalist safely tamper with specialists' judgments about the conclusions to be drawn from the facts? How feasible is it for one man to repeat the time-consuming processes of evidential appraisal other officials, presumably competent, have previously completed? The Ombudsman is free to answer those questions

[75] Powles (note 11), at 774.

as he may wish, for, as the Minister of Justice has said, it is "for him to decide whether he is in a position to disagree on the merits."[76]

The Ombudsman seems not to have been greatly frightened by the responsibility thus thrust upon him. His reports are full of cases that show his duplicating the work of others and arriving at independent conclusions (sometimes different from, sometimes in accord with those of the cognizant officials).

Case No. 228 is illustrative. A home had been damaged by flood waters. The Earthquake and War Damage Commission acknowledged that the householders' loss was "extraordinary disaster damage" within the meaning of the statute it administers. The Commission paid an amount the claimants regarded as inadequately compensatory. In the course of time, the issue of damages was inquired into by an independent loss assessor, an architect, an arbitrator, and the Commission itself, one after another; then a minister was unsuccessfully asked to intervene. After all that effort had left the claimants still dissatisfied, the matter came to the Ombudsman. The main factual question was whether the house had been habitable and in good repair before the flood or whether, instead, its uninhabitability after the flood was attributable to its having been in a poor state for a long time. "After a prolonged and careful study of all the relevant facts," the Ombudsman finally concluded that the Commission's judgment could not be criticized. He added: "As a consequence of further representations made to me by the complainant and his solicitor, and because I could not escape the suspicion that the complainant's parents had in fact suffered an injustice, I undertook a complete review of the case on two separate occasions and, despite the most anxious consideration, I was unable to find that there existed any justification for departing from the conclusion I had originally reached."[77]

[76] Hanan (note 13): "Naturally in many fields he cannot be expected to substitute his own view of the merits of the case for that of the department concerned. For instance, he cannot be expected to come to an independent view on a difficult engineering problem or a public health problem even though they impinge upon an individual citizen's rights or interest.

"In those cases his concern is to ensure that the proper procedure has been adopted; that the citizen's interests have been taken into account; that all the facts have been before the department; that precedents have not been too inflexibly applied, and so on.

"He can nevertheless ask the department to justify its decision if he chooses, and it is a matter for him to decide whether he is in a position to disagree on the merits."

[77] Ombudsman's Report 1965, at 57–58.

In Case No. 327 the complainant was a historian who had edited a volume—*The Richmond-Atkinson Papers*—published by the Government Printing Office. A thousand copies were printed at a cost of nearly $30,000. At a retail price of about $20, the Government Printer doubted that the book would appeal to general readers or be gobbled up by the lending libraries. He therefore restricted the number of review copies to two, much to the indignation of the learned editor. No author in the history of man has been wholly satisfied with his publisher's promotional efforts, but this is probably the only time a high government functionary was petitioned to weigh the validity of the publisher's judgment. The Ombudsman, when asked, confidently concluded that "having regard to the nature of the work, the time, money, and labour which had been expended on this publication, and the likely appeal of the work to the serious reader, as well as the historian," the Government Printer should have been more energetic and generous in drawing attention to the book.[78]

Case No. 916 involved a rural mail carrier who asked the Post Office to pay him £40 above the agreed contract price because protracted road construction work had exposed his delivery vehicle to abnormal wear and tear. When his application was rejected, the contractor brought his unhappiness to the Ombudsman. He prompted the Post Office to reconsider the matter and to make an *ex gratia* payment of the amount sought.[79]

Cases like the trio just discussed are entirely different from those in which the Ombudsman finds that administrative misconstruction of a statute has distorted factual analysis,[80] or in which he can perceive that facts have not been adequately explored and should therefore be investigated further by the administrator,[81] or in which he must in-

[78] Ombudsman's Report 1964, at 35.

[79] *Ibid.*, at 57.

[80] E.g., Case No. 754, Ombudsman's Report 1964, at 30: An educational subvention was refused a student of architecture because he had previously failed to complete courses in engineering for which a different grant had been given him. The Department said that provisions of the legislation then in force precluded any further financial aid. The Ombudsman, having studied the relevant legislation, concluded that its terms did not support the decision. The Department considered his views and agreed that no adequate statutory authority supported the ruling it had made.

[81] E.g., Case No. 36, Ombudsman's Report 1963, at 8: A horticulturist had developed a new type of plum he hoped to introduce into Australia. The Department of Agriculture sent a report to Australia which the complainant alleged was misleading. The Ombudsman was satisfied by the evidence that the report "had contained an

vestigate allegations that an inequitable result has been reached,[82] or in which the motives of the decider are called into question.[83]

This second cluster of cases, like the first, involves highly particularized inquiries, relating to the special facts and circumstances of each complaint. The Ombudsman is not, however, looking at the same issue that the administrator has decided, to see whether he entirely agrees with the decision. Rather, he seeks answers to wholly distinct questions —is the administrative decision vitiated by incorrect analysis of applicable law, or by slipshod work that means the job remains only half done, or by improper motivation?

While the Ombudsman's recommendations in the area of fact finding and choice between one result or another seem well considered, friendly writers have remarked that some "raise matters in which there is clear room for difference of opinion as to which is the correct decision having regard to the conflict of public and private interest that is involved. Sooner or later disagreement on such an issue will bring the Ombudsman up against a determined Department or Minister"—

---

assessment that was not warranted by the Department's experience up to the time the report was sent." He therefore recommended that the Department make a reassessment and prepare a further report. The Department did reassess the plum and a more favorable report was then sent to Australia.

[82] E.g., Case No. 1687, Ombudsman's Report 1965, at 22: A foreign student in a New Zealand university complained that the Department of External Affairs had ended his financial support. He had failed in six out of ten subjects, but the complainant said the failures had been caused by personal problems that no longer existed. He thought that his problems should have been more sympathetically considered by those who had examined him, and that their disappearance had not been taken adequately into account by those who passed upon his request to be given a second chance. He thought other foreign students had been treated more kindly. The Ombudsman investigated to make certain that the factors relied upon by the complainant had been known to and weighed by the departmental committee when it decided to terminate the complainant's award. Upon satisfying himself that the committee "had good grounds for so deciding," the Ombudsman held the complaint to be unjustified.

[83] Case No. 135, Ombudsman's Report 1965, at 22–23: The widow of a founder of "what is now a very large industry" was left in desperate financial circumstances by her husband's untimely death. She thought she should have some monetary compensation because the Forest Service, Ministers, and others had fought her husband's effort to establish and nurture an infant industry. The Ombudsman's "investigation was prolonged because of the complexity of the issues involved and the consequential necessity to marshall a substantial amount of background material." In the end, he said, "I concluded that the Forest Service, in opposing the establishment and development of the industry, did so on the basis of genuinely held and at the time defensible opinions, and I found no evidence that it had been motivated by less worthy considerations. As a consequence, I was unable to make any recommendation."

and when that happens, questions will begin to arise about the scope of his power.[84]

This has, in fact, already occurred. The State Services Commission, which controls appointment, classification, and compensation of public servants much more fully than does the United States Civil Service Commission, has twice proposed that the Ombudsman should be excluded from handling complaints about salaries, grading or employees' performance, and ranking of public service jobs. "We have to see each of these problems in relation to many others," a member of the Commission observed recently, "while the Ombudsman sees a complaint in isolation. If he were to deal with the proper evaluation of a public servant's position for purposes of fixing suitable compensation, or with the relationship of one occupational category to another, he would need the assistance of an entire personnel agency—and he would then be doing the precise work entrusted to this commission, which has more experience than he does and just as much detachment and independence."

Conflict has not, however, come to a head. The Government has not yet responded to the State Services Commission's advice. The Ombudsman has thus far not supplanted the Commission's judgment about the merits of any matter, but has confined himself to inquiring into the soundness of its underlying procedures.

The man of compassion. One of the most endearing qualities of the Ombudsman is his sympathetic attitude toward persons perplexed by life, rather than victimized by officialdom. He once referred to himself as the "Auditor-General of human relations accounts," and has said that he attempts to provide the individual attention larger organizations must subordinate to considerations of speed and efficiency.

An elderly and necessitous New Zealand lady who resided in South Africa complained, in Case No. 856, that Treasury regulations prevented her receiving adequate remittances from the estate of a mentally incompetent brother upon whom she depended for support. The Ombudsman found that her problems were not, as she had alleged, caused

[84] Aikman and Clark (note 10), at 52. But compare Sawer, (note 5), at 9: The Scandinavian ombudsmen (unlike New Zealand's) "are not empowered to criticize the exercise of discretions where there is no question of excess or abuse. This comes as a surprise to many British Commonwealth observers because . . . many of our complaints against bureaucracy concern unwise use of lawful powers rather than abuse of discretion."

by the Treasury, but by the circumstances of the incompetent's estate. He could quite properly have stopped there, but he did not. "It seemed clear to me," he wrote later, "that if this lady could take appropriate proceedings in the New Zealand Courts she would have a reasonable case for an order to be made under the provisions of the mental health legislation and she might well be granted more money than she was now receiving. I asked the Law Society of the district concerned to nominate a solicitor to act for her . . . and I placed this solicitor in direct contact with the lady concerned. Proceedings . . . are reported to be making steady progress."[85]

This kind of service with a smile shines through many cases.

In Case No. 1573, for example, he helped obtain a new electric blanket and a supplementary assistance grant of ten shillings a week for a chronic invalid and was able to advise about the possibility of making home repairs with the aid of public funds.[86]

A tax statute provides a "housekeeper's exemption" when a widowed, divorced, or unmarried breadwinner must engage a housekeeper to look after his family. The Ombudsman, receiving complaints from harassed taxpayers who needed housekeepers but were not covered by the statute, found the Commissioner of Inland Revenue sympathetically inclined to grant equivalent relief on hardship grounds.[87]

A complainant wished to bring his family to New Zealand from England, but could not obtain a permit entry for his mentally retarded stepson. Under New Zealand's well established policy, denial of the permit was entirely proper, though the care and maintenance of the stepson in New Zealand had been suitably assured. The Ombudsman, despite the policy whose validity and application he did not question, requested "a further serious review in the light of the special circumstances of this particular case," and the Minister finally approved the stepson's entry "on condition that the case should not be treated as a precedent."[88]

[85] Ombudsman's Report 1965, at 45.

[86] *Ibid.*, at 41.

[87] See Cases No. 569 and 581, Ombudsman's Report 1964, at 50, 51 (complainant, legally separated but not divorced, had custody of three small children; complainant, deserted by his wife, employed housekeeper to look after his family of five children); Case No. 1085, Ombudsman's Report 1965, at 30 (complainant's wife had been hospitalized for several years, while housekeeper cared for two small children).

[88] Case No. 79, Ombudsman's Report 1964, at 39.

The Ombudsman, acting as a mediator, helped a farmer obtain an adjoining property that had been acquired by a Department whose "conduct of negotiations for the purchase had been quite proper."[89] A foreign teacher found his way through the meshes of currency regulations after the Ombudsman communicated the problem "personally and unofficially" to the Governor of the Reserve Bank, who is not within the Ombudsman's jurisdiction.[90] He cleared the path for re-entry of a former resident whose own carelessness rather than official obtuseness had been the cause of difficulty; the complainant wrote, afterward, that "the extreme courtesy and kindness attending on my requests have further encouraged my return to New Zealand."[91] He responded to the wail of a complainant who had been baffled by the procedures for obtaining a sickness benefit; "every time I apply," the sick man had said, "I get another form to fill in."[92] He sided with swimmers who were indignant because their safety had been too little regarded when the Marine Department approved a water-ski lane in a certain harbor.[93] He aided a public servant to overcome the stigma of a long past and seemingly unfair dismissal on "security" grounds.[94]

These episodes might well be characterized as social casework, and a tenable argument could be made that the Ombudsman is too high (and too highly paid) a dignitary to be a caseworker. But the cases are only incidental to his main work. They do not preoccupy him. His humane response to offbeat problems serves not only to contribute to his "clients' " contentment, but also to remind other public administrators, en masse, that human happiness is the objective of government.

Principles and guidelines. In the end, however, the Ombudsman's more important contributions to good government are made in cases that generate new principles, new procedures, new policies rather than merely new results in the odd instance—though, needless to say, the "odd instance" may sometimes generate a decisional principle for the future, too.[95] His proposals are rarely dramatic. New Zealanders have

89 Case No. 300, *ibid.*, at 25–26.

90 Case No. 1675, Ombudsman's Report 1965, at 21.

91 Case No. 1660, *ibid.*, at 34.

92 Case No. 378, Ombudsman's Report 1964, at 60.

93 Case No. 15, Ombudsman's Report 1963, at 10.

94 Case No. 986, Ombudsman's Report 1965, at 70.

95 See, e.g., Case No. 987, *ibid.*, at 42: A purchaser of a newly constructed house owned by the State subsequently discovered structural defects. The State agency

not been oppressed by bad government from which only a good knight can rescue them. The Ombudsman's job is to tidy up and improve an already commendable administration of the public's affairs.

So, for example, in Case No. 29 he found no substantiation of various complaints about treatment in public hospitals. But, while investigating, he discovered that "patients were not always aware of the full extent and likely consequences of certain types of serious gynaecological operations," and he therefore proposed a brushing up of methods for giving full information to patients beforehand. For the future protection of both doctors and patients he recommended, too, a revision of the form of consent to undergo a surgical operation; the form then in use, he thought, was needlessly vague.[96]

Similarly, he has urged specific clarification of informational circulars and instructions whose obscurity may have misled affected persons; and he has done so even when finding no basis to criticize decisions that had evoked complaints to him.[97] The desirability of adequate and accurate information has, in fact, been a major theme in the Ombudsman's reports to Parliament.[98] The message perhaps needs

---

refused to pay the cost of remedying the conditions, saying that the house had been purchased "as is" and without any warranty as to its condition. Having investigated the purchaser's complaint, the Ombudsman thought that "any person who purchased a new house, which had been built to the specifications of, and under the supervision of, a Government Department, should be entitled to expect that such a house would be constructed in accordance with good building practice, that any defects in construction should have been discovered by inspection and remedied prior to the house being taken over by the Corporation from the builder . . ." This view finally prevailed, and the defects were made good without cost to the complainant. While no new policy was announced, one can scarcely doubt that action in this case created an equitable principle that will be applied consistently in future cases of the same kind, should they arise.

[96] Ombudsman's Report 1963, at 9.

[97] E.g., Case No. 137, Ombudsman's Report 1963, at 10–11 (information to old-age pensioners concerning suspension of benefits during absences abroad); Case No. 879, Report 1964, at 41–42 (elimination of ambiguity in registration form for conscientious objectors to military service); Case No. 167, Report 1963, at 11 (adding precise information in publicity materials concerning commencing date of family benefits).

[98] Ombudsman's Report 1964, at 11: "A significant number of complaints would never have arisen except for defective or inadequate publicity or lack of notification by Departments relating to the rights or obligations of citizens. This is a matter that calls for unremitting attention and care by Departments, and particularly by those departments dealing directly with members of the public generally who cannot be expected to have a detailed knowledge of their rights and duties or to employ experts to advise them.

"Most Departments are reasonably 'publicity conscious' and attempt to disseminate widely useful information about their requirements . . . and what they can offer . . .

to be received in that august body even more than in administrative agencies. If New Zealand's experience resembles America's, the funds appropriated for what some unsympathetic legislators persistently regard as "publicity agents" and "useless publications" are rarely adequate to support well designed public education activities.

Sometimes the Ombudsman has urged administrations to free themselves from self-imposed chains, when generally sound regulations and procedures have prevented the exercise of intelligence.[99] Sometimes, on the other hand, he has proposed the forging of new or stronger chains.[100] Sometimes he has found that even though a particular decision

However, I have found that there is a tendency to allow pamphlets to become obsolete and not to withdraw, replace, or amend them—to the discomfiture of the public. I have also found too many cases where ambiguous or misleading statements have been incorporated in pamphlets designed to guide members of the public . . ."

[99] Case No. 622, *ibid.*, at 62, is illustrative. Persons in receipt of certain social welfare benefits had until recently been allowed to collect their "order books" at any time up to seven days in advance of the date on which payment of the first "order" (a cash voucher) was due. The Social Security Commission changed this rule because some welfare recipients cashed the orders in advance and, in thousands of other cases, the recipients' circumstances changed before the orders became cashable. So it issued a regulation that order books should be issued only on the date when payment was due. A mother of four young children called one afternoon at the appropriate office to collect her order book for the family benefit. She was told she would have to return the next morning, the date on which the first order was due for payment. She thought this unreasonable and complained to the Ombudsman, writing: "I left the office feeling near to tears and knowing that these Civil Servants regarded me as a nuisance for daring to question departmental red tape. Goodness knows life is frustrating enough trying to bring up four youngsters to be decent citizens without these petty restrictions —no wonder so many mothers give up trying!" The upshot of the matter was that the Chairman of the Commission apologized to the complainant and re-instructed the staff not to enforce the new procedure with unthinking rigidity in the early stages before people knew and understood it.

[100] E.g., Case No. 330, Ombudsman's Report 1964, at 71 (gossip by payroll clerks concerning the circumstances of other public employees; notice published in *Public Service Official Circular* calling attention to regulations governing disclosure of information and threatening severe disciplinary action); Case No. 695, *ibid.*, at 41 (the passport of a foreigner who had been denied a N. Z. entry permit had been passed by a N. Z. official, without the owner's knowledge or consent, to an Australian consulate, which had then canceled a previously granted Australian visa. While cooperation of New Zealand and Australian consulates is desirable in the interest of the passport owner, the Ombudsman thought that where transferring a passport was contrary to the owner's interest, "different considerations should apply and, without impairment of other aspects of collaboration, the transfer should not normally be made without the consent of the owner." The Secretary of External Affairs concurred, and instructed N. Z. overseas posts accordingly); Cases No. 224 and 274, *ibid.*, at 55 (new practice instituted of giving information to unsuccessful bidders on government supply contracts); Case No. 183, Ombudsman's Report 1963, at 11 (necessity of investigating allegations made to one Department concerning improprieties in another).

could be sustained, the Department had relied on an imprecise statutory interpretation that would cause future wrong if uncorrected.[101] Sometimes he has found that too narrowly drawn a regulation has caused individual hardship offset by no social gain, and he has then proposed appropriate revision for the benefit of persons not yet affected.[102]

Because procedural norms are not firmly established in New Zealand, the Ombudsman has had opportunity to contribute to development of the right to be heard.[103] He has also addressed himself to problems of bias and to the need of giving reasons for results reached.[104] Like every other ombudsman, he has said that complainants come to him simply because they do not understand the official action concerning them.[105] Many, when the matter had been clarified by the Ombudsman, expressed appreciation and acknowledged that they had no cause to complain. Hence the Ombudsman, echoing his fellows in other countries, has adjured administrators to explicate

[101] Case No. 460, Ombudsman's Report 1964, at 61: Recipient of a weekly family benefit applied for its capitalization (that is, for a lump sum payment instead) in order to add to the family dwelling house. The application was denied because the applicant's husband's income was adequate and because the dwelling in question was situated on the husband's farm. The Ombudsman upheld the denial on the first ground, and so informed the complainant. He concluded, however, that "there existed no adequate statutory authority to decline an application on the ground that the property was situated on a farm and that the complainant derived his livelihood from that farm." After considering the matter, the administrators agreed with this conclusion.

[102] E.g., Case No. 63, Ombudsman's Report 1963, at 8–9: Financial support was given, under a valid regulation, to students who passed from New Zealand secondary schools into one of the universities. Complainant's daughter, however, had spent her final school year at a reputable Australian institution and was therefore deemed ineligible to receive a grant. The regulations recognized overseas schooling only if the student's parent had been transferred overseas in the course of employment. The Ombudsman thought that "the regulation should be based not on the exigencies of the father's employment, but on the standard of education received by the student." The Director of Education substantially agreed, and undertook to seek a change in the regulation accordingly.

[103] E.g., Case No. 1163, Ombudsman's Report 1965, at 32 (contested registration of trade names and trademarks). And compare *The Citizen and Power: Administrative Tribunals* (1965) at 13, where the Department of Justice wrote that the lack of a defined procedure "has become much less important now that we have an Ombudsman . . . In the light of his experience he would be fitted to indicate areas where a right to a hearing could be given. Experience is essential since it does not seem possible to designate a priori the situations where a right to a hearing is called for."

[104] As to bias, see Cases No. 365 and 641, Ombudsman's Report 1964, at 9–10, 27, 74.

[105] See Ombudsman's Report 1963, at 4; Report 1964, at 4, 76.

themselves—not only, he has added, because doing so will lessen the discontent of affected parties, but also because it will aid review and, in a more subtle way, will provide "an incentive to the authority to found its decision on reasons which will stand up to criticism."[106]

So far as has been observed, administrators have not wholeheartedly followed this advice in any country where an ombudsman has tendered it. The negative result probably reflects a well founded fear that explanation of every decision would either prove an intolerably burdensome task for already overworked staffs or would become so routinized as to be meaningless. A middle course might be worth considering. Perhaps the administrative authority should be directed to explain a decision when specifically requested to do so by an adversely affected party; and, reasons having been stated, the authority should stand upon them and not others were the decision subsequently to be attacked. A requirement of this type would probably not produce an unmanageable workload. Yet it would eliminate whatever genuine uncertainties or misunderstandings might exist and would force administrators to act on grounds that "will stand up to criticism." This possibility remains to be explored in New Zealand and elsewhere.

The most perplexing and maybe the most important single problem with which the Ombudsman has thus far grappled is how to reconcile the competing desiderata of uniformity and efficiency on the one hand and flexible judgment on the other.

Administrators' susceptibility to what John Stuart Mill called "the despotism of custom" has troubled the Ombudsman almost from the beginning of his office. "Our laws contain many provisions empowering Departments or organisations to exercise discretion in individual cases," he wrote in 1963, "but I have found that sometimes the Department or organisation concerned follows a firm rule of practice. I am concerned to see that this discretion is genuinely exercised on the merits, as Parliament must have intended when it passed the law in question, although in a large Department delegation is necessary, and this creates problems."[107]

Discretion, he said on another occasion, "must not become sub-

[106] G. Powles, "The Procedural Approach to Administrative Justice," [1965] *N. Z. L. J.* 79, 81.

[107] Ombudsman's Report 1963, at 5–6. And see also Case No. 326, *ibid.,* at 12; Case No. 96, *ibid.,* at 14.

merged in convenient rules of practice tending to reduce administration to routine"—though at the same time he had to recognize that when thousands of individual decisions are to be made, "there must be rules and directives" to assure consistent results.[108]

His 1964 report to Parliament returns to the problem. Exercising discretion is not hard, the Ombudsman thought, when the same person or group can make every decision. "The real difficulties arise," he said, "when so many decisions must be made that the power to make them has to be delegated, and the more widely the power is delegated, the greater the difficulties become. If the discretion is wide, there is clearly the danger that varying decisions might be given by different delegates even where the facts are similar, and this would cause justifiable dissatisfaction on the part of the public. On the other hand, if the authority that delegates lays down too many rules of practice or defines too closely the standards of judgment to be used by the delegates in making decisions, these decisions may in effect cease to be truly discretionary"—for then decisions must be made "according to the book" instead of "according to conscience." The Ombudsman found no easy solution that he could embody in a rule of his own devising. He could only "highlight the problem, so that both delegating authorities and delegates may realise the dangers and weigh them before the former lay down rules, and the latter make, in accordance with rules, decisions in cases having special features distinguishing them from the general run of cases that the rules were laid down to cover."[109]

The administration of social security laws, necessitating thousands of determinations by officials throughout the nation, has been a prime example of the perceived difficulties. The Ombudsman has acknowledged that rules of practice are necessary to achieve administrative uniformity, whose absence would cause the collapse of public confidence in the Social Security Commission and its staff; further, inconsistent results in similar cases might be regarded by the Ombudsman as "discriminatory" within the meaning of the Act, and therefore subject to criticism by him. And yet, he has insisted, administrative rules must be understood to be rules of guidance only, not mandatory directives that abrogate "the duty to exercise discretion in individual cases." Being an honest man, the Ombudsman added: "I fully realize

108 Powles (note 11), at 782.
109 Ombudsman's Report 1964, at 5–6.

that the question of when to make an exception to an established rule —of when the circumstances are such as to warrant such an exception —can give rise to the old question of uniformity, and we are in danger of going round the circle again." He thought, however, that the appropriateness of exceptions could be determined by reasonable methods of administration, and that the opportunity to make them must be preserved.[110]

These balancings of imponderable values are at least as difficult in the United States as in New Zealand, and probably even more so because of the greater number of determinations that have to be made.[111]

Legislative recommendations. Since 1937 a Law Revision Committee has sought to aid Parliament to identify problems, discover legislative solutions, and modernize existing statutes. The Committee, though unsalaried and unstaffed, has accomplished much good work; but it meets only twice annually and is incapable of keeping close watch over the daily operation of every statute in the books. Were it not that the Department of Justice, the Solicitor General, and the Law Draftsman aid its labors, the Law Revision Committee would be much less effective than it is.[112]

The Ombudsman Act, Section 19, adds the Ombudsman to the ranks of available legislative advisers, for it directs him to call attention to the desirability of reconsidering any law he believes has produced "unreasonable, unjust, oppressive, or improperly discriminatory results." The Ombudsman, as he himself has noted, "can never therefore wholly answer a complaint by stating that what has been done has been done in accordance with law; he is required to go further and satisfy himself that the law itself is fair and just."[113]

[110] *Ibid.,* at 76. The Chairman of the Social Security Commission, to whom these remarks had been addressed, replied (at 77) that the Commission had "always reserved the right to treat a case on its individual merits in spite of any general policy rule" and had been conscious that a general rule may have no merit in "particular circumstances."

[111] See e.g., Note, 48 *Calif. L. Rev.* 822 (1960).

[112] The Committee consists at present of the Minister of Justice as chairman, four representatives of the New Zealand Law Society, a member of each of the four New Zealand law faculties, a nominee of the Opposition, the chairman of the Statutes Revision Committee of the House, two lawyers especially qualified by past experience, the Solicitor General, the Law Draftsman, and the Secretary for Justice. Its work has been illuminatingly described in a pamphlet published by Minister of Justice Hanan in 1965, entitled *The Law in a Changing Society*. Most of its activity has in fact been in the so-called "private law" area.

[113] Powles (note 11), at 778.

In one of his reports the Ombudsman has written about his general approach to legislation. A statute or legal rule or practice, he asserted, must be shown to operate oppressively or invidiously against a class or category and not merely against an individual, before he would be justified in recommending an amendment.[114] The proposition is easier to state as a generality than to apply when specific problems arise, for the Ombudsman has undoubtedly furthered new legislation to deal with instances of seemingly isolated hardship.[115] Ad hoc statutory amendments would probably occur even more frequently than now were it not for the fact that New Zealand's high-ranking public servants possess the capacity and will to be guided by conscience in unusual cases.[116]

[114] Ombudsman's Report 1965, at 70.

[115] E.g., Case No. 1211, *ibid.*, at 18: The complainant was a teacher in a school that had been down-graded (for salary classification purposes) when enrollment dropped below a certain level. The relevant legislation, which had been in force for more than thirty years, allowed a teacher to retain his former salary for two years after down-grading, during which time he could seek a new post in a school with the same grading as before. The complainant was actively in the market for such a job, but no suitable vacancies occurred during the two years of grace. When that period had elapsed, his salary was substantially reduced, as the applicable statute undoubtedly required. The affected teacher deemed this an unreasonable result that Parliament could not have envisaged. When the Ombudsman represented the case to the Director of Education, "he agreed that the complainant's contention was sound, and undertook to promote legislation giving the Director discretion to extend the two-year period of grace in such circumstances. The special legislation was later enacted, and the complainant's former salary was retrospectively restored."

While the report of Case No. 1211 does not suggest that any similar cases were pending, several comparable situations had recently come to the attention of the Department of Education; Case No. 1211 was therefore regarded as a sort of test case. Still, the matter before the Ombudsman was a one-man hardship problem.

[116] E.g., Case No. 507, Ombudsman's Report 1964, at 37: The complainant, a low-paid hospital worker, was subpoenaed by the accused in a criminal case. He attended court on two consecutive days, but was not called. He lost two days' pay, a hardship for him. The applicable statute provides that witness fees and expenses are to be paid by the party who called the witness, unless the party is a legal aid recipient (which was not the case here). The defendant who had subpoenaed the complainant had been convicted and was now imprisoned, penniless. The complainant asked the Ombudsman "if you could assist me with this problem or suggest who I could apply to for compensation for loss of wages for which I would be very thankful?" The Ombudsman simply transmitted the complaint to the Secretary for Justice, asking for a report and "the benefit of your comments so that I may determine whether or not the matter is one which I ought to investigate." The Secretary for Justice inquired into the facts and the law, which clearly contemplated no payment of public funds to persons in the complainant's situation. Without any prodding by the Ombudsman, the Secretary nevertheless thought it unfair that the complainant should be out of pocket. He therefore sought the Finance Minister's authorization (which was given) to pay the complainant £4, the sum he would have received had the accused obtained legal aid. The Ombudsman, upon being informed, wrote the Secretary that this deci-

When broader changes seem feasible, the Ombudsman is unlikely to have access to all the policy considerations that shape legislative choice, nor are all interests affected by a general statute likely to be involved in the particular matter he has been investigating. These practical limitations upon his theoretical power have been noted by the Ombudsman himself.[117] Nonetheless, he has sometimes almost too boldly leapt to conclusions about proper statutory objectives or about the need for minor changes to close what he regarded as legislative gaps.[118] Occasionally his reports have half suggested that legislative stimulus has been provided by a complaint forwarded by him, though other influences may perhaps in fact have been more significantly operative.[119]

The New Zealand office is still too young to permit a firm appraisal of its legislative utility. Conversations with Cabinet and House members as well as public servants create the impression that thus far the Ombudsman has been uninfluential as a lawmakers' guide. If this be the fact, his experience parallels that of the Scandinavian ombudsmen, who have undoubtedly enjoyed their greatest successes when dealing with specific cases, while achieving little when proposing new laws.

---

sion "seems in full conformity with equity and conscience"—and thus the matter was closed, with satisfaction to the complainant and without statutory change.

[117] See Case No. 800, Ombudsman's Report 1965, at 23–25, involving an attack upon an allegedly discriminatory and unjust statute that limited to three years the appointment of hospital consultants. The complainant was the New Zealand Association of Part-time Hospital Staff, which said that the livelihood of consultants was placed in jeopardy every three years in a manner unlike that applicable to any other group. The Ombudsman "studied a great deal of material . . . , but I could not be satisfied that in this case I had been able to undertake a sufficiently careful inquiry . . . Furthermore, the case had been presented to me by the association—just one group of the medical profession—whereas I strongly suspected that the substance of the case had implications which affected the medical profession throughout New Zealand. For these reasons I did not consider it appropriate for me to continue the investigation or attempt to form any opinion thereon."

[118] See, e.g., Case No. 1000, Ombudsman's Report 1964, at 52 (expressed opinion that provision of Income Tax Law allowing a tax deduction in respect of fees paid to a non-profit educational institution while providing no similar deduction for fees paid to a school carried on for private pecuniary profit, seemed objectionable); Case No. 1101, Ombudsman's Report 1965, at 31 (indicated a need to remedy what, on first impression, he regarded as a defect in Motor-Vehicle Dealers Act, to extend the classes of creditors protected by a required dealer's fidelity bond).

[119] Case No. 772, Ombudsman's Report 1965, at 31, may be illustrative. The matter arose under a rather technical section of the bankruptcy act. The Ombudsman was led "to ask the Secretary for Justice whether there might be a gap in the law that needed closing." The Secretary replied after a time that the problem of the supposed gap and what, if anything, should be done about it was to be considered in the course of a review of the bankruptcy legislation, then already in progress.

5|The Impact of the Ombudsman's Work

Public attitudes. The very first thing to be said about the impact of the Ombudsman's work is that it has been appreciable outside the public service as well as within it. An ombudsman's achievement cannot be measured solely by the frequency with which he criticizes administrators. He serves equally well when he dampens hostile suspicions and helps create the public confidence upon which democratic government must be based. The Ombudsman has done much to reinforce that base.

Those who sponsored an ombudsman's office in New Zealand never regarded it as an offset against an implacable and corrupt bureaucracy. Nor have the Ombudsman's operations exposed implacability or corruption hitherto unsuspected. His first year's efforts revealed no evidence of moral obliquity in the public service—"mistakes, carelessness, delay, rigidity, and perhaps heartlessness, but nothing really sinful."[120] His 1965 report brought the record up to date. "Again it is pleasing to note," he wrote, "that no complaint of actual malpractice has been found justified."[121]

The Ombudsman has, in sum, protected the public service, not merely attacked it. He has found it "necessary to advise a few complainants, in quite forceful terms, that they should cease groundless attacks on Departments or officials."[122] Among them have been the obsessively suspicious and the chronically querulous, whose burdensomeness is greater than their numbers; their turning to the Ombudsman has been a boon to the administrators against whom they have complained. "Most of our hardy perennials have left us to go to the Ombudsman," commented one Department Head who is not among the Ombudsman's adorers, "and I'll say this for the man: he has ticked off some of them in a way we never would have dared do ourselves." Said another senior administrator: "The Ombudsman doesn't set out

120 Powles (note 11), at 773.

121 Ombudsman's Report 1965, at 5. Report 1964, at 8: "Although a few complaints have alleged malpractice, investigation has cleared the officers or Departments concerned, and recommendations have been confined to matters of administration." Compare Case No. 157, Report 1964, at 44–45, finding an allegation of malice on the part of a revenue agent to be unfounded, but nevertheless making constructive recommendations concerning the conduct of future investigations.

122 Report 1964, at 5.

on witch hunts. We don't believe he has taken sides against us. If he thinks a complainant is just trying to get at the Department, he gives him no encouragement. What's more, he has helped to quiet a few cranks, though he has told them just what we had been telling them before."

The "quieting" reflects the complainants' awareness that their allegations have been investigated thoroughly and independently. The Ombudsman's communications to complainants are lengthy—exceptionally detailed, patient, and explanatory. They seem calculated to persuade, not merely to announce. Apparently they have had the desired effect, for persons whose complaints have been rejected have often expressed appreciation of the Ombudsman's activity in their behalf.[123] This is all the more remarkable because many complainants exhibit the human tendency to lay on any shoulders but their own the blame for disappointments they have suffered.[124]

Apart from his utterances in individual cases, the Ombudsman has also found occasion to say cordial things about particular administrative agencies whose proceedings frequently come to his notice.[125] He is not an apologist, glossing over administrative imperfections. Rather, he expresses what is too often ignored, namely, that most public servants do in fact serve the public well most of the time, and deserve to be thanked for performing hard jobs faithfully.[126]

[123] Ombudsman's Report 1963, at 3–4; Report 1964, at 4.

[124] See, e.g., Cases No. 7, 179, 474, Ombudsman's Report 1964, at 18–20.

[125] See, e.g., Ombudsman's Report 1965, at 6: "By far the greatest number of complaints related to social security. This is only to be expected as social security touches the lives of the majority of citizens and the decisions made sometimes govern, and always affect, people's standard of life. Moreover, there is no special right of appeal against the decisions of the Social Security Commission. It is, I think, greatly to the credit of the Social Security administration that, of the 82 complaints that were investigated during the year, only three were found to be justified, and, of these, two were rectified and the remaining one did not warrant any recommendation . . .

"The Department of Inland Revenue is, of course, a tempting target . . . The Department has made outstanding efforts during the year to modify its procedures and to improve its public image, and I am glad to see the justification of the forecast I made in my last annual report that the proportion of the complaints in respect of this Department would show a substantial fall."

[126] But compare Aikman and Clark (note 10), at 53: "Compared with the enormous number of decisions actually made during the period on which the Ombudsman has reported, the actual figure of justified complaints is insignificant . . . It is difficult, however, to resist the feeling that the Ombudsman in his publicity has placed a little too much stress on his victories rather than on the cases where the Department or organization had acted perfectly properly . . . The hope may be expressed that as the

None of this is calculated to help bureaucrats win popularity contests, nor is that its purpose. The Ombudsman's favorable reports may, however, nurture respect for public service, thus facilitating the future recruitment of able personnel and the retention of high morale by those already employed. His reports may also help teach the public at large that fallibility in law administration is not necessarily, though of course it may be, a mark of dishonor or incompetence in the law administrator—whether the fallible law administrator be dubbed judge or bureaucrat.

Changes in administrative methods or attitudes. The effect of the Ombudsman upon administrative organs cannot be summarized in a word. Some establishments appear to be virtually unconscious of his existence. In others, superior officers have used him as a bogeyman, to frighten their subordinates. A few, as the Ombudsman has asserted, may have become "pervasively 'Ombudsman conscious.' "[127] In any event it is probably fair to say, in the words of a veteran professional observer of Wellington officialdom: "The Ombudsman has gingered up the public service even when no formal changes have occurred."

Here, for example, is the full text of a memorandum sent by a Permanent Head of a Department to all his Section chiefs, on the subject of "The Making of Decisions":

> 1. Several months ago the Ombudsman spoke in public about the "cold, impartial and often implacable application of the rules."
>
> 2. Thinking of the public service generally and of this department in particular I believe that there are some grounds for this comment. I wish to ensure that in future we as a department do not offend in this respect.

Ombudsman becomes more established he will find it more possible to publicize those cases in which the Public Service was not at fault."

Compare, however, the State Services Commission's annual report to Parliament for the year ending March 31, 1965: "The reports of the Ombudsman have also shown, and done much to bring home to the general public, that a sense of responsibility and fair play exists among public servants."

[127] Ombudsman's Press Release, April 29, 1965, at 4: "The Office of Ombudsman has now been functioning long enough for the Departments to become pervasively 'Ombudsman conscious', and I have seen in a few departmental files coming before me some reference to the possibility of a complaint to the Ombudsman if something or other is or is not done."

Confirmation came from the Permanent Head of one of the largest Departments, who said that he had personally heard, during staff conferences concerning pending matters, such expressions as, "Oh, I wouldn't do that—you'll have the Ombudsman on you."

3. When you are making decisions or submitting recommendations will you please place yourself under scrutiny from this angle. You can do this without running the risk of becoming flabby.

Assuredly such a communication is not wholly inconsequential, even though its consequences are not measurable.

Another Department Head, already deeply committed to simplifying and perfecting his departmental procedures, remarked that he sought to convey to the staff his own awareness of the Ombudsman's concern with similar matters. "The Ombudsman," he acknowledged, "gives me added leverage. Big organizations do not move evenly in all their parts. Some parts need more shoving and hauling than others, and I can use the Ombudsman's cases to help me when I have to shove. Last week, for instance, I wrote a district office that during the past six months five of the seven complaints involving the Department had come from that branch. I told the local director that he had better get busy to review his office's procedures."

One may fairly suppose, too, that superior officers who have been embarrassed by underlings' inefficiency will act vigorously to prevent its recurrence. This is not a matter of new methods or new policies, but simply of keeping subordinates up to a mark already well defined. A number of complaints to the Ombudsman have indicated, for example, unwarranted delay in completing staff action on pending matters. Upon learning of the complaints, high officials have felt called upon to apologize handsomely, though they themselves had not previously been involved in the episodes.[128] Not desiring to eat humble pie as a steady diet, they probably instituted internal controls to forestall tardiness in future cases.

The Ombudsman has publicly claimed that his decisions have encouraged "departmental officers to take great care in the exercise of discretionary powers which, before the Office of Ombudsman was instituted, were final and not open to challenge or redress."[129] Most officials, when asked to comment, denied behaving differently because the Ombudsman might later examine their judgment. Since knowing oneself and recognizing one's own motivations are among the most

[128] E.g., Case No. 140, Ombudsman's Report 1963, at 10 (Department of Labour); Case No. 281, Report 1964, at 46 (Department of Inland Revenue); Case No. 1061, Report 1965, at 53 (Department of Works).

[129] The assertion was made in an address delivered at Christchurch, April 27, 1964, reproduced as an appendix to Powles (note 11), at 785.

difficult of all feats, these subjective responses may be somewhat discounted though not wholly ignored. An official of high rank thought that his conduct had been unmodified, but that his subordinates had been impressed by the Ombudsman; some of his subordinates thought conversely that the Ombudsman had made no difference to them, but that their chief had been beneficially influenced. Against one Department Head's explosive "Work methods and attitudes haven't been affected a jot!" can be set another's milder "In this Department we think we always were sensitive to private rights and interests; but our people are busy, and there's a temptation to brush aside the troublesome case that interferes with seemingly more important matters. The staff really does take a bit more care now." A district office director, responsible for supervising action on thousands of cases each year, asserted unequivocally: "The Ombudsman hasn't made an ounce of difference. We never ask ourselves, What would the Ombudsman think about this case?" His superior, responsible for reviewing the district office decisions, said equally distinctly: "Yes, the Ombudsman has affected what we do. We refer many more cases than before to our legal counsel. This has slowed up our operation. We haven't been as ready as we used to be to act on the equitable side, you might say. We are being more legal, but that isn't always favorable to the citizen, you know. We are becoming somewhat more formal, less quick to do rough justice, and I think the Ombudsman is the reason. But whether he has influenced us for the better or the worse is a different question."

In a meaty though somewhat tendentiously phrased remark concerning public administration, the Ombudsman has summarized a main justification of the work he has been doing. Repeated review within an administrative agency, he asserted in 1964, is no guarantor of the final decision's fairness and wisdom. The first decision, even if made at a relatively low official level, "tends to generate its own defences within a Department . . . The official bias is towards the maintenance of the original decision, and accordingly an objector must generally bear the onus of demonstrating manifest error if he is to secure the reversal of a decision within the Department that made it." Many of the cases which had been rectified while the Ombudsman's investigation was still at a preliminary stage had been considered inside the administrative agency several times previously without result. But when he presented the case anew to the same agency, "a genuine review" occurred. Rationalizing a determination made by a staff member and forcing affected persons to prove its unsoundness are among "the inevitable concomitants of any extensive administrative system with its accompanying hierarchies and rules. The conclusion is therefore that some form of responsible and independent representation in proper cases is not only desirable but necessary if the private citizen is to receive proper consideration at the highest levels within Departments."[130] Elsewhere, the Ombudsman has praised top officials for having in general "shown a broad-minded and high-principled willingness to do justice to the cases of individuals regardless of prior decisions which may have been taken by lower echelons in their departments"; the matters coming to his office showed, he thought, that "in the lower ranks of a large department things can happen which are regarded as questionable when brought to the attention of the head of the department concerned."[131]

The conclusions thus declared can be amply supported by reported cases.[132] Without suggesting naughtiness or using emotive words like bias, one can safely generalize that most people—including administrators—avoid the extremely hard work of critical thinking if they can. One easy way to avoid it, when deciding cases, is to match up one case

[130] Ombudsman's Report 1964, at 7.

[131] Powles (note 11), at 780.

[132] See, e.g., Case No. 1027, Ombudsman's Report 1964, at 57: Claim for accrued annual leave was denied, and denial was sustained successively by departmental representatives in local and central offices; re-examination after Ombudsman investigated showed that a clerical error had been made, and the complainant was then paid, with apologies. See also Case No. 241, *ibid.*, at 66–68: The Government Superannuation Board rejected a request by a former schoolteacher. Complainant asked her member in the House of Representatives to intercede first with the Minister of Education, then with the Minister of Finance (who was also chairman of the Superannuation Board); the complainant herself saw the Minister of Finance and the Superintendent of the Board—all to no avail. The Ombudsman, after lengthily investigating her complaint, reported in detail to the Minister of Finance (as Board chairman), criticizing both the Board and the Department of Education. After considering this report, the Board accepted the Ombudsman's recommendation that the rejection be rescinded.

Compare Case No. 952, *ibid.*, at 24–25: Complainant had sought unsuccessfully for three years to obtain the Customs Department's review of denial of an importer's license; upon re-examining the case after an inquiry by the Ombudsman, the Comptroller of Customs made a fresh decision that the complainant and the Ombudsman regarded as "doing substantial justice." And see Case No. 829 (note 58 above), involving the desirability of procedural regulations to protect Education Board officials against summary dismissal; while the problem had been noted by some staff members of the Department of Education, they had neither done anything about it nor brought it to the attention of superior officers, who did not even know of its existence until informed by the Ombudsman.

with another that has gone before, noting superficial similarities and ignoring subsurface differences. That is what has caused the difficulties in some of the matters about which complaint has been made to the Ombudsman.

In at least some administrative agencies the Ombudsman's letters have made the highest officials aware of matters that would not otherwise have come to their notice at all. One of these officials, recognized in Wellington as an especially conscientious and hardworking administrator, remarked, however, "There's another side to that coin that has to be looked at. I am now giving personal attention to cases I used to see rarely, because they involve no policy problems, but only the proper application of old policies that the staff supposedly understands. The only reason I see them now is that they have been forwarded here by the Ombudsman after complaint to him, and I have directed that all correspondence from or to the Ombudsman must go through me personally. That is all well and good; I have agreed with a few complainants that their problems have not been handled by the Department as they should have been, and I have given satisfaction in those cases. But of course the time I devote to these matters is taken away from something else. Since I haven't limitless energy or hours at my disposal, a judgment has to be made in the end as to whether I should be doing one kind of work or another."[133]

Some Departments rather resent the Ombudsman's contention that results are fairer when cases proceed through his office instead of through normal administrative channels. One Permanent Head, somewhat vexed because the Ombudsman's report had listed six valid complaints about his Department, declared: "Not one of those six had ever previously been submitted for review by the Department's central offices. If we had had an opportunity to pass on them, they would have been decided just as they were when they came to us as complaints via the Ombudsman. They appear as black marks in the record solely because the bloke chose to write to the Ombudsman instead of to us." Another Permanent Head bitterly resented the Ombudsman's saying that complaints had been "rectified" or "justified" when in fact the

[133] Possibly still another course remains open: The top administrator should be able to find someone besides himself in his large Department who could review complaint cases scrupulously and intelligently, leaving the Head free to deal with issues of broader significance.

action complained of had been correct in the light of the information the complainant himself had supplied. "When additional information came to hand through the subsequent complaint to the Ombudsman, we granted the relief sought—just as we would have done if the complainant had approached us directly. We would have done right without the Ombudsman. He makes us look bad in order to make himself look good, as preserver of the citizen against the bureaucrat," the official sourly concluded.

Education for the future. The immediately preceding discussion has dealt chiefly with repairing errors and omissions. The most valuable work the Ombudsman can do lies in the field of prevention. If his views are to have a maximum educational influence upon the conduct of the public's business, they must reach those whom they seek to guide.

Occasionally this occurs indirectly but forcefully through instructions to subordinates from a superior officer who has adopted the Ombudsman's opinion as his own.[134] More often, unfortunately, knowledge of the Ombudsman's ideas is narrowly disseminated. A middle-level officer in a major Department complained recently: "I am told that the Ombudsman's reports are eye-openers. They haven't opened my eyes. I never see them. We don't know about his cases even when they involve this Department. I understand he does a lot of good cerebration on principles, but his messages don't reach me. Either he is in an ivory tower or I am." A number of officials in field offices were asked whether they had received reports or circulars or instructions that reflected the Ombudsman's judgments. They recalled none, though acknowledging that new instructions from the head office might have been influenced by the Ombudsman without acknowleding the fact.

The Ombudsman's powers to publicize his work and his conclusions are ample. Section 25 of the Ombudsman Act directs him to make an annual report to Parliament, "without limiting his right to report at any other time." Rules the House of Representatives adopted for his guidance in 1962 say that he "may from time to time in the public interest . . . publish reports relating generally to the exercise of his

[134] E.g., Case No. 1165, Ombudsman's Report 1965, at 67 (Police Commissioner circulated an instruction to the national Police Force of 2,700 men, embodying the Ombudsman's view concerning proper conduct of certain investigations).

functions under the Act or to a particular case or cases investigated by him, whether or not the matter to be dealt with in such a report may have been the subject of a report to Parliament."[135]

As yet, not enough copies of the annual report have been printed to allow for general circulation among public servants. Only 1,385 copies of the 1965 report were published; 1,600 copies have been authorized for the future. A single copy has gone routinely to each of the Departments and other organizations to which the Ombudsman's jurisdiction attaches. Though additional copies could have been obtained through the Government Printing Office, no great effort seems to have been made anywhere to see that field offices and lesser officials were exposed to the Ombudsman's thinking.

He himself has sought to widen the circle of acquaintanceship by holding semi-annual press conferences and by accepting speaking engagements when possible.[136] He has also participated in current training courses organized by the State Services Commission for the benefit of senior officers. He must at present walk a tightrope between too great silence and too much speech. Some of his supporters urge chary utterance because they believe publicity is most effective if sparingly used; others are impatient because the public is still inadequately informed about his availability and because his recommendations usually reach only the officials immediately involved, thus limiting their educational force. His detractors, too, push in different directions. On the one hand they say he speaks too often, "acts as though he were a sort of messiah," "turns up to give talks at ladies' societies and school graduations like a blooming junior politician"; and on the other hand some anti-administrationists blame him for not stimulating the citizenry to complain more frequently than it does.

Whether or not the Ombudsman's public relations are ideally balanced, more might advantageously be done in the future than in the past to bring his work to the appropriate notice of civil servants in a broad range.

Implications for Parliament. Section 11(3) of the Act declares that a committee of the House of Representatives may at any time refer to the Ombudsman, for his investigation and report, any petition or

[135] Parliamentary Papers 1962/208.

[136] Aspects of public relations work are discussed in Ombudsman's Report 1964, at 16; Report 1965, at 9–10. And see Aikman (note 12), at 417.

related matter before the committee, so far as it lies within his jurisdiction. Only three such referrals had occurred until mid-1965. Two of these remained inactive because they pertained to subjects outside the Ombudsman's statutory powers. Still, a parliamentary committee without an investigating staff of its own and having no power to peer at the files should be able to make good use of the Ombudsman as time goes on.[137]

In addition to the trio just mentioned, the Ombudsman says he has also received a "trickle of cases" from individual members of the House, usually in situations calling for extensive research or for examination of many documents. Apart from these, numerous others must have been referred in fact though not in form by members who diverted constituents from their own offices to the Ombudsman's. The Social Security administration, among others, has noted a very marked reduction in the number of inquiries and representations addressed to it by members of the House. Ministers have also remarked that in recent sessions members have questioned them less frequently concerning particular cases, apparently because constituents have chosen to complain to the Ombudsman instead of to the legislators. At least two members of the Cabinet, and probably others, have sometimes urged members to present grievances to the Ombudsman, after they themselves had been unable to reach an accord.

Many members of Parliament, according to some of their leaders, have gladly abandoned the role of "constituents' grievance man." "Why shouldn't we use the Ombudsman for this work, since he is an official chosen by Parliament and we have given him the capability of getting at all the facts?" a prominent member asked. "Passing complaints to him leaves us free to do our primary job, a job nobody else has power to do," another said.

Other members, however, believe they gain popular esteem by handling complaints themselves. "When I take care of a local resident's problem," one member candidly states, "I show him how diligent I am,

[137] Compare Northey (note 5), at 140: "This is a useful power in that the Commissioner can be expected to make a more detailed and possibly more intelligent investigation of the complaint, but it may, if it were to be used extensively, weaken parliamentary supervision of the administration and the member's sense of responsibility to the citizen. The power to send complaints or petitions on to the Commissioner might be treated by some members as an easy method of disposing of an awkward problem."

and he tells his friends. If I ask a Minister a few sharp questions that the press gallery picks up, I impress my constituency. I'd be a fool to let the Ombudsman have all the glory instead."

Whether or not the fact be welcomed by the members of the House, the volume of grievances addressed to them seems to be diminishing. Nothing, of course, prevents a complainant's going to his member or petitioning Parliament after the Ombudsman has rejected a complaint or has not dealt with it to the complainant's satisfaction. In all probability the grievance business will pass more and more into the Ombudsman's hands in the first instance, with Parliament still able and willing to be, as traditionally it has been, the last resort for the disappointed. Legislators, thus freed from spending endless hours on constituents' errands, may in the long run gain greater capacity to influence larger public policies.[138]

6 | Concluding Observations

New Zealand's Ombudsman has been a striking personal success. True, he has not won over all unbelievers, among whom are a few powerful figures in the House of Representatives; but, on the other hand, some previously skeptical members have more recently suggested that his power should be extended. Both major parties have thus far supported him strongly, and he is distinctly not a "political issue."

Among administrators, a few describe him in biting language. At least two Department chiefs actively desire to be excluded from his jurisdiction. Many more of the Departments, however, appear genuinely to admire the Ombudsman's accomplishments. While almost all were perturbed by his having occasionally concerned himself with general administration as distinct from particularized grievances, they thought his judgments on the whole had been balanced and constructive. Temperamental differences have created irritations felt in some quarters and not in others. "Our work would be faster, cheaper, and better all around if we could keep that fellow out of our hair," grum-

[138] The present state of members' power to shape legislation is well discussed in R. N. Kelson, *The Private Member of Parliament and the Formation of Public Policy: A New Zealand Case Study* (1964).

bled one chief official. "Some Heads think the Ombudsman is a nuisance because he makes them justify themselves all the time. What's wrong with that? It's a good idea to keep us on our toes," another Permanent Head cheerily remarked. "The man is an empire builder, and his empire isn't really worth building. He repeats work that has already been done carefully or, if a complaint does involve something new, the complaint that went to him should have come to us," said a hostile official. "When the Ombudsman began, we wondered whether he was going to be a blasted thorn in our side; but now we are glad to have him," said a friendly official. "For one thing, people will complain to him when for one reason or another they won't complain to me, and this gives me an added opportunity to police my own Department. And for another thing, when he goes over something we have done and says he finds nothing wrong, he takes the wind out of the sails of the Doubting Thomases."

Conversations with representatives of various non-governmental organizations create the strong impression that the Ombudsman has been well received by various economic and community groups. In general, those who were consulted knew little about the details of what the Ombudsman had done. They simply thought it a good idea to have someone at hand who could inquire into exercises of administrative authority, in view of the broad scope of governmental activity in New Zealand.

A non-resident whose opportunities to observe were necessarily limited cannot offer a confident conclusion of his own. But he can report and endorse the appraisal of Sir Ronald Algie, a former law teacher who is now the respected Speaker of the House: "The ombudsman system probably would not work well everywhere. It works well in New Zealand because we have a fine public service. Corruption is so rare as to be deemed virtually non-existent. Officials generally seek to serve rather than to defeat citizens. They give cases careful consideration, though of course that doesn't mean they invariably reach the best possible result. Our Ombudsman may stimulate officials to be even a little bit better than they have been. But the ombudsman system is succeeding here precisely because, really, there isn't a staggering lot for it to do."

four

Norway

Norway's parliamentary ombudsman for civil administration—its Stortingets Ombudsmann—began discharging his duties on January 1, 1963. The accomplishments of so youthful an institution—as yet neither fully tested nor, indeed, finally shaped—cannot be appraised confidently. The Norwegian method of handling citizens' disagreements with public administrators may nevertheless be described; and an attempt at preliminary evaluation may be useful while the pre-ombudsman past is still freshly in observers' minds.

1 | The Genesis of the Ombudsman System in Norway

Other Scandinavian countries long preceded Norway in deciding to appoint an official to serve as an overseer of public administration—Sweden in 1809, Finland in 1919, Denmark in 1954. Even in Norway an ombudsman had since 1952 watched against abusive treatment of military personnel.[1]

[1] The Military Ombudsman handles an average of 350 complaints per year, all of them involving disagreements between inferior and superior ranks; most of his "clients" are conscripts. He has power only to criticize and suggest, rather than command. An important part of his activity is serving as the top point of the "representatives' committees" which function in every detachment of thirty-five or more men, to advise the commanding officer about matters of interest to the lower ranks. The Military Ombudsman is supposed to carry further the matters not resolved to the satisfaction of the various "representatives' committees." He has no jurisdiction whatsoever over matters not directly involving relationships within the armed forces. Thus, for example, he is not concerned with military procurement contracts or

No special crisis drew attention to the desirability of matching the Military Ombudsman with an ombudsman to safeguard the citizenry against civil servants. On the contrary; an Expert Commission on Administrative Procedure, whose recommendation in 1958 gave the ombudsman idea its greatest impetus, proposed the new system simply as a safeguard against the possibility of excess, not as a weapon against abuses believed to be widespread.[2]

The Commission's simultaneous proposal of an extensive statutory prescription of administrative procedure aroused no immediate response, but the suggestion that Norway emulate the other Scandinavian countries in having an ombudsman for civilians attracted lively interest. Official spokesmen for the legal profession and businessmen's associations strongly endorsed the idea, though these groups explicitly declared that the ombudsman was unlikely to have significance for them in any immediate sense; he would benefit the "little man" rather than the members of powerful bodies like theirs. The labor movement as a whole was indifferent, though some of its leaders now profess to have been proponents of the ombudsman plan. Organizations of Norwegian civil servants (whose counterparts in Denmark had bitterly opposed the appointment of an ombudsman only a few years previously) were quiescent and may even have lent some support; one of their leaders recalled recently that "we had had connections with our

---

controversies between military and civilians. He is assisted by two staff attorneys and by an advisory committee of six, to whom he may refer matters of "a fundamental character or of public interest." He visits military installations from time to time to observe the conditions of service (such as sanitation and recreational facilities) and to talk personally with service personnel.

For further discussion see A. Ruud, "The Military Ombudsman and His Board," in D. C. Rowat, ed., *The Ombudsman: Citizen's Defender* 111 (1965).

2 The chairman of the Expert Commission was Terje Wold, President of the Supreme Court. Chief Justice Wold subsequently explained the Commission's recommendation of the ombudsman system as follows: "It seems unavoidable at the stage of economic and technical development which, regardless of politics, has been achieved in all modern societies, that ever larger and broader powers shall be bestowed upon administrative authorities." T. Wold, "The Norwegian Parliament's Commissioner for Civil Administration," 2 *J. Int. Comm. Jurists* no. 2, 21 at 24 (1960). Then he indicated that he and the Commission shared the opinion of Professor W. A. Robson that "the greater the powers given to the executive, the greater the need to safeguard the citizens from their arbitrary or unfair exercise." Robson, *Administrative Law,* in M. Ginsberg ed., *Law and Opinion in England in the 20th Century* 198 (1959). For further discussion see A. Os, "The Ombudsman for Civil Affairs," in D. C. Rowat (note 1), at 95.

Danish friends and had found out from them how much the Ombudsman had done for civil servants, to their surprise—and so we were and still are all for the institution." Governmental agencies seemed to be resigned rather than actively hostile. Many of them expressed belief that already existing judicial and parliamentary controls were adequate. A few rather resented the suggestion that their work might be seriously flawed by arbitrariness or carelessness, against which new protections might be needed. But no unit of the central government voiced outright opposition.

Finally, in 1960, the Cabinet itself put forward a bill to create a parliamentary commissioner for civil administration, explaining that an ombudsman would provide quick, cheap redress for persons who were aggrieved by administrative actions and, at the same time, would perhaps protect public employees against "quarrelsome persons." He might also "lessen the burden of work for the members of the Storting, who now constantly get complaints from private persons concerning the activities of some administrative authority." In laying the bill before the Storting, the Government added: "With the standard our administration has today, it is indeed not likely that the Ombudsman will find basis for criticism in any considerable number of cases. Experience both in Sweden and Denmark has shown that only in a relatively small number of the complaints, is basis found for further procedure. But the system may to some extent contribute to a higher degree of vigilance in the public administration. And through a longer period of time its effect may be to strengthen the confidence in the public administration and to create a feeling of security in the individual as to his relations to the public administration."[3]

Nearly two years of discussion preceded introduction of a partially redrafted Cabinet proposal in 1962. During subsequent debate in the Storting,[4] Minister of Justice Jens Haugland, presenting the Cabinet's views, stressed that the ombudsman was not to be a "super organ within the central administration," but would simply "protect the interests of the individual against all the mistakes that we know are bound to occur within a large administration." Leading the discussion

[3] The quoted matter is a translation from pp. 3–4 of a paper prepared in 1963 by Audvar Os of the Royal Norwegian Ministry of Justice and published by that Ministry in mimeographed form as Doc. No. 71, *The Ombudsman in Norway*.

[4] The Storting's debate is summarized under the topic heading "Grievance Commissioner to Probe Complaints against Government," in 19 *News of Norway* 95 (June 21, 1962).

for the then dominant Labor Party, Representative Jakob Pettersen characterized the proposed ombudsman as "a sort of social worker for persons who feel they have been treated unfairly by governmental officials," and said that he would need "infinite patience and a good sense of humor" as well as sound judgment and legal knowledge. Representative Lars Ramndal, speaking for the minority Liberal Party, declared that Norway fortunately possessed a conscientious, capable civil service, but that mistakes must inevitably occur in all human institutions and that an ombudsman could lessen the risk of occasional misinterpretation of statutes or lapses in official judgment; moreover, the ombudsman might greatly help "personnel in exposed positions" by sifting out "unsubstantiated complaints from habitual querulents."[5]

It was following low-pitched discussion of this tenor that the Norwegian Parliament unanimously approved adoption of the ombudsman system. Nobody argued an urgent need. The machinery of government was merely to be slightly refined rather than drastically remodeled.

In light of previous expectations, the popular response to the new institution was surprisingly intense. The first Ombudsman took office on January 1, 1963. During 1963 he registered 1,257 cases; during 1964 the figure declined slightly to 1,060. During his first year in office Norway's Ombudsman, dealing with the smallest population of any of the Scandinavian countries, handled more complaints than did any of the similar officials in Sweden, Finland, and Denmark in that same year.[6]

[5] Representative Ramndal's words probably received especially close attention. Though his party then held only twenty-odd seats in the 150-member Storting, he had earned noteworthy personal influence there. As chairman of the Storting's Justice Committee he had himself been the recipient of many complaints against administrative acts and had become in the course of time, in the eyes of both the press and the public, an "unofficial ombudsman." Administrators found him a responsible inquirer concerning the complaints he had received, for he sought sound results rather than political ammunition. But Mr. Ramndal never pretended that he had either the professional training or the staff that would enable him to perform the work of an ombudsman in addition to that of a legislator. He was among the first, if indeed he was not himself the first, to propose having an ombudsman in Norway.

[6]

	Pop. in millions	*Cases docketed 1963*
Norway	3.7	1,257
Sweden	7.6	1,224
Denmark	4.7	1,130
Finland	4.6	1,029

In both Finland and Denmark the complaints include those filed by military per-

2|Choosing the Ombudsman

The Act of June 22, 1962, creating the Stortingets Ombudsmann,[7] provides in Section 1 that the parliament is to choose the ombudsman after each general election, to serve four years until the next election unless sooner removed by vote of two thirds of the Storting.[8] Section 1 also states that he "must have the qualifications demanded for a judge of the Supreme Court"—which means, as a bare minimum, that he must be thirty years old and have earned a first-class law degree ("laudabilis") from a Norwegian university. Although the Storting may lay down general rules concerning the Ombudsman's duties, he is otherwise to discharge the responsibilities of his office, according to Section 2, "alone and independently of the Storting." His salary and pension rights are not fixed in the statute, but will presumably be adjusted as may be needed to induce acceptance by the person the Storting chooses; at the outset they have been placed on a parity with the compensation and perquisites of a Supreme Court Judge.

The first Norwegian Ombudsman is Andreas Schei, a member of the Supreme Court at the time of his election.[9] A respected lawyer who had served lengthily in various posts before becoming a judge, Mr. Schei was a non-partisan choice acceptable to the entire Storting.[10] He

---

sonnel; the ombudsmen in those two countries have jurisdiction over both civil and military administration. Like Norway, Sweden has a Military Ombudsman. His jurisdiction is, however, slightly broader than the Norwegian Military Ombudsman's, since he deals with military expenditures (such as procurement contracting) in addition to military personnel matters.

[7] Lov om Stortingets Ombudsmann for forvaltningen, 22 juni 1962, Nr. 8, *Norsk Lovtidend* 479–482 (1962).

[8] This eventuality is regarded as so unlikely that, according to one veteran legislator, "if the time ever came when two thirds of the Storting would be ready to discharge an ombudsman, they would probably simply abolish the office rather than bother to abolish the incumbent."

[9] Section 13 provides that the Ombudsman "must not hold any public or private appointment or office without the consent of the Storting." While the matter has not been stressed publicly, Judge Schei has in fact been allowed to keep his seat on the Supreme Court, from which he took a three-year leave of absence.

[10] A leader of the Storting has privately described the election process as follows: The name of a prominent law professor was put forward, but it was clear that he did not want the post. The Chief Justice had informally suggested Mr. Schei's availability and qualifications. Mr. Schei was not a politician; "a politician wouldn't have had a chance." He was not connected with the majority Labor Party, but had not declared

began his work in an atmosphere notably free from rancor—and, so far as a non-Norwegian can judge such matters, he has lost none of the support that was his in the beginning.

3 | Limitations upon the Ombudsman's Powers

The Ombudsman's province, Section 4 of the governing statute declares, "covers the Government administrative organs and civil servants and others in the service of the Government." This does not, however, include authority to deal with Cabinet decisions, the functions of courts, or the Auditor of Public Accounts. His duty, "as the delegate of the Storting" and in accordance with the rules it may lay down, is, under Section 3, "to endeavor to ensure that the public administration does not commit any injustice against any citizen." Debate preceding the enactment made crystal clear the Storting's disinclination to abandon any of its own powers; the Ombudsman, the Storting's agent, was not expected to act in matters to which his principal had already turned attention.

A | Matters Acted upon by the Storting

The Storting on November 8, 1962, promulgated rules for the Ombudsman's guidance. Rule 5(3) bars the Ombudsman from dealing with any complaint if the subject to which it pertains "has already been considered by the Storting, the Odelsting, or the Standing Committee on Parliamentary Control."

A few words of explanation concerning Norwegian parliamentary organization may clarify this rule's meaning.

---

which party he did support. The Election Committee informally inquired of all parties in the Storting whether anyone was opposed to Mr. Schei. Everybody seemed happy about him. The Election Committee unanimously nominated him. He was then elected by secret ballot. He had previously made clear his unwillingness to surrender the opportunity of returning to the Supreme Court, and that was taken into account when the Election Committee recommended him. Some of those who voted for him believed that he would find being the Ombudsman both more honorific and more interesting than being a Supreme Court judge, but the Storting had to leave the choice to him in order to get the man it wanted for this job.

The Storting consists of 150 members. After each general election it selects thirty-eight of its own members to sit in the Lagting, while the remaining 112 comprise the Odelsting. Legislative proposals affecting citizens' rights and duties must originate in the Odelsting, where they are usually offered by the Cabinet as Government-sponsored bills. They are considered separately in the Odelsting and the Lagting and must be adopted by both.[11] The Storting sits unicamerally, however, for many purposes, such as making appropriations, enacting new taxes, passing on constitutional amendments, and ratifying treaties. In the rare occurrence of impeachment of a member of the Storting, the Supreme Court, or the Cabinet, the Odelsting commences and prosecutes the proceedings while the Lagting sits with the Supreme Court as the adjudicating body.[12]

The Cabinet consists of the heads of the fourteen ministries.[13] Although nominally a council of advisers chosen by the King, they must be persons acceptable to the majority of the Storting, since they are answerable to it and are subject to interpellation at stated hours.[14] Cabinet minutes and other reports of Government actions are referred to the Standing Committee on Parliamentary Control (sometimes called the Protocol Committee), which may bring to the Odelsting

[11] A measure upon which agreement is not reached between the two divisions can be debated in a plenary session of the Storting and can then be passed if a two-thirds majority approves.

[12] Only eight impeachment proceedings have occurred in Norway, the most recent in 1927.

[13] The ministries are Foreign Affairs, Church and Education, Justice and Police, Municipal and Labor Affairs, Social Affairs, Industry and Handicraft, Fisheries, Agriculture, Communications, Finance and Customs, Commerce and Shipping, Defense, Wages and Prices, and Family and Consumer Affairs. Various more or less independent boards and directorates are subject to partial control by ministers; among these are such important bodies as the Directorate of Price Controls, the State Board of Waterways and Electricity Supply, and the National Tax Assessment Board. A number of governmental activities are, however, carried on entirely outside the ministries, though in some aspects subject to a measure of ministerial influence. The Bank of Norway, which is the central agency for directing and controlling banking activities, is the prime example. Certain other credit agencies—such as the Fisheries Bank and the National Mortgage Bank—have independent managements, but they are subject to audit by the Auditor of Public Accounts and they also seek appropriations of public funds by the Storting. Some publicly owned and operated business operations, like the State Wine and Liquor Monopoly and the State Grain Corporation, similarly function without ministerial superintendence, though answerable to the Storting for their activities and sometimes in need of public financing.

[14] See I. Wilberg, "Some Aspects of the Principle of Ministerial Responsibility in Norway," 8 *Scand. Stud. in Law* 243 (1964).

any matter in which the Government has apparently exceeded its legal authority.

Rule 5 tells the Ombudsman to abstain from acting whenever a matter has been "considered" by the Storting as a whole, by the Odelsting alone, or by the Standing Committee on Parliamentary Control. It fails, however, to define how much parliamentary attention is needed in order to constitute a matter's having been "considered" within the meaning of the rule. The Ombudsman has taken no chances. He has regarded a matter as having had parliamentary consideration if it has passed through the legislative halls at all, no matter how swiftly and, one is tempted to say, no matter how unconscious the legislators were of its presence.

Thus, for example, he has refused to deal with a complaint about which a member of the Storting had addressed a question to a Minister during the Question Hour.[15] He has similarly rejected a complaint about a ministry's action that necessitated expenditures for which the Storting subsequently appropriated funds (though without actual notice of the issue raised by the complainant).[16] In the same vein he declined to inquire into a complaint that a ministry had improperly rejected a bid for public property, after the Storting had consented to the sale of that same property to another purchaser, though apparently without accurate knowledge of the complainant's grievance.[17]

[15] Case No. 1963–20: The complainant alleged that the Director of Roads had improperly denied him an appointment as engineer because of his age. A member of the Storting had raised a question, which had been answered during the Question Hour by the suitable Minister. A supplemental question had been asked by the original questioner, and that was the end of the Storting's consideration. The complainant's name had not been mentioned in the Storting, but the Ombudsman thought it clear that his was the case involved. In these circumstances, the Ombudsman regarded the matter as having been "considered" by the Storting, within the meaning of Rule 5. Interpellations are a means of the Storting's controlling governmental activity, he said, and Rule 5 makes no distinctions among the ways in which the Storting can deal with a case.

[16] Case No. 1963–43: The complainant asserted that the Ministry of Fisheries' had improperly subsidized the sale of certain fish and had thereby caused him economic injury because he had to reduce the price of his unsubsidized fish in order to meet the resulting competition. The Ombudsman noted that the cost of the subsidy had been included in the Government's budgetary proposals, which had subsequently been submitted to and adopted by the Storting. The Ombudsman held that the subsidy system must therefore be regarded as having been approved by the Storting and as having been removed from his jurisdiction.

[17] Case No. 1963–10: The complainant alleged that the Ministry of Defense had carelessly dealt with his application to purchase certain land, which had subsequently been sold to a municipality. The Storting routinely gave its consent to the transaction,

The Ombudsman himself recognizes that drawing the line is not easy; he has been especially troubled by the question of whether an interpellation, without more, constitutes legislative consideration of a problem. Some of his most enthusiastic supporters think he may have been too ready to abstain from looking at cases laid before him. Moves are afoot to clarify his jurisdiction in this respect, apparently in the belief that the Storting's prerogatives will not be undermined if the Ombudsman inquires into matters which could have had but in fact did not have legislative attention.

A related problem arises in connection with the Section 4 command not to deal with "decisions made by the Cabinet," which are in theory political decisions subject to parliamentary reaction. In a number of cases complaint has been made to the Ombudsman that slipshod work in a ministry caused the Cabinet to act unwittingly in a manner harmful to the complainant. In all such instances the Ombudsman has said, in essence, that he cannot go behind the Cabinet decision and that anyone who wishes to attack it must direct his complaint to the Standing Committee on Parliamentary Control.[18] He has added, how-

---

as is required when public lands are sold. Its approval constituted consideration of the matter to which the complaint pertained and therefore took the case outside the Ombudsman's jurisdiction. Whether the Storting had had adequate information before it and, if not, whether the Ministry's failure to state all the pertinent facts had been decisive of the result, was not for the Ombudsman to say; this was for the Storting itself to judge.

A somewhat similar problem appears in Case No. 1963–16: An organization, *B*, complained that the Ministry of Wages and Prices had dealt unsatisfactorily with *B*'s request that increased costs be taken into account in setting new price levels. Subsequently the Ministry had proposed, and the Storting had approved, an extension of an existing regulation that would otherwise have expired with the passage of time. The Ombudsman rejected the complaint because the Storting had already adopted a law that, by continuing the previous regulation in force, dealt with the subject matter. The question raised by the complaint was really directed at the basis of the Storting's legislative action.

The Norwegian refusal to inquire into the departmental recommendations upon which a parliamentary decision has been based may be contrasted with the New Zealand ombudsman's readiness to inquire, described in Chapter 3, above.

[18] Case No. 1963–36 is illustrative: *A* complained to the Ombudsman that a vacancy in a public office, for which he would have applied if the vacancy had been properly advertised, had been improperly announced following Cabinet action upon the basis of a ministry's misinformation. The complaint was against the ministry rather than against the Cabinet's decision as such; but the Ombudsman held that the complaint pertained to the basis upon which the Cabinet had acted and must therefore be addressed to the Standing Committee on Parliamentary Control.

ever, that should a complaint concern a procedural crudity, important in itself and not because it had affected the decision finally made by the Cabinet, he would regard the case as within his power.

B | The Functions of the Courts

Section 4 also instructs the Ombudsman not to concern himself with "the functions of the Courts of Justice." Rule 3 has similarly directed him to ignore the Labor Court (which passes on disputes arising under collective bargaining agreements) and tribunals established to deal with landlord and tenant controversies. The ouster of jurisdiction is complete; he is to take no interest in either the courts' judicial functions or their administrative activities, such as issuance of marriage licenses.

The Norwegian Ombudsman's powerlessness in respect of judges resembles that of the Danish Ombudsman. By contrast, both the Swedish and Finnish ombudsmen have authority to consider complaints against the conduct of judges and other law administrators, without differentiation. Because the Norwegian Ombudsman's jurisdiction is so completely and so explicitly excluded, his relationships with the courts have been entirely amicable.

The emergence of the Ombudsman as a watchman against abusive civil administration has, however, drawn attention to the fact that judges in Norway are not closely watched by anybody at all. Leading jurists are beginning to give considerable thought to the question of whether conventional appellate processes constitute fully adequate safeguards against unseemly judicial manners or inattentiveness.

This is not to suggest that Norwegians lack confidence in their judges. On the contrary the prestige of the judiciary is extremely high, and the power judges wield in public affairs is correspondingly great.

Vacant judgeships are announced for public competition. Appointees are drawn chiefly from senior civil service posts, higher ranking public prosecutors, and the practicing Bar; the average age at initial appointment is about forty-five in the lower courts and forty-eight in the Supreme Court. Thus, unlike many European countries, Norway does not have a "career judiciary" in which the judges enter without experience and in which they advance to more responsible work as years pass. The Norwegian judges have had considerable exposure to the world's affairs before assuming office, as well as a good formal education in their youth.[19]

Like their American counterparts they have achieved a sort of judicial supremacy by setting aside legislative enactments considered to be at variance with the Constitution, though neither the Constitution nor any other positive law has in terms conferred this power.[20] Review of administrative determinations is also similar to that in the United States. The ordinary law courts have developed their own power to invalidate unauthorized actions, those brought about without observance of prescribed procedures, or those based on an erroneous view of the law or in disregard of the evidence. "This applies," an able Norwegian lawyer has written, "to decisions taken on every step of the administrative ladder—from the smallest local board to the King in Council; any country court may, for example, declare an act by the King to be invalid."[21]

But, as a practical matter, nobody can do anything about the way a judge comports himself. If convicted of a serious crime or if (as has virtually never been attempted) physical disability or financial irresponsibility were to be proved in a civil proceeding brought for that purpose, a judge could be forced into retirement before reaching the mandatory retirement age of seventy. Complaints that might warrant far less drastic action than removal from office—about courtroom manners, slowness in disposing of cases, and so on—do arise from time to time. When addressed to the Minister of Justice, he can theoretically investigate them with a view to issuing a warning; but as a matter of long-standing practice complaints are in fact simply sent to the man complained against, for his information.[22] When addressed

[19] Appointees to the Supreme Court and to the presidencies of Courts of Appeals must have earned a first-class degree ("laudabilis") in law. All other judicial appointees must have earned at least a second-class degree ("haud illaudabilis"), but most of them have in fact graduated in law with a first-class degree. Royal Norwegian Ministry of Justice, *Administration of Justice in Norway* 110 (1957).

[20] *Ibid.*, at 108.

[21] A. Os, "Administrative Procedure in Norway," 25 *Int. Rev. Admin. Sc.* 67, 76 (1959).

[22] Theoretically, too, a judge might be prosecuted and fined in a higher court for misconduct in office. Section 324 of the Norwegian Penal Code defines as an offense a public official's "intentionally failing to perform any service duty or . . . in spite of warning, performing his duty negligently . . ." Section 325 also provides punishment for, among other things, being "guilty of improper behavior toward any person during

to the Norwegian Bar Association, as occurs several times a year, complaints about rudeness or slowness have been forwarded to the affected judge, with a request for comment by him. In no instance has a judge refused to answer. Nothing further has been done in these cases, but the Bar Association believes that its manifestation of interest has significantly influenced individual judges' future behavior.

C | Municipal Affairs

Section 4 of the governing statute directs the Ombudsman to concern himself with "Government administrative organs," which, being interpreted, means the organs of central government as distinct from local administration. Sharply distinguishing between what is central and what is local in modern Norway is, however, virtually impossible.

The country is large—a thousand miles between northern and southern extremities, with a coast line variously measured at up to 12,000 miles—but thinly inhabited except around Oslo and in the southeastern counties.[23] The scattered population makes difficult a purely local provision of services and benefits such as doctors and clinics and, even, roadways. Hence many activities that might elsewhere be considered suitable for municipal administration have a substantial ingredient of central planning, financing, and supervision.

Local government has nevertheless continued ebulliently in some respects. In very recent years consolidations of previously separate municipalities have produced a manageable number of viable units; until 1963 the recognized "cities" had included one with a population of only 132. Slightly more than five hundred cities and rural districts now exist, each with power to impose taxes on income and property, to borrow money, and to maintain an administrative staff under control of an elected municipal council. They are responsible for providing, among other things, care for handicapped and neglected children and for the aged; health services; attention to problems of alcoholism; housing programs; primary education; building super-

---

performance of public service." Although nobody can recall the enforcement of these provisions, a judge's behavior is no doubt weighed by the Ministry of Justice when the question of promoting the judge to a more responsible post arises.

[23] The population density as a whole is thirty per square mile, about a twentieth of the British figure, for example.

vision; licensing and inspection of hotels, restaurants, and sellers of intoxicants; and the conventional local services such as sanitation and fire protection (but not including police, which has been entirely nationalized). Some municipalities administer rent control programs, operate public utility systems, and provide extensive recreational facilities. All this sounds like a very large area into which the Ombudsman is not to intrude. The first impression, however, is not exact.

All local governments are grouped into eighteen counties, plus the cities of Oslo and Bergen, each of which comprises a county in itself. Heading each county is a governor (fylkesmann), appointed by the central government and having permanent tenure. The county governments, which are themselves supervised by the Ministry of Municipal and Labor Affairs, must approve many municipal decisions such as those involving loans, major purchases and sales of property, and building or land use control. The governor may veto any local action deemed by him to conflict with existing laws and regulations. Various local welfare programs are superintended by central governmental agencies. The counties, with central guidance and help, may provide services which are beyond the capability of the separate localities, such as construction of hospitals and roads.

No doubt enough has been said to show the difficulty of identifying what is purely local administration. A student of Norwegian municipalities has concluded that the scope of local governmental authority "from an American viewpoint is very limited."[24] Few major decisions, he asserts, are free from central control. "Levying taxes, borrowing money, budgeting and accounting procedures, land use planning, public and cooperative housing, building inspection, welfare and rehabilitation programs, and education are some of the local activities," he adds, "which are regulated by central government laws and regulations or controls accompanying State loans and grants." When an adventurous municipality launches a voluntary program of its own without central financial help, "national legislation often appears to require and regulate the program throughout the country."[25]

[24] S. M. Wyman, *Municipal Government in Norway and the Norwegian Municipal Law of 1954* at 24 (1963).

[25] *Ibid.* Mr. Wyman remarks that local officials have conferred together about seeking to escape from central control. "However, although the distaste for control is certain, Norwegian municipal officials have had as much trouble as their American counterparts agreeing upon which local activities do not need the financial support

Despite the intertwinings of local and central authority, the Ombudsman does have to disentangle the threads. The legislative history of the governing statute shows that municipal administration, no matter how vague its contours, was to be set apart, differently from Finland where the Ombudsman's jurisdiction embraces every level of public administration.[26]

At the same time the statute did not entirely insulate local government from the Ombudsman's attention. In any administrative matter involving deprivation of personal liberty he was authorized to intervene whether the administrator involved was municipally or nationally employed.[27] And the statute also left open the possibility that later rules might authorize the Ombudsman to inquire into proceedings at the local level if they were to bear on a case already within his grasp because of complaint against a national administrative organ.[28] Rule 2 as finally promulgated by the Storting has in fact authorized him to look into any municipal agency's decision whenever "relevant to the consideration of a case with which he is dealing."

Despite this further blurring of the line between local and central affairs, the Ombudsman found that ninety-eight of the complaints addressed to him in 1963 and seventy-one of the 1964 complaints fell outside his jurisdiction because they pertained to purely municipal matters.[29] Storting members are already discussing enlarging the

---

of the national government." This comment recalls President Eisenhower's effort to clip the wings of the federal government and to "return to the states" the powers and functions that were rightfully theirs. A commission of state governors, asked to make recommendations to the President, could find nothing that they agreed should be returned to the states (and, thus, to their budgets).

26 The Cabinet, in presenting its proposal in 1960, had said, in part: "It seems right to proceed with some care, and consequently natural to delimit the main province to the governmental administration. Subsequently experience may show the necessity for a general extension of the Ombudsman's province to the municipal administration." Os (note 3 above), at 9.

27 Section 4 of the governing statute reads in part as follows: "The Ombudsman can deal with any administrative matter, including municipal administrative matters, concerned with the deprivation of personal liberty or connected with the deprivation of personal liberty."

28 Section 4 provides in part: "In the rules issued to the Ombudsman the Storting may determine . . . 3. that in connection with dealing with the individual case the Ombudsman may also take up the hearing of the case by the municipal administrative organ which has dealt with the case at a lower level."

29 Some of the matters rejected by the Ombudsman might have been judicially reviewable had the complainants chosen to go to court. See Wyman (note 24 above), at 12.

Ombudsman's power so that he may act on local complaints as freely as on national matters.

Municipal spokesmen with whom the issue was discussed in 1964 were opposed to expanding the Ombudsman's scope. They thought existing review mechanisms entirely adequate. They were embittered, too, by the opinion of some Oslo circles that local officials, even more than national, needed the Ombudsman's superintendence. Still, their opposition to coming under the Ombudsman's scrutiny seemed not to be very fiery, though some of them wistfully mentioned the possibility of having a local ombudsman to deal with local affairs.

D | Discretionary Acts

The Ombudsman is meant to be a safeguard against abusive public administration. Does this mean that he is to protest again exercises of power with which he disagrees, or only against actions so grossly erroneous as to be illegal?

The Cabinet, when initially proposing adoption of the ombudsman system, clearly sought to avoid creating a super-administrator who would remake decisions he deemed unsound. It proposed that the Ombudsman's "right to criticize the substance of decisions shall be limited" to issues of "legality in the broader sense"; when an administrator has exercised discretion, the Ombudsman, like the courts, should strike only at a decision regarded as invalid because arbitrary or motivated by unauthorized considerations, but should "not express his point of view on the reasonableness and adequacy of the decision."[30]

Many disagreed. The Cabinet's proposal, they said, would give the Ombudsman and the judiciary exactly the same power to deal with discretionary acts. They wanted him to have far more.

The parliamentary committee in charge of the bill finally reported a somewhat intermediate view. It accepted the Cabinet's position that the Ombudsman "should not be granted a *general* authority to express his view on administrative discretion," but at the same time the committee said he should be able to "review and give his opinion" concerning decisions "found to be clearly unreasonable or otherwise clearly in conflict with fair administrative practice."[31]

[30] The Cabinet's proposal is quoted in Os (note 3), at 19.
[31] *Id.,* at 20.

The statute as enacted states the matter slightly differently in Section 10: "If the Ombudsman is of the opinion that a decision is invalid or clearly unreasonable, he may make a statement to this effect." The Rules subsequently adopted by the Storting, however, recalled the words of the committee report rather than of the enactment, for Rule 9 states in part: "If the Ombudsman considers that a discretionary decision is manifestly unreasonable, or otherwise clearly in conflict with fair administrative practice, he may so declare."

This brief recapitulation sufficiently indicates that the Ombudsman has no blanket authority to reconsider all governmental actions with which citizens are dissatisfied. No man, not even an ombudsman, can be omnicompetent. He cannot facilely revise the physician's diagnosis, the bridge builder's specifications, the pharmacologist's determination that a drug compound may be deleterious to health, while simultaneously "exercising plain common sense" about the innumerable matters about which honorable, rational, and informed persons have reached diverse conclusions. The most he can do is to ascertain whether the judgment in each instance was of the kind authorized—in sum, whether it was based on the considerations contemplated by the empowering statute, whether it was understandably related to the pertinent information, whether it was accompanied by whatever procedural niceties the situation may have demanded.

During the first year of his activity many of the Ombudsman's inquiries proved fruitless because they bore upon administrative determinations lying well within the permissible range of reasonable judgment. At the outset the Ombudsman had been unable to distinguish readily between an attack on a discretionary decision because "manifestly unreasonable or otherwise contrary to proper administrative practice" (with which he is supposed to deal) and, on the other hand, disgruntlement that a discretionary decision had not fulfilled the complainant's fondest hopes (which have not been entrusted to the Ombudsman's care). At the year's end, however, the Ombudsman saw the differentiation more distinctly. "As the lines of policy in the work have become firmer," he wrote, "it has been unnecessary to ask the administrative authorities to comment on as many complaints involving discretionary decisions as had been referred to them in the beginning. Normally there will be insufficient reason to refer a case to the administrative organ unless the complaint alleges procedural errors or urges particular facts as its basis."[32]

Meanwhile, though at pains not to declare a judgment to be "manifestly unreasonable" simply because he thinks it may be imperfect, the Ombudsman has in fact been acting as a mediator between the citizenry and the administration in many cases that are probably outside his power.

Case No. 1963–71 is illustrative. Farmer *A* had asked the Ministry of Transport to extend a bus service so that it would pass his farm, thus enabling him to bring his milk to market. When the ministry refused, *A* complained to the Ombudsman. The ministry, responding to the Ombudsman's inquiry, informed him that the bus service in question already operated at a deficit, which had to be covered by a public subsidy; the ministry was unwilling to face an increased deficit. The decision was rather clearly within the ministry's power. The Ombudsman nevertheless pursued the matter. He asked the bus company how much added expense would be involved in driving to *A*'s farm and how much added revenue would be gained by carrying *A*'s milk. He proffered the bus company's data to the ministry and suggested that the ministry might perhaps wish to reconsider. The ministry did so. Extended service has now been provided every other day, with the ministry's agreeing to increase the bus operator's subsidy if necessary, which seems unlikely if Farmer *A*'s milk shipments prove to be as ample as he hopes.

Sometimes, too, his eye has caught a bit of evidence that may need fresh appraisal. For example, in Case No. 1963–58, a diabetic, *D*, complained that the Ministry of Social Affairs had denied his application for various disability and public assistance benefits. The Ministry, when asked for comment, sent the Ombudsman a file containing medical analyses and other reports showing that the rejection of *D*'s request was well within the range of permissible judgment. The Ombudsman noticed amidst the papers, however, a statement that *D* had necessarily incurred additional heavy expenses because of his disease. The Ombudsman put the matter before the Ministry once more, asking whether that circumstance had been fully considered. The Ministry took another look at the file, made a grant to *D* to help him meet his

[32] 1963 Ombudsman's Report, at 9.

expenses, and the Ombudsman closed the case, saying that investigation of the complaint had disclosed no basis for action by him.

Because he has in actuality been able and willing to induce reexamination of matters involving administrative discretion with which he cannot himself deal directly, the Ombudsman's good offices are likely to continue in heavy demand.

4|What the Ombudsman Does Do

Much of the preceding discussion has focused on things the Ombudsman is not expected to do. The important thing, of course, is what he does do.

As already remarked, he is a watcher of national administration—"Government administrative organs and civil servants and others in the service of the Government."[33] As to them he "can deal with cases either at the request of a person or on his own initiative."[34] The record shows that he has ranged very widely among public agencies, though the Ministry of Social Affairs and the Ministry of Justice and Police have, between them, accounted for more than half of all the cases he dealt with on the merits in 1963 and 1964.

The cases shown in Table IX were but a fraction of those docketed. The way in which the Ombudsman treated matters brought to his

[33] Act of June 22, 1962, Sec. 4. The statute contemplates the possibility of the Storting's later determining "whether a particular institution or function shall be regarded as being Government administration or part of the service of the Government"—presumably with a view to removing from his ken various government businesses (like the Aardal and Sundal Aluminum Works) and services (like the Postal Savings Bank) whose accounts are already publicly audited and which make few decisions of a formal or semi-formal nature. Thus far, however, nothing has been taken out of the category so broadly stated in the statute. Conversely, Section 3 of the Storting's regulations has removed possible doubt about the Ombudsman's ability to deal with certain borderline matters by explicitly declaring them to be a part of "Government administration."

[34] Sec. 5. A complaint to the Ombudsman "must be signed and must be submitted within one year from the date on which the official act or circumstance subject of the complaint took place or was discontinued," and it must come from someone who "considers himself to be unjustly treated by the public administration," so that a complaint cannot be made about impersonal wrongs (Sec. 6). These limitations upon complaints enable the Ombudsman to slough off ancient, unmeritorious, and anonymous cases; but nothing prevents him from taking up "on his own initiative" a matter brought to his notice by a defective complaint.

Table IX. Organs involved in cases dealt with on the merits

Ministry	1963	1964
Social Affairs	101	90
Justice and Police	99	127
Transport	37	33
Church and Education	31	26
Finance and Customs	23	31
Municipal and Labor Affairs	22	10
Agriculture	21	21
Wages and Prices	13	3
Fisheries	9	4
Defense	7	3
Commerce and Shipping	5	3
Industry and Handicraft	5	4
Foreign Affairs	3	0
Family and Consumer Affairs	0	0
Other Administrative Bodies	26	13

notice is set forth in Table X on the next page, which reveals that approximately two thirds were dismissed without reaching the merits.[35]

Special note may be taken of the many cases dismissed because administrative channels remained open. While the governing statute is silent as to the necessity of exhausting administrative remedies, the Storting's later instructions declare that the Ombudsman should insist upon a complainant's utilizing available administrative relief unless "particular reasons" warrant taking up a complaint at once.[36]

[35] Many dismissed cases required substantial work in the Ombudsman's office before the ground of dismissal became apparent. Correspondence and file analysis were often necessary, and in some instances formal opinions had to be written, as in matters that were ultimately rejected because they had already received some measure of legislative attention. Unlike those reached on the merits, however, the dismissed cases stopped short of asking officials for their opinions and justifications of the matters involved in complaints.

[36] Rule 5 provides: "If the complaint concerns a decision which the complainant according to administrative law or practice has a possibility to bring before a higher administrative organ for reconsideration, the Ombudsman shall not deal with the complaint unless he finds particular reasons for doing so without delay. The Ombudsman shall advise the complainant of the possibility of his having the decision reconsidered by an administrative organ. If the complainant is barred from demanding

Table X. Disposition of docketed matters

	1963	1964
Complaints received	1,257	1,060
Cases initiated by Ombudsman	18	16
Total docketed	1,275	1,076
Dealt with on the merits	402	368
Added information asked of complainant	5	0
Dismissed	868	708
a) Outside jurisdiction	393	293
Judicial activities	147	101
Considered by Storting	20	7
Cabinet decision	13	5
Municipal matters	98	71
Other (private affairs, etc.)	115	109
b) Filed tardily	97	52
c) Administrative remedies available	128	136
d) Insufficient foundation	91	61
e) Withdrawn by complainant	48	40
f) Anonymous or incomprehensible	20	3
g) Not real complaints (inquiries, etc.)	91	123

A second large group of dismissals is attributable to "Insufficient foundation," reflecting the Ombudsman's statutory power to "determine whether there are sufficient grounds for dealing with a com-

---

such reconsideration because he has exceeded the time limit allowed for doing so, the Ombudsman shall decide whether, in view of the circumstances, he should nevertheless deal with the complaint."

Two conditions have led the Ombudsman to deal with the merits even when administrative review remains available: "One is that the complaint is clearly without justification, so that nothing can be gained by suggesting that the complainant first utilize his right to appeal . . . The other is when the urgency of the matter renders it unreasonable to require the complainant to return to the administrative appellate channel. If the decision is unfavorable to the complainant, he is nevertheless informed that he still has a right of administrative appeal." 1963 Ombudsman's Report, at 8.

A Ministry of Justice official added during a discussion in 1964: "Even when the Ombudsman writes a prisoner that he must go through administrative channels before his complaint will be acted on, he may simultaneously say to us informally, what about this or that point in his complaint? So we have a rather clear impression of the Ombudsman's reaction even when, technically, he has not yet acted on a case."

plaint" (Sec. 6) and his authorization to "dismiss a complaint which he finds obviously unfounded" (Rule 7); some such authority is a desirable protection of ombudsmen against mentally or emotionally unstable complainants.

The table shows also that the Ombudsman has infrequently found reason to proceed on his own motion—eighteen self-initiated cases in 1963, sixteen in 1964.[37] As yet no cases have been referred to him for special report to the legislature, a possibility envisaged by Rule 5: "On cases which the Ombudsman receives from the Storting or Odelsting, he shall present his opinion to the Storting or Odelsting." Persons close to the Ombudsman have expressed hope that such referrals will never occur. They foresee that a special report concerning a matter investigated at legislators' behest would become the subject of partisan debate and in the end might damage the Ombudsman's non-political image.

The sources of complaints are diverse, but civil servants (including schoolteachers) have comprised one of the largest groups. They have brought to the Ombudsman their unresolved grievances about appointments, promotions, salary classifications, determination of pension rights, and other employment conditions.[38] The inmates of penal insti-

[37] Self-initiated cases thus far have been no more spectacular in nature than in numbers. Examples: (1) An aspirant to a teaching post wrote a newspaper that the final date for applying for a certain vacancy had been the very date on which the existence of the vacancy had first been officially announced. The Ombudsman inquired. The Ministry of Education acknowledged having made a mistake that would be guarded against in the future. (2) A lawyer wrote a newspaper about a ministry's slowness in responding to his communication. The Ombudsman inquired. Two days later the lawyer received his answer. (3) A publicly employed physician wrote a newspaper that he planned to work only a limited number of hours in the future because income taxes ate up all his additional earnings. The Ombudsman asked the physician's superiors to speak to him concerning the performance of his duties. The physician was spoken to. He said that he had been misunderstood.

[38] A top-ranking officer of a civil servants' organization remarked recently: "Discretionary decisions about promotions and nonpromotions are going to be the most important things from our point of view, even though the Ombudsman can perhaps only comment and not criticize. We have always been able to take up grievances with a committee of the Storting, but what would happen there was too predictable; political considerations would make it most unlikely that a Government action would be criticized. Therefore very few of our people bothered to go to the Storting. Now they will give the Ombudsman a try. Many of the cases submitted to him will not be manifestly unreasonable, and so he will probably not interfere. But we have the feeling that ministries are already taking more care in personnel matters than some of them did before the Ombudsman was around to ask them questions."

Political considerations occasionally intrude offensively into the career civil service, according to a number of Norwegian observers. The non-political director of a scientific department reports, for example, that inquiry has been made of him con-

tutions have been another large category; they accounted for 4.5 percent of the complaints received in 1963 and 16.1 percent of those filed in 1964, thus proving once again the value of word of mouth advertising. Attorneys have signed about 3 percent of the complaints, though they are thought to have prepared many others that were filed directly by their clients. Attorneys are also believed to have referred many "querulents" to the Ombudsman, thus relieving themselves of an unwelcome burden by transferring it to the official grievance bureau.

Table XI categorizes complaints so far as has seemed possible. It does not show the character of the individual complainants outside the indicated categories. Almost without exception, spokesmen for organized groups in Norway speak rather patronizingly about the users of the Ombudsman's services, describing them as "little people" or as "the ordinary man in the street" or as "persons too poor or too ignorant to have a lawyer" or as "men who are outside organizations that know where to go" or, simply, as "cranks." These characterizations fit the facts in many and probably most instances, but examination of the Ombudsman's records reveals well established business firms and substantial citizens among his clients, along with the small

Table XI. Sources of complaints

	1963		1964	
	Complaints	Percent	Complaints	Percent
Civil servants	113	9.0		
Prisoners	57	4.5	171	16.1
Attorneys	36	2.9	31	3.0
Mental hospitals	15	1.2	17	1.6
Organizations	14	1.1		
Undifferentiated	1,022	81.3	841	79.3
Total	1,257	100.0	1,060	100.0

cerning the partisan affiliations of subordinates he has recommended for promotion. The chief of a civil servants' union flatly expresses his union's belief that appointments to key positions are too often influenced by party considerations that distort judgment about the candidates' other qualifications.

fry, the bewildered, and the chronically combative. Among them, too, have been many claimants of disability benefits and other forms of social insurance. Contrary to the practice in other Scandinavian countries, in Norway these cases are not usually referable to a special administrative tribunal; consequently they consume much more of the Norwegian Ombudsman's time.

When acting on a complaint, the Ombudsman wields no awesome authority. Unlike the ombudsmen in Sweden, Finland, and Denmark he cannot direct that a civil servant be prosecuted or subjected to a disciplinary proceeding.[39] His is the power of reason alone, unaided by the power of compulsion or punishment. Section 10 of the governing statute says, simply, that "the Ombudsman has the right to express his opinion in matters which come within his province" and that "if the Ombudsman is of the opinion that a decision is invalid or clearly unreasonable, he may make a statement to this effect." Rule 9 of his instructions adds that he may also, if circumstances justify, advise an administrative organ that "compensation should be paid unless a new decision can rectify the matter."

The Ombudsman's capacity to counsel rather than command seems adequate for Norway's needs and consonant with its traditions. The repute of public servants, both local and national, is extraordinarily high. True criminality in governmental circles is generally believed to be a rarity, unlikely to concern the Ombudsman.[40] And while Norway's penal code like Sweden's and Finland's defines as a crime an official's acting inattentively, negligently, ignorantly, or rudely,[41]

[39] He may, however, under Sec. 10, "inform the public prosecutor or the appointing authority" of steps he thinks should be taken. Whether steps are then taken remains to be decided by someone other than the Ombudsman. He has not yet had occasion to give information of this type.

[40] Public confidence was somewhat shaken in 1963 by disclosure of an apparent impropriety, involving a single official in the Ministry of Industry. The scandal came to light during the lone month (August–September, 1963) that the Labor Party had been out of power between 1935 and 1965. This has led to speculation that if the doors of governmental closets were flung wide open, some other skeletons might be found.

On the other hand, even completely unconfirmed gossip about police corruption and the like was not heard in 1964. A high-ranking police officer did make a "confession." Some years ago, he said, a traffic policeman had investigated an accident involving the motor car of an American Embassy attaché. Upon learning that the attaché's diplomatic immunity precluded proceedings against him, the policeman terminated the investigation. The American then gave the policeman an unsolicited gift of two cartons of cigarettes. This was the only instance of "police corruption" that anyone interviewed in Oslo or elsewhere could recall.

[41] See note 22.

Norway has not emulated the Swedish and Finnish ferocity in prosecuting judges and other public employees for their minor lapses.[42] Hence the Ombudsman's inability to initiate criminal proceedings is no great deprivation. A review of the action taken upon the complaints before him shows that he has been able to exert a significant influence even though possessing no powers of enforcement. This can be demonstrated both statistically and anecdotally.

The statistics indicate that as of March 1, 1965, investigation had been completed and the files closed in 715 cases dealt with on the merits since January 1, 1963. In 510 cases nothing was found that led to a change in the decision or that called for comment by the Ombudsman. In 95 cases, however, the administrators changed their decisions while the complaint was under consideration, thus obviating the need for further action by the Ombudsman; the Ombudsman has followed the mild policy of informing administrators when his investigations have unearthed new facts or considerations, so that doubtful decisions may be re-examined by those who made them in the first place. In 110 additional cases the Ombudsman voiced a criticism or made a request to the administration, either in terms of the specific action against which complaint had been made or in more general terms for the future.

In only two out of 110 instances, so far as can be ascertained, has the Ombudsman's advice not been fully accepted. In one of these a schoolteacher had requested the Ministry of Education to grant compensation for additional transportation expense involved in his serving at a place distant from his home, after several previously scattered schools (including the one to which he had been assigned) had been consolidated at a central location. The request was denied. Having investigated the teacher's complaint, the Ombudsman concluded that the Ministry was statutorily obligated to compensate the complainant. He recommended that the Ministry compute the amount to be paid. The Ministry adhered to its view that no payment was due, leaving the teacher free to sue to recover the damages the Ombudsman (but not the Ministry) agreed he had suffered.[43] In the second case, a man

[42] For discussion of the Swedish and Finnish practices under similar statutes, see Chapters 5 and 2.

[43] Apparently the teacher and his organization decided not to pursue the matter further.

If the Ministry had paid as advised by the Ombudsman, its having done so might

previously held in a treatment center for alcoholism was arrested on fresh charges soon after his release. A person detained for alcoholism is, under Norwegian law, first committed to a workhouse; subsequently, if found to require more extended therapy, he may be transferred to a different place of detention. In the present instance the rearrested person was sent at once to the treatment center, for which he had acquired a lively distaste. The Ombudsman agreed with the complainant that he had been lodged in the wrong institution. The Ministry of Justice acknowledged not having observed the letter of the law, but expressed no remorse for having popped the recidivist into the treatment center at once instead of by way of the workhouse (which happened to be five hundred miles away). Thus far neither the Ombudsman nor the Ministry has surrendered. The Ombudsman can, however, do nothing further except report the matter to the Storting or urge the Ministry to seek an amendment to the present statute pertaining to detention of alcoholics.

The minor setbacks just described are more than offset by administrators' acceptance of the Ombudsman's counsel. Like the defeats, the triumphs are not spectacular. None the less they suggest, in the aggregate, that the Ombudsman has served a need that was real despite its not having been widely felt before he began his work. This may perhaps best be illustrated by reviewing classes of cases with which he has dealt.

Social insurance cases. Controverted claims for pensions or disability benefits flow through the Ministry of Social Affairs at the rate of more than ten thousand per year. While the Ministry's decision is accepted as final in most instances, a few disputes remain unresolved. Judicial review has always been available to dissatisfied claimants, but recourse to the courts has been rare. As shown by Table IX, however, recourse to the Ombudsman has been fairly frequent; a case may be

---

(at least in theory) have been held improper when its accounts were subsequently scrutinized by the Auditor of Public Accounts. While the Auditor's criticism would then be, in form, a criticism of the Ministry, it would in fact be a criticism of the Ombudsman. This is an anomaly in the Norwegian system, for while the Auditor of Public Accounts may in no instance be criticized by the Ombudsman (see Section 3 above), the Ombudsman's judgment is thus subject to being reviewed by the Auditor. The possibility of conflict between these two officers seems more theoretical than real, however, since the Auditor is not likely to disallow a payment made by an administrator who had simply followed the Ombudsman's recommendation based on his analysis of law.

taken to him even though a judicial remedy is available but as yet unsought. He has infrequently found fault with the Ministry's conclusions, though he has in a few cases stimulated reconsideration that has led the Ministry itself to change some previously unacceptable decisions.[44]

The way he has handled the cases before him has earned the Ministry's hearty respect. "We think he is only an amateur in the social insurance field," one high official said somewhat loftily, "but he is a very intelligent amateur. He asks good questions. He hasn't the power to make us change any decision, but we would certainly reopen any case whose result he criticized, and we would probably want to change the decision ourselves."

Another Ministry official, leafing through the files of cases about which the Ombudsman had inquired, noted one matter in which the Ombudsman had made five supplemental requests for information about the medical details of a disability insurance case before finally becoming persuaded that the administrative decision was just. "That experience was enough to convince me," the official remarked, "that the Ombudsman was not an easy man to distract. We sent out a general instruction to record the medical information in the disability case files more carefully than had been done in the past, so that the foundation of an essentially medical judgment about a man's physical fitness to earn a living would be readily apparent."

Only time will tell whether this "administrative reform," brought about by the Ombudsman's pertinacious questioning, will cause more trouble than it cures. Elaboration of the medical reports will no doubt be useful to those who review challenged decisions. On the other hand it will also very probably retard the pace of administrative action on all cases, those that will give rise to no later dispute as well as those that will remain controversial. Today's reform may prove to be tomorrow's red tape, subject to being criticized because it prevents speedy decision. At any rate, as of this moment, the Ombudsman's

[44] For an illustrative case see Case No. 1963–58, at pages 170–171 above. In another instance, Case No. 1963–7, the Ombudsman acted upon a complaint about the Ministry of Social Affairs' refusal to give retroactive effect to its own determination that a pensioner's benefits had been incorrectly computed; the Ministry proposed to increase the pension payments for the future only. The Ombudsman discussed the case with the pension authorities and then, as his report undramatically notes, they changed their decision.

influence has been felt in a way meant to be protective of claimants' interests.

Deprivation of personal freedom. Many countries, not least the United States, have been somewhat cavalier about detaining persons believed to be mentally ill. While hospitalization is of course not punitive in purpose, it does nevertheless cause loss of personal freedom. It should therefore be decided upon circumspectly, with close attention to the rights of involuntary patients. The Ombudsman has already found occasion to remind Norwegian health authorities that a patient's liberties must be respected.

Thus, in Case No. 1963–69, he censured a hospital administration for having detained a person in its psychiatric ward for more than three weeks without the patient's explicit consent, which the Ombudsman held to be legally requisite. And in Case No. 1963–70 the Ombudsman denounced procedural lapses in the involuntary commitment of a mental patient, further criticizing a subsequent lack of candor in dealing with the patient's attorney when he had sought to inquire into his client's plight. In Case No. 1963–46 notes made by a mental patient during his hospitalization were taken from him, apparently as an aid to diagnosing his condition, and were withheld from him when he sought their return. The Ombudsman agreed that a patient had no right to see doctors' notes or reports concerning his case, which might properly be withheld from him on medical grounds. But this did not warrant denying a patient access to his own writings, which he had a right to retain if he wished. As a result of the advice thus given by the Ombudsman, a previously general practice was changed for the future.

The Ombudsman has also looked into cases at the municipal level involving needlessly brusque decisions to isolate persons believed to be infectiously ill. He has inquired closely, too, into detention of alleged juvenile delinquents and into institutionalization of children neglected by their parents.

The importance of such cases transcends the individual instances. The liberty of all is exalted when the liberty of the community's most defenseless members is scrupulously protected. The Ombudsman's work in this area is likely to have intangible consequences of great value.

Complaints of prisoners. Prison administrators regard the ombudsman system as a mixed blessing. It adds to their work because prisoners take advantage of the opportunity to voice grievances ("it's an outlet for their aggressions," as one penitentiary warden said), thus forcing the administrators to explain and justify their acts. On the other hand, accessibility to an ombudsman tends to lessen some of the tensions of prison life. On balance, Norway's prison administrators say that the psychological values of the Ombudsman outweigh his disadvantages for them.

From the prisoners' point of view, Norway's adoption of the ombudsman system has been pure gain. Their complaints have not been overpoweringly numerous—57 in 1963, 171 in 1964—but since the population of all the lockups, jails, workhouses, and penitentiaries of Norway is somewhat less than 1,800 on the daily average, with fewer than 300 serving sentences of nine months or more, the proportion of complaints to prisoners is high. Most of the complaints have been rejected, though some have produced substantial changes in administrative practice.[45]

More significant than the outcome of particular cases has been a heightened effort on the part of the administrators to render objectively rational decisions. "A prison is an authoritarian society, not a democracy," an experienced director remarked recently, "and we who have the authority must guard against exercising it too freely just because we can do so without challenge." Another added: "If one of the inmates sends us a request or a complaint, we have always been able just to say 'No' and that was that. But now, with the Ombudsman in the picture, it's not enough. If he asks us why we said 'No', we have to give him a detailed explanation and we can't simply rest on our authority as we can with a prisoner. So now we try to think the matter through more carefully, to avoid being embarrassed by inability to explain ourselves if questioned later."

[45] Illustrations: (1) An unruly prisoner can be disciplined locally by the prison director and, additionally, by a later decision of the Ministry of Justice to prolong a sentence, within limits. By order of the prison director, prisoner *A* had been placed in solitary confinement for thirty days for an infraction of rules. Two months later he was notified by the Ministry of Justice that he would be detained for fourteen days beyond the completion of his original sentence. He complained to the Ombudsman against what he regarded as "double punishment" for the same misconduct. The Ombudsman found no ground for criticizing the Ministry, but he persuaded it that prisoners should be given a fuller explanation of the range of disciplinary measures that might be utilized by the authorities and, moreover, he encouraged the Ministry

Procedural refinements. Many of the Ombudsman's decisions have little consequence beyond the case immediately involved. When, as has happened, he suggests re-examining whether a teacher who had undertaken additional instructional duty has been suitably compensated in line with existing regulations, no new principle emerges though an isolated mistake may have been averted. When, on the other hand, the Ombudsman expresses dissatisfaction with an administrative agency's procedures, his views are likely to have a future projection far beyond the immediate case.

Case No. 1963–25 is illustrative. A physician complained that the Director of Health had denied a permit for the registration and use of Medicine *X*. The Ombudsman, having been informed that *X* was a "cancer cure" of no demonstrable value, found the challenged administrative judgment to be free from fault. He noted, however, that the system of administrative appeal in matters of this kind was defective and should be changed. A decision of the Director of Health is appealable to the Ministry of Social Affairs. When, as in the present instance, the decision turns upon considerations of medical science, the Ministry asks the Directorate of Health for advice, since all the Ministry's medical expertise is concentrated in that body. Hence the Directorate of Health plays a major part in deciding appeals from its own decisions. The Ombudsman proposed that new means should be found for giving the Ministry the expert assistance needed for sound and unbiased action on appeals in the future.

The Ombudsman has also given strong reminders that administrative procedural regulations are binding upon administrators as well as

---

to coordinate its punitive measures more closely with those decided upon by the prison administrators. (2) Penitentiary inmates earn a small daily wage, part of which is withheld until their release or until the prison director considers it is needed by the prisoner's family or for other worthy puposes. While in detention Prisoner *B* received a tax refund of about $20. The director refused to turn it over to him to be spent as he might choose. Upon *B*'s complaint, the Ombudsman suggested that the director had no power to control prisoners' funds other than those earned by prison work. As a consequence, prison administrators no longer interfere with an inmate's receiving windfalls and private funds, which may then be spent outside the prison as the recipient may choose. (3) Prisoner *C*'s application for release on probation, for which he was eligible, had been denied without the giving of any reason. The Ombudsman suggested, and the authorities agreed, that in the future a person denied the privilege of early release should be told the reason for the adverse decision. (4) Prisoner *D* complained that the coffee was too diluted; he was found to be an accurate analyst, and the strength of the coffee served the prisoners was increased.

upon the public, and may not lightly be ignored. Thus, he severely criticized the Ministry of Justice for not carefully following its own regulations in filling a prison staff vacancy.[46] The Ministry, impressed by his observations, promptly sent a circular letter to all subordinate units, drawing attention to the criticism and commanding scrupulous observance of prescribed procedures in the future.

The small irritations of organized society. The attractions of living together are sufficiently great to make urbanization more popular than hermitage. At the same time, living together creates frictions that sometimes take the joy out of life. Reducing those frictions one by one may not be the most impressive feat of social engineering imaginable, but it is a worthy activity in itself. The Ombudsman has proved himself to be adept in this work.

For example, in Case No. 1963–34 a craftsman whose initial license had expired and who had obtained a new one complained that the licensing authority would not return his expired certificate, which he wanted to preserve because of its sentimental value to him. The administrators had paid no attention to his plea. They never returned old licenses, but kept them in the licensee's file as part of the administrative records. Sentimentality must yield, they said in effect, to the administrative passion for archives. Why not make a photostatic copy of the original license, keep the copy in the files, and let the sentimentalist have the original for such enjoyment as it might give him? the Ombudsman asked. We never thought of that, answered the administrators.

In Case No. 1963–12 an insolvent debtor still enmeshed in bankruptcy proceedings needed a trading license, previously issued to him and still perfectly valid, in order to commence a new business activity. But the license was among the papers tied up in the bankruptcy pro-

[46] The case in question is No. 1963-28, involving a civil service union's complaint that an appointment had been made upon recommendation of a nominating committee, not constituted in accord with the Appointment Regulations for Prisons. The Ombudsman was unable to conclude that the error had affected the result, and he therefore declined to criticize the particular decision. But he did make clear his disapproval of nonobservance of an agency's own regulations. His view clearly parallels that of American courts, which denounce disregard of administrative regulations, but still weigh whether the disregard was prejudicial in the particular instance. Compare Vitarelli v. Seaton, 359 U.S. 535 (1959), and Accardi v. Shaughnessy, 347 U.S. 260 (1954), with Olin Industries. Inc. v. NLRB, 192 F.2d 799 (5th Cir. 1951), *cert. denied,* 343 U.S. 919 (1952).

ceedings and would not be returned to the licensee until they had run their course. Could not the Ministry of Trade arrange to give the licensee the immediate use of his license? We never have done that, answered the Ministry; the license will be restored as a matter of course when the bankruptcy proceedings end, and that is the way we have always handled cases like this. But since the licensee really needs his license now, could not something be done to help him right away? Well, yes, answered the Ministry, on second thought we really can't find any good reason not to give the fellow what he has asked.

Case No. 1963–21 involved a man who had been locked up overnight for being drunk and disorderly. When he had sobered up sufficiently to be released, the police discovered to their embarrassment that meanwhile they had given his personal possessions to another man of the same name who had been released from detention a few hours previously. The happy recipient of this largesse could not be found. When the outraged owner of the property complained to the Ombudsman that the police were unduly slow in compensating him for the loss occasioned by their carelessness, the Ombudsman moved quickly to remind the police about their obligations.

In Case No. 1963–11 a citizen temporarily away from Norway complained that an embassy official had refused to send money home in his behalf and, to make a bad matter worse, had called him a scoundrel or had described his proposal as a scoundrelly trick. The Ombudsman agreed with the embassy official that he had no duty to repatriate the Norwegian's funds (which seem to have been derived from questionable currency transactions). But when it came to name-calling, the official went beyond the bounds of propriety. Norwegian diplomats, the Ombudsman intimated, must be urbane in manner as well as correct in action.

A farmer complained in Case No. 1963–23 that a clergyman who occupied an adjacent State-owned farm had interfered with his enjoying the use of an access road. The road crossed a portion of the clergyman's farm, over which the neighboring farmer had an ancient easement. The Ministry of Church and Education had acknowledged the complainant's right to cross the clergyman's farm, but only "so far as possible taking into account the running of the farm." The complainant was irked from time to time to find the roadway blocked by the clergyman's large tractor. So he complained to the Ombudsman. The

Ombudsman told the Ministry that the complainant's easement was unqualified. He thought that the Ministry had better build a garage or parking space for the tractor, which seemed to be the main source of difficulty. He also suggested that the Ministry should reimburse the legal expenses the complainant had incurred in establishing his rights. The Ministry acquiesced, the complainant declared himself satisfied, and peace descended upon the valley.

In fairness to administrators, one must remark that they are often victims, and not invariably the generators, of unnecessary friction. The Ombudsman has sometimes been able to relieve suffering officials, too. One local administrator spoke feelingly not long ago about a resident's having complained to the Ombudsman against his neighbor's conduct, a matter clearly outside the Ombudsman's jurisdiction. "If there were no other reason to be glad about this new system," the official said with a sigh, "I would be glad just because this habitual complainer has switched his attention from me to the Ombudsman. The Ombudsman will never get rid of him, I'm willing to bet, but at least the fellow has stopped coming here every other day." Spokesmen for several ministries expressed similar contentment that the pressure of "querulents" was now less intense than in pre-Ombudsman days. A high-ranking police officer commented that "perhaps the Ombudsman can protect us against the people who are always dissatisfied, no matter what you do for them nor how you do it."

Obviously, the Ombudsman cannot eliminate all the petty irritations of organized society. But he has apparently reduced them here and there, and that in itself is a gain.

5 | The Ombudsman's Work Methods

The Ombudsman has thus far had only four law-trained assistants at any one time, and only three for a considerable period.[47] While work

[47] The controlling statute (Sect. 14) provides simply that "the personnel employed in the office of the Ombudsman shall be appointed by the chairman of the Storting on the recommendation of the Ombudsman. Their salaries shall be fixed in the same manner as for the Storting's personnel." The Ombudsman expects that work in his office will prove to be a "high prestige job." He would like to keep his assistants for about five years, after which he hopes they may be appointed to judgeships (as has

methods are still not finally shaped, a fairly stable pattern can be discerned.

Staff work. An incoming complaint is registered and is then at once passed to the Ombudsman himself for first reading. Next, usually without comment by the Ombudsman, it goes to the Chief of Office, who assigns it to one of the three staff lawyers according to ability and pertinent experience.

The staff lawyer is free to seek information by telephone or letter. When the complaint is that an administrator has been unduly slow in disposing of a case, a telephone inquiry is usually made at once and the complainant is then immediately informed how matters stand. The staff lawyer can also request that relevant administrative documents be sent to the Ombudsman's office for examination.[48] Carbon copies of all outgoing correspondence are placed in a current file for almost daily reading by the Ombudsman himself and by all staff members, who sometimes suggest possible sources of information.

If, after analyzing the documentary materials and other information at hand, the staff member believes that the administrative agency's comments should be sought, he must prepare a letter for the Ombudsman's signature, which is reviewed first by the Chief of Office and then by the Ombudsman personally; this is a serious step that cannot be taken upon the staff member's initiative alone, for it approximates a determination that a prima facie case has been made out against the administration.

---

already occurred in one instance). The pay scale of the Ombudsman's staff is somewhat better than that for comparably experienced personnel in the ministries.

[48] Section 7 of the governing statute empowers the Ombudsman to "demand information necessary for the performance of his duties from Government appointees and officials and from any other persons in the service of the Government. Similarly he can demand the presentation of records and other documents." The section also authorizes resort to the compulsory process of courts to obtain information needed from non-governmental sources. The "records" and "documents" referred to in this section do not include staff memorandums and similar internal working papers; they remain in the administrative organ's sole control in order to encourage candor and informality in communications between subordinates and superiors. The Ministry of Social Affairs, however, regularly sends its entire file to the Ombudsman whenever his office asks for documentary materials. Like all other ministries, it asserts that the Ombudsman has no right to see internal working papers, but it has no objection to his seeing them as a matter of privilege.

For additional discussion of this matter, see A. Schei, "The First Year of the Norwegian Ombudsman," 45 *Nordisk Administrativt Tidsskrift* 134 (1964), translated by J. M. Torgersen and distributed in 1966 by Institute of Governmental Studies, University of California, Berkeley.

Preparation of a remark or criticism by the Ombudsman must often be preceded by extensive legal study, involving analysis of statutes and legislative history. No suggestions or conclusions emerge from anyone in the Ombudsman's office other than the Ombudsman himself. As in the other Scandinavian ombudsman organizations, the Ombudsman's personal opinion, not an institutional judgment, is sought. The success of the Ombudsman's work, the Chief Justice of Norway has asserted, "will entirely depend upon his personal authority and the respect and esteem he enjoys."[49] Nobody in Norway seems inclined to dissent from the judgment.

Office consultations. Some five hundred office consultations occurred during 1963 and nearly four hundred in 1964. Some were with complainants who had been requested to provide further information or to comment on information otherwise acquired. Most of the office conferences were with persons who wished to make a complaint, but had not yet done so in writing as required by Rule 4 of the Storting's instructions to the Ombudsman, either because they were ignorant of the rule or because they felt they could explain themselves better orally. The Ombudsman's staff helped many callers to prepare written complaints; in a few complicated matters they sent would-be complainants to free legal advisers so that adequate complaints could be drawn.

Adversary hearings. No practice has developed of conducting adversary hearings in which the complainant and the accused official confront one another. In only one instance did such a hearing occur, and then with striking results.

Two customs officers complained in Case No. 1963–40 that the Ministry of Finance and Customs had notified them on May 22 that they were to be suspended on June 1 because of alleged intoxication while on duty. They heatedly denied the charge and said they had had no chance to defend themselves against it. The chief evidence, shown to the Ombudsman upon his request, consisted of a statement by a disinterested foreign traveler, supported by her companion; this, the Ministry said, clearly justified disciplining the officers without the necessity of further proceedings. The Ombudsman, still unpersuaded that a fair decision had been made, requested the Ministry to postpone the officers' suspension while he considered their complaint. The

[49] T. Wold, "The Norwegian Parliament's Commissioner for Civil Administration," 2 *J. Int. Comm. Jurists* No. 2, 21 at 28 (1960).

Ministry acquiesced. Then the Ombudsman invited the two aliens to attend a hearing in his office, at which were also present the two customs officers and a representative of the Attorney General. The travelers testified before the Ombudsman that they had been summoned to the customs office to pay duty. While there they had noted several bottles of liquor on or near the officers' desk, and one of the officers had had a strange manner. The witnesses had drawn the inference that the officers had been drinking out of the bottles, though no drinking had occurred in the witnesses' presence. The customs men were able to show convincingly that the liquor was not theirs for personal consumption, but had been confiscated by them in the course of performing their duties and had been properly disposed of afterward. The Minister, informed by the Ombudsman about the impressions gained at the adversary hearing, quickly rescinded the order of suspension. The customs officers returned to their posts with unblemished records.

The Ombudsman took two further steps. He requested the Minister to note the weakness of relying on written evidence without affording affected persons an opportunity to meet it; the ministry agreed to impress this point upon all subordinate bodies having power to initiate disciplinary actions. Then he proposed to another ministry, just then engaged in preparing a revision of the civil service laws, that the law should specifically require disciplinary measures to be based upon well tested and clearly persuasive evidence, not upon mere suspicion or unconfirmed accusations.

Inspections. Unlike his counterparts in other countries—and indeed, unlike the Military Ombudsman in his own country—the Norwegian Ombudsman does not routinely inspect institutions and offices whose work may give rise to problems deserving his attention. The governing statute declares in Section 8 that he "shall have access to service establishments, offices and other premises of all administrative organs and all enterprises which come within the province of his office." This is taken to mean that when he is investigating the circumstances of a particular case, he may visit the authority concerned—as might be useful, for example, if an inmate of an institution were to complain about some offensive aspect of life there. But the statute has not been regarded as imposing a duty to undertake inspections regularly nor as granting the power to become a steady caller.

The Ombudsman has as a matter of fact visited a few penal institutions since taking office, apparently only for the purpose of gaining visual impressions for later reference. He does not contemplate spending much time away from his office.

Public relations. Unlike Sweden and Denmark, where the press has followed the ombudsmen's activities with keen interest, the Norwegian newspapers have paid little attention to the Ombudsman. Newspapermen express sympathy with his purposes and, in fact, claim considerable credit for having mobilized public support for creation of his office. But journalists have thus far not pursued the Ombudsman with ideas of their own or with requests for current information.

This seems to be entirely to the taste of the Ombudsman, a modest and shy man. He told the newspapers at the very outset that they must give him time, and he declared recently that he desired his dealings with the press to "work out as quietly as possible" because "it is very important, in developing relationships with the administration, not to make administrators feel the Ombudsman wants to run to the newspapers as soon as something happens."

Some journalists may be becoming a trifle restive. One said not long ago: "It's hard to become excited about what the present Ombudsman is doing. He has had a couple of interviews, but all he did was give out a few statistics and they aren't very newsy. Of course he has to do his job in his own way and we haven't yet criticized him for being different from the ombudsman in Denmark; but that may come, that may come."

The Ombudsman has said, in any event, that he will respond to any journalistic inquiry that may be made. He has no obligation to seek more active press coverage of his work, for Section 10 of the governing statute says explicitly that he is to decide "at his own discretion whether and in what form he should notify the public of his action" in cases he has investigated.

Recognizing that the functions of his office must be professionally understood whether or not discussed in the daily newspapers, the Ombudsman has labored energetically as an educator. During his first eighteen months in office he delivered about thirty "lectures" (his own description of his speeches) before groups of civil servants, bar associations, conferences of rural police officers, and similar organizations. One has the impression that now, having gained experience, he intends to attempt more actively than in the past to bring his work to the notice of the public at large.

Annual reports. The governing statute (Sec. 12) requires the Ombudsman to submit an annual report to the Storting and permits him to make a special report if he "becomes aware of negligence or errors of major importance or consequence". The Storting's supplemental instructions in Rule 14 specify that the annual report should review cases "considered by the Ombudsman to have general interest" and should also record the Ombudsman's discovery of defects in existing statutes or regulations. The names of complainants and those complained against may be omitted, business secrets must not be revealed, information "subject to professional secrecy" must not appear, and the discussion of any case in the report must "contain an account of what the administrative organ or the civil servant concerned has stated in his defence."

The required annual report is clearly meant to be not only a repository of information about past events, but also an actively used guide to future conduct. The Ombudsman looks upon it as a teaching device, as it were. Its circulation is, however, rather limited. The first annual report was printed in an edition of 2,000, of which about six hundred were delivered to the Storting. Ministries and other administrative bodies were asked how many copies they would like to have for their internal distribution. Only a few more than four hundred copies were disposed of in this manner. A general mailing list of libraries, scholars, foreign readers, and the like accounted for approximately fifty copies. Those remaining were placed on public sale. "The report," one of the Ombudsman's aides acknowledged, "proved not to be a best seller."

In the autumn of 1964 few copies were to be found in a random sample of governmental offices and organizations having considerable contact with public affairs. Sometimes the document seemed to have been regarded as purely ornamental. A provincial governor, for example, disclosed that since two copies of all Storting papers are regularly sent to his office, he had received two copies of the Ombudsman's report—to which he pointed with pride as they reposed in a bookcase in obviously mint condition, untouched by human hands or eyes, his own or his subordinates'.

Measuring the circulation of the Ombudsman's opinions solely by the circulation of his report would, however, lead to a false conclusion. As previously noted, his views have been scantily reported in the newspapers and thus do not become known to rank and file officials informally. But a number of ministries have upon their own initiative dispatched special letters or bulletins to their own staffs, embodying advice or instructions shaped by the Ombudsman's actions in individual cases. The Ombudsman's opinions in police cases have been touched upon in the monthly circulars sent throughout the country by the Ministry of Justice and Police; and other administrative bodies have been equally ready to increase awareness of the Ombudsman's rulings by discussing them at staff conferences as well as in written communications. In sum, knowledge of the Ombudsman's attitudes seems to be reasonably well disseminated, though as yet his opinions have by no means saturated the marketplace of ideas.

Advisory opinions. A number of administrative organs have requested the Ombudsman's advice in advance of their having acted. He has declined to render advisory opinions, partly lest he be blocked from later comment and partly lest he become overburdened by the work of legal adviser to the government. He does, however, provide information concerning other similar cases already handled by his office.

A unit of the Ministry of Justice functions specifically as legal counselor of ministries and administrative organs. Its chief disclosed in 1964 that his office has received numerous inquiries concerning the implications of the Ombudsman's opinions. He believes that many officials have made a conscious effort to conform faithfully to the Ombudsman's suggestions not only in a particular case but in other matters to which the same principles might apply. And he notes an increasing volume of requests for advice about how to dispose of problems without risking the Ombudsman's criticism. This suggests, of course, that the Ombudsman's work really has had impact upon the conduct of public affairs.

6 | Concluding Observations

The dominance of the Labor Party during a virtually unbroken span of thirty years preceding the 1965 elections had created a paradox in Norway. On the one hand a comfortable feeling of stability existed; the government was a known quantity, and everything seemed to be proceeding as usual. On the other hand nervousness had developed about the supposedly corrupting effects of long continued power and about the insensitivity an unchallenged Establishment might develop. Enthusiasm for the Ombudsman reflected, at least partly, widespread longing for an external check upon too solidly entrenched governmental organs and upon too complacent politicians—a sentiment that played a part, too, in the Labor Party's electoral defeat in 1965.

Whether the Ombudsman can do as much as some people hope and expect is highly problematical. Every democratic society is tempted to look for easy solutions of difficult political problems. The Ombudsman system, now experiencing a considerable vogue, is one of those easy solutions that does not solve. In actuality, an ombudsman is not a countervailing power in society. His criticisms alone cannot remake or undo malfunctioning governmental machinery. He cannot impose his contrary will on resistant officials. He can be effective precisely to the extent that governmental organs share the values he seeks to nurture and precisely to the extent that they welcome having an impeccably objective eye peering over their shoulders at what they do. He is, in short, most useful in a society already so well run that it could get along happily without having his services at all. Norway is such a society.

The Norwegian Ombudsman seems to have enjoyed considerable initial approval. This is not because Norwegian public administration was an Augean stable awaiting Hercules, in the person of Andreas Schei. Norwegian government was in the main so efficient, so fair, and so well intentioned that the Ombudsman has had to deal only with occasional aberrations instead of with major deficiencies beyond his capabilities. What he has done, he has done well. His suggestions have produced better results than would otherwise have occurred in some scores of individual cases, and have presumably stimulated administrative self-improvement that is incalculably important.

In another sense the simple fact of his existence may have made palatable, to some sectors of the public, governmental decisions that might otherwise have been borne sullenly and suspiciously. Speaking of his own experience, a highly regarded Norwegian lawyer recently said: "Official decisions have always been appealable. I know from personal observation, both when I was in government service and since, that administrative appeals are almost invariably handled objectively within the ministries. But the people in general fear that one official in a ministry is going to support his colleague regardless of the merits. That suspicion, latent or recognized, has been a factor to be reckoned with in this country. Now the Ombudsman gives the people someone to whom they can take their complaints with confidence that he won't simply look for a way to justify the actions they want to challenge. I do not myself think he will discover many administrative faults. But I also think that people will believe him when he says that the administrator behaved properly, and I do not think that the people would as readily believe a ministry when it said precisely the same thing."

A somewhat similar opinion was expressed by a high official of the Ministry of Justice. Describing the Ombudsman's explanatory opinions as "soul medicine work," he added: "For myself, I am convinced there was no real need for the Ombudsman. Administrative judgments in this country are moderate and responsible, mistakes are not so frequent that we have to have a super-watchdog to guard against them. Still, I have to admit that the public is glad to have the Ombudsman in the background. Rightly or wrongly—wrongly, in my estimation—the people think that administrators are going to become fairer and quicker and all that. Things haven't been bad in the past and they won't be much different in the future. If the people think they are different, though, then the Ombudsman may make government more acceptable and more popular even though there may be no real change."

A generalized belief that all has been well is probably no more accurate than a generalized belief that all has been bad. Certainly instances of administrative face-saving do occur in every government, though not necessarily basely.[50] The detached position of the Ombudsman should indeed enable him to brush aside mere apologetics and to look coolly at problems if he finds they exist—and if they are small enough to be grasped by a generalist. Without supplanting the courts, and certainly without eliminating the need for political controls and administrative self-policing, the Ombudsman seems likely to add significantly to Norwegian well-being.

[50] The chief of a major Norwegian correctional institution remarked candidly that a recent suggestion by the Ombudsman had been applied without difficulty because the inmate to whom it pertained was being released, by coincidence, just when the suggestion was received. Otherwise, the chief said, he might have "lost face" because other inmates would have learned that he had been overruled. He added that his superiors were "very, very careful" before reversing any of his decisions, lest his authority be shaken. "Relationship with the inmates here is a delicate matter," he added, "and a lot of caution has to be exercised not to upset a balance it would be hard to restore."

five

Sweden

1 How It All Began

Much of the Swedish Constitution of 1809 has been forgotten; its delineation of royal powers and parliamentary structure has little relevance to today's realities. But the office it created, that of the Justitieombudsmän, has lived and grown. It has inspired similar establishments in Finland, Denmark, Norway, and New Zealand, and has added the word "ombudsman" to the international vocabulary.[1]

When, in 1713, Swedish King Charles XII appointed a representative, an ombudsman, to keep an eye on the royal officials of that day, he simply responded to the passing moment's need. He was bogged down in seemingly endless campaigns at the head of his army and in diplomatic negotiations that followed them. And so, very possibly ignorant that an overly occupied Russian monarch was facing much the same problem, he commonsensically commissioned a trusted subordinate to scrutinize the conduct of the tax gatherers, the judges, and the few other law administrators who acted in his name at home.

What had begun as a temporary expedient became a permanent

[1] Historians, intent upon demonstrating that there is nothing new under the sun, have sometimes discerned resemblances between the ombudsman and the Roman tribune of the people, the "censors" in seventeenth-century American Colonies, or even the Control Yuan that functioned in China during the Han Dynasty, 206 B.C.–A.D. 220. See, e.g., W. Haller, *Der Swedische Justitieombudsman* 16–27 (1964). But the nineteenth-century Swedes who created their ombudsman were probably not antiquarians, nor have the later creators of ombudsmen looked further than Sweden for inspiration.

element of administration, under the title of Chancellor of Justice. A century passed. The fortunes of the monarchy ebbed and then again grew large, but at last regal government was bridled and Sweden took hesitant steps toward representative democracy. Nothing would do then but that the Parliament should have its own overseer of administrative behavior. The king had his man; let Parliament have its man too, as a safeguard against royal officers' disregard of law. In 1809 a constitution, hastily composed during a period of domestic and international strife, defined new relationships between monarch and subjects. Among other things, it provided for a watchman over the law's watchmen who, unlike the already existing king's inspector, would report his discoveries to Parliament.

Yet, despite the antiquity of the office and the present enthusiasm for the ideas that underlie it, the scope of the Swedish ombudsman's power and his means of employing it are inadequately understood abroad. Foreign discussions have sometimes so romanticized this highly worthy Swedish governmental institution that a fresh look at actuality may now be useful.

2 | Sweden's Governmental System

In order to understand the role of Sweden's ombudsman, one must first understand the Swedish governmental structure as a whole. It little resembles that of other twentieth-century constitutional monarchies with which Western jurists are familiar. A country about the size of California with less than half of California's population governs itself admirably by means deemed outmoded elsewhere.

The Swedish king no longer exercises political power though, in form, all important governmental decisions are his. The decisions he purports to make are in fact those of the seventeen Councilors of State who are generally characterized as Cabinet ministers (in truth only the Prime Minister and the Foreign Minister officially bear ministerial title). Ministers, chosen by the Prime Minister alone, need not be members of the Parliament, though all are entitled to address it. Most importantly for purposes of the present discussion, ministers do not head large administrative departments for whose functioning they bear ultimate responsibility. Ministries are small bodies, rarely with as many as a hundred employees, including the lowliest clerical and custodial personnel. Their function is not so much to administer as to plan. They prepare Government bills and budgetary proposals; they promulgate regulations when specifically empowered by Parliament; they issue directives that may guide but do not necessarily command administrators;[2] they allocate funds and make appointments, and they entertain appeals that, in some classes of administrative matters described below, may be addressed to the king. Action on these appeals is taken nominally by the King in Council, but the collective decision is almost invariably a routine confirmation of a minister's judgment, for the weekly sessions of the King in Council dispose of literally hundreds of matters within perhaps half an hour. Important issues are of course dealt with by more leisurely intra-Cabinet discussions, as well as by searching consultations between ministerial officials and others whose expert opinions or interested views may be relevant. The significant point to note here is, simply, that except for the Foreign Office ministries are not themselves administrative bodies nor in any immediate sense responsible for administration by others, though they assuredly influence administration by deciding appeals. The Cabinet or an individual minister may occasionally be under political fire for acts of administrative bodies structurally subordinate to him because their budgets pass through his ministry and appeals from them to the king are considered by him; but when this occurs, a minister may hunt with the hounds, joining in verbally castigating the administrators or promising to investigate them.

As for Parliament, its two chambers must approve and may amend proposals submitted by the Government—that is, by the Cabinet. Its 382 members—among whom are many local officials, a number of teachers, a few civil servants, and a handful of lawyers—may themselves initiate proposals only during the first fifteen days of each annual session. Parliament does not investigate individual administrators or the conduct of public administration in general; the Constitution, indeed, actually forbids parliamentary consideration of specific administrative acts, though discussion of general principles is permis-

[2] See N. Herlitz, "Swedish Administrative Law: Some Characteristic Features," 3 *Scand. Stud. in Law* 89, 93–94, 100 (1959). And compare F. Schmidt and S. Strömholm, *Legal Values in Modern Sweden* 26–30 (1964).

sible.[3] As a result of such a discussion Parliament does at times request a ministry (or a ministry can decide on its own initiative) to create a "commission" to consider problems that may call for new legislation. Members of Parliament may serve on a commission of inquiry, along with specialists drawn from any source, the secretariat being provided by the suitable ministry. Commissions, let it be stressed, are not primarily investigators or critics of the past. They are students of what should be done in the future by general legislation. A commission report, when presented (probably after several years of deliberation), is circulated by the ministry for comment by all concerned. The report and the reactions to it may shape a later Government bill. The work of a Swedish commission rarely resembles American congressional investigations that, while nominally in aid of legislative understanding, are more often than not thinly veiled assaults upon administration of laws already in force.

If, then, Swedish public administration is subject to scant ministerial or parliamentary control, where does supervisory power lie? For a foreigner unattuned to the unwritten subtleties of Swedish government, that question is extremely difficult to answer. One is tempted to say outright that supervisory power is non-existent, each official being answerable only to The Law and his own conscience rather than to some higher official. No doubt that answer would ignore the realities of human relationships, for most persons find life easier when they follow orders than when they assert independence. Nevertheless, to a degree far beyond the generally accepted concepts of modern administration, a Swedish official is bound to apply statutory law as he alone believes it demands. If his belief differs from others', his is the one that counts. In some fields, however, Parliament empowers the king (that is, the king's ministers) to prescribe how statutes should be interpreted; thus uniformity may be nurtured.

In structure much of the responsibility for carrying out the commands of statutes and the Cabinet policies that sometimes elaborate

[3] Article 90 of the Swedish Constitution provides in part that "matters relating to the appointment and removal of officials, the decisions, resolutions, and judgments of the executive or judicial authorities . . . shall in no case or manner be subject to consideration or investigation by the Riksdag, its chambers or committees, except as literally prescribed in the fundamental laws."

Compare S. Jägerskiöld, "The Swedish Constitution: A Survey," 58 *J. Indian L. Inst.* 1, 5, 17 (1963).

them has been laid on "central administrative boards," each dealing with an indicated field—as, for example, social welfare, prisons, health, housing, social insurance, forestry, fisheries, and agriculture. Each board has at its head a Director General, appointed by the Cabinet for a term of years or for life; the board members are full-time senior officials, sometimes with the addition of part-time representatives of special interest groups. When boards have overlapping concerns (as might occur, for instance, in connection with forestry and agriculture), they are expected to cooperate; no ministry can make them do so. The boards do not, however, have direct access to Parliament. Their budgetary demands come under ministerial scrutiny, as do their recommendations of new substantive legislation. So a strong measure of political control remains, for the boards are not free to make their own grand designs. Moreover, as has already been suggested, individual decisions of central boards may as a rule be appealed to the King in Council, so that a ministry may occasionally upset a board's judgment in a particular case. Reversal of a board's action in one case does not, however, bind its behavior in the next, for the board remains duty-bound to obey The Law (as it conceives The Law to be) instead of obeying the Minister. One may suppose, realistically, that no official enjoys being reversed on appeal, so that reversals do no doubt shape future decisions in fact. Moreover, a rebellious or opinionated official is unlikely to be promoted rapidly, so here again the realities of life make for considerable uniformity of decision despite the officers' seeming freedom from ministerial control. In short, a minister may possess a substantial measure of informal authority beyond what appears on the pages of law books.

Theoretically, a central board's independence is shared by the board's subordinates. An underling who thinks The Law is on his side may disregard a contrary view in superior quarters. If he does so, his superior may detest him, but may not discipline him severely.[4] The

[4] A 1964 case involving the central administration of the Swedish prison system suggests how difficult it is truly to centralize administrative responsibility. The governor of a prison ordered an assistant to assume certain duties. The assistant refused. The governor then asked the Legal Division of the prisons administration whether he could discipline the assistant in some way. The Legal Division instructed him not to do so because, among other things, the disobeyed order had not been in writing. The prison governor then complained to the Ombudsman that the central administration was not doing its duty. The Ombudsman proceeded to investigate this complaint by a subordinate official that his superiors would not support him against one of his own subordinates.

serious punishment of all but the most minor civil servants—and especially the ultimate punishment, removal from office—is left largely in the hands of courts of law. An official may thus be penalized for wrongdoing, but, for practical purposes, only by a judicial decree after a formal trial and not by the methods of personnel administration ordinarily utilized by sizable organizations.[5]

What has been said about civil administration is true, equally, of judicial administration in all its ramifications. Judges are not hierarchically organized so that the decisions of a higher tribunal control the work of the lesser courts. Each judge applies The Law as he sees it. He may of course be influenced by the reasoning of other jurists whom he respects. He nevertheless remains free to determine whom he does respect, and how strongly. He and he alone is responsible for the correctness of his judgments.

Similarly, each public prosecutor must do his duty according to The Law. True, a Supreme Prosecutor sits in Stockholm, attempting to harmonize the actions taken by prosecutors throughout the nation. But he is more counselor than commander. The Law gives the orders.

How, one may well ask, can this individualistic system of public administration, perhaps well suited to a day when communities were scattered, communications were slow, and problems were few, meet the needs of a highly organized society? In part it does so simply because the individuals within the system are well educated, conscientious, and uplifted by professional morale; Sweden has long had a thoroughly justified pride in its able and honorable public servants.[6] Furthermore, for all the folklore about "the stubborn Swede," willful adherence to opinion is not commonplace among officials; they seek

[5] See S. Jägerskiöld, "Swedish State Officials and Their Position under Public Law and Labor Law," 4 *Scand. Stud. in Law* 103 (1960). A superior's imposition of an administrative disciplinary measure (such as transfer to a new assignment) is subject to de novo review by the Supreme Administrative Court. In 1963 the Court received 28 cases of that kind for review. Sweden has some 180,000 civil servants and officials, and additional thousands of public employees of other grades.

[6] As has occurred in many other countries, however, Sweden now faces a real risk that talents needed in its public service will be drained off by other respectable and more remunerative callings. In times past officials were compensated highly not only in esteem but also in salary. The respect given them remains high, but not their income. Since 1900 the real income of workers in industry has increased about 250 percent; that of agricultural workers nearly 400 percent. The median real income of salaried employees has risen proportionately. During that same period the real income level of civil servants has remained stationary, so that, relative to others, the financial position of public officers has been declining. The possible impact of this decline upon the prestige of the civil service cannot be wholly ignored.

consensus rather than dissent and are therefore receptive to other officials' views even when not, in theory, forced to accept them. Thirdly, to a degree far beyond the usual, Swedish officials function in the proverbial goldfish bowl. Their files are, with stated exceptions, open to the press and the public at large, so that reckless or too highly personalized patterns of action can perhaps be discerned and criticized more readily than in other countries; even papers bearing upon matters still under consideration are available to inquirers.[7] Fourthly, since each official must apply The Law as he understands it, care is taken to draft statutes that cannot admit of many diverse readings, and the "legislative history" of each bill is carefully compiled so that doubts will not later arise about the intended purposes of a new law; explicit statutory detail reduces the area of administrative choice and thus the risk of administrative aberration, but, perhaps offsetting this virtue, it increases the administrative rigidity sometimes denounced as "bureaucratic inflexibility." Fifthly, statutes sometimes explicitly authorize the issuance of regulations or general instructions that will diminish the range of individual officials' choice. Finally, individual administrators' judgments are, in varying degrees, subject to review by others, first within their own official establishment (such as a central administrative board) and then by appeal to the king, that is, to the cognizant minister.

When the volume of appeals became too great for effective consideration, Sweden in 1909 created a Supreme Administrative Court to which certain classes of cases (preponderantly those involving taxation) now go, instead of to the King in Council.[8] The Supreme Administrative Court has all the powers, in respect of the cases it is given to decide, that were formerly exercised by the King in Council; it can concern itself with issues of discretion as well as legality and can enter the finally dispositive orders it deems correct.[9] A separate Supreme

[7] For effective discussion of the scope of the publicity principle and its application, see N. Herlitz, "Publicity of Official Documents in Sweden," [1958] *Pub. L.* 50; H. Blix, "A Pattern of Effective Protection: The Ombudsman," 11 *How. L.J.* 386, 387–389 (1965).

[8] B. Lagergren, "Le Conseil d'Etat de Suède," 15 *Int. Rev. Admin. Sc.* 22 (1949). And see also N. Herlitz, "Swedish Administrative Law," 3 *Scand. Stud. in Law* 89, 95–99, 104–107 (1959).

[9] The Supreme Administrative Court has sixteen members, who sit in three divisions, handling more than four thousand cases annually. The nature of its work is revealed by statistics from recent annual reports, summarized in the table below:

Court for Social Insurance has similarly taken over the final power to consider appeals from administrative judgments in its field. While a decision by one of these high administrative organs disposes only of the immediate case, the tribunals are so greatly respected that, without formally recognizing the doctrine of *stare decisis,* administrators do in fact pay great attention to their well-indexed volumes of judgments rendered.

As for the ordinary courts of law, they have power to apply the penal law to administrators—and nothing more. They cannot command an official to do an act, nor restrain its being done. They cannot issue declaratory orders that constitute authoritative interpretations of applicable law. They have no role to play, in short, in securing sound administration or in forestalling bad administration. They can only punish an administrator for having violated the law.

That power, however, is broader than it seems, for in Sweden an official commits the crime of "breach of duty" if through "negligence, imprudence, or unskillfulness" he fails to act in the manner required by a statute, a valid regulation or direction, or "the nature of his office";[10] and the court, when it finds the "crime" of negligence or incompetence to have been committed, may punish it by fining, imprisoning, suspending, or dismissing the sinning civil servant.[11]

Activity primarily concerned	*Cases decided*	
	1962	*1963*
Agriculture	35	40
Communications	1,790	1,516
Culture & Education	59	62
Defence	2	4
Finance	1,628	1,746
Interior	282	376
Justice	215	140
Public Employment	34	20
Social Welfare	284	300
Trade	21	69
Totals	4,350	4,273

The backlog of undecided cases rose from 6,571 in 1961 to 7,127 in 1963. Of the undecided cases as of the end of 1963, 5,796 involved tax matters which provide the bulk of the business now flowing into the court.

An Administrative Court of Appeals initially considers appeals in certain classes of cases having to do with public finances, including tax controversies which are further appealable to the Supreme Administrative Court.

10 Swedish Penal Code, Chap. 20, Sec. 4.

11 A civil servant may also be required to pay damages to a private person he has injured; but a suit for damages cannot be privately initiated against a higher civil

The judges themselves, it may now be remarked, are also civil servants, subject like the rest to being prosecuted for carelessness and ignorance without more. Lower-level civil servants may be prosecuted in courts of first instance. The judges of those courts, along with superior civil servants and the heads of most Central Administrative Boards, are triable before a Court of Appeals. Appeals Court judges and the heads of a few Central Administrative Boards are triable before the Supreme Court. Ministers and members of the Supreme Court or the Supreme Administrative Court are triable only before a Special Court of Impeachment, which fortunately has had no occasion to convene for well over a century.[12]

In a technical sense the ombudsman fits into this system of individual instead of institutional responsibility simply as a prosecutor who can proceed against official wrongdoers (or non-doers) before the tribunals authorized to mete out punishment. The technicalities of the ombudsman's power do not, however, describe its actualities.

3 | The Selection of the Ombudsman

The Swedish Constitution declares simply that the ombudsman should be a person of "known legal ability and outstanding integrity."[13] He is chosen by forty-eight electors, twenty-four from each chamber of the Parliament, themselves reflecting the proportional strength of the political parties in that chamber. The electors have only fifteen days in

---

servant or against a judge. Only if the competent public prosecutor supports the claim against such an official can the possibility of assessing damages be considered. Compare S. D. Anderman, "The Swedish Justitieombudsman," 11 *Am. J. Comp. L.* 225, 228 (1962): "The statutory coverage is so broad that were citizens left free with this weapon, the resulting harassment of public officials would unduly limit their effectiveness in office."

A private civil action for damages can, however, be maintained against a lower civil servant even if the public prosecutor has declined to prosecute, having found no breach of duty. Civil suits of that nature are said to be extremely rare; for practical purposes one may conclude that the possibility of private redress hinges on the public prosecutor's appraisal of the action or nonaction which allegedly caused the injury.

[12] See S. Jägerskiöld, "The Swedish Constitution: A Survey," 5 *J. Indian L. Inst.* 1, 9 (1963).

[13] Art. 96, in an official English translation by Sarah V. Thorelli, *The Constitution of Sweden* (1954).

which to agree upon their choice. Because this leaves little time for exploration and discussion, at least preliminary canvassing of possibilities has sometimes been undertaken by the party leaders. As a matter of tradition, however, partisan considerations rarely weigh heavily. From the earliest days of the office the ombudsmen have usually been drawn from the judiciary. Neither the press nor the citizenry seems to have taken much interest in past elections or speculated about possible future candidates. Those finally chosen have had solid professional capabilities that were unlikely to have been noticed by the public at large; as one parliamentary leader put it, "The man we select does not lend distinction to the office; the office distinguishes him." The ombudsman now in office, Alfred Bexelius, had been a member of the career judiciary for thirty-four years and had served as Deputy Ombudsman before being elected to his present post.[14]

The Ombudsman's term of office is four years. His salary equals that of a Supreme Court judge. Parliament may remove an ombudsman during his term, though it has never done so. Re-election is possible, though service beyond three terms (that is, twelve years) is highly unlikely. An ombudsman who is not re-elected when his term expires may resume his previous career or may choose to be pensioned.

So far as can humanly be achieved, the Swedish system immunizes an ombudsman against the political pressures of the day. He has absolutely no responsibility to the Government (the Cabinet) or to any of its elements. He reports annually to Parliament. His parliamentary relationships are with the First Law Committee, which happens to be under the chairmanship of an Opposition member.[15] Such complaints as may be addressed to Parliament concerning the Ombudsman's work are channeled to that Committee. It may question the Ombudsman, but in recent times has apparently had no occasion

[14] The Deputy Ombudsman is chosen in the same manner as is the Ombudsman himself. He is answerable directly to Parliament rather than to the Ombudsman. In the original conception of the office the Deputy was to serve only during the Ombudsman's incapacity or absence, but in fact his work is now performed on a full-time basis. See U. Lundvik, "Comments on the Ombudsman for Civil Affairs," in D. C. Rowat, ed., *The Ombudsman:* Citizen's Defender 44, 48 (1965).

[15] In budgetary matters, such as provision for additions to his staff, the Ombudsman also has contact with the Bank Committee. And when consideration is given to changing the scope of the Ombudsman's responsibilities, the Constitutional Committee is involved. These are, however, such rare occurrences that, for practical purposes, the Ombudsman's parliamentary contact may be said to be exclusively with the First Law Committee.

to carry on any further discussion. The annual report is reviewed by the Committee—or, perhaps more accurately, by the Committee's secretary, usually a youthful judge on temporary assignment. Members may criticize the Ombudsman's past decisions or the general direction of his work, and these criticisms may possibly influence future activities; but the Ombudsman and members of the committee join in asserting unequivocally that at no time, directly or indirectly, has a parliamentarian sought to influence work in progress.

The leader of an Opposition party has privately commented that the Government needs no special mechanisms for controlling an ombudsman because, he says, the persons who are chosen to be ombudsmen "can be counted on not to rock the boat. They all have pretty much the same outlook as the ministers, they understand one another without having to send blueprints, and they aren't likely to try to make a lot of trouble for one another. After he has been around for a while, an ombudsman becomes Government-minded." In support of his thesis he remarks that no ombudsman has brought to light a single major scandal during the thirty-odd years of virtually continuous Social Democratic control over the Government.[16] So long a rule, in his opinion, would certainly have produced skeletons that a diligent searcher might have found hidden in political closets. When asked to comment on this remark, Ombudsman Bexelius answered sharply: "This office has had no part in cleaning up large scale corruption in public administration because, fortunately, it has not existed. If we had any reason to suspect it, nothing at all would stand in the way of our investigation."[17] His confidence is widely shared by Swedes. As an

[16] The Social Democrats have remained in power as the Government since 1932 except for one hundred days in 1936 and a period during World War II when a coalition cabinet was formed. They receive only about 50 percent of the votes, but the balance are spread among so broad a spectrum of opposition parties that parliamentary overturn has not been much of a threat.

Despite the long domination of the socialists, Sweden is not a very socialistic country. Of those employed at the time of the 1960 census, 89 percent were employed by private enterprises, 5 percent by producer or consumer cooperatives, 1 percent by municipal governments, and only 5 percent by the national government in all its aspects.

[17] In one of his writings, the Ombudsman expressed a similar thought: "Certainly, the things that the JO's office has accomplished during the past 150 years are not very great or sensational. There have not been any general clean-ups of corrupt officials. Neither has the activity of the commissioners involved them in a dangerous struggle against injustice, simply because—disregarding social injustices outside the field assigned to the office—corruption of justice has not existed. No, the activity of

admirer has put it, "The importance of the office cannot be measured by the scandals it has revealed but rather by the absence of any major scandals."[18]

4|The Ombudsman's Powers

The Ombudsman is by no means a superadministrator, empowered to overturn every error and to produce correct answers to all the difficult questions modern government confronts. The Constitution (Art. 96) says simply that, as a representative of the Parliament and pursuant to its instruction, he should "supervise the observance of laws and statutes" as they may be applied "by the courts and by public officials and employees."[19] Supervision, as Parliament's instructions make clear, does not include control over what judges or administrators do. The Ombudsman gives no orders. He cannot reverse a decision he deems improper; he cannot even direct the reopening of a case or the reconsideration of a judgment by the officials who rendered it. What he can do, primarily, is prosecute an official he believes to be guilty of the crime of "breach of duty," marked by his non-observance of statutory commands because he was careless, imprudent, or unskillful.[20] Similarly, he can commence disciplinary proceedings leading to a rebuke, a fine, suspension, or removal from office.

In aid of those powers the Ombudsman has practically unlimited access to official files and records; he may call on any official for an explanation of his acts; he may demand the opinions of superiors con-

---

the office has been on another plane . . ." A. Bexelius, "The Swedish Institution of Justitieombudsman," 27 *Int. Rev. Admin. Sc.* 243, 255 (1961). See also the same author's "The Ombudsman for Civil Affairs," in Rowat (note 14 above), 22, at 36–37.

[18] N. Andrén, "The Swedish Ombudsman," *Anglo-Swedish Rev.* 1, 7 (May 1962).

[19] Since 1915 the Constitution has also provided an ombudsman for military affairs, with the same qualifications and chosen in the same manner as the ombudsman for civil affairs. The Militieombudsman is to "supervise matters which by law are regarded as military, or affect employees remunerated from the appropriations for the armed forces." This work had previously been part of the Justitieombudsman's responsibilities. See H. Henkow, "The Ombudsman for Military Affairs," in Rowat (note 14), at 51.

[20] Before launching a prosecution, the Ombudsman is required, by parliamentary instructions, to afford the supposed offender a chance to justify or excuse himself.

cerning lowlier officials. He even has the right (which he almost never exercises) to be present as a silent observer during the deliberations of all courts and administrative bodies.

Because punishment for a past mistake is a rather antiquated way of encouraging sound administration, ombudsmen have for many years tended to lessen their reliance on penal sanctions and have instead developed the practice of "giving reminders" to erring officials. At first without explicit authorization by Parliament (but more recently with that body's full awareness and consent), the ombudsmen have commented on faults without launching prosecutions, in the belief that an admonition will influence not only the official immediately involved, but also others who may deal with similar matters in the future. Reminders vastly outnumber prosecutions by the Ombudsman. During the five years 1960–1964 inclusive, he initiated a total of only thirty-two punitive proceedings (twenty-seven prosecutions and five other disciplinary actions). During the same period he issued 1220 reprimands, suggestions, and the like. When admonishing, the Ombudsman does much more than simply rap the knuckles of an inattentive official. Rather, he prepares a reasoned opinion that, like the opinion of an American appellate court, may have considerable educational force. Behind the admonitory lecture lurks a thinly veiled threat to prosecute if the admonition be ignored.[21]

A few official matters are beyond the Ombudsman's reach. He has no power to deal with the Councilors of State—the Cabinet Ministers—who are subject to being impeached only upon the initiative of Parliament.[22] As a corollary of his incapacity to proceed against minis-

[21] Consider, as an example, the 1964 Report of the Ombudsman, at 164: A defendant, acquitted after prosecution for perjury initiated upon the complaint of a private person, afterwards complained to the Ombudsman that the trial court judge had not examined the complainant before the trial, as he should have done according to an applicable procedural rule. The judge, in response to the Ombudsman's inquiry, expressed belief that the rule imposed no such duty. Having reviewed the pertinent legislative history, the Ombudsman disagreed with the judge; he remarked that examining the complainant is especially important in privately initiated prosecutions of this character, and explained the possibly harmful consequences of failing to do so at an early stage of the proceeding. Then he added: "Since the examination did ultimately occur and there is no reason to believe that Judge Rune was improperly motivated in refusing to act or that he will hereafter fail to apply these rules, I leave the matter without further action."

[22] Members of the Supreme Court or the Supreme Administrative Court, by contrast with ministers, can be (but never have been) impeached by the Ombudsman. *Swedish Const.* Art. 101.

Many years ago the then Ombudsman, who had unsuccessfully sought to prosecute

ters, he cannot review the propriety of a judgment of the King in Council, upon appeal from an administrative decision; but this does not at all restrict his ability to deal with a matter that could still be appealed to that august body, for access to the Ombudsman is not blocked by any requirement that other remedies first be exhausted.[23] He does not have power over government corporations, engaged in economic operations for which conventional governmental procedures are thought to be unsuitable. Finally, the Ombudsman's power to inquire into cases concerning local government is limited.

Until 1957 the Ombudsman was competent to act only in matters of national administration. Drawing the line between national and local administration is not always easy in Sweden because municipal authorities have long shared in executing nationwide programs as the paid agents, as it were, of central administrative bodies. Despite considerable opposition at the time, Parliament instructed the Ombudsman in 1957 (pursuant to a constitutional amendment) to concern himself with what are traditionally local governmental affairs, with special regard for the municipalities' right of self-government. The popularly elected members of local assemblies remain wholly outside the range of the Ombudsman's attention. Moreover, acts of municipal administrators that can be appealed further within the locality or that are subject to correction by the local legislature or otherwise are not handled by the Ombudsman unless personal liberty is immediately endangered. These limitations are reinforced by the present Ombudsman's policy of being somewhat slower to criticize local administrators

---

a high official and whose appeal to the Supreme Court had been rejected, gave a strongly critical account of the matter in his next report to Parliament, concluding that the court's decision "places in a strange light the opinions which now prevail in the King's Supreme Court." A. Bexelius, "The Swedish Institution of the Justitie-ombudsman," 27 *Int. Rev. Admin. Sc.* 243, 251 (1961). As have his predecessors for the past hundred years, the present Ombudsman believes that he should not comment on Supreme Court decisions unless, as he has said to the author, it is "absolutely necessary."

23 The present Ombudsman has in fact suggested informally on several occasions that the doctrine of exhaustion of remedies should be made operative as to him, but Parliament has been unresponsive. At times a case has been appealed to the King in Council and simultaneously has been made the basis of a complaint to the Ombudsman. "In those situations," the present Ombudsman remarked, "the ministers tend to wait for me to do something and I tend to wait for them to do something. But usually I give in first and go ahead with the matter."

than those who are attached to national organs. Even so, a subtantial (and growing) part of the Ombudsman's work pertains to previously immune municipal affairs.[24]

5|The Nature and Sources of the Ombudsman's Work

The Ombudsman is more than a complaint bureau to which outraged citizens may turn. As Parliament's watchman, he can and does proceed on his own motion when problems come to his attention through newspaper stories, personal conversation, suggestions by officials themselves, or his own periodic inspection of courts and administrative agencies. Numerically, as Table XII below shows, citizens' complaints account for 86 percent of the cases docketed by the Ombudsman in recent years. The Ombudsman thinks, however, that his observations during inspections probably produce the most significant leads to official fault or carelessness, though they give rise to only 13 percent of his caseload.

Table XII. Sources of new cases docketed by Ombudsman

	1960	1961	1962	1963	1964
Citizens' complaints	983	983	960	1,224	1,239
Initiated on basis of newspaper stories	15	14	14	16	11
Initiated as a result of inspection or other information	211	83	189	156	179

The range of subject matters comprehended by these cases is impressive, as appears from even a cursory examination of Table XIII. In every year included in this summation, real or imagined derelictions by judges were the most numerous category of matters before the Ombudsman, while officials whose work is intimately connected with

[24] The classification of cases in the Ombudsman's annual reports prevents a completely accurate counting of what might be called purely municipal cases. Excluding all doubtful cases, however, one finds an average of 73 municipal matters dealt with in the three years 1957–1959, and an average of 130 during the next four years, 1960–1963.

Table XIII. Subject matters involved in docketed cases

	1960	1961	1962	1963	1964
Courts (excluding administrative courts)	210	171	178	241	226
Public prosecutors	123	171	81	108	130
Police authorities	190	101	168[a]	213[a]	208
Distraining authorities	40	35	44	55	43
Prison administration	111	123	106	146	163
Mental hospitals	91	110	123	102	114
Other hospitals	27	28	19	31	46
Care of alcoholics	24	16	21	18	31
Child and youth welfare	29	32	53	50	59
Real property controls	31	33	44	42	47
School administration	20	11	24	36	34
Tax authorities	35	37	66	53	55
State monopolies	8	13	14	17	22
Church authorities	20	32	14	19	12
National administration not included above	150	182	181	183	195
Municipal administration not included above	78	59	58	81	87
Miscellany—outside Ombudsman's jurisdiction	118	117	86	130	90

[a] Police matters were subdivided for the first time in 1962 into those pertaining to criminal law enforcement and those pertaining to other affairs (such as license issuance and revocation). The breakdown in 1962 was 99 criminal, 69 other; in 1963, 134 criminal, 79 other.

judicial administration were also frequently involved. On the other hand, the administration of social insurance and related "welfare state" activities was not a dominant element of the Ombudsman's caseload, nor were taxation disputes a major feature of his concern. These observations concerning the Ombudsman's work are emphasized here because both Swedish and foreign commentators have sometimes stressed that the ombudsman system is especially needed in societies with elaborate social welfare and tax administrations. The available figures suggest, on the contrary, that the Ombudsman plays a minor part in resolving the undoubtedly numerous controversies that arise between citizens and officials in those fields. Those controversies are dealt with by other means, especially designed for the purpose.

A mere counting of cases tells little about their significance and nothing about their disposition. We turn, therefore, to discussion of the Ombudsman's treatment of the matters before him.

6|Private Complaint Cases

Anyone can complain to the Ombudsman—a citizen about an official, an official about an official, a lawyer or the Bar Association about a judge, one judge about another, an organization in behalf of its members. Some of the Ombudsman's clients are steady customers—"querulents"—whose repeated communications may reflect emotional disturbance or mental disease, but must nevertheless be considered. Some 20 percent of all incoming complaints are weeded out instantly, with no action other than a notification that the Ombudsman perceives no cause to intervene. Many are "crank" letters, sometimes altogether incoherent or filled with fanciful tales of high-level conspiracies and persecutions.[25] Others pertain to private or public corporations over which the Ombudsman has no jurisdiction. Few are discarded because they reflect ancient grievances; the Ombudsman is willing to docket complaints about episodes that occurred as long as ten years ago.[26]

Of the approximately one thousand complaints each year, only about twenty-five are signed by lawyers either in their own behalf or in behalf of clients, though a few others may have been prepared by lawyers for their clients' signatures.[27] No artistry is needed. The Om-

[25] The Ombudsman's staff is aware, however, that one correspondent well known for his excited imaginings finally complained about an impropriety in the manner of collecting taxes. Investigation showed the complaint to be well founded, and corrective steps were accordingly suggested. Recollection of that instance encourages attentiveness to every complaint, regardless of its source.

[26] Experienced observers agree that "long-term cases" almost invariably have strong psychiatric overtones. The Ombudsman's tolerance of these old grudges reflects Sweden's ten-year statute of limitations in tort actions.

[27] Practicing lawyers in Sweden have a somewhat lesser role in the conduct of day-to-day affairs than do their American counterparts, perhaps simply because they

budsman's office deems one of its virtues to be its capacity to extract meaning from obscurely described—and, indeed, vaguely perceived—dissatisfactions. Roughly, the complainants include about seven hundred private citizens (many of whom file more than one complaint), the balance of the cases coming from organizations or officials.

From the complainant's point of view the great advantage of recourse to the Ombudsman is that no further effort (and no expenditure whatsoever) is demanded. The Ombudsman takes over the case as one to be pursued in the public interest. This, among other things, has often obviated the necessity of the complainant's utilizing remedies that may still be available to him within the judicial or administrative process.[28] True, the Ombudsman cannot quash an act he finds to be improper nor order additional moves to rectify the wrong done to the complainant. But many complainants are seemingly willing to surrender control over their own cases in the hope that criticism by the Ombudsman will induce some further and more favorable official step or even, in extreme cases, the payment of damages.

The processing of complaints may be described briefly. The Ombudsman personally reads the incoming complaints and, indeed, often opens the envelopes that contain them. This extreme manifestation of personal responsibility for the Ombudsman's work is linked with organizational problems to which later reference will be made. The opened letters, sometimes bearing the Ombudsman's suggestions concerning next steps, are docketed and are then taken to the Chief of Office, a permanent employee of long standing. He decides whether or not to request the official body involved in the complaint to forward the pertinent files for the Ombudsman's examination. He often hands

---

are less numerous. Fully qualified advocates number only about 1200, though other lawyers may carry professional responsibilities without using the title of advocate.

[28] This continues to be a controversial aspect of the Ombudsman system. In many instances the Ombudsman is burdened with cases that might well have been dealt with elsewhere, just as cheaply and conveniently. So, for example, a complaint concerning brutality by a policeman or prison guard may be lodged initially with the Ombudsman and will be inquired into by him even though the complainant has never reported the matter to the offender's superiors, who, had they been apprised of the matter, might themselves have investigated and then initiated suitable punitive action. Only if the superiors were insufficiently attentive to the complaint should the Ombudsman have to become involved. Without an all-embracing rule that available remedies must invariably be exhausted before recourse is had to the Ombudsman, his responsibilities could well be redefined to permit rejection of some classes of cases that now occupy his time prematurely.

over to the Deputy Ombudsman cases that may be disposed of at once. Others, with the relevant documents when they are received, are referred to a staff member for further analysis. Some but not much specialization exists within the staff. When the staff member is prepared for the next step—which may be dismissal of the complaint, a request for further information, or what not—he prepares a draft for approval by the Ombudsman or the Deputy Ombudsman. Staff members do not themselves communicate informally with officials to discuss the facts or the implications of the matters before them; they work exclusively with papers. The personalization of the Ombudsman's work again comes to the fore in this context, for several officials in 1964 recalled having received telephone calls from the Ombudsman himself, who then proceeded to ask questions about an apparently minor complaint received by him in that morning's mail.

By far the greatest part of the complaints are disposed of quickly after the official files have been received in the Ombudsman's office. In most of these instances the Ombudsman's staff assistant can perceive an allowable basis of the decision complained against. A letter to the complainant, signed by the Ombudsman or the Deputy, explains in some detail why the original official action seems unobjectionable. The Ombudsman has on several occasions urged Parliament to require courts and administrative organs to state reasons for their decisions, believing that had they done so in the past, many of the persons who had complained to him would have been satisfied with the actions taken. In his view, mystification engenders dissatisfaction which could be dispelled by official explications, but his recommendations have not yet been followed. At any rate, many persons who have filed vigorous protests seem to have been made content by the Ombudsman's reasoned explanations. The Ombudsman adds, with philosophical resignation, that even when the complainant continues to be unhappy with the outcome, he transfers his dissatisfaction to the Ombudsman so that future relations with the body complained against become less strained.

The present work method does, however, place on the Ombudsman's staff the burdensome responsibility of reviewing sometimes extensive documentary material to ascertain whether it lends legal, evidential, and technical support to a judgment reached elsewhere. Ombudsmen in other Scandinavian countries handle the matter somewhat differently. A complaint not dismissible on its face is sent to the affected official agency for comment; the agency's explanation is then forwarded to the complainant, who often accepts the reasons stated; only if the complainant questions the adequacy of the agency's answer does the Ombudsman's office demand all the pertinent papers for independent analysis. Thus unnecessary shuffling of papers back and forth is avoided.

Even the more cumbersome Swedish system does, nevertheless, manage to dispose of the bulk of the complaints reasonably quickly. During the first six months of 1964, for example, the Ombudsman closed 666 cases. Of these, 51 percent had been in the office for less than a month; 12 percent, one to two months; 6 percent, two to three months; 14 percent, three to six months—a total of 83 percent disposed of within six months after docketing. Signs of strain are nevertheless apparent in the backlog of cases remaining undecided at the end of a year; this number has mounted from 240 at the beginning of 1961, to 278 (1962), 385 (1963), 430 (1964), and 447 (1965).

Most complaints can be dismissed because their invalidity is at once clear or is disclosed by staff examination of the relevant documents. The Ombudsman's statistics do not reveal directly how many complaints led to affirmative steps by him, but one may infer from the figures shown in Table XIV on the next page that only a small number have been found to be justified; the estimate offered informally by experienced persons is "roughly 10 percent" of the total received.

Redress for injured individuals is, in a sense, only a by-product of the Ombudsman's activity. His primary interest is in securing sounder government in the future. If, however, the Ombudsman concludes that a license has been wrongfully denied or that private property has been illegally seized or that a privilege has been arbitrarily withheld, the official whose action has been criticized does almost invariably take steps to put the matter aright, even though he cannot be commanded to do so. Furthermore, the Ombudsman sometimes directly suggests that an official pay damages to a wronged complainant, intimating that failure to do so will indicate the official's adherence to a position the Ombudsman deems so clearly illegal as to be a prosecutable offense.[29]

[29] This practice has led to considerable criticism of the Ombudsman, who has been charged with using the threat of prosecution to induce acceptance of his opinion concerning debatable propositions of law. Compare S. Jägerskiöld, "The Swedish Ombudsman," 109 *U. Pa. L. Rev.* 1077, 1089–1090 (1961): "In the most extreme case after the Ombudsman had stated that he would abstain from prosecuting the

Table XIV. Ombudsman's disposition of docketed cases

	1959	1960	1961	1962	1963	1964
Referral to other authorities	13	15	17	4	12	3
Withdrawn by complainant	8	5	12	15	10	12
Dismissed without inquiry	184	263	190	217	287	381
Dismissed after inquiry	619	669	592	620	746	722
Prosecutions	5	8	7	4	6	2
Disciplinary proceedings	0	2	0	2	1	0
Admonitions or other remarks	247	271	208	192	275	283
Proposals for new legislation or rules	8	5	16	2	14	7

A less debatable exercise of authority occurs when the Ombudsman, having found injury done to a citizen by an unidentifiable official, suggests that the Government should pay damages out of the public purse—as, for example, when a person has been assaulted by a policeman who cannot later be singled out from the mass. The Ombudsman's recommendations in this type of case have not invariably been accepted, but they at least partially take the place of the cumbersome legislative measures often needed in similar circumstances in the United States.[30]

judges of a court of appeals if they would pay compensation to a citizen whose case they had decided (wrongly, it was said), the judges informed the Ombudsman that while they adhered to their earlier opinion, they would voluntarily pay the damages demanded because they did not want to be subjected to the inconvenience of a prosecution. Thus we have the remarkable outcome that qualified judges of an appellate court were forced to submit to consequences which only an adverse judgment on their conduct should have produced, despite the fact that the judges held fast to an opinion contrary to that of the Ombudsman." The same episode, involving the Stockholm Court of Appeals, is noted more approvingly by S. D. Anderman, "The Swedish Justitieombudsman," 11 *Am. J. Comp. L.* 225, 235 (1962).

[30] Compare W. Gellhorn and L. Lauer, "Congressional Settlement of Tort Claims against the United States." 55 *Colum. L. Rev.* 1 (1955).

In another and more important respect, the Ombudsman may help wronged individuals. Release from improper detention is not easily achieved in Sweden, where the writ of habeas corpus has no precise analogy. Persons in custody may perhaps sue those who have restrained their liberty, but the possibility that their custodians may later be punished or be compelled to pay damages is considerably less alluring than immediate freedom. The Ombudsman, if persuaded that a conviction has been wrongfully obtained or that a sentence is excessive, has sometimes successfully sought pardons or shortened terms of imprisonment when avenues of direct judicial redress had been closed by the elapse of time.[31] And he has seen to it, too, that persons held against their will to receive treatment for alcoholism or psychiatric problems have someone to whom they can cry for help.[32]

In another type of case the Ombudsman may relieve an individual from uncertainty that in the United States could be resolved by a declaratory judgment, a procedure not available in Sweden. An example is afforded by a controversy that arose when a fish and game warden threatened a fisherman with prosecution if he would not cease using certain nets. The fisherman, believing (but not being absolutely sure) that his conduct was within the law, had either to surrender or risk being penalized. He halted his fishing as commanded, but simultaneously complained to the Ombudsman that the official had arbitrarily interfered. After investigation the Ombudsman ruled against

[31] What has been said about the Ombudsman's attention to these cases should not be taken as suggesting that others in Sweden are insensitive to matters of that nature. On the contrary, the Minister of Justice himself twice weekly receives without prior appointment any caller who wishes to present a plea for clemency or other relief in behalf of someone in official custody.

[32] In one case somewhat difficult to classify the Ombudsman concluded that a patient should be ousted from a mental institution against his will. First hospitalized in 1921 as a dangerous schizophrenic, the patient was found to be no longer dangerous in 1935 and was told that he could depart. He refused to do so unless the doctors would certify him to be "perfectly healthy," which they were unwilling to do. The patient was left completely at large, except that he had to be in bed in the hospital ward at ten o'clock each night. From 1935 to 1958 the patient remained in the hospital, "on strike" (as he said) and refusing to participate in work programs. In 1958 the patient complained to the Ombudsman that despite his being in good mental health, he had been detained by the hospital authorities. The Ombudsman expressed the opinion that the doctors should have excluded the patient from the hospital in 1935 and at all times afterward, since whether or not he was as "perfectly healthy" as he believed, he was by the doctors' own accounts well enough not to take up hospital space. So the patient was sent away, still without his desired certificate. Now living comfortably as an old-age pensioner, he often pays social visits to the officials with whom he became acquainted during his long strike against authority.

the complainant, thus in effect providing the declaratory judgment for which Swedish law makes no provision. To be sure, his opinion has no binding force, since if the matter were later brought before a court, the issues would be for the judges to decide. In actuality, however, his analysis of the applicable law, whether favorable to the complainant or to the official, is likely to be accepted as finally dispositive of the point in question.

In the main, in any event, personal redress is not a likely outcome of complaints to the Ombudsman, though no doubt many an individual has gained keen inner satisfaction when the Ombudsman has given a a judge or an official a rebuke or "reminder." Arrogance unfortunately can be a widespread occupational disease among judges. It stings even when it does not monetarily wound those who encounter it. The Ombudsman has spoken sternly, for example, to judges who have badgered witnesses and lawyers without committing reversible errors, and this has perhaps been a form of personal vindication of the complainants as well as a suggestion for the future.[33] "There is no reason why a judge cannot behave like a gentleman," the present Ombudsman remarked in a recent conversation. He believes that his and his predecessors' "countless reminders" have gained force by repetition and have definitely influenced the behavior patterns of all civil servants, including judges.

These remarks would mislead if they were to suggest that most grievances—or, even, the most important grievances—are brought to the Ombudsman. The contrary is assuredly the case.

Even in areas with which he is accustomed to deal, matters are in the main settled finally without recourse to him. So, for example, the Central Medical Board in 1962 acted upon 1,560 complaints concerning the administration of mental hospitals under its control, and in

[33] An individual complaint may generate a more sweeping inquiry. In 1964, for instance, a complaint asserted that a judge had insulted a witness and had conducted a needlessly noisy hearing. The Ombudsman telephoned acquaintances in that district to inquire informally about the judge's handling of cases. Upon learning from several sources that the judge had a reputation for irascibility, boisterousness, and disregard of the sensibilities of persons in the courtroom, the Ombudsman decided to investigate more extensively than the original complaint might have warranted, with the likelihood of prosecuting rather than simply admonishing the intemperate judge. "His loss of respect in the community," the Ombudsman commented, "will be offset by increased respect for the court, because the people will know that the State will not allow judges to behave in that manner."

1963 it disposed of 1,878 complaints of that nature; in those years, the complaints to the Ombudsman from the same sources numbered 123 and 102, respectively.

Moreover, spokesmen for many major elements of Swedish life indicated flatly during interviews in 1964 that the Ombudsman had no significance for them or their members despite their having frequent and important contacts with other public authorities. Among those consulted were such diverse groups as associations of retail enterprises, civil servants, school teachers, labor unions, shipping concerns, forest owners, insurance companies, agriculturists, heavy industries, and banks. Even among the unorganized elements of society, such as those who use free legal aid services and those who are touched by social insurance or public health administration, recourse to the Ombudsman is so rare as to be all but disregarded. Nobody among those interviewed intimated that the Ombudsman was useless, even though wholly unused by the particular group to which the speaker belonged. All agreed, in fact, that the Ombudsman is, as one man said, "a good safety valve for the community" when no other means of securing suitable official attention may exist. They also agreed, however, that regularized methods of obtaining specialized review have been brought into being in modern times, so that the citizen with a problem is no longer helpless beneath a bureaucratic thumb, as perhaps once he was. "In olden days," a representative of a large economic interest declared, "everybody needed the Ombudsman because there was no place else to turn when an official or a judge did something outrageous. The officeholders had all the power and people couldn't stand up against them. Nowadays if we have a problem, we usually have a good route to follow in order to get suitable attention. In my opinion, not very many normal people are likely to complain to the Ombudsman. As a generality, he gets the unduly combative, the hypersensitive, the off-beat types, while others look for more direct channels and then go through them."

While this is undoubtedly an overstated opinion, it seems essentially sound. Swedes do like the idea behind the Ombudsman and are happy to have his office as a protection in reserve. But a general bureau of complaints is an inefficient means of dealing with modern government's many complexities. Sweden's sophisticated citizenry chooses to use sophisticated review procedures when they are available.

7 | The Ombudsman's Inspection

In times when judges were few, governmental activities were limited, and officeholders were measured by tens rather than by tens of thousands, direct and frequent inspection by the Ombudsman may have been practicable. The idea of personal inspection by him continues even today, despite changed conditions. As a matter of tradition the Ombudsman is expected to inspect every official establishment, including every court, at least decennially. Far from proclaiming the impossibility and the questionable value of this assignment, the Ombudsman asserts that periodic inspections are the surest guarantors of his success. He valiantly attempts to cover the whole of Sweden by devoting six weeks of each year to field trips among courts and administrative agencies. In truth, he has been unable to absent himself from his office for so long a period. As a consequence, general inspection (whatever may be its true worth) does not exist in fact, though many Swedes in and out of public office prefer to ignore reality and to assume that the Ombudsman is, as it were, constantly peering over official shoulders.

While inspections are perforce less frequent and perhaps less searching than popularly supposed, they do occur in substantial numbers. On very short notice, and sometimes on none at all, the Ombudsman and members of his staff appear in an office to examine its records. In trial courts the docket book is reviewed to ascertain whether cases are being brought to trial seasonably. The files of twenty-five civil cases and twenty-five criminal cases are drawn at random, to be reviewed on the spot and to be sent to Stockholm for more leisurely analysis if the judge's record-keeping or observance of the laws seems questionable. Prosecutors' records are checked to ascertain whether suspected persons' rights have been observed during investigations and whether defendants have been prosecuted without delay. Institutions—prisons in particular—are physically examined in respect of sanitation and the like, and inmates are invited to present grievances. In the main, inspection means looking into the files since most governmental operations are not subject to direct sensory perception. Informal conversation relieves the boredom of this rummaging through piles of papers, and makes possible an exchange of information that may be valuable to both the inspectors and the inspected.

One must consciously avoid idealizing the inspection process. Inspections do not in fact reach every corner of the nation. An experienced officer in a community distant from Stockholm could recall no inspection during his thirty years of service; time has not as yet allowed a thorough examination of all the municipal and communal affairs that came within the Ombudsman's jurisdiction in 1957; in some fields of national responsibility—as has already been remarked, social insurance and health administration are notable examples—inspections by the Ombudsman are virtually unheard of. Having said that much, one must add that the Ombudsman and his staff do apparently accomplish surprisingly much during their field trips, despite the broad range of specialized activities this nonspecialist group must seek to understand.

The chief administrative officials of two large provinces,[34] interviewed separately while the memory of the Ombudsman's most recent visitation was still green, used almost identical words in evaluating the inspection process. "The Ombudsman's staff," they said, "sometimes picks up mistakes we have been overlooking. They question things we have been taking for granted." In each instance the official drew from his desk the report the Ombudsman had sent by way of reviewing his inspection—seventeen pages, in one instance—with the recipient's own underlinings and annotations, and with indications that segments of the report had been brought to subordinates' attention. The storage of "Secret Documents" bearing on civil defense, the time delay in acting upon licenses because applications passed through too many hands, the inadequate consideration of alternatives to detaining a juvenile delinquent, the proper way to measure the running of a six months' stay of judgment when an appeal has been taken from the provincial

[34] Twenty-five provinces (or counties or districts) are headed by governors appointed by the Cabinet, who may be removed but who are in practice permanent. They are staffed by civil servants, the most important of whom is the Province Secretary. The provincial administrations have many direct responsibilities as the regional executors of national authority. They also serve as reviewing bodies to which appeals may be taken from activities of agencies of the roughly 1000 communes, such as the committees dealing with child welfare and public assistance. Appellate decisions of the provincial governments are in turn reviewable by the Supreme Administrative Court or, in some fields, by the King in Council.

government to the King in Council, the extent to which the province could delegate to a municipal agency the power to hold a supposedly dangerous alcoholic in custody, and the nonobservance of certain requirements concerning placing stamps on documents were among the topics discussed. This is a mixed bag of rather small game. If provincial governments need reminders about such things, one wonders whether the widely separated visitations of the Ombudsman should be relied upon as the chief means of supervision and stimulation.

Judges and prosecutors with whom the matter was discussed in 1964 endorsed even more strongly than provincial administrators the utility of the Ombudsman's inspections. A provincial prosecutor, responsible for supervising a number of police chiefs and prosecutors whose offices he himself inspected at least biennially, thought the Ombudsman's visits a desirable guarantor of his own vigilance. "I might become too good friends with my police chiefs in the course of time, you see," he explained—thus recalling the ancient question, who will watch the watchman? An unusually outspoken judge who had at one time crossed swords with the Ombudsman asserted that inspections sometimes brought to light oft-repeated miscarriages of justice, citing an instance in which a judge had long and rigidly applied a statute that had been repealed, a fact he learned only when the Ombudsman prosecuted him for negligence. Even such glaring judicial oversights may not be challenged by appeals to higher courts because, the judge asserted, the advocates outside the major cities cannot be relied upon for the professional skill needed to keep courts on the right track; the judges themselves, prodded by the Ombudsman as well as by the appellate courts, must (he said) assume responsibilities that may elsewhere be borne by the parties' lawyers.

Another judge, whose words were echoed by a colleague, spoke especially warmly of the opportunity an inspection gave him to discuss troublesome problems with a highly respected jurist. "Sometimes," he remarked, "I have to apply complicated procedural rules that are somewhat unfamiliar, and it helps me to know how the Ombudsman regards them or to learn what he can tell me about the way other judges are dealing with that matter. And sometimes I hear that a statute is being interpreted in different ways in various parts of the country, and I have found that discussion with the Ombudsman or one of his assistants may be clarifying." Still another judge commented: "The present Ombudsman is really a kind fellow, and I don't think that many judges are afraid of him. But they respect him enough not to want to be criticized by him, and so the fact that he may drop in to have a look at their records tends to make them more careful in their work." He added, however, that after a recent inspection had led to the Ombudsman's suggesting a change in handling default cases, "all six of the judges in this court agreed together to adopt the Ombudsman's suggestion, though all of us thought we were right and he was wrong. That happens more often than you would think. Theoretically we are not obliged to accept his advice, but it is easier to do so than to make a fight over it. I'm not sure that this always produces good results."

One broadly experienced trial court judge was markedly less ecstatic than many others about the inspection process. The defects discerned in the case files were, in his judgment, "just the small change of judicial administration—somebody was brought to trial eight days after arrest instead of after seven days, things like that". Then he added: "All this talk about personal contact is exaggeration. Most of the contact is with assistants, not with the Ombudsman. And, anyway, a personal contact that occurs once every ten years isn't much of a contact."

At the same time, while minimizing the significance of the Ombudsman's visits to the courts, the judge made a further highly suggestive comment: "Just as a public service I am a member of the Child Welfare Committee of this city. I am the only law-trained person there, and I have the devil's own time getting the Committee to do its work properly. What the Child Welfare Committee needs is an inspection by the Ombudsman about every other month."

This highlights a deficiency in the present system, which imposes on the Ombudsman so large a task of supervising everybody that he cannot efficiently supervise anybody in particular. Sweden acutely (though no doubt less acutely than many other countries) needs additional provision of regularized supervisory activity, educative work among officials on the job, continuity and coordination of work by the wielders of widely dispersed authority, and sustained attention to organization and methods. The Ombudsman, with the best will in the world and with the utmost devotion to duty, cannot fill that need; but the very fact of his inspections may create undue complacency.

An example is supplied by a recent inspection of one of Sweden's thirty major tax collection offices. After a general inspection that included an examination of the files, the Ombudsman reported, in two pages, that all was well from the legal point of view and that the work of that office was being performed faithfully. No doubt this was an accurate appraisal. What it omits is an expert evaluation of the entire tax collection system, in which uniformity is cumbersomely achieved by inflexible statutory commands that even specify in detail the headings to be placed at the top of columns in the ledgers. The Ombudsman can perhaps say whether the tax collector is obeying those commands, but he is not well equipped to say whether the commands are suitably formulated, whether mechanization should replace handwork, whether computerization of tax records would be advantageous, whether, in short, the tax collection office is as efficient as modern management can make it be.

Using the Ombudsman as a general handyman instead of using technical inspectors for technical matters is an anachronism. In the nineteenth century the ombudsmen then in office made tremendously valuable social contributions by reporting what they, and they alone, perceived in governmental establishments. The modernization of Swedish penology, for example, is widely attributed to ombudsmen who were outraged by conditions in isolated prisons they had inspected. Today the Ombudsman's are not the only outside eyes that look upon the jailers. Every prison in Sweden is inspected monthly by the regional director of the National Prison Board.[35] Annually it is inspected by a team of specialists—a structural engineer, an auditor, and so on. In between, traveling inspectors of the National Prison Board examine sanitation, kitchens, hospital quarters, and so on. Notwithstanding the change from the days when nobody cared about what happened to convicts behind walls, the Ombudsman continues personally to inspect prisons, though with understandably less spectacular results than his predecessors achieved.

Another demerit of the present inspection system is that it may focus attention on some facet of an office's work without taking into account other responsibilities that happen not to have come to notice during a hurried visit. The experience of a large provincial prosecutor's office

[35] The National Prison Board directs and supervises all penal institutions. In 1963 these institutions had a daily average population of 5,163; 12,773 new prisoners were admitted during the year. The Board (composed of a director general and four division chiefs) employed 2,900 persons, of whom only 132 worked at the Board's headquarters in Stockholm.

is illustrative. That office, which was then exercising supervisory authority over police as well as prosecutors, was inspected in 1963 for the first time since 1939. For several days two members of the Ombudsman's staff examined official files; for a few hours the Ombudsman himself conversed with the provincial prosecutor concerning problems of law enforcement. In the end, the Ombudsman had only one sharp criticism: the provincial prosecutor had failed ever since 1957 to require policemen throughout the province to undergo special training in the duties that would fall to them in case of war. The Ombudsman, observing a statutory direction that such training should be given, advised the prosecutor to mend his ways promptly. Within a few months more than a hundred policemen were summoned from their posts throughout the county and were instructed in what they should do if war were to come (and they were to survive its coming). "I wasn't going to argue the point," said the prosecutor, "because he was right in describing that statute. The only trouble is that we are terribly shorthanded here. I have been complaining for years about the understaffing of the police forces in the eighteen districts for which I am responsible. When we called in those men for war training, of course we had to take them away from doing other things the laws say we should do. We didn't suddenly have more men or more time. We simply used the men and the time differently, as the Ombudsman had said we should do. But if he were to come back now, he could criticize us for having left something else undone instead."

Another frequently heard criticism of the present inspection system is that it stimulates over-attention to paperwork at the expense of other activities. Since the Ombudsman is chiefly interested in documentary materials, both when he is making an inspection and when he is investigating a complaint, exactitude in record-keeping and amplitude of writings may at times be indulged in not to protect the persons to whom records and writings pertain, but to protect the record-keepers and writers. How much of this is a conscious or unconscious reaction to the Ombudsman's power to demand data, is hard to say. One senior officer thinks that formality and detailed paperwork are part of Sweden's tradition, not at all confined to governmental offices. He adds, however, that this tradition "is very strongly reinforced, I think, by the civil servant's awareness that he may be prosecuted for any omission. That slows up everything because not only do civil servants take pains to see that every comma is in precisely the right place, but they also like to distribute responsibility over two or three other people whenever they can, and it takes time to obtain approvals." This exaggerated care may cause considerable hardship to those it purportedly safeguards. The Ombudsman has several times called attention to delays in completing psychiatric observations of persons under arrest, who may have remained in custody for as long as six months simply to ascertain their mental competence. A qualified observer, asked whether this did not reflect a shortage of psychiatrists, replied: "It's partly that, of course. But much of it is just the doctor's feeling that he needs to write a treatise on each case, so that nobody can subject him to criticism if his report is ever reviewed by someone else."[36]

Still, even if the Ombudsman's inspections are not the unmixed blessings and triumphal processions many Swedes think them to be, they do produce some genuine accomplishments. So, for example, his inspections made the Ombudsman aware of diverse methods used by courts in determining whether tests showed an impermissible concentration of alcohol in the blood of automobile drivers. Driving under the influence of liquor is a stringently policed and heavily punished crime in Sweden. A suspect is tested while in police custody, but since the test occurs at some time subsequent to the driving itself, inferences must be drawn as to what it would have shown if the blood sample had been taken earlier. The Ombudsman, discovering that judges used a number of seemingly reasonable but nonetheless different formulas in this "counting back" from the blood tests, asked two well qualified scientists to help him analyze hundreds of case files drawn from various courts. Some of the courts, this analysis showed, in utter good faith committed serious technical mistakes. The Ombudsman then distributed to the judges and prosecutors a memorandum suggesting, in ac-

[36] The Ombudsman's report for 1964, at 82, discusses a number of complaints concerning detention of persons for psychiatric observations beyond the normally allowable period of six weeks. As early as the 1940's, the Ombudsman noted, his predecessors had voiced criticism of this practice. Since then, efforts had been made to increase the available institutional resources, so that the Ombudsman felt that he need take no further initiative at this time. He repeated "certain previous suggestions aiming at temporary improvement, such as using medical personnel from outside the prison organization, simplifying the procedure, and shortening the reports." The present lengthy detentions "are incompatible with basic principles of legal security" and every possible effort should be made to eradicate "one of the darkest chapters in modern Swedish life." Asked for comment on this problem, an officer of the National

cord with the scientific advice available to him, how blood tests should be interpreted in the future. The need for harmonizing and improving judicial practices in this regard might never have been recognized—or, at any rate, not recognized so quickly—had the Ombudsman not detected the problem in the course of making inspections.

In another instance the Ombudsman encountered, during an inspection, the question of whether the plaintiff in a divorce action could prove the defendant's chronic alcoholism by summoning as a witness a person who had had official contact with the defendant. The answer to that question was far from clear. The Ombudsman concluded that a court could properly receive testimony by the official in some circumstances, which he set forth in his annual report for the future guidance of judges who had previously been in doubt.[37]

Furthermore, the possibility that a dignitary of highest rank may concern himself with individual injustices has a no doubt beneficially sensitizing effect upon those empowered to restrict freedom of the person.[38] In many instances persons may be too ignorant or too inert to assert their legal rights. In such cases official malpractices come to light through inspections, if at all. A moving testimonial to the significance of this fact came from the lips of an administrator in a northern area who dealt with child welfare problems. In that connection his administrative agency could seize parents for non-support of their children and put them into forced work programs;[39] it could take

---

Medical Board told an interviewer in 1964: "In one of our mental hospitals with 1100 patients we have three full-time psychiatrists and one half-time man. They are kept so busy writing reports they have little time left over for diagnosis or therapy."

[37] For additional illustrative material, see Lundvik, "Comments on the Ombudsman," in Rowat (note 14), at 32.

[38] Personal liberty has always been one of the Ombudsman's paramount concerns, and some of his major accomplishments have pertained to custodial practices he found to be improper. See Anderman (note 29 above), at 234; Jägerskiöld (note 29 above), at 1098.

[39] Power to commit parents to "workhomes" was ended by a statute that took effect on July 1, 1964. Routine inspections of the files of a "workhome" in 1958 had revealed to the Ombudsman that some of those detained had not received charges or been heard before adverse decisions were made. In other cases, "the real reason for failure to pay for support was not lassitude or indifference but rather, for instance, an overwhelming burden of support with regard to the family or physical or mental defects . . . The cases often concerned chronic alcoholics, who ought to have been taken care of by the sobriety wards. Physical examinations were practically never made before deciding the case." A. Bexelius, "The Swedish Institution of the Justitieombudsman," 27 *Int. Rev. Admin. Sc.* 249 (1961). The Ombudsman, while critical of the

children from homes in which they were neglected; and it could detain juvenile delinquents. Discussing an inspection that had occurred in 1963 the administrator characterized certain of the Ombudsman's criticisms as "superficial," "petty," "reflecting inexperience." He was then asked whether this meant that the Ombudsman's inspections served no purpose. "No, indeed, it does not mean that," the administrator answered with great feeling. "I can tell you this: if I had a child of my own under the jurisdiction of an official body like this one, I would certainly want to have an outside check on it. And I can't think of a better one than the Ombudsman. I said that, in my opinion, the Ombudsman doesn't have experience in the fields in which we in this office have to face real-life problems every day, and this causes him to overlook some of our difficulties when he makes suggestions about how we should do our job. But he has the job of protecting human rights. He has plenty of experience there—vastly more than we have. It is far better for him to be an expert in his own field than in ours, if it comes to making a choice. We can stand being reminded that freedom is a part of the welfare we are supposed to be thinking about." Three other officials, present during the interview, indicated hearty agreement with their colleague's spontaneous utterance.

Others have independently confirmed that an even remotely possible future inspection by the Ombudsman does influence present behavior, especially in matters involving detention of the person. "How do you think the Ombudsman would like *that?*" a superior was quoted as having barked at a junior whose recommended action was being rejected. Discussing a colleague's proposal to make an arrest on somewhat inconclusive evidence, an official said: "I told him I wouldn't want to have such a case in my files if the Ombudsman were to come around to look at them, and that was the end of that." A young prosecutor acknowledged being conscious of saying to himself with considerable frequency: "I must be careful with this case, because it is just the kind the Ombudsman looks for." A former judge declared: "I can't point to a specific matter, but the Ombudsman entered into my thinking. He was a supervisory shadow, if I may put it so." A more youthful

---

particular institution that had been inspected, did not initiate any prosecutions. Instead, much more constructively, he called upon the Cabinet to formulate general instructions for the guidance of all the scattered authorities that bore responsibilities in this field. His recommendation was followed.

judge added: "The Ombudsman seems to me to personify the law, the omnipotent force in Swedish administration." A prison governor who had not experienced an inspection for nearly ten years said: "Often when I'm making a decision, I ask myself, How would the Ombudsman decide things? It has a good effect on me."

Having heard similar remarks uttered frequently and with seeming sincerity, an interviewer must conclude that many officials do regard the Ombudsman as a vigilant watchman—even though, in all probability, the watchman will not complete his rounds within the next decade. Some of them, one suspects, are really consulting only their own inner conscience, to which they have attached the Ombudsman's title.

8 | The Relationship of the Press to the Ombudsman's Work

The Swedish press plays a large part in the Ombudsman's work, both in stimulating his activity and in publicizing its consequences.

The Ombudsman, as has been observed, may initiate investigations on his own motion. Sometimes editorial exhortations bring issues to his notice. Sometimes direct "tips" by journalist lead him to make further inquiries. More frequently, newspaper stories written without the Ombudsman in mind suggest to his practiced eye the possibility of discovering "news behind the news." He has been especially vigilant to discern the civil liberties implications of matters that may be reported simply as interesting episodes of the day.

Thus, for example, in 1957 he plucked from the daily press an account of a Lutheran pastor's having torn down posters advertising an evangelical meeting of which he disapproved. In Sweden the clergymen of the tax-supported State Church perform such civil functions as recording deaths and births, and are therefore regarded as officials within the Ombudsman's reach. Dissatisfied with the pastor's explanation of his attempt to exclude a religious competitor, the Ombudsman suggested that the pastor's bishop should reprimand him. When the bishop demurred, the Ombudsman prosecuted the pastor for interfering with religious freedom and the right of peaceable assemblage; the pastor was convicted and fined. In 1963 the Ombudsman again locked horns with the State Church when a pastor refused to permit funds to be collected in his parish for certain activities in which female clergy participated. A statute enacted in 1958 had for the first time made possible the ordination of women as pastors of the State Church. Seeking to interfere with the operation of the new law, the Ombudsman said, was a breach of duty; and since the anti-feminist pastor remained obdurately unrepentant, the Ombudsman launched another prosecution, leading to conviction and fine.

Just as the press makes business for the Ombudsman, so too does he make business for the press. The sweeping principle of Swedish law that the public's files should be open to the public indiscriminately means, among other things, that complaints mailed to the Ombudsman can be read by journalists, as can his subsequent correspondence with officials, their explanations and excuses, many of the documentary materials that bear on the cases, and of course the reports of the Ombudsman's own actions. A reporter for the Swedish news association visits the Ombudsman's office every day to examine the incoming mail, which in fact the reporter sometimes sees before the Ombudsman himself has had a chance to read it; and copies of all outgoing correspondence are also available for his perusal. The reporter brings roughly a third of the incoming complaints to the attention of members of the news association, either as items of local interest, as "human interest" stories, or as matters of sufficient general importance to claim the attention of the metropolitan press. While the newspapers do not publish everything that comes to their notice, complaints are frequently publicized before having been investigated.[40] Time after time civil servants, when discussing the Ombudsman's work, bitterly denounced this practice as unfair to them because, though 90 percent of the complaints are later found to be unsound, an official's subsequent exoneration is often less prominently reported than the original accusation against

[40] The largest Swedish daily newspaper during August and September, 1964, printed a number of stories based entirely on current and as yet wholly unevaluated complaints. The following are examples: The Ice Hockey Federation accused taxation authorities of having exceeded their powers; a civilian lawyer attached to the United Nations peace-keeping organization in the Congo accused taxation authorities of discriminating against non-military personnel in applying tax regulations to persons temporarily abroad; an advocate in a small city in central Sweden accused a just retired district judge of having committed various improprieties, of which detailed examples were set forth, and of having conducted judicial affairs so that "the office of the court resembled a castle accessible only to persons with a specially designed key."

him. The Ombudsman, taking note of the officials' dissatisfaction, publicly suggested in 1961 that the civil servants' organizations and the newspaper publishers' association should negotiate an agreement concerning press coverage.[41] But the suggestion has thus far been ignored. The publishers' association denies any unfairness, pointing to its policy, binding on all members, that news reports should be delayed until a person whose reputation may be involved has had opportunity to tell his side of the story. The policy is morally enforceable by the association's "court of honor" to which injured individuals may complain. The "court"—composed of a Supreme Court justice, journalists, and publishers—cannot award damages, but its judgments (some thirty-odd each year) are said to be regarded as "sentences" upon an improper publication. They are widely reprinted and are thought to be influential. This, the newspapers feel, is adequate protection of civil servants who may be recklessly or simply mistakenly accused. The civil servants vigorously dissent.

Another and less noticed consequence of publicizing complaints is its deterrent effect upon some persons who might otherwise bring matters to the Ombudsman's attention.[42] The legal adviser of a leading bank, for instance, described what seemed to be an official impropriety, but added that the bank's officers, after considering the likelihood of publicity were a complaint to be made, decided not to report the occurrence to the Ombudsman. A lawyer, representing a large commercial interest, spoke of episodes apparently suitable for consideration by the Ombudsman but not communicated to him: "We can look out for ourselves without his help and we simply don't like to get mixed up in a newspaper controversy."

One has the impression that the Swedish press rather conscientiously seeks to avoid needless embarrassment to complainants; for example, a complaint by a person who has been detained as an alcoholic will be published without using the complainant's name. Moreover, in many instances the newspapers do not identify by name or specific title the official complained against; they tend to discuss problems and not persons. Perhaps no more can be asked. In any event, Parliament has

[41] A. Bexelius, "Hur JO-Aämbetet arbetar," [1961] *Statsvetenskaplig Tidskrift* 219.

[42] The Ombudsman does not register anonymous complaints. In a few instances, however, matters revealed by anonymous complaints have later been investigated by the Ombudsman, ostensibly on his own motion.

shown no enthusiasm whatsoever for legislative proposals, made from time to time, that publicity should be withheld until the Ombudsman has completed his action upon a complaint.

Relations between the Ombudsman and the press are cordial, though newspapers do not hesitate to criticize his judgments or to urge more vigorous attention to this or that area of public administration. Responding to journalistic complaints against officials' reticence, the Ombudsman has strongly upheld the newspapers' right to know.[43] Of course this has endeared the Ombudsman to newspapermen. As one leading editor exclaimed, "We look upon the Ombudsman as the responsible guardian of our freedom of the press, so we are eager to cooperate with him."

Thanks to that cooperation, the Ombudsman's criticisms and suggestions gain greatly added circulation. Editors with whom the matter was discussed acknowledged that they tended to emphasize cases with "human interest angles" while underplaying concededly more important matters that were "technical." A few of the most highly respected daily papers do give considerable attention to the superficially unexciting topics the Ombudsman has dealt with, thus adding to citizens' and officials' awareness of the Ombudsman's recommendations. At times they have built their own "editorial crusades" upon ideas provided by the Ombudsman's findings. All in all, the press has been a useful stimulator of Swedish interest in what might elsewhere be regarded as dull information. A journalist who had himself written much about the Ombudsman commented with satisfaction: "Sweden is blessed by having good civil servants. The public has come to expect high quality performances by them. When even a minor civil servant makes a serious error, our readers think that finding out about it is like reading a good detective story. It is a scandal and they want us to tell them all about it. And that is exactly what we try to do."

[43] In 1962, for example, the Ombudsman criticized a hospital administration because it withheld from newspapers the names of applicants for a vacancy in an important position; the applicants had specifically requested confidentiality in order to avoid embarrassment to them. Similarly, in August of 1964 the newspapers reported with obvious satisfaction that the Ombudsman had demanded from the municipal government of Lycksele an explanation of its not answering reporters' questions about who had applied for an appointive post. Two of the three applicants had requested that their names not be disclosed. The local authorities had honored this request in order to protect the applicants against possible unpleasantness in their present employment. The Ombudsman obviously thought this an inadequate justification of silence, since in Sweden the right of privacy has been so largely subordinated to the right of publicity.

9|The Ombudsman as Unofficial Adviser

While the Ombudsman is known chiefly as critic and reformer, he serves also, much less conspicuously, as cherished adviser.

Many judges and officials seek the Ombudsman's opinion concerning matters upon which they have not yet acted. Quite properly, he declines to give rulings concerning hypothetical as well as real cases. He does not purport to be General Counsel to the Civil Establishment. He recognizes, too, the danger of advising how to dispose of problems whose facets may have been only partially revealed. Hence, more resolutely than some of his predecessors, he flatly rejects formal requests for an expression of opinion about pending cases.

He has been helpful, on the other hand, when a judge or other public official has asked by telephone or letter whether the Ombudsman has encountered a particular problem in the course of his work. In such instances the Ombudsman makes available the knowledge he has gained through the past performance of his duties. This, in a sense, simply projects the conversational exchanges that may occur during an inspection, when the Ombudsman gives and receives information about the conduct of public business. It serves as a species of preventive therapy, for it encourages uniform statutory interpretation and the utilization of correct procedures. A number of judges spoke warmly of the benefits they had received from the Ombudsman's informal advisory service—a service he does not mention in his annual reports or stress in his comments elsewhere.

10|Relationship of the Ombudsman to Other Public Watchmen

The preceding discussion, focusing as it has done on the Ombudsman alone, may have suggested that he solitarily watches over Swedish law administration. In fact the Ombudsman's powers and duties are shared with others.

The Chancellor of Justice. Of most interest among the Ombudsman's fellow watchmen is the Chancellor of Justice (Justitiekanzler). His office is the direct lineal descendant of the King's ombudsman whose creation in the eighteenth century led to the nineteenth-century demand for a parliamentary counterpart.[44] Today, though nominally still a "representative of the Crown" and, according to the Constitution (Art. 27), the "Supreme Ombudsman of the King," the Chancellor of Justice holds a non-political post for life. Neither a member of the Cabinet nor responsible to any minister, he is in fact entirely independent. Like the Ombudsman, he heads his own staff, separate and apart from all others. Unlike the Ombudsman he submits no report to Parliament. The absence of that report is the chief vestigial remnant of the Chancellor's having once upon a time been the monarch's agent.[45]

His functions are more varied than the Ombudsman's.[46] But in one important respect they are exactly parallel. About a quarter of the Chancellor's and his small staff's time is devoted, as is the Ombudsman's, to receiving complaints from citizens and officials about judges and other officials;[47] to inspection trips; to investigating, on his own motion, matters discussed in the press or elsewhere; to admonishing, sermonizing, formulating general recommendations, and prosecuting those whose blunders are egregious or whose acceptance of guidance is halfhearted. If one were to ask why two men, one called Justitieombudsman and one called Justitiekansler, should do exactly the same work in exactly the same way affecting exactly the same people, but without even a tenuous structural link between them, the only possible response would be Justice Holmes's "Upon this point a page of history is worth a volume of logic."[48]

[44] Compare S. Rudholm, "The Chancellor of Justice," in Rowat (note 14), at 17.

[45] Instead of reporting to Parliament, the Chancellor of Justice makes a report nominally to the King, in fact filed with the Ministry of Justice. The report is a public document and, as such, can be examined by the curious. But it is not printed for general distribution.

[46] They include appearing as counsel in civil cases in which the State is defendant (twenty-five to fifty annually), acting in the King's behalf on letters addressed to the monarch by "supplicants" (of which there are only a few), exercising a somewhat vague supervision of enrolled advocates (who are members of a self-governing organization that renders usually final disciplinary judgments), giving advice concerning legal questions to the King in Council (that is, the Cabinet or a Minister; roughly, two hundred such matters annually), expressing opinions on legislative proposals before the Cabinet (a responsibility, or perhaps one should say an opportunity, he shares with many others), and prosecuting publishers who have abused the privileges recognized by the Freedom of the Press Act of 1949.

[47] The Chancellor of Justice has said that when superior officers in one of the central administrative boards have reason to call for an investigation of one of their subordinates, they are more likely to turn to him than to the Ombudsman because, thanks to history, he is a "part of the Government" while the Ombudsman is linked with Parliament.

[48] N.Y. Trust Co. v. Eisner, 256 U.S. 345, 349 (1921).

The activity of these two officers overlaps considerably, even though the Chancellor handles many fewer cases than does the Ombudsman. Analysis of the Chancellor's reports indicates that over a five-year span he has annually docketed an average of 260 new cases based on complaints or his own discoveries concerning the conduct of officials also subject to the Ombudsman's supervision.

Table XV. Chancellor of Justice cases that overlap Ombudsman's

	New cases filed	Decided	Balance at year's end
1960	235	230	69
1961	168	207	36
1962	264	220	80
1963	300	276	104
1964	335	338	101

The absence of friction or contrariety of results in the work of these two important officials is a tribute to their personal flexibility and the Swedish genius for reasoned discussion. Neither man is the superior of the other; a person who has complained unsuccessfully to one may with perfect propriety turn to his counterpart; no statute prescribes coordination of inspections and investigations. In short, all the preconditions of strife are present. Very occasionally the Chancellor and the Ombudsman do disagree in their legal reasoning, thus providing bemused administrators a choice of different guide lines. They attempt, however, to minimize confusion by private discussions over the lunch table several times weekly. The Chancellor of Justice before initiating an investigation on his own motion is likely to telephone the Ombudsman to inquire whether an investigation is already afoot. The two officials exchange notes concerning the "querulents" who may write to both of them simultaneously.[49] One stands aside for the other when a prosecution is in the offing. And so they rub along, officially wholly unrelated and yet in fact collaborators holding equal rank in the gov-

[49] The precise extent of duplication of complaints is not known, though the Ombudsman and the Chancellor confirm that they have many clients in common, who write to them simultaneously or successively. The Chancellor notes that chronically aggrieved persons file multiple complaints with him in the course of a year, so that the individual complainants are substantially fewer than the complaints received.

ernmental hierarchy, acting separately as general superintendents of law administration.

The Military Ombudsman. In 1915 the Ombudsman's work was divided. The Militieombudsman, a second parliamentary ombudsman chosen in the same manner and with the same general powers as the Justitieombudsman, was created to deal with all matters pertaining to the military. His jurisdiction extends not only to the conduct of the armed forces themselves, but also to all officials whose salaries are paid out of military appropriations, thus including defense procurement. Marking off the boundaries of the new ombudsman's duties in this way recognizes that modern military activities are a central element of civilian life and not merely the province of a small caste of professional soldiers. The Ombudsman's absorption in civil administration was thought to necessitate a separate officer to guard citizens against abuses in military administration.

The Military Ombudsman functions within his sphere much as the Ombudsman does in his. The two officers are mutually independent. They refer cases to one another when complaints have been misdirected or when an investigation by one of them discloses matters of interest to the other.

Most of the Military Ombudsman's business is an outgrowth of his own inspections. Complaints usually provide only about 12 percent of his annual caseload of approximately 650, though during World War II, when general mobilization affected a large part of the population, complaints were much more numerous. Like the Ombudsman, the Military Ombudsman can admonish a named person, make general recommendations, or prosecute an official wrongdoer. The prosecutions are, in the main, for matters that in the United States would probably not be deemed suitable for the criminal courts at all, but, rather, for some form of administrative discipline—an official connected with defense industries who had been careless in handling secret documents, a commissioned officer who had insulted a noncommissioned officer, a commander who had punished draftees for having been drunk at a time when they were off duty and not on military premises, and so on.

Together the Military Ombudsman and his colleague on the civil side are supposed to cover the entire area of Swedish public administration. Of the two the Ombudsman has been far the more active. The two offices are not in conflict, since the dividing line between their respective jurisdictions is clear and neither has sought to expand his empire by encroaching upon the other. Because, very occasionally, problems of classifying complaints may arise or the two offices may confront common questions of statutory interpretation, the Ombudsmen confer together informally and irregularly. Additional coordination of their activities has thus far not seemed needed.

The Public Prosecutors. In a strictly technical sense, the Ombudsman is only a public prosecutor. Other prosecutors are supposed to enforce penal laws within a defined geographical area. The Ombudsman is supposed to enforce them within a defined occupational area, namely, the public service.

Actually, even within that relatively narrow area, he does a far smaller share of the work than is commonly known. The prosecutors have not been freed from responsibility for making other officials toe the mark. They have been superseded by the Ombudsman and the Chancellor of Justice as prosecutors of judges and of very high officials. But as to the generality of Swedish public servants, the local prosecutors have the same power as the Ombudsman to prosecute for ignorance, carelessness, bad manners, and slothfulness, as well as for more serious venality. The Ombudsman may initiate a half-dozen prosecutions in the course of a year,[50] and the Chancellor of Justice and the Military Ombudsman may commence another eight or nine; not all result in convictions. According to available judicial statistics, however, courts of first instance in 1961 convicted 125 civil servants of having committed crimes in their official capacities.[51] The figure was 129 in 1962 and 107 in 1963.[52] These totals show beyond doubt that less exalted prosecutors have independently brought to the courts many cases of the types with which ombudsmen deal.

In theory a public prosecutor can only prosecute. He supposedly cannot content himself with scolding or advising as do the Ombuds-

[50] See Table XIV.

[51] Of these, only four were for conduct such as bribery or embezzlement that would constitute a serious crime in all countries. The remainder were for relatively minor acts of omission or commission, usually under the heading of "breach of duty." Twenty-two acquittals occurred.

[52] The convictions usually led only to imposition of fines. The courts did, however, order the dismissal or suspension of 16 officials in 1961, 13 officials in 1962, and 17 officials in 1963. An undetermined number of these removals from office seem to have been related to misconduct unconnected with official activities. The materials available in the Central Bureau of Statistics are not altogether clear in this respect.

man and the Chancellor. One distinguished scholar asserts flatly that ombudsmen are different from other law enforcement officials chiefly because "unlike the public prosecutors, they are not subjected to a legality principle in the sense of being obliged to prosecute when they consider that a breach of duty has been committed."[53] In reality, public prosecutors do not choose to prosecute every case, any more than do the other guardians of official rectitude. In the great bulk of cases reported to them by irate citizens in the local community, the prosecutor does exactly what the Ombudsman does when he thinks that a "reminder" will accomplish as much as a more formal punishment. Some prosecutors freely acknowledge using the telephone more frequently than the criminal courts to correct what they regard as administrative improprieties. Statistical evidence strongly supports the view that obligatory prosecution is not a "legality principle" or, if it be one at all, weighs only lightly on practical men. In 1961 the Swedish police investigated 1,079 alleged crimes by civil servants and concluded that accusations were well founded in 519 of these cases. In 1962, 1,208 investigations produced evidence of offenses in 666 cases. Prosecutors control and guide police much more closely in Sweden than in the United States (in many places, indeed, the chief of police and the prosecutor were one and the same person until a statutory change occurred in 1965). Hence, one may fairly conclude that prosecutions were technically justifiable in virtually all the cases the police had reported. Since prosecutions were in fact commenced in only a minor fraction of those cases and since prosecutors do not habitually altogether disregard police reports, one must conclude that other less drastic steps were taken instead. A confident assertion to this effect is impossible because the Supreme Prosecutor of Sweden recently stated that prosecutors must only prosecute, not admonish; if they believe that prosecution would be too drastic a measure, they have been explicitly instructed to refer the matter to the Supreme Prosecutor; he recalls receiving only about ten such referrals each year. Harmonizing the statements of the Supreme Prosecutor and his subordinates is beyond the capacities of a foreign interviewer.

Conflict between the Ombudsman and other prosecutors is rare. If a local prosecutor already has in hand a matter about which complaint has also been made to the Ombudsman, the Ombudsman defers to the

[53] S. Jägerskiöld, "The Swedish Constitution: A Survey," 5 *J. Indian L. Inst.* 1, 13 (1963).

prosecutor. Prosecutors, for their part, do not eagerly seek means of tweaking the Ombudsman's nose; they are not organizationally subordinate to him, but, like other officials, they are subject to his scrutiny. When a prosecution has been ordered by the Ombudsman (who rarely prosecutes personally), the order is obeyed without debate.[54] The public prosecutors, collectively, receive and act upon about as many complaints against civil servants as does the Ombudsman. As far as a foreign interviewer can discover, no atmosphere of rivalry or competition (or, one is tempted to add, even awareness that many cooks are engaged in stirring the same broth) has developed in any quarter.[55]

11 | The Ombudsman's Relations with the Courts

The Ombudsman's power over the courts is especially interesting to Americans, who think of judicial independence as the very foundation of the rule of law and who tend to equate judges' "independence" with their being unsupervised except by other judges. The Ombudsman acknowledges that foreigners often wonder whether his work undermines the independence judges should have. But he has no fears on that score. "I myself come from the ranks of judges," he has written, "and can assure that I have never heard a Swedish judge complain that his independent and unattached position is endangered by the fact that the [Ombudsman] may examine his activity in office."

Many judges of all ranks and of different degrees of experience, when interviewed in 1964, confirmed that the judiciary does not feel

[54] If a prosecutor were to reject a case the Ombudsman deemed clearly prosecutable, the Ombudsman could, in fact, prosecute the prosecutor for breach of duty. That type of clash seems never to have arisen.

[55] One prosecutor did express uneasiness about dropping a case without prosecution when a breach of duty has been found. "I can't believe that prosecution is the sensible step in every instance," he declared. "The other day a man very angrily complained right at this desk about having been treated offensively by a clerk in the post office. I called up the clerk's superior and he promised to speak to the clerk about it, warn him to watch his step in the future. That is all I did. I think it was the best way to handle the thing, though I daresay the clerk was guilty of an offense. But now, if the complainant still wants to make an issue of it, he can go to the Ombudsman and complain not against the clerk but against me for not doing my duty as a prosecutor. Well, I don't much like that possibility. I am having to gamble, you see, that nobody will complain or that, if someone does, the Ombudsman will agree with my informal approach. If I just went ahead and prosecuted every case, nobody could say a word against me."

imperiled. One judge of long service, possibly more philosophic than his brethren, commented: "We have grown up in this system. None of us has ever known any other. We are used to the idea back of the Ombudsman. If we had been encountering it for the first time, perhaps it would have made us uncomfortable. But as things stand, I doubt that any Swedish judge feels any loss of independence when the Ombudsman looks at what he has been doing."

Abstractly, the Ombudsman is not concerned with the content of courts' decisions (which, in any event, he cannot revise in any way), but only with the question of whether a judge has been acting illegally. Since illegality, in the Swedish view, covers so extensive a territory, consideration of the judge's decisions may be an inescapable necessity. To suggest the most extreme possibility along this line, the Ombudsman could even prosecute, for the crime of breach of duty, judges who had rejected his views in prosecutions commenced at his behest; he could not disregard the decisions he opposed, but he could proceed against the deciders. This has in fact never occurred. So far as one can tell, judges have not the slightest worry that it ever will occur. Even so, part of the Ombudsman's work does involve review of the judges' decisions, not only their conduct.

The distinction can be made plainer by illustration. Poor judgment rather than poor judging was involved when, a few years ago, an appellate judge was found guilty of having accepted compensation to help a lawyer prepare documents for use in litigation; the judge was not himself related to the litigation and no corruption of justice entered into the case, but the defendant was simply accused of improper behavior in acting as a lawyer's assistant. The Supreme Court, before which his trial occurred, convicted him and imposed a heavy fine. At about the same time three trial court judges were successfully prosecuted because they had heard and decided a forfeiture case without first giving an interested person the prescribed formal notice; the judges had thought that formalities could be waived because the interested person's legal representative was actually present in the court when the case was reached. In this instance, by contrast with the example previously discussed, the Ombudsman was acting as a critic of judicial work rather than of a judge's personal behavior.[56]

Cases like this do indeed cause a few judges to speak rather wasp-

[56] The judges' decision on the merits of the forfeiture case, incidentally, was affirmed on appeal. Moreover, the person from whom the required notice had been

ishly about the Ombudsman, whom they regard as sometimes a shade too censorious and self-righteous. On several occasions in widely scattered localities judges recounted with pleasure that the Ombudsman had had to eat humble pie at least once. Acting upon a private complaint during his first month in office, the Ombudsman had said that a court official had improperly attached the complainant's property in order to secure the payment of personal taxes. Conformably with the Ombudsman's advice, the impounded property was returned to its owner. Later, a Supreme Court judge convinced his friend the Ombudsman that he had misinterpreted the applicable statute. Meanwhile, the tax debtor had dissipated the previously attached property and had been unable to pay his taxes in full, so that the public treasury was the loser. The Ombudsman bravely acknowledged his own error by reporting it to Parliament and, at the same time, paid out of his personal funds the amount of the lost revenue. This episode, not at all discreditable in itself, has gained currency among judges, as though they welcomed being reassured that the Ombudsman can err just as they do.

Most judges, however, seem genuinely enthusiastic about the Ombudsman, whom they regard as an able jurist and a good human being. No judge who was interviewed in 1964 suggested that the present system of supervision should be abandoned.

12 | Appraising the Ombudsman's Work

The Ombudsman has in recent years been so rapturously regarded abroad that his achievements have not often been evaluated. What he is supposed to accomplish is taken as the equivalent of what he has in

withheld did not recover the property in controversy, nor were any damages awarded in the proceeding against the judges. The judges were, however, fined approximately half a month's salary. One of them still becomes almost explosively red in the face when discussing the matter. He thinks, moreover, that his work in the community was made more difficult for a time by reason of his having been convicted as a malefactor, though the difficulty was not long-lived because, as he said, the public had no choice in the matter. He also thinks that press publicity about complaints to the Ombudsman against a judge tend to be harmful to judicial administration even after the judge has been exonerated, because the newspapers (he says) "blow up the charges out of all proportion." Despite all this, he characterizes the Ombudsman as "really a very pleasant fellow" and regards his work as highly useful.

fact accomplished. The following paragraphs attempt to appraise rather than merely describe. The underlying observations were perforce incomplete; scientific accuracy is not claimed.

Securing uniformity in law interpretation. The doctrine of stare decisis does not compel lower courts in Sweden to follow the lead of the higher courts. This intensifies the risk, present in all legal systems, that principles and statutes may not be applied harmoniously throughout the country. This possibility becomes still greater when courts and other tribunals fail to write fully explanatory opinions tightly related to the facts of the cases under discussion.

One of the Ombudsman's important accomplishments is achieving uniformity. He does so by expressing his own opinion so effectively that courts and administrators voluntarily follow his lead. Indeed, until the Ombudsman has sought to resolve differences, many judges and administrators have been unaware that the differences had occurred; they have not consciously disagreed with other authorities, but have been ignorant of their views.

The Ombudsman has remarked on many occasions that differing applications of a single rule of law do not necessarily connote illegality; all of the interpretations may be defensible though some must be deemed incorrect. When the Ombudsman becomes aware that various authorities have been applying a law in different ways, he may first ask many agencies or individual officials to explain to him their interpretation of the statute or rule; then he may make an independent study of the pertinent legislative history; and finally, usually by setting forth his opinion in his annual report, he presents his own view of the law. His opinion, though assuredly not more binding than an opinion of the Supreme Court of Sweden, is highly persuasive. It brings home to scattered administrators the carefully considered thoughts of a respected jurist who has made a nationwide survey of present practices, and most law appliers seem to welcome what he can tell them.[57]

Some scholars have contended that the Ombudsman should not

[57] Compare Jägerskiöld (note 29), at 1092–1093: Although the Ombudsman's interpretations "are not legally binding on courts or administrators, and it is generally realized that they may be erroneous and that a court may disavow them, a certain presumption exists that these interpretations are correct. The annual reports of the Ombudsman are carefully studied as evidence of the law. Thus, although it is not in itself a fault to act contrary to those opinions, it is nevertheless true that if an official can show that he has acted in accordance with such a statement by the Ombudsman, he has a considerable chance of being absolved from blame."

function as an oracle, but only as a prosecutor in pursuit of officials who have done wrong. They point out that his pronouncements about law may ultimately be rejected by courts; this, they say, may accentuate confusion, which could be avoided if the Ombudsman were to remain silent except when he is ready to prosecute. The Ombudsman has answered that his interpreting the law is often a necessary first step toward ascertaining whether a judge or civil servant has acted wrongly. Having made his interpretation, he sees no reason to keep it a secret from those who might be helped by knowing it. And so he publishes his views even when he has found no breach of duty.

The Ombudsman's 1962 report shows several good examples of this practice, clustering about the seizure of defendant's property in connection with litigation. Property may be sequestered for use in evidence (for example, a negotiable instrument alleged to be illegally possessed) or as security for the payment of damages and costs. Having reviewed the report of a commission upon whose recommendation certain changes in procedural law had been enacted, the Ombudsman concluded that several judges had been acting mistakenly in sequestration matters, though not in circumstances warranting prosecution. In all the specific cases that had led to his examining the general problem, the Ombudsman noted, the judges had now discarded their original interpretations and had said that they would in future adopt his.

Officials in many parts of Sweden spoke warmly of what they characterized as the "service" the Ombudsman has rendered them by thus clarifying difficult legal issues. A local police administrator, for example, declared: "The new law of criminal procedure when it came into force a few years ago was less clear, we thought, than statutes usually are. It caused us a lot of difficulty, and I think we would be in it still if the Ombudsman hadn't given us some standards we could apply in connection with seizure and arrest. The law prescribes time limits for various actions, and the police and the prosecutors were terribly confused about how to measure the limits; in fact there were nearly as many opinions about the implications of those rules as there were police officers and prosecutors. Then the Ombudsman sent out his interpretations and did a lot to create a common practice all over the country."

The other side of the coin is, obviously enough, that the Ombudsman's legal analysis may sometimes be faulty. He works on many matters, aided by only a small staff. Even the ablest lawyer makes mistakes. A Stockholm prosecutor, one of the few outspoken critics of the present ombudsman system, calls the Ombudsman's pronouncements "a sort of one man lawgiving that is anachronistic in the twentieth century. It may have been all right in the seventeenth century. But who in modern times would think of creating a high court with only one member? Every appellate court reflects mankind's experience that two heads are wiser than one. Only in the case of the Ombudsman does it miraculously occur that one head is wiser than many."

The generalist in a specialized world. The possibility of error increases when a person whose training and experience are entirely in the law is called upon to be a compendium of governmental wisdom, as is the Ombudsman. Many of the earlier ombudsmen concentrated upon courts and court-related activities; during the first one hundred years of the office, according to its present occupant, 71.4 percent of the prosecutions commenced by ombudsmen were directed against judges, prosecutors, and police. As recently as 1951 the then Ombudsman issued 140 admonitions to those groups and only 33 to all other (and far more numerous) governmental personnel.[58] The growth of important law administration outside the courts made this distribution of the Ombudsman's attention seem glaringly inappropriate. Responding to urging by Parliament and by scholars, the present Ombudsman has striven mightily to cover the entire field of government.

One does not gain the impression that the Ombudsman ascribes to himself an all-encompassing wisdom. He does not, however, limit himself to legal questions. He feels free to offer suggestions looking toward administrative improvement.[59] Often those suggestions, the product of a fresh look by an intelligent eye, gain immediate and deserved acceptance.[60] Sometimes they lead to a negotiated settlement

[58] These figures are derived from C. Petrén, "Justitieombudsmannens uppsikt over förvaltningen," [1953] *Förvaltningsrattlig Tidskrift* 79, 86–87, cited and quoted in Anderman (note 29), at 236.

[59] For example, he recently rejected a complaint against a prison administrator who had disciplined a prisoner for disobeying a valid prison regulation. At the same time, noting that the prisoner was a Finn and that the prison population included other Finns who could not read Swedish, the Ombudsman suggested that the prison regulations be printed in a Finnish translation in order to avoid future misunderstandings.

[60] For example, in 1964 he proposed to a national inspection agency that it tighten its rules for protecting employees who complained to it concerning improper

when the administrators find the Ombudsman's initial proposals unacceptable but nevertheless concede that changes of some sort should be made.[61]

Still, "common sense" does not solve every problem. Government becomes increasingly complex and specialized year by year, responding as it must to the complications and specializations of human affairs. The Ombudsman, no matter how intelligent and diligent, cannot be expected to grasp all the implications of every branch of civil administration. While respecting him personally and giving him credit for a high measure of success, officials do at times remark that the Ombudsman "just did not understand our problem."[62]

---

working conditions. The question arose when a young hairdresser was discharged after her employer had read a letter which her father had written to the inspection agency concerning his daughter's work place. While Swedish law concerning public access to official files had to be taken into account, the Ombudsman thought that additional safeguards could be devised for the future. The inspection agency agreed.

[61] A few years ago a prisoner complained that the prison governor had forbidden his subscribing to a certain weekly magazine. The governor, who had legal power to restrict prisoners' privileges in order to maintain prison security, explained that this magazine caused unrest among prisoners by sometimes printing articles about prison conditions. He was upheld by the National Prison Board. The Ombudsman then questioned whether the prohibitory rule was valid, pointing out that the other prison governors had not deemed it necessary. Finally, the Board proposed that prisoners should be allowed to have the magazine in question unless the governor were to find a particular issue to be dangerous, in which case he could restrict distribution of that specific issue. This compromise satisfied the Ombudsman and the prison governor. A high official of the National Prison Board referred to this episode as one that "shows we do not ignore the Ombudsman's word even when we disagree with it. His view has great weight. Mostly we think his judgment is very good. He tells us in advance about the 'possibility' of his decision and we have a chance to comment before a final decision is made, and sometimes we work out a decision that seems to us a bit better than the 'possibility.' "

[62] Some examples, plucked from interviews and without any representation that the criticism of the Ombudsman is in each instance justified: (1) Ombudsman reprimanded school authorities for giving a "bad conduct mark" to a student newspaper editor who had printed an article not approved by faculty adviser, saying that this was infringement of freedom of the press; some educators think that the Ombudsman fails to grasp the difference between irresponsible adolescents within an educational framework and more mature journalists in the great world. (2) An apparently drunken man was picked up by the police and put in a cell to "sleep it off." Relatives clamored for his release, saying that he was ill, not drunk. The police, who had heard that tale before, were unmoved. Soon afterward the man died in a hospital, to which he had been taken tardily. Autopsy showed the cause of death to have been the illness of which his relatives had spoken. The Ombudsman did not criticize what the police had done, but urged that, in future, the chief of police should be personally called when apparently serious drunkenness problems occurred, so that he could decide whether special measures should be taken. Said the head of the police force in a large city: "If the Ombudsman's advice were followed, I would never have a

Whether or not that rather soft impeachment is sustainable, the Ombudsman does indeed seek to be a sort of social statesman in many fields that specialists find full of perplexities. His 1964 report deals, among other things, with detention of children under eighteen pending trial on delinquency charges, psychiatric examinations, provision of police protection for persons who have received threats of violence, and creation of medical facilities other than hospitals to which police and other officials may speedily refer acutely ill persons for diagnosis and emergency treatment. Other recent reports have discussed such diverse matters as custody of children of persons divorced by agreement, provision of needed legal services for impecunious or ignorant defendants, and revocation of automobile drivers' licenses. An outside observer cannot escape wondering whether a general practitioner should be expected to cope with so broad a range of ills, without the aid of more elaborate technical resources than the Ombudsman can command.

Attentiveness to the Ombudsman's recommendations. Earlier sections of this paper have commented upon the judicial and administrative response to the Ombudsman's "reminders." The more specific his recommendations are—the more, that is, they are tied to the facts of particular episodes—the more likely they will be accepted and acted upon. When he makes general proposals of statutory change or large-scale administrative revision, his suggestions receive respectful consideration, but they are not at all assured of being adopted.

In the past the Ombudsman addressed his legislative proposals

---

night's sleep. It's a fine idea, but it won't work." (3) A customs officer was prosecuted at the Ombudsman's behest because he had "covered up" for an informant who, under a pledge of secrecy, had given a tip that led to a smuggler's being apprehended and convicted. In the smuggler's trial and in official documents the customs officer had, in effect, represented that the detection of the smuggler had come about through official activity alone. The Ombudsman prosecuted for breach of duty. Said one official: "If we are not to be able to use tips from informers—and we certainly won't have many tips if we cannot protect our sources—this job will become pretty nearly hopeless. If the Ombudsman had to catch smugglers instead of officers, he would understand that." *Note:* In the last cited example, the court before which the customs officer had been tried said that the defendant had "behaved incorrectly," but, because of the pressure of events that had influenced his behavior, he could not be held guilty of breach of duty. The Court of Appeals affirmed the acquittal. The Ombudsman did not appeal further, saying that appeal to the Supreme Court should be undertaken "only where important questions of principle are at stake. The courts have confirmed that [the customs officer] handled the matter incorrectly. There is, therefore, no need to review the decision of the Court of Appeal." 1964 Report, at 15.

directly to Parliament through his annual report. At present he usually sends them first to the Cabinet or to a particular minister, and then later informs Parliament of what he has done. Some sticklers for the niceties of parliamentary organization criticize this on the ground that the Ombudsman is an agent of the Parliament and not of the Government. But the Ombudsman's practice does seem to secure quicker and surer attention to his ideas than if he simply dropped them into Parliament's lap.

Even when instant acceptance does not occur, the Ombudsman's proposals may give direction to later events. He has, for example, long urged that administrators should be required to give reasons for their decisions, and he has often developed the theme of due administrative procedure.[63] In doing so, he followed a path previously marked by the distinguished Swedish authority on Administrative Law, Professor Nils Herlitz. At first the Ombudsman's recommendations were quietly ignored, perhaps chiefly because administrative agencies advised they were impracticable. Undaunted, the Ombudsman patiently repeated his advice, which gained support in many private quarters. In 1964, after years of work, an official commission, appointed by the Ministry of Justice (on Professor Herlitz's suggestion) to study the desirability of an administrative procedure act, submitted a report embodying many of the principles the Ombudsman has urged. If a statute finally emerges from all this, it will not properly be attributed to the Ombudsman (who, indeed, would not himself claim credit), but it will at least perhaps have been hastened by him.

In the sphere of governmental activity, the Ombudsman may be said to resemble a law revision commission charged with noticing the need for changes in laws that do not constantly interest pressure groups, political parties, or the press. Earlier ombudsmen's efforts to humanize

[63] In 1964, for instance, he pointed out the desirability of higher authorities' giving opportunity for comment on decisions by lower administrative authorities. A person seeking permission to purchase farm land, as required by the Land Acquisition Act of 1955, has three chances to succeed, first by asking a local farm committee for the permit, then by appealing to the Agricultural Board from an adverse decision, and finally by asking the King in Council (realistically, the Minister of Agriculture) to review unfavorable action by the Agricultural Board. But, unless he makes a special effort to see the file containing a decision adverse to him, he is not apprised of the grounds upon which his application has been denied. The Ombudsman proposed that in the future an adverse decision should be fully communicated to an applicant, whose exceptions to it should be received and considered by the next higher level of authority.

Sweden's prisons furnish a notable example; even as recently as a dozen years ago a need was perceived for additional statutes that would bring scattered institutions within the reach of uniform rules. Statutory improvement of various aspects of judicial organization and administration may also be ascribed to suggestions by ombudsmen.

Without minimizing the ombudsmen's good works as law reformers, one must nevertheless conclude that their annual reports have been extremely minor forces in shaping Sweden's legislation. "Parliament does not sit up and take notice whenever the Ombudsman has an idea about statutes," said one veteran member, "nor does the Government. The ministries think they know what's what without his telling them." "That is perfectly true," another member of Parliament agreed, "but I would add that if the Government doesn't pay any particular attention to his ideas, somebody in the Opposition is almost sure to do so. That at least keeps the idea alive. Sometimes a suggestion the Ombudsman initiates might lead, much later, to a motion in Parliament that brings results. Taking a broad look at the matter, though, I would have to say that the Ombudsmen have been better suited to applying existing law than to persuading Parliament to enact new law."

Unfairness to officials. As has been described elsewhere in this paper, the Ombudsman has in late years initiated few prosecutions. Instead he has admonished officials who, in his opinion, have made mistakes. His annual reports, as well as the materials regularly available to the newspapers, identify the errant officials and explain why they have been censured. This practice, while seemingly milder than prosecution, has been strongly criticized. Civil servants, a well-known writer has said, may have to "stand . . . in the pillory not only for grave faults but also for minor lapses which are in fact more or less excusable—an example will be made of them in order to show how administive work should be carried on."[64] Since those in the pillory have not been tried and found guilty, the soundness of the Ombudsman's strictures has not been judicially tested. Some officials, noting that the Ombudsman's prosecutions are far from uniformly successful, suggest that his judgment may be equally fallible when he "gives a reminder." They question whether he should castigate an official whom he has found no cause to prosecute; they think he should keep condemnatory

[64] N. Herlitz, "Swedish Administrative Law: Some Characteristic Features," 3 *Scand. Stud. in Law* 89, 124 (1959).

opinions to himself, except in so far as they may be formulated so generally as not to bring shame to a named individual.[65]

The Ombudsman rather shrugs off these objections. His instructions from Parliament, he has observed, tell him to prosecute iniquitous, grossly negligent, and dangerous official behavior, not every picayune fault he may detect. The courts, moreover, will convict only when an official's mistake has been so blatant as to warrant imposition of punishment; so the Ombudsman thinks prosecution is a waste of everybody's time when in his own estimation punishment would be inappropriate even though an impropriety has occurred. Further, he says, an official aggrieved by the Ombudsman's treatment of him is always at liberty to complain to Parliament and to seek redress there.[66] Finally, the Ombudsman remarks that anyone who is outraged by having been castigated has only to say so—in which case the Ombudsman will "cooperate" by prosecuting instead of simply criticizing.[67]

In truth, the fault lies with Swedish law rather than with the Ombudsman. Neither the Ombudsman nor a disagreeing official can go to court to resolve differences of opinion, except in the unwieldy and unwelcome form of a prosecution for crime. Many official acts may be wrong without being criminal, just as the judgments of lower courts are often wrong (at least in the eyes of appellate courts) though rendered in the utmost good faith. The Ombudsman's effectiveness would be greatly diminished were he forced to remain silent about non-

65 For an especially well balanced presentation of this point of view, see Jägerskiöld (note 29), at 1088–1091.

66 This has occurred in a very few instances, never (so far as anyone can recall) with any response by Parliament, though perhaps the Ombudsman may have been asked questions in private. The Ombudsman's independence from parliamentary pressures is rather scrupulously maintained.

67 The Ombudsman's 1964 Report, at 115, discloses an example of this readiness. A prosecutor had promised a witness immunity from prosecution for tax evasion in order to induce him to testify concerning a fraudulent transaction from which he had profited. The defendant's lawyer questioned the propriety of the prosecutor's conduct. After consulting the Bar Association and the Supreme Prosecutor, the Ombudsman announced that the prosecutor, whom he named, had behaved wrongly, motivated by zeal rather than wickedness. Shortly afterward the prosecutor, in an article in a legal periodical, defended what he had done. The Ombudsman, remarking that the author's dissenting opinion perhaps suggested an intent to resume the practice the Ombudsman had found to be objectionable, asked whether the prosecutor would like to be prosecuted so that the courts could pass on the matter. Given a week to think about this generous offer, the prosecutor finally decided that perhaps it would be best to drop the argument then and there. For further discussion, see Lundvik, "Comments on the Ombudsman," in Rowat (note 14), at 46–48.

criminal wrongs. On the other hand, methods might well be sought to permit access to the courts in those instances when a conscientious official thinks the Ombudsman has erred.

One assuredly unintended consequence of the present system, with its harsh choice between prosecution and denunciation, is that it accentuates the timidity of some public servants. Although official excesses must be guarded against, modern Sweden like all other modern countries needs a great deal of official enthusiasm, vigilance, and devotion; if it were ever true that that government is best which governs least, nobody believes this to be sound doctrine today. A civil servant of highest rank and great experience, particularly in provincial administration, remarked in relation to the Ombudsman's fault-finding: "My observation over the years has been that the men who are trying hardest to get things done are the ones most likely to be criticized. We have suggested that the Ombudsman should look at a man's whole record before prosecuting or denouncing him, because that would give some basis for saying whether or not he really is a bad actor. But the Ombudsman says this is none of his business; he is interested only in the act, not the actor. The upshot of that is that officials who want to be sure not to get into trouble don't try to find the quickest and simplest ways to do their jobs, but the safest. I have rarely heard of anyone's being held up before the public as a horrible example because he was not being vigorous enough. Nowadays the civil service needs vigor, but it isn't really encouraged to have it."

A police chief, whose general attitude toward the Ombudsman was markedly favorable, asserted that the Ombudsman's naming policemen who had made non-criminal mistakes was unfair to them and socially unsound as well. "A policeman has to act on the spur of the moment," he said. "Of course if you are sitting at a table afterward, with plenty of time to look at the laws and regulations, you may be able to show that he didn't do things correctly in some respect. But the policeman didn't have a chance to make a long study; he had to react quickly. I heartily agree that the Ombudsman ought to be constantly in every policeman's mind, a part of his conscience. But I don't think that the policeman ought to feel that a heavy hand is always about to fall on him. I'm afraid that that is what is happening. Sometimes policemen are not doing their whole duty, not because of laziness or bad discipline or anything like that, but simply because they are playing it safe."

A lesser police official in another city repeated this thought, commenting that he had heard fellow officers say explicitly that they had not taken steps they thought appropriate because they were unsure about the Ombudsman's views. "None of those fellows worries about being punished for doing too little," he added, "but he knows he can get into plenty of trouble for doing too much."

A prison administrator remarked that many prisoners had been badly disturbed a few nights previously by the shouts of a fellow prisoner who had been denied a further dosage of sleeping pills; "when, next morning, I asked the guard who had been on duty why he had not tried to make the fellow shut up, he said, 'Why should I put my neck on the block? He is just the kind who would complain, and then I would be the one who had to defend myself.' "

The chairman of a municipal agency dealing with problems of alcoholism pointed to what he said had been a widely publicized criticism of a similar agency in a nearby community as an example of the Ombudsman's value. Then, almost as an afterthought, he remarked, "That criticism caused me a lot of trouble, though. My own committee became so cautious I had difficulty getting anything at all done, even the good things that needed doing very badly. The Ombudsman is necessary, but he also slows down the pace of our work. It is awfully hard to find the right balance."

The Burgomaster (a judge) of another city agreed that finding the right balance is indeed difficult. He put the matter this way: "The Ombudsman inhibits action by civil servants in much the same way as statutes influence citizens in general. Some citizens go right up to the line of permissibility that a statute has drawn. Others hang back, stopping far short of the line rather than run the risk of going across it. That is the way with officials. Some of them won't take a chance of getting into trouble and so they don't do things they probably could do—and should do—without being criticized."

Since the subtle motivations of human behavior are difficult to ascertain individually let alone en masse, these characterizations of official attitudes have not been scientifically verified. An effort was made, however, to ascertain whether the Ombudsman's admonitions have enough impact on the individual's career to justify regarding the admonitions with fear and trembling. Extensive inquiries lead to the conclusion that the Ombudsman's finding fault causes some temporary pain and perhaps some loss of self-esteem in most instances, but that it rarely leaves permanent scars if the offense was not willful.

The same high official who had suggested that the Ombudsman discouraged vigor in civil servants also remarked: "Most of my friends who have risen to the top jobs have been prosecuted at one time or another. With us," he said with a chuckle, "it is a kind of family joke." The head of a metropolitan police department, himself a lawyer like most Swedish police administrators, first noted that no policeman had been prosecuted for a serious fault during at least the past eighteen years, and then went on: "The press keeps such a close eye on us that a headline saying the Ombudsman has criticized the police is almost the equivalent of a prosecution. A criticism by me doesn't impress my subordinates nearly as much as one by the Ombudsman." But, he added, "when it comes to making promotions and assignments, I rely on my judgment, not the Ombudsman's, and I don't automatically lower a man's standing because the Ombudsman found fault with him." That kind of statement was made by a number of other high-ranking officials, including a provincial prosecutor, who asserted: "I would put it this way. A man who has been prosecuted or criticized by the Ombudsman is hurt in his public image, but not in his professional image. He might feel a bit awkward at the Rotary Club lunches for a few weeks perhaps, but his future career would not be affected."

Be that as it may, judges and civil servants talk much and freely about the hurtfulness of being included in the Ombudsman's list. Whether or not the hurt is as real as they believe it to be, their feelings about it seem to be genuine.

The Ombudsman as a protector. The Ombudsman serves importantly as a protector of the innocent as well as a smiter of the wicked. By finding no fault in 90 percent of the cases about which complaint has been made, he sets at rest what might otherwise be continuing rumors of wrongdoing. He may even be an insulator against the heat a hostile press has engendered.[68] His rulings serve to chart paths that

[68] In 1963 a child was atrociously murdered in Stockholm by a "sex maniac." The murderer killed again in similar circumstances before he was apprehended. The police were severely and frequently criticized in letters printed in the newspapers. Then the police master requested the Ombudsman to ascertain whether the police had been negligent or otherwise censurable. The newspapers, apprised of this, immediately

can be followed safely in the future. When he identifies inadequate staffing as a cause of undesirable delays for which hard-working officials have been unjustly blamed, he may help achieve needed organizational reforms; as a court president said, "Advice from outside often succeeds after we judges have failed to get what is needed." And sometimes, especially in his reports of inspections, the Ombudsman gives praise that does much for public servants' morale.

Ungenerously compensated for work of social import, civil servants in every country often hear themselves denounced and only rarely lauded. That is not the greatest possible inducement to take up a career of public service. While the ombudsman system is designed primarily to mete out blame rather than to give credit where credit is due, deserved protection and, occasionally, applause for the public's employees are desirable by-products of the Ombudsman's activities.

Circulation of the Ombudsman's views. The theory underlying much of the Ombudsman's work, especially when he admonishes and instructs, is that his views will be known generally within all ranks of officialdom. He prepares his opinions, as he has said, not in a peremptory way, but with fully stated reasoning. This, he expects, will not only inform the person whose fault he has disclosed, but also other officials, thus "preventing a repetition of the faulty procedure. In this manner, knowledge of the substantive law is disseminated due to the fact that all important decisions [by the Ombudsman] are accounted for in the annual reports. Most officials read the reports, at least as regards their own administrative field."[69]

Though the Ombudsman's annual report does indeed have an extraordinarily large readership, most officials do not in fact ever see it, let

---

ceased their agitation, leaving the police department in peace while the Ombudsman looked into the matter.

More than a year later the Ombudsman issued a 120-page report. He did find deficiencies in the organization of the detective work at the time and he criticized several police officers by name for not having adequately reported information they had received; their pieces might have fitted into a whole so that the main outlines of the picture could have been perceived more quickly by their superiors. But no cause for prosecution or further action was found, nor were any general recommendations made since the police department had already taken steps to improve its efficiency.

[69] A. Bexelius, "The Swedish Institution of the Justitieombudsman," 27 *Int. Rev. Admin. Sc.* 248 (1961).

alone read it. The report is printed at present in an edition of only 3,400 copies. Many of these go to Parliament, scholars, libraries in Sweden and abroad, journalists, and others who are not in the public service. About 2,000 copies are sent directly by the Ombudsman's office to judges and administrators. When one recalls that Sweden employs approximately five hundred judges in active judicial service, with two or three hundred others on temporary detail to special commissions, ministries, and the like; some hundreds of prosecutors; and nearly 200,000 civil servants, one must conclude that access to the annual report is not easily had by all.

This conclusion is readily confirmed by direct observations, of which the following are a random sampling: the report does not reach a regional administrator of social insurance, a provincial agricultural director, the acknowledged head (though not the ceremonial head) of a sizable city administration, police officers in general, local temperance and child welfare committees; many courts with plural judges receive one copy of the report; each provincial government receives six copies for the use of all its officials in all of its branches; in some offices in which the reports for the current and past years are displayed on bookshelves, they are in such unsullied condition that they have clearly never been passed from hand to hand. Furthermore, the reports had not been indexed for the past fifty years until, in 1965, an index was published for the period 1911–1960. Infrequent indexing makes continuing reference difficult even when copies are available.

This is not to suggest that the annual report remains unused. One can see, in some offices, indices prepared personally by conscientious readers; some copies are generously underlined and annotated; junior officials speak frequently of their impatience to see reports which their seniors are still studying. Since the Ombudsman's reports are not sprightly, being written in a rather heavy official style and without much appeal to the eye, the diligence with which many people read them is remarkable.

In the end, nevertheless, the Ombudsman's opinions would be little known were it not for their circulation in secondary sources. The role of the press has already been discussed. The newspapers can be depended upon to report the more flamboyant, easily understood matters. Technical rulings and, even more significantly, the generalizations that should emerge from specific cases must be circulated by more specialized publications. For example, a private organization reports some of the Ombudsman's decisions affecting social insurance; otherwise, they apparently remain unknown to administrators outside Stockholm. The National Social Board sends to eight hundred communal child welfare committees a circular letter which, among other things, informs them about current Ombudsman opinions, but without permanent form or indexing. A newspaper especially aimed at members of local temperance committees performs a similar service in connection with problems of alcoholism. A provincial agricultural administrator has no awareness of the Ombudsman's observations unless they lead the National Board of Agriculture to revise its standing instructions; in that event, the new instruction might (but need not) mention the reason for the change. A provincial prosecutor and police chief may dispatch bulletins and recommendations to local offices within his province, but he himself is scantily informed about current criticisms and suggestions concerning the activities of other provinces. Matters dealt with in the Ombudsman's inspection reports, but not afterward included in his annual reports, may never be known elsewhere. Thus, other provincial prosecutors were not apprised that one of their colleagues had been "given a reminder" to reactivate police training for wartime duties, nor did other provinces receive the instruction given to one of them concerning stays of execution pending the taking of an appeal to the King in Council. A provincial governor declares himself too busy to read the Ombudsman's report except as he sees bits of it in the newspapers, but he is "confident that the senior civil servants do read it and in time it trickles down to the rest"; he therefore sees no need to circulate the document or particularly relevant portions. A police officer of middle rank, in command of uniformed police in a large district, says that not much ever "trickles down" to him in any form from any source, but he does recall a recent circular letter from the provincial police chief. "I think that kind of distribution usually stops with the higher ups," he said wistfully, "though I enjoy reading about the Ombudsman in the papers now and then." The head of a major police force says that pertinent portions of the annual report are abstracted by a subordinate soon after it is delivered; the portions selected for further distribution are circulated among other members of his official family; if they call for instructions by him, he includes suitable paragraphs in the daily orders that are addressed to all under his command; for the rest, knowledge about the Ombudsman's activities depends upon a trade publication (*Swedish Police*) and "just plain gossip, which is probably the best circulator of them all." The National Prison Board, after careful study by the legal division, sends out to all its units a circular letter analyzing especially interesting decisions by the Ombudsman, but the circular does not purport to be comprehensive; when decisions necessitate a specific change in existing practices, the Board issues its own orders accordingly, since (unlike some other administrations) it has clear legal power to give binding directives to all branches of the penal system.

This partial catalogue suffices to show the chanciness that attends distribution of the wisdom the Ombudsman has produced. A better circulation system seems highly desirable, though the present somewhat haphazard methods have succeeded in producing surprisingly great awareness of the Ombudsman's work. What to a foreigner's eye appears somewhat chaotic may, indeed, merely be the normality of administration in a country accustomed to wide dispersal of authority.

Organizational problems. The Ombudsman performs all his duties with the aid of half a dozen law-trained assistants who work on a full-time basis, a few "specialists" who may be engaged for short periods to concentrate attention on a particular branch of administration, a handful of clerical employees, and a Deputy Ombudsman who was originally conceived of as a temporary replacement when the Ombudsman was ill or on leave, but who is now active throughout the year. The Deputy has entire responsibility for the matters on which he acts.[70] He is, in fact, a second parliamentary ombudsman who functions independently, but so much in the Ombudsman's shadow that everyone in Sweden prefers to believe he does not exist at all.

So small a group cannot supervise all officialdom. After several years of deliberation a special commission, appointed by the Minister of Justice upon Parliament's request, proposed at the close of 1965 that the workload be made manageable by assigning to the Military Ombudsman the responsibility of looking into complaints against judges, prosecutors, prison officials, probation officers, land surveyors, and policemen when investigating crimes. Retaining his former jurisdiction over the armed forces, the Military Ombudsman would simply

[70] Compare Lundvik, "Comments on the Ombudsman," in Rowat (note 14), at 48.

become a second Ombudsman, on a parity with the existing Justitie-ombudsman.[71] Each of the Ombudsmen would have a Deputy, who could replace him during three months of each year. As of the end of August, 1966, these proposals had not yet been approved by the Parliament.

The "personal touch" by a great father figure is what everyone wants to preserve. In reality, as earlier portions of this paper have shown, Sweden already has more than one ombudsman and seems to be no worse for the multiplicity. The Military Ombudsman created in 1915, the Chancellor of Justice, and the Deputy Ombudsman do ombudsman's work—as do, in a somewhat unheralded way, the public prosecutors throughout the country. This fact has rarely been looked squarely in the face. The ancient, more romantic conception of a knightly ombudsman riding forth to battle singlehandedly against every official wrong has prevailed. The 1965 proposals suggest that one knight may not constitute an adequate army in modern times.

For one who thinks in American terms, the ombudsman system seems a useful device for achieving interstitial reforms, for somewhat countering the impersonality, the insensitivity, the automaticity of bureaucratic methods, and for discouraging official arrogance. To rely on one man alone—or even on a few men—to dispense administrative wisdom in all fields, to provide social perspectives, to bind up personal wounds, and to guard the nation's civil liberties seems, on the other hand, an old-fashioned way of coping with the twentieth century. Ombudsmen, no matter how accomplished they may be, cannot replace all other mechanisms that make for governmental justice and wisdom. They must be viewed as supplementers of, not as substitutes for, legal controls.

[71] "Riksdagens Justitieombudsmän," *Statens Offentliga Utredningar 1965:64, Justitie departementet.*

|six|

Yugoslavia

Yugoslavia, with a population of nearly twenty million, occupies a territory slightly larger than the United Kingdom. Professedly "communist" in philosophy, increasingly "democratic" in practice, it recognizes that the supposed interests of the State do not preclude attention to individual rights as well. In recent years Yugoslavia, like the United States, has earnestly sought efficient means of examining complaints about public administration. This chapter sketches some of the measures that protect citizens against official abuse or mistake.

1|Political Structure

The Socialist Federal Republic of Yugoslavia comprises six republics —Bosnia-Herzegovina, Croatia, Macedonia, Montenegro, Serbia, and Slovenia—which are markedly diverse in language and tradition. Each republic, like each of the components of the United States of America, has a separate constitution and a considerable measure of governmental autonomy. Municipal bodies or "communes" exercise political power at the local level. Though varying greatly in size, all communes (numbering 577 in 1964) have the same legal status and organizational structure.[1] The communes in three of the six republics have grouped themselves into forty "districts" (as of 1964) to fit their

[1] The median population of communes in 1964 was only about 25,000. Only nine communes had more than 100,000 inhabitants, while 209 had fewer than 20,000.

respective economic, geographic, and cultural circumstances; the districts—communities of communes, as it were—provide cooperative governmental services with greater resources than a single locality can command.

A | Representative Assemblies and Executive Councils

Each level of government has an elected representative assembly.[2] The assemblies in turn elect the chief executive officials within their respective geographical jurisdictions.

At the national level, the Federal Assembly elects the President and Vice-President. The President designates an Assembly member to be President of the Federal Executive Council. The President of the Executive Council then proposes other assemblymen for election to that body, which also has additional ex officio members (including the presidents of the executive councils of the six republics). The Executive Council is defined by Article 225 of the Constitution as "the organ of the Federal Assembly which is entrusted with political-

[2] The communal, district, and republican "assemblies" are bicameral bodies; one chamber is directly representative of the electorate, while the other is a "council of producers," supposedly reflecting the interests of diverse economic groups. The Federal Assembly has had a more complex structure since the adoption of the 1963 Constitution. The Assembly consists of the Federal Chamber, representative of the entire citizenry; additional members are chosen by each republican or autonomous provincial assembly from among its own members, to keep an eye on ethnic and republican interests and to function as the "Chamber of Nationalities" in a few special circumstances, such as debate upon proposals to amend the Constitution. The four other chambers—the Economic Chamber, the Chamber of Education and Culture, the Chamber of Social Welfare and Health, and the Organizational-Political Chamber—are created by Article 165; their members are elected by the communal assemblies. Each of the chambers has 120 members, except the Chamber of Nationalities, which has sixty. The Federal Chamber has some independent powers, as, for example, in connection with foreign affairs (Art. 178). Each of the other chambers has autonomous powers of self-administration, inquiry, and debate, but when it comes to enacting legislation each of the chambers must act "on terms of equality" with the Federal Chamber. While the Federal Assembly thus appears to be a six-chamber organization, it might more accurately be described as an aggregation of bicameral bodies; the Federal Chamber works successively, as it were, with different partners according to the subject matter under consideration. A leading Yugoslav constitutional scholar explains: "Whereas the Federal Chamber as general political representative takes part in the main in all the jurisdictions of the assembly, the chambers of the working communities equally with the Federal Chamber examine matters and pass bills and other acts only in their jurisdiction." J. Djordjević, "Preface to Constitution of the Socialist Federal Republic of Yugoslavia," in VII *Collection of Yugoslav Laws* xi (Institute of Comparative Law, Beograd, 1963).

executive powers within the framework of the rights and duties of the Federation"; and it is declared to be "responsible for the execution of the Federation's policy" as established by the Assembly. But most members of the Executive Council are not, like British Cabinet Ministers or members of the American Cabinet, themselves the heads of governmental departments; they are coordinators, policy-makers, planners, and proposers of new legislation. Similar executive councils exist in each republic to oversee the public business of that governmental unit. The representative assembly itself performs the related tasks at the district and communal levels.

B | Administrative Organs

Apart from the representative and executive bodies just described, administrative agencies exist in each politico-territorial unit. At the federal level the Constitution mentions only two "state secretariats," the Secretariat of State for Foreign Affairs and the Secretariat of State for National Defense. But Article 233 contemplates that "federal secretariats and other federal administrative organs" will be created "to discharge the affairs of the state administration in the jurisdiction of the Federation." Article 235 provides that, within its own area of responsibility, each administrative agency "shall autonomously discharge affairs," subject to constitutional and other legal limitations. Under Article 236, the top administrative officials are chosen and are subject to being dismissed by the Federal Assembly, upon the Executive Council's proposal.

The same type of administrative structure appears at each of the subordinate levels of government. Each level is, however, independent of the others. That is, the administrators in even the lowliest commune are theoretically not under the command of a higher official in the capital of the republic or the nation; with rare exceptions, they are subordinate only to their own executive council or municipal assembly. This is true even though, as the Constitution directs, they may be enforcing federal and republican laws.[3] Each commune remains a self-

[3] Const. Art. 101: "The communal authorities shall attend to the enforcement of federal and republican laws and shall directly enforce them, unless the Constitution or law has placed their enforcement in the jurisdiction of the district, republican or federal authorities."

governing "institution of political authority" rather than an agent of some other authority.[4]

2 | Economic and Social Organization

Despite the elaborate governmental machinery whose outlines have just been briefly described, and despite social ownership of the chief means of production, Yugoslavia in recent times has left economic and social decision-making, to a very marked degree, in non-governmental hands. Political organs, according to the now prevailing view, should not themselves direct production or manage "creative social processes." These tasks, it is said, should be undertaken by so-called "working organizations," which are in essence self-managing cooperatives made up of the persons directly linked with an economic establishment or other activity.

Some of these organizations are very small; for example, every apartment house with three or more flats is autonomously managed by a "house council" elected by the tenants, although the house itself belongs to the State. Some, on the other hand, are extremely large. For example, the national railway system is a "working organization," to a considerable degree self-managed by those engaged in railroading. Other self-managing bodies include not only ordinary manufacturing and commercial concerns, but also organizations regarded in other countries as governmental, such as those that give postal service, provide water supplies, or execute social insurance programs for the aged, the sick, and the disabled.[5] A marked trend toward bigness can be discerned; as in the West, business in Yugoslavia is becoming highly concentrated.[6]

[4] J. Djordjević, "Introduction to the Local Government," in *II Collection of Yugoslav Laws* 10 (Institute of Comparative Law, Beograd, 1962).

[5] The minimum content of Yugoslavia's social insurance programs has been determined by federal laws, with room for additions by the several republics. The investment and protection of the insurance funds and the formulation of administrative methods and policies remain in the hands of the self-managing insurance organizations.

[6] An official newspaper reports the following, synthesized from 1964 financial reports: From 1962 to 1964 the number of industrial and mining enterprises with invested "capital" of a million dollars or less decreased from 2,317 to 2,012. At the

A | Relationships Between Self-Managing Enterprises and Administrative Organs

The organs of government are responsible for preventing the self-managers from becoming self-aggrandizers without regard for the general interests of society or in defiance of the principles of the established order. Moreover, government makes major decisions about the directions in which new capital is to flow (although current credit financing is in the hands of banks, which are themselves self-managing organizations). To a far greater degree than most Americans imagine, however, Yugoslavia, like the United States, relies on "private initiative," "free enterprise," and "competition" to get things done; it acts, as does the United States, on the hypothesis that entrepreneurial decisions will usually be in accord with the public interest and that considerable freedom from "regimentation" is good for business and thus for the community. So a "working organization," wielding purely economic power and having no capacity whatsoever to apply legal coercion, may make determinations that profoundly affect many interests—the interests of those who work in the organization and share its prosperity, its customers, its suppliers, and so on—unless and until government intervenes. Sometimes intervention is even more cautious than in the United States.[7]

In their relations with governmental administrators, organizations are in precisely the same position as individual citizens. They are subject to being regulated and their acts are subject to scrutiny to assure compliance with law.[8] Corporations and other organizations in

---

same time, the biggest enterprises showed a large numerical increase. One hundred sixty industrial enterprises held 56 percent of the total industrial capital of Yugoslavia, and four "giants" accounted for 40 percent of the total. One fifth of the enterprises achieved four fifths of the total income from industrial operations. A "further, more and more rapid concentration of the economy" was predicted. *Borba,* June 4, 1965, p. 5, col. 7.

[7] See, e.g., *Borba,* June 1, 1965, p. 6, col. 3, reporting that the Workers' Council of the Belgrade Railway Transport Enterprise had decided to terminate freight service at twenty railway stations on the main line because they handled too little business to make the service profitable. A new timetable also omitted mention of fourteen stations to which passenger service had previously been given. So far as appears, these entrepreneurial decisions required no governmental approval before or after the event; the Workers' Council giveth service and it also taketh it away, according to its own judgment.

[8] Compare L. Vavpetić, *Introduction to the Yugoslav Law on General Administrative Procedure* 21 (1961): "Even in relation to such organizations public adminis-

Yugoslavia, in short, resemble the private interests in America that find themselves from time to time facing administrators as opponents, as petitioners for subsidies or other aid, as critics of old policies, or as advocates of new policies.

B | Friction Between Enterprises and Administrative Officials

Whatever may be its virtues, nobody has ever contended that the free-enterprise system works perfectly, that individual enterprisers are invariably law-abiding, that every manager of business affairs is wise, or that short-term personal advantage is always subordinated to more enduring interests. Yugoslavia, again like the United States, has found that working organizations (free enterprises under a different name) sometimes behave antisocially—as, for example, when 55.5 percent of those included in a 1965 survey were discovered to be disregarding a price-freeze imposed to halt inflation.[9]

Yugoslavia has found, too, that perhaps well intended decisions may produce unintended undesirable results—as, for example, when organizations in which unskilled workers predominate have fixed their wage scales according to "the policy of equal bellies," thus eliminating the hope of higher personal earnings as an incentive to acquire skills needed in the enterprise.[10] It has also observed that regulatory con-

---

tration agencies must see to removing, by means of subsidiary legal intervention, possible social and legal irregularities committed by the organs of such organizations and resulting from the lack of social discipline. This function requires the agencies of public administration to observe strictest legality in their work, since the care for observance of legality is their main task."

[9] *Politika,* April 30, 1965, p. 6, col. 3. The Market Inspectorate inspected 1,354 economic organizations to check compliance with a price-freeze legally promulgated on March 22. Seven hundred fifty of those inspected were found to be violators.

[10] See e.g., J. Borkic, "Income and Production," *Borba,* May 26, 1965, p. 5, col. 1: In Bosnia and Herzegovina, university graduates have average earnings less than three times greater than those of unskilled workers. "The spans in earnings (not in starting bases), if connected with the results of work cannot and, even, must not be small. They cannot be looked at in a static way, from today to tomorrow, but from the standpoint of the extent to which they ensure future movement, development, and progress. Without a stimulation of qualified labor there can be no rapid modernization in technology, no incentives to the development of rationality, inventions, and so on. It is not difficult to make a correct ideological and political evaluation of the importance of stimulating work, particularly of skilled labor, in a country that is entering upon the world industrial stage, on which it claims its place. In fact, it is clear that without a more modern technology we will not be able to participate in the international competition for work, and ultimately there can be no rise in living

trols, introduced to prevent managerial abuses, are not self-executing, but require a good deal of policing in order to become effective—as, for example, when self-managing enterprises have maintained hiring and firing policies declared by law to be objectionable.[11] And it has noticed that the most enthusiastic adherents of free enterprise are not at all averse to dipping into the public treasury when prosperity eludes them; like American tobacco farmers, they want the profits but not the losses that self-management may bring.[12] Malfunctionings like these create pressure for governmental corrective activity. This may in turn produce further, although different, malfunctionings leading to demands that government keep its hands off business and that the bureaucracy be cut down to size.[13]

---

standards. Looked at from this angle, stimulation of skilled labor is something communists will have to think over. They cannot and must not be satisfied with the existing home peace and a compromising evasion of this problem. It is a comforting fact that certain big enterprises—the Zenica Steelworks, the Banovici Mines, and so on—have turned over a new leaf in this respect. . . . The organizations of the League of Communists cannot satisfy themselves only with the encouragement to 'common producers' and with the fact that the earnings of skilled personnel are neglected, since it is on their knowledge, skill, and interest that the advancement of technology and of the organization of work depends. . . ."

[11] See S. Mehmedi, "Irresponsibility of the Responsible Ones," *Komunist,* May 27, 1965, p. 4, col. 1. Unlawful discharges by enterprises in the province of Kosovo-Metohija numbered 674 in 1964, partly, but not entirely, it is thought, because of "a lack of law experts in work organizations." Even in large organizations with ample personnel, however, violations of the law occurred, sometimes with the specific approval of the self-management bodies. In one enterprise, ten workers were dismissed without notice and 648 persons were newly employed without observance of requirements, while two major executives were engaged "without even having competed for the job" as the law demands. For discussion of the supposedly useful but infrequently used grievance machinery in such matters, see A. S. Kahl, "Labor Law and Practice in Yugoslavia," *Bur. of Lab. Stat. Report No. 250,* at 54–56 (1963).

[12] See, e.g., *Borba,* June 2, 1965, p. 4, col. 1, reporting proceedings in the Republican Assembly of Montenegro, which heard the Republican Secretary for Finance discuss failure of industrial productivity to keep pace with increased industrial employment. He remarked also that certain enterprises which had been operating at a loss for some time "disproportionately and unrealistically increased personal income of the employed," instead of cutting wages and salaries; then the enterprises turned to the government for additional subsidies to offset their deficits.

[13] See, e.g., the Croatian Republican Assembly's discussion of the Executive Council's proposed "social plan" for 1965, as reported in *Borba,* Jan. 7, 1965, p. 4, col. 1. Deputies complained that not enough of the national income was being channeled into the hands of "work organizations," but was instead going into governmental organs. This, according to one speaker, "merely nourishes illusions that certain problems will continue being solved independently of the producers themselves." When the 1964 social plan had been adopted, he said, "the Assembly had clearly suggested that the oversized republican administration should be reduced to normal limits. However, this year again considerable funds are to be earmarked for the administra-

C | Inherent Limits on Self-Management

In truth, even if bureaucrats were to disappear entirely, the complexities of modern economic life might preclude absolute self-management. In most affairs of any consequence, many different entities manage various pieces of an interrelated whole, often without close attentiveness to what the other self-managers are doing.[14] When that happens, managing oneself may not produce the desired results. The City Transport Enterprise of Belgrade, for example, managed itself into enlarging its garage facilities and into increasing the number of buses available in that busy city. But a few weeks later it had to withdraw twenty-five vehicles from the streets and feared that service on some routes might have to be terminated altogether, because tires had become unprocurable. Its domestic supplier was unable to obtain needed raw materials. "We have told all the influential bodies—the Jugobanka, the Federal Economic Chamber, the Council for Communications—about the situation," the director asserted. "Besides, we have also concluded contracts in time, and that is all we can do." About two thousand tires had been imported by the government, but had been sold to intercity freight haulers instead of to local bus enterprises.[15]

---

tion, so that the impression is gained that the administration we have today is again being emphasized as indispensable."

See also *Borba,* May 22, 1965, p. 5, col. 1, editorially denouncing certain local governments for having blocked a large enterprise's decision to allocate fairly big sums of money to research work and exploration for new ore deposits. This was "an infringement on the independence of the given enterprise."

[14] See, e.g., N. Djurić, "Export Even to the Domestic Market," *Borba,* June 4, 1965, p. 5, col. 1: "Recently the director of a well established hotel enterprise, which takes in $400,000 annually from foreign guests, seriously criticized the supply system. There is no good quality meat to be had, he says, because all the good meat is exported. 'We cannot obtain first class fruit, and we dare not even mention this to the producer or merchant, since the goods available are immediately sold to another customer' . . . Much earlier, countries with developed tourist traffic, among them Switzerland, Italy, and Austria, established that sale of goods through tourism is a profitable business. Instead of exporting to the London or Munich markets, everything is exported, so to speak, to hotels . . . However, in exports there must be a continuous response to every market demand. Therefore it would be absolutely senseless to underestimate exports on account of tourism . . ."

[15] *Borba,* Jan. 15, 1965, p. 8, col. 1. The scarcity of foreign exchange is a problem with many ramifications in Yugoslavia. In the interview quoted above, for example, the director added: "The Enterprise mostly uses imported vehicles. Therefore it needs imported parts. Every year we are given money for that purpose. Last year we were

Moreover, while calling loudly for less governmental "interference," Yugoslav business enterprises often call equally loudly for more governmental "action" to produce conditions they deem favorable. This is usually done with honest unawareness that what is one man's "action" is likely to be another man's "interference." Thus, Yugoslavia's coal producers, wishing to mechanize the mines and to provide new housing for miners, welcomed a legislative inquiry into the funds of other organizations engaged in sales and distribution; the alleged prosperity of the coal dealers was "indicative of a siphoning of funds from the economy to the commercial network." The "action" the coal miners wanted (that is, tighter control over the middlemen) would of course be "interference" from the distributors' standpoint. At the same time, the mining industry was urging a sharp lowering of its contribution to social security funds and of customs duties on imported mining equipment, although, inevitably, other industries would then have to make higher payments to take up the slack.[16]

These are random comments upon, rather than a description of, business activities in Yugoslavia. Perhaps, nevertheless, they adequately suggest a cardinal fact of life in that country: economic power has been significantly dispersed, thus leaving in non-governmental hands the capacity to make important choices.[17] As a consequence, open clashes of interests remain possible, "coordination" is not rigid in every phase of existence, and controversy between officials on the one hand and "private parties" with substantial resources on the other is a socially acceptable possibility.

3 | The Yugoslav Law on General Administrative Procedure

The Yugoslav Law on General Administrative Procedure, which became effective in 1957, is an extraordinarily comprehensive effort

---

granted foreign currency amounting to 140 million dinars for the purchase of spare parts. This year, with more vehicles to maintain, we need about 186 million in foreign currency. The Jugobanka tells us we have been granted only about 23 million. If no change occurs, we are going to have to take still more buses out of service."

16 *Politika,* Jan. 9, 1965, p. 7, col. 2 (report from the Federal Economic Chamber).

17 See generally L. Sirc, "State Control and Competition in Yugoslavia," in *Communist Economy Under Change* 125–194 (1963).

to regulate administrative adjudication. It deals not at all with the making of new rules or the conduct of public affairs in general. But Article I(1) flatly states that all public officials, at whatever level of government, must "proceed according to this law whenever, applying rules directly, they decide in administrative affairs on rights, obligations or legal interests of individuals, juristic persons or other parties."[18]

The Yugoslav Administrative Procedure Act—YAPA—contains 298 articles, embodying 761 sections that seek to anticipate every problem an administrative adjudicator might encounter.[19] Apart from its details, YAPA declares a number of general principles that underlie all its sections. Among them the following seven bulk large:

1. *The principle of legality.* Decisions must rest on a statutory foundation; when a determination has been left to administrative discretion, "the decision must be made within the limits of the power and in accordance with the intention for which this power has been given."[20]

2. *The principle that citizens' rights, consonant with those of other citizens and the public at large, must be protected.* While parties to administrative proceedings presumably safeguard their own interests,

[18] The quotation of the statute is from the translation of Professor Leonidas Pitamic, published by the Yugoslav Institute of Comparative Law in 1961. The leading English language commentary on the statute is by an internationally respected member of the Belgrade University law faculty, N. S. Stjepanović, "The New Yugoslav Law on Administrative Procedure," 8 *Am. J. Comp. L.* 358 (1959). See also Vavpetić (note 8 above). Professor Stjepanović, describing the statute as the Yugoslav Administrative Procedure Act, has referred to it by the abbreviation YAPA, a practice followed in the present article.

[19] See, e.g., Art. 109(3): "Persons present at an action of the procedure must not carry arms or dangerous instruments"; Art. 180(3): "Dumb witnesses who know how to read and to write shall swear by signing the wording of the oath, and the deaf witnesses by reading this wording. To a dumb or deaf witness who knows neither to read nor to write, the oath shall be administered through an interpreter."

[20] Art. 4(2). As to this provision, Prof. Stjepanović comments: "Provisions granting discretionary powers do not always clearly define the limits and purposes of such powers, but these may be determined in each concrete case from the context, motives, and other elements of the relevant provision. A very important practical consequence of this is that in Yugoslavia a successful administrative suit may be started even against a discretionary administrative decision, and not only on the grounds that it contravenes essential provisions of administrative procedure, or of incompetence, improper evaluation and incomplete finding of fact, or excess of powers, but also on the ground of abuse of powers, when the decision rendered is contrary to the purpose for which such discretionary power was granted." Stjepanović (note 18 above), at 362.

YAPA also directs that officials must enable private interests to "obtain their rights as easily as possible," though the officials must see that rights are not asserted "contrary to the public interest or to the detriment of the rights of others." "Public interest" is to be determined by reference to previously announced legal prescriptions and directives.[21]

3. *The principle of "material truth."* All relevant facts—all facts "important for a lawful and correct decision"—are to be determined. The responsibility for discovering the facts rests on the official, even where through ineptitude or otherwise the immediately interested parties have failed to produce all the relevant evidence.[22] In appraising the evidence, the decision-maker must act on the basis of "his own conviction" after "conscientiously and carefully estimating each proof separately and all proofs as a whole and on the basis of the result of the entire proceeding."[23]

4. *The right to be heard.* Except in special cases authorized by law (chiefly those in which a favorable decision can be made without further proceedings), every party must be given an opportunity to present evidence and argument.[24]

[21] Art. 5(1). As to this, Prof. Stjepanović remarks: "A directive is a binding politico-administrative instruction of a *general nature,* not a concrete order or command governing an individual case; it must be consistent with law and other provisions and within the powers of the agency issuing it. A directive is binding on administrative agencies of the politico-territorial unit by whose representative and executive body it was issued, but it is not binding upon citizens and courts. Citizens may start a suit against, and competent courts may invalidate administrative acts issued in conformity with such directives if they are contrary to law or other provisions based on law." Stjepanović (note 18), at 363.

[22] Art. 6. Prof. Stjepanović observes that a decision "based on incompletely or incorrectly ascertained facts" may be amended, revoked, or annulled in a reopened proceeding (YAPA, Arts. 249–259), and may also be subjected to judicial review in an appropriate proceeding. Stjepanović (note 18), at 364.

[23] Art. 8. The quoted statement sounds much like the "substantial evidence on the whole record" rule enunciated by American courts and legislatures. See Universal Camera Corp. v. NLRB, 340 U.S. 471 (1951). The impression is strengthened by YAPA Article 159(2), which relieves administrative fact finders from observing formal rules of evidence, but not from attention to "proofs." The section adds: "Everything that is useful to ascertain the state of affairs and suits to the particular case can serve as proof, as are documents, witnesses, experts, and inspections."

[24] Art. 7. Other articles spell out a party's rights in greater detail. See, e.g., Article 143, which refers not only to presentation of evidence but also to cross-examining adverse witnesses. Prof. Stjepanović regards Article 7 as reflecting "the conception that a citizen, organization, or other party to a proceeding is a subject of procedural rights, not an object of procedure." Stjepanović (note 18), at 365.

5. *Independence in deciding.* The official who decides a case is directed to "establish independently the facts and circumstances" and to apply to them whatever rules may have been laid down. He must of course observe general instructions that guide the service of which he is a part, but he is not to be given (and he need not observe) orders about a concrete case.[25]

6. *The right of appeal.* The Yugoslav Constitution itself guarantees in Article 68 that decisions of "state organs and organizations which deliberate on [a person's] rights or his lawful interests" shall be appealable. The Administrative Procedure Act confirms that guarantee by providing in Article 10 that, in general, an appeal may be taken from an initial decision to the next higher-level administrative authority; no second administrative appeal is allowed, although judicial review may be sought when the single administrative remedy has been exhausted.[26] The Act also provides that an appeal may be taken from an administrative agency's failure to pass upon a case within the prescribed time limits; in such an event, the agency's inaction is taken as the equivalent of an adverse decision, appealable as a matter of course.

7. *Finality of decision.* A no longer appealable decision conferring definite rights on a party cannot later be "set aside, cancelled, or altered" except in highly unusual circumstances prescribed by law. Administrative determinations bind those who make them as well as the citizens whom the determinations affect.[27] Yugoslav scholars re-

[25] Art. 9. Prof. Stjepanović asserts that "independence of administrative agencies in administrative proceedings approaches the independence and autonomy of a law court in deciding civil and criminal cases." Stjepanović (note 18), at 366. While that statement no doubt reflects the aspiration of the statute, Prof. Stjepanović later adds a realistic reminder that "the extent and degree to which an officer conducting and deciding in administrative proceedings will be able to give effect to his independence depends on the degree of his professional qualifications, moral and political maturity and elevation, as well as on his personal legal status." *Ibid.*

[26] Articles 222–248 deal at length with appellate procedures. The appellate agency's power to amend a decision to render it more favorable to a party is very broad; the power to amend it to the disadvantage of an appellant is very narrow. The appeal is, in short, actually an appeal and not a de novo proceeding in which (as in Poland) the appellant risks an even less satisfactory result than the one against which he has protested.

[27] Art. 11. Articles 249–270 describe the circumstances in which a decision may be annulled or amended Prof. Stjepanović adds the comment that regardless of these provisions a decision which imposes an obligation on a party (as contrasted with one conferring a right) may be opened up at any time "under the condition that the new

gard this as a major contribution to stabilizing social relations and reinforcing legal security.

Other general propositions, spelled out by detailed sections of the statute, are the right of a party to be represented by an attorney or "legal proxy";[28] the impermissibility (with very narrowly stated exceptions) of conducting proceedings from which the public has been barred;[29] the impropriety of action by an official who is or might be believed to be biased;[30] and the duty to issue written decisions that disclose the reasoning on which they rest.[31]

How thoroughly the fine words of the statute are reflected in the daily round of administrative activities is unclear. Reality is not invariably governed by texts.[32] Yugoslav administration has been pushed ever more strongly into the hands of small local communities, many of which must in the nature of things lack personnel suitable for delicate adjudicatory work. The decisions of local officials, it is true, may be quashed by a higher authority on appeal. The local officials look for guidance, however, not to professional administrators, but to small-bore politicians who may or may not sympathize with legal limitations upon governmental power.[33]

---

decision shall reduce or alleviate the obligation of the party and that it shall not violate any legal prescription or right of a third person." Stjepanović (note 18), at 368.

[28] This right (conferred by Articles 53–63) seems rarely to be exercised. Article 13 provides, in any case, that the official in charge of a proceeding must himself "see that the lack of knowledge and experience of the party and of other participants in the procedure turn not to the detriment of the rights which they have in the procedure according to the law."

[29] Arts. 150, 151.

[30] Arts. 42–48. An official who participated in making a decision from which an appeal has been taken may not participate in the appellate proceedings. Disqualification because of relationship to the parties is absolute. A party may challenge an official for reasons set forth in the statute "and also when other circumstances render his impartiality evidently doubtful."

[31] Arts. 205–213.

[32] For example, Article 37 of the Constitution provides: "A maximum work week of 42 hours shall be guaranteed . . . In exceptional cases . . . the working time may for a limited period be longer than 42 hours in the week if the particular nature of the work so requires." Ever since the 42-hour week was thus constitutionally "guaranteed," Yugoslav coal miners have in fact worked a steady 53-hour week. The coal was needed, a personnel shortage existed, and so, for a "limited period" that has extended over the years, the Constitution has quietly been subordinated to the law of economic necessity.

[33] Compare Vavpetić (note 8), at 28: "Another characteristic of the Yugoslav state organization consists in a close horizontal connection with and considerable

In any event, unlike Poland (whose Code of Administrative Procedure covers much the same ground as the statute now under discussion), Yugoslavia has not chosen to stake everything on its administrators' uncoerced adherence to prescribed procedures. More fully than any of the other Eastern European countries, it has empowered its courts to pass upon "administrative contests" or, as Americans would say, to engage in judicial review of final administrative acts.

4 | Judicial Review

The Yugoslav theory of judicial review is straightforward. Administrators and judges alike are duty-bound to achieve a *legal* application of public power. The administrators, initially charged with effectuating social policies, have been authorized to issue prohibitory orders, to grant permits, and to use other appropriate means to the desired ends, but only to the extent and in the manner prescribed by law. The judges have the responsibility of deciding finally whether legal commands have been obeyed by the persons to whom the commands were addressed, whether those persons be individuals, organizations, or state officials. The judges could not perform their duty of being the arbiters of legality if administrative agencies were free to reach their own conclusions about what is legally allowable, or if court judgments could be re-examined by anyone other than another court.[34]

---

dependence of administrative agencies from the executive and representative authorities within the same politico-territorial unit. Owing to this connection, regulation of internal organization of administrative agencies of politico-territorial units, appointment and discharge of managing officers, caring for the necessary material means of administrative agencies and partly determining the legal bases of their activities, as well as direction of their work, especially political direction, are within the powers of representative and/or executive authorities of such politico-territorial units."

[34] Yugoslav judges are rather strongly entrenched, in a professional sense. Article 138 of the Constitution states that no judge shall "be called to account for an opinion given in the performance of judicial functions." A Disciplinary Court composed of justices of the Federal Supreme Court can censure or discipline lower court judges, but has rarely had occasion to do so. The Federal Executive Council, under Article 228 of the Constitution, shall "propose to the Federal Chamber the election and removal of the presidents and judges of the Supreme Court of Yugoslavia . . ."; the constitutions of the various republics contain similar provisions concerning the possible impeachment of Republican Supreme Court judges. No such impeachment has ever occurred. The "independence of the judiciary" is widely regarded as an

The Constitution provides in Article 159 that "the legality of individual final decisions by which state organs or organizations exercising public powers decide on rights or duties shall be judged by courts in administrative litigation," although federal law may "in exceptional cases" preclude judicial review.[35] Two aspects of this constitutional provision deserve special notice. First, the courts' power extends only to final decisions that have already determined rights or duties; that is to say, the courts are not in a position to enjoin an administrative agency from engaging in a threatened course of wrongful conduct or to command the administrative performance of a duty. The courts can annul or reverse a completed administrative act, and in some instances can even award damages, but they can rarely shape the act affirmatively.[36] Second, the courts review only the "legality of individual final decisions," which means that they do not have capacity to deal with administrative regulations or other dispositions apart from an adjudicated case.[37] When an administrative decision is based upon a rule or regulation, however, the courts can consider whether the underlying rule or regulation is itself authorized by law, since this is a precondition to the legality of the decision under review.

---

established fact, though communal court judges seem not to have achieved much prestige or to have earned widespread admiration; they are, on the contrary, often referred to sneeringly as "too much mixed up in local politics."

For further discussion of the judiciary, see F. R. Lacy, "Yugoslavia: Practice and Procedure in a Communist Country," 43 *Ore. L. Rev.* 1, 11–15 (1963).

35 Professors, judges, and administrators with whom preclusion of judicial review was discussed in 1964 were almost unanimous in stating that "about 90 percent" of all types of administrative proceedings are subject to judicial review. A notable exception has been determination of a voter's eligibility. A Supreme Court judge hazarded the guess that this and certain other exceptions might no longer be permissible, because the Constitution of 1963 provides in Article 150, in part: "The constitutional courts, pursuant to law, shall also safeguard the rights of self-government and other basic freedoms and rights established by the constitution whenever these freedoms and rights have been violated by any decision or action and other court protection has not been provided." Sentiment in favor of enlarging the area of judicial review has long been freely expressed by scholars and, indeed, by some administrators in Yugoslavia. In mid-1965 the Administrative Disputes Law was amended and supplemented to make explicit the judiciary's power to review all official actions that allegedly invade the "basic rights and freedoms" individuals have been guaranteed by the Constitution. See Official Gazette of the SFRY (Socialist Federal Republic of Yugoslavia), No. 21, May 5, 1965.

36 In a few circumstances, a court can itself enter a judgment on the merits, notably when an administrative agency has failed to observe a previous judicial decision in the same matter.

37 As to the power of the newly created Constitutional Court to pass on administrative regulations, see Section V below.

Despite the two limitations just noted, judicial power in Yugoslavia is broader than in many countries (though somewhat narrower than in the United States). The courts pass on the validity of administrative procedure as well as on the substance of administrative decisions, and they do so with apparent vigor. At the same time, as is true in the United States as well, the courts defer to the administrators' "expert judgment" concerning the merits of particular cases that could reasonably be decided either way. That is, the courts rarely re-try the facts of a case, but focus their attention upon the observance of procedural requirements and upon the administrators' adherence to whatever substantive norms have been laid down by law.

Judicial review occurs at a high level. A special chamber, or panel, of each of the Republican Supreme Courts decides the "administrative contests" relating to determinations by republican, district, or communal administrators. Appeal lies in limited circumstances to the Federal Supreme Court, where a three-judge panel also directly receives challenges against the acts of federal organs.[38]

Oral proceedings in connection with judicial review are rare. Appellants are sometimes represented by counsel, but need not be.[39] A Supreme Court judge recently expressed belief that many appeals are

[38] Article 239 of the Constitution provides that "the Supreme Court of Yugoslavia shall . . . decide on administrative litigation against administrative decisions passed by federal organs or organizations discharging public powers on the territory of Yugoslavia."

[39] As is true in most countries, legal advice is not always readily available to those who may need it most. Yugoslavia has adopted an interesting expedient in this respect. Once each week every judge stationed in a court of first instance schedules a free legal clinic. The judges not only give counsel, but also draw up petitions and complaints as may be required. The "clients" are said to number usually from five to twenty. The judges who advise their "clients" about possible administrative litigation do not risk the embarrassment of having to pass upon the same matters later when sitting judicially; the trial court judges have no official contact with "administrative contests," all of which go directly to one of the supreme courts.

In a recent interview, a member of the Federal Executive Council (Svetislav Stefanović) was quoted as deploring the present unavailability of "advocateship" and as having asserted that "it will be necessary to elaborate and improve as soon as possible the method for extending legal aid to our citizens through appropriate legal services in the organs of socio-political communities and organizations, to define more precisely and determine the place and role of advocateship as an independent social service, as one of the important forms of legal aid." *Borba,* April 22, 1965, p. 4, col. 5.

As a matter of fact, many communes have already set up legal aid services that include representation by professional advocates when litigation is necessary. These services are not, however, well distributed throughout the country, and they seem virtually never to be available in connection with administrative disputes.

prepared by lawyers, but are signed only by the appellants themselves because, he cynically suggested, "the lawyers don't want the income tax collectors to notice how many clients they are serving." Court costs are low. When an "administrative contest" has been filed, the court notifies the organ concerned, asks that the pertinent files be sent to the court, and invites the organ's answer to the appellant's contentions. The judges and their assistants then proceed to examine the case without further participation by those whom it concerns.

The volume of review proceedings is substantial. The six Republican Supreme Courts, according to informal accounts, annually decide in the neighborhood of 33,000 cases. Approximately 11 percent of all the challenged administrative determinations are flatly annulled. Another 24 percent are remanded to the administrative agencies for further proceedings, after the correction of errors the courts have discerned. The Federal Supreme Court passes each year on about 14,000 administrative matters, of which 2,000 come to it directly from federal administrative agencies, the remaining 12,000 being appeals from Republican Supreme Court decisions in administrative contests.[40] While the precise percentage of Federal Supreme Court judgments favorable to the complainants against official acts has not been ascertainable, some estimates run as high as 70 percent. Without accepting the accuracy of that figure, Yugoslav jurists believe that reversals and remands assuredly occur frequently enough to demonstrate the genuineness of judicial review.

Despite the large number of cases that do come before the courts, judicial review touches only a few of the matters decided by administrative agencies. Persons in a good position to guess, as it is necessary to do when comprehensive statistics are unavailable, say that administrators annually render several million judgments of the kinds judges might conceivably be entitled to review. If this guess be sound, only about one out of a hundred final administrative adjudications is carried

[40] A Federal Supreme Court judge who sits regularly on administrative appeals asserted during a conversation in early 1965 that "the great majority of our cases involve infringements of prescribed procedures" and that "the most frequent subject matter we deal with is social insurance of one kind or another, with housing problems coming next."

The volume of appeals from Republican Supreme Courts to the Federal Supreme Court may decline in future years. A recent statute (SFRJ No. 16/65) substantially restricted the right of appeal to the Federal Supreme Court in order to strengthen the doctrine of "republican supremacy."

to court. Moreover, judicial review extends (as has already been noted) only to orders entered in adjudicatory proceedings, and therefore does not touch the mass of other citizen-official relationships that may at times be less than satisfactory. Hence, while Yugoslav judges do indeed contribute importantly to fair administration, their work, standing alone, is an incomplete safeguard against administrative error or impropriety.

Before examining safeguards outside the courts, one must, however, take note of a new development whose impact is just beginning to be felt.

5|The Constitutional Court

The Yugoslav Constitution of 1963 has created a Constitutional Court, which, "as the safeguard of constitutionality, shall secure legality in accordance with the Constitution."[41] The Constitutional Court can pass on the constitutionality of all federal laws and regulations, can determine the conformity of republican law with federal law, can resolve jurisdictional disputes between federal organs and republican organs, and can decide how to protect "basic freedoms and rights established by the Constitution" if they have been jeopardized by "an individual decision or action of the federal organs."[42]

Apart from passing on specific constitutional challenges, the Court is also directed to "keep itself informed" about the possible need of affirmative steps for "attainment of constitutionality and legality," and it is told to "offer to the Federal Assembly its opinions and proposals to pass laws and to undertake other measures" deemed necessary "to protect the rights of self-government and the other freedoms and rights of the citizens and organizations."[43]

[41] Const. Art. 146. The tribunal is composed of a president and ten judges, elected by the Federal Assembly for a term of eight years, with the possibility of re-election for a second term but no more; during their terms of office, the judges are virtually irremovable. Const. Arts. 202, 243.

[42] Const. Art. 241.

[43] Const. Art. 242. According to a number of seemingly authentic personal accounts, Marshal Tito and his immediate associates in the pre-1963 government (which was far from closely confined by constitutional concepts) were readily won to the idea, unprecedented in Eastern Europe, of having a constitutional court with

Moreover, when the Constitutional Court determines that a non-statutory "general act"—that is, an exercise of delegated legislative power—does not comply with the federal constitution or laws, the court "shall annul or set aside the provision or act or regulation."[44] Thus the Constitutional Court may inquire into the validity of administrative programs, policies, and prescriptions, as distinct from individualized determinations already subject to judicial review. Because the Constitution sometimes makes generous promises, the Constitutional Court's control over both substantive and procedural administrative rulemaking is at least potentially extensive.[45]

Each of the six republics has created a similar tribunal to deal with questions related to its own constitution. Local or republican laws must conform with both the republican and the federal constitutions. As to republican constitutional questions, the republican constitutional courts have the last word; as to federal constitutional questions, the federal constitutional court is the final authority. In this, the resemblance to the American constitutional system is obvious.[46]

The Yugoslav Constitutional Court, however, differs from the United States Supreme Court in important respects. It is not an appellate tribunal at the highest point in a hierarchy of courts. It is not confined to dealing with "cases" or "controversies," but is expected to

---

the sweeping authority just indicated. One leading jurist recalled recently: "Tito and the others were easily convinced. Indeed, they didn't need to be convinced that the Constitutional Court was a good idea; they took to it right away. Where we had trouble was with the lawyers and with the members of the Supreme Court. They were almost impossible to win over, either because they didn't want constitutional litigation in any shape or form or because they wanted it to be added to the Supreme Court's jurisdiction. Many of us favored a separate tribunal because we thought it could concentrate on its single responsibility and would carry greater weight with the Federal Assembly, have more prestige than the regular courts."

[44] Const. Art. 247. In addition, Article 150 provides in part: "Constitutional Courts shall decide on . . . the conformity of other regulations and general acts with the constitution and law."

[45] See, e.g., Const. Art. 66: "Every arbitrary act violating or restricting the rights of man by whomsoever committed is unconstitutional and punishable . . ." Art. 67: "Every person shall be entitled to equal protection of his rights in proceedings before . . . administrative and other state organs and organizations which decide on his rights and obligations." Art. 69: "Everyone shall be entitled to damages for the unlawful or faulty execution of an office or action by a person or officer of a state organ or organization carrying on affairs of public concern."

[46] For a fuller discussion of federal-republican constitutional relationships, see J. Djordjević, "The Constitutional Courts of Yugoslavia," 14 *Yugoslav Law* no. 4, at 6 (1963).

deal with constitutional questions in the abstract, without reference to particular applications in specific instances. Its attention may be drawn to issues of constitutionality and legality not only by those immediately affected, but by the Federal Assembly or a republican assembly, by the Federal Executive Council or its republican counterparts, by the federal public prosecutor, or by the republican constitutional courts, as well as by the Supreme Court of Yugoslavia or other supreme courts "if the point of constitutionality and legality ensues in court proceedings."[47] Then, to top all this, "A point of constitutionality and legality may be raised by the Constitutional Court of Yugoslavia on its own initiative."[48] The Constitutional Court, in sum, does not merely rule upon the merits of contested matters, but is itself expected to promote attention to constitutional and legal restrictions upon governmental power.

At the beginning of 1965 Blazo Jovanović, President of the Federal Constitutional Court, told an interviewer how that court functions.[49] In its first full year of activity, the Constitutional Court received over 1,400 "petitions referring to individual acts" and over 150 "demands for evaluation of constitutionality and legality of various acts." As for the former, the Constitutional Court took no action because power to review administrative determinations pertaining to individuals is lodged in the regular courts. Hence, it simply referred "concrete cases" to the appropriate reviewing authority. President Jovanović remarked, however, that "the Constitutional Court of Yugoslavia does examine the petitions in these individual instances, not to make decisions about them, but to watch for trends." The Constitutional Court is said to have "undertaken a few successful interventions" in the fields of housing, labor relations, and social welfare to eliminate for the future certain general problems illustrated by particularized cases.

As to "normative acts" (general statutes, regulations, decrees), the Constitutional Court had been pleased by its own effectiveness. In fifteen instances, after the Court had taken preliminary steps to ex-

[47] Const. Art. 249. Article 149 imposes on all lower courts a direct duty to bring constitutional questions to suitable notice: "Whenever a court deems that a law which it must enforce does not conform to the Constitution, it shall propose to the competent supreme court to institute proceedings to assess the conformity of such a law with the Constitution."

[48] Const. Art. 249.

[49] The interview is reported in *Borba,* Jan. 1, 2 and 3, 1965, p. 3, col. 1.

amine constitutional questions, the bodies that had issued the possibly invalid normative acts withdrew them at once. "This is a very positive thing," President Jovanović asserted, "since the purpose of the Constitutional Court is not to hold as many public hearings as possible, but to eliminate violations of constitutionality and legality."

The Court did annul some acts after formally declaring them to be contrary to law, chiefly because they were ultra vires or because they were improperly retroactive.[50] Its decisions in these matters pertained technically only to the particular statute or regulation then under the Court's consideration. But President Jovanović noted approvingly that its rulings have in fact been applied more broadly when a number of governmental bodies within Yugoslavia have adopted similar laws. "It would be quite normal," he said, "that, once the Constitutional Court has assumed an attitude towards one of such acts, the other bodies should alter, that is, adapt their acts to the viewpoint of the Court, and we expect them to do so . . . The decisions of the Constitutional Court are morally binding also for other bodies that have passed identical or similar acts, since the decisions of the Constitutional Court express its attitude in principle towards identical cases."[51]

The republican constitutional courts have also begun to function, albeit with small caseloads.[52] President Josip Hrncevic of the Constitutional Court of Croatia has reported that his court received during 1964 more than a hundred petitions concerning alleged violations of individual or organizational rights, but had rejected them because they

[50] Const. Article 154 provides, in part, that "no regulation or other general act shall have retroactive force," unless a statute specifically contemplates retroactivity in certain situations. In no event can a penal law or regulation be validly given retroactive effect, since Article 49 states that "no one shall be punished for any act that before its commission was not defined by law or by prescript based on law as a punishable offence, or for which no penalty had been provided." And Article 154 adds: "Criminal offences and economic misdemeanors and offences shall be ascertained and the penalties for these acts executed according to the law in force at the time when they were committed, unless a subsequent law is more lenient towards the offender."

According to President Jovanović, the Court's own analyses suggest that "almost two thirds of auxiliary legal acts" have been marred by offensive retroactive features.

[51] The legal effect and enforceability of the Constitutional Court's judgments is discussed further in Djordjević (note 46 above), at 11, 15.

[52] The Constitutional Court of Montenegro, for example, made its first constitutional ruling on December 28, 1964, when it held that the residents of four small villages had been subjected to an illegal "self-contribution" in connection with raising funds for a new schoolhouse. "This means that all the citizens of these villages who paid self-contribution can ask for their money back." *Borba,* Dec. 29, 1964, p. 4, col. 7.

should have been addressed to administrative agencies or to other courts. Too many citizens, President Hrncevic asserted, "apply to this Court when they are dissatisfied with a regular court's decision or have failed to use an administrative remedy. Their belief that the Constitutional Court is a 'court above all courts' is not justified. No one—and that means the Constitutional Court, too—has the right to take over the jurisdiction of the regular courts of law or to alter their decisions."[53] Still, the Constitutional Court did have some legitimate business to do, though its content may seem strange to American constitutional lawyers.[54] Moreover, the Court had concluded, after examining official gazettes, that many local governments were enacting retroactive measures and were not publishing their regulations suitably.[55] The Court informed the Croatian Assembly and, according to President Hrncevic, "demanded that measures be undertaken for the respecting of the constitutional norms." The effectiveness of the Assembly's response to that demand has not been disclosed, although some reason exists for believing that the Assembly may have been too busy with beams in its own eye to warrant its worrying about motes in others'.[56]

Yugoslavia's experiment with constitutionalism is still too young to have produced conclusive results. The new tribunals, duty-bound to ring alarm bells when constitutional frontiers have been invaded, have not yet fully demonstrated their vigilance or proved their willingness to defend the boundaries at all costs. Even so, the very existence of the constitutional courts does tend to keep the spotlight focused on legality. Legal experts have been commissioned to review the large body of pre-1963 statutes and subordinate legislation to ascertain their conformity with the 1963 constitution. Hasty enactments of the past

53 President Hrncevic's remarks are reported in *Borba,* Dec. 31, 1964, p. 4, col. 2.

54 "During the next two months we shall have a number of hearings, to examine the legality of the Metkovic assembly's decision concerning application of the minimum amount of agro-technical measures, to examine republican laws relating to election and recall of the members of managerial bodies, and to examine an individual's right to choose a medical establishment and his own physician." *Ibid.*

55 Const. Art. 152: "Laws and other regulations and general acts shall be made public before they take effect."

56 President Hrncevic, referring to conditions in Croatia, is quoted as having said: "Our legislation is still incomplete and unharmonized. In a rather disorderly state of legislation, it is not always easy to find one's bearings and to say what is law and what is not. If we add to this the unskillfulness and the bureaucratic inertia of a certain number of the administrative and other personnel, this is one of the main causes of the poor work in preparing laws and protecting citizens' rights."

may be refined as a consequence of this work.[57] Furthermore, those who now promulgate rules and regulations will no doubt be more fearful of illegality than were some of their more impatient, blunter predecessors in the post-war period.

All this is to the good, but it would be absurd to say that every Yugoslav official has been so inspired, enlightened, or frightened by the Constitutional Court that problems of ultra vires acts are about to disappear. A senior Yugoslav jurist was much nearer to the mark when, in a recent conversation, he mused: "The Constitutional Court is making a good beginning, but it is really too early to know how it will end. We Yugoslavs live in a normative society, one that constantly makes pronouncements about how things should be. When it comes to constitutional principles, we need to remain aware of the difference between our aspirations and the way things actually are."

6 | Non-judicial Correctives

In Yugoslavia, non-judicial correction of administrative errors is not a trackless jungle, but a jungle so heavily crisscrossed by paths as to bewilder the wayfarer. Appeal to a second layer of officialdom is the first suitable step, prescribed by law and constitution. It is orderly, understandable, and widely used. After that, each to his taste. Some

[57] *Politika,* June 3, 1965, p. 6, col. 3, reports that the Legal Council of the Federal Executive Council, under the chairmanship of Belgrade University Professor Jovan Djordjević, had just completed re-examining federal laws in order to achieve constitutional compliance. The Legal Council proposed a permanent "Legal Institute" that would "study, much more thoroughly than so far, the way in which individual laws are being applied and the way the legal system established by the Constitution is being realized." The Legal Council also advocated codifying various laws in both the "public law" and "private law" fields in order to contribute to "institutionalizing" and "stabilizing" the legal system.

Federal Executive Councilor Stefanović has been quoted as saying that federal laws and regulations "in the field of internal affairs" had been revised in keeping with constitutional principles, in order to "make possible a more effective protection of the rights and liberties of man and citizen, and considerably restrict the discretionary rights of the responsible organs." He also remarked: "Of course, in other laws as well, for example, in the Law on Travel Documents, in the Law on Movement and Stay of Foreigners, and so on, we have endeavored, as much as possible at the present stage of our development, to safeguard and guarantee the process of democratization of social life and the position of man in it in accordance with the basic principles of the Constitution." *Borba,* April 22, 1965, p. 4, col. 5.

who still feel abused or unsatisfied by administrative action turn to their own "working organization," trade union, or other group to take up their cause. Others write to the newspapers.[58] Others prefer to lean upon members of the Assembly or upon a locally eminent personage. Some ask the prosecuting attorney to flex his muscles. Others, relatively only a few, may have heard about the Bureau of Petitions and Proposals,[59] and may decide to find out whether it really does accomplish anything. Some, unwilling to waste time with subordinates, go directly to the top of the power structure to beg that things be set right. Oddly enough, however, all the paths seem at present to meander in essentially the same final direction, namely, toward the lowest level of governmental activity, the commune.

A | The Public Prosecutor

In the days before Yugoslavia seceded, as it were, from the Stalin Empire, Russian administration provided an admired model. So it came to pass that post-war Yugoslav prosecutors were charged with the duty of enforcing law against citizens and, at the same time, like the Russian Procuracy, were supposed to ensure that public officials carefully applied state policies (and, thus, operated legally).[60] General supervision over public administration was not strongly and successfully performed, however, by Yugoslavia's prosecuting attorneys, whose prestige, professional qualifications, and perceptivity were highly variable. When Russian influence waned in Yugoslavia, nobody

[58] A sampling of topic headings will suggest the content of grumblings expressed in the press: Carelessness in a hospital; An institution's ignorance of regulations concerning providing food for children (*Borba,* Dec. 30, 1964, p. 6, col. 3); Judge criticizes Belgrade's failure to create juvenile disciplinary centers required by Criminal Code of 1960 (*Borba,* Jan. 4, 1965, p. 6, col. 6); Housing problems in Tutin; Crvenka has no coal; Shortage of stamps in Gujilane (*Borba,* Jan. 7, 1965, p. 6, col. 2); The railway station in Leskovac is dirty; Troubles over a village road (*Borba,* Jan. 15, 1965, p. 6, col. 2); Woman fined for no reason by railway official; A parcel which took eight days to reach its destination (*Borba,* May 22, 1965, p. 5, col. 3; p. 6, col. 2); Work of the Vrecar Assembly's committees and commissions should be open to the public; Wrong distribution of flats in Vozdovac (*Borba,* June 3, 1965, p. 6, col. 2).

[59] See Section VI(C) below.

[60] For discussion of the Russian prototype, see G. G. Morgan, *Soviet Administrative Legality: The Role of the Attorney General's Office* (1962); and see also Chap. 8 of this book.

argued strenuously that the procuracy system had proved its worth and should be retained despite its Soviet origins.

Although the public prosecutor has now been relieved of general supervisory responsibility, Yugoslav law still recognizes him as a guardian against defective administration. Article 223 of the Administrative Procedure Act authorizes the prosecutor to seek review of any administrative decision "by which the law has been infringed to the benefit of an individual or of a juristic person and to the detriment of the social community." Further, Article 261 empowers him "to present a demand for the protection of legality" when he thinks a nonreviewable decision has disregarded applicable laws; his "demand" must be considered by an authority competent to act upon appeals or, if no such authority exists, by the Executive Council itself. So, for example, a dispute concerning passport issuance (one of the matters the courts cannot review) could be reopened at the prosecutor's behest.

Authorities with whom the matter was recently discussed asserted unanimously that the public prosecutor's unofficial role is even larger than his official role. He can, to be sure, prosecute wrongdoing officials for committing crimes in office; he can protect the public interest by appealing; he can require that another look be taken at a supposedly closed matter. Those powers are, however, infrequently called into play. Above and beyond exercising his legal authority, he apparently often intervenes informally on behalf of citizens embroiled in controversy with administrators. One highly placed official, familiar with the world outside Yugoslavia, put it this way: "I wouldn't say that our public prosecutors are exactly like the ombudsmen in Scandinavia, but some of the prosecutors do listen to citizens' complaints and then follow up rather effectively, even though without any real power to command. They ask a question here, make a suggestion there, and their remarks can carry a lot of weight. When a prosecutor becomes convinced that an administrative abuse has occurred, he may quietly inform a higher authority about his opinion and then the higher authority is likely to use its power to change the result. This isn't written in the law. It isn't institutionalized. It isn't uniform, because not every prosecutor has close relations with either citizens or officials. But the prosecutors are definitely still in the picture, when it comes to informal controls over public administrators."

B | Legislative Bodies

Since the adoption of the 1963 Constitution, Yugoslavia's national legislative body has been more effectively interested in public administration than previously. Article 205 of the Constitution empowers the standing committees of the Federal Chamber to "require federal officers to explain the state of affairs in their respective departments of administration and to present reports concerning the enforcement of federal laws and other federal regulations and concerning other matters in the jurisdiction of the pertinent administrative organs, and to answer questions either orally or in writing, and to give other information and explanations." To effectuate that power, a standing committee "may hold inquiries and hearings and to this purpose may require data, files and documents from all the state organs and organizations."[61] Each standing committee has its own staff, or secretariat. The similarity of Yugoslav Assembly committees and United States congressional committees is strikingly evident.

The Yugoslav legislative investigating committees have acted on their own initiative, on citizens' proposals, or on the basis of newspaper articles suggesting the need for action. Thus far the committees have chiefly concerned themselves with looking into allegedly imperfect management of various public enterprises and with weighing the merits of proposed statutes. Although they have by no means been perfunctory in examining officials' administrative programs,[62] they have not been disposed to deal with individual complaints that administrators have flouted the will of the legislature or have adopted needlessly oppressive policies. Hence they have not been a major means of repairing errors or smoothing ruffled feelings.

61 Const. Art. 206. Individual Assembly members as well as committees have been given broadly stated powers of inquiry. Article 198 states in part: "Every deputy shall have the right to question the Federal Executive Council or the officers in charge of the federal administrative organs on matters pertaining to their work and on matters in the jurisdiction of the organ concerned." Article 199 adds: "Every deputy shall have the right to require information from the federal officers in charge of autonomous federal administrative organs. The officer in question shall give the required information."

62 See, e.g., *Borba,* Dec. 25, 1964, p. 3, col. 1: The Federal Chamber refused, upon recommendation of its Organizational-Political Questions Committee, to take up a new tax proposal of the Federal Secretariat for Finance because it contained "formulations which would render difficult the realization of the rights of the citizens in proceedings before the organs of administration." The Federal Secretary for Finance then agreed that the proposal needed redrafting.

Some leading Yugoslav scholars of public administration believe, nonetheless, that the committees are likely to evolve into "watchdogs" and to engage in "continuous legislative oversight," as have their American equivalents. The standing committees of the Federal Chamber, according to the scholars, already show signs of wishing to superintend the administrative process in the same sporadic manner as American legislators, who devoutly believe in the separation of all governmental powers except their own.[63]

Militating against that development is the Yugoslav practice of preventing the accumulation of seniority. If American legislative organization, with its insistence upon preferment for those who have had the lengthiest service, seems at times to be one of built-in obsolescence, Yugoslavia's system is assuredly one of built-in inexperience. Deputies are chosen for a single term of only four years, and may not be immediately re-elected to the same chamber in the same assembly. This, according to a prominent commenator, "derives from the idea of socialist democracy according to which as many citizens as possible should take their turn in deliberation in social affairs."[64] Giving everyone his chance to sit in the seats of the mighty has a certain surface charm, of course; but it does not make for a sophisticated legislature, able and willing to match its experience against the administrators' expertise.[65]

C | Bureau of Petitions and Proposals

Article 34(7) of the Yugoslav Constitution of 1963 provides that, as a means of achieving "social self-government," all citizens possess "the

[63] For examples of congressional participation in administration, see W. Gellhorn and C. Byse, *Administrative Law—Cases and Comments* 174–195 (4th ed. 1960).

[64] Djordjević (note 2 above), at viii.

[65] For a reflection of the legislators' lack of self-assurance, see *Borba,* June 2, 1965, p. 4, col. 1, reporting a Federal Assembly discussion of a committee report concerning the work of local representative bodies. The reporter gained "the impression that the deputies are 'shy' to speak about [the problems] and to make any definite judgments (the majority of them are new and were only recently elected, so that yesterday one could often hear them say: 'Excuse me, I am new and am not completely familiar with the matter')."

The same report indicates that 80 percent of one group of local assemblymen included in a recent survey were found not to read official reports; many of the assemblymen were frequently absent from sessions. One is inclined to suppose that a "professional" may be more diligent than an "amateur" legislator; but of course a similar survey among professional legislators might produce some disquieting statistics, too.

right to petition and present proposals to the representative bodies and other organs, to receive an answer to them, and to undertake political and other initiatives of general concern." Every administrative organ and every representative assembly has developed some sort of mechanics for receiving petitions, complaints, suggestions. To reinforce the stated right to petition for redress of grievances, the national Executive Council created its own Bureau of Petitions and Proposals, through which complaints and suggestions might be channeled by Executive Councilors or anyone else who might choose to use it. The director of the Bureau is appointed by the Council and is answerable directly to it. The executive councils of the several republics soon emulated the federal model.

The underlying theory has been that the Bureau of Petitions and Proposals will remain quiescent so long as anything remains to be done within the administrative organ immediately concerned. A complaint to the Bureau about a matter still susceptible of being considered or reviewed administratively will simply be referred to the appropriate administrator. But when all the appeals have been concluded and all of the administrative pronouncements have been made, those who are dissatisfied with the outcome may yet bring their petitions and proposals to a high governmental establishment.

Actually, the Bureau has not yet been generally recognized as the best means of gaining desired changes in administrative acts or programs. Its powers are scanty; its spirit is mildly educational rather than aggressively decisive; and its personnel have not been either professionally or politically distinguished. Hence one forms the impression that the Bureau of Petitions and Proposals is far from being the champion most likely to be sought out by an individual in search of help against the mass.

Nonetheless, the Bureau does participate in numerous affairs, sometimes with substantial results. During 1964, according to figures informally stated by the director, the Bureau dealt with approximately fifteen thousand cases of all kinds, the bulk of which involved dissatisfaction with particular determinations. Of these, more than three thousand had to do with labor matters, chiefly allegations that applicable laws had been disregarded in imposing discipline (discharge, suspension, demotion). About four thousand cases arose from public land disputes, disagreements concerning the value of property taken for public purposes, and so on. Another four thousand had to do with housing problems, particularly the ranking of names on the lengthy waiting lists of those wishing apartments when available. A large (though not precisely ascertainable) number pertained to pensions and social insurance. Complaints ran the full range—outright illegality, rude behavior, undue slowness, poor planning, faulty judgment.

A central office staff of eight and a field staff of twelve handle the cases as they come, with some degree of specialization according to subject matter. Having no power to command, but only to inquire and suggest, the Bureau first seeks an official explanation of the action complained against. It then usually arranges what it characterizes as a "public discussion" of the grievance. This is not, as the term might suggest, a mass meeting, but is a conference that may be attended and observed by anyone interested. Especially in the area of worker-management relations, the sessions as described by the director sound very much like an effort to conciliate. "A lot of things come out that can't be brought to a court's attention," the director commented during an interview in late 1964, "because the rules of evidence wouldn't allow it. We get the subjective feelings of the people involved, and when everything is out in the open, satisfactory results can somehow be brought about through the public discussions." The director's estimates indicate that "satisfactory results" were achieved in slightly more than 80 percent of the labor cases, in about a third of the social security cases, in perhaps 10 percent of the expropriation cases, and virtually never in the cases involving distribution of living quarters.

Such uneven consequences of the Bureau's intervention arouse doubt as to whether the merits controlled the outcome, since one can scarcely believe that labor administrators are almost invariably wrong-headed while housing administrators are almost invariably right-minded. Persons with whom the matter was discussed in Yugoslavia tended to feel that discrepancies in the results reached simply reflected the relative "hardness" of the various subject matters. In the labor cases, they said, it is easy to feel sympathy with even an undeserving worker, so agreement can be reached on "giving him a second chance" without anyone's admitting having been wrong. In the social security cases, Yugoslav law allows discretionary evaluation of so many factors (the applicant's participation in the war effort, his having been wounded, his having been or not having been a collaborator, and so on) that considerable decisional flexibility remains after all the legal elements of the case have been resolved; hence a settlement may continue to be practicable even when a determination has already been sustained on appeal. In expropriation cases, a little leeway exists because sometimes a satisfactory trade of properties can be arranged, instead of the outright purchase that had been contemplated. But when it comes to the housing cases, change is virtually impossible because the supply of apartments is too small, the demand is too large, and re-arranging the names on the waiting list will set off a chain reaction of complaints by those whose own place will be affected by any change.

To this somewhat skeptical account one must in fairness add that a distinguished and well informed Yugoslav scholar believes that administrators pay considerable attention to the Bureau's "gentle prodding." The Bureau, he remarks, "is reluctant to say to an official, 'You should not have done such and such.' Instead it asks, 'Why did you do such and such?'—which isn't very much pressure, but still does get results. Many officials are a bit insecure. They worry about their reputations. They think that the Bureau can get the attention of important people on the inside—after all, it is the agent of the Executive Council—and so the officials are likely to listen to what the Bureau wants them to hear."

A prominent judge agreed, and added: "Some of the complaints that go to the Federal Assembly and to members of the Executive Council shouldn't be ignored, but they are really too trivial to justify the Assembly's or the Executive Council's intervening in one instance after another. Take the matter of public servants treating citizens rudely. That is a big problem with us, a daily problem. It has to be ended, finally, by inner responsibility, by a feeling of what is the right relationship between officials and the public. Somebody has to encourage the development of that feeling. The Bureau can help, though of course the main reforming pressure has to be absolutely local, right at the scene, so to say. Anyway, the Bureau can do more than others in the federal government, simply by being in touch with officials more often. So when complaints of that kind go to the Council or to the Assembly, they are likely to be referred over to the Bureau. And the Bureau has been doing some good work to change the spirit of the public servants."

In at least one other respect the Bureau of Petitions and Proposals has contributed substantially to improved public administration. When numerous complaints have fallen into a discernible pattern, the Bureau has occasionally called upon a specialized body to propose changes in administrative procedures. An "Institute of Administration," maintained by the Republic of Serbia to perform the functions of an Organization and Methods Office, provides technical and scientific advice to communal, district, and republican administrative organs. Its contacts with the federal Bureau of Petitions and Proposals appear to be cordial and fruitful. The Bureau has sometimes asked the Institute of Administration to analyze repeated complaints concerning case-handling. The Institute, a service agency with no coercive powers at all, has then considered whether improved procedures or organization might eliminate future dissatisfaction of the same kind.

Recently, for example, slowness in making payment of child welfare allowances caused considerable distress. When the Bureau inquired into the circumstances, the administrators replied that payment had been delayed only because the applicants themselves had been tardy in presenting certain required proofs. The Institute of Administration, whose advice was sought at that point, was able to show that entitlement to the welfare payments could be fairly established by four documents instead of by the dozen or more papers the administrators had been demanding. Administrators and clients alike benefited from the simplified procedures that were thereupon adopted.

The members of the Executive Council are expected to—and, in fact, do—refer to the Bureau of Petitions and Proposals virtually all the complaints they receive, unless they are plainly referable to another organ. This not only relieves them of work, but also makes possible the Bureau's analyzing the flow of grievances and suggestions in order to detect general problems. Individual members of the Federal Assembly are permitted (though not required) to refer to the Bureau the complaints infrequently sent them by constituents. The Yugoslav League of Communists, which at one time dealt somewhat imperiously with government organs, no longer presumes to handle complaints and suggestions about administration, but routinely refers them to the cognizant administrative organ or to the Bureau of Petitions and Proposals.

7 | The Power House

The two most powerful recipients of complaints, the President and Vice-President, maintain their own grievance bureaus, wholly independent of the Executive Council's complaint-processing machinery. The cases that come to their offices—the power houses of public administration—outnumber those of the Bureau about three to one.

It goes without saying that President Tito cannot participate personally in action upon the nearly thirty thousand written complaints addressed to him in the course of a year; nor can he conduct approximately a thousand "oral hearings"—more accurately, office discussions—that occur each month in connection with individual grievances not yet reduced to writing. The Vice-President's lighter caseload—five thousand written complaints, and six thousand oral complaints annually—is still much too large for personal attention. Nevertheless, everyone inside and outside official ranks seems persuaded that the federal government's chief officials take a keen interest in grievances.

Both of these powerful men are aided by large staffs—"bureaus," as they are quite suitably called—whose work focuses on grievances. The presidential and vice-presidential assistants do not simply route letters to appropriate recipients. They inquire into the circumstances of most of the matters and follow through to a final determination. As a matter of fact, the Vice-President has himself become aware of an extraordinarily large number of individual complaints; a rather careful staff estimate, based on a random sampling of files, supports the statement that the then Vice-President had had personal contact with about a fourth of all the complaints, written and oral, that had come to his office during 1964. President Tito is more fully insulated.

The flow of essentially petty business into these two exalted offices can be attributed partly to past military comradeship as well as to present recognition of the national leaders' commanding stature. Yugoslavs who fought together to liberate their homeland have maintained strong ties of sentiment, often wholly unconnected with political ideology; indeed, the bonds among former Partisans sometimes irk younger people who mutter that "the old school tie," Yugoslav style, leads to preferment of valiant but otherwise undistinguished persons, to the disadvantage of the younger generation. At any rate, former comrades in arms are prominent among those who have written to the nation's chieftains.

The Yugoslav War Veterans' Federation is not, however, the sole source of presidential and vice-presidential business. A quick riffling of complaint letters in one day's incoming mail revealed some addressed to the recipient by his first name, others that referred to previous contacts, a few that might be regarded as coming from old constituents. Most, however, seemed simply to reflect the writers' belief that quick and just results could best be achieved by "cutting through red tape" and going directly to the top of the governmental structure. They pertained to almost every imaginable administrative activity and to a few that were unimaginable—as, for example, one that insisted upon an immediate personal wage increase and another that asked the Vice-President to help the complainant replace his wife, who had abandoned his two small children.

Incoming complaints in the presidential and vice-presidential offices are docketed at once. A preliminary examiner weeds out those that are unmeritorious on their face, and prepares a suitable reply for signature by a superior. Matters that appear worthy of further attention are referred to the bureau chief and, in his judgment, to his own chief. Considerable staff analysis of the pertinent law and facts may precede the bureau chief's next step. That step is almost invariably to request further inquiry and reports—usually, however, not by the administrative organ immediately involved in the grievance, but, rather, by the president of the representative assembly (republic, district, commune, as the case may be) within whose geographical jurisdiction the administrative organ is functioning. More often than not this is a municipal body; that is to say, the President or the Vice-President of the Socialist Federal Republic asks the president of the assembly of a small commune to look into the case locally.

A communication of this nature is not likely to be ignored, but a follow-up letter is sent if response is delayed. The results have rarely dissatisfied those who act for the President and Vice-President. If, however, feeling persists that the grievance has been inadequately dealt with, a matter may possibly be referred to the public prosecutor or to the president of a republican executive council, to exert supervisory power over unresponsive persons at the local level.

The extraordinary thing about the procedure is that the two exalted political offices infrequently establish direct contact with an administrative organ. In cases involving indubitably federal action at a high level, the offices may address themselves to administrators. Far oftener they remain exclusively in the channels of representative government. In fact, when a satisfactory conclusion has been reached, the complainant usually learns it not from the presidential or vice-presidential offices, but, at their suggestion, from the president of the local legislative body. "This is sound politically," a very important official explained recently, "and it brings the citizen into contact with government at the proper level, so that maybe next time he will know where to go when he has a problem. We are not trying to get credit for solving all the complainant's difficulties. If he has a deserving case, he ought to learn that he can get it attended to without coming here."

When asked why his office dealt with grievances at all instead of simply informing each grievant that his complaint had been forwarded elsewhere for suitable attention, the same person replied: "If that were done, the complainant would say, 'Just another bureaucrat.' That is the same reason we never tell a complainant that he should go to court instead of coming here. If a citizen wants to petition here instead of somewhere else, it is not for me to tell him he shouldn't have bothered me. Naturally, we can't personally investigate every little disagreement in every corner of the country; but we can make sure that someone does do so, promptly enough and thoroughly enough to satisfy us that the job has been done. That is *our* action on the petition, and it wouldn't be the same at all if we had simply informed the grievant that he should deal with another organ altogether.

"Another reason this office pays attention to grievances," he went on, "is that they point to difficulties in various parts of the country. We analyze them before passing them along to be investigated. They give us a basis for estimating social needs and for thinking about organizational changes. For a political man, analyzing these letters and understanding the problems they suggest are really essential. In a way, they amount to Government's closest touch with the ordinary people."

The citizens are justified in believing that the President and Vice-

President (through their respective aides) work quickly. A sampling of completed cases in 1964 showed none that had been in the office for longer than two weeks before being forwarded with specific directions for further action elsewhere; some bore the Vice-President's initials, showing that he had given them his personal attention, within three days of having been received; in "emergency cases," such as one involving a threatened eviction, investigation had been immediately initiated by telephone.

One who cherishes administrative structure may regard the Yugoslav practices as somewhat unsettling. They make for a certain formlessness and, in a sense, indiscipline because complaints may be "processed" in so many different ways and may engage the attention of so many uncoordinated authorities. In fact, the same high official just quoted acknowledged that many a determined complainant had written both to his office and simultaneously to other organs and individuals, all of whom had then become involved in handling the complaint duplicatively. When asked whether established channels might not make for efficiency and responsibility, he answered strongly: "We don't believe in closing any channel to anybody. If that is inefficient, well, it is just a cost of Yugoslav democratization and we don't regard it as a very high one."

8 | Concluding Observations

Yugoslavia and the United States are significantly alike in outlook, patriots in both countries to the contrary notwithstanding. Of course the countries have differences as well as similarities. Yugoslavia, self-labeled as "communist," deplores the Unted States because it is "capitalist," and vice versa. Adjectives aside, both countries are seeking the good life for their people and both are essentially pragmatic in their searching. In both Yugoslavia and America doctrinal orthodoxy frequently makes way for experimentation or, if one were to phrase the matter disapprovingly, for expediency. Neither country, as a consequence, is quite as pure as it likes to think nor as depraved as the other one believes it to be.

As the preceding pages have sought to show, Yugoslavia today places heavy emphasis on administering law fairly. The individual instance is regarded as important in itself, just as in America. Rough and ready justice, impatiently disregarding the risks of mistake or prejudice and slow to acknowledge committed errors, is not now acceptable in Yugoslavia as once it may have been.[66]

Whether the present protective mechanisms will produce the desired results is more doubtful.

A | Emphasis on Localism

Yugoslavia's current governmental thinking is placing ever greater emphasis on local controls, as a phase of "democratization." If administration is supervised by communes, so runs the theory, the people themselves will suppress the bureaucrats' domineering propensities. The concept of local self-government appeals strongly to almost everyone, not to Yugoslavs alone. The realities of human experience in nation after nation strongly suggest, however, that many of the most glaringly oppressive, most blatantly discriminatory, and most shockingly illegal acts of public administration occur at the commune level amidst an uncaring populace. Without reference to conscious corruption and favoritism, municipal governments have been notoriously susceptible to bossism, special interest pressures, and shortsightedness. Small administrations, rarely being able to avail themselves of developments in administrative science (specialized staffing, internal organization, mechanization, and the like), may lack the efficiency that reduces the chances of error. Municipal imaginativeness, moreover, is necessarily hemmed in by narrow geographical limits and by the demands of immediate problems; hence short-run considerations often lead local populations and their elected representatives to deal cavalierly with the future—for example, with guarding against water pollution, preserving natural beauty and resources, providing recreational facilities for coming generations, or elevating the standards of education.[67]

[66] Federal Executive Councilor Stefanović, commenting on recent legal developments, said: "In practice we must fight for the consistent application of the constitutional and legal principles and norms which guarantee equality before the law. It is on this plane that we have the most frequent case of flouting and disrespecting law, because of which our citizens rightly react and seriously criticize those who are called upon to render that impossible." *Borba,* April 22, 1965, p. 4, col. 5.

[67] In four of the six republics constituting the federation, personal income of schoolteachers is lower than the average wage scales. This reflects local indifference to educational needs. At the end of 1964 moves were afoot to force some federal

Yugoslav communes are not unique. They are not little idylls of democracy, pockets of purity in an otherwise naughty world. Local electorates and those who speak for them have no insights denied to others; often, on the contrary, they lack insights others possess. Yugoslavia's constant pressure to localize administration and its supervision, apparently inspired by genuine desire to return government to the people, may prove a dubious means of strengthening legality and safeguarding personal rights. It may, instead, simply encourage their fragmentation.

B | Belaboring the Bureaucrats

The stress on localism is matched by an almost obsessive clamor against "bureaucracy." Perhaps pre-war public administrators, perpetuating an arrogant tradition of the Austro-Hungarian Empire that had included much of Yugoslavia until 1919, tyrannized the citizenry instead of serving it. Perhaps post-war survivors of the civil service could not adapt their methods and attitudes to the needs of a revolutionary "people's government." Perhaps the desire to find suitable peacetime posts for the deserving veterans of the war of liberation necessitated deprofessionalizing the public administration. Possible explanations and justifications for a depreciatory attitude toward civil servants come readily enough to mind, but the continuingly bitter derogation of bureaucracy is more difficult to understand. In Yugoslavia "bureaucracy" is an exceedingly harsh epithet, not a description. It may be and is attached irrelevantly to almost any attitude the speaker wishes to deplore.[68]

---

regulation of minimum salaries for teachers, because communes persisted in denying the necessary budgetary support. See N. Pesić, "Measures for Improving Educational Workers' Situation," *Borba,* Dec. 24, 1964, p. 1, col. 3.

[68] For example, *Komunist,* May 27, 1965, p. 1, col. 4, speaks eloquently about the ethnically diverse structure of the population in Bosnia and Herzegovina—Croats, Serbs, Moslems. Efforts to overcome past hostility and divisiveness have been vigorous, but unifying the rural districts has been difficult because of lack of recreational and library facilities. The matter is worsened, the authoritative periodical adds, by "*bureaucratic* and careerist abuses of national color and national, that is, ethnic feelings." Another example: *Komunist,* April 29, 1965, p. 8, col. 1, extensively reports a Belgrade University students' question-and-answer session with Veljko Vlahović, Secretary of the Central Committee of the Yugoslav League of Communists. A student question: "What is the relationship between political and scientific criticisms?" Mr. Vlahović: "Political criticism, in internal relations, is aimed against

Without losing anything of value Yugoslavia may, if it chooses, make "bureaucracy" a term of opprobrium and may pin it, as a locally recognized badge of infamy, on anti-social tendencies. Then some other non-pejorative word can be found to describe large-scale modern organization for executing a public policy. At the moment, Yugoslavia seems to be doing more than engaging in that kind of semantic digression. It seems to be persuading itself that amateurism in government is in itself a positive good, while professionalism is to be watched with sharpest suspicion, if not to be abolished altogether. Brief incumbency in official posts has become not only a policy but a constitutional principle.[69]

A sort of gadgetry has begun to mark administrative organization, as though the accumulated experience of public administration throughout the world were an illusion and scientific management of large enterprises, a bourgeois fallacy. So, for example, in discussion of the federal budget for 1965, proposals were seriously advanced that the personnel of all administrative organs should be reduced by a flat 5 percent without any examination of each individual organ's activities and needs; half of the salaries thus saved would be divided up among the remaining staff members, while any organ that slashed its staff even further could then give the entire savings as a bonus to the survivors.[70] Instead of considering how to strengthen governmental

---

bureaucracy and all the obstacles which bar the way to the strengthening of democracy and self-management . . . By such an orientation, political criticism paves the way for scientific criticism, facilitates the process of freeing science from various forms of backwardness and conservatism."

[69] Const. Art. 236: "The federal secretaries of state, the federal secretaries, the secretary of the Federal Executive Council, and other federal officers designated by law shall be nominated and dismissed by the Federal Assembly . . . An officer who has held one of the enumerated offices for four years may be appointed to that office for no more than an additional consecutive four years if justified reasons so require. Upon the proposal of the president of the Federal Executive Council, the assembly shall first determine by a majority vote whether or not the reasons given for making an exception to the principle of limitation of renomination are justified." But the "principle of limitation" does not apply to President Tito, whom the Constitution specifically excepts from its application and who is therefore eligible to succeed himself time after time.

[70] *Borba,* Dec. 26, 1964, p. 1, col. 8. As of July 1, 1965, each federal organ was instructed by the Federal Executive Council that it should formulate a program truly reflective of "the substance, character and volume of the work . . . and that the professional structure of the personnel should be fixed accordingly . . . It was also stated that the funds for personal salaries should be so distributed that personnel are paid in proportion to their work and not only according to the estimated work at

units that render public services, important persons debate how they can be cast adrift as self-managing organizations.[71]

These remarks are not directed to the question of whether Yugoslavia correctly perceives its administrative needs; a casual visitor cannot presume even to guess which kind of government or non-government is best suited to Yugoslavia. The purpose of these comments is simply to suggest that administrative observance of legality in substance and procedure, administrative exercise of sound judgment, administrative sensitivity to persons as well as to programs pre-suppose *administrators*—men and women whose insights and aptitudes have been shaped by sustained experience or special training, or both. If destroying "bureaucracy" extends (as it seems in a fair way to be doing in Yugoslavia) to destroying administrators as well, securing justice will become more, not less, difficult.

individual places of work." *Politika,* June 3, 1965, p. 6, col. 1. No information is yet available concerning the consequences of attempting to put public servants on a piecework basis.

[71] See *Borba,* Dec. 29, 1964, p. 1, col. 1, reporting a plenary session of the Organizational-Political Chamber of the Federal Assembly, considering which activities —education? medical care? labor exchange? culture and the arts? scientific research? —should or should not remain within the governmental structure. The editorial commentator remarked at the close: "In connection with all this, it is necessary to liquidate the resistance which is being manifested, not only in the traditional 'bureaucratic mentality' of some people in the institutions, but also in the fairly strong étatistic concepts regarding the institutions; it is necessary to overcome petty-bourgeois and other negative and sometimes even reactionary tendencies which . . . are objectively holding back the process of further assertion of the system of social self-management."

seven

Poland

New societies—either those without an immediately relevant past (as in some parts of Africa) or those that have revolutionarily repudiated what they have been (as in Eastern Europe)—are unlikely to be instantly attentive to the niceties of administrative procedure. So many urgent decisions must be made and so few persons are empowered to make them authoritatively that deliberation tends to become equated with "bureaucratic delay," while efforts to contest decisions may be viewed as challenges to authority itself. Those who exercise power come to feel that their will, unconfined by external restraints, is the bedrock of the new society's order and that they, rather than those who cry out for "law and order," are truly upholding the values their society cherishes.

If the resulting administrative absolutism long remains, government perforce becomes fully dictatorial. Unchallengeable decisional processes may as often reflect whimsy, favoritism, or even corruption as they do principled adherence to prescribed norms. Justice to the individual takes a low place in the hierarchy of social values, because the quest for justice inevitably imposes restraints upon those who exercise power in the name of the state.

If, on the other hand, the new society grows beyond its uncertain beginnings, if it acquires confidence in its stability and its future, if it seeks popular trust and support rather than mere outward submissiveness to the will of a governmental elite, then means are sought to regulate public administration—not to curb the power of administrators to do good, but to curb their capacity to be despotic, erratic, or simply incompetent without being challenged. Bridling previously unbridled administrative authority is seen to be preservative of the state as well as of the individual human beings whose often conflicting and always diverse interests the state must somehow serve.

Perhaps unduly influenced by the political rhetoric of our times and the over-easy generalizations of editorialists, many intelligent Americans suppose that the peoples of countries in the "Eastern Bloc" are governed despotically, with small opportunity to voice (let alone to seek redress of) grievances. A study of administrative processes in Poland in the autumn of 1964 shows that at least in that member of the Eastern Bloc this supposition is ill-founded.

The present paper makes no pretense of describing or evaluating all the features of Poland's "people's democracy." Rather, it deals narrowly with the citizen's opportunity to challenge an official action that offends him. The means of protecting individuals' interests will be considered under six headings: the Code of Administrative Procedure, the right to complain to higher authority, the power of the Public Prosecutor, the press and radio, the Supreme Chamber of Control, and the Party.

1|The Code of Administrative Procedure

The new Polish Code of Administrative Procedure became effective on January 1, 1961.[1] In pre-war years and, indeed, after World War II Poland had nominally functioned under an administrative procedure law patterned after that then in force in Austria. Thus, unlike the Soviet Union, Poland had previously been exposed to the idea that

[1] Valuable English language discussions of the Polish law appear in W. Dawidowicz, "Administrative Procedure: Remarks Concerning Some Institutions in Poland," 30 *Rev. Int. des Sciences Admin.* 7 (1964); B. Helczynski, "The Polish Code of Administrative Procedure," 6 *Law in Eastern Europe* 38–77 (1962); J. Katz-Suchy, "Administrative Procedure in Poland," 4 *J. Indian L. Inst.* 359 (1962). The Code is available in an official translation into French, *Code de Procedure Administrative de la Republique Populaire de Pologne* (1961), published in Warsaw under the authority of the Council of Ministers. Discussions that led to the Code began as long ago as 1957. An official commission to draft the Code was created by the Prime Minister in 1958. It named Professors Emanuel Iserzon and Jerzy Starosciak as Reporters and Professor Maurycy Jaroszynski as Co-reporter. See J. Starosciak, *Prawne Formy Dzialania Administracji* (Warsaw, 1957).

persons immediately affected by administrative determinations should have some means of controlling administration.

With few exceptions, the new Code governs proceedings in "individual cases" involving the rights and duties of identifiable persons or organizations. It does not apply to the "normative activities" of administrative organs, that is to say, the promulgation of general rules that pertain to the future.

The Code begins with a statement of "general principles" which Professor Stefan Rozmaryn, chairman of the commission that prepared the new law, has characterized as not merely pious expressions of hope, but as binding directives to public administrators. Their content is admirable. For example, administrative organs must act only on the basis of law in force (Art. 4), must in all their proceedings take every necessary step to develop the relevant facts and end the matter with proper regard for both "the social interest and the legitimate interest of the citizen" (Art. 5), must conduct their proceedings in such a way that public confidence in official agencies will be strengthened (Art. 6), must safeguard citizens against disadvantage because of their ignorance of the law and to that end must provide necessary explanations and guidance for interested parties (Art. 7), must afford all parties suitable opportunity to comment on the evidence and proposals prior to rendering a decision except when summary action is necessitated by "imminent danger to life or public health or by the necessity of avoiding irreparable material injury" (Art. 8), must explain the reasons underlying their decisions "in order so far as possible to achieve compliance without recourse to coercive measures" (Art. 9), and must put their decisions into writing (Art. 11).

These generalities are given a sharper focus by specific procedural requirements, strikingly similar in their essence to those developed by American legislatures and courts. Problems of bias and disqualification of an official or an administrative organ are suitably treated (Arts. 21–24); the interest necessary to commence or to participate in a proceeding is spelled out (Arts. 25–28); methods of giving notice (Arts. 36–45), obtaining testimony and offering proofs (Arts. 70–81), and conducting oral hearings when required by law (Arts. 82–89) are prescribed. Records are not kept in the form of stenographic transcripts of testimony, but the proceedings are nevertheless suitably recorded (Art. 63) and the records are open to parties and their representatives, who may take notes and make copies if they desire (Art. 68). The administrative organ may admit into evidence "everything which can help to clear up the case and is not contrary to law" (Art. 70), which is not unlike what American judges have said is "substantial evidence."[2] The administrative organ must receive and must consider all the evidence in the case (Art. 71), though irrelevant testimony can be excluded at a hearing if, upon request of the affected party, the record shows what was excluded (Art. 88). The decision, when rendered, must show to whom it is directed, its legal foundation, whether and in what manner it may be appealed against, its date, and the full name and official position of the person who issued it. Moreover, if the decision rejects a party's requests in whole or in part, or if it settles a controversy between parties, or if it imposes obligations upon a party, it must set forth its legal and factual reasoning (Art. 99). Decisions once rendered cannot readily be rescinded or revised (Arts. 12, 127–142). Without further descriptive detail, one can fairly state that the Polish Code of Administrative Procedure embodies conceptions of administrative justice widely supported by non-socialist jurists.

Enforcement of these excellent provisions is another matter. Decisions by ministers and "central offices" are altogether unappealable (Art. 187). As to other cases, the Code prescribes a single appeal, in every instance to the administrative organ immediately superior to the one which made the decision, unless a special appellate body has been provided for a particular type of case (Art. 110). The appellate process is uncomplicated; the appellant must only express his dissatisfaction with the original decision, without detailing its alleged shortcomings (Art. 111). Moreover, the appellant need not discover the correct appellate body, since he files his appeal with the organ of first instance, which is then obligated to see that it reaches the right hands (Art. 112) and that other parties are suitably notified (Art. 114). The appellate organ can, if need be, receive (or direct the organ of first instance to collect) further evidence (Art. 119). In acting on

[2] International Ass'n of Machinists v. NLRB, 110 F. 2d 29, 35 (D.C. Cir. 1939), aff'd, 311 U.S. 72 (1940): "[I]t is only convincing, not lawyers' evidence, which is required . . . The evidence must be such as a reasonable mind might accept, though other like minds might not do so." NLRB v. Remington Rand, Inc., 94 F. 2d 862, 873 (2d Cir. 1938): The findings of an administrative adjudicator must be "supported by the kind of evidence on which responsible persons are accustomed to rely in serious affairs."

the appeal, the superior organ can affirm, reverse, modify, or entirely rewrite the decision under attack (Art. 120), and can, indeed, "render a decision less favorable to the appellant when the decision appealed against is contrary to law or social interest" (Art. 121). This summation of the appellate process shows that "appeal" is rather a misnomer. A party cannot ask a superior organ to pass upon his assignments of error in the proceedings below. He can ask merely that a second organ reconsider the entire case on the merits, and he must run the risk that the final outcome may be even less satisfactory to him than was the initial decision.[3]

Nor has any general opportunity been provided for judicial review once the "administrative course of instances" has been completed (when, that is, two levels of administration have examined the case). Social insurance controversies are referrable to a special court, manned by full-fledged judges. "Penal administrative proceedings," which have few precise American counterparts (they comprise such matters as police detention of disturbers of the peace at night), may also be carried to courts by a sufficiently resolute objector to the administrative action. Other disagreements between citizen and official remain wholly within the administration, no recourse to independent judges having been provided. This has not been unremarked by Polish legal scholars, most of whom have declared strongly in favor of judicial review at some stage as a necessary guarantor of administrative legality.[4]

[3] See Dawidowicz (note 1 above), at 10–11.

[4] Among the "Don Quixotes of legality" are such outstanding Administrative Law specialists as Professors Emanuel Iserzon of Lublin, Jerzy Starosciak of Warsaw, Waclaw Brzezinski of Krakow, Jozef Litwin of Lodz, and Marian Zimmermann of Poznan. A search through the pages of *Panstwo i Prawo* (State and Law), Poland's leading scholarly periodical in the field of law, reveals a number of articles in recent years advocating judicial review, none opposing it.

The significance of judicial review may be gauged by the outcome of cases considered by the High Court of Social Insurance. During the first quarter of 1964 the court acted on 2,441 appeals. Of these 19 were dismissed without reaching the merits 1,500 of the challenged decisions were affirmed; 222 were modified; and 700 were reversed altogether. Reversal or modification thus occurred in 29.9 percent of the appeals, a figure strongly supporting the value of review. And compare Katz-Suchy (note 1 above), at 363: "Practice shows that the securing of the rule of law in the judiciary is always much easier than in the every day activities of the administrative authorities. Bureaucracy often becomes the greatest enemy of the rule of law. It does not suffice therefore to lay down general provisions of conduct or provide a strict division of competence. It frequently happens that even with the best intention an official violates law for reasons which in his view are justifiable and apart from criminal intent abuse is sometimes practiced on the alleged ground of State interest."

The scholars' opinion is not clearly echoed in administrative circles. Some highly placed government officials privately expressed belief that judicial review of administrative legality would be desirable and that it will come into being in the course of time. On the other hand, a number of local administrators with whom the matter was discussed in 1964 held the contrary opinion; they asserted that judicial review would simply add to the time and expense of proceedings without in fact increasing the likelihood of sound conclusions.

Whatever may be the outcome of the debate over judicial review, the present lack of any external means of enforcing the Code of Administrative Procedure has created a certain pessimism within Poland concerning the Code's significance. A number of well informed observers, in and out of official positions, have characterized it as an aspiration rather than a reality, and have intimated that Polish administrators are for the most part ill-equipped to understand and apply the Code's commands. These critics say, too, that the persons for whom the Code's protections are intended are often unaware of their rights and therefore they do not adequately restrain administrators who cut procedural corners.

A necessarily brief study by a foreigner cannot produce conclusions deserving instant acceptance. My own impressions, for whatever they may be worth, are somewhat more favorable than those just indicated. True enough, the Code did not change night into day on the date it became effective. Many Polish officials, especially but not exclusively in small towns and rural communes, are poorly trained and educated. Poland lost 22 percent of its population through enemy action during World War II, being by far the hardest hit of all countries in that respect; not in actual numbers, but in proportion to national population, Poles killed in action or murdered in captivity outnumbered Americans 155-to-1 and Soviet citizens 6-to-1. Among Poland's losses were an even larger percentage of the intelligentsia and the professionally trained personnel from whom the ranks of higher governmental posts were filled; and among those who survived the war, some chose not to remain in the new Poland or were driven from their posts during the period of post-war revolutionary change. Hence official traditions have had to be created anew rather than merely revived. After the Code had been enacted, but before it went into effect, sturdy efforts were made in Warsaw to provide suitable training programs for officials at every level of government. But neither direct schooling nor instructional handbooks reached every administrator—nor, for that matter, did every administrator warmly welcome the new order of things, which imposed time-consuming and laborious "formalities" upon the somewhat rougher practices that had previously been acceptable.

A study of early experience under the Code confirmed fears that its provisions were imperfectly applied. The staff of the Procurator General (to whom further reference will be made in later pages) drew the files of 27,000 closed cases from 428 separate administrative authorities scattered throughout the country; the sample comprised 40 percent of all the cases decided by those agencies during the third quarter of 1961. Defects of one sort or another were found in 82 percent of the cases analyzed. In a few instances, indeed, agencies acted upon matters entirely outside their competence. Most of the errors, however, involved non-observance of procedural norms—as, for example, failure to give adequate notice of the commencement of proceedings (10.95 percent), failure to conduct required hearings before decision (2.57 percent), failure to incorporate all relevant documentation in the case file (5.78 percent), failure to fulfill formal decisional requirements such as providing information about opportunity to appeal or referring to the legal basis of the decision (16.9 percent), and failure to decide within the prescribed time limits (8.5 percent).[5]

This far from satisfactory beginning spurred further efforts by central governmental officials to achieve compliance with the Code. Under the auspices of the Council of State,[6] conferences occurred in 1962 with officials of the voivodship level—that is, with the responsible administrators of the provincial governments, of which there are seven-

[5] This information is derived from T. Kolodziejczyk, "Z Prawem na Bakier," 19 *Rada Narodowa* nos. 38 and 39 (Sept. 22 and 29, 1962).

[6] The Sejm (Parliament), elected for a four-year term, chooses from among its 460 members 17 to serve as the Council of State as a sort of collective head of the state, as well as the executive committee of the Sejm with power to act for that body when it is not in session. The Council of State also gives guidance to the "people's councils," the local representative bodies that function at various territorial levels.

In addition to the Council of State, the Sejm has nineteen standing committees that have special responsibility for keeping themselves informed about the work of the various ministries and central agencies of government.

S. Rozmaryn, *La Pologne* (Comment Ils Sont Gouvernés no. 8, 1963), is an excellent introduction to and description of Poland's governmental structure. And see the same author's *The Sejm and People's Councils in Poland* (1958).

teen plus five large cities having the same status. Each province has supervisory responsibilities with reference to the powiats (or districts, of which there are 391 altogether) and gromadas (or small communes, totaling well over 5,000) within its territory. The provinces were urged to undertake further intensive training at the lower administrative levels and this has in fact occurred, partly with the assistance of instructors supplied from Warsaw by the Council of State. The law professors of Poland, too, have contributed valuably to stimulating attentiveness to the "rule of law." Their former students, now in official posts, have begun to put their professors' views into practice.

While perfection is unlikely to occur in Poland (any more than in, say, the United States), considerable improvement is now discernible in administrative procedure. A 1964 survey of all types of cases decided during a current three-month period by the authorities in the village and rural communes, the districts, and the provincial offices of three widely separated provinces showed a laudable degree of compliance with the Code's requirements. In fact, observance of procedural niceties has now advanced to such a degree that attention can be paid to further refinements of administration. Thus, for example, the analysts found very slight disregard of prescribed time limitations in the current sampling, but they began to feel that administrators were prone to regard the permissible maximum of two months as an admissible minimum and were therefore taking far too long to decide some matters that called for quickly rendered judgment; hence effort has now turned to encouraging a discriminating sense of time's passage, instead of merely mechanical observance of a calendar. Similarly, some officials had seemingly become so absorbed in the Code of Administrative Procedure that they had lagged in their awareness of substantive law; as a consequence, one of the ministries directed officials from twenty-two localities to undergo further training in the basic laws they were under a duty to apply.

Sensitivity to the commands of the Code, all observers agree, is still not uniform throughout the country. Some of the provincial governments have been more education-minded than others, and this is reflected in the quality of local official actions. In Lodz, reputedly one of the best of these administrations, sixty teams of lawyers gave instruction concerning the Code between its enactment in 1960 and its becoming effective in 1961. The Legal Section prepared a commentary on the Code that made clear its application to various proceedings. The presidium—or, as it were, the executive committee of the provincial legislative body—from time to time has distributed among administrators a discussion of its action upon grievances recently filed with it, and thus all administrators have been encouraged to learn the lessons to be derived from imperfect case-handling in other official organs. While these instructional endeavors do not alone explain the favorable results in Lodz (Poland's second largest city, which is educationally and economically better situated than some other Polish voivodships), one may find significance in the declining volume of citizens' complaints that the provincial government receives concerning alleged errors by lower-level officials. In the first six months of 1960, 3,500 complaints of that kind were lodged, as against only 1,700 in the first six months of 1964. The complaints filed during the first half of 1964 totaled only 70.4 percent of those filed during the comparable period in 1963. Since the citizenry's awareness of and insistence upon its rights has grown rather than lessened during these years, the sharply reduced volume of complaints is all the more suggestive of increasingly effective, sensitive, and "correct" public administration.

2|Citizens' Complaints to Higher Authorities

As has been noted above, the "administrative course of instances" consists of a decision by a competent administrative body followed by complete re-examination of the matter by the next higher level of authority if an "appeal" is taken (or, to describe the process more realistically, if a request for reconsideration is filed). Since the second decision may still be deemed unsatisfactory by the affected parties and since, indeed, some administrative judgments of great concern to private interests may not be subject to hearings and appeals at all (for example, changing the location of bus stops and providing service to shippers and passengers), opportunity to complain further has been provided.

Aggrieved citizens have been given the constitutional right, without any indicated exception whatsoever, "to submit complaints and grievances to any State organ," and all officials are directed to deal with them "speedily and fairly" while avoiding delay or exhibiting "an indifferent or bureaucratic attitude" (Art. 73, Polish Constitution of 1952). This constitutional expression had been preceded at the end of 1950 by a joint resolution of the Council of State and the Council of Ministers.[7] This resolution not only announced the citizen's absolute right to complain to and about every State organ, but also commanded the chief of every official organization to schedule a weekly occasion when grievances could be personally presented to him without any prior formality.

Following that resolution and an accompanying instruction by the Prime Minister, all major public offices created special units to handle complaints. Pent-up dissatisfaction with things as they had been was instantly reflected in a flood of complaining letters and petitions. According to a highly placed official of the Council of State, a million grievances were addressed to that body, to the Prime Minister, and to the Council of Ministers in 1955 alone; many of these were undoubtedly duplicates, so that the total of individual complaints was not so high as the recorded total, but, even so, the volume is impressive. Perhaps the point should be made explicitly, however, that complaints pertaining to governmental operations in Poland include all the complaints that in the United States flow into private business offices. The children's clothing that shrank too much when washed, the plumbing in the apartment house that needs overhauling, the unsatisfactory meat supplied by the butcher, the undue delay in receiving the newly purchased television set whose delivery had been promised before the first of the month—all such matters are in Poland the business of the State, since the State has entirely displaced the businessman.

The new Code of Administration Procedure sought to add an element of efficiency without undermining the informality of the grievance machinery. Part IV of the Code is entitled "Complaints and Motions."

[7] The Council of State has been described above (note 6). The Council of Ministers is the supreme executive body, accountable to the Sejm (or to the Council of State when the Sejm is not sitting). It consists of the chairman, that is to say, the Prime Minister, five vice-chairmen, twenty-three ministers who head branches of state administration, and the Chairmen of the Planning Commission, the Small Production Committee, the Science and Technology Committee, and the Work and Wages Committee. The Sejm, or Parliament, is nominally supreme and can in theory overrule the Council of Ministers. The ministers are appointed and are removable by the Sejm.

Recalling the constitutional provision mentioned above, the Code adds that the duty to receive and consider "complaints" (about what has been done) or "motions" (proposals about what should now be done) rests not only on conventional administrative bodies, but also on State economic organizations and on "professional, self-governing, cooperative, and other social organizations" that deal with "individual matters relevant to State administration" (Art. 152). Disciplinary action is threatened against officers who handle citizens' communications slowly or formalistically (Art. 153). The Council of Ministers was instructed (Art. 156) to issue regulations concerning the manner of receiving and acting on complaints; this task was performed on October 13, 1960, even before the Code became effective.

Complaints in individual matters need not come from the immediate parties, but can be lodged by any person "acting in his own interest or that of others, and also in the public interest" (Art. 151). They can pertain to "negligence or an irregularity on the part of organs or their staff members in performing their duties, to violation of law or disregard of legitimate interests, and to undue delay or a bureaucratic attitude in disposing of matters" (Art. 157). Motions can be aimed at "organizational improvement, strengthening the rule of law, increasing the efficiency of work and preventing abuses, protecting public property, and better satisfying the needs of the population" (Art. 169). The grievant need not put a proper label on his communication; labeling is the duty of the recipient, as it is also his duty to see that the communication promptly reaches the appropriate hands if it has been misaddressed (Arts. 152, 161, 171), giving the communicant suitable notification of what has been done or advising him what he should do further in his own interest (Art. 161). The Code defines at length the proper channels through which complaints and motions should flow (Arts. 159–62, 170). Fundamentally, complaints are to be dealt with by the organ immediately superior to the one complained against; thus, for example, a complaint against a determination made by a district "people's council" (a local legislative body with considerable administrative responsibility) would go to the provincial people's council; a complaint against a minister would go to the Council of Ministers; and a complaint against the head of a central office would go to the minister in charge of that activity. A superior organ can assign a complaint to a disinterested subordinate organ, or to the superior officer of a subordinate official, with notice to the complainant that this has been done and with a direction to the assigned organ to report the action finally taken (Art. 162). Both complaints and motions are to be disposed of within two months unless special problems, of which the communicant has been notified, necessitate longer consideration (Arts. 167, 172, 173).

The question at once arises whether these and related provisions of the Code are simply window dressing. They add nothing to the citizen's legal rights except, perhaps, a statutory command to answer his complaint or motion within two months. The Code gives no assurance that the action taken upon grievances will be fair; the range of administrative discretion remains what it was before, and the means of forcing administrators to stay within the permissible range has not been amplified. This had led some commentators to feel that the machinery for bringing citizens' views to official attention has only psychological significance.

True enough, the grievance machinery has not added to the citizens' legal protections. Strong reasons exist, nevertheless, for believing that, in some areas of Polish official activity, complaints and motions are taken very seriously as useful means of avoiding injustice, elevating administrative attitudes, and regularizing the State's decisional processes.

In 1955, as noted previously, hundreds of thousands of complainants turned to the State's highest organs for redress against lower-level administration. By 1964 the volume of cases coming to the Council of State and the Council of Ministers had diminished dramatically. More and more effort has been made to strike at the causes of complaint, using individual communications as indicators of problems to be dealt with comprehensively. Responsibility to supervise subordinates in order to encourage sounder initial determinations has been pressed downward in the governmental hierarchy. The Council of State's staff spends less time than it did formerly on inducing corrective action and more time on advising people's councils in the provinces and districts about how to execute their duties properly. Repeated complaints about a particular organ or type of problem lead rather quickly to a general investigation. Efforts have been made to strengthen the Section on Organization and Law within each provincial administration, so that attention to problems of legality may be constant.

The Council of Ministers' Office of Letters and Complaints receives at present some 20,000 new cases yearly, a decline of 20 percent since 1961. These include discussions of general problems (such as what adjustments in working schedules should be made when "daylight saving time" commences in the summer), inquiries about the reasons for increased charges for electric power, and suggestions about the location of new industries, educational facilities, and the like. As for complaints as such, the Council is primarily competent to dispose of complaints against the presidium of a provincial people's council or against an individual minister. During 1964 the Office of Letters and Complaints dealt directly with only some 500 complaints and 6,000 suggestions or proposals ("motions", in the terminology of the Code of Administrative Procedure), the other incoming matters having been referred to ministers or other governmental units competent to consider them.[8] A staff of seventeen professional staff members, who have received law degrees or alternatively have had many years of administrative experience, are assigned to handle correspondence or to carry on discussions with the thirty-odd persons who come directly to the office each day. Their work undoubtedly does affect the well-being of individual complainants, though the interest of the office is likely to go beyond the particular case to the problem it suggests.

For example, several complaints by old-age pensioners concerning their difficulties in gaining delivery of gift parcels from abroad led to consultations with the Ministry of Finance, which then greatly simplified the methods by which gifts can be received without payment of customs duties. Similarly, three tenant farmers whose crops had been ravaged by deer complained when they were denied benefits under a statute providing indemnification against depredations by wild animals. Investigation by the Office revealed that the cognizant Minister uniformly withheld indemnity payments in the fairly frequent cases of this kind because the statute spoke in terms of granting relief to "agri-

[8] As has been found to be true in every country, some "querulents" write repetitively and irrationally about personal problems not within the domain of government at all. Such communications are not forwarded, but the communicants are informed that no action is being taken. A high official added, conversationally, "If somebody who once owned a factory that has now been expropriated were to write us and say, 'To the Devil with the whole system,' I dare say we would not regard this as a 'complaint' upon which someone would have to make a decision. But except for a case like that or one that reflects a pretty plain problem of insanity, we will either take action ourselves or direct the appropriate office to do so."

cultural owners" who suffered losses; since the tenant farmers were not "owners" of farmlands, the Minister rejected their claims though acknowledging that their crops had indeed been damaged. The Office believed that this was a too restrictive (though tenable) interpretation of the benefactory statute. Accordingly, it persuaded the Minister to adopt new regulations providing for State payments to farmers whose agricultural produce had been destroyed, whether or not they happened to own the underlying soil. In yet a third case, some fifteen owners of parcels of land near the center of a large city complained against denial of permits to build single family residences for their own use on the land they held. The denials had been motivated, the Office found, by the municipal authority's belief that the centrally located land would soon be needed for expansion of public facilities and should therefore not be devoted to residential purposes. In this instance the Office saw no reason to intervene beyond gaining assurance that other plots of land suitable for home building would be made available to the owners of the centrally located properties, if they wished to effect an exchange rather than merely sell their real estate to the city. While the outcome no doubt fell short of satisfying the complainants, the attention given their problem was by no means cursory and the result seems entirely consistent with land use principles that have evolved in non-socialist as well as socialist countries.

Similarly careful work seems now to be common within various ministries and provincial administrations. The Ministry of Agriculture, for example, directly disposes of something more than a thousand complaints monthly, pertaining to such diverse matters as land titles, soil classification for purposes of fixing taxes, obligatory delivery quotas, and assignment of vacant State-owned lands. The percentage of decisions favorable to grievants is low, perhaps as little as 3 percent overall. But close discussion of the steps taken within the Ministry strongly persuades one that the cases are carefully examined without an adverse predisposition. Moreover, the Ministry emphasizes the desirability of correct decisions at lower levels by dispatching twelve inspectors to various parts of the country to tone up subordinate administrations when complaints suggest that their work has not fully won local confidence. Further, grievances of a similar type from scattered areas are taken as a signal that substantive rules, policies, or standing interpretations may be defective. Incoming complaints are painstakingly classified so that their possible significance may be perceived, and a legal staff is charged with responsibility for re-examining existing standards of decision in the light of what the complaints may show.

The Ministry of Communal Affairs and Housing considers thousands of complaints annually; a staff of thirty professional administrators in the Bureau of Complaints is unable to keep abreast of the inflow. In one area alone—that of whether the occupants of a flat have more space than they need for themselves and should therefore share it with others—approximately one thousand new cases are filed every month. Each one involves difficult factual determinations and highly charged emotions, for the occupants are in essence seeking to defend their right of privacy. A Vice-Minister sets aside a day each week for discussing cases personally with those involved; this in itself serves to encourage care and tact on the part of lower-ranking officials, who are aware that resentful citizens have direct access to the top level of administration. In the end, the complainants prevail in about 10 percent of the cases considered.

In Poznan, Poland's fifth largest city and one of those with the rank of province, the presidium of the People's Council dealt with 1,904 complaints during the first half of 1964. After action by that body, only 24 complainants remained sufficiently dissatisfied to take the matter any further. In the somewhat larger city of Lodz, 1,743 complaints were received by the presidium during that same period. Of these, 744 were acted upon favorably, 759 were found to be groundless, and 240 were still under consideration at the close of the period. A member of the presidium, discussing these figures and noting the high percentage of favorable determinations, remarked: "We tend to be more pro-complainant than some of the administrators. After all, we have to have an open meeting with the electorate every three months, and then we have to account for what has been going on. We have to face the music. The administrators don't. It's as simple as that." The presidium and its professional staff members who look into complaints can in fact be freer than subordinate administrators to ponder equities (or, perhaps one should say, humanities) rather than legalities. So, for instance, one recent case involved a young mother and child, accepted as lodgers by an aged woman who had overlooked obtaining the required permit. The old lady died soon afterward and the young mother was then told by the office in charge of vacant rooms that she must leave, since she had no right to occupy the quarters she had been renting. The administrator who made that harsh decision decided correctly according to the applicable law. The presidium overruled him simply on equitable grounds, as it were, without criticizing the action he had taken.

The conclusion may reasonably be drawn that regularized processes for acting on grievances do genuinely add to the citizens' protections in Poland. Matters are being investigated quickly.[9] And to a marked degree they are being examined seriously, rather than being treated simply as papers that must be shuffled about in order to create a spurious impression of care.

That is not to say, however, that the grievance machinery is a perfect safeguard against stupidity, wrongheadedness, or worse. In the first place, the complainant outside of formal proceedings governed by the Code of Administrative Procedure has no effective opportunity to join in examining the issues his complaint may have brought to the fore. He delivers his grievance into the hands of officialdom and then hopes for the best. He petitions for grace and favor, as it were, rather than participating as a protagonist in governmental processes that concern him. Subjectively, he may feel like a contestant; objectively, he finds no contest in which he can join.

In the second place, the grievance machinery may mask as readily as it may reveal the problems that have begotten complaints. On every side in Poland, in office after office, one learns that the allotment of living quarters has engendered the bulk of complaints. Citizens fight for preferred places on the waiting lists. The shortage of available housing certainly has been and still is acute. Its inception is understandable. The devastation of Polish cities during World War II was immense. In Warsaw, 85 percent of the living quarters were destroyed;

[9] In Poznan in 1964, 1.4 percent of the complaints received were not finally disposed of within two months. Similar observance of time limitations was noted in other major centers and ministries. In Warsaw the People's Council, not content with the two-months rule, has created its own time schedule for making rejoinder to questions and complaints. Some must be answered instantly, others within a stated number of days related to subject matter. The Council's ire was aroused, and its new schedule was formulated, when it learned that a complaint concerning the breakdown of heating equipment in a State-owned apartment house during the winter had not been dealt with quickly; the official to whom the complaint had been referred had blandly explained the delay by saying, "I didn't think there was any rush. After all, I have two months for acting on complaints."

other centers of population suffered lesser though still gigantic losses —80 percent in Wroclaw, 55 percent in Poznan, 55 percent in Gdansk, for example. Poland's pre-war population was about 27 million. Despite the war-related deaths of 5½ million men, women, and children, the population stood at 24½ million in 1949. By 1961 the figure had grown to 30 million and by 1965, to well over 31 million. The combination of housing destruction and population expansion would have been enough to create a housing crisis. To these factors was added yet a third, namely, rapid urbanization. In 1949 only 36.2 percent of the Polish population lived in cities and large towns; in 1961 the figure had become 48.5; in 1964, slightly more than half. In such circumstances the lack of adequate housing is readily understandable. One wonders, however, whether steps to attack the problem were taken as rapidly and as forcefully as conditions demanded and whether concentration on procedural issues may not have diverted attention from the main question—much as, in the United States, three decades of preoccupation with the procedures of the Federal Communications Commission may have retarded inquiry into the wisdom of giving away radio and television channels to private entrepreneurs. At any rate, Poland's directed economy has not produced nearly enough new housing to prevent hardship twenty years after the war's end. As a consequence, Poles compete with one another to get and to keep the accommodations that do exist. Those who are disgruntled file complaints by thousands. Some succeed. Every winner in the struggle for living space is, however, matched by a loser, so that the sum total of social satisfaction remains static no matter how conscientiously complaints may be examined. More and more housing rather than more and more grievance machinery is needed. By great effort Poland manages annually to add about 300,000 rooms to the supply of available housing. Yet this just about keeps abreast of the increase in population year by year.

The third reservation about complaint handling is that the integrity and the utility of existing methods vary according to subject matter. An outside observer, unfamiliar with Polish realities, can state his own strong personal impression that the officials who discharge more or less conventional governmental duties are serious and honorable. At the same time he must report a widespread and often expressed belief among Poles that venality is commonplace in government circles; the contrast between Polish and Scandinavian attitudes in this respect is indeed striking. The usually offered examples of supposed corruption in Poland's high places almost invariably pertain to the State's economic enterprises. As to these, enough has appeared in the public press to support the expressed distrust. Whether the corruption is as general as some informants charge or whether it exists chiefly among those engaged in running the businesses that are elsewhere privately managed for profit, one cannot confidently say, though one can say definitely that evidence of improprieties on the part of "gentlemen of the law" is indeed hard to find. At any rate, when the public lacks respect for those to whom complaints might otherwise be submitted, the grievance machinery is likely to grow rusty from disuse. The grievance procedure presupposes that decisions are determined by the force of reason, and it has no value when potential users believe, rightly or wrongly, that external considerations will be the true determinants.

Finally, a word must be said about the continued grip of neo-Stalinist elements upon the State's security apparatus. Westerners sometimes believe that Communist countries are monolithic. In Poland, at any rate, this is far from true. Within the party organization, conservative and progressive elements compete for control much as they do in the Republican Party and the Democratic Party in the United States. At the moment in Poland a somewhat uneasy advantage lies with what might be characterized as the liberals, but, just as arch-conservatives in the Congress of the United States have retained some important posts, so also in Poland some key positions remain in other hands. This appears to be especially true in respect of police administration and related activities that are thought to affect internal security. As in the United States during periods when extremists have been in charge of "loyalty" and "security," moderate elements have been frightened into being silent when they should be outspoken. One can never say whether fearfulness is altogether justified, but it indubitably exists in Poland. And yet nobody complains very loudly about its causes.

Several persons with whom a foreign visitor wished to converse in late 1964 declined to talk in a hotel room lest listening devices be concealed there. In cafes they preferred to sit in the center of the room rather than along its walls. Two important officials indicated willingness to be interviewed, but not in their own offices where conversation with an unvouched for American would be too widely noticed. Experiences like these are not at all typical; most officials did talk freely in their offices, in hotel rooms, and at restaurants without the slightest nervousness, and other Poles to whom these experiences were recounted have expressed incredulity. Still, uneasiness remains sufficiently apparent to make one aware of its reality for many persons who nevertheless make no open complaint. One of the most offensive things encountered in Poland in later 1964 was incessant interference with the mails. Many letters addressed to or mailed by me disappeared without a trace; others were delivered after being resealed with tape bearing the cynical legend, "Received in a damaged condition at the post-office." To one who had received letters from the same correspondents in many countries without ever before having had the envelopes become unsealed, the high percentage of "damaged condition" in Poland was incredible. The censorship, moreover, is—like most censorship—unutterably stupid. A letter concerning decisions of an American educational institution's trustees was regarded by the censors as undeliverable in Warsaw, though a carbon copy of the letter reached the addressee in another city. A letter from Warsaw to an American agent concerning property matters in the United States was confiscated, apparently as a threat to Polish security. These were not isolated examples. Still the Poles, who are not an unusually reticent people, voice no complaint—and this despite Article 74(2) of the Polish Constitution, which in specific terms guarantees the privacy of the mails. When an outspoken Communist was asked to comment, he shrugged his shoulders and replied: "We Poles are very busy people, you see. We are far too busy to write letters complaining about things we know aren't going to be changed anyway." Another high official was asked to help arrange an appointment with someone in the Ministry of Internal Affairs, so that inquiry could be made concerning the handling of complaints against uniformed policemen (not the secret police). He strongly argued against making the effort, believing that it would be unsuccessful in any event and adding, "Even if they did give you an appointment, they wouldn't satisfy your curiosity. But the very fact that you were curious would make them actively curious about you, and you might find some unexpected difficulties after that."[10]

None of this is meant to suggest that Poland has reverted to being a police state. The contrary is true, for since Stalinism was ousted in 1956, the stress on legality has meaningfully enhanced personal security. What has been said is, merely, that many Poles are still unconvinced that, as the Constitution assures them, they may freely and safely complain about any and all governmental behavior of which they disapprove.

3|The Prokuratura

The prokuratura, or procuracy, is the office of the public prosecutor. Its province is much wider than that of an American district attorney or prosecuting attorney, whose function it is to conduct legal proceedings against alleged violators of penal statutes. The prokuratura, by contrast, is charged with the duty of achieving legality, not only on the part of citizens but on the part of the state, and not only in respect of criminal law as such but in respect of the legal system as a whole. At the head of the prokuratura is the Procurator General (or General Public Prosecutor), appointed by the Council of State and removable by it alone. Formal removal has never occurred, though one Procurator General is said to have been quietly nudged out of office. In any event, he is in theory an entirely free agent. He in turn names procurators (public prosecutors) throughout the nation, those who serve in his own office in the capital as well as those who serve in the lowliest district, so that the procurator is everywhere at least hypothetically immune from the local political pressures that might be mobilized by officials whose acts he scrutinizes. The system was inspired by the Soviet Union's example. Whether it works well in Poland is an issue

[10] Information subsequently received suggests that the Ministry of Internal Affairs would probably not have been the appropriate place in which to inquire, in any event. Complaints against uniformed police are governed by the Militia Act of 1955 (Dekret o milicji obywatelskiej) and by the Order of the Council of Ministers, published in *Monitor Polski* no. 19 (1955). These vest control over the "militia" in the presidiums of People's Councils. A citizen's complaint against a policeman is referred to the commanding officer of the province or district, to be investigated. The commander must inform the presidium about the action taken on each complaint.

concerning which Poles themselves sharply disagree. On balance the prokuratura seems to have substantial accomplishments to its credit, but it is far from being as strong a shield against official disregard of citizens' rights as theory makes it out to be.

The duty of the public prosecutor to protect the rule of law against official infraction was enunciated in the Constitution itself; Article 54 states that the Procurator General is (among other things) "to guard the people's rule of law . . . and to assure respect for citizens' rights." A statute enacted on July 20, 1950,[11] authorized and directed the prokuratura to watch over the legality of administrative acts other than those performed by the State's supreme organs. To that end the prokuratura was empowered to call for information about the conduct of public business, to participate in meetings of all people's councils and their administrative agencies, to instruct superior officers to control the acts of officers subordinate to them, and, even, to participate in administrative proceedings that had not yet been concluded.

The Code of Administrative Procedure, building on this statutory base, asserts that the procurator has the right to ask the competent administrative organ to commence proceedings looking toward elimination of an illegal condition (Art. 143). He may participate in an administrative proceeding at any stage "in order to assure that the procedure and the disposition of the matter conform to law" (Art. 144). Where a final decision has already been rendered, he may ask a superior administrative organ to reopen the proceedings or to force an amendment of the decision in defined circumstances (Art. 145). Action on such a request must be taken within thirty days (Art. 146). and meanwhile the superior organ may and in practice usually does suspend operation of the challenged decision (Art. 148). If a matter is still subject to appeal, the procurator may take an appeal with the same rights as are enjoyed by the immediate parties (Art. 149). The Procurator General, but not his subordinates, may make respresentations even to the highest organs of state administration, which are instructed to examine the objections voiced by him and to respond to them promptly (Art. 150).

These seem on the surface to be formidable powers. One might suppose that persons who think their rights have been trampled upon

[11] Procurator Organization Act, [1950] *Dziennik Ustaw P.R.L.* no. 38 (Poland).

by despotic bureaucrats would direct their complaints to the prokuratura, in the hope that that awesome body would spring to action in their behalf. In fact, the prokuratura does not appear to be an extremely active watchdog.

The reasons are various. At the district (powiat) level, everyone agrees that many offices are simply inadequately staffed; normal criminal law enforcement keeps the district attorneys fully occupied; they are too busy to participate in what may be protracted administrative proceedings or to learn about all the laws and regulations that bear on questions of legality. Furthermore, as one official candidly remarked, "A young man can make a name for himself by demonstrating his brilliance in the course of trying a criminal case. But how can he show how brilliant he is in the section of general supervision? Finding good men for the district prosecutor's offices is a hard job, at best. Finding them for the work of supervising administration has just been impossible."

Even so, many persons agreed during conversations in 1964 that district prosecutors do accomplish useful results in behalf of individual complainants. This may be done almost casually, perhaps by a telephone call while the complainant is still present in the prosecutor's office. Informal intercession of this type is not revealed by statistical tables, but it may nonetheless be a valuable protection against slovenly administration in areas remote from central supervision.

The prokuratura does have a "Section of General Supervision" in each of the provincial offices and in the national office. "General Supervision" is somewhat a misnomer, for no one of the offices is sufficiently staffed to undertake truly comprehensive oversight of public administration. A senior officer commented: "Understaffing of the prokuratura is a fact of life at all levels, but if the prokuratura were to try to supervise the legality of everything that is done in every field of government (and that means just about everything in this country), then the staff would have to be limitless." In most of the provincial offices the staff of this section consists of six or seven attorneys. In the national office, the available staff is only slightly larger. Instead of attempting to cover the entire field of government by routine examination of administrative operations, the Section of General Supervision tends now to select particular target areas in a given year and to review actions within those areas with some degree of intensity.

At times this meshes closely with what might otherwise have been a criminal law investigation. Thus, a nationwide study of land acquisition cases was launched a few years ago in response to rumors of bribery in some instances; all offices of the prokuratura joined in reviewing the files of 40,000 closed cases. The review led to some prosecutions of bribe-givers and bribe-takers, and it led also to the introduction of new administrative safeguards designed to forestall future corruption. More recently a conversation, overheard in a railway train, about the poisoning of edible fish led first to informal inquiries and then to a full-scale study of the administration of measures against river pollution in ten provinces.

Another important activity of the prokuratura is reviewing the legality of normative acts—the local legislation promulgated by people's councils as well as the regulations issued by ministries and other administrative organs. According to the present Procurator General, his staff reviewed the staggering number of 117,346 resolutions of people's councils and their presidiums in the calendar year 1963; in 813 instances the prokuratua made representations that apparently induced changes before the resolutions were adopted. During the same year the prokuratura complained to higher authorities concerning the content of 812 enactments that had already been put into effect.[12] How carefully studied this review of subordinate legislation can be, when so great a volume of work must be done by so small a staff, is problematical. In any case, the number of objections noted shows that the review process does have practical results.

Despite preoccupation with the matters just discussed, the prokuratura does react when complaints are lodged with it by persons aggrieved by an assertedly illegal act. Complaints reach the prokuratura by mail, telephone, and personal visitation. If all administrative remedies have not yet been exhausted, the complainant is advised what further steps he should take in his own behalf. Though the prokuratura itself has the right to participate in administrative proceedings, nobody can recall an instance when this actually occurred. So long as self-help is possible, the prokuratura will leave a complainant to his own devices.

But when the administrative course has been run, the prokuratura

[12] These figures are derived from K. Kosztirko, "Praworzadnosc, Opinia Spoleczna, Prokuratura" (Law Compliance, Public Opinion, Prosecuting Attorneys), 21 *Rada Narodowa* no. 19, 4 (1964).

may feel that the complaint deserves investigation. Since the prokuratura is concerned exclusively with legality and not with policy, with permissibility and not with wisdom, many complaints are discarded as probably not cognizable by this office. Sometimes repeated complaints from different areas about the same general topic stir an interest that would otherwise lie dormant. In general, nevertheless, one gains the impression that the prokuratura is not eager to enlarge its clientele and that individual complaints are not major objects of concern.

When the prokuratura does decide to step in, however, its representations may achieve a great deal. Recently, acting on its own motion, the Warsaw prokuratura examined the decisions of each of the "Social Committees" which function in Warsaw's seven boroughs as an arm of the Warsaw People's Council in the war against alcoholism. The prokuratura found many procedural defects in the Committees' decisions, as well as indications that unsuitable personnel had been used. The procurators' findings, presented to the People's Council, led to new directives to the Social Committees to guide them in future cases and also brought about systematic training in the medicolegal aspects of proceedings against alcoholics.

An experienced procurator estimated that representations are made in behalf of individual complainants in more than 5,000 cases annually, taking the country as a whole. The figure seems high, in the light of information obtained in scattered localities. In the city of Poznan, for example, the prokuratura recalls receiving only about 500 individual complaints yearly, of which only 5 to 7 percent led to active measures in support of the complainant's position; the People's Council in that same city asserted that not a single matter had been brought to its attention by the prokuratura during the second half of 1964, but this does not mean that no cases had arisen in Poznan, since the prokuratura often addresses itself directly to the administrative unit with whose action it has disagreed and the matter may end there if the unit accepts the prokuratura's advice. Interpretation of the available statistics is also complicated by the fact that individual complaints may be absorbed into larger-scale investigations or may stimulate studies of general issues while they themselves may be virtually ignored as separate matters. In any event, whatever may be the precisely accurate figure, one may reasonably believe that the prokuratura has a substantial role.[13] This belief has been confirmed by officers of the Polish Bar Association, who assert that advocates do turn to the prokuratura in behalf of clients and do frequently obtain effective assistance in protecting personal interests.

The prokuratura's accomplishments are particularly noteworthy because that agency has little power to command acceptance of its views concerning legality; it must rely chiefly on persuasion. A certain spinelessness in the early years of the prokuratura's existence led one author in 1956 to entitle his article concerning the function of general supervision, "When Everything Means . . . Nothing"; and another author in that same year wrote, "Let us be frank—up to now nobody has taken the procurators' offices seriously."[14] The revolt against Stalinism in 1956 apparently emboldened the prokuratura to voice its opinions, and in recent years it has gained considerable success in inducing administrative changes. A respected scholar, himself experienced as a procurator, has asserted that during the five years 1956–1960 the prokuratura's demands were satisfied in 95 percent of the cases considered.[15] Persons now connected with the prokuratura put the current figure somewhat lower, but none estimated it as less than 85 percent except perhaps in the Ministry of Internal Affairs.

The prokuratura rarely relies on the implied threat of prosecution in order to force acquiescence by officials. Unless deliberate wrongdoing underlies an asserted illegality, the procurator is likely to do no more than give advice he hopes will be followed in the future. A procurator

[13] Kosztirko (note 12) reports that the "legality of administrative decisions" was investigated in 83,508 cases in 1963, and that objections were voiced to actions taken in 2,329 of these, while suggestions were made in 1,564 others. J. Paliwoda, *Nadzor Ogolny Prokuratury* (The Prokuratura's Function of General Supervision) 101–102 (Warsaw, 1961), gives the following table of "complaints" and "interventions" by the prokuratura. He regards these two classifications of actions in particularized cases as having essentially the same significance in carrying out the function of general supervision:

Year	*Complaints*	*Interventions*	*Total*
1956	655	3,348	4,003
1957	2,143	2,197	4,340
1958	3,248	2,945	6,193
1959	3,650	2,964	6,614
1960	5,790	3,936	9,726

[14] Quoted in Helczynski (note 1 above), at 73.

[15] Paliwoda (note 13).

told recently of investigating a complaint that local officials had illegally consented to the construction of a private residence on land earmarked for other purposes. No evidence of bribery or other improper motivation was uncovered, though the consent was found to have been unmistakably wrong. "What could we do, though?" the prosecutor asked. "The house had already been built and we couldn't very well demand its destruction. So we simply said that the officials shouldn't do this sort of thing again." When informed that some Scandinavian countries would in these circumstances prosecute officials for maladministration even without a showing of corruption, the procurator responded: "Our problem in Poland is to train our administrators to a high enough level of efficiency to justify prosecuting them for inefficiency. As matters stand now, we just have to put up with it and try to undo mistakes so far as possible."

A number of persons, well situated to know the facts, have questioned whether the Procurator General is sufficiently aggressive in his dealings with ministers. Clearly he has no power to compel a minister to comply with his wishes; he can only offer an unsolicited opinion about the legality of ministerial decisions. The minister can brush the opinion aside if his own advisers disagree with it or if, as concededly sometimes happens, he deems legality to be less important than his own policy. Theoretically the Procurator General need not regard a ministerial rebuff as the last word. He holds an extremely high office, independent of any ministerial control. Nothing prevents his bringing disagreements to the attention of the Council of State or the Council of Ministers. In actuality, he does so very rarely if ever. This somewhat supine policy has been excused on the ground that a minister probably consults the Prime Minister before flouting the Procurator General's advice about legality, so that the minister can be confident of being upheld by the Council of Ministers if the matter were to be carried there. The excuse has left critics of the prokuratura unsatisfied. Some Polish legal circles believe that the work of the prokuratura will never be wholly effective until the Procurator General has been empowered to present for final review by the Supreme Court those matters in which his counsel is ignored by the officials (no matter how lofty their position) to whom it has been addressed; others advocate the creation of a special administrative tribunal to which he can turn; few think that he has a firm grip on Polish administration as matters now stand.

4|The Press and Radio

In every sophisticated country the mass media think of themselves as gadflies, not solely as recorders or as entertainers. They have the function of uncovering the deficiencies of government, the delinquencies of individual officials, and the disorders of the body politic, so that a well informed public can press for suitable corrective action. In a society that discourages critical re-examination of philosophical premises, the mass media are unlikely to be insistent challengers of the status quo. They can nevertheless be vigilant critics of the way things are being done in daily life. In Poland, to perhaps a larger degree than in Western democracies, the press and radio have accepted the role of people's tribune and have undertaken to help the little citizen struggle against being crushed by big government. So energetic have they become that some detached observers regard the press as more influential than the prokuratura in securing suitable official action on grievances.

Journalistic participation in complaint handling has been formally recognized in the Code of Administrative Procedure. Complaints and suggestions forwarded to officials by editorial offices are to be considered and disposed of in the same manner as those that come directly from affected parties; and, upon the editors' request, information must be promptly given about the action taken (Art. 175). Articles and other material published in newspapers must be treated as complaints or motions if the editors forward them as such; and the competent organ must then tell both the editors and, so far as possible, the persons whom the matter concerns what the organ does with the forwarded material (Art. 177). Radio, television, and motion pictures are equated with newspapers in the present context (Art. 179).

The press and radio take themselves very seriously as founts of information and righters of wrongs. Some officials remark rather bitterly that they take themselves much too seriously and have an inflated sense of their own importance. But nobody denies that they are indeed important, whether or not as important as they believe.

Their activity began soon after creation of the Polish People's Republic twenty years ago, when governmental organization was in a state of acute confusion. *Zycie Warszawy,* a leading Warsaw newspaper, then commenced informing its readers where to go for official services and decisions of various kinds. This led quickly to correspondence about highly particularized problems.

Today that newspaper assigns seven journalists and a legal adviser to its Bureau of Reader Complaints. One day a week is set aside for personal consultations with the staff lawyer, and on that day scores of persons await their turn in the free legal clinic the newspaper provides; twenty-five were counted in the queue when an unannounced visit to the office occurred in late 1964. The journalists in the Bureau answer questions themselves, by telephone or by letter, when information about standard governmental matters is all that is needed.

A reader complaint is ordinarily simply forwarded to the competent organ with a request that suitable action be taken. Those that might embarrass the complainant are forwarded without attaching his name, with a request that reply be made to the newspaper. Complaints that make for interesting reading may be published in the paper. If an official rejoinder is not promptly received, the letter is clipped out and sent to the competent organ with a demand for a response as contemplated by the Code of Administrative Procedure. The staff may itself investigate a complaint and may then publish its own account of the matter, coupled with a call for corrective action—or, in some instances, with a vindication of the officials who had been attacked. At times a large-scale inquiry may be touched off by repeated complaints, and in such situations the newspaper has found the prokuratura to be a cooperative source of needed information, as occurred when reporters delved deeply into labor law administration. In return, the newspaper has brought to the prokuratura's attention cases in which it thinks citizens have been treated shockingly, and the prokuratura's action in these cases has struck the editors as highly effective.

The editors assert that they have never themselves received criticism or been placed under outside pressure in connection with their publication of critical letters, articles, or editorials. Very probably they exercise a prudent degree or self-censorship without having to be ordered to do so; at any rate, stories about the Ministry of Internal Affairs have seemingly not been deemed newsworthy. The editors make no extravagant claims about the success of their service to readers, acknowledging that few officials admit becoming more careful in their work because they fear journalistic vigilance; but they believe that the Bureau of Reader Complaints does have a real impact on public administration, regardless of the administrators' unwillingness to say so.

Examination of a single issue of *Zycie Warszawy*—that of November 12, 1964—shows the range of journalistic treatment of letters to the editor. That day's columns contain an attack on the postal authorities for selling stamps that do not adhere to envelopes and also for delay in delivering money orders sent by mail. They record a reporter's inspection of a large tenement house about whose disrepair a reader had complained. After describing numerous unsatisfactory or dangerous conditions, the newspaper laid the blame at the door of House Administration Authority No. 7, remarked ominously that other complaints had been received about that same body's inactivity, and concluded: "This administrative organ does not suitably care for occupants, who are being denied the minimal necessities and conveniences." A reader inquired whether, as a full-time employee of a state owned enterprise, he could legally render services as a radio and television repairman after working hours and without a license. His attention was drawn to applicable laws and regulations, whose contents were precisely summarized (after having been obtained from the officials concerned with such matters). A doctor complained that he had been misclassified for salary purposes; the newspaper reported its opinion that the complaint was unsound in the light of official rulings over a period of years, which had been made available to it by the Minister of Health in response to the editors' inquiry. A patient complained that he had had to go to a clinic three times before being able to consult an oculist; his efforts to make an appointment in advance had been fruitless, so that he had wasted much time and effort. The newspaper looked into the practices of health clinics in general, found that most of them did make future appointments upon request, and concluded that the complained against clinic was unduly rigid in its rejection of "the widely accepted practice." Finally, the paper published a highly sarcastic editorial based on investigation of a reader's complaint. The local tax collector had seized personal property of Mr. Reader to satisfy a claim for past due real estate taxes. Mr. Reader "had twenty-six reasons for thinking that he had no outstanding obligations to the National Treasury, the first of these being that he had never owned any real estate." When Mr. Reader stormed into the appropriate office, he was told that the whole thing had been an unfortunate mistake attributable to his having the same name as the delinquent taxpayer; so, armed with a certificate of blamelessness, he proceeded to reclaim the property that had been seized. The editorial continued: "You think it's over? Not at all. The financial section said it was quite ready to return Mr. Reader's property—provided he would pay 30 zlotys, the cost of executing the distraining order. So the citizen who was victimized by mistake was now told to pay for the mistake, too." The editorial concluded with a few pungent observations that seemed likely to penetrate even the most impervious bureaucratic hide.

Lacking the time and facilities for a follow-up study, one cannot confidently assert that the publication of such a mélange has significant consequences. Officials to whom the question was put expressed belief that complaints in which newspapers show an interest do receive rather more thoughtful attention than others, because, as one of them put it, "nobody likes being exposed to public notice."

At any rate, the demand for this kind of journalism seems to be considerable. Jerzy Parzynski, an able Krakow editor who holds a doctor's degree in law, surveyed forty-one major newspapers throughout the country and found that thirty-seven have a staff lawyer who answers readers' letters and receives personal callers. At the time of his survey, some six or seven years ago, he estimated that 72,000–84,000 persons obtained oral advice from newspaper lawyers in the course of a year, and that 80 percent of the matters under discussion pertained to governmental problems (the balance being made up chiefly of family law and criminal law questions). Parzynski's own paper, *Echo Krakowa*, receives about 4,000 written complaints and suggestions annually. He himself confers with 30 callers a month, and the number of personal interviews rises year by year. The columns based on correspondence and its aftermath apparently hold the public's interest. "Followership" is suggested by reaction to an article in which Parzynski, commenting upon an official's apparently illegal act, reminded his readers that complaints of illegality can be filed directly with the prokuratura. Krakow's procurators confirm that the very next day they received 300 new complaints.

Apart from the daily press, periodicals that appeal to special segments of the population similarly serve citizens and prod administrators. A women's weekly receives something more than 60,000 letters yearly concerning legal problems, many of them in the nature of complaints. A journal catering to the peasantry is said to be the most vitriolic commentator of all; one official made the wry remark, "The editors of that paper don't write with pens. They use needles exclusively."

The question must sooner or later arise whether newspapers and magazines are suitably staffed to fill the social need manifested by the demands for their help. They fell almost by accident into the job of operating legal clinics. The questions presented are so numerous and so assorted that no one man—or two men—could be expected to give consistently good counsel about them all. Sometimes the published answers to questions have caused needless alarm or raised false hopes. But whether or not the press is the best possible response to the need for legal advisers, it does seem to be a substantial contributor to the resolution of citizens' grievances.

The radio performs related but not precisely the same work; television is omitted from the present discussion simply because it has not yet become the chief channel of communication throughout Poland, though no doubt it will soon expand even further than it has already done. Unlike the newspapers, the radio authority does not have a daily forum in which complaints can be aired. A program that reaches an impressively large listening public, "Wave 56," builds its weekly broadcast around problems disclosed by complaints; but the complaints become generalized or fictionalized in the course of being transmuted into scenarios, so that the program, while it apparently has prophylactic value and often stimulates campaigns having desirable social consequences, is not adapted to securing justice in individual instances. Nevertheless the Polish radio's Bureau of Letters and Complaints receives some 150,000 complaining letters yearly from about 140,000 different correspondents.

Statistics are tricky when they pertain to too broad categories. The large figures just given include all manner of things besides criticism of administrative decisions. They include, for example, an indeterminate number of denunciatory remarks about the music played over the radio. But the bulk of the correspondence does pertain to complaints and perplexities related to public administration, and a full-time staff of fifty persons devotes itself to analyzing, forwarding, following up, and responding to these missives—and also to interviewing approximately 2,000 persons who choose to present their problems personally.[16] Leszek Mikolajczyk, the sociologically minded director of the Bureau of Letters and Complaints, has interestingly analyzed the sources of letters. In general, those who complain to the radio are society's weakest members, educationally and economically, the ones least able to look out for their own interests, the ones most likely to be baffled by the complexities of governmental organization. More letters come from poorer parts of the country than from the rich and highly industrialized sections, possibly because higher quality administration in the industrial areas lessens the grounds for complaint. The radio programs themselves do not apparently generate complaints. Complaints are fewest from the communities where radio ownership and, presumably, listenership are greatest. Since ownership of radios and television sets, though very widespread in Poland, is perhaps still an indicator of relatively favorable economic status, this reverse correlation is further evidence of the comparatively lowly condition of the Bureau's clients, taken as a whole.

The Bureau's analysis intimates another proposition deserving thought, namely, that a large volume of complaints may possibly reflect progress and a rising level of expectations rather than governmental inadequacy. Consider, for example, the incidence of complaints about housing conditions. One might suppose that these would come from the areas of greatest decay and most acute shortage. The contrary appears to be true. Warsaw, which has had a dynamic home building program, has produced four times more housing complaints to the Bureau, per capita, than has the rest of the country; Poznan and Lodz, two other cities in which marked enlargement of the housing supply has occurred, also far exceed the nationwide level of complaining about living conditions. Similarly, when a program looking toward the rehabilitation of dilapidated housing occurs, the volume of complaints about slowness in making repairs and improvements within the affected area suddenly spurts far beyond what it was when nothing at all was being done to relieve bad conditions. Until three years ago a district in

[16] Forty-seven percent of the complaints are forwarded to competent organs of administration, with a request that a reply be made directly to the complainant (with a copy to the Bureau) or that the Bureau be given information on the basis of which it can itself respond to the complainant. The staff answers the remaining letters without referral to any official body. If the letter shows on its face that it is a duplicate of a complaint sent elsewhere, the complainant is simply told that the Bureau intends to take no action in the matter.

eastern Poland had 1,100 kilometers of roads, only 40 kilometers of which were paved. Its inhabitants uncomplainingly though perhaps not happily made their way through mud or dust as had their ancestors for a thousand years. Then the State announced plans to pave another stretch of 40 kilometers. Instantly the Bureau began to receive complaints: if paving can be laid over there, why not over here, too? These examples do not prove that complaints are invariably signs of health, but they do strongly suggest that sometimes they may signify growing pains and not disease.

5|The Supreme Chamber of Control

By a constitutional amendment in 1957,[17] Poland acquired a new means of supervising administrative organs. The Supreme Chamber of Control, or State Control Commission, was created as an agency of the parliament (the Sejm), and charged with the duty of examining into budgetary and economic questions related to administrative operations of local as well as central governmental organizations. Its president is appointed by the Sejm; he and his deputies are free from any ministerial control, being answerable only to the parliament. The Chamber, with a staff of about a thousand investigators, accountants, management specialists, and other functionaries, acts as a sort of Inspector General. Its representatives periodically visit each public organ and enterprise (even each university) to ascertain whether its affairs are conducted efficiently, legally, and with suitable regard for applicable fiscal controls. Budget estimates must be submitted for its analysis before being presented to the parliament for final endorsement. Accounts must be approved by the Chamber of Control, which can and does bring its criticisms to the attention of the parliament, the responsible ministers, and, in grave cases, the public prosecutor. A recent major prosecution for diversion of foodstuffs into forbidden commercial channels was directly an outgrowth of a Control Commission inspection.

This brief summation of the Supreme Chamber of Control's duties

[17] Constitution of 1959, Chap. 3a, Art. 28a-d, added by Law of Dec. 13, 1957, [1957] *Dziennik Ustaw P.R.L.* no. 61, item 329 (Poland).

demonstrates that, in American terms, it performs the functions of the Bureau of the Budget and of the Comptroller General as well—though, because of Poland's system of state ownership, the Control Chamber works in a far broader field than do its American counterparts. The Chamber also strongly resembles the Austrian Rechnungshof, or Court of Accounts, a parliamentary organ that over the years has expanded the conception of fiscal control until it encompasses virtually all questions of official legality, capability, and integrity. The resemblance is not wholly accidental, since until 1920 Poland did have an Austrian-influenced Supreme Chamber of Control that functioned much like the present body.

Confident evaluation of the Control Commission's activity as a whole is difficult. Some of the inspection work seems to be done in a routine manner, with exasperatingly close attention paid to petty formalities and not much grasp of the basic problems with which administrators cope. Many inspectors inquire into legality only as it may bear on costs; wholly unauthorized proceedings, requiring additional administrative staffing, might arouse the Control Commission's concern because they would add to an organ's expenditures, while no concern whatsoever might be felt about official illegalities hurtful to citizens but without budgetary disadvantage to the State. In some instances, according to responsible persons, investigations have not been pressed to a conclusion because of intercession by friends in high places who have had access to the chiefs of the Supreme Chamber of Control; supporters of the Chamber regard this as a scurrilous invention, but not everyone is a supporter.

For the present, the Supreme Chamber of Control seems to be of little use as a shield against oppressive or inept official actions that have an immediate impact on individuals. This may not be true forever, if the organization continues in existence. The Austrian Rechnungshof, to which reference has just been made, does at times receive and act upon complaints by citizens, investigating the permissibility of governmental operations even when budgetary issues are not implicated in any way. So, too, does the Comptroller General of Israel; in that country fiscal accountability (which is the Comptroller General's concern) appears to be sufficiently broad to include anything done by a person on the public payroll. Having in mind the well-known tendency of central organs of inspection to build ever larger empires and to intrude farther and farther into the functioning of the bodies they inspect, one may anticipate that sooner or later the Supreme Chamber of Control may respond to individual complaints more eagerly than is true today. Its legislatively declared purpose—to be a guardian of legality, economical management, administrative purposefulness, and integrity—is certainly broad enough to justify its becoming a more significant feature of Polish official life.

6|The Party

In Poland the Communist Party goes by the name of the Polish United Workers' Party. Two non-Marxist parties, the United Peasant Party and the Democratic Party, are allowed to function as additional members of the "National Unity Front," pledged not to seek restoration of capitalism though not bound always to agree in detail with the dominant United Workers' Party concerning the rate or manner of change necessary to build a more perfect society. The three parties offer in each election district a list of candidates who support the National Unity Front; since 1956 the number of candidates must exceed the number of seats to be filled, so that the voters do have a modicum of personal choice, though obviously within a very narrow political spectrum. In both the 1961 and the 1965 elections for the national legislature, the United Workers' Party returned 255 deputies, the United Peasant Party 117, and the Democratic Party 39; the remaining 49 seats were filled by persons who claimed no formal party affiliation. The three parties cooperate through an inter-party consultative body called the Coordinating Committee of the Political Parties, but they have separate conventions and maintain at least a token independence. Hence one cannot accurately describe Poland as a one-party state.

Nevertheless, Poland is, in a realistic sense, politically unicellular. Conversation about politics invariably involves repeated references to "The Party." Nobody ever has occasion to ask which party is meant. For practical purposes only one party has the power to shape the course of events.

The relation of The Party to governmental problems of the kind discussed in this paper seems to be changing. Less than a decade ago,

The Party's massive headquarters in Warsaw included an Office of Letters and Complaints that functioned to all intents and purposes as though it were itself a branch of administration. Officials about whose acts complaint had been made were ordered to deliver files to the Office for its examination; the staff of the Office eventually returned the files, often with "advice" about what should next be done in the matter complained of; lines of supervision and coordination of authority became confused, subordinates being bewildered when the White House (as Communist headquarters is sometimes called) gave instructions inconsistent with those of their nominal chiefs.

Today this is much altered. The Party's Office of Letters and Complaints has been closed. The number of functionaries at headquarters has been greatly reduced. Complaints are still addressed to The Party; nobody has any doubt about the seat of ultimate power in Poland nor about the unofficial primacy of Wladyslaw Gomulka, who, holding no executive post in the government, is the First Secretary of the Central Committee of the United Workers' Party. But when complaints come, they are in most instances, according to a Party official, "routinely referred to the appropriate governmental body without any comment." The Party's present task, he remarked, is "to prod administrators rather than to supplant them."

The dividing line between prodding and administering is not always sharply defined. The Party still does speak directly to administrators, telling them to answer letters or, in supposedly clear cases, to give a complainant what he wants. Since those who speak for The Party are not necessarily conversant with all the technicalities, what is "clear" to them may seem opaque to others, and this is when the danger of undue partisan pressure is greatest. Perhaps the risk of improperly applied "influence" is lessened only by the fact that most important official posts in Poland are filled by Party members who would resist, in their own behalf and in behalf of their subordinates, pressures exerted by lesser Party members.

Away from the capital, the relationships between The Party and the administrators seem to reflect personality differences more than they do conceptions of governmental responsibility. Where The Party's spokesmen are strong and the administrators are weak, "political leaders" reign as they do in some American cities and states. Where the local administration takes a professional pride in its work, the likelihood of frequent partisan intrusion is seemingly not oppressively great at present. Even in those areas, however, administrators concede that "consultations" occur between officers of The Party and local officials, looking toward the "guidance" of the latter in discharging their responsibilities in specific situations as well as in the general course of business; but these consultations are said to be far less frequent than they were only a few years ago. Amenability to "guidance" is perhaps a fact of political life wherever one party dominates the community. As was said by a presidium officer in one of Poland's strongest provinces, "It's worthwhile to have good relations with The Party because it makes up the election list, and of course we would like to be renominated when the time comes."

A number of well-informed observers, interviewed separately, commented that The Party supports the proposition that fear of reprisals should not deter the voicing of complaints against officials. The Code of Administrative Procedure asserts that "Nobody can be exposed to prejudice or criticism because of having filed a complaint or motion, or having supplied material to a publication in the nature of a complaint or motion, if he has acted within legal limits" (Art. 155); the exception suggests that while malicious distribution of falsehoods will not be condoned, otherwise complainants are not to be imperiled. Despite this statutory assurance, almost everyone agrees that timidity does discourage the filing of some complaints and that occasionally the timidity may be well justified.[18]

The danger of subtle discrimination against complainants is, of course, not peculiar to Poland or to the Communist countries. Reluctance to press for redress of grievances is reflected in such wholly American slang as "You can't fight City Hall" and "It doesn't pay to stick your neck out," while many a lawyer has bottled up his feelings about the behavior of judges or court clerks lest he find himself the object of future hostility expressed through the withholding of minor courtesies and through galling insistence upon usually ignored technicalities.

The Party's declared policy is that the channels of complaint must be kept open as an aid to identifying social maladjustments and designing timely corrective action. So frequently was this policy reflected

[18] Journalists and radio officials believe that one of the reasons citizens write to them instead of directly to administrative organs is that the writers think this lessens the risk of reprisal. The newspaper or the radio bureau, the writers may quite correctly suppose, will stand behind their correspondents if officialdom threatens them.

in conversations with officials at every level of government that one can scarcely doubt the reality of its existence. Even unmeritorious complaints, it was stressed, have their value, for they may reveal areas of inadequate understanding to which The Party should direct increased educational efforts to stave off wider discontent.

Persons who think they have suffered because of having complained against officials have been urged to tell The Party about their difficulties. At that point The Party attempts to find out whether the complainant's subsequent troubles are in fact attributable to his past criticism of administration. Proving prejudice is a notably difficult task, and not many cases have been sufficiently clear to justify disciplinary proceedings against officials. A few administrators have, however, been disciplined, and much was made of these examples in the hope that they would serve as a warning to all. In most instances, however, seemingly scrupulous investigation by The Party has not uncovered adequately persuasive evidence that officials had engaged in reprisals. A very high officer was asked what happens then. He answered, wholly seriously and with every appearance of candor: "Usually in these cases the man who says he has been hurt points to some change in his job status as proof of the discrimination—he has been discharged or demoted or given an assignment he doesn't like. Most often The Party's investigation shows that he simply isn't a good worker and that he probably deserved everything he got. But unless The Party has absolute confidence—*really* absolute confidence—in the person who took the action, the fellow who complained will be reinstated in his old job or, what is more likely, be given an even better job some place else. The Party takes the view that it is better to give a possibly undeserved advantage to an incompetent man than to let anyone else suppose he is in trouble because he complained to the government or wrote a letter to a newspaper."

7 | Concluding Observations

This review of a citizen's ability to oppose an official's decision shows that a Pole is by no means wholly defenseless. On the contrary, he has a rather generous assortment of ways for recording his dissatisfaction. The protections accorded him are genuine and are apparently meant for use, not merely for display.

To a Western lawyer the protections seem nevertheless to be markedly deficient in two major respects: first, the virtual absence of judicial review and, second, the relegation of a complainant to the status of a petitioner, without opportunity to participate effectively in the proceedings his complaint may have launched.

As for the first of these, much of the discussion in Poland seems based upon a misconception of judicial review at least as it has developed in the United States. Polish administrators fear judicial review because, they say, judges are untrained in administration and are uninformed about the economic and other subject matters with which the administrators deal. This is of course perfectly true. It is, however, irrelevant if judicial review be confined to issues of administrative propriety, leaving untouched the entire area of administrative judgment within the limits defined by law. In some European countries, the administrative courts to which challenged official decisions are brought for review may often go much farther. They may act at times, in truth, as super-administrators, empowered to re-examine the merits of a matter with a fresh eye. To a Pole, "judicial review" usually connotes something of that sort. To an American, accustomed as he is to judicial review by ordinary law courts rather than by specialized administrative courts, it connotes something much narrower.

Poland, despite many pre-war associations with France, is now well outside the influence of the legal patterns prevailing in Western Europe. It is free, therefore, to experiment with judicial review (as have Bulgaria, Hungary, and Yugoslavia) to fortify its conceptions of legality without undermining its administrators' capacity to effectuate policies beyond the experience of law-trained judges. Unless some official body—the courts or some other—be authorized to decide finally whether an administrator's action is legal, the rule of law in Poland may be short-lived. Though the prokuratura may remonstrate against illegalities in law administration, the administrator's capacity to reject the remonstrance and the prokuratura's powerlessness to enforce it make this a somewhat thin shield against oppression.

The "administrative course of instances" is a rather short course, as an American might measure such things. Once the course has been completed, the affected citizen can no longer present and argue a case that concerns him. He can ask someone else to look into the case, but he has no real chance to point, to explain, or to counter what the investigator may be told. Because of differences in the subject matters dealt with in Poland and the United States, this may not be so serious as it seems to an American lawyer used to administrative procedures that stress opportunity to participate extensively in gathering and appraising evidence as well as in argumentation. Polish administrative proceedings rarely involve as complex issues as are encountered in major regulatory cases in America. Still, they may be of considerable moment to those concerned.[19] The opportunity to participate, not the absolute necessity of doing so in every instance, should be more generously provided than it is today.

The seemingly inadequate chance to be a contestant and not simply a supplicant is, in a sense, a characteristic of Polish administrative organization that far antedates the present political structure. What is true as to individual controversies is true also as to more generalized matters. No law or custom requires that the promulgators of subordinate legislation (such as a minister or the presidium of a People's Council) provide opportunities for public hearing or other types of discussion before issuing new normative acts having the force of law. A possible expansion of the Code of Administrative Procedure is now under consideration, looking toward the creation of procedural requirements in rulemaking as well as in adjudicatory proceedings. Steps in that direction would be consonant with Poland's insistence that it relies on democratic methods to achieve a Marxist society.[20]

Despite the reservations just suggested, the objectives of the present Polish controls over administration seem praiseworthy, and their accomplishments, substantial. The system is still in a state of becoming; it is not yet fully and finally shaped, but is changing its contours as experience dictates.

One must be cautious not to apply to another country more severe

[19] See, e.g., J. Jonczyk, "The Problem of Protection of Personal Values in the Law of Labour," 18 *Panstwo i Prawo* no. 5 (1963).

[20] A highly respected senior scholar of the law has recently proposed that some types of subordinate legislation actually be submitted to a direct referendum and that "obligatory universal consultation" be required in all instances, with publication of drafts and opportunity for all interested persons to comment before a new regulation be promulgated. See M. Jaroszynski, "The Decentralization of the Rulemaking Function as a Democratizing Factor," 4 *Problemy Rad Narodowyck* 30 (1965).

tests than one applies to one's own. Every candid American recognizes that governmental affairs are not invariably handled as they should be. Goals are stated and efforts are made to attain them, but performance falls short of the mark often enough to necessitate constant search for improved methods and new safeguards; furthermore, legitimate aspirations sometimes compete with one another instead of coinciding, as when some American lawyers urge the importance of cheap and speedy administrative procedures while other lawyers simultaneously and equally strongly insist upon the need for more deliberate methods. So it is in Poland. Today the protection of individual citizens against overbearing wielders of public power seems to be accepted as an unqualifiedly desirable goal. The goal is not always achieved, and probably never will be. But a serious search has been made to develop suitable means for reaching the end. Enough progress has been made to justify hopes that still more will be forthcoming.

eight

The Soviet Union

When drastically different from one's own, a foreign legal system may seem unsystematic if not, indeed, virtually non-existent. An American lawyer looking at Soviet law must therefore take care to adjust his eyes, lest failure to find precise resemblances lead him to overlook general equivalents.

Administrative lawyers must perhaps be especially careful. Until relatively recently public administration as a scientific discipline has not held the interest of Soviet professional circles. Perhaps as a consequence, controls over it have been devised somewhat haphazardly. In the early postrevolutionary period, in fact, Lenin described administering public affairs as a simple task, well within the grasp of anyone who can read and write. Lulled by such imaginings, Soviet leaders were not quickly attentive to the complex administrative problems created by Soviet social development.[1]

Conventional methods of internal superintendence were certainly not ignored; subordinates have made reports, inspectors have made their rounds, technical teams and "efficiency experts" have visited in-

[1] Compare M. E. Dimock, "Management in the USSR—Comparisons to the United States," 20 *Pub. Admin. Rev.* 139, 140 (1960): ". . . the pathology of bureaucracy increases with size and complexity and the Russians have been slow to cope with it largely because their dogmas prevented their anticipating and learning to deal with it." In some areas "the Russians are notoriously poor administrators by American standards," though, paradoxically, they have "scored outstanding triumphs" in others. "This unevenness is due in part to their system of priorities: they do well the things they consider most important at the time and defer until later things that can wait."

See also I. N. Ananov, "Science of Administrative Law in the Soviet Union," 24 *Int. Rev. Admin. Sc.* 355 (1958).

stitutions and other official establishments, a bureau of audit has sent agents to check accounts without warning. A leading scholar has characterized the system as "a formidable proliferation of central administrative controls" on an unparalleled scale, and asserts that Soviet officials function in an environment in which every decision is "subject to the possibility of check, recheck, and counter-check."[2]

The close policing of administration just described has been aimed at assuring the suitable discharge of the official's obligations to the state he serves, rather than at assuring fairness to individual interests. Supervising the relations between administrators and individuals, reconciling public and private interests, guarding against abusive exercises of power, involve different mechanisms of control and special difficulties. This paper will attempt to sketch some of the Soviet efforts to cope with those difficulties.

1|The Legislature

In theory the Supreme Soviet (the elected assembly) is indeed supreme. In form it creates and directs the organs of the state, designates the Council of Ministers as well as its own Presidium, and can summon any public official to account for the conduct of his office. Even an individual deputy can, according to the Constitution, require a minister (or the entire Council of Ministers) to respond within three days to an interpellation concerning any aspect of public affairs. Investigating committees may be named to inquire into the acts of public administrators, without limitation. Decrees and decisions of subordinate bodies can be freely annulled by the Presidium of the Supreme Soviet if deemed illegal. Hypothetically, then, the legislature is a major protector against administration that adversely affects the citizenry.[3]

The protection is more apparent than real. Soviet legislators, elected on a single slate of carefully picked candidates who are unopposed at

[2] M. Fainsod, "Recent Developments in Soviet Public Administration," 11 *J. Pol.* 679 (1949).

[3] See, generally, P. Romachkine ed., *Principes du Droit Soviétique* 68–73, 124–125 (1963). The statements in the text have to do with the legislature of the Union of Socialist Soviet Republics. The legislatures of the republics comprising the U.S.S.R. have similar powers under the respective republican constitutions.

election time, have rarely been notably critical or aggressive. Their votes have been remarkable for their unbroken unanimity. Most of the deputies are amateurs; those who are not high-ranking Communist Party officials serve usually for a single four-year term and then return to their customary occupations.

This is not to say, however, that the Soviet deputies are wholly inert. They do sometimes criticize economic maladministration that has affected the immediate well-being of the citizenry. They do sometimes stimulate and participate in discussion of general issues of concern to their constituents.[4] And they sometimes act, much like American congressmen, as their constituents' guides through bureaucratic mazes.[5] Persons with whom the matter was discussed in Moscow in late 1964 agreed that a deputy would probably not be able to reshape an administrator's view of the merits, but they agreed, too, that a citizen's protest, request, or question would receive very prompt and respectful administrative attention if transmitted through a member of the Supreme Soviet. Legislators, then, do serve in fact (though not so fully as in theory) as a means of arousing administrators to look closely at individuals' problems.

2 | Judicial Review

The judicial power has been broadly stated in the Soviet Union. The courts are directed to protect the "political, labor, residential, and other personal and property rights and interests of the citizens of the

[4] See Romachkine (note 3), at 68: A proposed pension law was significantly redrafted after public meetings had drawn attention to inadequacies. Originally containing 46 articles, the measure as finally enacted had 61 articles; apart from the 15 articles that had been added, 7 articles had been entirely redrafted.

[5] Compare Romachkine (note 3), at 73: "O. Kvitko, for example, a teacher by profession, deputy from the Donets region, delivered 64 speeches before her constituents during her four year term, received on those occasions numerous important suggestions concerning the construction of new industries, electrification in cities and towns, extension of public services, cultural matters, aid to pensioners, and so on—propositions which, transmitted to the Supreme Soviet and its standing committees, were taken into account when new laws were being formulated. During the same period this woman deputy received 1200 personal callers, whom she aided in handling their personal affairs."

USSR that are guaranteed by the USSR Constitution and the constitutions of the Union and Autonomous Republics."[6]

Here again the words promise more than the deeds fulfill, for Soviet judges seem not to exercise very active control over public administration. Regulations promulgated by those empowered to issue rules are virtually immune from direct attack in judicial proceedings,[7] though a court might not aid in enforcing a regulation it deemed to be invalid. Penal sanctions have been freely used to discourage administrative miscalculations and carelessness, but infrequently in respect of administration aimed squarely at individuals.[8] Privately initiated actions for damages growing out of an official abuse cannot be brought until the abuse has been established through penal or disciplinary proceedings against the official—proceedings the victim of the alleged abuse can neither commence nor share in conducting. A careful analyst of Soviet law concluded some years ago: "Protection by the Courts against violations of laws committed in execution of executive power is . . . of doubtful practical value."[9]

That conclusion seems somewhat harsh in its unqualified form. In some fields courts may be asked, actually, to examine administrative decisions in much the way American courts engage in judicial review. Electoral privileges, some types of controversy about housing, taxes, compulsory delivery of agricultural produce, and, above all, the enforcement of administrative fines are among the subject matters with which Soviet courts may deal.[10] Certain phases of labor relations directly touching individual workers, especially those concerned with dismissal from jobs by state managers, are also referrable to the courts for independent review.[11]

[6] Article 2(b), Judiciary Act 1958, translated in *Fundamentals of Soviet Criminal Legislation, the Judicial System and Criminal Court Procedure* 40 (Moscow, 1960).

[7] See G. G. Morgan, The "General Supervision" of the Soviet Procuracy," 2 *J. Int. Comm. of Jurists* no. 2, at 117 (1960).

[8] See M. Fainsod, *How Russia is Ruled* 413 (1963).

[9] D. A. Loeber, "The Soviet Procuracy and the Rights of the Individual against the State," 1 *J. Int. Comm. of Jurists* no. 2, at 59 (1957). A prominent American scholar, Professor Harold J. Berman, has expressed to the author his opinion that the courts have become more active and more significant in this sphere in recent years.

[10] See Loeber (note 9), at 63; G. G. Morgan, *Soviet Administrative Legality: The Role of the Attorney General's Office* 1, 2 (1962).

[11] See, generally, G. Langrod, "Court Control of Administrative Legality in the U.S.S.R.," 26 *Int. Rev. Admin. Sc.* 202 (1960).

Without exception Soviet scholars with whom judicial review was discussed in 1964 believed that it should be broadened beyond the limitations then resting upon it. A casual American inquirer, not knowledgeable about the full range of individual matters that may be administratively determined, cannot precisely indentify the gaps in judicial power that need to be filled. Many regulatory activities that give rise in the United States to conflict between administrative officials and private interests have no precise Soviet counterparts, simply because no comparable private interests exist; hence, no occasion arises either for administrative decision or for judicial review in those areas. Conflicts and contests among state-owned enterprises are adjudicated by a state arbitration system (Gosarbitrazh) that takes the place of both judges and administrators. The shortcoming of judicial review most frequently cited in the Soviet Union is the citizen's inability to challenge subordinate legislation—"normative acts," "ordinances," "regulations," "resolutions and decrees" that command or restrict. These, as a later portion of this chapter will show, are subject to review by a non-judicial organ, the Procuracy, instead of by the courts.

3| Administrative Procedure

No Code or "Fundamental Principles" of Administrative Procedure governs the methods of U.S.S.R. agencies that deal with the citizenry. A draft code had been prepared on the eve of World War II, but was put aside when more urgent problems faced the nation. Interest in regularizing administrative procedure has not revived to any great degree, despite the emergence of comprehensive codes in Czechoslovakia, Poland, and Yugoslavia.

Scattered conversations in 1964 gave the impression that procedural reform ranked low on the list of things Soviet administrative lawyers wished to accomplish. Codification of substantive administrative law was regarded as much more pressingly needed. "The body of our administrative law is now so large," a leading Soviet academician said, "that we can't even discuss it as a whole. We have to try to organize it in its several parts, simply to find out what substantive laws and regulations now exist. We constantly exhort administrators to adhere to the law, but they—and even we ourselves—have difficulty learning what it is at times. So we want to codify the law now in force, if for no other reason than to be sure we can identify it and then consider possible improvements."

As for the individual's opportunity to participate effectively in proceedings affecting him, prominent jurists asserted almost in unison that despite the absence of any general law on the subject, statutes addressed to particular organs do nevertheless provide suitable procedures (including the right to be heard) in various classes of cases. One of them added, while others nodded in agreement: "Anyway, how important is the right to be heard before a decision? Under our system, anyone who thinks himself concerned can interrupt the proceedings at any point, before or after a decision has been made, and can insist on having his say. In my opinion, we probably have too much instead of too little opportunity to be heard. But I don't advocate restricting the individual's initiative. It's a good check. We don't want a rigid system like Poland's, where you have sixty days in which to take this step, thirty days in which to take that one."

In one highly important realm, in any case, the Soviet legal system has rather fully utilized procedures that are congenial to Western lawyers. Since 1961 "administrative fines" can be imposed legally only after opportunity for a hearing that closely resembles an ordinary judicial trial. Violations of traffic, sanitary, fire prevention, factory safety, transportation, and other administrative regulations are punishable by money penalties. Minor fines can, indeed, be assessed on the spot by traffic policemen, fire department inspectors, and the like. Slightly larger fines can be levied by a higher-level officer. Such cases are then, on demand subject to complete re-examination by an "administrative commission," which also serves as the tribunal of first instance to consider more serious allegations. An administrative commission utilizes what Americans recognize as "formal administrative procedure"—notice of charges, confrontation of witnesses, opportunity to present proofs and argument, and so on.

Despite their general lack of interest in procedural prescriptions, Soviet jurists seemed to regard "administrative commissions" as highly desirable shields against summary determinations that, no matter how purely motivated, might be unjust because ill-informed. Similarly formal procedures are, however, insufficiently widespread to constitute as much of a safeguard as they are thought to provide in countries that stress the concepts of "due process" or "fair play."

4|The Right to Complain

Since at least 1936 Soviet citizens have had a generally worded statutory right to complain to almost everybody about almost anything. History tells us that exercising the right has not always been the height of prudence.[12] But even during the period of Stalinist repression, complaints apparently continued to be welcomed and to be handled objectively so long as they did not touch Communist Party interests or the political police.[13] Today, in any event, criticism is encouraged and efforts are made to bring complaints into the open, not to unmask the complainer but in order to come to grips with the grounds of dissatisfaction.[14] Still, despite the continuance of what must sometimes be galling officially enforced restrictions on individual liberty (as, for example, in connection with meetings and publications), complaints have been somewhat limited in scope. As was said recently, one "cannot know how much the experience of more than forty years with the restraints established by Soviet authorities has conditioned Soviet citizens to refrain from testing the toleration point of licensing officials."[15]

Be that as it may, the one legally prescribed and universal administrative protection is the citizen's right to complain. He may complain not merely that he has suffered a legal wrong, but also that he has been unwisely or unfairly treated; he may complain not merely that a decision has been made adversely to his interests, but also that a general policy or practice has been adopted, distastefully or disadvantageously

[12] Compare J. N. Hazard and I. Shapiro, *The Soviet Legal System* 62 (1962): From the late 1930's until Stalin's death in 1953, complaints that suggested criticism of even junior officials (let alone of Stalin) were highly hazardous to the complainer. While a citizen could quarrel with economic inefficiency, he "had to be careful lest he be thought to be masking political criticism in economic terms."

[13] H. J. Berman, "Human Rights in the Soviet Union," 11 *How. L. J.* 333, 338–339 (1965).

[14] The present position is that "the complainant is protected against any repressive measure so long as the complaint does not contain calumnies." Romachkine (note 3 above), at 142. The cited volume is an authoritative publication of the Institute of State and Law, Academy of Sciences of the U.S.S.R.

[15] Hazard and Shapiro (note 12 above), at 63.

to him; he may complain not merely that something has happened that undesirably affects him, but also that the public interest has been jeopardized by something not affecting him at all. A determined person may spread his complaint far and wide, and may press it in whatever quarter he may choose.[16]

Actually, the recipient of a complaint, if he is not himself the cognizant official, ordinarily passes it along through the correct channels for consideration.[17] Whatever emotional satisfaction the complainant may experience from writing to a well-known personage, the simple fact is that the complaint will usually be forwarded within three days to the administrative organ immediately superior to the one complained against, with notice to the complainant that this has been done.[18] Most of the republics have provided statutory time limits within which various types of complaints must be considered and answers sent to the complainants. Every ministry and important institution in the

[16] Among the often chosen quarters are the more influential newspapers. They are chiefly important, in the present context, as general supporters of legality, rather than as righters of individual wrongs. But they do concern themselves with individual cases to some extent. *Pravda,* the Communist Party newspaper in Moscow, receives between 200 and 300 letters daily, many of them recognizably complaining about administrative determinations. A staff unit deals with the complaint letters, distilling from them the basis for news stories and editorials even when the letters themselves are not published. A news section entitled "On the Traces of Letters" is devoted to things that were or were not accomplished after *Pravda* had forwarded complaints to the proper organs; in many instances, according to *Pravda* spokesmen, "matters are solved operatively through direct contact by us with, for instance, the manager of an establishment. We ask him what's what, and sometimes the necessary action is taken even without forwarding the complaint." A regular television program is based on letters which criticize shortcomings in official or economic bodies, and radio programs use newspaper letters also. *Pravda's* department for dealing with readers' complaints and criticisms is said to have counterparts throughout the U.S.S.R. For a fuller discussion of the role of the press, see B. A. Ramundo, "They Answer (To) *Pravda,*" 1964 *U. Ill. L. Forum* 103.

[17] A Justice of the U.S.S.R. Supreme Court recently remarked that about twenty callers present themselves at that tribunal's headquarters each day, "asking for advice about legal matters, usually as a basis for making a complaint. Our staff gives them whatever help is feasible and tells them where they really should go."

[18] The head of a public health administration, interviewed in 1964, asserted, however, that the recipient of a complaint often does do more than simply refer it to the proper quarter. In his own experience, he said, referral of a complaint had sometimes been accompanied by questions and often by a request to be informed about the action finally taken on the complaint. "I have received complaints through the republic's Ministry of Health, the Minister of Health of the U.S.S.R., the Moscow city soviet [i.e., the local legislature], the newspapers, and many others," he added, "And have rarely felt that they had entirely washed their hands of the matter as soon as they had forwarded the complaint to me—and this, too, even though the matter may really have been none of their business in the first place."

national establishment is required to name a special unit to examine and act upon complaints; the statute prescribes that where no unit exists, the chief of the organization or establishment must himself determine complaints. Moreover, hours for a designated official's receiving personal callers are fixed in every administrative organ, so that a written complaint may be followed by an oral presentation.

In summary, the complaint is, in essence, the citizen's means of administrative appeal. He asks that a step already taken be retraced. The shortcoming in the system is that the complainant has little control over his case. He petitions within the governmental hierarchy and hopes for the best. Such rules as have been laid down for acting on complaints are not enforceable at his behest, nor (subject to the exceptions outlined in earlier pages) can he readily turn to the courts for aid. How well the system functions in practice is difficult to ascertain, for the results of Soviet public administration are not reflected in reports and statistical analyses readily made available to a foreign visitor. Perfunctory handling of citizens' complaints is known to have been strongly criticized by Soviet writers in 1960.[19] Although the criticism sufficiently shows that some complaints were being dealt with dilatorily and "bureaucratically" (a very derogatory word in the Soviet vocabulary), one has no way of knowing whether these deficiencies were widespread.

An answer to this question may be intimated by the citizenry's increasingly heavy reliance on the Procuracy instead of on complaints to administrative organs, when seeking to upset an objectionable determination. The Procuracy, to which we now turn, may be said to be the common man's complaint bureau. Once it has become interested in the subject matter of a complaint, it assumes the role of a party—and, at that, a much more powerful party than the original complainant could hope to be.

5 | The Historical Background of the Procuracy

Origins. The Procuracy in the Soviet Union is, among other things, responsible for prosecuting lawbreakers and for keeping an eye on the

[19] Hazard and Shapiro (note 12), at 91.

courts.[20] Its most important activity, in the context of the present discussion, is exercising "general supervision" over public authorities in order to guard against abuses of law. An authority on Soviet law describes the Procuracy as combining the "functions of our [American] Department of Justice, congressional investigating committees, and grand juries."[21]

Its roots are buried deeply in the pre-Soviet past: Peter the Great created a Procurator General in 1722, characterized him as the "eye of the Tsar," and bade him not only to enforce laws and edicts, but also to protect the population from overbearing officials.[22]

In the course of time the procurators became merely prosecutors; the leading American writer on the Procuracy says that for fifty years before the Communist regime "the Tsarist Procuracy had engaged for the most part in purely judicial functions similar to those of its European counterparts."[23] In 1922, however, "the young Soviet government reached back into the past and revived the supervisory functions of the Procuracy in an effort to promote observance of legality

[20] The procurator may present his opinion concerning legal issues while litigation is still in progress, in civil as well as criminal proceedings; the Procuracy has the standing of a party, representing the interests of the state, and in that capacity has the right to appeal to a higher court, like any other party. But the Procuracy's powers go farther. Procurators may conduct a post-audit of the judges' work, as it were. After a court judgment has become final, the Procurator General of the Soviet Union and his deputies can demand that the proceedings be reopened for consideration of a "protest" against the decision previously rendered; and lower-level procurators have a similar power, limited in point of time, with reference to the acts of some judicial organs. Pending action on the protest, the Procurator General or the procurator of a republic may suspend execution of the judicial order whose reconsideration has been sought. Procurators' protests and appeals are infrequent; they affect fewer than 5 percent of court decisions, apparently. The Procuracy has unlimited access to court files, and the Procurator General may participate in the executive sessions of the Supreme Court of the Soviet Union in order to draw the court's attention to what he deems to be legal errors.

Private persons may petition the Procuracy to exercise its power to cause a reopening of no longer appealable judgments. In this respect the Procuracy may become the protagonist of an individual who has been the victim of mistake or has been wronged by defective procedures. Somewhat similar practices in Finland and Sweden are described in Chapters 2 and 5, above.

[21] H. J. Berman, "The Dilemma of Soviet Law Reform," 76 *Harv. L. Rev.* 929, 939 (1963). And see also the same author's *Justice in the U.S.S.R.* 238–247 (1963).

[22] The history of the Procuracy is set forth in G. G. Morgan, *Soviet Administrative Legality: The Role of the Attorney General's Office* 10 et seq. (Stanford: Stanford University Press, 1962). This is the chief English language discussion of the Procuracy, past and present.

[23] *Ibid.*, at 21.

in its sprawling bureaucracy and to ensure the conformity of local enactments with central decrees."[24]

Development. Direct supervision of the acts of all agencies exercising "Soviet authority" in order to assure legality was not an encompassable task. Physical inspection of a power plant or a penal institution might bring to light some administrative disregard of law; looking at the impalpabilities and imponderables underlying economic and social decisions was a different matter entirely. Professor G. G. Morgan has well presented the Procuracy's limited range of vision when attempting to be the State's all-seeing eye or, as a Procurator General himself put it, when seeking to embrace the unembraceable.[25]

The function of general supervision never entirely lapsed, but at times it took a very subordinate place; procurators then devoted themselves to zealous enforcement of criminal laws while carefully failing to observe their fellow officials' abuses. Infringements of personal rights tended to be ignored; attention was concentrated on protecting the State's supposed interests. This was notoriously so during the late 1930's, when Andrei Vyshinsky was Procurator General. A Deputy Procurator General has recently revealed that Vyshinsky failed to protect his own subordinates when they protested against the excesses of the security police; as a consequence, 90 percent of the provincial procurators lost their jobs, and many were executed.[26]

[24] *Id.*

[25] *Soviet Administrative Legality,* at 48–74.

[26] See N. V. Zhogin, "On Vyshinsky's Distortions in The Theory and Practice of Soviet Law," Eng. trans. in 17 *Curr. Dig. of the Sov. Press* no. 19, 20 at 21 (June 2, 1965). Morgan (note 22), at 112–113, notes that, interestingly, the Stalin regime nevertheless re-emphasized the Procuracy's general supervision function at the very height of the wholesale illegalities of the purges. "General supervision," he comments, "was not revived to challenge infringements of the Soviet regime on the rights of individuals and groups. The Soviet Procuracy was and is an arm of the government, the tool of the Party to aid in the implementation of the latter's policies . . . General supervision was resuscitated . . . to assist in bringing *efficiency* into the government machinery. An administrative apparatus that dealt in irregularities and illegal enactments could not be depended upon to execute the new policies that the regime was seeking to introduce. Thus, increased emphasis was laid upon protesting the illegal enactments of agencies and officials that endangered the 'stability of laws' and threatened to create disregard for the laws that would thereby endanger the implementation of Party policies. Therefore, the Procuracy could engage in the exercise of general supervision with the aim of promoting regularity and efficiency in governmental operations at the same time that the group directing the Procuracy, the rulers of the Soviet regime, were simultaneously employing the Procuracy and other bodies to exterminate large numbers of putative opponents of the policies of the regime. There was never any role for general supervision in challenging the illegalities

General supervision came strongly to the fore again after Stalin's death in 1953. A new statute on procuracy supervision, adopted by the Presidium of the Supreme Soviet in 1955, directed the Procurator General and his subordinates to keep a close watch on correct, uniform application of law throughout the Soviet Union, "without any regard whatsoever to local differences or to local influences of any kind."[27] Though in this respect the statute may have done little more than codify already existing grants of power and assignments of responsibility, it has certainly revitalized the general supervision function. Post-Stalin leaders have sought to restore respect for law. To that end they have fortified personal rights against invasion by officials.[28] Although serving as the citizens' shield is in fact much more difficult than serving as the State's sword, the Procuracy has apparently been seriously responsive to the shifted emphasis of its work. During the past decade it has considerably reinforced "socialist legality," as following pages will show.

Organizational structure. The Procuracy's head, the Procurator General, is elected by the Supreme Soviet for a term of seven years and is removable only by it. His immediate deputies are appointed by the Presidium of the Supreme Soviet upon his recommendation. All other procurators are appointed for five-year terms by the Procurator General directly or by procurators subordinate to him. Each of the fifteen federated and twenty autonomous republics, each of the approx-

---

and abuses committed by the rulers of the country." And compare Loeber (note 9 above), at 95–99.

[27] See Regulations on the work of supervision performed by the prosecutor's office in the U.S.S.R., 7 *Curr. Dig. of the Sov. Press* no. 23, at 3–5 (July 20, 1955); "Regulations on Supervision by the Procuracy in the Soviet Union," *Socialist Legality* (Sotsialisticheskaya Zakonnost) no. 7, at 1 (July 1955).

[28] Compare Morgan (note 22 above), at 129–130: "Since Stalin's death, there have been a number of actions that have been taken in the Soviet Union to improve the status of 'socialist legality.' These include various amnesties, reducing the power of the secret police, discontinuing administrative exile to Siberia, abolishing the harsher features of various laws, modifying the criminal laws, etc. The general supervision function of the Soviet Procuracy has been a part of these changes, although the developments affecting this operation have not been as dramatic as those concerning, for example, the diminution of the role of the secret police . . . Although one could hardly maintain that the 'Rule of Law' has become a permanent feature of Soviet governmental life, it is evident that the regime is utilizing general supervision to watch over the enactments and actions of governmental agencies and organizations at *all* levels. The Soviet regime in the post-Stalin period wishes stability of its laws and depends partially on the Procuracy to ensure observance of them."

imately 120 regions, each of the approximately 2,000 "raions" or townships, has a procuracy office with a section of general supervision.

The procurators at the lower levels owe their allegiance not to local political leaders but to the hierarchy of procurators leading to the Procurator General. Independently of other authorities (including courts), the Procuracy controls its own affairs, subject only to being countermanded by the Supreme Soviet or its Presidium if the Procurator General's instructions are themselves deemed to be illegal.[29]

Procurators at times past may have been ill-trained to discharge professional responsibilities.[30] The present level of competence is seemingly high. Professor H. J. Berman has written that "in general the Procuracy is on a higher level than the courts in prestige, in quality of work, and in independence of local Party influence."[31] The 1955 definition of the Procuracy's function of general supervision specifies, in any event, that procurators must have had "higher legal education,"

[29] Despite the apparently thick insulation against local pressures, procurators are said at times to have been "drawn into a network of close 'family relations' with local officials." See Fainsod (note 8 above), at 412; see also Morgan (note 22 above), at 15. Some thoroughly reputable Soviet legal scholars think that detachment of the procurators from local governmental control is an undesirable anomaly, running counter to the general trend toward greater autonomy in place of strong central government. The highly respected Professor A. I. Denisov of Moscow University is a proponent of this view, which will no doubt be considered by the Judicial Committee of the Council of Ministers, now studying preparation of a new constitution; Prof. Denisov is a member of the committee. Professor S. G. Berezovskaia, a prominent writer on the Procuracy, opposes decentralization of that organ lest its freedom to deal with official illegalities be weakened. Economic organizations and other locally powerful groups might, she fears, be able to bring strong pressures to bear on local procurators who were unwilling to overlook "technicalities."

[30] Compare Morgan (note 22), at 15–16, asserting that not until the late 1950's did the Procuracy begin "to be staffed to any extent with legally trained personnel so that it could function as planned at the time of its revival;" one of the causes of earlier inadequate staffing, he contends (p. 106), was the Stalinist purging of about half the experienced personnel and their replacement by factory workers and others of known "loyalty," but limited legal knowledge. Professor Morgan's statements about the professional quality of Procuracy personnel are not endorsed by all American scholars familiar with developments in the Soviet Union, and they have also been challenged by Soviet critics. Professor Morgan, in a letter to the author dated January 31, 1966, says: ". . . my conclusions were drawn solely from the complaints in Soviet legal publications . . . Throughout your paper I can see that the statements I encountered in the Soviet legal works were sometimes at odds with what officials told you personally. I think this may be due to the fact that their press is primarily used to set forth shortcomings and to call for improved efforts—whereas the well-functioning operations and procedures get no specific attention." Without entering into the controversy on this point, one can nevertheless hazard the guess that the Procuracy at various times in the past has probably needed more good lawyers than were then available.

[31] H. J. Berman, Book Review, 57 *Am. J. Int'l L.* 689, 691 (1963).

and a course entitled "Procuracy Supervision in the U.S.S.R." has been introduced into the law schools' curriculum; in-service training courses, conducted by jurists who are otherwise independent of the Procuracy, have also been strongly developed in late years.

The salary scale for procurators is relatively good—"equal to the salaries of scientists," as some legally trained civil servants remarked rather enviously in 1964—and the budget is provided by the Soviet government. Local pinch-pennies are therefore in no position to affect procurators' incomes.

All of this suggests an autonomous, professionally oriented organization operating outside the framework of Party control. This impression is inaccurate because, according to some who have closely studied political realities in the Soviet Union, persons appointed to serve as procurators must in fact still be "cleared" by the relevant level of the Communist Party hierarchy; moreover, a branch of the Secretariat of the Central Committee of the Party is said to maintain continuous contact with the Procuracy and other organs of law administration, in order to assure their acting conformably with Party policies. Hence, the seeming independence of the Procuracy may perhaps be a façade rather than a bulwark.[32] Some of the persons interviewed in the Soviet Union seemed to take seriously the Procuracy's self-contained structure and, whether as a matter of wishful thinking or otherwise, appeared to believe that it enabled procurators to function with professional detachment. Their opinion is not shared by all, either in the Soviet Union or abroad.[33]

[32] Writing of an earlier period, but in terms that may have contemporary significance as well, Professor Fainsod has said: "But above and beyond the law, as well as through the law, the procuracy and the courts continued to function as an instrument of the Party dictatorship. Party directives provided the political guide lines that regulated the scope of judicial discretion and determined the direction of the work of the procuracy. . . . Both the procuracy and the courts are revealed as arms of the Party dictatorship, dedicated to carrying out its policies and reflecting its changing demands. The norms which the legal organs enforce operate from time to time as restraints on arbitrary action by administrative subordinates, but they do not restrict the Party leadership itself. The ultimate reality is one of servility and subservience rather than of an independent legal system binding rulers and ruled alike." M. Fainsod, *Smolensk Under Soviet Rule* 178, 192 (1958). And see also E. Zellweger, "The Principle of Socialist Legality," 5 J. Int. Comm. of Jurists 164, 183–186 (1964).

[33] But compare H. J. Berman, "Human Rights in the Soviet Union," 11 *How. L. J.* 333, 339 (1965): ". . . it remains true that the Procuracy is helpless to enforce Soviet Law against the wishes of the Party leadership, and, moreover, that its efforts are usually directed primarily against those abuses that the Party leadership desires to eradicate."

6|The Procuracy's Review of Subordinate Legislation

As already noted, Soviet courts have only a limited power to determine the validity of statutes or of subordinate legislation. The Procuracy provides the main prescribed method of review. At every level of governmental functioning, the rules, decrees, ordinances that have been issued by delegates of legislative power must be submitted to the scrutiny of the cognizant procurator's office.

Scope of power to review. Perhaps the point should be clearly stated at the outset that the Procuracy's power to supervise legality does not reach to the "collective organs" at the top of the governmental structure. The supreme soviets—that is, the legislatures—of the U.S.S.R. and of the republics that comprise the union are beyond the Procuracy's grasp.[34] So are their presidiums, or executive committees. So, too, are their respective councils of ministers, which are theoretically subject to complete and continuous legislative oversight by the supreme soviets and their presidiums.[35] That still leaves a considerable range of official activity under the Procuracy's scrutiny, for the Procurator General is declared to be responsible for supervising "the strict execution of the laws by all ministries and institutions subordinated to them, as well as by public servants . . ."[36]

Utilization of the power to review. Exercises of authority at very high levels have been successfully challenged. The Ministry of Finance, the Ministry of Internal Affairs, directorates attached to the Council of Ministers, the State Bank, the Minister of Health—these and others have been told that they had issued illegal decrees or instructions, and the offending pronouncements have then been canceled.[37]

[34] If a republican legislature (supreme soviet) were to enact a law deemed to be violative of the national constitution or in conflict with a national law, the Procurator General should, according to Soviet sources, report the matter to the Supreme Soviet of the U.S.S.R. or to its Presidium. I was given no examples and do not know whether such reports have in fact ever been made.

[35] A former Deputy Procurator General, discussing control over decrees of the Council of Ministers of the U.S.S.R., remarked that the Procurator General could, if he chose, make a report to the Supreme Soviet of the U.S.S.R. concerning any action of the Council of Ministers he deemed to be beyond that body's competence. He acknowledged, however, that no such report had ever been made, and he seemed not very much inclined to believe that one ever would be.

[36] Const. U.S.S.R., art. 113. But compare J. Stone, "A Retrospect on Soviet Marxist Theorizing on State and Law," 10 *U.C.L.A.L. Rev.* 754, 768 (1963).

[37] See Morgan (note 22), at 224, for illustrations.

Moreover, local legislatures and officials at lower levels (where no doubt legality is most likely to be disregarded) have often been brought up short when their acts have limited personal rights, and not merely when some "state interest" was at stake. In recent years, for example, local decrees that hampered citizens' freedom of movement in search of congenial employment have been denounced,[38] as have public works hiring policies that discriminated against non-residents,[39] forbade employment of persons dismissed from other jobs,[40] or declared scientific research workers to be unemployable after the age of forty.[41] Regulations restricting farmers in selling their cattle and produce in neighborhood markets have been upset, as have local legislatures' attempts to levy on the assets of economic enterprises that were beyond their authorized reach.

The procedure of review. The procedure for achieving these results is not elaborate. The issuer of every written pronouncement or order intended to have legal effect must submit it to the cognizant procurator's office—local, regional, republican, national, as the case may be—as soon as it is issued. The procurator in charge of that office may "protest" it if he deems it to be illegal in any respect, whether in form or in substance. His protest must be examined by the issuer within ten days.[42] Meanwhile, the protested enactment is not suspended unless its issuer so chooses; neither the procurator nor the courts can, as it were, issue a temporary injunction against its being enforced.

[38] Hazard and Shapiro (note 12), at 70–71. Compare Edwards v. California, 314 U. S. 160 (1941).

[39] Hazard and Shapiro (note 12), at 161.

[40] *Ibid.*, at 162.

[41] *Id.*

[42] Procuracy Statute, Sec. 13, cited in note 7 above. Morgan (note 22), at 213, summarizes statements made in 1956 by the then head of the Department of General Supervision of the U.S.S.R. Procuracy, to the effect that time limits had often been ignored in the past without objection by the procurators. "Some heads of establishments," it was said, "take advantage of this situation and in a 'number of instances' try to delay consideration of a procurator's protest so that the illegal resolution may be put into effect, making any discussion of the protest futile." Without pretending to have made a scientific or penetrating inquiry, I did attempt to ascertain whether this condition still existed as of the end of 1964. Sources inside and outside the Procuracy expressed strong belief that the prescribed time limit was now rarely being exceeded. They said, too, that procurators complained to higher authorities when lower-level officials had been dilatory in acting on protests; offending officials had in fact been disciplined and dilatoriness had thus been discouraged. In at least one case, I was told, an official had been prosecuted for having ignored a procurator's protest.

Penalties for its violation must, however, be held in abeyance while the protest is pending.[43]

If the procurator's protest is accepted, the offending pronouncement is rescinded altogether or is modified to meet the procurator's objection. If the issuer rejects the protest, the procurator may "appeal" to the issuer's superior when the superior is within the same geographical jurisdiction as the procurator's office. Otherwise, the dissatisfied procurator passes the matter to the office next higher in the procuratorial hierarchy, which (if it agrees with the procurator below) revitalizes the objection by filing its own protest with the office or official superior to the original issuer.[44] A leading Soviet authority, S. G. Berezovskaia, characterizes this as a "transfer" of a protest, but it seems in essence to be an appeal from one official level to a higher.

This process may continue from the lowest to the very highest—until the Procuracy's view prevails, or until a higher procurator decides that a lower procurator's protest was ill-grounded, or until the end of the line is reached without acceptance of the Procuracy's opinion concerning the permissibility of the protested act. When all has been said and done, no procurator, not even the Procurator General, has the power to command rescission or modification of an assertedly illegal pronouncement. He can only state an opinion, hoping that his prestige and presumed professional capability will lead to its being received favorably.

Effectiveness of review. One may easily enough be skeptical about the efficacy of so routinized a system. Experience in Britain and America with continuous, ex parte review of administrative regulations has not encouraged any overpoweringly strong enthusiasm for this particular control device.[45] Yet a personal inspection of procurators'

[43] Procuracy Statute, Sec. 13, cited in note 27.

[44] An experienced procurator said recently that a rejected protest, when passed to a higher level, often bears, as a sort of informal endorsement, the legal opinion of the president of the local court; the local procurator has enlisted the judge's opinion to add weight to his own.

[45] See W. Gellhorn and C. Byse, *Administrative Law* 189–195 (4th ed. 1960), for discussion of relevant English and American experience. See also J. A. G. Griffith and H. Street, *Principles of Administrative Law* 84–91 (3rd ed. 1963); C. T. Carr, "Legislative Control of Administrative Rules and Regulations," 30 *N.Y.U. L. Rev.* 1045 (1955); B. Schwartz, "Legislative Control of Administrative Rules and Regulations: The American Experience," 30 *N.Y.U. L. Rev.* 1031 (1955). And see Ore. Rev. Stat. §171.705–.710 (1963), creating legislative review of complaints concerning administrative rules.

offices persuaded a prominent Soviet jurist, well and favorably known outside her homeland, that regulations, ordinances, and the like were then being subjected to persistent, searching scrutiny. The jurist informed me in late 1964 that she had recently visited numerous local procurators, selected randomly and without prior notice, for the assigned purpose of noting and criticizing such defects as she might discover by reading files and observing current activities. She found that the minutes of meetings of official bodies and establishments as well as their formal enactments were being promptly received.[46] Most procurators, she concluded, regarded review of these documents as a primary responsibility and were discharging their duties with creditable professionalism.

This favorable appraisal of what the Procuracy is now doing accords with others. According to Professor Berezovskaia, who recently surveyed action taken on protests, 96 percent of the initial protests have ultimately been "satisfied," either by the issuing authority or by a higher body to which an appeal had been taken.[47] After reviewing the unsuccessful protests in detail, she concluded flatly that they had rested on shaky analytical foundations and had been properly rejected. The extensive range of questions that may possibly have to be considered makes this, nonetheless, a reasonably satisfactory showing.[48]

[46] One may note, in passing, that many Soviet republican statutes direct procurators themselves to attend meetings of local executive bodies, in order to nip threatened illegalities in the bud. This is regarded by the leading Russian authority on the Procuracy as an excellent means of supplying and receiving information and as a valuable preventive measure. See S. G. Berezovskaia, *Okhrana prav grazhdan sovyetskoy prokuraturoy* (The Protection of the Rights of Citizens by the Soviet Procuracy) 67, 68 (1964). Preventive work by procurators may be especially important in local organs, which are not served by "jurisconsults"—legal experts who are employed in the more important governmental bodies and enterprises to review all rules and regulations before they are put into effect. Procuracy Statute, Sec. 16, cited in note 27, provides a foundation for preventive activities, for it empowers procurators to make recommendations to public organs and institutions "to eliminate future violations of law and factors leading to violations."

An illuminating review of the Berezovskaia book by Prof. G. G. Morgan appears in XVII *Soviet Studies* 113 (July 1965).

[47] About nine out of ten protests are accepted locally, according to informal estimates frequently repeated in conversation. Most of the others go up the ladder for attention at higher levels.

[48] Since 1923, according to a scholarly estimate, 450,000 laws and decrees have emanated from the highest Soviet Union organs, not counting ministerial orders and the like. Many thousands have had to do with specific administrative matters. The immensity of this body of law obviously complicates the procurators' task of checking questions of ultra vires, along with all other legal issues that may be suggested

The present system does, however, have deficiencies that even the more euphoric Soviet jurists recognize. For one thing, local procurators (like all other occupational groups) are varyingly able, diligent, and aggressive. An unobservant man may overlook imperfections that a keener legal eye would discern. And an unconfident man may not speak up boldly about the imperfections he does discover.

Some with whom this topic was considered in 1964 remarked that protests about "technical illegalities" have occasionally been withheld by procurators intent upon courting local good will. Furthermore, local officials can embarrass an unpopular procurator by rejecting his protests, thus forcing him to go to his superiors for help. "A procurator who bombards higher offices with protests he hasn't succeeded in getting accepted on his own level, won't be regarded as very competent in his post," a realistic observer commented, "and since he knows that to be so, he may refrain from making a protest he fears may be rejected. No procurator ever acknowledges that he has been timid for the sake of his own reputation, but that is the way things happen in life."

A more serious shortcoming is the present impossibility of forcing suspension of a regulation whose validity has been protested. Those who look on the procurators as watchdogs of legality think that a regulation should become wholly inoperative when denounced by an examiner especially trained to ascertain its legality. Since 96 percent of the procurators' protests are ultimately given effect, continued application while protests are being considered means that many illegal edicts are at least temporarily enforced (though, to be sure, they cannot be enforced by imposing penalties on violators).

Another defect, according to enthusiasts for Procuracy control, is inability to deal with acts of the councils of ministers of the federated republics. While nobody is known to advocate the Procuracy's questioning the legality of what the Council of Ministers of the U.S.S.R. chooses to do, the republican councils are thought to be fair game for the lawyers. The councils are not invariably under effective control

---

by the rules and regulations under review. Life is made bearable, however, by the fact that most local bodies tend to have narrowly defined statutory powers, so that determining their competence does not often require recourse to the vast accumulation of general law.

by their nominal superiors, the republican legislatures; they are not always well informed about matters of national law and national policy; they are sometimes moved by considerations of local interest that obscure the claims of broader policies. In some republics, procurators at times attend sessions of the council of ministers in order to offer informal advice concerning legal questions that may arise; they cannot, however, formally challenge actions taken contrary to the tendered advice. Some reformers believe that the power to protest should be clarified and extended.[49]

7 | The Procuracy's Review of Administration

While rules, regulations, and formally enunciated policies are subjected to regular scrutiny in the way just discussed, their day-to-day application presents fresh problems. Theoretically the Procuracy supervises all official actions, to assure that governmental performance harmonizes with legality. In momentary flushes of enthusiasm or overconfidence, years ago, the Procuracy did attempt to exercise truly comprehensive supervision—even to the extent, for example, of examining the adequacy of maintenance work done in tractor stations (a "legal question" because the law requires that custodians of state property take good care of it). Lapsing back into bad habits of regarding themselves as the overlords of all administration, procurators very recently looked into the daily work of a railroad station manager and into the cleaning of freight cars after use. Nowadays supervision is usually more selective.

Inspection campaigns. In many instances the procurator of a republic prepares a plan to check on the administration of a particular law deemed to have special public importance. His plan spreads downward through the regional to the local offices of the Procuracy. Then it is executed simultaneously by all offices. Thus a coordinated, searching

[49] But note especially that Morgan (note 22), at 142–148 and 211–212, gives examples of procurators' protests that have in fact been lodged against these types of enactments. He also points out (at 241–245) that even when protests as such have not been made, procurators have advanced "proposals" that amount to challenging the legality of enactments of higher governmental organs.

inquiry is made into law observance within the chosen field of governmental activity—such as, for instance, adherence to labor laws or safety regulations.

Sometimes administrative fulfilment of procedural requirements is tested by investigating a problem common to many separate agencies and organizations. Thus, administrative mechanisms for handling complaints have been looked into systematically, as has also administrative observance of laws requiring that negative decisions be accompanied by an explanation. In at least one republic the procurators inquired into whether the top officials of establishments, institutions, and organizations were in fact personally accessible to callers, as directed by a law requiring them to keep a fixed schedule of visiting hours.

In addition to these rather focused and purposeful inspection campaigns, procurators do still engage in "complex investigations" which have no particular object, but are intended, as one learned author has said, to "determine legality with reference to the given object in its totality."[50] Although discontinuance of these general fishing expeditions seems not to be flatly advocated in the Soviet Union, their practical accomplishments appear to have been few. They have been defended on the basis of their supposed "educational effects," "the interest they arouse among many persons," and "their making local officials more aware of the control function"—intangible results that cannot well be appraised by an outsider, but that in any event should be achievable by some means other than the blunderbuss.

These massive campaigns do not, at any rate, preclude more episodic investigations into the conduct of public affairs. A deputy procurator of one of the republics reportedly said as recently as 1959 that "up to now the question of the limits of general supervision of the Procuracy has not been worked out theoretically and practically."[51] To suggest that both the theory and the practice of supervision have since become fully established would be foolhardy. But it is not too much to say that at least the contours seemed plainly discernible in late 1964.

First, a few words about the Procuracy's powers in the area of law observance as distinct from law promulgation.

The Procuracy's powers. Procurators have power to demand—and

[50] Berezovskaia (note 46 above), at 99.
[51] Quoted in Morgan (note 7 above), at 122.

officials are under a duty to produce—all documents deemed to bear on an investigation into legality.[52]

They may "carry out investigation on the spot pertaining to law observance in connection with complaints or other information concerning trespasses of law." Alternatively, they may direct the heads of public establishments to investigate and, if need be, reform subordinate bodies and officials.[53]

They may themselves appeal from an administrative order that imposes obligations or disadvantageous consequences on an individual; and pending the appellate body's action on the procurator's appeal, the challenged execution of the administrative penalty must be held in abeyance.[54]

When a procurator detects what he believes to be an official departure from legality, he may seek redress by initiating criminal, administrative, or disciplinary proceedings as may appear to be suitable in the circumstances, and "when necessary, may take steps toward securing compensation for material damage, resulting from a trespass of the law."[55]

As to places of detention, the procurator is under an affirmative duty to make "systematic" visits and to become "directly acquainted with their administration," with the object of halting acts contrary to law.[56] He has "unlimited access," the right to see documents and to conduct personal interviews with detained persons, and to call for the testimony of staff members.[57]

These powers are clearly more compelling than those utilized when examining the legality of written pronouncements. There, the procurator has authority to receive a copy, to analyze its legality, and to

[52] Procuracy Statute, §§ 11(2), 12 cited in note 27.

[53] *Ibid.*, §11(3)(4).

[54] *Ibid.*, §13.

[55] Procuracy Statute, §15. The power to prosecute, according to an informed observer of Soviet law administration, adds great potency to the procurator's advice about questions of administrative legality. An official who responds too casually to a procuratorial protest or proposal may, so it is said, "find himself a defendant in a criminal case." And see further, as to the possibility of prosecution for "official crimes," Berman (note 13 above), at 335–336.

[56] Procuracy Statute, § 33.

[57] *Ibid.*, §35. According to authentic non-Soviet testimony, procurators do regularly visit penal institutions, where they receive prisoners' complaints (to which, as a recently released prisoner stated to Professor Berman, the procurators "responded very vigorously" by prodding prison authorities into compliance with applicable laws and regulations).

express an opinion in the form of a "protest." Here, he is given tools for digging below the surface of official conduct in order to ascertain the realities of what is happening.

Skeptics assert that the primary purpose is not to protect individual citizens against officially inflicted wrongs, but is to protect the interest of the State (and the Communist Party) in maintaining control over the Soviet Union's vast administrative machinery. That may arguably be true, but the fundamental law pertaining to Procuracy powers does nevertheless heavily stress *individual* rights. Section 14 obligates the procurator to receive and act upon complaints by private persons; Section 36 requires that a prisoner's complaint addressed to a procurator must be delivered within twenty-four hours, must be promptly examined and acted upon by the procurator, and must receive a written response showing the procurator's judgment concerning the matters in question.

Moreover, since the 1961 reform of the procedure leading to imposition of "administrative fines," procurators have regularly attended the executive sessions of the administrative commissions empowered to penalize violators of various regulations. So far as could be gauged by an interviewer in 1964, this was not at all a pro forma matter. Procurators participate in discussions in order to forestall official illegalities, not to lend a spurious air of regularity to proceedings in which they have no direct interest. One can never exactly measure the results of preventive activity, but serious observers strongly believed that procurators were often interceding effectively in behalf of citizens who might otherwise have been roughly dealt with by commissioners. While procurators are empowered to attend sessions of every public organ, pressures of time prevent their dashing from one meeting to another without pausing for breath. They do, however, concentrate on the work of the administrative commissions, where the citizen is most likely to be the direct object of an official decision and where the moderating counsel of a lawyer may therefore be most important to affected individuals.

The Procuracy's handling of complaints. Complaints provide a large part of the business that flows into local procurators' offices, which handle the bulk of the caseload in the first instance.[58] A top-level proc-

[58] The office of the Procurator General of the U.S.S.R. annually receives and determines perhaps a thousand administrative cases involving central governmental

urator of many years' experience estimated that 60 to 65 percent of the general supervision matters dealt with locally are direct outgrowths of individual grievances. Chiefly, these pertain to housing, pension, and labor law matters.[59]

When, as often occurs, the complaint to the procurator shows on its face that established procedures for administrative review have not yet been used, the procurator may at times do no more than forward the letter to the proper recipient; the Procuracy's own rules require that the complainant be advised of what has been done.[60]

Several persons connected with the Procuracy stated, however, that even when available administrative remedies had not been exhausted, procurators frequently did something additional. One of them said: "I often telephone without forwarding a complaint at all, and sometimes I write my own opinion, sending it along with the complaint. The other day, for example, I telephoned the director of a large factory and told him about what seemed to be a violation of a worker's rights. We call that an 'oral protest by the procurator.' The director agreed with me, and that closed the matter then and there. In some instances, I haven't telephoned but have myself gone to an establishment to look for other violations, when a complaint has suggested to me that a pattern of illegality might be present instead of just an isolated error."[61]

---

agencies, according to one informed source. In 1964, a former Deputy Procurator General characterized its chief work, however, as "leading the activities of the field staff, which is responsible for hundreds of thousands of cases." Morgan (note 22), at 191–192, states that there are no published examples of the Procuracy's checking on complaints concerning the way higher officials or agencies have executed the laws. My Soviet informant concerning casework by the Procurator General's staff said flatly that complaints against high-level officials are, in fact, checked. I have no independent knowledge of the matter.

59 The Procuracy's duty to supervise law observance extends beyond ministries and administrative agencies as such, reaching as well to "their subordinate establishments and enterprises, . . . cooperative and other public organizations . . ." Procuracy Statute, §3, cited in note 27.

60 If the procurator decides to do nothing at all (as he may if the complaint seems plainly unmeritorious), he must tell the complainant why.

61 Compare Morgan (note 22), at 204: In connection with allegedly illegal acts not reflected in formal written papers, "the procurator takes steps to eliminate the violations of law by proposing (in writing or orally) to the violator that he rectify the violation, and in some instances raises the question of instituting criminal prosecution or proceedings in disciplinary action against him. For example, if the director of an enterprise illegally refuses to pay a worker his wages, give him his labor book, or give him a certificate necessary for him to get another job, or if the director of a school illegally refuses to admit a pupil, or if a hospital director illegally refuses to admit a sick person for treatment, the procurator in writing or orally (sometimes by

Added light on complaint handling is shed by Professor Berezovskaia's recent authoritative study.[62] She remarks, first, that a complaint to a procurator need not be filed within whatever time limits may have been prescribed for direct administrative review of a challenged act. Nor need a complaint be in any particular form, written or otherwise; formal requirements, it has been thought, might discourage recourse to the Procuracy by those who may most need its help. No fee is payable in respect of a complaint, but once it has been filed with the procurator, it cannot be withdrawn by the complainant; the procurator may pursue it as far as he sees fit. Often an individual complaint becomes merged in a broader investigation, the procurator not being bound by the specific claims the complainant has put forward.

While Professor Berezovskaia thinks that the Procuracy has often done commendable work, she candidly notes serious shortcomings in some offices: superficial analysis; inadequate use of complaints as potential indicators of wide illegality; failure to formulate principles for appraising safeguards against future violations; merely formal attention to a complaint—as, for example, a procurator's forwarding a citizen's grievance to a competent body and then making no further inquiry when informed that "action has been taken"; failure to comply with the Procuracy's own regulation that no complaint should be rejected without a statement of reasons; unwillingness to take the responsibility of deciding that a grievance is ill-founded as a matter of law, and saying so without "sending persons from Pontius to Pilate"; unreadiness to recognize sheer litigiousness and querulousness when they occur, because the procurator fears that he himself might be accused of insufficient concern for protecting citizens' rights.

These remarks by an admirer of the Procuracy's achievements sufficiently suggest the importance of the human element in the Soviet protective machinery. The machinery runs imperfectly when its operators are inept. The same must be said, of course, about all countries'

---

telephone) explains to the officials the impropriety of their actions . . . If the violator refuses to rectify the violation and there are no grounds for initiating a criminal case, the procurator protests the act or action of the violator to the agency to which the latter is subordinate."

When a complaint has been handled informally, the Procuracy's regulations require that both the complaint and the remedial activity it has induced be recorded in a special "reception diary." Berezovskaia (note 46), at 78.

[62] See Berezovskaia (note 46), at 70–94.

efforts to assure the justice and legality of administrative acts. Whether Soviet personnel deficiencies occur sufficiently frequently to jeopardize the complaint handling system as a whole is a question that cannot be answered here. Professor Berezovskaia, who impresses an interviewer as markedly an enthusiast but not at all a mythologist, thinks that the shortcomings in performance are the exceptions and not the rule.

Extent of procurators' participation in individual cases. In every system of review, a line has to be drawn between examining the challenged administrative action to ascertain its validity and, on the other hand, doing the administrator's job over again while pretending simply to check whether it had been done adequately the first time.

Drawing that line—or paying attention to it, once it has been drawn—has sometimes seemed to be beyond the capacity (or, perhaps, inclination) of some American judges.[63] The task has been at least as hard for Soviet procurators, who have occasionally been tempted to become superadministrators. One's notions about wisdom sometimes intertwine with one's professional judgment about permissibility, unless considerable self-restraint is exercised.

Moreover, some of the procurators, acting under the guise of "general supervision" and not under the guise of prosecuting malefactors, have directed their attention to what citizens were doing instead of to what administrative agencies and other organizations were doing. To the extent that they addressed themselves to the citizenry, the procurators took over the functions of other administrators to whom primary responsibility for law administration had been assigned.

The top-ranking officials of the Procuracy seem to be very clear in their own minds about what procurators should and should not do. A Deputy Procurator General long in charge of general supervision, G. Toropov, repeatedly stated that his subordinates should avoid becoming administrators themselves, while remaining critical analysts of what the immediately responsible administrators have done.[64] Proc-

[63] See, e.g., National Labor Relations Board v. Walton Manufacturing Co., 369 U.S. 404 (1962), reversing the decision of an appellate court that had displaced the Board's choice between two fairly conflicting views of what had been proved.

[64] As to "generally supervising" law observance by the citizenry, for example, compare Morgan (note 7), at 128: "Toropov maintains that trying to exercise such supervision 'in practice' would result in undesirable consequences, to substituting the procurators for the appropriate administrative agencies. Thus, individual citizens

urators have been told forcefully not to meddle in economic and operational affairs, which are beyond their professional competence; when procurators involve themselves in such matters, they have been warned, they supplant the control and auditing agencies that should be relied on to do the primary work. As recently as 1964, however, Mr. Toropov acknowledged that some procurators continued incautiously to weigh the merits of administrative action instead of simply adjudging its legality; rather than pursuing complaints about law violation, they were attempting to perform work others were obligated to do initially.[65]

This particular criticism of procurators, it will be noted, is that some of them have been doing too much, not too little. In any event, the fact seems to be that most procurators do follow up complaints they receive, at least to the extent of ascertaining whether the administrator has acted legally and sometimes to the far greater extent of ascertaining whether he has acted correctly according to the procurators' notions of correctness. A jurist who is a lecturer to newly appointed procurators put the matter succinctly: "We try to teach them that they must, above all, be determiners of what the law requires or allows. That is the purpose, and the only purpose, for which they are supervisors. They are not supposed to be nursemaids, patting the hands of people who are unhappy whenever things are not entirely to their liking. And they are not supposed to act as though they know more about everything than anybody else. They should try to be specialists in legality, not specialists in all affairs."

The People's Control Committee. The procurators of the Soviet Union have by now probably become increasingly observant of the limits upon their competence. An extremely powerful body, the "Con-

---

might not pay the agricultural or income tax, make compulsory deliveries of agricultural products to the State, etc., on time. Toropov says that this is undoubtedly a violation of the law, but asks rhetorically whether in such instances the Procuracy should intervene directly 'and make definite demands of individual citizens.' He replies that it should not, for then it would be replacing the appropriate financial agencies in which the law vests checking on the timely payment of taxes and compulsory deliveries by citizens, 'applying sanctions provided by law in certain instances to the defaulters.' The Procuracy is not to 'stand aside' from supervision over the observance of the laws concerning State taxes and compulsory deliveries, but its duty consists of exercising supervision over how the *financial agencies* are executing the requirements of the law which compels them to be checking constantly on whether citizens are paying their taxes and making deliveries on time."

[65] G. Toropov, "An Important Condition for Improving the Work of Public Control," *Socialist Legality* (Sotsialisticheskaya Zakonnost) no. 2 (Feb. 1964).

trol Committee of the Party and the State," functioned from late 1962 until December, 1965, specifically to serve as a managerial overseer.[66] Then it was replaced by the "People's Control Committee," with apparently the same responsibility of supervising economic and financial aspects of state and other organizations. That committee's expanding activity tends to push procurators back into their own niche.

This is not to suggest that the Communist Party's interest in superintending administrators was aroused for the first time in 1962. Party members—a sort of elite corps comprising only 5 percent of the population—had long been, as Professor M. E. Dimock has put it, "watchdogs, checking on professional civil servants and keeping them in line."[67] The Party's statutes direct its members "to inform leading Party bodies, up to and including the Central Committee, of shortcomings in work, irrespective of person" and "to carry out the Party policy among the non-Party people, . . . to combat bureaucracy, and to verify fulfilment of Party and Soviet directives."[68] Many non-members in the past are said to have complained to Party organs about acts of governmental officials; and the Party often, though unsystematically, offered its "recommendations" to officials, who were unlikely to ignore advice from so influential a source. Procurators themselves, when they found that they had bitten off more "general supervision" than they could chew, are known to have turned to the Party for help, in preference to calling upon their own superiors.[69] What occurred in

---

[66] For discussion of the Control Committee, see Romachkine (note 3), at 82–83, 127–133. And see also W. Dabrowski, "Le Côntrole Général du Procureur de la Légalité de l'Action Administrative en URSS," in M. Mouskhely ed., *L'U.R.S.S.* vol. 2 at 141 (1964).

[67] Dimock (note 1), at 144.

[68] Quoted in Loeber (note 9), at 65.

[69] Morgan (note 22), at 235, provides an excellent example: "The Vinnitskii raion procurator learned of violations of labor legislation in a local garment factory. Acting on such information he checked the 'observance of legality' in the factory and submitted a proposal to the factory management contemplating elimination of the violations. However, sometime later, the procurator again was apprised of violations of law in the factory. This time the procurator made a thorough check in the factory; a general meeting of workers and employees was called, and the procurator described the violations he had uncovered. Various speakers in the meeting 'subjected the administration to sharp criticism for violations of labor legislation,' along with the factory committee, which was accused of a poor job of ensuring observance of labor laws.

"The procurator simultaneously submitted a proposal to the raion Party committee concerning the violations disclosed in the garment factory and raised the question of punishing the factory director. The raion Party committee responded by imposing

1962 was therefore not so much the Communist Party's becoming involved directly in public administration as it was systematizing an already existing involvement.

After the Party's Central Committee had strongly criticized existing control mechanisms, the Presidium of the Supreme Soviet, the Council of Ministers, and the Party jointly created a new organ of surveillance, the Party-State Control Committee, to supervise enterprises, establishments, and administrative organs of all kinds. Accountable ultimately to the Council of Ministers and the Central Committee of the Communist Party, the Control Committee functioned through extensions of itself (that is, through subordinate committees) at every level of government. Cooperating committees were elected in economic enterprises, workshops, collective farms, trade unions, pensioners' organizations, councils of workers' wives, and even apartment houses, to bring to the attention of the suitable Party-State Control Committee any matter the cooperators might think should be investigated. At the end of 1964 an informed Moscow source asserted that 4,500,000 Soviet citizens were directly engaged, without salary, in furthering the work of control committees. The committees were said by then to have become universally operative, from the smallest unit to the very top, constituting a people's control system operating outside official channels.

The assigned duty of control committees was "to aid the Party and the Government achieve the Communist Party's new program" by systematically checking "the actual execution of the directives of the Party and the administration" and assuring observance of "the discipline of the Party and of the State."[70] To that end, control committees could demand all sorts of documents, could compel officials to justify what they had done or had not done, could report adverse findings to higher authorities, and, most significantly, could suspend decisions and forbid actions they deemed to be illegal or prejudicial to State interests. In fact, a control committee could actually discipline and

a 'severe Party penalty' on the director and demanded immediate elimination of the violations of law. A subsequent Procuracy check in this factory disclosed no further violations."

[70] Romachkine (note 3), at 128.

even remove or demote persons whom it regarded as responsible for mismanagement or other deficiencies. The Party-State control was thus unabashedly concerned with managing rather than with reviewing; it concerned itself with purposes, policies, practicalities, not simply with proprieties.[71]

All of these powers and activities seem now to have been transferred to a post-Kruschchev creation, the People's Control Committee.

The impact of all this on the Procuracy's work has not yet been fully measured. Problems of coordinating the controls have already been experienced, since the division between legalities and managerial shortcomings is indistinct in the Soviet Union, which defines as crimes many things other countries regard simply as regrettable mistakes.[72] In some localities procurators and control committees have worked together, making simultaneous inspections and exchanging information that has come to hand.[73] In other places, apparently, an uneasy feeling has developed that multiple controls have engendered administrative irresolution and conflicting pressures. This uneasiness is accentuated by awareness that various technical and fiscal inspectorates, as well as trade union inspectors, may also tread in the path already trod by procurators and the Control Committee.

One may suppose that if the importance of the Control Committee's work is heavily emphasized by the Soviet Union's leaders, procuratorial concern about managerial matters will greatly lessen. This may free procurators from work for which they are not professionally trained and may enable them to concentrate on investigating the merits of individual grievances.

[71] But compare *N.Y. Times,* Dec. 7, 1964, p. 2, col. 2, quoting *Pravda* as asserting "The essence of the Leninist style of party leadership is that it is not a leadership of an administrative but of a high political type. The party ensures political guidance of all governmental and public organizations. But it does not assume their functions, functions of direct administration."

[72] In some circumstances, for example, failure to carry out plans and assignments for delivery of industrial goods has been a penal offense in the U.S.S.R., as has producing goods that fell below prescribed quality standards. Procurators in the past, though seemingly not now, have spent much time looking into the operation of lagging economic enterprises in an effort, so it was said, to investigate the legality of the management, though what was really in question was its efficiency. Compare Morgan (note 22), at 173. Compare "Economic Crimes in the Soviet Union," 5 *J. Int. Comm. of Jurists* 3 (1964).

[73] Compare Toropov, note 65 above.

8 | Some Concluding Comments

This chapter is not based on extensive field observations, examination of files and original documents, evaluation of inaccessible statistics, or numerous conversations with persons who have dealt with the Procuracy as complainants or respondents. The most that can be claimed for the conclusions reached is that they rest in part upon substantial interviews with persons both well informed and seemingly well disposed to be candid. The writer's very limited credentials must be borne in mind when reading the paragraphs that follow.

In the space of only a few decades Western countries have changed from laissez-faire and rugged individualism to economic regulation and welfare statism. Most Westerners accept the change as an accomplished fact and think only about improving the new society rather than about reverting to the old one. Changes that cannot be reversed are not peculiar to the West. They may equally possibly occur in Soviet society. Specifically, legality as it bears on individual interests, quite apart from the supposed "interests of the State," may have become an abiding concern and not merely a momentary tactic.

Because personal rights have been trampled upon at times during the Soviet Union's history and because Communist tracts have sneeringly dismissed Western legal values, many non-communist observers regard recent Soviet developments with understandable skepticism. The present Soviet stress on legality, they plausibly suspect, might prove to be a device to further efficiency and to strengthen the regime, and not at all a genuinely felt resolve to advance the cause of justice.[74]

[74] Compare T. Napolitano, "Outline of Modern Soviet Criminal Law," 6 *J. Int. Comm. of Jurists* 54, 80 (1965), expressing skepticism concerning the "renovation" of Socialist Law in light of the Communist Party's domination over law administering organs. But see V. Mironenko, "Counsel for the Prosecution," 11 *Bulletin of the Institute for the Study of the U.S.S.R.* 33, 41 (Aug. 1964): "It may well be asked whether the Soviet *prokuratura* is now really helping to enforce Soviet laws or whether it is merely circumventing these laws to the Party's advantage. There is every reason to suppose that, generally speaking, the former is the case." But compare G. G. Morgan, "People's Justice: The Anti-Parasite Laws, People's Volunteer Militia, and Comrades' Courts," 7 *Law in Eastern Europe* 49 (1963), raising grave questions about tendencies that seem to run counter to the stress on justice and legal orderliness.

On the face of the matter, however, a true effort is in progress to protect citizens against mistake and abuse. The tools relied upon may be imperfect, but the objectives of their use seem laudable.

Indeed, the present "general supervision" of the Procuracy in the Soviet Union somewhat resembles that of parliamentary commissioners (or ombudsmen) in Scandinavian countries. Both the Scandinavian ombudsman and the Soviet procurator deal with problems of ultra vires; both of them act on citizens' complaints as well as on their own motion; both of them make recommendations concerning the desirability of new legislation to correct statutory deficiencies they have discovered;[75] both of them protest and advise, without power actually to command administrators; both of them can report to the highest organs when they think their advice has been improperly rejected; both of them can make proposals for improved administrative methods in order to forestall future lapses from rectitude;[76] both of them have special responsibility to inquire into the grievances of persons held in places of detention; both of them engage in educational activities aimed at developing rights consciousness and public awareness that redress of grievances can be sought;[77] and like the Swedish and Finnish ombudsmen, the Soviet procurator can launch a prosecution or disciplinary action against an official whom he deems to be gravely derelict.

The Scandinavians' work and purposes have justly aroused enthusiasm in the West. The larger-scale though similar Soviet undertaking perhaps deserves more favorable appraisal than now given by most Westerners. Quite properly recalling the Procuracy's flabbiness in past periods, when the hue and cry against "state enemies" swept aside the claims of legality, Western jurists need a lengthier demonstration before becoming altogether convinced that the newly turned leaf will stay

[75] See Procuracy Statute, §9, cited in note 27, authorizing the Procurator General to recommend new legislation, through the Presidium of the Supreme Soviet.

[76] *Ibid.*, §16. Institutions and organizations to which a procurator proposes means of eliminating future errors must study the proposal and act upon it suitably within a month.

[77] See Toropov (note 65): Procurators appear at meetings of social organizations, labor unions, collective farms, and the like to discuss their work, to receive grievances, and to give legal advice. They also appear frequently in newsprint and on radio and television.

turned.[78] Legality may again in the future be subordinated to the real or supposed needs of Party rule; administrative abuses may again become protected means of maintaining political domination, instead of being viewed as evils to be extirpated. But Westerners should at the very least keep their minds open to the possibility that a basic change has really occurred. When literally hundreds of thousands of citizens' grievances receive professional attention, often leading to redressive measures even in the remotest parts of a vast country,[79] one cannot dismiss lightly the present Soviet commitment to justice.

The Soviet Procuracy faces far greater difficulties than the Scandinavian Ombudsman in serving that commitment. The scope of governmental activity is, to begin with, so much greater in the Soviet Union than in a Scandinavian country that the occasions for citizen-official disagreements are grossly multiplied.

Then, too, officials who wield power in the Soviet Union have neither inherited a strong professional tradition as have Scandinavian civil servants nor, as yet, built up their own tradition of deference to law. Procurators have publicly deplored officials' poor training, their obtuseness in applying statutes, and their insensitivity to legal norms.[80]

A third difficulty is the simple factor of size. In a country with a small caseload of citizens' unresolved grievances, a single exalted personage, aided by a few technical assistants, can himself attend to every case. Apart from assuring uniformly high professionalism in complaint-handling, this has important educational consequences because all officialdom tends to listen when the exalted personage speaks. In the Soviet Union, by contrast, the work must be done by many hands in many places, with varying degrees of skill and enthusiasm and collateral impact. Admonitory utterances by superior to subordinate proc-

[78] Compare J. N. Hazard, Book Review, 78 *Pol. Sci. Q* 479, 480 (1963): "Those who protect citizens from arbitrary officials because it makes for efficient government relax controls more quickly in danger than those who provide protection because it is right to do so . . . Scandinavia does well with an almost similar institution, and this suggests that it is not without merit. Its failures come more from attitudes toward government . . . than from inherent weakness in the structure of the Procuracy."

[79] See, e.g., Morgan (note 22), at 223, showing that violations of personal, property, and other rights of citizens were being upset by procurators in Armenia at the rate of forty per month in 1960.

[80] See K. Grzybowski, *Soviet Legal Institutions* 261 (1962); and see also Morgan (note 22), at 223, quoting a Ukrainian procurator as calling for "raising the legal training of soviet officials themselves."

urators show that the Procuracy shares every big organization's difficulties in inspiring and coordinating a numerous, widely dispersed staff. The Procuracy, one observer has declared, has the disadvantage of being an "authoritarian organization susceptible to red tape, lack of initiative, and indifference to the material results of the work, unless the personal interest of the officials concerned is affected."[81]

Finally, the Soviet Union's procurators are in a sense less supported, more isolated than their Scandinavian analogues. A Scandinavian ombudsman is concerned with legality as is a Soviet procurator, but many other organs join with him to assure law observance by public servants. The ordinary law courts, special administrative courts, administrative tribunals with formal procedures—all are involved simultaneously in receiving and acting upon reports of controversy between citizens and officials. The Soviet procurator, by contrast, carries upon his own shoulders almost the entire burden of appraising the legality of official determinations.

This point has been perceived within the Soviet Union itself. Professor M. S. Strogovich, a highly respected authority on the Procuracy, has advocated allowing procurators to seek quick judicial review of allegedly illegal acts by administrators.[82] During an informal conversation in 1964 a group of well regarded legal scholars went even further in the direction of urging judicial review. Immediately affected persons, they said, should themselves have greater access to the courts for the purpose of challenging official determinations.

American specialists in Soviet law do not unanimously believe that expanded judicial review would benefit the Soviet citizenry.[83] One

[81] Loeber (note 9), at 100.

[82] See Morgan (note 22), at 250.

[83] Morgan (note 22), at 251, doubts that judicial review would be significant because "the courts are also completely under the domination of the Communist Party of the Soviet Union." Berman, who thinks it misleading to describe the courts as "completely" dominated without differentiating among subject matters and, indeed, degrees of domination, nevertheless says (note 31 above, at 690–691) that "it would not substantially improve matters—from the standpoint of civil liberties—to shift some of the powers of the Procuracy to the Soviet courts. Indeed, it would worsen matters . . ." But compare I. Shapiro, Book Review, 63 *Colum. L. Rev.* 969, 971 (1963): ". . . no propaganda concerning an alleged return to 'socialist legality' can obscure the fact that a Soviet citizen aggrieved by the enactment of an illegal ordinance or regulation or by an arbitrary act of a Soviet official must look to an agency of the executive for his remedy. Perhaps, given the totalitarian nature of the Soviet regime, it would be too much to expect the Soviet courts to act independently when

thing, however, is clear. If opportunity to take a case to court were more generously provided than at present, aggrieved persons could retain control over their own cases in a way not now possible. When a citizen complains to a procurator and the procurator decides to pursue the complaint, the case becomes the procurator's; the complainant has no further voice in the matter. The Procuracy's rules instruct the staff how to proceed, but the instructions are not enforceable by the citizen. If the complaint is handled carelessly, if the procurator is too readily convinced by what the challenged administrator tells him, if a local procurator's protest is pigeonholed without further action at some higher level within the Procuracy, or indeed if the procurator does nothing at all to investigate the matters complained of, the original complainant has no course of self-help he can readily pursue.[84]

Considerations like these have led practicing lawyers in the Soviet Union to become disenchanted with the present system of complaint handling. They use the system and they want to retain it, but they regret its exclusivity. In 1964 two leading spokesmen of the legal profession agreed that action within the Procuracy is often extremely slow, partly because a matter must sometimes pass through many levels before a decision is reached to file a formal protest in the name of the procurator. "Our chief objection," one of the speakers added, "is the bureaucratic nature of the Procuracy's consideration of the complaint. We have no opportunity whatsoever to meet the case put forward by the official; we don't know what he tells the procurator, and so we aren't sure that the procurator has a true picture before him. We haven't a chance to urge our view of the law, once the matter is in the procurator's hands. What we favor, and I am confident this view prevails among practicing lawyers, is a system of judicial review, with proceedings in which the complainant can play a part, and with an opportunity to obtain a definite judgment if the complaint is upheld."

---

reviewing a government decree or action, but the enlargement of the role of the Soviet courts in this area would be a greater step in the direction of the 'rule of law' than would greater vigilance on the part of the Soviet Procuracy."

[84] Berman (note 13), at 338, comments on a complainant's having pursued a claim for redress "through all the intermediate stages from a West Russian village to the Deputy Procurator General of the USSR in Moscow"; but one gains the impression that similar pertinacity is rare.

Impressed by the Soviet Union's present means of correcting official lapses and at the same time convinced that seemly judicial review of administrative determinations is socially valuable, one can only hope that the Procuracy and the courts will not come to be thought of as mutually exclusive. Both can play vital roles in redressing citizens' grievances. Both can share, even more constructively, in stimulating administrators to strike at roots from which future grievances might grow.

nine

Japan

Friendly observers often remark that the Japanese have superbly cultivated the trait of patience. Less amiable critics argue that the cult of submissiveness—inherited from the feudal past—holds the Japanese in its grip. Neither characterization is entirely true, for no single description can fit a population of nearly a hundred million. But whether because of patience or because of submissiveness or because of many reasons in combination, the Japanese people as a whole seem less inclined than Americans to engage in open contest with public officials. Since 1945, however, Japanese civilians have become increasingly conscious of their rights—and increasingly inclined to assert them. Though "rights consciousness" has as yet neither swept the entire nation nor greatly changed traditional disinclination to pursue legal remedies, it has encouraged the quest for informal means of dealing with citizens' grievances. Mediatory devices of considerable importance have emerged.

1 | The Existence of Formal Remedies

A | Types of Formal Review

The newly developed informal methods of settling citizen-official controversies supplement rather than supplant legal remedies available to those who choose to use them.

Judicial review. After World War II, administrative determinations became subject to broad judicial review in the ordinary courts. Japanese judges still cannot command or enjoin official acts quite so extensively as can American courts. Their powers under present statutes are nevertheless impressive. In fact, however, recourse to the courts is infrequent. During 1960, 1961, and 1962, for example, only 2,448 cases involving public administrators—an annual average of 816—appeared on Japanese judicial dockets; and these included every type of controversy from patent registration (the largest single category) to election procedures and tax matters.[1]

Although direct quantitative comparisons are unfeasible because of differences in population size and in the content of underlying statutes, a glance at American judicial statistics may lend perspective to the Japanese figures. In the fiscal years 1962, 1963, and 1964, United States courts were asked to review 2,858 old-age, survivors, and disability claims cases (an annual average of 953).[2] This single category of federal administrative activity thus outnumbered all the cases that found their way into Japanese courts from both national and local levels of administration.

Administrative review. Administrative redress is little more popular than recourse to the courts. Opportunities for formal review have been greatly expanded in recent years, notably by the Administrative Review Act of 1962, which supplemented existing laws applicable to specific

[1] The stated figures are derived from *Japan Law Times* Report No. 166, at 23 (1964). The percentage distribution of subject matters was as follows:

Patent cases	23.6
Agricultural land use	22.5
Taxation	18.3
Public personnel	7.6
Eminent domain	5.6
Election procedures	3.2
Miscellaneous	19.2

These totals, one may note in passing, apparently far exceeded those for immediately preceding years. A statistical compilation published by the Administrative Management Agency, *Gyosei Kanri Nenpō* (Annals of Administrative Management) no. 9, at 343 (July 1961), shows that during the seven years 1953–1959, inclusive, only 841 applications for judicial review of administrative acts were filed. Of these, 435 were appeals from decisions; 406 were requests for judicial help other than actual appeals. The yearly average was only 120 cases of all types included in the compilation, which may have been slightly different from those included in the figures for later years.

[2] Figures supplied by Department of Health, Education, and Welfare, May 28, 1965.

categories of cases and replaced the thoroughly outmoded statute of 1890; the new statute permits appeal or petition for reconsideration in virtually all types of official proceedings affecting private persons. Comprehensive statistics are unavailable, but scattered data suggest that the 1962 statute has been little used. In the area of the Tokyo Metropolitan Government, embracing a population of about eleven million, only some twenty matters are filed under the new review law each month.[3] In Osaka Prefecture, with a population of six and a half million, officials could recall no cases at all under the Administrative Review Act of 1962, though they were aware of four or five hundred appeals under statutes applicable to special matters such as tax administration. Officials of Miyagi Prefecture (population, one and three-quarters millions) were confident in mid-1965 that no formal administrative appeals had ever occurred there. Fragmentary figures obtained from the Secretariat of the Supreme Court indicate that throughout the whole nation only 241 cases of all types were filed under the 1962 law during the six months ending March 31, 1963.

Although direct comparisons with American litigation statistics are impossible, still one may note with interest that formal proceedings to review the determinations of customs officers were begun in the United States in 128,317 cases during the fiscal years 1962, 1963, and 1964 (an average of 42,772 in that single category).[4] Contested administrative proceedings akin to those contemplated by the Japanese statute of 1962 arise yearly in at least 10,000 other cases in American federal agencies.[5] These large figures do not include the cases heard by state agencies; comparable cases would, in Japan, appear in the national total.

B | Inadequacies of Formal Review

Expense and delay. A few Japanese officials smugly assert that judicial review is infrequently sought because administrators never err. Others

[3] During March, 1965 (for which detailed figures are at hand and which was characterized as "a typical month") 16 appeals, objections, and petitions for reconsideration were received. During that same month, 23 cases were finally concluded. The backlog of pending cases at the end of March was, however, 1,148; this suggests that filings of appeals must have been at a much higher rate at some point in the past than at present.

[4] Figures supplied by Administrative Office of the United States Courts, May 19, 1965.

[5] Report of Subcommittee on Administrative Practice and Procedure, S. Rep. No. 119, 89th Cong., 1st Sess., at 6 (1965).

seek more persuasive explanations.[6] Expense and delay are often cited. Lawyers' fees and court costs in Japan seem reasonable, judged by American standards. Many Japanese nevertheless regard litigation as a prohibitively expensive means of determining conflicts. A litigant is expected, moreover, to pay a portion of court costs and attorney's fees in advance, and this may conceivably inhibit attack upon governmental actions of debatable legality. Free legal assistance, which is generously provided to impecunious persons involved in criminal law matters, is rarely available in civil litigation. Nationally subsidized legal aid, administered by the barristers' organizations, has apparently never been granted to a would-be challenger of administrative determinations, although it has supported a few tort actions against policemen and other officials.

Slowness of judicial action is certainly a problem in Japan, as in America. In Tokyo, for example, the courts began the month of March, 1965, with a backlog of 107 cases involving metropolitan administrators, and ended with 113, seven new cases having been commenced during the month while only one was decided. This kind of decisional strangulation is said to be endemic.

Although expense and delay may thus genuinely stimulate Japanese reluctance to take grievances to court, they scarcely tell the entire story. Cultural tradition is an additional factor. Juridical dispute, not truly popular anywhere in the world, has long been distasteful to Japanese even more than to most people. Chinese scholars are said to have commented on that fact many centuries ago, and prominent Japanese judges are among those who trace the past into their compatriots' present patterns of behavior. Moreover, many still living Japanese were schooled to think of law almost exclusively as a definition of their duties, and not as a means of achieving citizens' goals—as something for use against them rather than for use by them. This conception has restrained older persons from seeking the courts' assistance in ordinary private controversies as well as in public law disputes.[7] The post-war generation may possibly prove to have a very different outlook.

[6] For especially perceptive analysis, see T. Kawashima, "Dispute Resolution in Contemporary Japan," in A. T. von Mehren ed., *Law in Japan* 4 (1963).

[7] During 1961, 1962, and 1963, the number of civil cases filed in Japanese courts of general trial jurisdiction averaged 131,926. The number of comparable filings in New York courts in the fiscal year 1963–1964 was 289,286, not including cases filed in "small claims courts" or courts of specialized jurisdiction, many of which resemble

Inability to obtain counsel. Unavailability of counsel is yet another factor contributing to the comparatively infrequent use of Japanese courts. The entire practicing bar of Japan numbers only about 7,400. Chicago, with a population only slightly larger than that of the city of Osaka, supports some 13,000 practicing lawyers; the United States as a whole has approximately 200,000 private practitioners.

Of course, multitudinous lawyers may not be an unmixed blessing. And assuredly a happy society can be achieved without constant litigation. If the existence of many lawyers were to lead simply to litigiousness, then countries like Japan could count themselves fortunate to have a small Bar. A numerous legal profession, however, does much more than provide courtroom advocates. It tends to infuse the entire population with understanding of and respect for legal institutions. Its guidance enables laymen to avoid frictions by identifying and respecting other people's rights.

In part because Japanese lawyers are so few, they are little consulted for advice. Chiefly they are sought out only when the client has himself concluded that litigation is necessary; this self-diagnosis is as risky as a patient's turning to a surgeon only after he has determined his own need for surgery. A larger number of lawyers in Japan could provide representation in formal proceedings which often should be, but now seldom are, commenced. Perhaps also they could reduce some of the hurts to individual members of society, hurts unnoticed by others because those upon whom they have been inflicted have borne them silently.

Feudalism and fear. Still operative in Japan, although diminishing in intensity, is a tradition of deference to authority that forestalls complaints. Centuries of feudalism dictated uncritical obedience to overlords. In pre-war times, officials were distinctly masters of the public at large. Today, in democratized Japan, officials are public servants, no longer masters. In some quarters, nevertheless, the atmosphere of

---

cases included in the Japanese total. The population of New York state in 1960 was about one-sixth that of Japan. The major courts of New Jersey, with a population of six million, received 50,847 new civil cases in 1963–1964—more than a third as many as were filed in Japan by a population sixteen times larger than New Jersey's. These figures, however, need refinement. Most of the American court cases never came to trial, but were settled along the way. Hence the extent to which Americans use the courts really to decide disputes rather than as a tactical step toward negotiations and voluntary agreements is unclear. Compare D. F. Henderson, *Conciliation and Japanese Law* (1965).

olden days lingers on. Some officials still think of themselves as superior beings, and some citizens share their thought. In a status-conscious society (which Japan assuredly is), inferiors do not easily disagree with or complain against their superiors. Hence, to the extent that officials are exalted, they tend to be unchallenged. The prevalence of this attitude in present-day Japan is not precisely measurable, but many seemingly alert Japanese believe it to be widespread, especially though by no means exclusively in rural areas.

In its most acute form the citizen's disinclination to challenge public administrators is marked by positive fear of reprisals or other untoward consequences. Numerous persons (including officials, practicing lawyers, professors, and judges) expressed belief that many a questionable administrative determination is unresisted simply because the affected person thinks that a victory over the administrator might cause future hostility. Though perhaps unjustified, this attitude toward public authorities is apparently widely shared.[8]

Similarly, fear that the police "may pay a visit to say thanks" (in the words of a phrase widely used to suggest the intimidatory tactics of gangsters) seems to have discouraged complaints against policemen's behavior. Most observers appear convinced that Japan's policemen, unlike those in the pre-war period, are on the whole respectful of citizens' rights. But occasional untoward episodes reinforce timid persons' doubts about the wisdom of voicing grievances.[9]

[8] The attitude described in the text is said to be especially prevalent in connection with tax matters. Some objective evidence suggests that tax officials now in office are suspect not because of what they themselves have done, but because of their predecessors' behavior. Taxation offices today are, on the whole, more conscientious than many other public agencies about providing information concerning opportunity to appeal. Officials would have no reason to take pains to make this information available if they intended to react vindictively whenever a taxpayer might choose to utilize the appeals procedure. Moreover, the tax appeals body in at least one prefecture seems to re-examine initial determinations with no predisposition to uphold them. See note 13.

[9] For example, a feature article by T. Ushiomi, "A Fortress of the Critical Spirit," *Asahi Journal* 37–38 (June 6, 1965), reviews a publication of the Japan Federation of Bar Associations concerning civil liberties cases in which it had been involved. One of these concerned a citizen of Niigata who had written the prefectural police chief that police attached to the Oyamada police station had been inept or uninterested in maintaining surveillance of a criminal suspect. The Oyamada police had thereupon detained the letter-writer (as can be done without making a formal arrest) on suspicion of having committed the crime of undermining police authority. In the presence of newspapermen the head of the Oyamada police said that he was considering referring the matter to the prosecutor for suitable action. The publicity that followed had injured the complainant's standing in the community. The Niigata Bar Association, after an independent investigation, concluded that the original complaint

While businessmen are unfrightened by the police, who tend to be extremely considerate in dealings with persons well established in the community, many seem afraid to disagree with other public officials. Importers, for example, apparently avoid challenging the judgment of customs officers, in the belief that acquiescence in an incorrect determination is less harmful in the long run than a reversal of the decision by higher authority. As one business executive put it, "Today may be bad enough, but tomorrow would probably be worse if I tried to do too much about today."

Of course this attitude is not universal. A group of Chamber of Commerce officials were questioned on this point. After lengthy discussion among themselves, they stated a consensus: Hesitation about appealing from adverse rulings is markedly lessening, although still a factor particularly when continuing relationships are involved, as in subsidy, licensing, and tax matters. Another businessman, commenting on this conclusion, remarked: "I agree that hesitation to go beyond an official is present, but I think it is not caused solely or maybe not even chiefly by fear. It is more a matter of cultural psychology. A lot of businesses look to the government for help. The relations between the two become close. The businessman might beseech the official to do something or to change his mind about something he has already done, but he wouldn't embarrass him by taking an appeal to another official or by going to court. Why, that would be almost like brother suing brother."

Without pretending to be scientifically informed, a foreigner in Japan becomes convinced that fear of public administrators is a factor of some importance. An official publication commented as recently as 1964 that "in the local districts of Japan there still remains the traditional feudalistic mentality that it is not profitable for people to make complaints against any maladministrations," partly because of a lingering belief that "the public office is too dignified for people to reach near" or "we must be compelled to bear silently, if the public office is opponent."[10]

---

had indeed been well founded and that the action subsequently taken against the complainant "was aimed at hiding police inefficiency as well as at getting even with the citizen."

[10] Administrative Inspection Bureau (Administrative Management Agency), *System of Good Offices of Administrative Complaints* 1, 3 (1964). In country districts, one

Three converging currents tend to diminish this kind of thinking. First, citizens of the post-war era have become increasingly aware that well-being does not depend upon remaining in the favor of an autocrat or a highly placed benefactor.[11] Second, modern officials do not regard an appeal from one of their determinations as a personal affront, any more than a judge views as an insult the taking of an appeal to a higher court. Third, governmental organizations have in recent years made positive efforts to bring grievances out of hiding. But to the extent that old-fashioned citizens still regard officials as "okami"—superior beings—the use of appellate mechanisms is forestalled.

Distrust. Another psychological factor that discourages resort to review procedures is simple disbelief in the objectivity of the deciding officials. "What is the use of taking an administrative appeal?" a prominent attorney recently asked resignedly. "After all, the top administrators who act on the appeal are the very same people who laid down the policy the junior administrators simply obeyed when they made the decisions complained about, so of course the top men are going to uphold the results." A professor of administrative law, speaking about the same problem, remarked: "Everybody knows that organizational loyalty is likely to forestall an objective re-examination of a challenged decision." In June of 1964 the Tokyo Metropolitan Government sought information from three thousand men and women constituting a scientifically selected sample of Tokyo's population. They were asked, among other things, whether they themselves had complaints against governmental agencies. Forty-two per cent of the respondents answered affirmatively, but five out of six of those who acknowledged having complaints had never voiced them. Of these

often hears seemingly authentic accounts of petty reprisals by officials who dislike being opposed. A farmer near Maebashi, for example, spoke feelingly of having once raised a question concerning food inspection; the next inspection consumed half a day instead of only a few minutes, and though the inspector made no remark, the farmer says he received a clear message that questions cause trouble.

[11] Readiness to complain does seem to bear some relationship to the level of education, which is rising constantly in Japan. In March, 1965, the Prime Minister's Office published an opinion survey on the topic, "Citizens' Awareness of Local Administration." Question 10 was "Have you ever filed complaints?" Only 10.6 percent of the entire sample answered affirmatively. But of those whose last educational experience had been in a university, 20.0 percent had filed complaints at one time or another; 13.3 percent of those who had been high school students had done so; only 10.2 percent of middle school and 3.6 percent of primary school graduates had ever been complainants.

noncomplainers, 42 percent explained their silence by saying "it would be no use filing complaints." A national authority recently declared a similar belief that administrative appeals are rarely productive.[12]

Accurate statistical analysis of the functioning of the Administrative Review Act is impossible. Some estimates place reversals, modifications, and remands of initial administrative decisions as high as 20 percent, a figure which, if correct, would indicate a considerable degree of objectivity; but few people with whom the matter was discussed believe this to be the fact.[13] In any event, as Japanese scholars were quick to point out when the new law was adopted, the present statute contains few protections against official bias and does not provide extensive procedural safeguards against mistake.[14] Though the Administrative Review Act of 1962 is a marked advance toward regularizing official judgments, it has not yet captured the confidence of the Japanese people.

[12] Administrative Inspection Bureau (note 10) at 6–7: "Procedural factors" involved in recourse to the Administrative Review Act of 1962 "inevitably produce hostile sentiments between citizens and administrative organs. Moreover, review rarely brings about a final solution until court action is tried. These conditions force citizens to spend much time and money, placing unbearable burdens on their shoulders. To make the matter worse, it cannot be disregarded that they leave undesirable sentiments (anti-bureaucratic or anti-governmental sentiments) accompanied by hostile situations."

[13] Detailed figures provided by Hyogo Prefecture (of which Kobe is the main city and which has a population just under four million) suggest that perhaps no single pattern of action exists. The results of all appeals and petitions for review filed between late 1962 and mid-1965 may be tabulated as follows, with many diverse subject matters grouped according to the department of government immediately concerned:

Department	*Cases filed*	*Rejected, dismissed, withdrawn*	*Appeal succeeded*	*Pending or referred elsewhere*
Civil Engineering	121	119	0	2
Construction	1	1	0	0
Agriculture & Forestry	4	0	0	4
Sanitation	2	0	0	2
Welfare	181	140	40	1
Tax	370	131	208	31

If one had looked at only the first four categories, he would have had to conclude that appeals were altogether useless. But, going further down the list, he would discover that 22 percent of appellants concerning pensions, health insurance, and the like had prevailed, and that a staggering 56 percent who sought review of tax determinations had succeeded in overturning them.

[14] See, *e.g.*, S. Tanaka, "The Administrative Appeal Laws," and I. Sonobe, "A Reflection on the New System of Administrative Review," summarized in the Japan Public Law Association's *Public Law Review* for 1963, at 234, 235.

2|The Uses of Personal Influence

Perhaps even more than citizens in Western societies, the Japanese have traditionally relied on influence and personal acquaintances to achieve their ends in matters public and private. This tradition still lives, although the identity of the "men of influence" has changed. Members of the national, prefectural, and local legislatures are now powerful figures; and professors and successful businessmen carry considerable weight. On the other hand, the large rural landowner, formerly a potent figure, has disappeared from the social scene, and military leaders no longer command civil servants. But today, as in the past, "the face of an important man says strong words to Japanese officials." Many persons, confronting situations that would send an American hurrying to a lawyer, look for "face" that may come to their support.

Some have asserted that, like fear of officials, this is a rural rather than an urban attitude. The basis of the differentiation, however, may be that a country man, a stable member of a stable community, is likely to know and be known by an important man. The impersonality of his environment may limit the city dweller's ability to use influence, but his desire to do so remains.

In order to gain understanding of administrative practicalities in Japan, I put this simple hypothetical case to professors, lawyers, businessmen, and others whom I interviewed in 1965: "Mr. X is the proprietor of a very small restaurant. He desires to hang a large sign over the street near his establishment, to advertise its presence. He applies to a suitable official for permission, which is brusquely denied. He thinks that he has seen similar signs elsewhere and that he should be allowed to carry out his business plans. What would he do?" Time after time, those who were not themselves officials immediately responded that Mr. X would seek to enlist the help of someone important or, failing in that, would simply give up.[15] "He should go to the most influential person he knows and tell him the problem," said a leading

[15] Without making any inquiry into the facts, many officials to whom this case was stated replied at once that the decision on Mr. X's application must have been correct or it would not have been made. They had to be reminded that the question under discussion was not whether Mr. X should prevail, but was, rather, what he would do after an initial rebuff.

professor. "Then, if that person believed him, he would act in his behalf, to right his wrongs. But if Mr. X doesn't live in an old and established neighborhood where everyone knows everyone else, he would probably just accept the wrong." With minor variations, this proved to be the most frequent comment, sometimes elaborated by the speaker's reminiscences about using his own "face" in another's interest.[16]

The "influential man" system of public administration does, however, have readily apparent disadvantages. Emphasizing as it does the intermediary's supposed power rather than the merits of the affected party's case, it adds to the widespread distrust of official action by suggesting that personalities are more significant than substantive principles and notions of justice. Although frank discussion with numerous Japanese officials leads one to conclude that even strong pressures rarely succeed in persuading a public administrator to act in utter disregard of law, many seemingly reliable anecdotes clearly indicate that discretionary judgments can be and often have been much affected by the intercession of important men. Since the permitted range of discretion is likely to be broad in Japan, influence may induce action that, while perfectly legal in itself, might not otherwise have occurred. Moreover, the speed and courtesy with which a case is handled seem to depend to a great extent on who is interested in the outcome.[17]

[16] Few persuasive sociological data are available to test the supposition stated in the text above. But statistics printed in the March, 1965, edition of *Voice of Citizens,* an official publication of Toyonaka City, are suggestive. Toyonaka City (population 266,000) is a particularly modern, service-minded, rather well-to-do satellite of Osaka. Since 1962 it has very vigorously pushed the development of a "Citizens' Room" to which grievances can be brought, with assurance that appropriate operating officials will suitably consider them. In January and February of 1965, 3,216 Toyonakans were asked: "What do you think is the best way to deal with complaints or requests in connection with city government?" Responses from 2,558 showed the following: Go to official directly, 29 percent; go to Citizens' Room, 53 percent; ask an influential man, 11 percent; give up, 7 percent. Even with an effectively functioning, strongly publicized Citizens' Room and the relatively favorable status of many Toyonakans, the influential man still had a considerable following. Moreover, the city government itself, in constructing its questionnaire, apparently anticipated that "influence" would be a quantitatively significant response.

[17] A reflective civil servant, discussing this point, mused: "People look for an influential intermediary not so much because they suspect us officials of being dishonest as because they expect we will be slow or unimaginative. They think we like to do routine work in a routine way, without any eagerness to serve the common man efficiently, though full of polite efficiency when an important man asks for

While evidence of actual corruption among Japanese civil servants is scant (on the contrary, officials appear to have markedly high professional morale), a rather widespread suspicion of their probity is nurtured by the influential man approach. The intermediary's assistance is often delicately acknowledged by valuable gifts, by cash payments, by reciprocal favors, or by contributions to an elective official's campaign fund. Some ordinary citizens apparently suppose that shares of these donations pass from the influential man to the men he appears to influence. Despite the fact that the decision might have been precisely the same had the citizen personally presented the problem through ordinary channels, the influential man is credited with having brought about the result, sometimes by means best left unknown. Thus the idea develops that venality is more prevalent among administrators than in fact seems to be the case. This is especially dangerous in a society as complicated as Japan's, in which economic and social conditions necessitate ever-widening regulation in the public interest. Americans, recalling the lessening of confidence in governmental processes caused by "influence peddling" during the Truman and Eisenhower Administrations, will appreciate how debilitating the loss can be.

Related to and yet going beyond possible corruption is the issue of favoritism. Influence exists in infinite degrees. Those who are themselves influential can usually command other influential support, and so the strong grow stronger in a society in which influence shapes results. The notion that all dealings with government involve a nobly deserving citizen on one side and a malevolent bureaucrat on the other is of course absurd. Often the true contestants are, simply, private interests with competing aspirations. Often, too, the "malevolent bureaucrat" is merely a poorly armed guardian of individually powerless persons who need protection. Too heavy an accumulation of influence on one side may distort the work of the official arbiter or

---

service. The behavior of some public officials, I'm sorry to say, gives a good deal of support to that theory."

On the other hand, one of the just-quoted speaker's colleagues, asked whether an influential man could obtain speedier decisions than an ordinary citizen, denied that this would generally be true and added: "As a matter of fact, influential intermediaries often make for slower action. Because they do not know all the facts, they have to go back to the principal for additional information, sometimes more than once. If the principal had come to us directly, we could probably have disposed of all the questions during the first conference."

protector. Thus, for example, a belief exists in Tokyo that deserved approval of new industrial products, such as food additives, has been blocked or delayed by pressures in behalf of already established businesses, eager to ward off competition. Similarly, governmental hesitancy to grapple with problems of air and water pollution is widely ascribed to the influence of powerful industrial groups.[18]

Public policy has no predestined shape. It is formed by competing pressures and the choices they necessitate. Hence nothing is intrinsically wrong with choosing, for example, to encourage manufactures by ignoring pollution, despite its dangers and discomforts for the public at large. The point made here is, simply, that many Japanese have become increasingly conscious that when choices lie within administrative power, officials may be more accessible to some persons than to others, so that not all opinions and needs receive the same degree of attention. Influential men do not maintain a twenty-four hour, day and night service available to everyone. Even when, by personal acquaintanceship or through a chain of introductions, the ordinary citizen can approach an influential man, he may hesitate to ask for assistance because the use of another's "face" may entail uncomfortably heavy obligations. So the ordinary citizen—handicapped by being unable to find an influential spokesman, or by being unable to find as influential a spokesman (or as many) as someone else has

[18] Pollution problems, though acute, have thus far been approached very gingerly. The monthly deposit of soot and dust as measured in some parts of Osaka, for example, is 43 tons per square kilometer, as against a clinical finding that 14 tons is the very outside limit of tolerance from a human health standpoint. Sulphurous acid gas, measured at seventy places in Osaka Prefecture, was found present in the atmosphere beyond the "permissible doses" in most parts of the prefecture. The Osaka Municipal Health Research Institute reports that almost all streams in the prefecture are polluted beyond the "permissible degree" health officials have agreed can be overcome by suitable cleansing measures. In Niigata, deaths, paralysis, and blindness followed a 1965 outbreak of "Minamata disease," so named because in earlier years many fatalities and crippling illnesses had occurred along Minamata Bay, apparently as a result of drinking water polluted by mercury believed to be of industrial origin. At the same time, a local fishing industry faced destruction because the fish of that area had been killed, presumably by industrial wastes; four large chemical factories discharge waste into the sea nearby. All the above examples are drawn from *Mainichi Daily News* (Kansai Edition), June 14, 16, 1965, at 3. Later, the chief of the Niigata prefectural hygiene department was reported as having ascribed the mass outbreak of "Minamata disease" to waste lye discharged from factories along the Agano River. *Mainichi Daily News* (Kansai Edition), June 23, 1965, at 3. Soon after, an as yet incomplete survey showed that 205 persons in Niigata suffered paralysis or loss of hearing, with five deaths, apparently because of "organic mercury poisoning" of the local waters. *Japan Times,* June 28, 1965, at 4.

found, or by being unable to express his appreciation adequately—often finds the traditional indirect approach to officials somewhat unpalatable. These deficiencies have led to an increasingly intense search for less objectionable ways of bringing citizens' grievances and views to official attention.

3|The Administrative Management Agency

Of chief interest among Japan's efforts to adjust citizen-official conflicts by informal means is the work of the Administrative Inspection Bureau of the Administrative Management Agency (AMA).

The AMA was created by statute in 1948, nominally as an adjunct of the Prime Minister's Office, to examine the operations of national administrative organs and other agencies that serve as delegates of the national government or are subsidized by it. The Director General of the AMA is a member of the Cabinet and is given adequate investigative powers.[19] The Agency achieves its primary purpose of assuring the efficient and legal conduct of governmental affairs by inspecting various phases of administrative activity and, when appropriate, by recommending improved procedure or organization to the appropriate authorities.[20]

The object of making inspections, the Director General has said, is not to lodge accusations based upon past faults, but to induce sound administration in the future. To that end, the Administrative Inspection Bureau conducted more than two hundred nationwide field studies between 1948 and 1965, in addition to a number of localized inspections. About twenty national inspections annually are now con-

[19] Admin. Mgt. Agency Act, 1948, Sec. 4, empowers the Director General to call upon government departments for data and explanations as he may deem necessary; he may make on-the-spot investigations of any government agency; he may inform heads of departments about the results of his inspections when he deems it necessary to do so; he may call for reports about steps taken to comply with advice given as a result of inspection; and he may tell the Prime Minister when he thinks that any government agency needs to be instructed to improve its operations.

[20] The leading sources of information, in English, about this work are a pamphlet published by the AMA itself, *Administrative Inspection by Administrative Management Agency* (1963), and S. Yamamoto, "Operation of the Japanese Government's System of Administrative Inspection," 9 *Kwansei Gakuin University Annual Studies* 59 (1960).

templated. The specific objectives sought have often been of a "housekeeping" character, such as consolidating various intraorganizational communications, utilizing business machines, rationalizing procurement, maintaining property, deploying personnel, and coordinating the work of related administrative units. Some of the inspections, however, have dealt with matters of more immediate interest to private parties, such as enforcing building construction restrictions, subsidizing small and medium-sized businesses, licensing irregular aviation transportation services, and eliminating overlapping and obsolete regulations concerning motion picture projection rooms. The AMA estimates that 70 percent of several thousand of its recommendations have been unqualifiedly accepted, while many other recommendations have led to partial improvement or have been accepted in principle, subject to budgetary additions or statutory amendments.[21]

Almost by accident, this agency of intra-governmental self-criticism has developed a second purpose and a second personality. It has become the chief national organ for receiving, investigating, and seeking to redress citizen's grievances. For Japan the agency may indeed prove to serve some of the same purposes as do ombudsmen in Scandinavia, and may ultimately supplant the "influential man" as the individual's ambassador to officialdom.[22]

The Beginning. Noting that individual cases might shed light on general problems already under investigation, the AMA in early 1955 announced willingness to use its "good offices" in connection with complaints pertaining to administrative organs then being inspected. Rather to its surprise, hundreds of complaints reached the agency

[21] As to the future effectiveness of the AMA's general inspection activities, compare the well-reasoned prediction of Yamamoto (note 20), at 77: ". . . we may forecast a general tendency that public services may become more specialized . . . Accordingly, it will be difficult adequately to inspect specialized branches of public services without special knowledge and experience concerning them. A small number of inspectors and short study and training courses will not suffice to provide the special knowledge and experience needed to cover the entire range of public services requiring inspection."

[22] The late Professor Shotaro Yamamoto seems thus far to have been the sole Japanese scholar deeply interested in grievance handling by the Administrative Inspection Bureau. See his "Ombudsmen in Japan," 12 *Kwansei Gakuin University Annual Studies* 73 (1963), and his "Gyoseiho ri okeru Kinku no Gensoku" (Principles of Balance between Administrative Actions and Individual Rights), 14 *Ho to Seiji* (Journal of Law and Politics) 549 (1964). No other published work, in Japanese or in English, has been discovered.

during the balance of that year. By 1960 the number of annual filings approached 10,000—in an operation that had not yet been authorized by law. In May of that year the major parties represented in the Diet agreed that the Administrative Management Agency Act of 1948 should be amended to permit AMA inspectors to "perform the necessary good offices for the purpose of resolving" complaints pertaining to central authorities or other bodies carrying on administrative functions delegated by the national government.[23]

Although the AMA's Bureau of Administrative Inspection, with eight regional and forty-one district offices, has a branch in every prefecture, complainants living at a distance from the nearest office had difficulty discussing their problems with the Bureau. In 1961 the Director General of the AMA attempted to solve their problem by promulgating a regulation calling for the appointment in every locality of unpaid "local administrative counselors" to receive citizens' grievances or requests and to forward to the Bureau those deserving its attention.[24]

The success of the new system of local volunteers linked with a permanent governmental organ is reflected in the gigantic caseload that has developed as the Local Administrative Counselors have increased from 822 in 1961 to 3,605 in 1965. As the following table shows, the number of cases handled by the Bureau of Administrative Inspection grew from 11,507 during 1960–1961 to 20,516 in 1961–

Table XVI. Volume of cases handled by Administrative Inspection Bureau (Yearly figures cover the period April 1–March 31, the Japanese fiscal year)

	1960–61	1961–62	1962–63	1963–64	1964–65
Number of Counselors	0	882	1,770	2,690	3,605
Cases received by Counselors	0	9,149	24,653	35,778	43,320
Cases received directly by Bureau	11,507	11,367	7,960	10,906	12,227
Total cases received	11,507	20,516	32,613	46,684	55,547

[23] Sec. 2(13) of the AMA Act. The development is discussed in an AMA pamphlet, *System of Good Offices of Administrative Complaints* 3 (1964).

[24] The local administrative counselors receive a few stamped postcards and only 3,000 yen ($8.40) yearly for expense money, far too little to cover their necessary out of pocket expenditures.

1962 (when counselors first served) and reached 55,547 in 1964–1965 after the staff of counselors had been expanded.

Local administrative counselors. Utilizing local cooperators as in the present instance has precedents in Japan, where post-war democratization has drawn many private citizens directly into governmental activities that in other countries are handled either by full-time public employees or by altogether nongovernmental organizations. Thus, to suggest only a few examples, locally respected men and women have been officially designated as Civil Liberties Commissioners, Welfare Commissioners, Agricultural Commissioners, and even as "Worries Advice Counselors." Until the AMA's creation of Local Administrative Counselors in 1961, however, no volunteer cooperator had been concerned with the entire sweep of public administration.

Selecting, training, inspiring, and supervising 3,605 counselors have not been tasks easily (or, as yet, perfectly) performed. In order to assure the cooperation of municipal authorities and to take advantage of their acquaintance with potential appointees, the Bureau solicits and almost automatically accepts the personnel recommendations of local governments. The results of this recruiting have been favorable on the whole, although lethargic, self-important, personally ambitious, or otherwise unsuitable counselors have at times been appointed and have been retained lest their sponsors be gravely offended. The term of appointment is only one year, but the Bureau has never exercised its power to discontinue a counselor's services after the term has expired.[25] The main problem in any event will probably be to prevent rather than to create a high turnover rate of counselors, for the Bureau cannot afford to lose the momentum of cumulative experience in grievance handling.[26]

[25] In one instance a counselor in Nagano was very quietly asked to resign after involvement in an election scandal had impaired his usefulness. In several prefectures Bureau offices report having "given instruction" to laggard counselors with such frequency that the laggards have finally resigned, having themselves concluded they were not up to the demands made upon them.

[26] Analysis of the nationwide list of Local Administrative Counselors in office on August 20, 1964, shows that only 58.5 percent of those who had been first appointed in 1961 were still serving three years later. The list of counselors provided by the Tohoku Regional Office (Sendai), embracing six prefectures, also permits a suggestive analysis of turnover. Of the 455 counselors in office in that region on April 1, 1965, 20.4 percent had been newly appointed in 1965; of the counselors who began serving in 1961 and 1962 only 43.5 percent and 54.5 percent, respectively, remained on the list in 1965.

The qualifications laid down by AMA regulations are few. Local Administrative Counselors are supposed to be "well acquainted with local conditions," to "enjoy public confidence," to have "deep interest or understanding and enthusiasm for cooperating" in handling administrative grievances, and to "have sufficient knowledge and ability" to perform their duties. As for negative restrictions, the counselors are supposed not to be in a position which might cause the office of Local Administrative Counselor to be politically or personally exploited, they should be physically capable, they must not have been dismissed from past public service or convicted of serious crime, and they must not be dedicated to violent overthrow of the government. Despite so little specific guidance, local authorities have done surprisingly well in recommending persons able and willing to engage in unspectacular, time-consuming work for their fellow citizens.

The counselors (of whom 92 percent are men) are mature persons. As of August 20, 1964, only 17.3 percent were younger than fifty and almost half were over sixty. More than a quarter of the entire group have been engaged in agriculture and forestry, and many are retired educators, business executives, or civil servants.[27] A large number function simultaneously as unpaid cooperators in other public programs. Some dozens of "senior citizens" now serving as local administrative counselors were interviewed by me recently. Their dedication and capability suggest that Japan has been fortunate in mobilizing talents that might otherwise lie dormant in retirement.

These diverse, scattered representatives of the Bureau of Administrative Inspection have been trained in only a superficial manner, apparently on the theory that the counselors will learn best by doing. Upon appointment, each new counselor receives explanatory pamphlets; a bimonthly Bureau newspaper is distributed, as is a yearly "casebook" briefly describing typical cases and the action taken on them; and each Bureau field office holds a semi-annual conference of the counselors in its territory in order to discuss experiences and explore ideas. Individual counselors may also visit the Bureau to talk with inspectors about matters of concern to their local clients.

[27] Among the other chief occupational identifications, stated in percentages of the whole group, are commerce and industry (15.3), religious (7.6), housewives (6.3), association directors (5.7), salaried business executives (5.2), and public officials (4.3). Lawyers, physicians, teachers, printers, fishermen, tax accountants, innkeepers, and many others make up the ranks.

"We don't have a difficult job," a new counselor recently remarked cheerily. "All we do is listen to complaints and mail them on to the Bureau. You don't need much training to do that." But the job must entail more than the speaker indicated if the system is to work well, since the Bureau's professional staff is far too small to permit it to act on every matter that comes to the counselors.[28] The counselors themselves must take substantial responsibility for winnowing out the utterly groundless complaints and for adjusting others on a local level so far as possible. The abler and more experienced counselors have already assumed these functions. Of the 43,320 cases filed with local counselors during the twelve months ending April 1, 1965, 13,937 (or 31 percent) were disposed of without being referred to the Bureau.[29] Perhaps because of the scanty training received, however, self-reliance is not widespread among the counselors. Ten percent of the counselors in Gumma Prefecture, for example, accounted for all of the cases that were handled without reference to the paid staff of the Bureau.[30]

Paradoxically, deficient training has caused many counselors and perhaps AMA inspectors, too, to undertake more activity than is theoretically appropriate, although much of it appears to have advantageous results. Under the law and regulations, the local counselors and AMA staffs should confine themselves to problems growing out of national administration or financing. They are directed, moreover, to

[28] The entire field staff of the Bureau in mid-1965 numbered 1,369, but of these only about 200 (scattered among 49 offices) were available for work on administrative grievances.

[29] One may note, in passing, that the statute creating the system of "good offices of administrative grievances" did not contemplate the appointment of local administrative counselors, let alone their serving as conciliators of controversies. The 1961 regulation that brought the counselors into being apparently anticipated that they would be no more than conduits through which complaints would flow. The growth of positive activity on their part has been an unforeseen development, but one not now likely to be ended.

[30] In Kyoto Prefecture almost exactly half of the cases filed with counselors were disposed of by counselors themselves, but according to Bureau spokesmen only "old and experienced counselors" dared to handle cases alone.

Quite apart from experience, another factor (not so polite to recognize) discourages counselors' activity, namely, expense. Traveling throughout a locality to investigate the facts of grievances or to consult public officials concerning them may be costly. The counselors are given only 3,000 yen for expenses (see note 24) and some cannot or will not dip into their own funds for more. Many of the counselors, too, are busy making a living. So when a case seems likely to require an expenditure of considerable time or money, a counselor may be inclined to pass it along to someone else even though he himself might be capable of handling it.

supplement rather than supplant pre-existing means of providing informal help to the citizenry. But the instructions and examples given by the Bureau of Administrative Inspection to local counselors obscure instead of clarify the jurisdictional boundaries.

Counselors are told to transmit to the suitable municipal officers complaints and requests pertaining to local affairs, without attempting to influence the officers' action.[31] Materials distributed by the Bureau to local counselors to show them how to do their jobs often run directly counter to this general advice. Active negotiation by counselors has been approved in the context of highly localized problems, such as obstruction of traffic by street vendors, air and water pollution, and faulty maintenance of city-owned housing.[32]

Similarly, the counselors are told to confine themselves to matters of public administration, and not to seek a cure for every social or personal problem mankind may experience. Disregarding its own admonitions, the Bureau approves of published case studies that admiringly describe successful efforts to cope with such non-administrative matters as ostracism of an unpopular neighbor or parental interference with a child's school attendance.[33] Welfare Commissioners appointed by the Ministry of Health and Welfare are responsible for bringing the special problems of needy citizens to the attention of appropriate officials. Presumably Local Administrative Counselors were not brought into being to duplicate the work of Welfare Commissioners. But illustrated stories in the Bureau of Administrative Inspection's newspapers feature achievements in that precise field.[34]

[31] The Japanese Constitution, in Articles 92 and 94, explicitly exalts "the principle of local autonomy" and the right of local public entities "to manage their property, affairs and administration" without intrusion by national organs.

[32] All these illustrations are drawn from the Administrative Inspection Bureau's *Annual Casebook* 7, 25, 26, 37, 48 (April 1963).

[33] *Ibid.*, at 15, 19. These matters lie specifically within the range of duties of Civil Liberties Commissioners, discussed in later pages.

[34] See, *e.g., Complaints Information* 1 (April 20, 1962), lauding a staff member for having obtained a subsidy to enable an unemployable paralytic to become a self-employed poultry raiser; *Administrative Counseling* 1 (March 1, 1965), reporting success in having persuaded a local welfare office to install a bath in the home of a badly crippled townsman unable to use the public bath house.

A Local Administrative Counselor, asked whether matters he had been handling were not in fact precisely those that Welfare Commissioners were supposed to take care of, said recently: "Yes, many of my cases are really welfare cases. But, you see, there are fifty-six Welfare Commissioners in my territory and there is only one of me. People know that if they discuss a problem with me, nobody else will know

In fact, jurisdictional boundary lines are not clearly perceived by either complainants or local administrative counselors. Believing that service to the public is more important than inter-governmental niceties or other limits upon counselors' activities, the Bureau has thus far actually encouraged (though nominally it has discouraged) the counselors to deal with whatever comes to hand. Moreover, a considerable number of local governments have seemingly welcomed national counselors' involvement in municipal affairs. One may readily suppose, too, that the clients are content with the present situation; once they have managed to identify the Local Administrative Counselor, they have eagerly sought his help in affairs almost as varied as is life itself. The concept of "good offices of administrative grievances" has had to be stretched beyond recognition to reach (as it has) the rice farmer who claimed damages from a bean curd factory for dirtying the water in his paddies, or the child born out of wedlock who needed advice about seeking an inheritance, or the local school that could not persuade a landowner to transfer property needed for enlarging the playing field, or the householder on whose property malodorous refuse was deposited by rainwaters because the city had failed to install a needed drainpipe. Recognizing that such matters are formally not the business of the local administrative counselors, Bureau officials nevertheless invite the counselors to handle whatever citizens bring to them during this assertedly "transitional" period. As a consequence, much time and effort are expended on matters outside the legal competence of the Bureau of Administrative Inspection.[35]

---

about it if I keep my mouth shut. But if they take up a problem with one Welfare Commissioner, all fifty-six are going to hear about it, you can be sure of that. Since most people don't want their troubles to be talked about all over town, they prefer coming to me."

[35] The precise amount of this extra-curricular activity is hard to state because one suspects that different standards of judgment are being utilized by those who compile statistics. In the Chubu Region (Nagoya) that comprises six prefectures, 18 percent of all cases received in the twelve months ending March 31, 1965, are said to have related to matters unconnected with national administration; one notes, however, that the range is from 31 percent in Aichi Prefecture to 9 percent in Mie Prefecture. Similarly in the Tohoku Region (Sendai), also comprising six prefectures, the over-all figure for the comparable period is given as 8.3 percent, ranging from a high of 14.9 percent in Fukushima Prefecture to a low of 1.3 percent in Iwate Prefecture. In Nagano Prefecture, 20.4 percent of the incoming cases were classified as falling outside the Bureau's competence; in adjacent Gumma Prefecture the figure was stated to be 8.6 percent. Such large statistical discrepancies suggest that perhaps the statisticians were not applying consistent measurements.

Perhaps as another consequence, reliance on the Local Administrative Counselor may gradually supplant reliance on "the influential man" to speak for perplexed or timid citizens. That development, if it does in truth occur, will be socially desirable, for the Local Administrative Counselor unlike the influential man will presumably be available to all—and at no cost. The danger to be guarded against is well-intentioned but ill-considered wandering into areas where even experts must move cautiously.[36]

Public knowledge of the system. If the Bureau and the local counselors are to serve the entire community well, the entire community must know of their existence and their functions. Mindful of that fact, the Bureau takes its public relations work seriously. It presents semimonthly playlets for rural broadcasting, distributes scripts for use by local radio stations, and even arranges for door-to-door delivery of handbills advertising its services.[37] The counselors themselves, according to individual taste and ingenuity, publicize their availability by speaking at meetings, posting signs, or persuading local governments to spread the word. One counselor, for example, noting that he him-

[36] Indications of incaution came frequently to light during recent conversations with local counselors. One counselor, for instance, had undertaken to investigate questions of land ownership complicated by the destruction of local records; another had become involved in a family's challenge to the authenticity of documentary evidence of a wealthy decedent's deathbed marriage; a third had come to the aid of a citizen whose house was being damaged by vibrations caused by heavy industrial trucking, but failed to propose measures that would have occurred at once to a lawyer.

[37] The leaflet quoted below is typical. It well indicates the wide-open nature of the invitation to bring grievances to official attention.

ADMINISTRATIVE COUNSELING

Haven't you any troubles or complaints about matters handled by public officials? For instance, matters concerning old age and war widow pensions, registration of land or houses, people's pensions, health insurance, laborers' accident insurance, agricultural land, transportation, traffic, postal service, roads, rivers, licenses or permits, national railroad service, telecommunication service, public corporations, etc.

Haven't you any grievances like the ones written below?

They are dealing with matters too slowly.
Public officials are very unkind.
No improvement has been shown after repeated demands for it.

It is the task of Local Administrative Counselors and Inspectors to handle any such complaints you may have. There is a counselor in every ward in [city]. He will be glad to receive your complaint at home. There will also be administrative counselings on the first Thursday of every month. Complaints will be received between 1:30–3:30 p.m. Counseling is free of charge and we will keep confidential all matters talked about.

[Then follows a list of the counselors, with addresses and telephone numbers.]

self always looked carefully at the envelope of any communication addressed to him by the city government, asked the city to stamp in the corner of all its outgoing envelopes a brief announcement about local administrative counseling. This device has worked so well that his clients now include many people outside his area who have received mail from his city.

Despite these efforts, knowledge of the administrative counseling system is less general than the Bureau is willing to acknowledge. The human mind seems doggedly non-absorptive of information concerning public affairs, even when the information is all but injected intravenously.[38] No doubt word of mouth advertising by satisfied customers will ultimately provide the best publicity, but ignorance remained widespread in 1965.[39] City governments, which have been involved in choosing the local counselors, were found to be reasonably in touch with what the Bureau and its aides do. On the whole, too, the cities were helpful in trying to increase general awareness of the services provided. Representatives of most other governmental agencies, including many whose own work might be brought to the notice of the Administrative Inspection Bureau by complainants, seemed extraordinarily unconscious that a major public program existed, let alone that

[38] The experience of Kyoto in this regard is instructive. Kyoto has been especially devoted to democratization of local government, having initiated many programs to draw citizens into policy-making and into the role of critics. Its officials are also markedly service oriented. The city publishes a newspaper as well as frequent reports that are delivered to all homes free of charge. These contain much information about available services. In March, 1963, a scientific sampling survey was made to determine the efficacy of the city's publications. The survey showed, among other things, that 98.6 percent of the households in Kyoto receive the official newspaper, and that someone in 95 percent of the families reads it. But only 26 percent of the readers say they read it carefully. The paper repeatedly stresses that the city provides "citizens' counseling" about administrative and other problems without charge, as it does also "legal counseling" for those who need advice about legal matters. After long publicity about these free services, only 58.5 percent of the Kyoto citizenry knew that citizens' counseling could be had and only 39 percent knew about the availability of free legal counseling.

[39] This conclusion was formed during a three-month period of questioning randomly chosen persons in many walks of life—including merchants, tax accountants, real estate men, and representatives of labor unions and chambers of commerce—as to whether they knew either about the Bureau's availability or about local administrative counselors. A negative response was commonplace. More striking than the man in the street's lack of information was the frequently encountered ignorance of public officials in ministries, prefectures, and branch offices of central organs; post offices and police stations could very rarely identify the local administrative counselor; many professors of public law were wholly uninformed.

it might have significance for them. Be that as it may, public knowledge of the Bureau's work is spreading. A program that produces nearly five thousand new cases a month is obviously known to more than a handful of initiates.

The sources and objects of complaints.[40] The chief clients of the Bureau and of the local counselors are individual citizens, but many corporations, associations, and even town and city governments are also complainants. Reflecting the lingering fear of officialdom referred to previously, some of the complainants beg to be shielded by anonymity.[41] Most of them seem to feel, however, that no untoward consequences will occur if their problems are presented through an official intermediary. Complainants have thus been bringing into the open problems they had previously kept to themselves because of disinclination to approach directly the officials concerned or to use the formal review procedures established by law.[42]

[40] Perhaps a word about vocabulary should be inserted here. Japanese, as a matter of ethnic tradition, regard *complaining* as unworthy. Hence, in everything to do with the matters under discussion in this paper, the Administrative Inspection Bureau avoids using the word "complaint." Even the word "grievance" comes very close to being tabu. Instead of having Administrative Grievance Commissioners, Japan therefore has Local Administrative Counselors, who receive "matters" and "requests" rather than complaints. For non-Japanese readers, the euphemistic approach need not be followed.

[41] In two interesting cases encountered in 1965, municipal governments asked the Bureau to raise questions about national administrative organs' requirements, but at the same time pleaded not to be identified when their problems were being pursued. They feared, they said, that future relationships with national officials might be affected—and grants in aid might then be harder to come by.

In its booklet *System of Good Offices of Administrative Complaints,* the AMA itself remarks (at 26) that "small towns and villages consult with the AMA, as they cannot complain to the other organs directly because they receive instructions in administrative affairs and subsidies from them." The same publication asserts that "a citizen who is discontented with a specific administration is in a very awkward situation as an individual, and he necessarily feels abnormal uneasiness, worry, a sense of pressure, and excitement when he wants to complain to a government office which has the giant organization and authority. And it can be seen from many letters of thanks that for a citizen in such a situation the administrative good offices of the AMA are his staff of life and that his delight stands above whether or not the good offices succeed."

[42] Some problems have been bottled up for a long time. In May of 1965, after four years of silent dissatisfaction, a businessman in Wakayama finally complained to the Bureau of Administrative Inspection that a permit had been given in 1961 to place a bus stop precisely in front of his lumber mill, located on a national highway. The permit had been issued by a national ministry without consulting local residents. Since a statute forbids parking of motor vehicles within ten meters of a bus stop, the lumber mill, its suppliers, and its customers were greatly inconvenienced by inability to load or unload trucks without becoming lawbreakers.

Moreover, the issues presented are substantially broader than those susceptible of administrative appeal or judicial review, both of which deal with narrowly defined illegality or injustice. The "good offices of administrative grievances" embrace all aspects of public service—or, for that matter, failure to render public service.

Comprehensive materials made available by the Administrative Management Agency indicate that during the fiscal years 1962 and 1963 roughly 23 percent of all cases received pertained to the Ministry of Health and Welfare, which administers many pension and social insurance programs. The next most frequent target of attack was the Ministry of Construction, which deals with the highway system, waterways, and other public works that involve the use of eminent domain and that bear on the citizens' convenience (17 percent). Then came the Ministry of Agriculture and Forestry (11 percent), often in connection with land use controls, and the Prime Minister's Office (8 percent), mainly in relation to police administration and civil service problems. Every ministry and most government corporations had at least a few dissatisfied users. Even under the broadest possible analysis, 11 percent of the cases pertained to no national governmental activity whatsoever.

The AMA has analyzed more than 40,000 of its 1963 cases which unquestionably bear on national administration. Just over half of them involved public works in one way or another—inadequacy of planning, inefficiency in completing construction, and so on. Assertions that officials had misconstrued or misapplied laws or ordinances, had misunderstood the facts, had utilized improper procedures, or had committed other more or less "legal" errors accounted for another 35.4 percent. The other types of problems were too varied to permit easy categorizing, but many of them clustered about matters of administrative organization, methods, and manners.

According to the AMA, only about a third of all the cases reflect discontent with what it has denominated as "juristical action," a term that encompasses such issues as the legally permissible content of administrative decisions or undue delay in formulating a judgment. Delay is said to be a more frequent cause of complaint than are the completed decisions themselves. Most complaints, the AMA has found, relate not to "juristical" but to "actual" action such as managing and maintaining public properties or rendering postal, telephone, or transportation services. Unsatisfactory behavior of public officials, such as unkindness or downright rudeness, is considered to be an instance of "actual" action.[43]

What happens to the cases. Cases that have come to Bureau offices or Local Administrative Counselors have had happy outcomes to an extraordinary degree. The Bureau of Administrative Inspection's records show that 48.1 percent of all cases during a recent nine-months' period (April 1–December 31, 1964) were resolved in the complainant's favor, either through changing an existing decision, obtaining a desired decision that had been withheld, or inducing governmental action. Slightly more than 46 percent came to naught, often because a complainant had simply misunderstood applicable laws and regulations. Bureau officials assert that in the bulk of these cases the complainant subsequently declared himself to be satisfied by the explanations given him. At the time these statistics were compiled, 4 percent of the cases were still under discussion with appropriate officials or required legislative as well as administrative action. Only 1.3 percent of the cases remained "unsettled" in the sense that the Bureau had given up after being unable to budge either side.[44] The figures just cited may not be precisely accurate, resting as they do on somewhat unstandardized reports from many sources.[45] But even if one

[43] Classification of cases presents obvious difficulties, since a complainant who is angry because an official was curt may direct his complaint to some substantive issue without revealing its real motivation. A close analysis of more than 27,000 cases received in 1962 did show, however, that only 732 (2.7 percent of the total) unmistakably had to do with officials' allegedly bad manners and another 69 (0.2 percent) with allegedly bad morals.

[44] Some of the "unsettled" cases should perhaps never have been accepted as cases in the first place. In one large city, for example, numerous complaints have been directed at industrial pollution of air and water. National regulation of these matters is rather superficial, with little direct administrative control. See Law No. 182, Dec. 25, 1958 (discharge of factory waters); Law No. 146, June 2, 1962 (emission of smoke). Enforcement has been left to ordinary penal processes or to litigation by immediately injured private parties. Notwithstanding the scantiness of public controls, Local Administrative Counselors, sometimes seconded by Bureau officials in that city, have sought to induce individual industrial enterprises to mend their dirty ways. Pressed to explain how this effort to influence private businesses fell within his organization's jurisdiction, a Bureau official answered: "Pollution has become important enough to be regarded as public, and there is a lot of agitation for a law to control it better, so I treat it as a public question." The unresponsiveness and irrelevance of the speaker's remark are apparent, as is the fact that his heart is in the right place even though he may not be a keen legal analyst.

[45] Figures for the Chubu Regional Office (Nagoya) for the entire year 1964 are at hand. They show why one hesitates to accept the Bureau's statistics at face value. In summary, the Chubu figures parallel the national record fairly closely: 45 percent of the cases were resolved favorably to the complainant; 51 percent were dismissed after the complainant became satisfied by the explanation given him or the Bureau

makes an allowance for inaccuracy in detail, the over-all record still seems highly impressive.

These gratifying results were not achieved without intensive staff work. The invariable first step is to analyze the complainant's dissatisfaction closely in order to determine which official has power to examine the problem. The Bureau usually then communicates directly with that official, so that he may explore the matter involved. A large share of the cases may be ended at this stage because the complainant's information as transmitted by the Bureau sheds new light on the problem or a questionable interpretation is changed when challenged. The Bureau reports that the officials seem ready to reconsider with an open mind when matters are presented in an informal, unembarrassing way. At times the Bureau has had to conduct rather extensive investigations of disputed facts, although it possesses no power to conduct trial-type hearings or to make independent findings. Often it has had to prepare extensive arguments concerning statutory interpretation, especially when an overly literal official has ignored the purpose behind the legislature's words.[46] In any event, the Bureau cannot command, but can only persuade. It acts to encourage officials to take another look, but cannot force them to look in a particular direction. Nevertheless, dealing with the immediately responsible official rather than with his superiors suffices in most instances to produce results the Bureau regards as sound.[47]

---

decided the complaint was unfounded; 3 percent were referred to central authorities with suggestions for budgetary, statutory, or organizational changes; 1 percent were unresolved for various reasons. One notes, however, that in Gifu Prefecture, one of the six prefectures in the Chubu region, 66 percent of the complainants were reported as having been victorious, a percentage not even remotely approached elsewhere. Mie Prefecture reported having sent 13 percent of its entire caseload to Tokyo because solution hinged on new laws or other high-level political action, while throughout the rest of the region only slightly more than 1 percent of the cases called for any such disposition. These very large and unexplained spreads of figures within a single administrative region cast doubt upon the reliability of the statisticians if not upon that of the statistics.

[46] In one recent case, for example, an official had denied industrial accident benefits to a worker injured while wielding a hammer to break rocks used in highway construction. If the worker were engaged in road building, he would be in an "industrial" occupation and therefore entitled to benefits. But the official ruled that the injured man had not been industrially occupied, since he was merely breaking rocks supplied by nature. The official was later induced to change his mind.

[47] Even complaints relating to an official's personal conduct—his asserted rudeness or his lethargic attitude toward work, for example—seem more often than not to have been disposed of by an apology and a promise of future rectitude, simply after

Cases move to a higher level either when the initially responsible official and the Bureau do not reach accord or when a useful result no longer lies within the subordinate's power. A problem in one prefecture involved the application of laws imposing different taxes on single-family residences and on commercial establishments. What should be the assessment on a building comprising both a store and the store-keeper's home? That question could be and was plausibly being answered in different ways by various tax assessors. The Bureau's concern was not to gain reversal of a particular decision but to induce superior authorities to lay down a rule that could be uniformly applied in the future. In another instance, a complainant was irked by a local post-master's insistence upon burdensome formalities before he would accept a check for 10,000 yen ($28). Investigation disclosed that the postmaster was blameless; he had merely complied with a regulation of the Ministry of Postal Services which required bank certification of checks for 10,000 yen or more. But since the regulation had been promulgated in 1940 when the value of the yen was substantially greater than now, the Bureau proposed to the Ministry that it consider amending a no longer functional requirement. Somewhat similarly, the Bureau, having pursued a resident's complaint concerning slow delivery of mail from a town less than four miles away, found that the local postmaster was carrying out orders. In conformity with old regulations he had dutifully dispatched the mailbags by a roundabout rail route with several intermediate changes, though in recent years a new highway had been built and a nationally owned bus line now connected the two localities twenty times daily. The Ministry of Postal Services was apparently delighted to learn from the Bureau that henceforth the news could be carried from Ghent to Aix more speedily than in the nineteenth century.

A sampling of recent cases from various parts of Japan may suggest both the diversity of subject matter Bureau representatives may encounter and the diversity of negotiations they may undertake.

---

informal conversation at the operating level. When an official denies misconduct but the Bureau continues to believe that impropriety of some sort has occurred, it can do no more than report its information to a superior officer, with a request that he admonish or discipline the supposed offender. Usually, the Bureau says, the superior then informs the subordinate that a complaint concerning his work has been received and that, regardless of the true facts in that connection, he should be especially careful to avoid giving even a pretext for a citizen's taking offense in the future.

In Nara, a complainant had repeatedly and unsuccessfully sought the Police Office's permission to use motorcycles to transport blood needed for surgical transfusions. Applicable rules required the use of motor cars for this purpose. The Bureau persuaded the Police to act favorably on the long-ignored request to use two wheels instead of four.

In Kumamoto, a landowner discovered in 1961 that land he had registered fourteen years previously under the Land Reformation Law of 1947 had been incorrectly described in the records of the Legal Affairs Bureau of the Ministry of Justice. When he sought correction, the original error was traced to the landowner's own representative, an "influential man" who had made a mistake when registering in the complainant's behalf. The Legal Affairs Bureau then refused to change its records. Through the "good offices" of the Administrative Inspection Bureau, the Legal Affairs Bureau was ultimately persuaded that a good-faith mistake had been made in 1947, that its correction had been sought as soon as the mistake had been noticed, and that no public purpose would be served by the landowner's stewing in his own juice.

An elderly worker in Yamagata supported a son who had returned to his parents' home totally disabled after being hospitalized for six years following a mine accident. Until 1955 the son had received accident compensation, which had then ceased for undisclosed reasons. The father thereupon sought public welfare assistance, which was paid for some time but was later terminated because of the father's misstatements when applying. The Bureau concluded that misstatements had indeed been made, but that a genuine need for assistance nonetheless existed. It brought its factual information to the attention of the Social Insurance Office, which reopened its file and ultimately resumed payments to the complainant.

The saddened heirs of a deceased farmer in Saga were made even sadder when they received a bill for estate tax on land that had been utterly swept away by a river flood some years previously. The heirs protested in vain to the tax official, who pointed out that the tax was levied on registered land and that the land in question was still registered. He was very sorry if the river's main channel now occupied the space where the land was supposed to be, but records are records and there was nothing he could do about it. The Bureau finally persuaded the land registration official to revise the records to fit the facts and the tax official to revise the tax assessment to fit the retrospectively altered records.

Other cases have been concerned with such earthy matters as the need for additional toilets in a railway station, the control of muddy water running out of an abandoned quarry used in years past by highway builders, and charges that the Japan Monopoly Corporation did not distribute a great enough variety of cigarettes in rural districts. Few of the many cases concerning the progress of public construction have been susceptible of ready solution, but at least some advance has been made toward mutual understanding. Occasionally, immediate steps have lessened hardship, as, for example, when the Bureau induced the Construction Ministry to reorganize a highway repair schedule that would have barred road traffic at a time particularly awkward for local farmers.

Unfortunately, the sense of triumphant achievement sometimes lingers only briefly. "I worked for weeks and weeks," a local counselor in Osaka recently wailed, "in order to persuade the Japan National Railway to install a warning siren at a crossing the residents said was dangerous. Now I'm receiving new complaints from other residents who insist that the neighborhood has been made too noisy." In Kyoto Prefecture, repeated criticisms of narrow, twisting highways led to extensive widening and straightening of the roads. At once complaints began to arrive from those whose land had been taken to make this possible. The Bureau, like all government agencies everywhere, has had to conclude that it can perhaps please some of the people all of the time and all of the people some of the time, but certainly not all of the people all of the time.

The hidden part of the iceberg. The Bureau's most striking weakness is its inability as it is now staffed to pursue the general implications of specific problems that come to its notice. Being the servant of justice in individual cases is a noble occupation, but righting wrongs on a whosesale basis might be more productive than the sort of hand tooled work the Bureau chiefly does at present. This may especially be true in a country where irritations are conventionally suffered silently. One suspects that many non-squeaking wheels in Japan need to be greased fully as much as those that do squeak.

The Bureau's office in Gumma Prefecture demonstrated the soundness of this suspicion in two rather interesting recent instances. A farmer had been directed to pay taxes on a strip of land that had once been his but had subsequently been expropriated for highway purposes. Upon the farmer's request the Bureau discussed the situation with the tax collector, who quickly contented the complainant by rescinding the tax levy. The Bureau suspected that somewhat similar cases might exist elsewhere in the prefecture. An incomplete check of available records by twenty local counselors soon disclosed that in Gumma Prefecture alone taxes had been levied upon some three thousand others who were former owners of land now belonging to the public. Not a single one of the three thousand had protested, though in some cases the amount collected in taxes had by then exceeded the compensation paid for the expropriated land. Thanks to the Bureau's inquiries, widespread regularization of land records and tax levies was achieved. In the second matter, a high school student who regularly traveled some distance to a Maebashi school complained that train and bus schedules were not synchronized. As a consequence she had to wait in the railway station for forty minutes each morning before being able to proceed by bus. Initial inquiry indicated that the bus schedule could be revised without causing hardship elsewhere along the line, and so a change was made to the complainant's satisfaction. On its own motion the Bureau examined train-bus connections at other places in the prefecture, with the result that over sixty adjustments were made to serve public convenience.

Both of these self-initiated efforts reflect credit on the Bureau's officials. Similar activities will, however, be rare because the work pressures on present personnel are already excessive.[48] In theory, sweeping investigations are not to be conducted at all by that part of the Bureau devoted to "good offices of administrative grievances." If needed, they are supposed to be carried on by the administrative inspection unit as such. But since the inspection branch is also overburdened, an energetic grievance-handler may be tempted to disregard the organizational system and to launch his own attack on a broad

[48] Local counselors, when asked in 1965 to comment on the existing system of grievance-handling, were prone to complain that cases move too slowly. The criticism was heard in too many districts to be regarded as a purely local problem. Too heavy a caseload may affect the Bureau's popularity as well as its efficiency. One local counselor observed: "We are urged to report grievances. We do so. Then we have to defend ourselves against the people who filed the grievances because someone doesn't get to work instantly on their cases. We tell them that there are too many cases and too few people in the Bureau, but they continue grumbling, anyway."

problem he has perceived. Nevertheless, he will not be able to yield to the temptation very often and still keep even remotely abreast of his current assignments.

Perhaps the Bureau attempts too much in cases such as those just described. The administration of land recordation and tax laws in Gumma Prefecture is not the Bureau's responsibility, nor is the superintendence of bus operations to assure adequate public service. These are the jobs of other official organs. The Bureau should be attempting to spur those others to perform their duties well, instead of trying to be a super-administrator who will complete the work the immediately responsible administrative bodies have neglected.

The Bureau often loses sight of its own goal by becoming engrossed in particulars. In 1965, for example, one of the district offices was approached by a committee of complainants against the discontinuance by a motor freight hauler of common carrier service in a certain area. The trucking company had rebuffed the complainants when they had pleaded for restoration of service. Enlisting the help of a unit of the Ministry of Transportation, the Bureau succeeded in inducing the trucker to resume operations. Everyone rejoiced, and there the matter ended. A continuing defect remains—inadequate public regulation of the abandonment of common carrier service. Nobody has yet recognized the problem of which the local episode was merely a symptom.

Proposals for strengthening future administration need not always be preceded by a field investigation. Good judgment, broad experience, and readiness to discuss ideas before announcing final judgments may in many instances suffice as foundations for sound suggestions. The ombudsmen of Scandinavia are supported by only small staffs and yet, in addition to helping redress past grievances, they sometimes provide sage advice concerning improvements in administrative method or policy. The Bureau is only beginning to realize its own potentialities as a guider of public administration.

This matter is related to but separate from the question of whether the Bureau should publicize its discovery of administrative mistakes and misdeeds in order to discourage similar future errors. Especially in the Scandinavian countries, the results of grievance-handling work are widely discussed in official reports as well as in the press. In those countries, publication of discovered faults is looked upon as a means of educating both officials and the public at large; the reports help create approved norms of governmental conduct. A different view prevails in Japan. As earlier discussion has indicated, Bureau officials think that officials can be persuaded to correct their own mistakes if allowed to do so quietly and without being put to shame in the process. If not pushed into becoming self-defensive, they will neither cling stubbornly to unsound opinions not attempt to disguise blunders. "Letting others know about wrongdoing," one of the Bureau's top officers suggested in 1965, "would not be looked upon at all favorably in this country. Having in mind the temperament of the Japanese people, we think that ease in settling grievances on the spot is more important than trying to use one official's unhappy experiences as a means of teaching other officials."

Even if speaking softly and privately be the best way to win complainants' cases, general conclusions should be drawn from particular episodes more consistently than has occurred in the past. The redressive aspects of the Bureau's work are being done with mounting effectiveness. The preventive, forward reaching aspects need further attention.

4|The Civil Liberties Bureau of the Ministry of Justice

A second important governmental agency concerns itself with controversies between citizens and public servants, if the controversies have a civil liberties aspect. The Civil Liberties Bureau of the Ministry of Justice has functioned since early 1948 to "investigate and collect information concerning cases involving violation of human rights."[49] It performs these tasks today through a small headquarters staff and through civil servants stationed in the Ministry's 49 Legal Affairs Bureaus in major population centers or in the 238 branch offices of those 49. Altogether, fewer than 250 persons are assigned preponderantly to civil liberties work, although other Ministry of Justice personnel may be involved sporadically. Supplementing these full-time officials are more than 9,000 unpaid Civil Liberties Commissioners, citizens of local standing who are supposed not only to report disregard of human rights, but also to create a climate in which rights may

[49] Ministry of Justice Establishment Law, Art. 11.

flourish.[50] Although the Civil Liberties Commissioners are appointed by a Cabinet minister to cooperate with an official organ, they also independently formulate policies and plan programs through their own legally recognized consultative assemblies.[51]

What the Civil Liberties Bureau and its adjuncts do. The Ministry of Justice identifies only a strikingly small volume of cases as having civil liberties implications. This is especially noteworthy because civil liberties cases are not, as in the United States, limited to governmental invasions of individual rights protected by constitutional provisions. The Japanese Constitution, unlike the American, contains many rhetorical flourishes that may be read as adjurations to the public at large, rather than to the government as such.[52] These provide a basis for discerning "human rights" or "civil liberties" issues quite apart from those pertaining to explicit constitutional protections.[53]

[50] The Minister of Justice appoints Civil Liberties Commissioners in each city, town, or village for three-year terms upon the recommendation of the mayor in consultation with the local legislative body. The commissioners must be "of noble character and broad view, well acquainted with the actual state of social affairs and much interested in the protection of civil liberties . . ." Before making an appointment the Minister must consult with the prefectural governor, the bar association, and the suitable Federation of Consultative Assemblies of Civil Liberties Commissioners. The permissible maximum number of commissioners is 20,000. Law for Civil Liberties Commissioners, Law. No. 139 of 1949, as amended by Law No. 268 of 1952 and Law No. 71 of 1953, Arts. 6(2)(3), 9, 10. No Civil Liberties Commissioner has ever been dismissed before expiration of his term.

[51] Article 16 of the statute cited in the preceding note contemplates the creation of "consultative assemblies" of the commissioners who function within a small district; these are to be linked into a "federation of consultative assemblies" within a larger area, usually a prefecture; and, finally, the "National Federation of Consultative Assemblies of Civil Liberties Commissioners" is to provide an all-Japan coordinating body. Three hundred consultative assemblies, forty-nine federations of consultative assemblies, and of course the all-Japan federation were in existence in 1965.

[52] See, for example, Art. 11: "The people shall not be prevented from enjoying any of the fundamental human rights." Art. 12: "The freedoms and rights guaranteed to the people by the Constitution shall be maintained by the constant endeavor of the people . . ." Art. 13: "All of the people shall be respected as individuals . . ." Art. 14: "All of the people are equal under the law and there shall be no discrimination in political, economic or social relations because of race, creed, sex, social status or family origin." Art. 24: "Marriage shall be based only on the mutual consent of both sexes and it shall be maintained through mutual cooperation with the equal rights of husband and wife as a basis . . ." Art. 25: "All people shall have the right to maintain the minimum standards of wholesome and cultured living . . ."

[53] The Japanese Constitution does explicitly protect, among other things, the right to petition, advocate, associate, or express; religious freedom; freedom of movement; collective bargaining; academic freedom; property; the sanctity of the home against invasion by unwarranted search and seizure; freedom of the person from arbitrary arrest, from torture, from forced confession, from double jeopardy, and from bondage. Art. 16, 18, 20, 21, 22, 23, 28, 29, 33, 34, 35, 36, 38, 39.

Indeed, neither the staff members of the Ministry of Justice nor the Civil Liberties Commissioners feel themselves limited to redressing violations of existing laws or ordinances, let alone violations of the Constitution. Thus, for example, the failure of the Ministry of Trade and Industry to prevent pollution of the Sumida River, whose malodorousness has been readily discernible in central Tokyo for many years, was seriously raised as a civil liberties question in 1964. The Civil Liberties Commissioners recognized that the Ministry had only a limited power to control pollution, but maintained that more should have been done to protect the health and welfare (the fundamental human rights) of residents affected by the river's stench.[54]

The Ministry of Justice seems content with this type of free-wheeling analysis by semi-official assemblages composed preponderantly of persons untrained in law or government.[55] For example, in 1965 the Kyoto office took up as a civil liberties problem a construction company's having caused damage to private homes by heavy work activi-

[54] Matters of this sort, involving the recognition of a previously unrecognized or only dimly perceived civil liberty, are discussed in the consultative assemblies or federations described in note 51, and their character is then determined by a majority vote of the commissioners present, without the necessity of approval by the Ministry of Justice. The commissioners are insistent upon preserving their independence of judgment.

[55] The occupational background of 9,219 Civil Liberties Commissioners in office as of January 1, 1965, approximately ten percent of whom were women, has been summarized by the Ministry as follows:

Farmers, foresters, fishermen	34.9
Religious activities	11.9
Commercial activities	6.3
Public officials	5.3
Company employees	5.0
Lawyers	4.1
Related to medical service	3.9
Manufacturing and processing	3.2
Education	2.7
Organization officials	2.6
Others	20.1

The lawyers, numbering only one out of twenty-five commissioners, are said to carry heavy weight in the assemblies, however. Most officers of federations appear to be lawyers, and special deference is said to be paid to lawyers' views about what is and what is not a violation of fundamental rights.

Training sessions for new members of this heterogeneous group last for a single day, supplemented by rulebooks and other written materials. Training is further supplemented, however, by frequent Bureau publications; newspapers, casebooks, and tracts of the commissioners' federations; periodic meetings with Ministry of Justice personnel; and the meetings of the commissioners' own organizations.

ties in their neighborhood. The city government was prodded into making threatening noises, and ultimately the building contractor was persuaded to pay more than $20,000 to those whose property had been affected by its alleged carelessness. While undoubtedly the situation was one calling for sympathy and corrective measures, many lawyers might find difficulty in classifying vibrational damage as an invasion of civil liberties unless every negligent or otherwise tortious act is to be regarded as interfering with somebody's life, liberty, or pursuit of happiness and thus with his fundamental human rights. This might be a perfectly useful theory if there were any way of limiting it before it had absorbed all of life, a possibility that has not as yet terrified the Civil Liberties Bureau. For instance, in 1964 the Bureau agreed with a group of Tokyo Civil Liberties Commissioners that sleepers' civil liberties were violated by noisy construction of a new expressway during the hours of the night, and subsequently persuaded the Ministry of Construction to cease work between seven o'clock in the evening and seven o'clock in the morning—an arguably sound decision, but one that seems no more related to civil liberties than do all the other thousands of governmental decisions to be made in an interrelated society that can rarely choose simply between good and evil, having usually to perform the infinitely harder feat of weighing one convenience against another.

Despite the somewhat Confucian tendency not to differentiate between positive law on the one hand and their own notions of morality and justice on the other, the guardians of Japanese civil liberties reported in 1964 a grand total of only 7,581 suspected violations of civil liberties. Only some 8 percent of these—604, to be precise—pertained to the execution of duties by public servants, and fewer than half of those 604 were placed in the category of "special cases" deemed serious enough to be brought to the attention of the Ministry's Civil Liberties Bureau itself.[56]

[56] All the figures used in the text were kindly provided by the Civil Liberties Bureau. They cover the calendar year 1964. Comparable figures for the immediately preceding years are shown below:

Year	*Total cases*	*Cases involving officials*
1963	5,056	522
1962	5,530	601
1961	6,464	623
1960	8,037	704

The modest totals just stated are misleading in some respects. In the first place, matters that arouse American civil libertarians may be passed over entirely in Japan. This is true, for example, with respect to action by customs officials who block the entry of motion pictures they deem to be unsuitable, despite Article 21 of the Japanese Constitution which provides in part that "no censorship shall be maintained." Similarly, though Article 23 of the Constitution says that "academic freedom is guaranteed," violent student interferences with academic freedom are commonly ignored in Japan, with the result that university campuses at times more nearly resemble battlefields than marketplaces of ideas. In the second place, the Civil Liberties Bureau has declared its unwillingness to deal with civil liberties violations that have an element of criminality. These, it says, involve "very delicate matters" it would like the courts to decide, though it itself has no means of bringing them before a judge.[57] Since many of the constitutional prohibitions (such as the prohibition of extorted confessions and of unwarranted searches) are reinforced by penal sanctions, the Bureau's self-limiting policy would greatly restrict its work if consistently applied.[58]

[57] While the Bureau or its adjuncts do have capacity to refer a civil liberties matter to the prosecutor's office for suitable action, this seems virtually never to be done as a matter of fact. Not a single prosecution occurred throughout Japan in 1964 as a result of the Bureau's work or referrals.

Even cases involving malicious acts are customarily approached in a mediatory frame of mind. Thus, for instance, an irrigation and land improvement organization of local farmers requested a national sanatorium in Kochi Prefecture to contribute to the costs of maintaining the local waterways. When no reply was received, the managers of the irrigation project closed the gates in the waterways, causing a flood that badly damaged the sanatorium. This was considered to be a civil liberties problem for reasons not altogether clear. In any event, officials of the Ministry of Justice first persuaded the project managers to open the gates so that the floodwaters would drain back into the irrigation channels; then they persuaded the sanatorium to contribute to the future expenses of maintaining the waterways; and nobody said or did anything about willful damage to national property.

[58] The Bar Associations seek to take up some of the slack in this respect, with varying degrees of vigor in the several prefectures. In 1964 the All-Japan Federation of Bar Associations itself handled 22 cases (1963, 35; 1962, 18) identified as civil liberties cases; it estimated that the prefectural associations' cases averaged about three each year (no nationwide figures are available). Requests for Bar Association assistance may have totaled a thousand throughout Japan, but the barristers sift them carefully before agreeing to render aid. Most of the cases, Federation officials say, involve policemen, prosecutors, and judges and pertain largely to criminal law administration such as extorted confessions and the suppression of evidence; but some have had to do with brutal treatment of prisoners, involuntary hospitalization, and even private wrongs such as defamation. The All-Japan Federation has also published pamphlets bearing on such topics as the rights of alleged juvenile delinquents and the

Violation of citizens' rights was found to have occurred in 45.7 percent of the civil liberties cases involving officials that were disposed of in 1964.[59] This figure contradicts the belief widely stated by many lawyers and public officials that the Civil Liberties Bureau tends to be unaggressive lest it embarrass the government in power. Yet the feeling persists that evidence of official misdeeds is not energetically sought by either the Bureau or the Commissioners.[60] When asked to comment, Ministry representatives in many parts of Japan answered simply and uniformly that public officials (including policemen) have been intensively trained in the post-war period to respect civil liberties; hence, they maintain, objectionable acts rarely occur.

Whatever may be the continuing degree of open or concealed disregard of citizens' rights, the officially sponsored protective mechanisms have proved themselves to be useful extra-judicial means of discouraging violations. Without power to do much more than advise and exhort, the civil liberties agencies have sometimes been able to alter obnoxious behavior patterns. Thus, for example, the once almost

---

right of a person detained as a suspect to consult a lawyer in private; these pamphlets, one of which was sponsored jointly with the National Federation of Consultative Assemblies of Civil Liberties Commissioners, have been circulated widely among the public and among suitable officials.

[59] The figures for recent years are as follows:

	Cases	*Violation found*	*Percent*
1960	666	276	41.0
1961	637	348	54.6
1962	697	324	41.9
1963	531	280	52.7
1964	599	274	45.7

[60] While this may not be true as to the Bureau and other branches of the Ministry of Justice, the Civil Liberties Commissioners are clearly not activists in this field. Of the 604 cases involving officials in 1964, only 45 were received through the more than 9,000 commissioners in office during that year. The sources of these cases were as follows:

Direct complaint to a bureau office	406
Newspaper reports	140
Commissioners	45
Referred by other official bodies	13

The Civil Liberties Commissioners seem to have had a larger, though still markedly secondary, role as sources of the non-official civil liberties cases docketed in 1964:

Direct complaint to a bureau office	5,123
Newspaper reports	492
Commissioners	1,280
Referred by other official bodies	82

universal infliction of severe corporal punishment by schoolteachers has been much diminished (though 55 violations were found in 1964); public transportation companies have been persuaded to discontinue offensively searching bus conductresses who might have pocketed fares; superior officials have severely disciplined their subordinates for rude attitudes toward members of the public; policemen have been reprimanded and transferred for crudities that were formerly almost the norm. Japan's unique experiment in creating a nationwide watchman over the state of civil liberties has accomplished enough to be accounted worthwhile.

At the same time, Japanese experience shows that the present system is deficient. The investigators of alleged violations need more power to get at the facts than they now possess. Since they have no means of compelling answers, all too often their polite questions go unanswered. Nor do they have the authority to state or to pursue forcefully the conclusions resulting from their investigations. Especially in a field like civil liberties where redressive steps are usually ineffective, the injunctive help of courts may be a valuable and sometimes an essential protection against threatened or repeated abuses; yet the Ministry's staff has no power at present to seek this or any other kind of judicial assistance. Finally, the guardians of civil liberties need much more budgetary nourishment than Japan has been willing to provide. To call the Civil Liberties Bureau a paper tiger would be harsh, but the Bureau's effectiveness is limited by its dependence on the gratuities of local and prefectural governments that sympathize with its work. Lack of funds forestalls entry into fields that cry for large-scale investigation[61] or for more imaginative attention than is involved in acting on an occasional complaint.[62]

[61] For example, complaints by persons in detention are few. Only 37 matters of all kinds came from Japanese prisons, jails, workhouses, juvenile delinquent centers, and so on in 1964; 7 were found to be justified. In other countries the number of similar prisoner complaints is far greater. Nobody has yet learned whether Japanese prisoners are so uniformly well treated that they have no complaints to make or whether, on the contrary, they are terrorized by the prison officials who read their outgoing mail or whether, perhaps, they are simply ignorant that even prisoners have rights.

[62] For example, Japan suffers acutely from hostility toward and active discrimination against minority groups, notably the "buraku-min" (people of the separate community—a pure-Japanese caste that has been relegated to an inferior status for three centuries), Koreans, and the aborigine Ainus. Altogether those who are subject to discrimination number more than three million. During all of 1964 the massive

Human rights counseling. Another activity of the Justice Ministry's branch offices has greatly benefited the public at large, though it is only tangentially related to civil liberties or even to relations between citizens and governmental organs. Noting that potential complainants were often unable to put the correct label on the problem that troubled them, and noting also that legal advice was often unavailable when needed, the Ministry's 49 Legal Affairs Bureaus, their 238 branches, and the 9,000-odd Civil Liberties Commissioners began some years ago to offer "human rights counseling" to all. In 1964, advice was given in the stupendous total of 162,141 cases concerning nearly everything under the sun. Only 340 matters were referred to the Research Section of the Civil Liberties Bureau for more extended analysis than could be provided locally.[63] The Civil Liberties Commissioners established their importance by handling more than half of this tremendous workload without the aid of the Ministry's local staff members.

While purists might wonder that so wide a range of problems is dealt with by persons officially concerned solely with civil liberties, continuation of this activity is pragmatically justified on several grounds. First, it may stimulate the conscience of communities that at times seem to deal more capably with things than with people.[64] Sec-

official civil liberties organization received only eight matters pertaining to discrimination. Candid Japanese recognize that the social cancer of group prejudice claims more victims than that every day. Responsibility in this area does not rest solely on the Civil Liberties Bureau and its aides, but this is clearly a field within its area of concern—and one that deserves more constant consideration than it receives.

[63] The variety of "human rights counseling" and its usually (but not invariably) non-governmental focus can best be indicated by using the Civil Liberties Bureau's case classifications, to which have been attached percentages of the total caseload computed on the basis of elaborate figures the Bureau has made available.

Type of case	*Percentage of total*
Civil matters in general	33.1
Family matters	24.3
Landlord-tenant	19.4
Agricultural land	5.0
Aid for everyday living	3.0
Criminal matters	1.7
Labor	1.7
Tax	0.8
Other	10.9

[64] Two examples drawn from many 1964 cases discovered in the files:

(1) A housewife, accused of having taken goods from a supermarket, was quickly absolved when the actual thief was detected. Meanwhile, however, a rumor about the woman's supposed misdeed had swept through the town and could not be caught.

ond, Civil Liberties Commissioners have become better known locally than have other volunteers and are therefore readily approachable.[65] In a society lacking in professionally trained legal advisers, much can be said in favor of using the advisory tools that lie at hand, even if they are not the finest precision instruments ever made. Third, sessions for "human rights counseling" are often specially arranged in ways that publicize the commissioners and officials involved and draw attention to the civil liberties area in general; "P.R." (as even the Japanese call their public relations work) must be regarded as an important phase of all endeavors to nurture love of liberty.[66]

The woman's health declined, her husband's small shop suffered a severe drop in business, her child was made unhappy in school. When asked for advice in 1964, the local Civil Liberties Commissioners and the Legal Affairs Bureau distributed more than 3,000 handbills that explained the circumstances and proclaimed the housewife's innocence. And everyone lived happily ever after.

(2) A farmer's wife became mentally disturbed. Her mother, practicing the psychiatric methods traditionally used in that village, wrapped the woman's hands and legs tightly, fed her hot peppers, and burned incense sticks close enough to her face to scorch her skin. The husband, concerned lest perhaps this treatment might not be the best available, asked a Civil Liberties Commissioner's advice. Ultimately the Commissioner and the Bureau arranged to have the farmer's wife committed to a mental hospital. They also undertook to explain to her mother and to other villagers that the husband should not be condemned for having been doubtful about the locally approved therapy.

[65] Report of the Civil Liberties Bureau No. 53, October, 1964, describes at 37 an opinion study made in July, 1964, by the Legal Affairs Bureau and the Federation of Civil Liberties Commissioners in Gifu Prefecture. Of the respondents (who were 82.4 of those questioned) 75.9 percent knew of the existence of civil liberties commissioners and 48.9 knew a commissioner by name; 77.1 percent knew of the existence and function of the Legal Affairs Bureau. A similar survey in Fukuoka Prefecture, reported in December, 1963, by that area's Legal Affairs Bureau and Federation of Civil Liberties Commissioners, showed that among those who responded to questions (80 percent of those who were asked), 72 percent knew of the existence of the Bureau and the Commissioners; 67 percent knew of their willingness to provide "human rights counseling;" but only 27 percent could actually name a particular civil liberties commissioner.

Awareness of civil liberties commissioners compares very favorably with the degree of public knowledge about local administrative counselors, discussed in earlier pages.

[66] The P. R. work of a single region, that based on Nagoya and embracing six prefectures, is reflected in the following summation of its activity in 1964: special counseling sessions, 708; lectures and movies, 298; conferences, 136; papers for general distribution, 272; other publications, 54; "P. R. car" (i.e., traveling information bureau), 34; street signs, 679; other activities, not specifically identified, 938. At the same time, in that same territory but independently of the Bureau, the Civil Liberties Commissioners were responsible for additional counseling sessions, lectures, radio talks, and pamphlets.

5 | Counseling by Local Governments and Prefectures

To round out the picture of governmental efforts to discover and deal with citizens' problems, mention must be made of local and prefectural counseling. Acknowledging that the Japanese people have not been notably expressive in the past, many governmental units in recent years have actively encouraged the voicing of grievances and raising of questions. Some cities occasionally station officials in department stores or in other busy areas where even the most hurried and harried housewife can lodge a complaint, make a suggestion, or ask for advice. A variant of this practice is "trip counseling" in more remote parts of the city by a mobile unit intended to attract the attention of passersby.[67]

Acting first entirely on their own initiative, but more recently in accord with urging by the Ministry of Local Administration, many cities have created "Citizens' Counseling Rooms" to receive complaints from citizens and to ensure action by the appropriate officials. The locally established counseling rooms, when well managed, not only help their intended clients but also serve as a coordinating agency for the various national counselors, who otherwise may do each other's work haphazardly, seemingly oblivious that other functionaries have duties related to theirs. For example, Suita City near Osaka takes pains to announce that Civil Liberties Commissioners will be in the Citizens' Counseling Room weekly to receive reports about human rights violations, while the Local Administrative Counselor will be present on another day to receive "complaints connected with national govern-

[67] The following, observed in a small city in western Japan, is representative: An open-sided, canvas-covered shelter big enough to hold two small desks and several chairs had been erected alongside a brightly painted car. On the side of the car and on the sidewalk in front of the temporary "office" were placards that read: "We are here to receive complaints and grievances from those who live far from City Hall and may have difficulty coming to a city office. Please bring in any opinions, grievances, or requests you may have concerning your City Government." Some cities take mobility one step further by having a "traveling city hall"; their mayors and other top officials periodically set up shop in schoolhouses or other public buildings in various outlying wards, on the theory that this will facilitate direct access. Nobody has calculated as yet whether the good will thus engendered is offset by the annoyance of those who have gone to City Hall to do business, only to find that City Hall has temporarily been deserted.

ment or government corporations or financial institutions," and yet another day is reserved for the Worries Advice Counselor, who will take up "social welfare, difficulties in everyday living, marriage, and other worries."

The adjacent city of Toyonaka (population 266,000) provides an even larger range of specific counseling services, and also helps to bring order out of the near-chaos of overlapping national activities.[68] Confirming the common sense conclusion that ordinary people are likely to have more frequent and more troublesome contacts with local than with national administration, Toyonakans in 1964 presented 2,762 matters that the Citizens' Counseling Room recognized as grievances of one kind or another, of which only thirteen concerned national government.

Nearby Amagaski (population 406,000) provides free legal counseling six days a week, using the part-time services of practicing lawyers and law professors from three universities. During 1964, 2,328 residents availed themselves of the service. The city also offers counseling by specially qualified consultants on "personal matters" such as family, tax, and mental health problems. Finally, it provides a so-called "public hearing" for anyone who is dissatisfied with governmental activity or inactivity in any field. Through its many publications the city also attempts to inform its citizens about the functions, identity, and addresses of counselors connected with national organs. Not all cities are as alert[69] or as successful as these in creating public confi-

[68] Toyonaka's services include weekly legal counseling by practicing lawyers, who receive a small honorarium from the city; they advised 342 Toyonakans in 1964 concerning "all kinds of disputes ranging from those having to do with housing and property to those arising out of traffic accidents." Then, in addition to "Citizens' Counseling" concerning city problems, "Administrative Complaints Counseling" concerning national affairs, and "Civil Liberties Counseling," the citizen could also receive "Counseling for Women," "Counseling for Children's Welfare," "Counseling for Fatherless Families," "Counseling for Physically Disabled or Mentally Ill Persons," "Counseling for Juvenile Problems," and, if anything remained, "Marriage and Worries Counseling." Finally, businessmen were referred to special "desks for counseling on business management, labor problems, and tax problems," and the Police Department provided a "desk for counseling on matters relating to police."

[69] While visiting City Hall in a moderately sized city, I asked in the "Citizens Section" whether anybody knew the name of the Local Administrative Counselor in that locality. I was referred to a second office where possibly I might obtain the desired information, and by the second to yet a third, which proved to be the Citizens' Counseling Room. The person in charge of the room did not know, but undertook to inquire by telephone. Finally it was discovered that the Local Administrative Counselor was a city official, immediately superior to the one who was

dence in their desire to serve.[70] Still, success is by no means a rarity. Moreover, many cities, though interested in complaints about past shortcomings, have stressed consultation with citizens while policies are fluid and plans as yet unshaped.[71]

The prefectural governments have recently been following the cities' lead both in establishing counseling activities and in eliciting expressions of public opinion. Some prefectures have established branch offices to receive complaints and requests; others engage in extensive "trip counseling," often in conjunction with representatives of the Administrative Inspection Bureau so that national as well as prefectural matters can receive attention in many places other than the prefecture's main city; and still other prefectures have recruited a volunteer corps of specialists—doctors, engineers, builders, and others—with whom particular types of problems can be discussed and who can then in turn advise the prefectural government.

All this activity will almost inevitably create a general change in attitudes and atmosphere. As thousands of ordinary citizens deal directly and satisfactorily with their government without the backing of powerful allies, still other thousands will be emboldened to follow

---

inquiring. Had it not been for an outsider's question, City Hall and its Citizens' Counseling Room might never have learned.

[70] One Local Administrative Counselor in a central city remarked in 1965: "I used to spend a day in the Citizens' Counseling Room every week, but very few people came because nobody likes to go near City Hall if he can help it. Last year I announced in the newspapers that I was going to move my own counseling activities to a room just above a public pawnshop. Now that I have gotten away from City Hall, plenty of people come to see me."

[71] Kyoto has been among the leaders in this respect. Since its veteran mayor has also long been president of an association of municipalities, its experience has become well known in other cities. Kyoto inaugurated a now widely copied "letter writing week," which has stimulated an outpouring of opinion. It has also effectively used a system of "monitors," some hundreds of citizens constituting a true cross section of the population; the monitors, who receive a very small stipend, commit themselves to respond to the city's inquiries about problems concerning which it wants a quick intimation of public opinion. Other types of opinion survey are frequently used and are carefully reported. The content of citizens' letters and counseling visits is well analyzed, and officials are fully apprised of what people think about their work and their programs.

When learning of the apparently sincere efforts that are made to recreate a sort of direct democracy in some Japanese cities, an outsider gains the impression that representative democracy has been losing ground because many local legislators are thought not to be monuments of personal integrity. But the Japanese are too polite to say this out loud to a foreigner.

their lead. Mistakes and shortcomings that might otherwise have remained unrepaired simply because their existence was unknown can then be set right.[72] This of course greatly benefits those immediately affected, but even more significantly though more subtly it strengthens society's underpinnings.

6|Some Concluding Observations

Japan has changed with extraordinary rapidity from a society in which citizens' voices were muted to one in which citizens are actively encouraged to participate. At every governmental level, praiseworthy steps have been taken toward genuine democratization. To be sure, progress in that direction has been far from uniform. Moreover, strong differences of opinion remain concerning the desirable pace and nature of change. Still, the current has flowed discernibly toward more rather than less participation by the citizen in decisions affecting his well-being.

Adding notably to that current have been devices aimed at facilitating the articulation of dissatisfaction. Self-centered, querulous men and women, constantly attentive to petty irritations and petulantly demanding others' help when patience and self-reliance should suffice, are obviously not the desired end products of democracy, nor are they the goal of present Japanese activities. Japan seeks not to stimulate selfishness and whining. It seeks, rather, to stimulate efficient and fair government. As a means to that end, it encourages citizens not to accept uncomplainingly what they believe to be inefficient or unfair,

[72] In Tokyo, for example, 3,000 out of 27,000 individual matters brought to the metropolitan government in 1964 could properly be classed as specific complaints. Of those 3,000, 47 percent were rejected, often with explanations that made acceptable what had previously been deemed objectionable. Of the complaints, 25 percent resulted in action immediately and wholly favorable to the complainant; 27 percent resulted in only partially favorable action or in no action because of legislative or budgetary considerations; but some of these cases were regarded as still likely to produce steps desired by the complainants. In the much smaller city of Sendai, a recent follow-up study was made of actions taken on 798 citizens' grievances, drawn from the files consecutively. The complaint was found to have been satisfied in 35.9 percent of the cases; the city expected to be able to give satisfaction in an additional 38.8 percent; and in only 25.3 percent had a flat rejection of the citizens' view occurred.

but to bring dissatisfactions into the open for dispassionate examination.

The Japanese efforts discussed in the present paper affect more people than comparable grievance-handling mechanisms in other countries. They may therefore especially merit the notice of heavily populated nations which, though impressed by the success of Scandinavian ombudsmen, have nevertheless hesitated to create informal complaint bureaus lest they be overwhelmed by their caseloads. Using citizen-cooperators to expand the personnel resources of the Administrative Inspection Bureau and the Civil Liberties Bureau has been a distinctively Japanese contribution to public administration. That device may be adaptable to the peculiar needs of other societies. In any event, Japan's experimentation with a bureaucratized instead of a highly personalized grievance machinery deserves to be closely watched. Interest in developing quick, cheap means of resolving disagreements between citizens and officials has become worldwide in recent years. Nobody in Japan believes that its programs as yet fulfill that country's needs, let alone constitute models fit for general adoption. But the programs have shown enough promise to justify their continuation at home and their attentive study abroad.

Japanese experience, valuably suggestive of new approaches, is also valuably suggestive that old approaches toward justice and efficiency must not be slighted. Although case-by-case settlement of administrative grievances is an absorbing and highly satisfying activity, the effort lavished on effects has distracted Japanese attention from the search for causes. The following examples illustrate this point:

(1) The Administrative Inspection Bureau happily reports having persuaded many low-ranking administrators to withdraw determinations based on imperfect understanding of relevant facts. The frequency with which this has occurred suggests malfunctioning administrative fact-finding processes. Improvement in ascertaining the facts in all cases would clearly be a far more significant reform than overturning the relatively few mistakes that happen to come to light.

(2) Similarly, thousands of the complaints now reaching the Administrative Inspection Bureau are found, upon examination, to involve nothing more than the complainants' mystification; had the complainants understood what the administrators had done, they would have been content (or, at least, resigned) from the very first. If admin-

istrators could be induced to explain their decisions when rendered, needless uncertainties and frictions would diminish.

(3) Slowness of administrative action is apparently an even more frequent cause of complaint than the content of completed administrative action. When a complaint about delay is received, officials usually hasten to mollify the complainant by dealing with his problem as speedily as possible. This may involve lifting his case to the top of the pile of papers on an administrator's desk, while action on other cases is correspondingly slowed; the complainant's satisfaction is purchased by time taken away from someone else, perhaps just as eager for action although less outspoken about saying so. Clearly, then, special favors for those who complain will never accomplish as much as an attack upon administrative organization or practices that beget decisional delay.

(4) Some of the cases that reach the Administrative Inspection Bureau involve suspicion that administrative judgment has been influenced by legally extraneous policy considerations. This suspicion, once aroused, is not readily quieted, because many Japanese officials seem even less ready than their Western counterparts to permit examination of governmental files. Little attention has been paid to the desirability of making public records accessible to the public, let alone to emulating some countries' statutory requirements that public business be done publicly. Changing Japanese law might be far more desirable than alleviating complainants' suspicions in individual cases.

Grievance work functions at its best when cases are regarded as manifestations of a problem and not simply as isolated episodes. One weakness of the highly decentralized Japanese system is its occasional inability to grasp the broad implications of complaints. Unsatisfactory service by a common carrier in a particular area, for instance, may possibly be only a local problem, but, equally possibly, it may reflect a gap in the nationwide regulation of common carriers. The present grievance-handling organization will perceive the local but may ignore the national significance of the matter. If a body such as the Administrative Inspection Bureau is to realize its fullest social potential, it will have to become a forceful general adviser concerning public administration and legislation. It cannot content itself with trying to cure ailing parts of the body politic. It must try so far as possible to keep the body healthily free from ailment.

This is too large an assignment, of course, for a single subordinate unit of government. The resources of others must be used fully. In this respect, Japanese experience may have negative lessons for others, because coordination and mutual reinforcement have not been among the more obvious accomplishments of the major organs concerned with the topics now under discussion. The courts and most administrative agencies possessing large adjudicatory and regulatory powers accept with lethargic resignation the public's dissatisfaction with their services. Nobody else has yet tried hard to discover whether that dissatisfaction is justified and, if it is, to strike at its roots. Individualized disagreements should be dealt with more frequently than now by tribunals with power to enforce a conclusion; but this will not occur so long as no attention is paid to popular belief that the tribunals provided by law are needlessly slow, heavily encrusted by complex procedures, and sometimes infected by bias.

In the realm of informal action, agencies with common aims must become aware of one another's activities in order to avoid unintended conflicts. Recently, for example, the complaints bureau in a certain prefecture was chivying administrators to hasten the completion of needed public works, long delayed by discussions with landowners concerning the compensation to be paid for property that would have to be expropriated. Those who favored the public works program argued that if agreement on price could not be quickly reached, procedures were provided by law for fixing just compensation. At the same time civil liberties officials, drawn into the battle by landowners who did not want to sell, were cautioning against the hasty use of governmental powers in order to acquire private property and were lauding the Japanese tradition of voluntary consensus. The administrators, thus caught in a crossfire of official advice, were little helped to achieve socially desirable results.

Present endeavors, in sum, are not free from fault. Yet their general worth can be acclaimed. Starting without the guidance of other countries' experience (and without much guidance from its own past experience, either) Japan has significantly stimulated attentiveness to informally expressed grievances of the citizenry. Its work in that respect may be a major breakthrough in the effort to humanize modern administration without impairing its efficiency.

|ten|

Common Strands in the Fabric of Controls

No crisis in public administration confronts the United States or any of the countries this book discusses. Among public officials in all nations that count themselves well developed, professionalism and probity are normal though not invariable. Were administrators thought to possess too narrow capabilities and too broad consciences, their authority should, as a matter of logic, be confined to utterly routine matters. Then they would have little room in which to err. But since this would leave correspondingly little room for achievement, no country has concluded that straitjackets looped with chains should be prescribed as uniforms for public servants.

Instead, the responsibilities committed to administrators have everywhere been enlarged. At the same time, efforts to suppress blunders (regardless of motives) have intensified. Insensitivity, often reflected in slowness, is no doubt the largest generator of dissatisfaction with officials; it may afflict the upright as well as the corrupt. Imprecision may appear in the work of usually careful craftsmen (even Homer is said to have nodded). Persons not in the least "power hungry" may misconceive the scope of their responsibility or its relationship to competing public interests. Scrupulously unbiased minds can faultily analyze issues of fact or law, as witness the frequency with which appellate courts reverse the decisions of respected judges. Taking note of all these possibilities, sophisticated societies constantly seek governmental equivalents of what industrialists call quality controls. That is to say, they are trying to maintain output at a desired level of quality without adding inordinately to costs.

Quality controls tend to be cumulative, not mutually exclusive. Procedural steps that administrators must take when contested matters arise can be carefully prescribed; as in Poland, this prescription can be coupled with provision for review at a higher level of administration. Hierarchic review within the administrative structure is entirely consistent with penetrating review by ordinary courts; the two exist side by side in countries as diverse as Yugoslavia and Denmark. Specialized tribunals, concentrating upon a single subject matter, may become sufficiently expert to be more than a match for expert officials, as has happened in Swedish courts that deal only with administrative decisions about social insurance and taxes. Audits of financial records, aimed primarily at fiscal regularity, shed light also on how officials go about their work and can therefore easily be linked with evaluation of operational quality, as in the Soviet Union and Finland. Mass communication media, going beyond merely recording the news of citizen-official conflicts, can actually investigate dissatisfactions with administrators and, as Polish law specifically provides, become protagonists in individual cases. Political leaders and other prominent personages can intercede in administrative matters as in Japan and Yugoslavia, perhaps disadvantageously if they inject themselves into controversies they have not sought to understand, but often beneficially because their expressed interest may induce serious re-examination of too hasty judgments.

None of these controls precludes another. All are well known and widely used in the United States. But they are only variably effective. Procedural prescriptions sometimes defeat their own purposes by causing delay and inflexibility. For many minor matters, administrative review can be too burdensome an undertaking even when (as is not always true) its impartiality is beyond suspicion. The cost and inconvenience of judicial review, whether by special or general courts, deter recourse to it by some whose causes may be just. Financial oversight may degenerate into a bookkeeper's passion for every detail without adequate attention to the truly significant. Because undramatic discontents with official acts do not arouse general interest in populous countries, mass communication media rarely agitate about particular grievances that have no scandalous overtones. Influential intercession, which doubtlessly does at times induce the repair of genuine errors and omissions, also stimulates nagging suspicions that officials can be prompted by irrelevancies; on balance, lessened confidence in public administration may more than offset the increased satisfaction brought about by the successful intervention of "friends at court."

To acknowledge these defects is not to say that the indicated quality controls never function well. Quite to the contrary, they often work efficiently, exactly as intended. Moreover, knowledge that the controls exist probably lessens the need for their being used. None of them should be abandoned. But, taken together, they still leave need for something more. The countries discussed in this volume have sought to fill that need. In one guise or another, they have empowered readily accessible, professionally qualified, wholly detached critics to inquire objectively into asserted administrative shortcomings. Institutionalizing the giving of expert criticism, accomplished by each of the countries in its own way, has distinctively contributed to strengthened public administration. Recapitulating the problems they faced may be instructive.

1|Personnel Issues

If external criticism is to succeed, the critics must command the respect of public administrators as well as of the public at large. How to find the right men for these important posts has been a major concern everywhere.

Required experience and training.

The statutory prescriptions and the experience under them point toward high standing as a jurist as a prime qualification for office. The Scandinavian countries are explicit. The ombudsman for civil affairs in each of those countries must be law-trained. Denmark says that he "must have legal education"; Finland, that he be "distinguished in law"; Norway, that he "have the qualifications demanded for a judge of the Supreme Court"; Sweden, that he be a person of "known legal ability and outstanding integrity." In the Soviet Union the Procurator General is the highest lawyer in a tremendous organization all of whose subordinate members must have had "higher legal education." New Zealand states no requisite occupational background for its ombudsman; the only man who has thus far occupied that post was an experienced lawyer before becoming an administrator and diplomat. No mention of prior legal training is made in Japan, where the head of the Administrative Management Agency (the main organ of external criticism) is a Cabinet member, or in Yugoslavia, where a policy of amateurism in government has argued against fixing educational or other prerequisites for the directorship of the Bureau of Petitions and Proposals.

The emphatic preference for lawyers has been well warranted. The matters to which external critics turn do not always involve questions of legality, but many do indeed require extensive analysis of statutes and rulings. Even when the issues are unrelated to law as such, a sensitive lawyer may be well suited to consider them because his training especially equips him to function as a generalist who can, in Anthony Sampson's phrase, peep over the partitions that separate many occupational specialists. Not every lawyer possesses this capability, of course; but a careful choice should provide an undoctrinaire critic capable of seeing relationships among problems, attacking complex factual issues, and seeking solutions without being hobbled by outmoded tradition.

A critic's personal attributes are no doubt more important than his past training. He need not be widely known when he begins his work, though obviously he cannot be a nonentity. The Finnish and Swedish ombudsmen, for example, have usually been drawn from the lesser judiciary or some other official post that has not at all put them in the public's eye. The first (and still incumbent) Norwegian ombudsman had been a veteran civil servant and Supreme Court judge, but was not a prominent public figure. The Dane had been a law professor. They and their counterparts elsewhere have gained recognition through their work after appointment. A Swedish legislator summarized the matter by saying: "The man we select does not lend distinction to the office; the office distinguishes him." Once having been appointed, the critic must draw heavily upon all his skills, negotiatory as well as analytical, to produce judgments that win a following and establish him as a man fully worthy of his high post.

How chosen.

Typically, administrative critics have been selected by legislative bodies. In New Zealand the ombudsman is appointed by the Lieutenant Governor, the Queen's delegate, but he acts only upon the recommendation of the legislature. The ombudsmen in Denmark, Finland, and Norway are elected by the respective parliaments. The Procurator General in the U.S.S.R. is at least nominally chosen by the national legislature. The Polish Procurator General is elected by the Council of State, the legislature's executive committee. The Swedish ombudsman is the choice of forty-eight electors drawn from the two chambers of the parliament and reflecting the proportional strength of all the parties represented there. The most nearly comparable Yugoslav official is appointed by the Executive Council, a body composed largely of members of the National Assembly. In Japan the director of the Administrative Management Agency is designated by the Prime Minister, of whose Cabinet he becomes a member.

The question at once arises whether partisan considerations do not govern the selections made. Undoubtedly in a one-party state the choice falls on a person whose professional objectivity is not likely to hinder his responses to the party's dominant views. In Japan, too, organizational commitments might conceivably blunt the edge of the director's criticisms of governmental operations. In Finland, whose ombudsman carries less weight nationally than do his colleagues in other countries, the election has traditionally been contested; the party that is in control at the time proposes a name, the opposition parties propose another, a secret ballot is taken without discussion, and the controlling party's nominee is the winner. The ombudsmen elsewhere have been the products of all-party consensus and have been elected without even token opposition. They seem to have been notably free of partisan entanglements, past or in prospect, and have been regarded throughout their respective countries as persons selected not because of "politics," but solely because thought to be well qualified—as, indeed, has been entirely true.

Tenure, emoluments, and assistants.

The officers chiefly discussed in these pages are expected to be bravely independent, untroubled by political pressures or personal insecurities. None of them, however, has an assured career in his present post. The ombudsmen in Denmark, Finland, Norway, and Sweden are chosen by each new parliament. The normal parliamentary term is four years. In New Zealand, each new parliament (chosen triennially) can select the ombudsman, but the incumbent carries on indefinitely unless and until a successor has been designated. Removal from office is easy (but not done) in Denmark and Sweden, more difficult in New Zealand and Norway, and impossible in Finland. The Soviet Union's Procurator General has a seven-year term, but his appointment can be terminated sooner; his position resembles, in this respect, that of the Polish and Yugoslav officials under discussion.

For posts like these, limited terms are probably preferable to lifetime appointments. The theoretical enhancement of independence that flows from security in office must be weighed against the possibility that a critic may lose verve and flexibility if too long involved in the same work. Moreover, since critical ideas sometimes gain respect because the critic apparently enjoys wide legislative support, a critic cannot continue to function well after losing lawmakers' confidence. If the risk of removability were in fact to diminish his detachment from political considerations, a critic's effectiveness would be badly dented if not wrecked. That seems not to have happened, at least in multiparty states where threats to the critic's independence of thought or action would stir a lively public debate.

Control of salary might be a means of bringing a critic to heel or of showing displeasure with his work. This is avoided in some countries by putting his compensation permanently on a parity with that of a member of the Supreme Court, as in Sweden and Denmark. The salary has been at a high level in all countries, as a materialistic indicator of the importance attached to the critic's office. Only in New Zealand has the amount of the compensation been left to the chief executive's discretion; and only in that one country has the salary been fixed a bit below the pay of the most important judges and a few other officials of loftiest stature.

A critic's independence could be undermined also by interfering with his choice of subordinates. This has been avoided everywhere. The deputy ombudsman in Sweden, who serves continuously, is elected in the same manner as the ombudsman himself, but all other employees are the ombudsman's personal choice. In Finland, too, a deputy ombudsman is elected by the national legislature; he serves only when the ombudsman is on leave or otherwise out of action. All subordinates are the ombudsman's own selections. In the Soviet Union the Procurator General recommends his chief deputies, who are appointed for five-year terms by the legislature's executive committee. All other procurators, throughout the entire Soviet Union, are appointed by the Procurator General or by persons who are accountable to him. Provision has been made for parliamentary election of a deputy ombudsman in Norway if the ombudsman himself be temporarily incapacitated, but this has not occurred. In all the countries studied the external critic has been empowered to select assistants who have his personal confidence. Their number and salary scales, established after consultation with parliamentary or executive organs, have in every instance thus far noted been regarded as satisfactory. Subordinates have been well paid in relation to other public servants of comparable experience, and suitable means have been found of making these jobs seem desirable. No external critic has been hobbled by being denied the staff he needs.

2|Bringing Critics into Action

External critics of administration do not freely concern themselves with every issue of public moment. None has been empowered, for example, to look askance at the work of main legislative organs. The Danish and Finnish, but not the Norwegian and Swedish ombudsmen, can inquire into and criticize the actions of Cabinet members; the New Zealand ombudsman cannot criticize a Cabinet action, but can criticize the departmental recommendations on which the action was based. The courts, as a branch of public administration, are subject to examination and criticism by the Swedish and Finnish ombudsmen, but not by any of the others, though procurators in the U.S.S.R. can seek review of judicial determinations they deem ill-advised. The acts of local government officials (but not of local legislative assemblies) have to a large degree come within the reach of the ombudsmen in the four Scandinavian countries. Procurators have considerable relationship to local administration as well as to broader governmental matters. In New Zealand the ombudsman can deal only with central government organizations and departments specifically listed in the statute that created him; elsewhere, power to look at governmental activities has been generically stated. In short, no single jurisdictional pattern emerges. Each of the external critics has had to devote considerable thought and energy to ascertaining whether a grievance does or does not touch upon matters within the scope of his assigned responsibilities.

Complaints.

The services of all the external critics can be sought by individuals or organizations, usually without any formality. Complaints, which are the main source of the critics' business, must be written and signed in the five countries that have ombudsmen, but not in any of the others. Only New Zealand requires the payment of a small filing fee, the thought being that this will discourage frivolous complaints; the experience there has not supported the belief that a charge should be made for voicing a grievance. In Denmark, New Zealand, and Norway a complaint will be rejected if not filed within a year after the occurrence complained about; in the Soviet Union and Poland, complaints about official action can be freely made and must be acted upon within two months; in Sweden, ancient grudges can be reflected in grievances relating to occurrences of nine or ten years ago; in Japan no formal restrictions prevent the filing of stale complaints, but in fact almost all complaints do relate to current difficulties. General experience supports the conclusion that complaints should be generously received with an absolute minimum of formality, but that a reasonably short statute of limitations serves the desirable purpose of sifting out cases no longer suitable for investigation. If, as may happen unusually, an over-age complaint really does seem to raise issues worthy of examination, the external critic can proceed on his own motion to inquire into those issues.

As a protection against becoming overburdened by repetitive, incoherent accusations that probably reflect a complainant's disturbed emotional state more than they suggest an administrative aberration, critics should be empowered to decline to act. In Norway, for example, the ombudsman can "determine whether there are sufficient grounds for dealing with a complaint" and can "dismiss a complaint which he finds obviously unfounded." The New Zealand ombudsman may withhold investigation whenever he thinks "a) the subject matter of the complaint is trivial; or b) the complaint is frivolous or vexatious or is not made in good faith; or c) the complainant has not a sufficient personal interest in the subject-matter of the complaint." Similar power to decline to act has been granted or assumed generally. This is a desirable safeguard against overloading the machinery, but the requirement of personal interest should not be strictly enforced lest it cut off the filing of grievances by public-spirited persons who are concerned about the conduct of civil servants even when the complainants have not themselves suffered because of it.

Exhaustion of remedies.

A tendency may be discerned to limit critics to matters that are not elsewhere reviewable. Thus, the New Zealand ombudsman cannot act upon a complaint concerning administrative action that is subject to full review in a special tribunal or a court. In the Soviet Union and in Poland a procurator who receives a complaint about a matter that may still be administratively reviewable simply refers the grievance to the appropriate administrative organ, advising the complainant that this has been done. In Denmark a complaint about a decision still subject to change by a higher non-judicial authority is not appropriately considered by the ombudsman. The Norwegian ombudsman has discretion to reject objections concerning matters that could be judicially or administratively reviewed. Japan and Yugoslavia take no note of formal remedies that may still be available to a complainant, but handle virtually any and all grievances as they are lodged.

Containing a matter within prescribed decisional channels is, in general, a sound move. It takes advantage of whatever specialized organizations may have been established to consider specified categories of cases. So long as suitable means remain at hand for reexamining an assertedly objectionable decision, the external critic's services are really not needed. He helps a complainant by explaining what steps can be taken to secure review, and in most instances that should be sufficient action at this juncture.

Absolutely precluding the critic's dealing with the grievance (as in New Zealand) is undesirable, nevertheless. Sometimes the opportunity to take an appeal, whether to a higher administrative body or to a court, cannot be grasped because of the expense and strain further proceedings entail. Sometimes, indeed, a complainant may care too little about the immediate case to wish to be bothered further, though at the same time he may quite properly think it to be worthy of attention by someone else who is paid for his pains. Denmark meets this problem in part by instructing its ombudsman to guide a complainant toward judicial review and by authorizing him to recommend that free legal services be provided. The British parliamentary commissioner for administration, who came into being in 1966, is not absolutely blocked from inquiring into a matter that may still be judicially reviewable; he has been given "discretion to act if he thinks that the remedy open in the courts is not one which the complainant could reasonably be expected to use." Some such discretionary authority to proceed, notwithstanding the theoretical availability of unexhausted remedies, is desirable if access to an external critic is to be fully meaningful.

Action on own initiative.

An external critic, as has just been said, should not be compelled to act on every complaint directed to him. He should, however, have freedom to act without receiving any complaint at all if his concern about official affairs has been aroused by other means. All the countries included in this study have conferred that authority. Nowhere has it been used over aggressively. Power to proceed in the absence of a complaint has been exercised by the external critics chiefly to inquire into problems of general public concern as distinct from individually focused conflicts.

Polish newspapers may themselves be complainants about alleged administrative faults that do not affect them in the slightest degree, but about which they have learned through letters to the editor. In most nations, however, journalists simply report the news. They do not become activists, devoted to correcting past errors and refining future proceedings. Since "nothing is as stale as yesterday's news," many a journalistic coup that aroused indignant murmurs may soon be forgotten without having produced more tangible results. If, however, an external critic has been empowered to do something other than mutter to himself at the breakfast table while reading the morning paper, a stronger follow-up may occur. The implications of news reports can and should be readily perceived by a critic continuously engaged in administrative oversight. In Sweden the press has itself occasionally pointed out those implications; editorials have called them to the ombudsman's attention and have prodded him to act upon them.

Inspection and general supervision.

In Sweden, Finland, and Denmark the ombudsmen have been directed to make periodic inspections of the governmental establishments within their jurisdiction. In the Soviet Union and Poland the procurators exercise the function of "general supervision," in the course of which they plan and execute systematic observation of selected governmental activities.

Field inspection is a necessary ingredient of any large-scale, dispersed undertaking. Responsible management could not exist without it. Inspection by generalists (such as external critics) does not fulfill the same purpose as inspection by persons more specifically qualified to understand the work processes that are being inspected. The generalist, one might say, can only inspect the inspectors. If they have done their jobs well, not much should remain to concern the generalist unless it be the reflection of a policy choice with which he finds fault.

The Swedish ombudsman strongly defends the value of his inspection trips. He believes that both he and the officials he visits learn much from all his journeys into the field. Elsewhere external critics have not stressed the importance of personal inspection as a tool. Visits to penal institutions, however, are a special category to which everyone gives a high rating. A prominent outsider's entry into the authoritarian society of a prison apparently has a tonic effect on both the prison population and the custodial staff. Injustices are invisible behind institutional walls. Most of those who may suffer from that species of injustice are somewhat inarticulate. These factors make especially desirable a personal appearance from time to time by an external critic (or his representative) who can penetrate the walls, hear grievances, and reflect society's continuing concern for all its members.

Review of rules and regulations.

Apart from grievances, self-initiated investigations, and personal inspections, the procurators in Poland and the Soviet Union regularly review the rules and regulations promulgated by the various authorities subject to their supervision. Normative acts—those that prescribe standards of conduct by imposing requirements or stating prohibitions —must be referred to the procurators as soon as promulgated. The procurators can then challenge their legality and demand that the promulgating authority examine them anew. The work, though unspectacular, seems to be done with considerable vigor. Many objectionable regulations have been wholly withdrawn or have been drastically amended in response to procurators' criticisms.

In Great Britain and in some of the American states administrative rules must be routinely laid before legislative committees prior to taking effect, so that their conformity with statutory grants of power can be considered. The value of this "pre-audit" has not clearly been proved, but neither has its worthlessness. If one can judge by the frequency of procuratorial faultfinding, pre-auditing is done seriously and with good effect in Poland and the Soviet Union. Elsewhere, the external critics do not ordinarily concern themselves with the validity of administrative rules until they have been applied in a controversial manner. Other than the most superficial pre-auditing would require far greater manpower resources than most of the external critics have had at their disposal.

3 | Conducting Inquiries

Hearings that resemble trials are almost never used by external critics as a fact-finding technique. In every country the critic has been statutorily empowered to examine official files, call for further investigation and report by officials, and summon persons for direct interviewing. Some of the statutes include formal sanctions for non-compliance with the critic's demands for evidentiary material. In point of fact, so far as can be learned, no sanction has been needed. The critics receive the information they need because, without exception, they have enjoyed the respect of all concerned.

In Finland, Poland, the Soviet Union, and Sweden the ombudsmen and procurators, as the case may be, are empowered to attend the executive sessions of official organs within their jurisdiction. Except in the Soviet Union the power is little exercised. The Soviet procurators do regularly attend sessions of administrative commissions that impose penalties on alleged violators of regulations and local ordinances; they are also present during many sessions of rulemaking bodies, in order to advise concerning the limits of their authority.

By and large, the basic method of inquiry is, very simply, to ask for an explanation of whatever has been complained against and, if the explanation does not remove all doubts, to look at the materials in the administrator's files. Personal conversation with the complainant or with officials sometimes occurs, but is less likely to be dispositive than are the official papers in the matter. The investigatory technique has proved adequate in the great mass of cases considered. It fails when the matter at issue is an unrecorded occurrence such as an asserted rudeness, act of police brutality, or solicitation of a bribe. In these situations, often unwitnessed except by the complainant and the official accused, the critics have had to proceed hesitantly. Since, however, the primary purpose of an external critic is to build for the future rather than to exhume the past, constructive suggestions about the avoidance of similar controversies may not be precluded by inability to reach a firm conclusion about guilt in the present instance.

Heavy reliance on the administrative files has had a side effect worth noting. In several countries officials assert that they have paid increasingly close attention to the desirability of preserving detailed records, so that were an external critic ever to ask questions about anything they have done, the files can provide complete answers. So far as this reinforces official care and accuracy, it is an obviously desirable development. If, as apparently has occurred in a few instances, adoration of the written word occupies so large a portion of the working day that accomplishments worth writing about become fewer and fewer, record-keeping is a menace. Differentiating between adequate files and too much paperwork is not always as simple as it may seem.

4 | The Aftermath of Inquiry

Finding out what has happened is not the end but, in a way, the beginning of an external critic's job. He is more concerned with advising about what should be done next than with allocating praise or blame for what has already been done.

Negotiated Settlements.

Although not an assigned duty, all of the external critics have sometimes sought informally to change official determinations not illegal or otherwise subject to criticism. An altogether permissible exercise of discretion may needlessly hurt. In these instances ombudsmen and others have served as mediators between aggrieved citizens and righteous officials, helping to negotiate adjustments that all can accept.

In Denmark, New Zealand, and Norway negotiations invariably commence at a high official level, apparently on the theory that top-ranking officials can look more coolly and uncommittedly than can their subordinates at decisions the subordinates have made. In Japan, on the contrary, the officials whose determinations have caused dissatisfaction are directly approached, apparently on the theory that everyone can be persuaded to change his mind for the better if his doing so will not embarrass him. Both theories work well. The external critics everywhere successfully suggest minor adjustments that overcome bureaucratic rigidity. The critics continue to take an interest in the human consequences of decisions they cannot criticize.

Review of discretion.

Theoretically, an external critic does not criticize the exercise of administrative discretion simply because he himself might have done the job somewhat differently had he been in the administrator's place. Criticism is appropriate only when the discretion is found to have been exercised for insupportable reasons. But this difference is hard to formulate in words and even harder to preserve in action. In some countries it is almost entirely ignored.

The New Zealand ombudsman, for example, can consider not only whether a challenged administrative action is illegal, but also whether it is unjust, oppressive, or, as the governing statute bluntly says, just plain "wrong." That comes close to an invitation to look critically at all administrative judgments no matter how broadly discretionary they may be; and the invitation has been accepted. In Norway, whose ombudsman has been told to concern himself with "injustice," and in Denmark, where the ombudsman can criticize "mistakes" and "unreasonable decisions" among other things, considerable latitude exists. The broad language just quoted is somewhat qualified by other statutory provisions; the Norwegian ombudsman, for example, has been told to bother himself only with discretionary decisions that are "clearly unreasonable or otherwise clearly in conflict with fair administrative practice." Nevertheless one gains the impression that the critics have not felt themselves unduly constricted in their ability to speak up when they feel like doing so.

In the Soviet Union procurators, like ombudsmen, have sometimes failed to disentangle the issue of permissibility from the issue of desirability. The superior officers of the procuracy have clearly directed their staffs to concentrate on legality and not to weigh the merits of challenged administrative actions. Procurators, it has been said, "are not supposed to act as though they know more about everything than anybody else." Some of them still do what they are not supposed to do.

Pursuing the implications.

The critics have contributed valuably to the improvement of public administration when they have perceived the case before them as a symptom of a general problem, rather than as a self-contained episode. This has happened frequently in Yugoslavia and in the five countries that have ombudsmen for civil administration, but much less frequently in countries where the critical function is performed by large, decentralized staffs. In Japan, for instance, manifestations of a problem in one locality may be handled there without any recognition at all that the problem may be nationwide. This makes for fragmentation of efforts to solve it, duplication of work, and failure to propose preventive measures that might lessen future difficulties. The same comment might be made about the supervisory activities of the Soviet Union's procuracy, dispersed as it is among 2,000 widely separated offices.

On the whole, however, the external critics have hotly pursued the implications and not merely the immediacies of the matters that have sailed within their reach. A critic's report may state explicitly that though the complaint itself has been found to be groundless, a refinement in case-handling technique has been proposed for use should similar problems arise again. Or a decisional standard, conceded to be within the range of administrative choice, may be commented upon adversely because it creates collateral difficulties that another approach would escape.

Often, too, a critic's analysis reveals that an administrator has acted blamelessly because he has simply obeyed a blameworthy statute. Proposals for legislative change reflect a critic's awareness that his responsibilities do not end when he has passed upon the merits of an aggrieved citizen's complaint. As the New Zealand ombudsman has written, he cannot wash his hands of a matter as soon as he discovers that "what has been done is in accordance with the law; he is required to go further and satisfy himself that the law itself is fair and just." Even in the Soviet Union, in which the legislative process has not traditionally been the heart of government, the procuracy was commanded in 1955 to distill from investigated complaints its own recommendations for new legislation to reduce the risks of future abusive administration. In Yugoslavia, somewhat similarly, intensified efforts have been made in recent years to bring administrative practices and the laws on which they rest into conformity with the lofty principles of a new constitution. Work of this character may be even more important, in its forward projection, than the redress of current grievances.

Explanatory decisions.

The ombudsmen in Denmark, Finland, New Zealand, Norway, and Sweden have been extraordinarily diligent and successful in explaining their conclusions. Their opinions, marked by closely reasoned analysis of the law and a careful summation of the pertinent facts, have had strong moral and rational appeal. The general acceptability of their conclusions supports Alfred North Whitehead's view that because reason does not always prevail, one need not despairingly conclude it never does.

Even more significant in some ways than opinions that induce officials to repair their errors are opinions that explain to complainants why their complaints are ill-founded. Most of an external critic's caseload consists of matters he finds to be free from fault or for some other reason not subject to criticism by him. A complainant whose complaint has been rejected, one might suppose, would be bitterer than before. The opposite seems to have been true in most instances. The ombudsmen's files are full of letters from previously aggrieved persons who express satisfaction despite not having been upheld. A thorough explanation seemingly does more than turn away wrath; it induces contentment.

Every country that has instituted a system of external criticism contemplates that the critic will not merely state conclusions, but will review the matter in full when he records his opinion. The practice is not, however, followed faithfully except by the five ombudsmen. Their explanatory labor, taxing and time-consuming though it be, accounts in considerable measure for the abundant public confidence they enjoy.

5 | Enforcing the Critics' Views

A persuasive opinion is a powerful instrument so long as it does in fact persuade. How can an external critic make an administrator pay attention if he is unpersuaded? The short answer to this question is that the giver of advice and suggestions presupposes the possibility of their being rejected; if their acceptance were enforced, they would be transmuted into edicts. External critics are advisers, not commanders. They rely on recommendation, not on compulsion.

Some of the critics do keep a club behind the door, nevertheless. The procurators in the Soviet Union and Poland can prosecute heedless administrators or can commence disciplinary personnel proceedings. The Swedish and Finnish ombudsmen are, as a matter of history, prosecutors who can hale officials into court on charges of negligence, laziness, or incompetence as well as on more conventional accusations of criminality in office. The Danish ombudsman may order a prosecution and the Norwegian ombudsman may recommend either prosecution or disciplinary action.

These powers, little used in any circumstances at present, are almost never exercised to make officials acquiesce in recommendations they honestly believe unsound. The three most recent national ombudsmen —the Danish, New Zealand, and Norwegian—have entirely avoided recourse to enforcement devices or threats, and none has seemed to suffer any lowering of prestige. The known instances of non-compliance with ombudsmen's proposals have been few in number, picayune in content. This has been true, too, in the other systems included in this study. Even wholly informal suggestions, made casually by telephone, seem to have had a large degree of acceptance in Poland, the Soviet Union, Sweden, and Yugoslavia.

Most of the external critics have discovered, in fact, that before they have so much as begun to think about the recommendations they might make when investigation had been completed, administrative bodies have often voluntarily withdrawn from positions that had been complained against. Officials themselves thus demonstrate that they understand and embrace the critic's conceptions of fair administration. Knowing that the critic's eye will peer at what has been done, an administrator takes a closer look than perhaps he otherwise might; he detects error unaided; and he initiates the suitable remedial measures without having to be pushed by the external critic. This voluntarism might be called a response to anticipatory persuasion, but certainly not to coercion.

To buttress their own persuasiveness external critics rely heavily on favorable public opinion. They make annual reports to their creators, usually the national legislatures, and may report additionally when they wish. Their reports record their criticisms and suggestions, and also set forth administrative non-compliance with their recommendations. This need rarely be done. More is accomplished by continuing efforts to persuade than by enlisting the forces of parliament on the critic's side.

The press in Sweden and Denmark gives heavy publicity to findings that reflect adversely on an official or an administrative unit. Elsewhere, far less journalistic fervor attaches to external critics' work. In Japan, as a matter of fact, the organ of external criticism goes out of its way not to publicize its triumphs over wicked officialdom, believing that administrators who are not shamed into being self-defensive can be induced to correct their own faults.

One small danger lurks in a newly created system of external criticism, especially if the need for the system has been exaggerated by its proponents: the critic may be (or feel himself to be) under pressure to "get results," that is, to find flaws in public administration.

If the critic constantly depicts himself as a St. George slaying dragon after dragon, officials who do not relish being regarded as dragons may themselves become just a bit critical. An external critic needs the admiration and support of administrative personnel as well as newspaper men.

6|A Final Word

Americans traditionally favor living under a government of laws, not of men. That aphorism expresses well founded belief that dictatorial or whimsical government flourishes when clearly established principles decay. But the aphorism expresses utter silliness when taken to mean that men are not the central ingredient of good government. Deficient laws can be surmounted by good officials; the best laws cannot surmount bad administration.

In the context of the present discussion, even the most carefully elaborated grievance-handling machinery will produce few satisfactions unless the men who operate it and the men upon whom it operates are worthy. No mystically golden light shines upon every move of ombudsmen, procurators, and other critics. The mere existence of their offices means little. The men in the offices are what counts. Whoever holds responsibility for dealing with citizens' complaints must measure up to a very big job because most assuredly the job of attacking administrative imperfections will not execute itself.

This means, among other things, that those who select an external critic must themselves fully believe in the critic's importance and must wish him to succeed as a citizens' protector. "Politics as usual" cannot be the slogan of those who search for an appointee as inspired and as inspiring as his function demands.

The matter does not stop there. Not only must the critic and the critic's selectors be good men, but also the officials with whom the critic works must in general be moved by the governmental ideals his appointment reflects. Recommendations by ombudsmen and similar critics are significant precisely because (and, really, little beyond the extent that) officialdom has already committed itself to sound principles. The critic can isolate aberrations; he can suggest better ways of reaching agreed ends; he can point out new applications of previously accepted concepts. Like the United States Supreme Court he can sometimes articulate society's previously incoherent "intuitions of public policy." What he cannot do is force resistant officials to embrace a philosophy newly created by him. Rather, he shares tenets whose validity the great mass of officials already acknowledge. If administrators' objectives and his, their conceptions of honorable service and his, fundamentally conflicted, the external critic could achieve little.

Finally, good government requires good citizens. They themselves significantly shape the service they receive. Repeated references to citizens' grievances naturally enough conjure up a picture of defenseless necks beneath the boots of brutal officials. Along with that picture a few others should perhaps be hung. Some would show citizens who have corrupted officials to advance their own selfish purposes. Some would show citizens who, in dealings with governmental agencies, have cut so many corners that the agencies have reacted by becoming suspicious and severe. Some would show citizens who constantly demand more and better services of every kind, and then balk at paying the taxes the services necessitate. Some would show citizens who, proclaiming that government employees lack capability, ambition, and integrity, indiscriminately withhold the respect and the appreciation that might encourage faithful public servants. And some would show citizens so deficient in self-reliance and at the same time so self-centered that every momentary frustration, uncertainty, or misunderstanding becomes a suitable object of complaint.

If the citizens shown in that series of pictures were typical of the people meant to be protected, an external critic would be well advised to flee. But were he asked to function in a society already basically healthy, the society and its critic of public administration would share a richly rewarding experience.

Index

Administrative courts: in Finland, 58, 67, 86; in New Zealand, 97; in Sweden, 200; in Yugoslavia, 271; in Poland, 299

Administrative Inspection Bureau (Japan): feudalistic attitude toward officials, 378, 395*n*; inutility of formal review proceedings, 380*n*; creation and functions of Administrative Management Agency, 385; inspection activities, 386; organizational structure, 387; volume of individual grievances handled, 387; local administrative counselors, 388; public awareness of available service, 393; sources and types of complaints received, 395; outcome of complaint cases, 397; work methods, 398; self-initiated activities, 401; failure to generalize, 403, 417; joint activity with prefectures, 415

Administrative Management Agency, *see* Administrative Inspection Bureau

Administrative penalties: in Poland, 299; hearings before imposition in U.S.S.R., 341; procurators' challenges, 357; procurators' participation in "administrative fine" proceedings, 358

Administrative procedure: improvements proposed by ombudsmen, 39, 136, 182; exercising discretionary power, 138; Norwegian commission on administrative procedure, 155; Swedish recommendations, 245; codification in Yugoslavia, 264; codification in Poland, 296; substantial evidence rule, 266*n*, 298; unregulated in Soviet Union, 340

Aikman, Colin C.: on inefficacy of parliamentary supervision of administration, 95; on ombudsman's ability to obtain evidence, 125; on conflict between ombudsman and official, 130; on need to publicize findings favorable to administrators, 143*n*

Algie, Ronald, on success of ombudsman system, 153

Anderman, S. D., on damage suits against public officials, 202*n*, 214*n*

Auditor General, *see* Control agencies

Austria, influence of: on Polish administrative procedure, 296; on State Control Commission, 328

Berezovskaia, S. G.: on procuracy's detachment from local control, 348*n*; on protest procedure, 352; on procurators' attending executive sessions, 353*n*; on action taken in response to procurators' objections, 353; on inspection campaigns, 356; on procedures for handling individual complaints, 360

Berman, Harold J.: on increased judicial activity in U.S.S.R., 339*n*; on complaints in Stalin period, 342; on procuracy functions, 345; on procurators' capability and prestige, 348; on Communist Party domination of procuracy, 349*n*; on U.S.S.R. judicial review, 369*n*

Bexelius, Alfred: election as Swedish ombudsman, 203; on infrequency of official corruption, 204*n*; on criticizing the courts, 207*n*; on journalistic treatment of uninvestigated complaints,

229; on value of ombudsman's opinions, 251
Brzezinski, Waclaw, advocate of judicial reviewability, 299*n*

Chancellor of Justice in Finland: appointment and removal, 50; powers, 51; prestige, 52; relations with Executive, 53, 56; participation in Council of State, 54; constitutional opinions, 55; power over judges, 57; action on closed judicial cases, 62; work division with ombudsman, 64; complaints received and actions taken, 65, 71; staff work and methods, 69; legislative proposals, 81; annual reports, 82, 84; press relations, 85
Chancellor of Justice in Sweden: creation, 195; relationship to legislative and executive branches, 232; responsibilities, 232*n*; action on complaints, 232; volume of work, 233; cooperation with ombudsman, 233
Christensen, Bent: on Danish ombudsman, 6*n;* on judicial review, 10; on review of discretion, 14; on ombudsman's initiative, 20
Civil liberties: Swedish ombudsman's impact, 77, 227; little stressed by Finnish ombudsman, 87; Norwegian ombudsman's concern with deprivations of liberty, 167; Swedish attention to custodial practices, 225*n*; judicial power in Yugoslavia, 270*n;* role of Yugoslav Constitutional Court, 273; Civil Liberties Bureau, Japanese Ministry of Justice, 404; liberties broadly defined in Japan, 405; Japanese inattention to discriminatory practices, 410*n*
Civil Liberties Bureau (Japan): in Ministry of Justice, 404; staff and duties, 404; liberties defined, 405; volume of cases, 407; types of matters handled, 408; outcome of cases, 409; inadequate investigatory powers, 410; general counseling activities, 411; public relations activities, 412
Civil Liberties Commissioner (Japan): selection and tenure, 405; consultative assemblies, 405*n*; occupational background and training, 406*n*; inactive in search for misdeeds, 409; important as counselors, 411; public knowledge of their availability, 412
Civil servants: opposed creating Danish and New Zealand ombudsmen, 5, 91, 103; as complainants, 25, 66, 92, 123, 174; endorsers of Norwegian plans, 155; effect of Norwegian politics on career service, 174*n*; Swedish civil servants' autonomy, 198; penal liability for inadequate performance, 59, 86, 164*n*, 201; objection to publicizing complaints, 228, 246; response to Yugoslav Bureau of Petitions and Proposals, 285; Yugoslav suspicion of professionalism, 292; qualifications in Poland, 300; distrust of Polish and Japanese officials, 312, 379, 383; procuracy supervision (U.S.S.R.), 357; inadequate training in U.S.S.R., 368; relations between Japanese officials and citizenry, 376
Comptroller General, *see* Control agencies
Control agencies: Revision Department (Den.), 41; Auditor of Accounts (Nor.) independent of ombudsman, 178*n*; State Control Commission (Pol.) — organization and powers, 327; Rechnungshof (Austria), 328; Comptroller General (Israel), 328; bureau of audit (U.S.S.R.), 337; People's Control Committee (U.S.S.R.), 362
Courts: disciplinary supervision over judges in Denmark 12, Finland 59, Norway 164, Sweden 216, 237, Yugoslavia 269*n;* judicial structure in New Zealand 96, Norway 163, Sweden 199, 202; judicial powers in Denmark 10, New Zealand 97, Norway 164, Sweden 201, Yugoslavia 269, Poland 299, Soviet Union 338, Japan 373, 410; Yugoslav judges as free legal advisers, 271*n;* Yugoslav Constitutional Court, 273; U.S.S.R. Supreme Court as legal clinic, 343*n;* judgments subject to procuracy examination and appeal, 345*n*; advocacy of more judicial review in Poland, 299; advocacy of more judicial review in Soviet Union, 369

Denisov, A. I., on detaching procuracy from local control, 348*n*
Denmark: ombudsman, 5; size, population, governmental system, 8; local government, 9, 11; judicial review, 10; disciplinary power over judges, 12; absentee voting, 16

Dimock, Marshall E.: on Soviet public administration, 336*n*; on Party members as administrative watchdogs, 363
Djordjević, Jovan: on Yugoslav legislative organization, 257*n*; on local self-government, 259*n*; chairman of Legal Council, 278; on rotating offices, 282
Documentary materials, *see* Public documents

Enajari, Risto, Finnish Chancellor of Justice, 53

Fainsod, Merle: on supervision of Soviet public servants, 337; on relations among local officials, 348*n*; on Communist Party's influence on law administration, 349*n*
Financial controls, *see* Control agencies
Finland: size and population, 48; relationship with Sweden and Russia, 49; Chancellor of Justice, 50; governmental structure, 53; judicial system, 58; provincial courts, 67; complaint handling by local prosecutors, 68; parliamentary powers over administration, 76; Supreme Administrative Court, 58, 86

Hanan, J. R.: on party discipline, 95; responsible for ombudsman plan, 101; on ombudsman's term of office, 104*n*; on ministerial responsibility, 106*n*; on ombudsman's over-extension, 109; on ombudsman's range of choice, 128
Hazard, John N.: on political criticism in U.S.S.R., 342; on motivation for protecting citizens, 368*n*
Herlitz, Nils: on the Swedish publicity principle, 200; influence on administrative procedure, 245; on exposure of civil servants, 246
Hrncevic, Josip, on Constitutional Court, 276
Hurwitz, Stephan: past career and selection as Danish ombudsman, 5; lectures and writings, 6; influence upon administration, 14; interest in penology, 18; on value of prisoner complaints, 19; public esteem, 33; on need to explain decisions, 38*n*

Influence: recourse to Yugoslav leaders, 287; United Workers' Party influence on Polish administration, 330; Communist Party influence on U.S.S.R. procuracy and on administrators, 349, 363; Japanese reliance on "face," 381
Information services: public need for, 134; Polish journalistic initiative, 321; educational efforts of U.S.S.R. procurators, 367*n*; "human rights counseling," Japanese Ministry of Justice, 411; local and prefectural informational activities (Japan), 413
Inspections: by ombudsmen in Denmark 18, Finland 78, New Zealand 124, Sweden 218; by procurators in Poland, 317; by procurators in U.S.S.R., 355; by Polish State Control Commission, 327; by Japanese Administrative Inspection Bureau, 385
Iserzon, Emanuel: draftsman of Polish Administrative Procedure Code, 296*n*; advocate of judicial reviewability, 299*n*

Jägerskiöld, Stig: on legal status of Swedish public servants, 199; on ombudsman's "reminders," 213, 247; on difference between prosecutor and ombudsman, 236; on legal effect of ombudsman's opinions, 240*n*
Jansson, Jan-Magnus, on Finnish lawyers, 49
Japan: judicial review, 373; formal administrative appeals, 374; costs of review proceedings, 375; unavailability of legal advisers, 376; feudal vestiges, 377; attitudes toward officials, 378, 382; educational level of complainants, 379*n*; Administrative Review Act, 374, 380, 380*n*; reliance on influence, 381; Administrative Management Agency, 385; inspections of administrative functioning, 385; individual complaint cases, 387; local administrative counselors, 388; public awareness of grievance mechanisms, 393; sources and objects of complaints, 395; outcome of grievances, 397; Civil Liberties Bureau, Ministry of Justice—structure and functions, 404; civil liberties commissioners, 405; outcome of civil liberties grievances, 407, 416*n*; human rights counseling, 411; local and prefectural advisory services, 413
Jaroszynski, Maurycy: draftsman of Polish Administrative Code, 296*n*; pro-

poser of new rulemaking procedures, 334*n*
Jovanović, Blazo, on functioning of Constitutional Court, 275
Judges, *see* Courts

Kastari, Paavo K., on Finnish constitutional "exceptions," 55*n*
Katz-Suchy, Julius, on administrative disregard of law, 299*n*

Lawyers: relations with ombudsman, 28, 43, 67, 175; legal profession in Finland, 59; legal profession in Sweden, 210*n*; support Norwegian plan, 155; bar association action on complaints against Norwegian judges, 164; availability of Yugoslav lawyers, 271*n*; Polish lawyers' use of procuracy, 319; Polish newspapers' legal clinics, 324; dissatisfaction with Soviet procuracy, 370; Japanese legal aid, 375; shortage of Japanese legal services, 376; Japanese Bar's participation in civil liberties matters, 408*n*
Legislature: structure and powers in New Zealand 93, Norway 160, Yugoslavia 257; Yugoslav legislative investigations, 281; inexperience of Yugoslav legislators, 282; Polish Sejm and Council of State, 301; Supreme Soviet in U.S.S.R., 337; legislature not subject to U.S.S.R. procuracy review, 350; declining confidence in Japanese representative system, 415*n*
Leskinen, Risto, past career and selection as Finnish ombudsman, 53
Letters and Complaints, Office of: in Polish Council of Ministers, 307; in newspapers, 322; in radio, 325; in United Workers' Party, 330
Liability for damages caused by official errors, 86, 201*n*, 213, 239, 274*n*, 357
Litwin, Jozef, advocate of judicial reviewability, 299*n*
Local Administrative Counselors (Japan): selection, 388; training, 389; activities, 390; intrusion into municipal affairs, 391; public relations, 393
Local government: relation to ombudsmen in Denmark 11, Finland 64, 67, 167, New Zealand 105, 115, Norway 165, Sweden 207; administrative responsibility in Yugoslavia, 268; grievance investigation in Yugoslavia, 289; Yugoslav emphasis on localism, 291; Polish provinces, districts, and communes, 302; U.S.S.R. procuracy's review of local legislation, 351; relation to Administrative Inspection Bureau personnel (Japan), 391; local fear of national officials (Japan), 395*n*; citizens, counseling services (Japan), 413
Loeber, D. A.: on judicial inactivity in Soviet Union, 339; on procuracy's organizational problems, 369

Mass communications: journalistic enthusiasm for Danish ombudsman, 34; inattention to prosecution of Finnish judges, 61; inattention to Finnish ombudsman's reports, 85; relations with Norwegian ombudsman, 189; relations with Swedish ombudsman, 227; Swedish publishers' court of honor, 229; Yugoslav reporting of grievances, 279; mass media's roles in Polish grievance procedures, 321, 331; mass media as complaint-handlers in U.S.S.R., 343*n*
Mental health: investigation of patients' complaints in Denmark 22, Finland 66, New Zealand 122, Norway 180, Sweden 215, 216; prolonged detention for psychiatric examination, 224
Merikoski, Veli, on legality and efficiency, 85
Mikolajczk, Leszek, analysis of Polish complaints, 326
Military affairs: in Denmark, 19; in Finland, 80; in New Zealand, 114; in Sweden, 205*n*
Military ombudsman: in Norway, 154; in Sweden, 205*n*, 234
Morgan, Glenn G.: on history of procuracy, 345; on function of general supervision, 346; on socialist legality, 347*n*; on procurators' training and ability, 348*n*; on challenged acts of republican ministers, 355*n*; on handling individual complaints, 359*n*; on U.S.S.R. judicial review, 369*n*

New Zealand: size, population, and governmental structure, 93; Petitions Committee, 95; judiciary, 96; administrative tribunals and appeals authorities, 97; ombudsman, 101; tax administration, 112, 132; State Services Commission, 131; social welfare administration, 138, 143*n*; Law Revision Commission, 139;

parliamentary relations with ombudsman, 150
Newspapers, *see* Mass communications
Northey, John F.: on ombudsman's qualifications, 92*n*; on New Zealand administration, 94; on Petitions Committee, 95; on filing fee, 122*n*; on legislators' use of ombudsman, 151*n*
Norway: military ombudsman, 154; expert commission on administrative procedure, 155; debate on ombudsman plan, 156; parliamentary organization, 160; ministries and cabinet, 160; courts and judges, 163; municipal and county government, 165; politics in civil service, 174*n*; auditor of accounts, 178*n*; effects of long Labor Party dominance, 191

Ombudsman institution: selection, tenure, compensation, and perquisites of ombudsman, 7 (Den.), 51 (Fin.), 104 (N.Z.), 158 (Nor.), 203 (Swed.); jurisdiction over national and local officials, 10 (Den.), 64 (Fin.), 105, 115 (N.Z.), 159, 165, 171 (Nor.), 205, 207 (Swed.); relations with courts, 12, 32 (Den.), 57 (Fin.), 110 (N.Z.), 163 (Nor.), 216, 237, 242 (Swed.); powers, 13 (Den.), 51 (Fin.), 118 (N.Z.), 159, 162, 176 (Nor.), 205 (Swed.); inspections, 18 (Den.), 78 (Fin.), 124 (N.Z.), 188 (Nor.), 218 (Swed.); access to documents, 18 (Den.), 51 (Fin.), 125 (N.Z.), 186*n* (Nor.), 200, 211 (Swed.); relations with military authorities, 19 (Den.), 80 (Fin.), 114 (N.Z.), 154 (Nor.), 205*n*, 234 (Swed.); self-initiated action, 20 (Den.), 75 (Fin.), 122*n* (N.Z.), 174 (Nor.), 208 (Swed.); complaint cases, 21 (Den.), 65, 71 (Fin.), 119 (N.Z.), 174 (Nor.), 210, 217 (Swed.); investigations made, 22 (Den.), 71 (Fin.), 173 (Nor.), 214 (Swed.); establishments affected, 24 (Den.), 78 (Fin.), 171 (Nor.), 208 (Swed.); issues determined, 24 (Den.), 127 (N.Z.); relations with civil servants, 25 (Den.), 91, 123 (N.Z.), 174 (Nor.), 228, 246 (Swed.); relations with legal profession, 28, 43 (Den.), 210 (Swed.); staff and work methods, 29, 30 (Den.), 69 (Fin.), 121, 123 (N.Z.), 185 (Nor.), 211, 254 (Swed.); time expenditure, 31 (Den.), 213 (Swed.); decisions, 33 (Den.), 72 (Fin.), 143 (N.Z.), 177 (Nor.), 214, 240 (Swed.); press relations, 34 (Den.), 85 (Fin.), 150 (N.Z.), 189 (Nor.), 227, 251 (Swed.); official reports, 35 (Den.), 82, 84 (Fin.), 149 (N.Z.), 190 (Nor.), 251 (Swed.); impact on public administration, 36 (Den.), 83 (Fin.), 144 (N.Z.), 192 (Nor.), 213, 226, 231, 248 (Swed.); procedural recommendations, 38 (Den.), 136 (N.Z.), 182 (Nor.), 245 (Swed.); legislative proposals, 40 (Den.), 81 (Fin.), 139 (N.Z.), 244 (Swed.); evaluation of success, 45 (Den.), 73 (Fin.), 153 (N.Z.), 192 (Nor.), 239 (Swed.); independence, 57 (Fin.), 203 (Swed.)
Ombudsman, Denmark: creation, 5, 7; influence of first incumbent, 6; selection, removal, and term of office, 7*n*; jurisdiction over national and local officials, 10; relations with judiciary, 12, 32; formal powers, 13; informal influence on decisions, 15; negotiated settlements, 17; inspections, 18; access to documents, 18; visits to military bases, 19; self-initiated action, 20; complaint cases, 21; investigations undertaken, 22; establishments involved, 24; issues determined, 24; civil servants' complaints, 25; sources of complaint, 27; relations with the bar, 28, 43; staff, 29; work methods, 30; time expenditure, 31; decisions, 33; public relations, 34; official reports, 35; impact on public administration, 36; need for administrative explanation and information, 38; legislative proposals, 40; evaluation of success, 45
Ombudsman, Finland: selection and removal, 51; powers, 51; prestige, 52; non-participation in Council of State, 55; independence, 57; power over judges, 57; action on closed judicial cases, 62; work division with Chancellor of Justice, 64; complaints—sources, volume, and action taken, 65, 71; staff and work methods, 69; effectiveness of advice given, 73; self-initiated action, 75; inspections, 78; relations with the military, 80; legislative proposals, 81; annual reports, 82, 84; impact on public administration,

83; press relations, 83; inactivity in civil liberties matters, 87
Ombudsman, New Zealand: creation, 101; selection, tenure, perquisites, 104; jurisdiction, 105; matters elsewhere reviewable, 110; military matters, 114; local government, 115; staff, 116*n*; powers, 118, 120; action on complaints, 119; work methods, 121, 123; self-initiated action, 122*n*; inspections, 124; access to official documents, 125; review of decisional merits, 127; as personalizer of government, 131; as stimulator of new methods and policies, 133; proposed procedural improvements, 136; legislative recommendations, 139; influence on public opinion concerning officials, 142; impact on public administration, 144; reports and educational efforts, 149; relations with legislators, 151
Ombudsman, Norway: genesis, 154; military ombudsman, 154*n*; volume of cases, 157; qualifications, selection, tenure, emoluments, 158; jurisdiction over national officials, 159; barred from matters considered by legislature or by Cabinet, 159, 162; no power over judiciary, 163; relation to local government, 165; limited authority over discretionary acts, 168; service as mediator, 170; establishments dealt with, 171; exhaustion of remedies, 172; disposition of docketed matters, 173, 177; self-initiated action, 174; sources of complaint, 174; powers, 175; outcome of cases, 177; action in social insurance contests, 178; deprivations of personal freedom, 180; prisoners' complaints, 181; procedural recommendations, 182; staff and work methods, 185; access to official files, 186*n*; office consultations, 187; inspections, 188; public relations, 189; annual reports, 190; advisory opinions, 191; evaluation of success, 192; impact on public attitude, 193
Ombudsman, Sweden: impact on civil liberties, 77; origin, 195; role as prosecutor, 202; qualifications, selection, tenure, and perquisites, 203; Deputy Ombudsman, 203*n*; relations with legislature, 204, 246; powers, 205; prosecutions and admonitions, 206, 241; relations with ministers and King in Council, 206; local administration, 207; self-initiated action, 208; nature of complaints received, 209; nature of complainants, 210, 217; no need to exhaust other remedies, 207*n*, 211; staff and work methods, 211, 254; redressive measures taken, 213; disposition of docketed cases, 214; intercession in closed penal cases, 215; admonition of judges, 216; inspections, 218; stress on documentation, 223; influence on administrative attitudes, 226; press relations, 227; advisory utterances, 224, 231, 240; relations with Chancellor of Justice, 223; with Military Ombudsman, 234; with public prosecutors, 235; with courts, 237, 242; legislative recommendations, 244; procedural recommendations, 245; overcaution induced by criticism, 248; effect of criticism on civil servant's future, 249; protection against ill-founded complaints, 250; annual reports and public relations, 251
Organization and Methods: Danish office of, 41; Serbian Institute of Administration, 286
Orr, G. S., on administrative adjudication and appeals, 98*n*, 99*n*
Os, Audvar, on judicial review, 164

Paliwoda, J., on functioning of Polish procuracy, 319
Parliament, *see* Legislature
Parzynski, Jerzy, on Polish newspapers' legal advice to readers, 324
Pedersen, I. M.: on Danish ombudsman, 6*n*; on explanation of decisions, 38*n*; on administrative procedure, 39*n*
Petitions and Proposals, Bureau of: creation in Yugoslavia, 282; activities, 283; staff and work methods, 284; effectiveness, 285
Poland: Administrative Procedure Code, 296; administrative appeals, 298; narrow judicial activity, 299, 333; depleted civil service, 300; the legislature (Sejm) and Council of State, 301; provinces, districts, and communes, 302; training in legal procedures, 302; complaints to higher authorities, 303; Council of Ministers, 304; volume and types of complaints, 304, 306; procedure for filing and considering complaints, 305; Office of Letters and

Complaints, 307; ministries' grievance handling, 308; housing problems, 310; security apparatus, 312; procuracy, 314; procuracy's help to complainants, 316, 318; review of local laws and administrative regulations, 317; extent of procuracy's general supervision, 319; press and radio action on grievances, 321; "Wave 56" radio program, 325; State Control Commission, 327; political parties, 329; United Workers' Party as administrative overseer, 330; protection of complainants, 331; rule-making procedures, 334

Police: response to ombudsman in Denmark, 37, 39; as investigators for Finnish ombudsman, 70; response to Finnish ombudsman, 73; New Zealand police appeal board, 100*n*; Norwegian freedom from corruption, 176*n;* disagreement with Swedish ombudsman, 243*n*; over-caution produced by criticism, 248; use of ombudsman as a shield, 250; knowledge of Swedish ombudsman's opinions, 253; Polish security administration, 312; fear of Japanese police, 377; infrequent involvement in Japanese civil liberties matters, 408

Powles, Guy: professional career, 92; on departmental answers to parliamentary inquiries, 95*n*; on ombudsman's duty to consider statutory changes, 139; on observed deficiencies of public administration, 142; on subordinate officials' failure to follow superior's lead, 147

Prisoners: complaints to ombudsmen in Denmark 19, 36, Finland 65, 80, New Zealand 122, Norway 175, 180; prison inspections by U.S.S.R. procurators and action on complaints, 357; infrequency of Japanese complaints, 410*n*

Procuracy: local prosecutors' action on complaints, 68 (Fin.), 235 (Swed.); functions in Yugoslavia, 279; study of Polish administrative procedures, 301; organization and functions in Poland, 314; review of delegated legislation, 317 (Pol.), 350 (U.S.S.R.); volume of Polish cases dealt with, 319; origins of Russian procuracy, 344; power relating to court judgments, 345*n*; function of general supervision, 346, 350, 355; structure and personnel in U.S.S.R., 347; training and salary, 349; attendance at local executive sessions, 353*n*, 354; review of administrative judgments, 355; inspection campaigns, 356; access to documents, 356; investigative methods, 357; individual complaint cases, 358; scope of action taken, 361

Public documents, files, and records, accessibility of: in Denmark, 18, 34; in Finland, 85*n*; in New Zealand, 125; in Norway, 186*n*; in Sweden, 200, 205, 208; in Poland, 315; in U.S.S.R., 357; in Japan, 385*n*, 410, 418

Public prosecutor, *see* Procuracy

Radio and television, *see* Mass communications

Ramndal, Lars, "unofficial ombudsman," supporter of Norwegian ombudsman plan, 157

Robson, John L.: draftsman of New Zealand ombudsman plan, 101; participant in United Nations seminar, 102

Robson, William A., on need for administrative safeguards, 155*n*

Romachkine, P., on legislative activities in U.S.S.R., 338*n*

Rozmaryn, Stefan: on principles underlying Polish administrative procedure, 297; on structure of Polish government, 301*n*

Schei, Andreas: selected as first Norwegian ombudsman, 158; on access to ministry's records, 186*n*

Shapiro, Isaac: on political criticism in U.S.S.R., 342; on U.S.S.R. judicial review, 369*n*

Soldiers, *see* Military affairs

Soviet Union: attitude toward public administration, 336; bureau of audit, 337; legislature (Supreme Soviet) and its powers, 337; inexperienced legislators, 338; judicial power, 338; administrative procedure, 340; imposition of administrative fines, 341; right to complain, 342; mass communications as complaint-handlers, 343*n*; official action on complaints, 343; procuracy origins, 344; procuracy power as to judicial proceedings, 345*n*; function of general supervision, 346, 350, 355; procuracy statute, 347, 358; procuracy organization and personnel, 347; Communist

Party influence on procuracy, 349; procuracy review of delegated legislation, 350; procuracy review of administrative actions, 355; procuracy's access to official documentation, 356; investigative methods, 357; handling individual complaints, 358; People's Control Committee, 362; comparison of procurators with ombudsmen, 367; judicial review, 369; legal profession's attitude toward procuracy, 370
Special Prosecutor of Judges, operations in Finland, 59
Starosciak, Jerzy: draftsman of Polish Administrative Procedure Code, 296*n*; advocate of judicial reviewability, 299*n*
State Control Commission, *see* Control agencies
Stjepanović, Nikola S., analysis of Yugoslav Administrative Procedure Act, 265*n*
Strogovich, M. S., advocacy of enlarged judicial review in U.S.S.R., 369
Sweden: constitutional history, 194; creation of Chancellor of Justice, 195; size, population, and governmental structure, 195; parliamentary organization and powers, 197; central administrative boards, 198; judges and prosecutors, 199, 235; socialism, 204n; military ombudsman, 205*n*, 234; provincial administration, 219*n*; functioning of Chancellor of Justice, 232; prosecutors' action on complaints against public servants, 235; intimidation of public servants, 248; proposed reorganization of ombudsman system, 254

Tito, President Josip Broz: attitude toward constitutional court, 273; handling citizens' grievances, 287
Toropov, G.: on procurators' function of general supervision, 361; on procurators' educational activities, 367*n*

United Kingdom: review of delegated legislation, 352; parliamentary commissioner's discretion to proceed despite available judicial remedy, 429
U.S.S.R., *see* Soviet Union

Vavpetić, Lado: on need for legality in public administration, 260*n*; on Yugoslav administrative organization, 268*n*

Welfare administration: little affected by Finnish ombudsman, 74; discretionary choices in New Zealand, 138; Norwegian ombudsman active in social insurance contests, 175, 178; Swedish social insurance court, 201; minor element of Swedish ombudsman's case load, 209; Yugoslav social insurance administration, 259; Polish social insurance court, 299*n*; frequent object of Japanese complaints, 396
Wild, H. R. C.: on entrusting tasks to courts, 98; on scope of appeal, 99*n*
Wold, Terje: on genesis of Norwegian ombudsman system, 155*n*; on conditions of ombudsman's success, 187
Wyman, S. M., on Norwegian local government, 166

Yamamoto, Shotaro, on Administrative Management Agency inspections and grievance-handling, 386*n*
Yugoslavia: population and size, 256; federal structure, 256; legislative and executive organization, 257; administrative organs, 258; "working organizations," 259; business self-management, 260; Administrative Procedure Act, 264; judicial review, 269; Administrative Disputes Law, 270 *n;* procedure in special chamber for administrative contests, 271; judgments rendered, 272; Constitutional Court, 273; federal-republican relationships, 274; Legal Council to reexamine federal laws, 278*n*; public prosecutors, 279; legislative oversight of administration, 281; Bureau of Petitions and Proposals, 282; presidential and vice-presidential grievance bureaus, 287; emphasis on localism, 291; hostility toward bureaucracy, 292; rotation in office, 293*n*

Zhogin, N. V., on Soviet procuracy during Stalin regime, 346*n*
Zimmermann, Marian, advocate of judicial reviewability, 299*n*